# FISHERIES DEVELOPMENT IN INDIA

# FISHERIES DEVELOPMENT IN INDIA

## The Political Economy of Unsustainable Development

(In Two Volumes)

(Volume–1)

Dr. Ramakrishnan Korakandy

PUBLICATIONS

KALPAZ PUBLICATIONS

DELHI-110052

Fisheries Development in India : The Political Economy of Unsustainable Development

Rs. 1800 (Set)



ISBN: 81-7835-632-5 (Set)
ISBN: 81-7835-633-3 (Vol. 1)



Published in 2008 in India by
Kalpaz Publications
C-30, Satyawati Nagar,
Delhi-110052
E-mail: kalpaz@hotmail.com
Phone : 9212729499

*Laser type setting by* Quick Media, Delhi
*Printed at* Vishal Kaushik Printers, Delhi

# DEDICATION

This book is dedicated to the loving memory of the late Professor N.K. Velankar, who was Consultant to establish the School of Industrial Fisheries during 1976-78, the late Professor (Dr.) P.G.K. Panikkar, former Director, Centre for Development Studies, Thiruvananthapuram, and Padmasree Professor (Dr.) M.V. Pylee, former Vice-Chancellor, Cochin University of Science and Technology, for their kind gesture in giving me an academic chair at the School of Industrial Fisheries in 1978 which sustained me all these years.

# CONTENTS

# PREFACE

Like 'socialism' in the last century, 'sustainable development' today is the most popular term in economic developmen thinking in both developed and developing countries. The concern for sustainable development, which is very acute tody, seems to have existed even during the times of Adam Smith. Adam Smith had spoken of the 'stationary state' in which the economic activity was at the peak and no further progress was possible. Smith had also cited the examples of China as a 'stationary state' in the eighteenth century enjoying high levels of prosperity and Bengal, the English Company's domain, experiencing a decline in its prosperity under the company's rule. Later writers like Malthus, Ricardo, Mill, Marx, Marshall, Keynes and many others also had expressed the possibility of the economy moving towards a 'stationary state' from where no further progress was possible.

The modern concept of 'sustainable development' has been popularised by the IUCN, WCED, UNCED, and a host of other agencies and individual writers during the second half of the last century. One of the most frequently quoted definitions of sustainable development is given by the WCED as "development that meets the needs of the present without compromising the ability of future generations to meet their own needs". The concept of sustainable development was institutionalised by the UNCED, which appealed to all nations to promote sustainable development in their territories, and other agencies in their area of jurisdiction. The concept has now undoubtedly acquired a multidimensional and multidisciplinary status with increased acceptance and importance.

The sustainable development of fisheries, is now a major concern for all nations because of their contribution to food supply, employment, national income, foreign exchange, public revenue, regional development, recreation, social welfare, etc. Sustainable development of fisheries, world-wide, is presently in the agenda of action programmes of the FAO. The chief instrument for promoting sustainable development of fisheries on a global scale proposed by the FAO in 1995 and adopted by the UN is the *code of conduct for responsible fisheires.*

Sustainable development of Indian fisheires is now very much in the planning process of the Government of India. The tenth five year plan document of India speaks of an "integrated approach for sustainable development of fisheries and aquaculture". It has also proposed measures for the effective utilisation of marine and inland fishery resources of the country by introducing new technology, better training, infrastructure, etc. There are also plans for the effective management of fish stocks and welfare of fishermen.

The present study, *Fisheries Development in India—The Political Economy of Unsustainable Development* was initiated while availing a sabbatical leave from the Cochin University of Science and Technology during 2006. The basic premise of this study is that fisheries development in India is not sustainable at present due to several ecological, economic, social, cultural, institutional and technological constraints. Sustainable development of fisheries in India needed the removal of these constraints, which is, however, considered difficult due to many interactions, interdependencies and externalities, which remind one about the working of the 'impossibility theorem' that is characteristic of many poor countries.

This study is presented in eight chapters. The first chapter explains the background and need for the study, its objectives, scope, hypotheses, methodology, database, limitations and utility of the study. Chapter two makes a survey of the general theoretical literature relating to sustainable development and the applied literature relating to fisheries development, both national and international. Chapter three presents the theoretical concept of sustainable development, including the definition, evolution of the concept through classical, neo-classical, Marxian, modern and post-modern era, measurement of sustainable development, factors behind unsustainable development and criteria/indicators of sustainable development. Chapter four outlines the major sustainability issues of global fisheries. Chapter five gives a detailed picture of the inventory of resources available to the fisheries sector of India and their development. Chapter six discusses the major sustainability issues of Indian fisheries and their indicators. Chapter seven makes an analysis of the political economy of unsustainable development of Indian fisheries. Chapter eight, being the last chapter, presents the summary and conclusions of this study.

The present study is quite unique in certain respects. It is perhaps the first theoretical study on sustainable development thinking in India and on the sustainable development issues of Indian fisheries, having both theoretical and empirical contents. In doing so, it has delved deep into the international literature relating to the general theory of sustainable development and sustainable development of fisheries in particular. This study has undoubtedly come to a very pessimistic conclusion about the sustainability of Indian fisheries—the impossibility theorem—the impossibility of achieving sustainable development, which may sound quite alarming. The present study with its sound theoretical backing and empirical support will be quite interesting for academics, administrators and others concerned with sustainable development theory in general and fisheries development in particular, world-wide.

**Dr. Ramakrishnan Korakandy**

# ACKNOWLEDGEMENTS

The passion for studying the sustainability issues of Indian fisheries had crept into my mind slowly during the last few years when I began to learn a little about the concept of sustainable development from text books on ecological economics and environmental economics. However, before long, I thought of putting my limited knowledge in some order, by venturing to write this book. Fortunately, in this effort, I have been assisted abundantly by many people and institutions. Here, I place on record my sincere gratitude to all those individuals and institutions. First of all, I note my deep gratitude to Prof. (Dr.) P.K.Abdul Azis, former Vice-Chancellor of Cochin University of Science and Technology, Prof. (Dr.) N.D. Inasu, Pro-Vice-Chancellor, Cochin University of Science and Technology and Prof. (Dr.) A.Ramachandran, Registrar, Cochin University of Science and Technology, for their kind assistance by way of granting me the sabbatical leave for undertaking this study during 2006. I also place on record my gratitude to the administrative staff of the University office for moving my request for leave in time.

Another major source of support for this study was indeed my colleagues at the School of Industrial Fisheries. Prof. (Dr.) Saleena Mathew, presently Director of the School, Prof. (Dr.) Madhusoodana Kurup, (presently also Adviser to Minister for Fisheries, Government of Kerala), Dr, K.T.Thomson and Sri John Mohan were quite helpful in supporting my request for sabbatical leave to undertake this study. I record my sincere gratitude to them for this. With this, I also place on record my gratitude to the administrative staff and students of the School of Industrial Fisheries for excusing me for my absence from the School during the period of this study.

Among the other institutions and people that helped me most for undertaking this study were the libraries and staff of some of the Schools and Departments of the Cochin University of Science and Technology, the Central Marine Research Institute, Cochin, the Central Institute of Fisheries Technology, Cochin, the Central Institute of Fisheries Nautical and Engineering Training, Cochin, and the Marine Products Export Development Authority, Cochin. In this regard, I am particularly thankful to Sri Edwin Joseph, Librarian, CMFRI, Cochin, and Smt. Shobhana

Devi, Librarian, Department of Applied Economics, Cochin University of Science and Technology.

I am equally grateful to Dr. (Mrs.) Ammini Joseph, then Director, School of Environmental Studies, Cochin University of Science and Technology, Dr.R .Sathiadhas, Principal Scientist, CMFRI, Dr. M.Ramachandran, Scientist, CMFRI, Dr. Saly, N. Thomas, Scientist, CIFT and Dr. Leela Edwin, Scientist, CIFT, for gaining me access to some of the books of the libraries of their respective institutions and to Sri M.K.R. Nair, Commissioner, Fisheries Development, Department of Animal Husbandry, Dairying and Fisheries, Government of India, New Delhi, Sri Mohana Pai, Department of Animal Husbandry, Dairying and Fisheries, Government of India, New Delhi, Sri V.Vishnu Bhat, Director, MPEDA, Cochin, Sri Vijaya Kumar Yaragal, Deputy Director, MPEDA, Cochin and Dr. G.R. Unnithan, Principal Scientist, CIFT, Cochin, for providing me timely information relating to the fisheries sector of India.

I am also to acknowledge here that I have benefited greatly from the published international literature relating to sustainable development theory and sustainable development of fisheries from the FAO and other western sources. I have quoted extensively from these sources to substantiate my arguments and they have been acknowledged at all points.

This long acknowledgement should undoubtedly mention my great indebtedness to my 'friend in need' Sriman K.V.Chandran, who again did the wonderful job of typing the scribbled manuscript of this work to give it the present shape. I am a little apologetic in noting here that I have caused enough trouble to my wife, Dr. Chandraprabha and son Amarkrishna, due to my failing health after taking up this study. I have only regret for their fate. A word of eternal gratitude is to Dr. K. S. Mathew, an old time friend and historian from the Jawaharlal Nehru University, New Delhi for perpetual succour.

Finally, I express my great gratitude to Kalpaz Publications, Delhi for taking up the job of publishing this book. With this I also express my regret for not being able to give it the required perfection.

**Dr. Ramakrishnan Korakandy**

# Acronyms

| | |
|---|---|
| ACMRR | Advisory Committee on Marine Resource Research |
| ADB | Asian Development Bank |
| ASEAN | Association of South East Asian Nations |
| BED | By- catch Exclusion Devices |
| BFDA | Brackish Water Fish Farmers Development Agency |
| BOBP | Bay of Bengal Programme |
| CAM | Coastal Area Management |
| CAMP | Coastal Area Management Plan |
| CBD | Convention on Biodiversity |
| CESS | Centre for Earth Science Studies |
| CFC | Chloroflurocarbons |
| CFP | Common Fisheries Policy |
| CIFE | Central Institute of Fisheries Education |
| CIFNET | Central Institute of Fisheries Nautical and Engineering Training |
| CIFRI | Central Inland Fisheries Research Institute |
| CIS | Common Wealth of Independent States |
| CMFRI | Central Marine Fisheries Research Institute |
| COP | Conference of Parties |
| CRZ | Coastal Regulation Zone |
| CSD | Commission on Sustainable Development |
| DDT | Dichlorodiphenyl trichloroethane |
| EBFM | Ecosystem Based Fisheries Management |
| EC | European Community |
| ECA | Ecologically Critical Areas |
| EIA | Environmental Impact Assessment |
| EU | European Union |
| EUS | Epizotic Ulcertation Syndrome |
| FAD | Fish Aggregating Devices |

| | |
|---|---|
| FAO | Food and Agriculture Organisation |
| FCCC | Framework Convention on Climate Change |
| FFDA | Fish Farmers Development Agency |
| FISHCOPFED | Federation of Fishermen's Co-operatives Ltd. |
| FRP | Fibre Reinforced Plastics |
| GDP | Gross Domestic Product |
| GESAMP | Joint Group of Experts on Scientific Aspects of Marine Pollution (of IMO-FAO-UNESCO-WMO-IAEA-UN-UNEP) |
| GMO | Genetically Modified Organism |
| GMP | Good Management Practice |
| GNP | Gross National Product |
| HACCP | Hazard Analysis and Critical Control Points |
| IAEA | International Atomic Energy Agency |
| ICAM | Intergrated Coastal Area Management |
| ICM | Integrated Coastal Management |
| ICSU | International Council of Scientific Unions |
| IFPRI | International Food Policy Research Institute (Washington) |
| IGBP | International Geosphere – Biosphere Programme |
| IISD | International Institute for Sustainable Development |
| ILO | International Labour Organisation |
| IMF | International Monetary Fund |
| IMO | International Maritime Organisation |
| IPCC | Intergovernental Panel on Climate Change |
| IUCN | International Union for the Conservation of Nature (now World Conservation Union) |
| KWBSP | Kerala Water Balance Study Project |
| LIFDC | Low Income Food Deficit Countries |
| LME | Large Marine Ecosystem |
| MATSYAFED | Kerala State Co-operative Federation for Fisheries Development |
| MPA | Marine Protected Area |

| | |
|---|---|
| MPEDA | Marine Products Export Development Authority |
| MRL | Maximum Residue Levels |
| MSC | Marine Stewardship Council (Washington) |
| MSY | Maximum Sustainable Yield |
| NACA | Network of Aquaculture Centres in Asia-Pacific |
| NCAP | National Centre for Agricultural Economics and Policy Research |
| NCD | Natural Capital Depletion |
| NCDC | National Co-operative Development Corporation |
| NEERI | National Environmental Engineering Research Institute |
| NFI | National Fisheries Institute (Washington) |
| NGO | Non-Governmental Organisation |
| NI | National Income |
| NIEO | New International Economic Order |
| NIO | National Institute of Oceanography |
| NMFS | National Marine Fisheries Service (USA) |
| NNP | Net National Product |
| NNW | Net National Welfare |
| NRC | National Research Council (USA) |
| NRTEE | National Round Table on Environment and Economy (Canada) |
| OAL | Over-All Length |
| OBM | Out Board Motor |
| ODA | Overseas Development Agency |
| OECD | Organisation for Economic Cooperation and Development |
| OPEC | Organisation of Petroleum Exporting Countries |
| PHC | Public Health Centre |
| PPM | Process and Production Methods |
| PSP | Paralytic Shellfish Poisoning |
| PSR | Pressure State Response |
| SAP | Structural Adjustment Programame |

| | |
|---|---|
| SD | Sustainable Develpment |
| SEAI | Seafood Exporters' Association of India |
| SPS | Sanitary and Phyto-Sanitary |
| SSE | Steady State Economy |
| TBT | Technical Barriers to Trade |
| TED | Turtle Exclusion Device |
| TEK | Traditional Ecological Knowledge |
| TNC | Trans-National Corporations |
| TRIM | Trade Related Investment Measures |
| TRIPS | Trade Related Aspects of Intellectual Property Rights |
| TURF | Territorial Use Rights in Fisheries |
| UN | United Nations |
| UNCED | United Nations Conference on Environment and Development |
| UNDP | United Nations Development Programme |
| UNEP | United Nations Environment Programme |
| UNESCO | United Nations Educational, Scientific and Cultural Organisation |
| US | United States |
| USITC | United States International Trade Commission |
| UT | Union Territory |
| VER | Voluntary Export Restrictions |
| VMS | Vessel Monitoring System |
| VRA | Voluntary Restraint Agreements |
| WCED | World Commission on Environment and Development |
| WCS | World Conservation Strategy |
| WCU | World Conservation Union (fomerly IUCN) |
| WHAT | World Humanity Action Trust (London) |
| WMO | World Meteorological Organisation |
| WSSD | World Summit on Sustainable Development |
| WTO | World Trade Organisation |
| WWF | World Wide Fund for Nature |

# LIST OF TABLES

# LIST OF APPENDICES

# 1

# INTRODUCTION

## 1.1. Theme and Background of the Study

The theme of this book is *Fisheries Development in India – The Political Economy of Unsustainable Development.* The sub-title of this book points to the prevailing crisis of unsustainable development in the industry and the complex ecological, economic, social, cultural, institutional, technological and other factors contributing to un-sustainability.

This theme was chosen for an in-depth study during a sabbatical leave granted to me by the Cochin University of Science and Technology in 2006. The motivation for choosing this subject for detailed investigation was the academic curiosity of knowing more about the concept of sustainable development and the practical value of this knowledge, if any, for promoting sustainable development of fisheries in India in particular and the world in general.

The concept of sustainable development has become very popular ever since the World Commission on Environment and Development (WCED) defined it as "development that meets the needs of the present without compromising the ability of future generations to meet their own needs" (WCED, 1987, p.43). It acquired operational significance when the United Nations Conference on Environment and Development (UNCED, 1992) made it part of Chapter 17 of Agenda 21 for implementation by nations. The concept got wide acceptance in the fisheries sector with the FAO drafting the Code of Conduct for Responsible Fisheries in 1995 and the UN giving its nod for implementation by states since then.

It must be noted here that the concept of sustainable development had received wide attention in the academic circles of the west even earlier and it has been at the center-stage of academic debate by a galaxy of economists, ecologists and ecological economists for more than two couple of decades earlier. The concept has been acclaimed for its theoretical rigour and appeal for implementation in a world of conflicting interests, such as between North and South or rich and poor nations. Its main appeal, it is claimed, is its harmonising spirit in a world of multiple conflicts. Ironically, the concept has also found enough critics who believe that the concept is quite 'deceptive', 'clever', 'vague', 'oxymoron', and a 'cliched platitude'. Keeping these in mind, it is more tempting and thought provoking to approach this concept and to apply this in the context of fisheries development in India and to study the political economy of unsustainable development.

### 1.2. Need for the Study

The need for the present study arose primarily from the complexity of situation prevailing in the fisheries sector of India which is passing through a serious crisis of unsustainable development and needing a course correction towards sustainability. The complex situation prevailing in the fisheries sector of India consisted of a number of ecological, economic, social, cultural, institutional and technological issues, which threaten the very survival of the industry. Interestingly, these are problems which are not typical of the fisheries sector of India alone, but common to the fisheries sector world-wide and indeed most primary producing activities of the world.

As a matter of fact, the fisheries sector of India, which produced nearly 6.40 million tonnes of fish in 2003-04, and contributed significantly to domestic food supply, employment, national income, foreign exchange earnings, public revenue, regional development, recreation and national welfare is indeed besieged by a variety of ecological, economic, social, cultural, institutional and technological issues which directly and through their interaction and interdependencies produce a number of negative externalities which threaten the survival of the sector. The fact that the fisheries sector of India is besieged by a variety of problems is common place, but to identify and measure the magnitude of the critical problems needs a special study, and the present study is directed to that end.

### 1.3. Objective of the Study

The primary objective of this study is to make clear the political economy of unsustainable development of fisheries in India.

In tune with this objective, the study seeks to identify, assess (measure) and discuss the impact of critical ecological, economic, social, cultural, institutional and technological factors (issues) affecting the sustainability of Indian fisheries. *Ipso facto*, this study also aims to suggest and review the feasibility of various measures for promoting the sustainable development of fisheries in India.

### 1.4. Scope of the Study

With its theoretical underpinning on sustainable development, the scope of this study is broad based, dealing with sustainable development thinking and its application to the fisheries sector of India. In terms of its textual presentation, it covers much of the global thinking on sustainable development, the sustainability issues of global fisheries, the Indian scenario and policies for sustainable development of fisheries in India.

### 1.5. Hypothesis of the Study

The main hypothesis of this study is that the sustainability of Indian fisheries is currently threatened by a number of ecological, economic, social/cultural/institutional and technological factors (issues) which act as constraints for the working of the industry. It further holds that the sustainable development of fisheries in India requires the removal of these constraints, which is, however, not quite easy, given the many interactions, interdependencies and externalities working in the sector, and against the sector, all of which remind one about the operation of the 'impossibility theorem'.

### 1.6. Methodology

The methodology followed in this study is fundamentally deductive, based on the received doctrine of 'sustainable development'. The epistemology of sustainable development essentially defines the concept, develops criteria/indicators for the measurement of (un)sustainable development, and evaluates the given economic system referring to these criteria/indicators. The present study has made use of this epistemology of sustainable development by first explaining (defining) the concept and then exploring the criteria/indicators of (un)sustainable development and finally noting the frequently cited factors that lead to unsustainability.

The existing epistemology of sustainable development focuses on the ecological, economic, social, cultural, institutional and technological parameters/indicators of sustainable development and evaluates growth/development in the economic system by referring to the multiple criteria/indicators, all of which correspond to the above factors. The present study has sought to explain the unsustainability of development in the fisheries sector of India by identifying/developing suitable indicators of unsustainability. The various indictors identified were sought to represent and explain the real issues/constraints for the sustainable development of the industry due to their interaction, interdependencies and externalities.

Having studied the epistemology of sustainable development and the unsustainable path of development of Indian fisheries, this study has suggested standard international solutions to remove the various constraints for sustainable development. Simultaneously, this study has also reviewed the feasibility of these solutions and reached valid conclusions about the impossibility of sustainable development of fisheries in India at present.

A rethinking on the concept of sustainable development has further prompted me to present the many prevailing criticisms against this concept and to question the mainline thinking on sustainable development, including the 'weak sustainability' hypothesis. Alternatively, the need for adopting a 'strong sustainability' hypothesis is also presented. Further, the importance of checks on population, production, consumption and trade is also noted for achieving sustainability in the larger context of life in this planet.

## 1.7. Data Base

The data base for this study predominantly consisted of the published information from national and international sources. The national sources consisted of, apart from published books and journals, the statistical Hand Books of the Government of India relating to fisheries and official statistics from MPEDA and other sources. The international sources consisted of chiefly the relevant publications of the FAO, and other published materials in the form of books, journals and the internet.

## 1.8. Limitations of the Study

One apparent limitation that one may possibly note against this study is that it did not make any single composite index (numerical estimate) of the degree of unsustainability prevailing in the industry. This is indeed not possible when the dimensions of unsustainability are vast and complex and many not amenable for quantification. It is, however, significant to note here that the various sustainability issues identified and the indicators studied, are quite sufficient to represent the nature of the unsustainability situation prevailing in the industry and this approach is very much in tune with the global approach to the study of sustainable development.

## 1.9. Utility of the Study

The utility of this study is partly academic and partly applied. As an academic exercise, this study is significant for its comprehensive coverage and approach to the study of sustainable development thinking. It is truly holistic and universal in this approach. As an applied study, it has charted the dimensions of unsustainable development both in Indian and global fisheries, which may be of much interest to fisheries management in India and the world alike. Its pessimistic conclusions, particularly the difficulties in achieving sustainable development, which reminds one about the working of the 'impossibility theorem' might be a little mind-bogging to all double-digit growth seeking economists and democrats, particularly in the third world. But that is, however, quite inevitable in the given political economy situation of the world today which is, to a large extent, its own making.

# 2

# A GENERAL SURVEY OF THE LITERATURE ON SUSTAINABLE DEVELOPMENT

## 2.1. Introduction

The objective of this chapter is to make a general survey of the literature relating to sustainable development of fisheries in India. In this regard, considering the global theoretical developments and the domestic need for bringing the global thinking on the subject to the forefront of academic discussions, this survey takes note of both the domestic (national) and foreign (international) literature. Moreover, since much of the discussions on sustainability and sustainable development had their roots in the recent works on ecological economics and some of the earlier writings in 'general' economics and 'welfare' economics, this survey also takes note of such other works. Accordingly, this survey is presented in two sections: the first dealing with the 'general' theoretical literature and the second dealing with the 'applied' fisheries literature. Both of these sections are further grouped as 'national' and 'international' literature. The emerging pattern in the 'national' and 'international' literature is noted in the summary section.

## 2.2. General Theoretical Literature

Included in this category are the general theoretical literature on sustainable development originating from national and international sources. A brief description of these are given in this section.

### 2.2.1. National Literature

The national literature on sustainable development, with any significant theoretical underpinning, is yet to develop. In the land of the Mahatma (M.K.Gandhi) who said that "there is enough in the world for everyone's need but not enough for everyone's greed", the concern for sustainable development is not yet very common in academic circles, and the literature on sustainable development is quite scanty. Quite a few of the notable studies with some import for sustainability are reckoned here.

Ghosh and Malhotra (1994) gave an overview of the implications of Agenda-21 for sustainable development.

Jaitly (1994) gave an overview of the post-Rio political economy issues and their implications for sustainable development.

Parikh (1994) made a case study of the linkage between trade and environment in India.

Sarkar (2000) offered a critical analysis of humanity's fundamental choice between eco-socialism and eco-capitalism and recommended eco-socialism for sustainable development.

Sanwal (2004) outlined the evolution of international policy and law with respect to sustainable development.

Koli (2005) considered the sufficiency of environmental laws to promote sustainable development.

Manonmoney (2005) wrote on the management of ecological (common property) resources in developing countries.

### 2.2.2. International Literature

The international literature on sustainable development is quite advanced and still growing. Much of this literature, as already pointed out, had their origin in the contemporary writings in ecological economics and some of the earlier works of classical, neo-classsical and modern economists. A few institutional works also have contributed to this literature. The tendency for the economic system to come to a critical pause or crisis had been pointed out by Adam Smith (1776), David Ricardo (1817) and T.R. Malthus (1820). J.S. Mill (1852) had outlined the possibility of the economy to prolapse to a 'stationary' state. Karl Marx's (1867) prognosis of the collapse of the capitalist economy is epochal. Lord Maynard Keynes (1936) had unravelled the tendency of the capitalist economic system to oscillate between prosperity and depression or 'full employment' and 'unemployment'. Joseph Schumpeter (1939) recognised the stagnation in the economic system as the end result of expansion and vanishing investment opportunities in the economy. Alvin Hansen (1951) also subscribed to the stagnation thesis (secular stagnation) which was popular in the post- second world war era in

Europe and America which experienced 'reaching' the frontiers of growth.

An outline of the classical, neo-classical, modern and post-modern explanation of the crisis of unsustainable development is proposed for the next chapter. A general listing of the many works dealing with sustainable development and related to definition, measurement, association with ecology, environment, society, culture, etc., is attempted here.

Hotelling (1931) outlined the economics of exhaustible resources and its impact on growth.

Pigou (1932) highlighted the loss of social welfare due to loss of environmental values to society.

Rachel (1962) portrayed the havoc to environment caused by reckless exploitation of natural resources for economic development.

Barnett and Morse (1963) highlighted the linkages between natural resource scarcity and the constraint for economic growth.

Boulding (1966) gave an account of the economics of the coming spaceship earth wherein production and consumption are constrained by the growing shortage of inputs under the 'closed' planet or the spaceship earth.

White (1967) traced the historical roots of our environmental crisis.

Daly (1968) established the relationship between economics and ecology and proved it (economics) to be a life-science.

Hardin (1968) illustrated the possibility of over-grazing of common lands and the resulting 'tragedy of the commons'.

Georgescue-Roegen (1971) explained the entropy law and its relationship with the economic process.

Lagault (1971) questioned the 'freedom of the seas' as a 'licence to pollute'.

Ward and Dubas (1972) pleaded for the care and maintenance of our 'small' planet, the 'only one earth'.

Meadows, *et al.* (1974) submitted the first report to the Club of Rome highlighting the 'limits to growth' and the predicament of mankind.

Mesarovic and Pestal (1974) submitted the second report to the Club of Rome showing 'mankind at the turning point'.

Horst (1977) pointed to the mysterious relationship between environmental quality and the gains from trade.

Talbot (1977) wrote on the need and interplay of conservation and economic efficiency as part of an approach to the materials policy of the state.

Ehrenfield (1978) worked out and pointed to the 'arrogance of humanism'.

Das Gupta and Heal (1979) wrote on the economic theory of exhaustible resources.

Sinden and Worrel (1979) noted the existence of 'un-priced values' and the practice of decision making without taking note of market prices.

IUCN (1980)) noted the need for a world conservation strategy for living resources for sustainable development.

Tisdell (1982) highlighted the economics, ecology and ethics of environmental conservation.

Daly (1984) outlined the need and mechanism for operationalising sustainable development by investing in natural capital.

Redclift (1984) wrote on the environmental crisis following economic development and the dilemma of choosing between red or green alternatives to combat the crisis.

Boulding (1985) wrote on the need to consider the world as a 'total' system.

Regier and Baskerville (1986) wrote on the need for sustainable re-development of regional eco-systems degraded by overexploitation and development.

The World Commission on Environment and Development (1987) published its report highlighting the strategies to be followed for securing 'our common future'.

Rees (1988) prepared the background paper defining sustainable development for the conference on planning for sustainable development at the University of British Columbia, Canada.

Svedin (1988) gave a brief illustration of the concept of 'sustainability'.

Tietenberg (1988) gave a brief outline of the sustainability issues and threats to growth.

Berkes (1989) edited the monograph on common property resources and their ecology and community based sustainable development.

Ehrlich (1989) wrote on the limits to substitution following meta-resource depletion and the need for a new economic-ecologic paradigm.

El Serafy and Lutz (1989) gave an overview of environmental resource accounting for *sustainable development.*

The Institution of Engineers of Australia (1989) prepared a draft 'policy' for sustainable development.

MacNeill (1989) outlined the strategies for sustainable development

Milbrath (1989) wrote on finding our way out and envisioning a sustainable society.

Pezzey (1989) gave an economic analysis of sustainable growth and sustainable development.

Simov (1989) questioned whether the 'concept of sustainable development' is a mere theoretical construct or an attainable goal.

Weiss (1989) wrote on international law, common patrimony and intergenerational equity, all in fairness to future generations.

Archibugi and Nijkamp (1990) edited the compendium on economy and ecology directed towards sustainable development.

Archibugi, *et al.* (1990) raised the challenge of sustainable development

Barbier and Markandya (1990) presented the conditions for achieving environmentally sustainable development.

Daly (1990a) gave out some of the operational principles of sustainable development.

Daly (1990b) also spelled out the 'steady state' and the 'growth' concepts for the twenty-first century.

The FAO (1990) highlighted the linkage between sustainable development and natural resource management.

Hueting (1990) gave a critique of the Brundtland Report (Our Common Future) showing it to be a matter of 'conflicting goals'.

James, *et al.* (1990) wrote on ecological sustainability and economic development.

Lombardini (1990) highlighted the interface of economics and ecology.

Lux (1990) argued how a moral philosopher (Adam Smith) invented economics and ended morality, culminating in the crisis of unsustainability.

Mac Neill (1990 a) elaborated the notion of sustainable development, economics and the growth imperative.

Mac Neill (1990 b) wrote on the need for sustaining the momentum on 'Our Common Future'.

Munn (1990) gave an environmental perspective towards sustainable development.

Pearce, *et al.* (1990) gave an outline of the economics and environment in third world and their bearing for sustainable development.

Peet and Peet (1990) argued to work with people's wisdom and for community based perspectives on sustainable development.

Rees (1990) outlined the ecology of sustainable development.

Robinson, *et al.* (1990) tried to define sustainable society, its values and principles.

Simonis (1990) traced the elements of sustainable development, which he presumed to be beyond growth.

The World Bank (1990) brought out its adjustment lending policies for sustainable development.

Christensen (1991) wrote on the driving forces, increasing returns and ecological sustainablity.

Costanza (1991) edited the compilation on ecological economics dealing with the science and management of sustainability.

Cumberland (1991) highlighted the role of intergenerational transfers in ecological sustainability.

Daly (1991a) gave an outline of ecological economics and sustainable development.

Daly (1991b) extended the notion of sustainable development from conceptual theory towards operational principles.

Deadman and Turner (1991) tried to establish linkages between resource conservation, technical change and sustainability.

El Sarafy (1991) conceptualised the 'environment' as 'capital'.

Goodland (1991) argued the case that the world has reached limits to growth.

Goodland, *et al.* (1991) wrote on environmentally sustainable economic development while building on the Brundtland report.

Jansen (1991) explored the linkages between structural adjustment and sustainable development.

Kuik and Verbruggen (1991) probed in search of indicators of sustainable development.

Norgaard and Howarth (1991a) outlined the linkages between economics, ethics and environment.

Norgaard and Howarth (1991b) highlighted the linkages between sustainability and discounting of the future.

Norgaard, *et al.* (1991) interlocked economics, ethics and environment.

O'Riordan (1991) outlined the politics of sustainability.

Pearce (1991) wrote on the sustainable use of natural resources in developing countries.

Perrings (1991) outlined the working of reserved rationality and the precautionary principle and the relevance of technological change, time and uncertainty in environmental decision-making.

Shrybman (1991) wrote on the 'trading away' of environment.

Tinbergen and Hueting (1991) argued the case that GNP and market prices give wrong signals for sustainable economic development and they disguise environmental destructions.

Toman and Crosson (1991) pointed out the need for balancing trade offs and imperatives between economics and environment.

Turner (1991a) edited the works on principles and practice of sustainable environmental management.

Turner (1991b) gave an overview of sustainability, resource conservation and pollution control.

Victor (1991) gave an outline of the indicators of sustainable development and some lessons from capital theory.

Brooks (1992) wrote on sustainability and technology.

Brown, *et. al.* (1992) wrote on saving the planet and how to shape an environmentally sustainable global economy.

Cline (1992) outlined the economics of global warning.

The Commission of the European Communities (1992) brought out the European Community programme of policy and action in relation to the environment and sustainable development.

Common and Perrings (1992) explored to work out a theory of ecological economics and sustainability.

The Commonwealth of Australia (1992) outlined the national strategy for ecologically sustainable development.

Costanza and Daly (1992) explained the significance of natural capital for sustainable development.

Daly and Ehrlich (1992) highlighted the linkage between population, sustainability and earth's carrying capacity.

Daly (1992a) outlined the steady state economics.

Daly (1992 b) wrote on allocation, distribution and scale, closely linking them and moving towards an economics that is efficient, just and sustainable.

Dean (1992) made a survey of the literature linking trade with the environment.

Durning (1992) raised the crucial question of 'how much is enough' and the threat of the consumer society to the future of the earth.

Ekins (1992) presented a 'four capital' model of wealth creation.

Haimes (1992) wrote on a holistic approach to natural resource management and sustainable development.

Howarth, *et al.* (1992) outlined the need for environmental valuation for sustainable development.

Low and Yeats (1992) raised the alarming topical sustainability question, 'do dirty industries migrate'?

Mitlin (1992) offered a guide to the literature on sustainable development.

Norton (1992) wrote on the inter-linkages between sustainability, human welfare and ecosystem health.

Pearce and Atkinson (1992) asked the question, 'are national economies sustainable' and sought to measure sustainable development.

Pearce and Warford (1992) sought to explain the 'world without end' and economics, environment and sustainable development.

Peat (1992) wrote about 'energy' and the ecological economics of sustainability.

Pezzey (1992) outlined the sustainable development concepts for economic analysis.

Redclift (1992) briefly outlined the meaning of sustainable development.

Solow (1992) sought to present an 'almost practical' step towards sustainability.

The UNCED (1992) brought out agenda-21, chapter 17 for the protection of the oceans, all kinds of seas, including enclosed and semi-enclosed seas and coastal areas and the protection, rational use and development of their living resources.

van Gragstak (1992) discussed the political economy of trade and the environment in the United States.

Young (1992) outlined the role of sustainable investment and resource use and their impact on equity, environmental integrity and economic efficiency.

Berkes, *et al.* (1993) explained the importance of traditional ecological knowledge, biodiversity, and resilience for sustainability.

Bishop (1993) wrote on economic efficiency, sustainability and biodiversity.

Daly (1993) outlined the perils of free trade and its impact on sustainable development.

Ekins (1993a) wrote on the 'limits to growth' and 'sustainable development' and the need for grappling with ecological realities.

Ekins (1993b) highlighted the need for making world trade environmentally sustainable without trading off the future.

Hawaken (1993) explained the ecology of commerce as a declaration of sustainability.

Levin (1993) edited the 'forum' perspectives on sustainability.

Meadows, *et al.* (1993) looked 'beyond the limits' for confronting global collapse and envisioning a sustainable future.

Munasinghe (1993) wrote on environmental economics and sustainable development.

Panayotou (1993) explored 'green market' as a basis for the economics of sustainable development.

Pearce (1993) explained the past practice and future prospect of valuation of the environment for sustainable development.

Pearce and Atkinson (1993a) wrote on measuring sustainable development.

Pearce and Atkinson (1993b) linked capital theory with the measurement of sustainable development and as an indicator of 'weak' sustainability hypothesis.

Pearce, *et al.* (1993) gave a blueprint for measuring sustainable development in the United Kingdom.

Prakash and Pearce (1993) sought to define sustainability as resilience while measuring sustainable development.

Prendergast (1993) wrote on engineering sustainable development.

Riedel (1993) explored biodiversity prospecting and using genetic resources for sustainable development.

Serageldin (1993) wrote on making development sustainable.

Solow (1993a) gave an economist's perspective on 'weak' sustainability which was quite regressive.

Solow (1993b) restated his position as 'an almost practical step toward sustainability'.

Tamanaha (1993) pointed out the folly of the 'social scientific' concept of legal pluralism which can wreck social harmony vital for sustainability.

Turner (1993) edited the work on sustainable environmental economics and management.

Beckerman (1994) expressed the doubt as to whether sustainable development is a useful concept.

Berkes and Folke (1994) pleaded for investing in cultural capital for sustainable use of natural capital.

Cropper and Charles (1994) highlighted the interactions of population growth and environmental quality.

Cumberland (1994) recognised the role of ecology, economic incentives and public policy in the design of trans-disciplinary pollution control instruments.

Daly (1994) offered 'parting' suggestions for the World Bank for fostering environmentally sustainable development.

Daly and Cobb (1994) wrote on redirecting the economy toward community, the environment and a sustainable future for the common good.

Daly and Goodland (1994) offered an ecological economic assessment of deregulation of international commerce under GATT.

Folke, *et al.* (1994) suggested investing in natural capital and explained 'why, what and how' about it.

de Groot (1994) studied the functions and values of protected areas and offered a comprehensive framework for assessing the benefits of protected areas to human society.

Ekins and Jacobs (1994) raised the question whether environmental sustainability and economic growth are compatible.

Goodland (1994) dwelt on environmental sustainability.

Jansson, *et al.* (1994) argued for investing in natural capital as the ecological approach to sustainability.

Kummer (1994) viewed the transboundary movements of hazardous wastes at the interface of environment and trade as a threat to sustainability.

Naem, *et al.* (1994) argued that declining biodiversity can alter the performance of the ecosystem and have implications for sustainability.

Norgaard (1994) attempted a co-evolutionary re-visioning of the future, following the betrayal of development and the end of progress.

OECD (1994) outlined the environmental effects of trade.

Owen (1994) studied the issues of land, limits, and sustainability, and gave a conceptual framework and some dilemmas of the planning system.

Panayotou (1994) outlined the economic instruments for environmental management and sustainable development.

Pearce and Moran (1994) highlighted the economic value of biodiversity.

Pearce and Atkinson (1994)) briefly explained the meaning of sustainable development.

Rees and Wakernagel (1994) traced the concepts of 'ecological footprints' and 'appropriated carrying capacity', and tried to measure the natural capital requirements of the human economy.

The Thailand Environment Institute (1994a) studied the internal linkages between trade and environment.

The Thailand Environment Institute (1994b) appealed for applying the polluter-pay-principle and noted it was time for action.

van den Bergh, *et al.* (1994) edited and outlined the concepts, methods and policy towards sustainable development.

Victor, *et al.* (1994) raised the significant question, "how strong is 'weak sustainability' hypothesis?"

von Moltke (1994) probed the implications of the World Trade Organisation for sustainable development.

World Bank (1994) reported on making development sustainable.

Baldwin (1995) raised the fundamental question, 'does sustainability require growth?'

Beltratti, *et al.* (1995) tried to link sustainability with the green golden rule.

Bromley (1995) edited the handbook on environmental economics.

Carraro and Domenico (1995) wrote on policy coordination for sustainability and the need for commitments, transfers and linked negotiations.

Common (1995) pointed out 'sustainability and policy' as 'limits to economics'.

Costanza and Patten (1995) made an attempt for defining and predicting sustainability.

Daly (1995) wrote in response to Wilfred Beckerman's critique of sustainable development.

Dean (1995) studied the linkages between export bans, environment and developing country welfare.

Ekins (1995) wrote on harnessing trade to sustainable development.

Ekins and Jacobs (1995) discussed environmental sustainability and the growth of GDP and conditions for compatibility.

Goodland (1995) once again outlined the concept of environmental sustainability.

Grossman (1995) tried to explain the interaction between pollution and growth.

Hammond, *et al.* (1995) tried to develop environmental indicators for a systematic approach to measuring and reporting on environmental policy performance in the context of sustainable development.

Jacobs (1995) wrote on sustainable development, capital substitution and economic humility in response to Beckerman.

Munasinghe and McNeely (1995) spelled out the concepts and terminology of sustainable development.

Munasinghe and Shearer (1995) sought to define and measure sustainability in relation to its biological foundations.

Nagpal and Folke (1995) outlined the visions of a sustainable world and the need for choosing our future.

Norton and Michael (1995) gave the ecological and economic perspectives of sustainability.

O'Connor (1995) studied the political economy and politics of ecology and raised the historical question – 'is capitalism sustainable?'

Panayotou (1995) studied the environmental degradation at different stages of economic development.

Pearce and Atkinson (1995) wrote on measuring sustainable development.

Rees (1995) conjectured whether reform or transformation will help in achieving sustainability.

Reid (1995) gave an introduction to sustainable development.

Scott (1995) sought to explain what sustains economic development.

Toman, *et al.* (1995) highlighted the linkage between neo-classical economic growth theory and sustainability.

Beckerman (1996) presented a skeptical view of sustainable development.

Bergh and Vanden (1996) outlined the theory, methods and applications in ecological economics and sustainable development.

Bruce, *et al.* (1996) discussed the economic and social dimensions of climate change.

Clayton and Radclife (1996) gave a systems approach to sustainability.

Costanza, *et al.* (1996) outlined the practical applications of ecological economics.

Daly (1996) showed that beyond growth there is the economics of sustainable development.

Dobson (1996) gave an analysis and a typology of environmental sustainability.

El Serafy (1996) wrote in defence of 'weak' sustainability as a response to Beckerman.

Faber, *et al.* (1996) outlined the role of science and ethics in sustainable development.

The International Institute for Sustainable Development (1996) made an independent assessment of the World Trade Organisation and sustainable development.

Lafferty (1996) outlined the politics of sustainable development and the global norms for national implementation.

McMahon and Mrozek (1996) discussed the principles of economics, entropy and sustainability.

Meadows (1996) wrote envisioning a sustainable world.

Opschoor, *et al.* (1996) wrote on the Brettonwoods intervention programmes and sustainable development.

Perman, *et al.* (1996) discussed the concepts of sustainability and sustainable development.

Prescott (1996) suggested the use of a 'barometer' of sustainability and explained 'what it is for' and 'how to use it'.

Rees (1996) discussed the need for 'revisiting' the concept of 'carrying capacity' and using area-based indicators of sustainability.

Rees and Wackernagel (1996) highlighted the importance of urban ecological footprints and why cities cannot be sustainable and why they are a key to sustainability.

Serageldin (1996) prepared a monograph on sustainability and the wealth of nations.

Stern, *et al.* (1996) wrote on economic growth and environmental degradation and the possibility of environmental Kuznets curve and sustainable development.

Atkinson, *et al.* (1997) wrote on the macro-economic and environmental dimensions of measuring sustainable development.

Costanza, *et al.* (1997) gave an introduction to ecological economics.

Dean and Gangopadhyay (1997) explored the association between export bans, environmental protection and unemployment, all having implications for sustainability.

Eskeland and Harrison (1997) examined the tendency of multinationals moving to greener pastures and the 'pollution-haven' hypothesis.

Flint (1997) examined the biological diversity of developing countries.

Folke, *et al.* (1997) highlighted the ecosystem appropriation by cities.

Goodland (1997a) outlined the biophysical objective and sustainability issues.

Goodland (1997b) discussed the 'universal' and 'rigorous' issues of environmental sustainability.

Lesser, *et al.* (1997) outlined the linkages between economic growth, environment and sustainability.

Markandya (1997) outlined the criteria for sustainable agricultural development.

Meadowcroft (1997) discussed planning, democracy and the challenge of sustainable development.

Norton and Toman (1997) hightlighted the ecological and economic perspectives of sustainability.

Pearce (1997) drew attention to the economics of global environmental challenges.

Pezzey (1997) recognised several constraints, viz. sustainability versus optimality, optimality versus inter-temporal concerns, and axioms versus data.

Rees (1997) explored the question whether sustainability is an 'oxymoron' term.

Rennings and Wiggering (1997) outlined the steps towards indicators of sustainable development and for linking economic and ecological concepts.

Victor (1997) gave an outline of some indicators for sustainable development, drawing some lessons from capital theory.

Vincent, *et al.* (1997) discussed the problem of resource depletion and sustainability in small open economies.

Ayers and Weaver (1998) discussed eco-restructuring and its implication for sustainable development.

Barbier (1998) outlined the concepts of sustainable development and natural capital and the economics of environment and development.

Heal (1998) explored the value of the future and its economic theory and sustainability.

Kageson (1998) discussed the concept of sustainable development, growth versus environment and whether there is a trade off between the two.

Lutz (1998) reviewed agriculture and the environment with perspectives on sustainable rural development.

Maravasti (1998) made an assessment of the international technology transfer systems and the new law of the sea.

Pearce (1998) brought out essays on ecological economics and sustainable development.

Pearce, *et al.* (1998) wrote on the measurement of sustainable development.

Strutt and Anderson (1998) explored whether trade liberalisation will harm environment and studied the case of Indonesia by 2020.

vanden Bergh and Hofkes (1998) made a survey of economic modelling of sustainable development.

World Resources Institute (1998) prospected for building a safe climate for a sound business future.

Achterberg (1999) highlighted the importance of basic income while planning for sustainability.

Beaton and Maser (1999) emphasised the need for reuniting economy and ecology in sustainable development.

Bromley (1999) outlined the importance of environmental resources in developing countries for sustaining development.

Daly (1999) outlined the 'steady-state' economics and the need for avoiding un-economic growth.

Dragun (1999) emphasised the linkages between trade liberalisation, agriculture and sustainability.

Dragun and Tisdell (1999) edited the studies on sustainable agriculture and environment, keeping in view the impact of trade liberalisation and globalisation.

Hanley, *et al.* (1999) outlined the economics of sustainable development.

Jacobs (1999) studied sustainability and markets with emphasis on the neo-classical model of environmental economics.

Kenny and Meadowcroft (1999) edited the studies on planning sustainability.

Loucks and Gladwell (1999) edited the studies on sustainability criteria for water resource systems.

Meadowcroft (1999a) outlined the politics of sustainable development, the emergent trends and the challenge for political science.

Meadowcroft (1999b) reviewed the planning for sustainable development and considered what can be learned from critics.

Redclift (1999) studied the pathways to sustainability, focusing on issues, policies and theories.

Rees (1999) analysed the scale, complexity and the conundrum of sustainability.

Tisdell (1999a) examined the 'weak' and 'strong' conditions for sustainable development.

Tisdell (1999b) studied economics, aspects of ecology and sustainable agricultural production.

Tisdell and Dragun (1999) discussed the impact of trade liberalisation on agriculture and sustainability.

Gilpin (2000) gave an overview of sustainable development.

Heal (2000) gave an account of markets and sustainability.

Panayotou (2000) outlined the interface of environment and growth.

Pearson (2000) gave a detailed perspective on sustainable development, its measurement and the interface of trade, environment and sustainability.

Sands (2000) discussed the issue of environmental protection in the twenty-first century and the relevance of international law to ensure sustainable development.

van Kooten and Bulte (2000) discussed the issues of sustainable development and conservation.

Salih (2001) sought to suggest a balancing act in the face of emerging globalisation, sustainable development and environment.

Khor (2002) gave an account of the impacts of globalisation and the challenges before the Johannesburg summit of 2002 for sustainable development.

Goodstein (2002) gave a neo-classical and ecological view of sustainability.

Bigg (2004) reported the sustainable development agenda presented by many 'civil society' organisations (NGOs) at the World Summit on Sustainable Development (WSSD).

von Moltke (2004) outlined the trade and sustainable development issues in the Doha Round meet of the WTO.

Jenkins (2005) outlined the socio-cultural dimensions of ecological economics and sustainable rural development.

Young (2005) enquired whether there are necessary or desirable institutional conditions for sustainable use of renewable natural resources.

Now, looking back and taking stock of the above review, it appears that the international theoretical literature on sustainable development is quite advanced and expanding. Starting with the incidental thoughts of classical, Marxian, neo-classical and modern writers in general economics and welfare economics, the literature has its boom in the writings of contemporary ecological economists and other institutional writers attached to OECD, World Bank, International Institute for Sustainable Development, etc.

The contemporary international literature on sustainable development focused primarily on definitions, measurement, establishing linkages between environment (ecology), economy (economics), society (culture), institutions, and sustainable economic order. The majority of studies found over-exploitation of the natural resource base (natural capital) as the main cause of unsustainability. Many of these studies argued for investing in natural capital for sustaining development. Some of the studies were found concentrating on technological change as the focal point for sustainability. Some recent studies favoured bioprospecting for sustainable development.

A good number of studies dealt with criteria and indicators of sustainable development. Many studies observed the prevalence of a trade off between environment and sustainability, environment and trade and between economic growth and sustainability. Some recent studies also probed the association between trade liberalisation (globalisation) and sustainability. Some studies even questioned the very concept of sustainable development. A general scanning of the international theoretical literature on sustainable development would also show a certain amount of continuity and progression in its mission, mode and strategy. A further scrutiny of this literature is partly attempted in chapter three.

## 2.3. Applied Fisheries Literature

The applied fisheries literature is classified and reviewed as national and international literature separately.

### 2.3.1. National Literature

The national applied fisheries literature, like the national general theoretical literature on sustainable development is very scanty. There is, however, some sign of growth since the 1990s. Some of the traceable studies are noted here.

Prakash, *et al.* (1990) studied the economic viability of aquaculture in sewage fed farms.

Das and Das (1995) made a review of fish disease in India.

Joseph, *et al.* (1995) made a case study of the impact of shrimp farming on the environment in India.

Krishna (1995) reported on technology transfer for sustainable shrimp farming in India.

Kutty (1995) reviewed aquaculture development and sustainability in southeast Asia.

Phillips (1995) studied the relationship between shrimp culture and the environment.

Sathiadhas, *et al.* (1995) suggested marine fisheries management for sustainable development.

Verghese (1995) highlighted the importance of aquaculture production to augment export of marine products from India.

Sathiadhas (1996) wrote on the economic evaluation of marine fisheries of India for sustainable production and coastal zone development.

The Supreme Court of India (1996) gave its verdict in the case related to unsustainable aquaculture activities in India.

Anonymous (1997) argued for ecology based fishery management in Aliyar reservoir in Kerala.

Devaraj (1997) explained the need for promoting ecofriendly mariculture in India.

Ayyappan and Jena (1998) suggested a sustainable farming practice for carp culture in India.

Devaraj, *et al.* (1998) explored the new economic policy and perspectives for marine fisheries research and development in India.

Kurien (1998) explained the importance of traditional ecological knowledge and ecosystem sustainability and tried to find new meaning to Asian coastal proverbs.

Paulraj, *et al.* (1998) made a case study of environmental and social issues in coastal aquaculture in India.

Vohra (1998) outlined the trends in fisheries development in Gujarat.

Devaraj, *et al.* (1999) reviewed coastal zone governance in Kerala in relation to national and international situations.

Devaraj and Vivekanandan (1999) discussed the challenges and opportunities in marine capture fisheries of India.

Gopakumar (1999) outlined the strategies for increasing inland fish production in India.

James (1999) gave an overview of environmental, socio-economic, legal and other implications of shrimp farming development in India.

Kutty (1999a) discussed aquaculture development in India from a global perspective.

Kutty (1999b) pointed out the imperatives of aquaculture development and sustainable environment.

Somvanshi (1999) discussed the resource potential and conservation measures in capture fisheries in India.

Krishna, *et al.* (2000) suggested group farming for sustainable aquaculture.

Parthasarathi and Nirmala (2000) discussed the economics and environmental issues of brackish water aquaculture.

Selvan and Ramaswamy (2000) studied the socio-economic and environmental impacts of shrimp farming.

Abidi and Biradar (2001) outlined the changing needs of fisheries education in India.

Ayyappan and Jena (2001) pleaded for sustainable freshwater aquaculture in India.

Bhatta (2001) gave an account of production, accessibility and consumption pattern of aquaculture products in India.

Bavenik (2001) explained the marine resource management conflict and regulation in the fisheries of the Coromandel coast of India.

Kumar, *et al.* (2001) gave an overview of performance, policies and programmes for fisheries sector in India.

Pandian (2001) edited the compendium on 'Sustainable Indian Fisheries' and gave a prelude for Indian fisheries policy.

Planning Commission (2001) brought out the report of the working group on fisheries for the tenth five year plan.

Rao and Ravichandran (2001) gave a perspective account of sustainable brackish water aquaculture in India.

Sakthivel (2001a) outlined the challenging tasks for sustainable fisheries development in the millennium 2000.

Sakthivel (2001b) discussed the need for a legal framework for sustainable aquaculture.

Somvanshi (2001) discussed the problems and prospects of deep sea and far sea fishing by India.

Sugunan and Sinha (2001) discussed the methods for sustainable capture and culture based fisheries in freshwaters of India.

Vivekanandan (2001) pleaded for sustainable coastal fisheries for nutritional security.

Anonymous (2002) reported on the state-wise status of shrimp culture in India reviewed at the expert consultation on sustainable shrimp farming in India held at Chennai during August 2002.

Katiha and Bhatta (2002) outlined the past trends, present status and future prospects of production and consumption of aquaculture products in India.

Korakandy (2002) noted the sustainability issues of Indian fisheries.

Planning Commission (2002) outlined the fisheries component of the tenth five year plan (2002-2007) of India.

Boopendranath, *et al.* (2003) edited the compendium titled 'Sustainable Fisheries Development' with focus on the Gujarat state of India.

Kumar and Kumar (2003) wrote on the food safety measures and their implications for fisheries sector in India.

Kumar (2003) gave a broad review of sustainability and management of aquaculture and fisheries.

Datta and Chakrabarti (2004) outlined the Indian scenario and management perspective for sustainable marine fisheries under globalised market conditions.

Divan, *et al.* (2004) pointed out the need for new dimensions in marine fisheries management for sustainable development.

The National Centre for Agricultural Economics and Policy Research (NCAP) and World Fish Centre (2004) brought out the strategies and options for increasing and sustaining fisheries and aquaculture production to benefit poor households in India.

Reddy, *et al.* (2004) reported on the prioritisation of fisheries research in India.

Sinha (2004) gave a conceptual analysis of large marine ecosystems (LMEs), ecologically critical areas (ECAs) and sustainable management of India's marine biodiversity.

Radhakrishnan and Vijyakumaran (2004) outlined the status of lobster fishery in India and options for sustainable management.

Somvanshi (2004) brought out the papers presented at the international symposium on *Large Marine Eco-systems: Exploration and Exploitation for Sustainable Development and Conservation of Fish Stocks* held at Cochin during November, 1998.

Ayyappan and Srinath (2005) discussed the sustainability issues of marine fisheries in India.

Boopendranath, *et. al.* (2005) edited another compendium titled *Sustainable Fisheries Development* with focus on Andhra Pradesh.

Devadasan (2005) outlined the CIFT initiatives for responsible fishing operations in India.

Kadekodi and Nayampalli (2005) explained the biodiversity degradation of Chilka lake.

Kurien (2005) gave a different perspective for fisheries co-management.

Korakandy (2005a) studied the political economy of coastal zone management in Kerala and its impact on the sustainable development of the coast and its fisheries.

Korakandy (2005b) offered some comments on sustainable development of Indian fisheries.

Korakandy (2005c) offered further comments on the sustainability of Indian fisheries.

Kurup, *et al.* (2005) brought out the souvenir *Sustain Fish 2005.*

Kurup and Manojkumar (2005) explained habitat conservation as the ultimate 'impulsion' for fisheries sustainability.

Kutty (2005) discussed the development of sustainable aquaculture systems.

Modayil (2005) explained the ways and means of ensuring sustainability in the open access marine fisheries of India.

Rajasenan (2005) sought to explain the dynamics and challenges in marine fishing in Kerala.

Roshada (2005) discussed the feeds and feeding connection in sustaining aquaculture development.

Srinath and Pillai (2005) reviewed the trend in marine fish production in India and outlined the approach to responsible fisheries management.

Somvanshi (2005) explained the advances in exploratory survey and fish stock assessment in the seas around India.

Velayudhan (2005) outlined the status of freshwater prawn farming in Kerala with special reference to sustainable development.

Vijayan, *et al.* (2005) discussed the disease related crop failures and factors affecting the sustainability of shrimp aquaculture in India.

Jyothishi and Parthasarathy (2007) outlined some of the sustainability issues of reservoir fisheries in India making a case study of the Tawa reservoir in Madhya Pradesh.

It appears from the above review of the applied national fisheries literature that the majority of them are dealing with the issue of aquaculture development, most of them advocating the promotion intensive aquaculture for enhancing fish supplies and others suggesting balanced growth, caring for the environment and its sustainability. A few writings dealt with the sustainability of marine fisheries, with respect to environment, technology, output, cost, etc. Quite a few studies were also dealing with coastal fishermen and their social life. What is quite dismaying about the domestic applied fisheries literature is the fact that scarcely any study discussed the sustainability issues systematically, following or evolving some theoretical or practical criteria for sustainability. The majority of these writings seems to have used the term *sustainable development* and *sustainability* in a very general sense with no definite understanding of the concept even after the turn of the last decade. Indeed the bulk of this literature is written in 'low visibility journals' (Jayashree and Subbaiah, 2001, p.306), A few writing have, no doubt, mechanically tried to recommend some of the received western institutional models in their prescription for sustainable development of Indian fisheries. The paper by Datta and Chakrabarti (Datta and Chakrabarti, 2004) is a good example for this. The domestic literature is by and large devoid of any theoretical rigour and comprehensiveness.

### 2.3.2. International Literature

The international literature on sustainability and sustainable development of fisheries is remarkably advanced and still growing. A brief note of the accessed literature is offered here.

Gordon (1954) outlined the economic theory of a common property resource (fishery) and pointed out the tendency for dissipation of profit in the long run and its eventual collapse.

Christy and Scott (1965) highlighted the tendency of open access fisheries becoming uneconomic in the long run and the failure of market and technological changes in arresting this tendency.

Wilen (1976) made a case study of the North-Pacific Fur Seal as a common property resource and the dynamics of its overexploitation.

Larkin (1977) questioned the validity and the 'maximum sustainable yield' concept as a tool for fisheries management.

Pearson (1982) explained the environmental policies and their trade implications for developing countries with special reference to fish, shellfish and vegetables under the UNCTAD regime.

FAO (1984) brought out the report of the FAO World Conference on Fisheries Management and Development, which spelled out its strategy for global fisheries management.

Bailey (1988) outlined the political economy of fisheries development.

Primavara (1989) discussed the social, ecological and economic implications of intensive prawn farming.

Mc Goodwin (1990) outlined the crisis in world fisheries with special reference to people, problems and policies.

New (1990) reported that shrimp farming was experiencing environmental problems, world-wide.

The FAO Committee on Fisheries (1991) discussed the issues of environment and sustainability in fisheries.

The Indo-Pacific Fisheries Commission (1991) brought out the report of the symposium on artificial reefs and fish aggregating devices as tools for the management and enhancement of marine fishery resources.

The Joint Group of Experts on the Scientific Aspects of Marine Pollution (1991) discussed the imperatives of reducing the environmental impacts of coastal aquaculture.

Pullin (1991) gave an overview of environmental issues in developing country aquaculture development.

Barg (1992) provided guidelines for the promotion of environmental management of coastal aquaculture development.

Folke and Kautsky (1992) considered aquaculture with its environment and the prospects for sustainability.

Hodgson and Dixon (1992) analysed the environmental and economic effects of sedimentation damages to marine resources.

The World Bank (1992) made a study of international fisheries research.

Christie (1993) attempted developing the concept of sustainable fisheries.

Cicin-Sain (1993) outlined the significance of integrated coastal zone management for sustainable development.

FAO (1993a) reviewed the changes in world marine fisheries, a decade after the passing of the Law of the Sea in 1982.

FAO (1993b) outlined the need for conservation and rational utilisation of living marine resources with special reference to responsible fishing.

FAO (1993c) highlighted the implications of UNCED for fisheries.

Hammer, *et al.* (1993) outlined the concepts of diversity, change and sustainability and their implications for fisheries.

Hancock (1993) brought out the studies on sustainable fisheries through sustaining fish habitat.

Orrego (1993) argued for the settlement of pending issues of the law of the sea and to move towards effective management of high seas fisheries.

Sherman (1993) gave an ecological perspective of large marine ecosystems as global units for marine resources management.

Sissenwine and Rosenberg (1993) reported the state of marine fisheries being at a critical juncture.

Willmann and Insull (1993) argued for integrated coastal fisheries management.

Appolonio (1994) advocated the use of ecosystem characteristics in fisheries management.

Charles (1994) outlined the move towards sustainability and the fishery experience.

Dyer and McGoodwin (1994) reviewed cases of folk management in world fisheries and suggested lessons for modern fisheries management.

Garcia (1994a) explained the 'precautionary' principle and its implication in capture fisheries management.

Garcia (1994b) outlined the precautionary approach to fisheries with special reference to straddling fish stocks and highly migratory fish stocks.

Gimbel (1994) edited the work suggesting limiting access to marine fisheries and keeping focus on conservation.

Harden (1994) prescribed ecologically sustainable development of fisheries.

Holden (1994) traced the origin, made evaluations and probed the future of common fisheries policy of Europe.

Ruddle (1994) examined the role of local knowledge in the folk management of fisheries and coastal marine environment.

The United Nations Environment Programme (1994) reported the impacts of climate on fisheries.

Anderson (1995) explained the role of individual transferable quotas (ITQs) as a technique for privatising open access fisheries.

Bagarino and Flores (1995) suggested the move towards sustainable aquaculture in south east Asia and Japan.

Caddy and Griffiths (1995) gave some environmental and institutional perspectives for the sustainable development of living marine resources.

Caddy and Mahon (1995) suggested reference points for fishery management.

Charles (1995) presented sustainability assessment and bio-socio-economic analysis as tools for integrated coastal development.

Doeringer and Terkla (1995) found the global economic structure, regulatory reform and fisheries trade in troubled waters.

FAO (1995a) outlined the precautionary approach to fisheries management, part one being guidelines on the precautionary approach to capture fisheries and species introduction.

FAO (1995b) outlined the code of conduct for responsible fisheries.

Government of Japan and FAO (1995a) revealed the key policy issues and measures for safeguarding future fish supplies.

Government of Japan and FAO (1995 b) outlined the demand and supply of fish and fish products in selected areas of the world and the perspectives and implications for food security.

Jentoft and McCay (1995) outlined user participation in fisheries management and the lessons drawn from international experience.

Lane and Stephenson (1995) gave a framework to link biological, economic and social objectives in fisheries management.

McGoodwin (1995) discussed the culture based conflicts in the use of the living marine resources and gave suggestions for resolving or mitigating such conflicts.

Pauly and Christensen (1995) outlined the primary production required to sustain global fisheries.

Pinkerton and Weinstein (1995) suggested that fisheries work or achieve sustainability through community based management.

Pomeroy (1995) recommended community based co-management institutions for sustainable coastal fisheries management in south east Asia.

Rogers (1995) expressed the fear that oceans are emptying and the 'fish wars' affect their sustainability.

Crean and Symes (1996) brought out the writings which show fisheries management in Europe in crisis.

Drummond and Symes (1996) made a rethinking on sustainable development as a realistic paradigm.

Dunn (1996) outlined the sustainability indicators for fisheries.

Fegan (1996) wondered whether sustainable shrimp farming in Asia is a vision or a pipe-dream.

FAO (1996a) outlined the precautionary approach to capture fisheries and species introduction.

FAO (1996b) explained the integration of fisheries in to coastal area management.

Garcia (1996) gave an updated review of the precautionary approach to fisheries and its implication for fisheries research, technology and management.

Info-fish (1996) brought out extracts on Kyoto declaration and plan of action for the sustainable contribution of fisheries to food security.

Korakandy (1996) gave a critique of the global theory of fisheries management and its implications for third world fisheries.

Macintosh (1996) suggested doing something positive for the environment of mangroves and coastal aquaculture.

Resources for the Future (1996) recommended the transition to a new 'industry' founded on 'rights based fishing'.

Ridmontri (1996) hypothesised that a temporal shrimp import ban could be good for 'resources'.

United Nations (1996) brought out the provisions of the agreement for the implementation of the United Nations Convention on the Law of the Sea of 10 December 1982 relating to the conservation and management of straddling fish stocks and highly migratory fish stocks.

Barg and Phillip (1997) explained the environmental sustainability of fisheries.

Charles (1997a) prepared an annotated bibliography of sustainability indicators with emphasis on fishery systems, coastal zones and watersheds.

Charles (1997b) outlined the path to sustainable fisheries.

Corbin and Young (1997) explained planning, regulation and administration of sustainable aquaculture.

FAO (1997a) brought out the review of the state of world fishery resources (marine fisheries).

FAO (1997 b) presented the technical guidelines for fisheries management.

FAO (1997c) provided the technical guidelines for inland fisheries.

Garcia (1997) explained the indicators of sustainable development of fisheries, land quality indicators and their use in sustainable aquaculture and rural development.

Garcia and Grainger (1997) considered fisheries management and sustainability as a new perspective of an old problem.

Garcia and Newton (1997) discussed the current situation, trends and prospects in capture fisheries.

Golding and Triplett (1997) described the environmental effects of aquaculture in the US as falling in the realm of murky waters.

Hancock, *et al.* (1997) edited the proceedings of the second World Fisheries Congress for developing and sustaining world fisheries resources and focusing on the state of science and management.

Jesdapipat and Piyawadee (1997) studied the impact of eco-tax on shrimp farming and mangrove protection in Thailand.

Mace (1997) published the keynote paper, 'Developing and Sustaining World Fisheries Resources: The State of Science and Management' prepared for the second World Fisheries Congress at Brisbane, Australia, during 28 July - 2 August 1996.

Nielson and Vedsmand (1997) gave the perspectives on fishermen's organisations in fisheries management (co-management) based on Danish fisheries.

OECD (1997) discussed the economic aspects of management of living marine resources for sustainable fisheries.

Roberts (1997) sought to provide 'ecological advice' for the global fisheries crisis.

Rojer, *et al.* (1997) sought to move towards policies for conservation and sustainable uses of aquatic genetic resources.

Springer (1997) explained the Canadian 'turbot war' with Spain as a unilateral action in defense of environmental interests.

Willmann (1997) made a preliminary assessment of certification and eco-labelling in marine fisheries.

ADB and NACA (1998) brought out the report of a regional study and workshop on 'aquaculture sustainability and the environment'.

Chesson and Clayton (1998) offered a framework for assessing fisheries with respect to ecologically sustainable development.

Downes and Brennan (1998) examined fisheries conservation and trade rules and sought to ensure that they promote sustainable fisheries.

Folke, *et al.* (1998) made a review of the 'ecological footprint' concept for sustainable seafood production.

Hammer (1998) outlined the adoption of an ecosystem approach to the conservation and sustainable use of biological diversity, also called as the 'Malawi principle'.

Loucks, *et al.* (1998) edited and published the report on self-management titled 'managing our fisheries, managing ourselves'.

The Marine Stewardship Council (1998) prepared the Arlie House Draft principles and criteria for sustainable fisheries.

Miles (1998) outlined the concept of ocean governance, its evolution towards the twenty-first century and the principle of sustainable ocean use.

Mooney (1998) suggested ecosystem management for sustainable marine fisheries.

NRTEE (1998) prepared a co-management guide towards sustainable strategies for oceans.

Nunes and Parsons (1998) outlined the dynamics of tropical coastal aquaculture systems and the consequences of waste production.

Pitcher, *et al.* (1998) edited the work titled 'Re-inventing Fisheries Management' which sought to discover old concepts and practices in fisheries management in Europe.

Pitcher and Pauly (1998) showed that rebuilding ecosystems, not sustainability, is the proper goal of fishery management.

Ric (1998) explained the crisis in world fisheries and the need to respond.

Sutton (1998) suggested harnessing market forces and consumer power in favour of sustainable fisheries.

WTO (1998a) outlined the background to the WTO work on trade and environment by the WTO.

WTO (1998b) discussed the market access impact of eco-labelling requirements.

Collect (1999) argued for a paradigm shift from unsustainable resource use to governance of marine ecosystem, noting the functions and role of the ethics of the sea.

Deere (1999) outlined eco-labelling and sustainability of fisheries.

FAO (1999 a) outlined the state of world fisheries and aquaculture.

FAO (1999 b) brought out the indicators for sustainable development of marine capture fisheries.

Edward (1999) outlined the influence of a century of macro economic changes on U.S. fisheries production.

Garcia, *et. al.* (1999) worked out a strategy for FAO and World Bank towards sustainable fisheries.

Gladstone, *et al.* (1999) explained the issues, needs and strategic actions for the sustainable use of renewable resources and conservation in the Red Sea and Gulf of Aden.

Hatcher and Robinson (1999) discussed the relationship between overcapacity, overcapitalisation and subsidies in European fisheries.

Lery, *et al.* (1999) reported the findings of a global study and an interregional workshop on economic viability of marine capture fisheries.

Long (1999) advocated the Marine Stewardship Council initiative and the development of a market incentive approach to achieving sustainable fisheries.

NMFS (1999) published the ecosystem based fishery management plan, being a report to the Congress by the Ecosystem Principles Advisory Panel.

NRC (1999) prepared the plan for sustaining marine fisheries of the U.S.

New (1999) outlined the third generation farming technology for sustainable shrimp farming in the tropics.

Pullin, *et al.* (1999) edited the proceedings of the conference on sustainable use of aquatic biodiversity and the need for data, tools and cooperation, held at Lisbon during 3-5 September 1998.

Sherman and Duda (1999) highlighted large marine ecosystem as an emerging paradigm for fishery sustainability.

Tsamenyi and Alistair (1999) discussed the international environmental instruments and their effect on the fishing industry.

Williams (1999) discussed factoring fish into food security and policy issues.

Andy and Elizabeth (2000) explained the Latin American fisheries, globalisation and the sustainability debate.

Anonymous (2000a) brought out the Australian Commonwealth Government Guidelines for the assessment of sustainable fisheries.

Charles (2000) suggested sustainability assessment for Novascotia's fisheries and to move towards a genuine progress index.

Cochrane (2000) outlined the reconciling of sustainability, economic efficiency and equity in fisheries and the one that got away.

Deere (2000) considered the net gains of linking fisheries management, international trade and sustainable development.

Coffey (2000) discussed European funding for sustainable development of 'fisheries dependent' regions.

FAO (2000 a) discussed the state of world fisheries and aquaculture.

FAO (2000 b) outlined the implications of globalisation for international fish trade and food security.

FAO (2000 c) discussed the demographic change in coastal fishing communities and its implications for the coastal environment.

Frank and Pascal (2000) discussed fisheries and the internationalisation of markets.

Garcia (2000) outlined the FAO definition of sustainable development and the code of conduct for responsible fisheries and the related principles, criteria and indicators.

Garcia and Stapples (2000) made a review of concepts and elements for a set of guidelines for sustainability indicators for marine capture fisheries.

Garcia, *et al.* (2000) discussed the FAO guidelines for the development and use of indicators for sustainable development of marine capture fisheries and an Australian example of their application.

Greiner, *et al.* (2000) outlined the incentive instruments for the sustainable use of marine resources.

Gudmudsson and Cathy (2000) discussed eco-labelling of seafood for sustainable production and its implication for fisheries management.

Miller (2000) noted the fluid sovereignty of third world states and its impact on development options and the politics of sustainable ocean management.

NFI (2000) outlined fisheries industry principles for responsible fisheries.

OECD (2000) reviewed the economic and policy implications of the transition to responsible fisheries.

Pajack (2000) discussed the need for thinking globally and acting locally in the 21st century for sustainability, ecosystem management and indicators.

Schmidt (2000) outlined the lessons learned from past experience regarding traceability in fisheries and pointed out what the consumer wants and the government needs to do.

Sumaila, *et al.* (2000) edited the proceedings of the international workshop on markets, global fisheries and local development, held at Bergen, Norway during 22-23 March 1999.

Symes (2000) gave a critical review of the common fisheries policy of Europe and the future for fishery dependent regions.

Wilson (2000) discussed the development challenges in trade associated with sanitary and phyto-sanitary standards.

WHAT (2000) brought out its second report on governance for a sustainable future, dealing with fishing for the future.

Charles (2001) gave a detailed account of sustainable fishery systems.

FAO (2001a) discussed ecosystem based fisheries management and the opportunities and challenges for coordination between marine regional seas conventions.

FAO (2001b) made a cross-country comparison of production, accessibility, marketing and consumption pattern of fresh water aquaculture products in Asia.

GESAMP (2001) discussed planning and management for sustainable coastal aquaculture development.

Pitcher (2001) argued that ecosystem goals can reinvigorate fisheries management, help dispute resolution and encourage public support.

Wessels, *et al.* (2001) explained product certification and eco-labelling for fisheries sustainability.

FAO (2002) reviewed and outlined the state of world fisheries and aquaculture with focus on selected issues facing fishers and aquaculture.

Greboval (2002) edited the report of the international workshop on factors contributing to unsustainability and overexploitation in fisheries, held at Bangkok during February 2002.

Aqorau (2003) outlined the obligations to protect marine ecosystems under international conventions and other legal instruments.

Bordal (2003) highlighted large scale industry perspectives for incorporating ecosystem considerations into fisheries management.

Delgado, *et al.* (2003) brought out 'Fish 2020' projecting the supply and demand for fish in the changing global markets.

Garcia (2003) discussed the ecosystem approach to fisheries.

Garcia and Moreno (2003) gave a global overview of marine fisheries.

Katherine (2003) outlined the anthropogenically induced changes in the environment and their effects on fisheries.

Keith and Sumaila (2003) discussed the need for incorporating ecosystem objectives in the management of sustainable marine fisheries, including 'best practice' reference points and use of 'marine protected areas'.

Schrank (2003) introduced the working of the subsidy in fisheries and its implications for sustainability.

Sinclair and Valdimarsson (2003a) edited the papers of the Reykjavik conference on responsible fisheries in the marine ecosystem held in October 2001.

Sinclair and Valdimarsson (2003b) brought out the Reykjavik declaration on responsible fisheries in the marine ecosystem.

Sinclair and Valdimarsson (2003c) outlined the need for ecosystem based approach to fisheries management.

Sissenwine and Mace (2003) gave an ecosystem approach to governance for responsible fisheries.

Annick (2004) outlined the need for compliance with international fisheries law.

Charles (2004) gave some general ideas relating to fishery sustainability.

Cunningham and Bostock (2004) edited the papers presented at the workshop and exchange of views on fiscal reforms for fisheries to promote growth, poverty eradication and sustainable management, held at Rome in October 2003.

FAO (2004) brought out the state of world fisheries and aquaculture, 2004.

Philippe (2004) explained the case of developing countries in the workshop on the implementation of international fisheries instruments and factors of unsustainability and overexploitation in fisheries held at Mauritius in February 2003.

Swan and Greboval (2004) edited the report of the international workshop on factors contributing to unsustainability and overexploitation in fisheries held at Mauritius during February 2003.

Ward, *et al.* (2004) explained measuring and assessing capacity in fisheries as a basic tool for sustainable development planning.

Looking back at this stage, the above note on the global literature on sustainable development of fisheries makes certain points clear. As noted earlier, the global literature is quite extensive and growing. Equally notable is the outstanding diversity of topics handled by them. They deal with a plethora of problems, ranging from sustainability of capture fisheries to aquaculture and environment, food safety and security, responsible fisheries, global economic structure, trade and sustainability, compliance with international law, FAO /World Bank strategy for sustainable development of fisheries, WTO, globalisation and sustainability, and a host of other issues. They also discuss the different dimensions of sustainability such as the ecological (environmental), economic, social (cultural), institutional and technological dimensions and their interactions. Some of the literature also deals with criteria, indicators, and mechanisms (incentives and controls) for sustainable development. Along with the growth in the global literature on sustainable development of fisheries, there appears to be an improvement in its quality with more focus on definitions, issues, dimensions, criteria, indicators, measurement, and strategic planning for sustainability. This seems to be particularly true of the institutional literature originating from FAO, OECD, World Bank, etc., especially after the UNCED in 1992. Incidentally, this literature is also quiet goal-oriented in maintaining global fish production and the trading system to ensure the 'sustained' flow of 'wild' or 'cultured fish' to the developed country markets.

The global institutional literature is, however, quite silent on the unsustainable developments in the fisheries of developing countries. It is, however, no fault of the global institutional literature. It is only fulfilling the dominant interests of the representing nations. There is, nevertheless, some dissenting note and bold thinking on the sustainability issues of developing countries as reflected in the writings of scholars like Miller (Miller, 2000, p.252). Notwithstanding the developed country-centered treatment of sustainable development issues in the global literature, its comprehensive coverage of ecological, economic, social, technological and institutional issues of production (capture and culture), processing (value addition), marketing (trade) and management of the industry makes it amenable for adoption and adaptation by developing countries as well for sustainable development planning in their fisheries. The major issues and treatment of the global literature will be further explained in the next chapter. The dissenting notes on sustainable development thinking will also be made clear in that chapter.

## 2.4. Summary

This chapter took note of the general theoretical literature and the applied fisheries literature relating to sustainable development of fisheries, both domestic and international. The domestic literature, both general and applied, were found to be quite scanty and underdeveloped in its structure and composition. The domestic applied literature on sustainable development of fisheries discussed predominantly the sustainability issues of aquaculture and the need for promoting specific aquaculture systems for sustainable development. Some of this literature also discussed the sustainability of marine fisheries with respect to their environment, technology, output, cost, etc. Quite a few of these studies also dealt with the coastal fishermen and their social life. The most shocking aspect of the domestic literature is, however, that scarcely any of them discussed the sustainability issues systematically following or evolving some practical criteria for sustainable development.

The international theoretical literature on sustainable development is found to be quite advanced and expanding. Its origin may be traced in the writing of Adam Smith, David Ricardo, T.R. Malthus, J.S. Mill, Karl Marx, John Maynard Keynes, Joseph A Schumpeter, Alvin Hansen and so on. The global theoretical literature, however, has its boom in the writings of contemporary ecological economists and other institutional writers attached to OECD, World Bank, International Institute for Sustainable Development, etc. The contemporary international literature focused mainly on definition, measurement, development of criteria and indicators, mechanisms (systems and institutions) for sustainable development, and establishing linkages between environment (ecology), economy (economics) and society (culture). The global literature is found to have developed in some good progression in its mission, mode and strategy.

The international applied literature on sustainable development of fisheries is also found to be extensive and growing. The global literature is quite outstanding with a variety of topics handled by it. It ranged from the sustainability of capture fisheries to aquaculture and environment, responsible fisheries, food safety and security, global economic structure, trade and sustainability, FAO/World Bank strategy for sustainable development of fisheries, WTO, globalisation and sustainable development, and a whole host of other issues.

The global literature, especially the institutional literature, originating from FAO, World Bank, OECD, etc. is found to be quite advanced in its formulation of criteria, indicators, and measurement of sustainable development of fisheries. It is found to focus on ecological, economic and social criteria of sustainable development. This literature is however, generally silent on the unsustainable development of fisheries in developing countries. Notwithstanding the developed country-centric treatment of sustainable development issues in the global literature, its comprehensive coverage of ecological, economic, social, technological and institutional issues of production, processing, marketing and management of the industry makes it amenable for adoption and adaptation by developing countries as well for the sustainable development planning of their fisheries. The slack in the growth of domestic literature, both general theoretical literature and applied fisheries literature, is, however, quite disturbing in view of its topical importance to the country.

# 3

# THE CONCEPT OF SUSTAINABLE DEVELOPMENT

## 3.1. Introduction

This chapter seeks to look at the various definitions of sustainable development, the development of the concept through the classical, Marxian, neo-classical, modern and post-modern thoughts, and to highlight the importance of measurement using criteria and indicators of sustainable development. This chapter also looks at the inter-face of unsustainability and reports on the frequently cited factors that lead to unsustainable development. A brief note on the policies for sustainable development is also offered. A summary of points discussed in the various sections are given at the end of this chapter.

## 3.2. Definition

A general understanding of the concept can be obtained from a scanning of the different definitions of sustainable development. Unfortunately, however, as rightly noted by Loucks and Gladwell, "the concept of sustainability can mean different things to different people" and "it seems to defy a precise definition" (Loucks and Gladwell, 1999, p.1). Referring to the complexity of the definition, Toman, *et al.* noted that "the issue of 'sustainability' figures prominently in contemporary discussions of natural resource and environmental management and economic development. However, the concept is not easily defined and is interpreted differently by economists, ecologists, philosophers and others. Even among economists there are significant differences of interpretation. Some treat sustainability as not much more than another way of espousing economic efficiency in the management of services derived from the natural endowment. Others claim that conventional economic efficiency criteria are inadequate for addressing sustainability concerns..." (Toman, *et al.* 1995, p.139). However, terms like sustainability and sustainable development are found used interchangeably along with other idioms like 'sustainable growth', 'sustainable biosphere' 'sustainable living', 'sustainable resource management' and 'sustainable cities', etc. (Meadowcroft, 1999, p.13). Of late, terms like 'environmental sustainability', 'ecological sustainability', 'economic sustainability', 'social sustainability' and 'cultural sustainability' have also become very common although each term has its own shade in the sustainability spectrum. Notwithstanding all these, a cursory listing of the many definitions and observations relating to the common theme of sustainability is made here.

Ciriacy-Wantrup referred it to "a safe minimum standard of conservation as a matter of resources and economic policy, to be achieved by avoiding the critical zone – that is, the physical conditions, brought about by human action, which would make it uneconomical to halt and reverse depletion" (Ciriacy-Wantrup, 1952, p.253).

Coomer noted that "the sustainable society is one that lives within the self-perpetuating limits of its environment. That society ... (is) not a 'no growth' society, ... It is, rather a society that recognises the limits of growth ...(and) looks for alternative ways of growing" (Coomer, 1979, p.1. words in parentheses added).

Pirages observes that "sustainable growth means economic growth that can be supported by physical and social environments in the foreseeable future. An ideal sustainable society would be one in which all energy would be derived from current solar income and all non-renewable resources would be recycled" (Pirages, 1977, pp. 10-11).

Howe, noting the "guidelines for a responsible natural resource policy" states that "...activities should be considered that would be aimed at maintaining over time a constant effective natural resource base ... and it implies not an unchanging resource base, but a set of resource reserves, technologies, and policy controls that maintain or expand the production possibilities of future generations" (Howe,1979, p.337).

IUCN emphasised its world conservation strategy thus: "the maintenance of essential ecological processes and life support systems, the preservation of genetic diversity, and the sustainable utilisation of species and ecosystems, with the overall aim of achieving sustainable development through the conservation of living resources" (IUCN, 1980).

Allen, summarising the IUCN world conservation strategy for sustainable development noted that:

1. Sustainable utilisation is a simple idea: we should utilise species and ecosystems at levels and in ways that allow them to go on renewing themselves for all practical purposes indefinitely.

2. The importance of ensuring that utilisation of an ecosystem or species is sustainable varies with a society's dependence on the resource in question. For a subsistence society, sustainable utilisation of most, if not all its living resources is essential... The greater the diversity and flexibility of the economy, the less the need to utilise certain resources sustainably, but by the same token the less the excuse not to ...

3. It is essential ... to ensure that ... people protect those parts of the biosphere that need protecting and modify the rest only in ways that it can sustain and

4. Sustainable development, is development that is likely to achieve lasting satisfaction of human needs and improvement of the quality of human life (Allen, 1980, pp. 18-23).

Allen also noted that (1) "development ... depends upon conservation, and that conservation depends equally upon development, and (2) conservation of the biosphere is a prerequisite for human survival and well-being ... Interdependence is an inescapable fact of life" (Allen, 1980, p.16).

Porritt emphasised that "all economic growth in the future must be sustainable, that is to say, it must operate within and not beyond the finite limits of the planet" (Porritt, 1984, p.120).

Talbot presented three objectives of the world conservation strategy thus:

1. to maintain essential ecological processes and life support systems,

2. to preserve genetic diversity

3. to ensure that the utilisation of living resources, and the ecosystems in which they are found, is sustainable (Talbot, 1984, p.4).

Tietenberg observed that "the sustainability criterion suggests that at a minimum, future generations should be left no worse off than current generation" (Tietenberg, 1984, p.33).

Repetto observed that the "core of the idea of sustainability, then, is the concept that current decisions should not impair the prospects for maintaining or improving future living standards... This implies that our economic systems should be managed so that we live off the dividend of our resources, maintaining and improving the asset base. This principle has much in common with the ideal concept of income that accountants seek to determine: the greatest amount that can be consumed in the current period without reducing prospects for consumption in the future" (Repetto, 1985, p.10).

Repetto also stated that: (1) "this does not mean that sustainable development demands the preservation of the current stock of natural resources or any particular mix of human, physical and natural assets. As development proceeds, the composition of the underlying asset base changes".

(2) "There is broad agreement that pursuing policies that imperil the welfare of future generations, who are unrepresented in any political or economic forum, is unfair" (Repetto, 1985, pp. 16-17).

Bartelmus noted that "the overall goals of environment and development are not in conflict but are indeed the same, namely the improvement of the human quality of life or welfare for present and future generations" (Bartelmus, 1986, pp.13-14).

Daly observed that "the market does not distinguish an ecologically sustainable scale, just as it does not distinguish between ethically just and unjust distributions of income. Sustainability, like justice, is a value not achievable by purely individualistic market processes" (Daly, 1986, p.320).

Burness and Cummings, responding to Daly's notion of sustainability said "in a pedagogical sense sustainability requires that all processes operate only at their steady state, renewable level, which might then suggest a return to a regulated caveman culture" (Burness and Cummings, 1986, p.323).

Clark and Munn noted that "a major challenge of the coming decades is to learn how long term, large-scale interactions between environment and development can be better managed to increase the prospects for ecologically sustainable improvements in human well-being" (Clark and Munn, 1986, p.5).

Clark and Munn further pointed out that "throughout most of history, the interactions between human development and the environment have been relatively simple and local affairs. But the complexity and scale of these interactions are increasing ... What was once straight forward questions of ecological preservation versus economic growth now reflect complex linkages – witness the feed backs among energy and crop production, deforestation and climate change that are evident in studies of the atmospheric 'green house' effect" (ibid, p.5).

Solow observed that "a society that invests in reproducible capital the competitive rents on its current extraction of exhaustible resources, will enjoy a consumption stream constant in time ... This result can be interpreted as saying that an appropriately defined stock of capital – including the initial endowment of resources – is being maintained intact, and that consumption can be interpreted as the interest on that patrimony" (Solow, 1986, p.141).

Barbier, speaking of the third world, noted that "... the concept of sustainable economic development as applied to the third world ... is therefore directly concerned with increasing the material standard of living of the poor at the 'grass roots' level, which can be quantitatively measured in terms of increased food, real income, educational services, health-care, sanitation and water supply, emergency stocks of food and cash, etc., and only indirectly concerned with economic growth at the aggregate, commonly national level. In general terms, the primary objective is reducing the absolute poverty of the world's poor through providing lasting and secure livelihoods that minimise resource depletion, environmental degradation, cultural disruption and social instability" (Barbier, 1987, p. 103).

Brown, *et al.* referring to global sustainability noted that "in the narrowest sense, global sustainability means the indefinite survival of the human species across all the regions of the world. A broader sense of the meaning specifies that virtually all humans, once born, live to adulthood and that their lives have quality beyond mere biological survival. Finally the broadest sense of global sustainability includes the persistence of all components of the biosphere, even those with no apparent benefit to humanity" (Brown, *et al.* 1987, p.717).

Differentiating between 'growth' and 'development' Daly said "by 'growth' I mean quantitative increase in the scale of the physical dimensions of the economy;... by development I mean the qualitative improvement in the structure, design and composition of physical stocks and flows, that result from greater knowledge, both of technique and of purpose" (Daly, 1987, p.323).

Goodland and Ledec noted that "sustainable development is here defined as a pattern of social and structural economic transformations (i.e. 'development') which optimises the economic and social benefits available in the present, without jeopardising the likely potential for similar benefits in the future. A primary goal of sustainable development is to achieve a reasonable (however defined) and equitably distributed level of economic well-being that can be perpetuated continually for many human generations" (Goodland and Ledec, 1987, p.36).

Goodland and Ledec also think that "sustainable development implies using renewable resources in a manner which does not eliminate or degrade them or otherwise diminish their usefulness for future generations... Sustainable development further implies using non-renewable (exhaustible) mineral resources in a manner which does not unnecessarily preclude easy access to them by future generations ... Sustainable development also implies depleting non-renewable energy resources at a slow enough rate so as to ensure the high probability of an orderly societal transition to renewable energy sources ..." (Ibid, p.37).

Pearce states that "the sustainability criterion requires that the conditions necessary for equal access to the resource base be met for each generation" (Pearce, 1987, p.13).

Tolba noted that "sustainable development has become an article of faith, a shibboleth: often used but little explained...In broad terms the concept of sustainable development encompasses:

1. help for the very poor because they are left with no option other than to destroy their environment;
2. the ideal of self reliant development with natural resource constraints;
3. the idea of cost-effective development using different economic criteria to the traditional approach; that is to say development should not degrade environmental quality, nor should it reduce productivity in the long run;
4. the great issues of health control, appropriate technologies, food self- reliance, clean water and shelter for all;
5. the notion that people-centered initiatives are needed; human beings in other words, are the resources in the concept" (Tolba, 1987, p.98).

Tolba also noted that "economic development and environmental quality are inter- dependent and, in the long term, mutually reinforcing. The rational management of the world's threatened natural resource base forestalls a loss in environmental quality and enhances sustainable economic growth" (ibid, p.150).

Turner, referring to the IUCN programme wrote that "the world conservation strategy... gave considerable prominence to the sustainability concept, although its precise meaning and practical applications were not presented in a detailed and operational form" (Turner, 1987, p.576).

The World Bank highlighted its mission to "... satisfy the multiple criteria of sustainable growth, poverty alleviation, and sound environmental management" (World Bank, 1987, p.10).

It further noted that "to a large degree, environmental management should be seen as a means of attaining the wider objectives of sustained economic growth and poverty alleviation, ... elevating concern about environmental matters ... and developing the capacity to implement sound practices for environmental management are both needed to reconcile, and, where appropriate, make trade offs among the objectives of growth, poverty alleviation, and sound environmental management...Promoting growth, alleviating poverty, and protecting the environment are mutually supportive objectives in the long run ... In the short run, however, the objectives are not always compatible ... That makes it essential, if environmental degradation is not to become completely unmanageable, to devise policies oriented towards economic growth, with special emphasis on improving the incomes of the poor ... Nevertheless, economic growth may also destroy the environment and further jeopardise the already tenuous lives of the poor ... Thus, although growth is imperative for alleviating poverty, it may also adversely affect the poor and the environment if inadequate attention is paid to the poor and their needs" (ibid. pp.5-7, 28).

WCED noted the following as fundamental to sustainable development:

1. we come to see that a new development path was required, one that sustained human progress not just in a few places for a few years, but for the entire planet into the distant future. Thus 'sustainable development' becomes a goal not just for the 'developing' nations, but for industrial ones as well.
2. sustainable development is development that meets the needs of the present without compromising the ability of future generations

to meet their own needs. It can contain within it two key concepts: (*a*) the concept of 'needs', in particular the essential needs of the world's poor, to which over-riding priority should be given; and (*b*) the idea of limitations imposed by the state of technology and social organisation on the environment's ability to meet present and future needs.

3. even the narrow notion of physical sustainability implies a concern for social equity between generations, a concern that must logically be extended to equity within each generation.
4. living standards that go beyond the basic minimum are sustainable only if consumption standards everywhere have regard for long-term sustainability. Yet many of us live beyond the world's ecological means, for instance in our patterns of energy use. Perceived needs are socially and culturally determined, and sustainable development requires the promotion of values that encourage consumption standards that are within the bounds of the ecological possible and to which all can reasonably aspire.
5. economic growth and development obviously involve changes in the physical ecosystem. Every ecosystem everywhere cannot be preserved in tact.
6. the loss (i.e. extinction) of plant and animal species can greatly limit the options of future generations; so sustainable development requires the conservation of plant and animal species (WCED, 1987, pp.4, 43-46).

The WCED also reported that "it is impossible to separate economic development issues from environment issues; many forms of development erode the environmental resources upon which they must be based, and environmental degradation can undermine economic development. Poverty is a major cause and effect of global environmental problems" (ibid. p.3).

Describing the dynamic nature of the concept, it noted that "this development involves a progressive transformation of economy and society. A development path that is sustainable in a physical sense could theoretically be pursued even in a rigid social and political setting. But physical sustainability cannot be secured unless development policies pay attention to such considerations as changes in access to resources and in the distribution of costs and benefits. Even the narrow notion of physical sustainability implies a concern for social equity between generations, a concern for social equality between generations, a concern that must logically be extended to equity within each generation" (ibid, p.43).

Turner again noted:

1. the precise meaning of terms such as 'sustainable resource usage', 'sustainable growth' and 'sustainable development' has so far proved elusive.
2. in principle, such an optimal (sustainable growth) policy would seek to maintain an 'acceptable' rate of growth in per-capita real incomes without depleting the national capital asset stock or the natural environmental asset stock.
3. it makes no sense to talk about the sustainable use of a non-renewable resource (even with substantial recycling effort and reuse rates). Any positive rate of exploitation will eventually lead to exhaustion of the finite stock.
4. in this (sustainable development) mode ...conservation becomes the sole basis for defining a criterion with which to judge the desirability of alternative allocations of natural resources (Turner, 1988, pp.5,12, 13,21).

Markandya and Pearce noted that "the basic idea (of sustainable development) is simple in the context of natural resources (excluding exhaustibles) and environment: the use made of these inputs to the development process should be sustainable through time ... If we now apply the idea to resources, sustainability ought to mean that a given resource stock of resources – trees, soil quality, water and so on – should not decline... sustainability might be redefined in terms of a requirement that the use of resources today should not reduce real incomes in the future" (Markandya and Pearce, 1988, pp.9-11).

O'Riordan thinks that "it may only be a matter of time before the metaphor of sustainability becomes so abused as to be meaningless, certainly as a device to straddle the ideological conflicts that pervade contemporary environmentalism" (O'Riordan, 1988, p.29).

This author, however, adds that "sustainability is a much broader phenomenon (than sustainable development), embracing ethical norms pertaining to the survival of living matter, to the rights of future generations and to institutions responsible for ensuring that such rights are fully taken into account in policies and actions" (ibid, p.30).

Rees considers it as a "positive socio-economic change that does not undermine the ecological and social systems upon which whole communities and society are dependent" (Rees, 1988).

Pearce, Barbier and Markandya observed that "we take development to be a vector of desirable social objectives, and elements might include: increases in real income per capita, improvements in health and nutritional status, educational achievement, access to resources, a fairer distribution of income, and increases in basic freedoms ..., sustainable development is then a situation in which the development vector increases monotonically over time...We summarise the necessary conditions (for sustainable development) as 'constancy of the natural capital stock'. More strictly, the requirement is for non-negative changes in the stock of natural resources such as soil and soil quality, ground and surface water and their quality, land biomass, water biomass, and the waste assimilation capacity of receiving environments" (Pearce, Barbier and Markandya, 1988, pp.4-6).

Tonn outlined the two principles of 500 – year planning for sustainability as: "Principle 1: Future generations should not inherit from present generations, unacceptable risks of death owing to environmental or other preventable catastrophes. Principle 2: Future as well as present generations may inherit constraints on their primary freedoms as sacrifices for enjoying the conditions of Principle 1" (Tonn, 1988, p.6).

Robinson, *et al.* defined it as "the persistence, over an apparently indefinite future of certain necessary and desired characteristics of the socio-political system and its natural environment. Both environmental/ ecological and social/political sustainability are required for a sustainable society" (Robinson, *et al.* 1990).

Caddy and Griffiths, quoting the FAO Committee on Fisheries, noted that "sustainable development is the management and conservation of the natural resource base, and the orientation of technological and institutional change in such a manner as to ensure the attainment and continued satisfaction of human needs for present and future generations. Such development conserves land, water, plant, and genetic resources, is environmentally non-degrading, technologically appropriate, economically viable and socially acceptable" (Caddy and Griffiths, 1995, p.3).

Loucks and Gladwell view "sustainable development as a relationship between changing human economic system and larger but normally slower - changing ecological systems. In this relationship human life can continue indefinitely and flourish, and the supporting eco-system and environmental quality can be maintained and improved. Sustainable development, then, is one in which there is an improvement in the quality of life without necessarily causing an increase in the quantity of resources consumed. But the idea of sustainable growth, i.e. the ability to get quantitatively bigger, continually, is an impossibility. Sustainable development, i.e. to improve qualitatively and continually, on the other hand, may be possible" (Loucks and Gladwell, 1990, p.29).

These authors also think that "sustainability is an integrating process (and) it encompasses technology, ecology, and the social and political infrastructure of society. It is probably not a state that may ever be reached completely. But it is one for which we should continually strive. And while it may never be possible with certainty to identify what is sustainable and what is not, it is possible to develop some measures that permit one to compare the performances of alternative systems with respect to sustainability" (ibid, p.24).

According to Prendergast "sustainable development is an effort to use technology to help clean up the mess it helped to make, and engineers will be central players in its success or failure" (Prendergast, 1993, pp.39-43). This author considers that "future technology will use energy and other natural resources more efficiently through conservation measures and switching over to renewable resources, waste minimisation, much greater recycling and reuse of resources and materials, more comprehensive economic/environmental assessments employing 'life-cycle' analyses and more effective and efficient management of resources" (ibid).

Referring to sustainability, Costanza, *et al.* noted that "probably the most challenging task facing humanity today is the creation of a shared vision of a sustainable and desirable society, one that can provide permanent prosperity within the biophysical constraints of the real world in a way that is fair and equitable to all humanity, to other species, and to future generations" (Costanza, *et al.* 1996).

Pearce noted that "sustainable economic development now becomes fairly simply defined. It is non-declining consumption per capita, or GNP or whatever the agreed indicator of development is. And this is how sustainable development has come to be interpreted by most of the economists addressing the issue ...The merits of this definition are, first, that it accords with the intutive idea that the meaning of words is to be found through observation of common usage of those words, and second, it is consistent with, though not identical to, the most widely used definition in the report that made the term so popular. That report is the World Commission on Environment and Development's report in 1987 on North-South relations and the global environmental problem" (Pearce, 1998, p.70).

Serageldin reminds that "sustainability is to leave future generations as many opportunities as we ourselves have had, if not more…leaving future generations more capital per capita than we have had, although the composition of the capital we leave to the next generation will be different in terms of its constituent parts than the capital we have used in our generation" (Serageldin, 1996).

According to Barbier, "sustainable development is ... directly concerned with increasing the material standard of living of the poor at the 'grass roots' level, which can be quantitatively measured in terms of increased food, real income, educational services, health care, sanitation and water supply, emergency stocks of food and cash, and so on, and only indirectly concerned with economic growth at the aggregate, commonly national, level. In general terms, the primary objective is reducing the absolute poverty of the world's poor through providing lasting and secure livelihoods that minimise resource depletion, environmental degradation, cultural disruption and social instability" ( Barbier, 1998, p.6).

Barbier also argues that "real improvements cannot occur unless the strategies which are being formulated and implemented are ecologically sustainable over the long term, are consistent with social values and institutions, and encourage 'grass roots' participation in the development process. As the primary objective is to provide lasting and secure livelihoods that minimise resource depletion, environmental degradation, cultural disruption, and social instability, this process can be viewed as an interaction among three systems - the biological and resource systems, the economic system, and the social system. The general objective is to maximise the goals across all these systems through a dynamic and adaptive process of trade-offs. To be truly useful as a concept of economic development, 'sustainability' must be applicable to all forms of economic and social activity, ranging from agriculture and forestry to industry and human settlements" (ibid, pp. 18-19).

Lesser, *et al.* observed that "the literature on sustainability is immense and growing. Unfortunately, the term 'sustainable' has become a ubiquitous adjective, attached to everything from energy policy to competition. Though this may popularise the term, it provides little guidance for policy makers. And despite the temptation to take the h*umpty-dumpty* approach to vocabulary, environmental policies that are 'sustainable' cannot be defined, nor can progress be measured, until there is agreement on the concept itself" (Lesser, *et al.* 1997, p.593).

Notwithstanding the above observation, these authors ventured to define sustainable development thus: "In its simplest form, 'sustainable development' is development that does not occur at the expense of future, whatever that means" (ibid, p. 563).

Perman, *et al.* noted that "in terms of usage, the concept of sustainability does not possess any single meaning or definition. In order to structure our thoughts and discussions on sustainability, it will be useful to classify in as simple a way as possible the alternative manners in which writers have treated the concept. At least five alternative conceptualisation can be identified.

1. (*a*) A sustainable state is one in which utility is non-declining through time; (*b*) A sustainable state is one in which consumption is non-declining through time.
2. A sustainable state is one in which resources are managed so as to maintain production opportunities for the future.
3. A sustainable state is one in which the natural capital stock is non-declining through time.
4. A sustainable state is one in which resources are managed so as to maintain a sustainable yield of resource services.
5. A sustainable state is one which satisfies minimum conditions of ecosystem stability and resilience through time" (Perman, *et al.* 1996, p.56).

Presenting a blueprint for measuring sustainable development, Pearce, *et al.* defined sustainability thus: "sustainability means making sure that substitute resources are made available as non-renewable resources become physically scarce, and it means ensuring that the environmental impacts of using those resources are kept within the earth's carrying capacity to assimilate those impacts" (Pearce, *et al.*, 1996, p.4).

Pearce, *et al.* further made it clear that "sustainable development is about ensuring that some measure of human well-being is sustained over time. Fundamental to this approach to economic development is the requirement that any action now which are likely significantly to impair the well-being of the future must be associated with actual compensation of the future. Otherwise, the future is worse-off compared to the present ...; the mechanism whereby current generation can compensate the future is through the transfer of capital bequests. What this means is that this generation makes sure that it leaves the next generation a stock of capital no less than this generation has now. Capital provides the capacity to generate well-being through the creation of the goods and services upon which human well-being depends" (ibid, p.15).

Bartelmus offered an operational definition of sustainable development thus: "the set of development programmes that meets the targets of human needs satisfaction without violating long-term natural resource capacities and standards of environmental quality and social equity" (Bartelmus, 1994, p.73).

Focusing on the human needs dimension, Bartelmus reminds that the Rio Declaration of the UNCED in its first principle noted that "human beings are at the center of concerns for sustainable development and all other principles were attuned to realise the goal of sustainable development with all its complexities and incoherence" (ibid, p.72).

Toman, *et al.* noted that "while there is not a 'text book' definition of sustainability that commands wide spread agreement , it is clear that a central issue is concern for the well-being of future generations in the face of growing pressure on the natural environment to provide a range of valued services (extractable materials, waste absorption, ecological system resilience, aesthetics). A second issue, given a concern for future well-being, is the capacity for the economic system to substitute other forms of wealth for diminution of 'natural capital'- the total repository of service capacities from the natural environmental – in order to maintain the welfare of future generations" (Toman, *et al.* 1995, p.140).

Cicin-Sain and Knecht observed that "sustainable development may be thought of as a new paradigm, new mode of thinking that serves as a guide to action. Achieving sustainable development entails a continuous process of decision making whereby certain questions are asked and the 'right' choices and decisions are made. Thus there is never an 'end state' of sustainable development, since the equilibrium between development and environmental protection must constantly be readjusted ...

The general goal of sustainable development is to meet the needs of the present without compromising the 'ability of future generations to meet their own needs ... or in other words, sustainable development is a process of change in which the exploitation of resources, the direction of investments, the orientation of technological development, and institutional change are made consistent with future as well as present needs ... Two ideas are underlined in this definition: (1) the concept of needs, especially those of the developing world, and (2) the idea of limitations on the environment's ability to meet present and future needs. Sustainable development requires that societies meet human needs both by increasing productive potential and by insuring equitable opportunities for all' (Cicin-Sain and Knecht, 1998, p.84).

Pearson, after a long and detailed discussion on sustainable development, states that it would be 'unproductive' to give yet another definition of sustainable development but identified three threads that bind the different interpretations of sustainability. He noted: "First, the concept of sustainability knits together ecological and environmental systems – natural resources broadly defined – with economic systems. Second, sustainable development reflects a concern for inter-and intra- generational efficiency and equity in the use and conservation of natural resources. Third, sustainable development implicitly acknowledges that past and present patterns of economic development have neglected economic-environmental interactions and emphasises that corrective measures must integrate environmental considerations into conventional economic planning and policy" (Pearson , 2000, p.484).

The myriad of definitions and observations noted above indicate the basic issues and approaches involved in sustainable development, world-wide. The issues identified primarily relate to (1) eco-system failure, i.e. the eco-system failing to provide inputs and services infinitely for production and consumption, both as a source of raw material and as a 'sink' for waste dumping (2) the economic system failing to provide optimum conditions for sustained production and consumption for want of proper incentives and signals to the players i.e. producers and consumers and (3) social system failing to fulfil the requirements of intragenerational and intergenerational equity criteria of sustainable development.

The basic approach to sustainability indicated in many of the definitions and observations are to make modifications in the producing and consuming systems with suitable changes in technology, social systems and institutions, all of which impact on the environment and affect sustainability. Since the mosaic of definitions and notes reproduced above are not explaining the fundamental logic of sustainable development, an attempt is made in the next section to briefly unravel the concept and its development over time.

### 3.3. Development of the Concept

The concern for the sustainability of the economic system was prevalent in all societies. The ancient Greeks were believed to have fears about the environmentally damaging nature of certain economic activities (Jones, *et al.* 2000, p. 26). Most ancient Greeks were said to be believers in the 'Gaia' principle which holds that "the automatic control system of 'Gaia' (Greek earth-goddess) has enabled her to survive many ecological catastrophes in the history of the Earth" (Sarkar, 1999, p.10). Ancient Indians had concern for the good of all creatures and the *vedas* advocated *Loko Samastha Sukhino Bhavanthu* (let all be happy) principle. In the last century, Vinobha Bhave had put it crisply as *Sarvodaya* (the upliftment of all). For the Mahatma, it further required that all ends to be sustainable must be sought through proper, truthful and non-violent means, *Ahimsa.* Leaving these purely spiritual or philosophical approaches to sustainability, the attempt in this section is to trace the core vision or thinking of the classical, Marxian, neo-classical, modern and post-modern view on the subject.

#### 3.3.1. Classical View

The sustainability of the economic system or the prospect for the economy to maintain the prosperity in the future as well had indeed become a subject matter of enquiry by Adam Smith in the Wealth of Nations. Adam Smith observed that "the annual produce of the land and labour of any nation can be increased in its value by no other means but by increasing either the number of productive labourers, or the productive powers of those labourers who had before been employed. The number of its productive labourers, it is evident, can never be much increased, but in consequence of an increase of capital, or of the funds destined for maintaining them...The productive powers of the same number of labourers cannot be increased, but in consequence either of some addition and improvement to those machines and instruments which facilitate and abridge labour, or of a more proper division and distribution of employment. In either case an additional capital is almost always required. It is by means of an additional capital only that the undertaker of any work can either provide his workmen with better machinery or make a more proper distribution of employment among them. When the work to be done consists of a number of parts, to keep every man constantly employed in one way requires a much greater capital than where every man is occasionally employed in every different part of the work. When we compare, therefore, the state of a nation at two different periods, and find, that the annual produce of its land and labour is evidently greater at the latter than at the former, that its lands are better cultured , its manufactures more numerous and more flourishing, and its trade more extensive, we may be assured that its capital must have increased during the interval between those two periods, and that more must have been added to it by way the good conduct of some, than had been taken from it either by the private misconduct of others or by the public extravagance of government. But we shall find this to have been the case of almost all nations, in all tolerably quite and peaceable times, even of those who have not enjoyed the most prudent and parsimonious government" (Smith, 1970, pp. 443-444).

Adam Smith also noted the possibility of the economic system reaching a 'stationary state' where no further progress is possible for want of technical improvements. Smith further recognised the possibility of growing unemployment leading to a stationary state. He wrote: "though the wealth of a country should be very great, yet if it has been long stationary, we must not expect to find the wages of labour very high in it. The funds destined for the payment of wages, the revenue and stock of its inhabitants, may be of the greatest extent; but if they have continued for several centuries of the same, or very nearly of the same extent, the number of labourers employed every year could easily supply, and even more than supply, the number wanted the following year…If in such a country the wages of labour had ever been more than sufficient to maintain the labour, and to enable him to bring up a family, the competition of the labourers, and the interest of the masters would soon reduce them to this lowest rate which is consistent with common humanity. China has been long one of the richest, that is, one of the most fertile, best cultivated, most industrious, and most populous countries in the world. It seems, however, to have been long stationary…China, however, though it may perhaps stand still, does not seem to go backwards … But it would be otherwise in a country where the funds destined for the maintenance of labour were sensibly decaying…This perhaps is nearly the present state of Bengal, and of some other of the English settlement in the East Indies. In a fertile country which had before been much depopulated , where subsistence, consequently, should not be very difficult, and where, notwithstanding three or four hundred thousand people die of hunger in one year, we may be assured that the funds destined for the maintenance of the labouring poor are fast decaying. The difference between the genius of the British constitution which protects and governs North America, and that of the mercantile company which oppresses and domineers in the East Indies, cannot perhaps be better illustrated than by the different state of those countries" (Smith, 1970, pp.173-176).

Adam Smith also remarked that a "progressive state is in reality the cheerful and the hearty state to all the different orders of the society. The stationary is dull; the declining, melancholy" (ibid, p.184).

The other classical economists like Malthus and Ricardo argued that the economy had a tendency to converge in the long run to a stationary state due to the scarcity of land resources, population growth and diminishing returns in production. In this state, as summarised by Perman, *et al.* "the majority of people would live at a subsistence level, closing off any tendency for population to rise. The long-run tendency towards the stationary state would be punctuated intermittently by periods of rising living standards and increasing population; these periods of material progress would be brought to an end by the diminishing returns that would inevitably follow as a consequence of the population increase..." (Perman, *et al.* 1996, p.51).

Gill summarises the Malthusian view as "any improvement in the standard of living of the mass of working men would immediately lead to an expansion of population and this, in turn, would bring the standard of living back to 'subsistence' level. As long as its passions and moral character remained unchanged, mankind was chained to the wheel of perpetual poverty" (Gill, 1972, p.20).

Gill recapitulates the Ricardian position thus: "The process continues until the population is so large, the pressure on land so great, and rents so high that (1) wages are at the subsistence level and (2) profits are so low that no capitalists wish to accumulate more capital. At this point, we have reached the 'stationary state'. Since wages are at the subsistence level, population will not grow. Since profits are very low, there will be no further capital accumulation and hence no further force to raise wages. The system has come to a dead halt. Only if there is some external change

– for example, an improvement in agricultural methods – will the movement begin again" (ibid, p.24).

The emergence of the 'stationary state' was better expressed by J.S Mill. According to Mill, "it must always have been seen, more or less distinctly, by political economists, that the increase of wealth is not boundless: that the end of what they term the progressive state lies the stationary state, that all progress in wealth is but a postponement of this, and that each step in advance is but an approach to it...The richest and most prosperous countries would very soon attain the stationary state, if no further improvements were made in the productive arts, and if there were a suspension in the overflow of capital from those countries into the uncultivated or ill-cultivated regions of the earth" (Mill, 1970, p.111).

Mill is, however, not enchanted, by the arrival of the 'stationary state' as an end state. Mill wrote, "I confess, I am not charmed with the ideal of life held out by those who think that the normal state of human beings is that of struggling to get on; that the trampling, crushing, elbowing, and treading on each other's heels, which form the existing type of social life, are the most desirable lot of human kind, or anything but the disagreeable symptoms of one of the phases of industrial progress" (ibid, p.113).

What the stationary state meant to Mill was a "stationary condition of capital and population" that is, a constant population and a fixed mass of capital. It did not preclude the possibility of technological change. As Mill noted, "the industrial arts might be as earnestly and successfully cultivated and the industrial improvements would produce their legitimate effects, that of abridging labour" (ibid, p.16). As noted by Perrings, "The concept of the stationary state of an economy-environment system implies only the zero physical growth of the economy. It does not imply that this represents a stable equilibrium" (Perrings, 1987, p.141).

For the classical economists, as Higgins put it, "the development of capitalist economies was a race between technological progress and population growth, a race in which technological progress would be in the lead for sometime but which would end in a dead heat, of stagnation" (Higgins, 1976, p.87).

Higgins further notes that "the classical concept of the 'stationary state'-which for the classical school was a historical phase and not just an analytical model-was essentially a concept of a mature economy. Adam Smith saw that the 'stationary state' might be one in which wealth would be 'very great' but nevertheless one in which 'there would be a constant scarcity of employment'. In the stagnation theory of Ricardo and Mill, however, unemployment plays no significant role; 'stagnation' in Ricardo's analysis referred to what Mill called gross annual produce, and what we would now call gross national product at full employment. The stagnation resulted from the natural tendency of profits to fall and the consequent choking off of capital accumulation. Ultimately, stagnation would result in a constant population; but capital accumulation may cease 'long before' population reaches its highest point. In Mill's stationary state, there would be no increase in either population or stock of capital, profit having reached the maximum necessary to prevent net dissaving by the economy as a whole. However, there might still be a rising standard of living due to improvements in the art of living and increased leisure through technological progress" (ibid, p.98).

Summing up the classical thinking it may be noted that the classical economists anticipated or envisioned a 'stationary state' where further economic expansion is stalemated by rising population, scarcity of fertile land, diminishing returns, unproductive capital accumulation and lack of incentive for technological change. The 'stationary state' of the classical school parallels the 'unsustainable' development of the present era in a historical framework, barring its ethical dimensions. The way out suggested is obviously a check on population growth, exploring new territories (colonies) for resources and markets, technological changes, etc. Of course, laissez- faire (free trade) was at the heart of classical thinking.

### 3.3.2. Marxian View

The unsustainability of the capitalist economic system was unequivocally established by Karl Marx. In Volume III of Capital published posthumously, Marx and Engels wrote: "The stupendous productive power developing under the capitalist mode of production relatively to population, and the increase, though not in the same proportion of capital values (not their natural substance), which grow much more rapidly than the population, contradict the basis, which, compared to the expanding wealth, is ever narrowing and for which this immense productive power works, and the conditions under which capital augments its value. This is the cause of crisis" (Marx and Engels, 1971).

The Marxian prognosis of the collapse of the capitalist system is summarised by Gill thus: "In Marxian analysis, the capitalist is seen as extracting a surplus value from labour which is the source of all value...In order to prevent wages from rising, however, the capitalist is forced to substitute machinery (constant capital) for labour. This causes unemployment and distress in the labouring class and reduces their wage demands, but (in a typical capitalist contradiction) it also harms the capitalist because machinery is not a source of surplus value. Thus, capitalism is capable of producing a fall in the profit rate and immiserisation for the working classes at the same time. These developments, along with the growing concentration of capital and the problem of capitalist crisis account for the eventual collapse of the capitalist system". (Gill, op. cit. p.44).

The inevitability of economic crisis under capitalism and its unsustainability as conceived by Marx is reported by Miller thus:

> "History has demonstrated that economic crises emerged and are recurring only under the capitalist mode of production. The cause of crises is to be sought in the nature of this mode of production and is determined by the laws and contradictions inherent in it...The most deep-seated cause of economic crises is the basic contradiction of capitalism-the contradiction between the social nature of production and the capitalist private form of appropriation. It reflects the contradiction between the productive forces and the capitalist relations of production" (Miller, 1974, pp.152-153).

The likely course of business cycles and the final collapse of the capitalist system as visualised by Marx is summarised by Higgins thus: "in the Marxist system economic fluctuations consist mainly of occasional booms, launched by investment undertaken to introduce new labour-saving techniques, which temporarily carry the economy above the trend line. But sooner or later, and usually sooner, the economy sinks back to its long-run trend, with its inevitable tendency for the rate of profits to fall. This trend toward a growing gap between potential and actual output shows up as deeper and deeper depressions, shorter and weaker booms.

Now everything the capitalist do to maintain profits in the face of this trend increases the misery of the working class. The increasing tendency towards monopoly has another effect that helps to pave the way for revolution; it leads to the disappearance of the middle class. In the late stages of *high capitalism*, capitalists become desperate indeed. Encountering increasing resistance at home, they turn to colonies for more ready exploitation of labour. Colonies also provide sources of cheap raw materials, new outlets for investment, and new markets in which monopoly positions can be established for the sale of final products. So valuable are these colonies in staving off the collapse of capitalism that the advanced capitalist countries fight imperialist wars for their possession ... All in vain. At best, these desperate measures of desperate men can bring only temporary respite. The rate of profit continues to decline, and capitalists cannot resist turning the screws on workers a bit more in the effort to save their way of life. Eventually the workers can stand it no longer; by sheer strength of numbers, they over throw the system through revolution" (Higgins, op cit. pp. 117-118).

Referring to the Marxian notion of unsustainability of capitalist development, Costanza, *et al.* note that "Karl Marx (1818-1883) addressed, among his multiple critiques of capitalism, how the concentration of land and capital among a small portion of society affected how economies worked. There is an extensive collection of literature written by scholars influenced by Marx. Some of this literature addresses the sustainability of development and how the ownership of resources affects the path of development...we now recognise that the initial distribution of rights to resources and to the services of the environment is critically important to resource and environmental conservation and the prospects for sustainability ... It has long been known that how economies allocate resources to different ends depends on how resources are distributed among people, that is whether they are owned by or otherwise under the control of different people. Peasants or others who work land and interact with biological resources owned by some one else have little incentive to protect them. Landlords can only counteract this lack of incentive by diverting their own labour or that of managers under them from other productive activities and employing it to monitor and enforce their interests in protection. This diversion of human potential would not be necessary, with a more equal distribution of control. Furthermore, especially wealthy landlords may have little interest in protecting any particular land or biological resource, for their descendants when they hold land in such abundance that their foreseeable descendants are certain to have an adequate share" (Costanza, *et al.* 1997, p.33).

Costanza, *et al.* further emphasised that "our understanding of the environmental consequences of concentrated ownership and control are rooted in economic thinking, especially that of Karl Marx. Questions of equity are extremely important to the process of environmental degradation and to the possibilities for sustainable development. The occupation and ecological transformation of the Amazon have been partly driven by the concentration of the ownership of land in the more productive regions of Amazonian nations and partly driven by the economic power and hence political influence of the rich that has enabled them to obtain subsidies to engage in large scale land speculation or cattle ranching. The ongoing efforts to establish international agreements on the management of biodiversity and climate change have been repeatedly forestalled by debates over the ownership and control of resources. But it is not simply a debate over fairness. The structure of the global economy and how specific economies interact with nature in the future will depend on which nations - the nations of origin or of the Northern commercial interests, the likely discoverers of new uses for here to fore unused species - receive the 'rent' from resources" (ibid, p.35).

These authors, however, point out that "Marx and his followers in communist countries have made a negative contribution to the allocative efficiency problem, even while highlighting issues of just distribution. Their ideological rejection of rent and interest as necessary prices, and their insistence on a labour theory of value that neglected nature's contribution were responsible for much of the environmental destruction in communist countries" (ibid, pp. 35-36).

Sarkar however, holds the thesis that "socialism failed in the USSR and Eastern Europe mainly because it encountered the limits to growth" (Sarcar, op cit. p.5). This author in fact thinks that "the theories of all varieties of socialism demand rapid development of productive forces and a high degree of affluence considered to be essential elements of policy of a (transitional) socialist or social-democratic regime and indispensable foundations of a future socialist society. Both elements are opposed to the requirements of a really ecological economy" (ibid, p.4).

Referring to the Marxist perspectives on environment and sustainability, Redclift notes that "a Marxist view of the environment needs to encompass a number of closely related, but separable, issues. In the first place it needs to address the issue of the way nature is transformed under capitalism, and the implication of this process for developing countries today. In this context, the question of commodity production is of paramount importance, and distinguishes Marxism from both neo-classical and Radical Ecology perspectives, ... Second, Marxist approaches to the environment are necessarily concerned with the distribution of environmental cost and benefits, not simply from a 'welfare' standpoint, but because the distributive effects of environmental change have important implications for the kinds of social movements which are likely to emerge from ecological degradation. Third, Marxists are concerned about the ideological content of environmental ideas, and their relationship both to bourgeois processes of legitimation and to central Marxist concepts such as alienation and the class struggle ...

... Together with radical ecologists, Marxists agree that the market allocates natural resources in an efficient way through time, ultimately destroying the basis of survival for future generations. Nevertheless, Marxists see the commitment to commodity production under capitalism as making ecological externalities inevitable. Indeed, it is part of the contradictory nature of capitalism that the environmental crisis presents a massive threat to the earning powers of entrepreneurs, as underwritten by the capitalist state ..." (Redclift, 1991, pp. 59-61).

To summarise, the unsustainability of the capitalist system is evident in the Marxian concepts of capitalist process of changing organic composition of capital, extraction of surplus value, the reserve army of unemployed workers, the immiserisation of labour, recurring economic crises, the revolt of the working class and the overthrow of the capitalist bourgeois class by the proletariat. As in the classical model, the Marxian model also attaches great significance for technological improvements, market expansion through colonial trade, etc. for escaping from the crisis of unsustainable development or stationary state. Moreover, it upholds intragenerational equity as the basis of socialism as required for sustainable development and contrary to capitalism.

### 3.3.3. Neo-classical View

The neo-classical writers of the late 19$^{th}$ and early 20$^{th}$ century appeared to be less concerned with the sustainability issues. This is quite likely as these writers were primarily concerned with the determination of market equilibrium (optimisation) by the forces of supply and demand.

W.S. Jevons who wrote in the middle of the 19$^{th}$ century, however, focused his attention on energy and in particular coal, the chief non-renewable natural resource used in production. He had warned of economic stagnation in Britain, caused by the rising scarcity and cost of coal. Alfred Marshall, who published the 'Principles of Economics' in 1890 discussed the core principles of supply, demand and prices under different market conditions. Marshall, however, gave his views on the properties of land and treated it with special care. Marshall, indeed, made a clear distinction between land (natural resources) and capital. Marshall wrote that "land is a permanent and fixed stock while appliances made by man ... are a flow capable of being increased or diminished ... These considerations lead us to repeat that ... a farseeing statesman will feel a greater responsibility to future generations when legislating as to land than as to other forms of wealth; and that from the economic and from the ethical point of view, land must everywhere and always be classed as a thing by itself" (Marshall, 1972). Later neo-classical writers had contributed significantly to the sustainability debate. This indeed is true of Joseph, A. Schumpeter, John Maynard Keynes and Alvin, H. Hansen, who perceived of secular stagnation as the end result of capitalist expansion. Keynes and Hansen attached great importance to public policy to combat the onset of depression.

The later neo-classical writers were, however, quite explicit in their treatment of the sustainability problem. They in fact, refuted the natural resource constraint felt by the classical writers and believed that the scarce, natural resources could be substituted by the abundant resources or indeed by the man-made resources of capital. They further held the view that technological improvements also raised the productivity of the resources and mitigate the constraint of scarcity of natural resource inputs.

As pointed by Perman, *et al.* "the neo-classical growth theory, developed in the twentieth century, almost entirely rejected the classical hypothesis of a long-run tendency towards a stationary state. The increasing share of output generated by manufacturing industry led economists to downgrade the importance they attached to land as a productive input. Indeed, neo-classical growth theory no longer posited the existence of any fixed factor; productive inputs were visualised as either growing naturally over time (labour input) or capable of being accumulated indefinitely (capital). An assumption of continuing technical progress was sufficient, in this framework, to generate the conclusion that economic growth (rather than merely same level of output) could be sustained perpetually" (Perman, *et al.* 1996, p.52). The above vision of the neo-classical school, had in fact, led to the emergence of two dominant, diametrically opposite, views (hypotheses) on sustainable development the 'weak' sustainability hypothesis and the 'strong' sustainability hypothesis.

#### 3.3.3.1. Weak Sustainability Hypothesis and Strong Sustainability Hypothesis

Daly and Cobb view 'weak' sustainability and 'strong' sustainability in terms of whether reproducible and natural capital are to be kept in tact together (weak sustainability) or separately (strong sustainability). Weak sustainability allows for a high degree of substitution between reproducible and natural capital, while strong sustainability assumes that they are complements rather than substitutes in most production functions (Daly and Cobb, 1994, p.72).

Barbier, *et al.* indicated weak sustainability when they stated that "as long as the natural capital that is being depleted is replaced with even more valuable human-made capital, then the value of the aggregate stock – comprising both human-made and the remaining natural capital – is increasing overtime" (Barbier, *et al.*, 1994, p.54). Strong sustainability on the other hand stresses that there are limits to substitutability between natural and man-made capital. These authors suggest that "it is difficult to ensure that future economic opportunities are maintained without imposing some conditions on the depletion of natural capital" (ibid, pp. 55-56).

According to Jones, *et al.* weak sustainability "allows diminishing levels of natural capital to be compensated for by more man-made capital and strong sustainability does not allow man-made capital to substitute for natural capital; the overall stock of natural capital must be maintained" (Jones, *et al.* 2000, p.27). Strong sustainability demands "constant or increasing stock of natural capital whereas weak sustainability requires only a constant or increasing stocks of all capital, subject to critical natural capital constraints"(ibid, p. 28).

The strong sustainability hypothesis is favoured by Daly and Cobb, among others, for several reasons. First and foremost, some natural resources are considered vital for production, and their loss would constitute a catastrophic event. They form critical natural capital. Similarly, there are natural resources for which there are no substitutes, e.g. wilderness.

The neo-classical paradigm of weak sustainability is associated with the names of staunch supporters like Robert Solow, John Hartwick and Julian Simon. The neo-classical position of weak sustainability is summarised by van Kooten and Bulte thus: "As resources become scarce, their relative prices will rise, which leads to conservation and substitution toward alternative resources and the development and use of new technologies ... Rising relative prices cause substitution away from those resources that are becoming scarce. Neoclassicals point out that there are two possibilities for sustaining growth. First, there is likely sufficient substitutability between reproducible capital and the non-renewable resource so that economic growth can be sustained while generating a continuous decline in the non-renewable resource stock" (van Kooten and Bulte, p.240).

Referring to weak sustainability, Pearce, *et al.* note that "unless there are special reasons for singling out one form of capital, the requirement for sustainable development then becomes one of passing on to the next generation an aggregate capital stock not less than the one that exists now ... This 'constant capital' rule is known as 'weak sustainability' in the sustainable development literature. Weak sustainability means that we are indifferent to the form in which we pass on the capital stock. We can pass on less environment so long as we offset this loss by increasing the stock of roads and machinery or other man-made capital. Alternatively we can have fewer roads so long as we compensate by having more wetlands or meadows or more education. Weak sustainability therefore assumes that the forms of capital are completely substitutable for each other...

On the weak sustainability interpretation of sustainable development there is no special place for the environment. The environment is simply another form of capital. This said, there is a crucial requirement for even weak sustainability to be achieved. This is that depletion of natural capital that are in fixed supply – non - renewable resources - should be accompanied by investments in substitute resources ..." (Pearce, *et al.* 1996, p. 15-16).

Pearce, *et al.* explain the strong sustainability position thus: 'Ecologists would point to the limited nature of substitution between ecological assets and man-made assets. There are two reasons for this. First, some ecological assets would seem to be essential to human well-being even if they are not essential to human survival – the experience of space and amenity for example. Second, since natural capital has to be interpreted widely, many assets are essential to human survival, at least in the longer run: the basic biogeochemical cycles for example.

We might therefore designate those ecological assets which are essential in either sense as being 'critical natural capital'. They are critical either to well-being or to survival. Some would argue that the ozone layer is an example of critical capital due to the profound ecological consequences that would arise from further significant ozone layer depletion. Others might cite the carbon cycle as critical capital, and hence global warming as a major threat. Loss of biological diversity is perhaps the most important loss of natural capital. The reason for this is that such losses may threaten the primary life support functions of ecological systems. Ecologists speak of the primary values of ecological systems as opposed to the secondary values which relate to the uses that human kind makes of ecological systems. Secondary values – uses such as food exploitation, timber supply, recreation, etc. - are contingent upon primary values. By and large, then, primary values relate to critical natural capital.

If the forms of capital stock are not easily substituted for each other, then the strong sustainability rule requires that we protect critical natural capital at least. A broader interpretation is that the overall stock of natural capital should not be allowed to decline. There are therefore two variants of the natural capital rule. The first speaks generally of conserving natural capital. The second highlights the role of critical natural capital and focuses on its conservation, with or without some overall rule for conserving overall natural capital" (ibid, pp. 16-17).

Going one step further, Pearce, *et al.* noted that "measuring sustainable development thus depends on the view taken about what is necessary to achieve it. On the weak sustainability rule we need to look at the overall stock of capital. On the strong sustainability rule we need to look at the overall stock of capital and pay special attention to the environment. Recall that environmental degradation was highlighted as the main way in which this generation threatens the well-being of the next generation. This gives added support for adopting the strong sustainability view" (ibid, p.17).

Other reasons for adopting this view as given by these authors are:

1. There is extensive 'uncertainty' about the way in which natural capital stocks work. We do not understand the full working of ecological systems. Uncertainty is always a reason for being cautious, unless society can be deemed to be indifferent to risk or positively to welcome it ('risk-neutrality' and 'risk-loving'). Indeed this uncertainty lies at the foundation of the precautionary principle whereby decision-makers do not wait for full scientific certainty before making decisions. The precautionary approach is especially important if the scale of change from natural capital loss is likely to be large.
2. When natural capital assets are lost it may not be possible to recreate them. This is the problem of 'irreversibility'. Once lost, such assets are lost for ever. By contrast, man-made capital can

be run down and then recreated, as can human capital (although the conservation of indigenous knowledge and crafts, for example, is important).

For these and other reasons, conserving natural capital is especially important to sustainable development (ibid, p. 17).

Based on the level of sustainability perspectives, environmentalists have been classified by Turner into four categories.

1. 'Cornucopian' technocentrists, taking an exploitative position supportive of a growth ethic expressed in material value terms (e.g. Gross National Product); it is axiomatic that the market mechanism in conjunction with technological innovation will ensure infinite substitution possibilities to mitigate long-run real resource scarcity.
2. 'Accommodating' technocentrists, taking a conservationist position, which rejects the axiom of infinite substitution and instead support a 'sustainable growth' policy guided by resource management rules.
3. 'Communalist' ecocentrists, taking a preservationist position, which emphasises the need for prior macro environmental constraints on economic growth and favours a decentralised socio-economic system.
4. 'Deep ecology' ecocentrists, taking an extreme preservationist position, dominated by the intuitive acceptance of the notions of intrinsic (as opposed to instrumental) value in nature and rights for non-human species (Turner, 1991, p.1).

The awkwardness of the weak sustainability hypothesis or infinite substitution possibility was highlighted by Daly, when he stated "if the two form of capital were good substitutes, then natural could be totally replaced by man-made, and the only limit to expansion of man-made capital would be the finitude of the containing system. But in fact man-made capital loses its value without a complement of natural capital. What good is the man-made capital of fishing boats without the natural capital of the fish population? Saw mills without forests? And even if we could convert the whole ocean into a catfish pond, we would still need the natural capital of solar energy, photosynthetic organisms, nutrient recyclers, and so on…

The neo-classical economists' emphasis on substitution to the eclipse of complementarity in technical relations among factors of production seems really quite extreme when one takes a hard look at the neo-classical production functions used in growth theory. Usually production has been taken as a function only of labour and capital. Resources are excluded. One wonders how the labour of the cook and the capital of his kitchen can produce a cake with no flour, eggs, milk, sugar, and so on. Substitution is one thing; breaking the law of conservation of mass is something else. More recently we find resources sometimes stuck in the Cobb-Douglas functions as a third factor multiplied with labour and capital, and therefore assumed to be substitutable by them.

We now need some greater-than-zero amount of eggs, flour, sugar and the like to make our cake, and that seems big step until we realise that the function says we could make our cake a thousand times bigger if the cook simply stirred faster and used a bigger oven.

Such absurdities reflect a strong animus in neo-classical economics to deny any significant role to nature in the generation of wealth. In fact, the large statistical residual of around 50 per cent (the Solow residual), the variation in production unexplained by variations in labour and capital, is attributed to technology – another human factor. The idea that natural resources could have been responsible is ruled out by the dogma that only human factors – labour and capital and (residually) technology – add value. There is no consideration of 'that to which value is added' and its differing receptiveness to receiving the value added by labour and capital…" (Daly, 1999, pp.639-640).

### 3.3.4. Modern View

The 'modern' view of sustainability may be said to have its beginning in the Conservation Movement that originated in the United States in the first decade of the last century. The principal advocates were the new elites of the scientific environmentalists operating under the progressive political ideologies formed in the United States at the turn of the last century. The champion was President Theodore Roosevelt and the intellectual leader, Gifford Pinchot, Chief Forester of U.S.A. President Theodore Roosevelt noted in 1908 that "the time has come to enquire seriously what will happen when our forests are gone; when the coal, the iron, the oil, and the gas are exhausted: when the soils shall have been still further impoverished and washed into the streams, polluting the rivers, denuding the fields, and obstructing navigation. These questions do not relate only to the next century, or to the next generation. It is time for us now as a nation to exercise the same reasonable foresight in dealing with our natural resources that would be shown by any prudent person in conserving and wisely using the property which contains the assurance of well-being for the family and its children. The nation behaves well if it treats its natural resources as assets which it must turn over to the next generation increased and not impaired in value" (Quoted by Gilpin, 2000, p.42).

Responding to the rapid disappearance of federal lands, Roosevelt used existing powers to transfer and convert remaining land to national forests. Roosevelt accelerated the pace of transfer and with broadened powers, reserved for future generations parks and mineral, oil and coal resources as well as hydroelectric power sites. During seven years (1901-1908 ), an additional 80 million ha of the federal domain were closed to commercial development. The new natural resource policy, as defined by Philip Wells, the law officer of the Forest Service, aims at the "use of foresight and restraint in the exploitation of the physical sources of wealth as necessary for the perpetuity of civilisations, and the welfare of present and future generations" (as quoted by Pearson, 2000, p.471).

Richard Ely defined conservation in 1918 as "the preservation of the unimpaired efficiency of the resources of the earth" (ibid, p.471).

Pinchot wrote that "conservation advocates the use of foresight, prudence and intelligence in dealing with public matters. It proclaims the right and duty of the people to act for the benefit of the people. Conservation demands the application of common sense to the common problems for the common good.... Conservation is the foresighted utilisation, preservation and/or renewal of forests, waters, lands and minerals for the greatest good of the greatest number for the longest time" (as quoted by O'Riordan, 1991, p.32).

Pearson noted that "the parallels between the Conservation Movement in the United States and current endorsements of sustainable development are many. Both stress the 'wise' use of natural resources and the avoidance of waste (inefficiency in modern terminology). Many in both movements attribute transcendent values in nature. Both are more than a little vague. President Taft's statement in 1910 resonates in current discussions of sustainable development: A great many people are in favour of conservation, no matter what it means. Nor did the international aspects of conservation go unnoticed. President Theodore Roosevelt writing in 1909 to invite the Prime Minister of Canada and the President of Mexico to the North American Conservation Conference, noted, 'it is evident that the natural resources are not limited by the boundary lines which separate nations...." (Pearson, 2000, pp. 471-472). One may also note here that the appeal to prudence and foresight as advocated by Pinchot is foreshadowing the contemporary principle of precautionary approach as recommended by the UNCED in 1992.

The emerging thinking on sustainability in the U.S. during the middle of the last century is reported by Pearson thus:

> "The early post-World War II era was marked by a great divergence of views. The Palay Commission, established by President Truman and reporting in 1952, was influenced by World War II and Korean war commodities shortages and found many causes for concern including evidence of moderate increases in the cost of raw materials...The Commission's recommendations included government stock-piling of strategic materials for defence purposes, and greater reliance on imported raw materials. The perspective was national, not global" (Pearson, op cit. p. 465).

Sir Arthur Pigou, the English economist, who wrote the *Economics of Welfare* in 1919 argued for state intervention to promote people's welfare. Pigou wrote "it is the clear duty of Government, which is the trustee for unborn generations as well as for its present citizens, to watch over, and if need be, by legislative enactment, to defend, the exhaustible natural resources of the country from rash and reckless spoliation. How far it should itself, either out of taxes or out of state loans, or by the device of guaranteed interest, press resources into undertakings from which the business community, if left to itself, would hold aloof, is a more difficult problem. Plainly, if we assume adequate competence on the part of governments, there is a valid case for some artificial encouragement to investment, particularly to investment, the return from which will only begin to appear after many years" (Pigou, as quoted by Gilpin, 2000, p.43).

A major turning point in the modern debate on sustainability was the publication of an influential book 'Scarcity and Growth' by Harold Barnett and Chandler Morse in 1963. These authors raised the natural resource limit issue and tested the hypothesis that if natural resources were becoming increasingly scarce, the real cost of extractive output would increase overtime. When tested against U.S. data for the period 1870-1957, these authors, however, found the opposite, that the trend in unit costs of extractive goods as a whole had been decreasing and not increasing for various reasons.

Another major critical point in the modern thinking on sustainability was the long-term price trend for natural resources in the early post-war years. This is related to the so-called Prebisch thesis, named after the prominent Latin American economist, which argued that because of different income elasticities of demand between raw materials and industrial products, and because productivity increases in raw materials tended to be passed forward in lower prices whereas productivity increases in industrial goods were passed back into higher factor incomes (due to competitive bargaining), there was a long term tendency for the terms of trade of commodity-exporting developing countries to deteriorate. The policy implications of this were import substitution and international commodity agreements to limit supply and shore up prices. The terms – of-trade argument and policy implications were not intended to promote conservation or sustainability as such, but it reflected the point that raw material prices were declining over the long run, as noted by Barnett and Morse earlier. This indeed, had exposed the unfavorable terms of trade for developing countries and their unsustainability in the long term. The import-substitution policy followed by large developing countries like India was a major shock for industrial countries in the seventies and eighties, forcing them to demand the 'opening up' of the markets of these countries in the post-*perestroika* era.

The threat to global prosperity was continuing. One new view expressed in the 1970s, as vividly put by Pearson, was that "the conflation of poverty, population growth, and pressure on natural resource base in the context of high energy prices, might not only limit economic growth but combine to cause economic and environmental collapse. The 1970's increase in energy prices coincided with accelerated population growth in developing countries as mortality rates fell sharply with the introduction of improved sanitation and health services ...the poor in developing countries are caught in a vicious cycle of deforestation, soil erosion, ever shorter fallow periods for traditional agriculture and the use of dung for cooking and not for fertilizer for crops, all of which were exacerbated by high prices for commercial fossil fuels and all of which tended to reduce productivity of natural resources and compound poverty..." (Pearson, op. cit. p.466).

This new perspective is considered important for three reasons by Pearson. "First, it shifts the focus of the prevailing 'limits' debate away from industrial country growth to development in the Third World. In doing so it contributes to a widespread view, still held by many, that sustainable development is mainly an issue for developing countries. Second, it emphasises that poverty itself can be a cause of environmental degradation and that sustainable development requires meeting the needs of the 'present' generation, an idea picked up in the Brundtland Report. In this sense, a revitalisation of intragenerational equity concerns - help for the poor - is not only an ethical issue but a necessary condition for long-term economic growth. Third, there is a recognition that abuse of the natural resource base, occasioned through poverty and population pressure, might not only place a 'limit' on economic growth, but cause a pronounced 'decline' in economic welfare. In that event, adequate protection of the natural resource base is not a luxury but a pre-requisite for sustainable income and development" (ibid, pp.466-467).

The connection between poverty and resource degradation was well documented in the U.S. in the beginning of the last century. Referring to the southern Appalachian mountains at that time, Pinchot wrote that "these people, poor as the mountain farmer is apt to be, were obliged to use without reserve all the resources of their scantily productive lands. They were therefore in the habit of cutting all trees that could be used or sold as fuel, fencing, or saw-logs. They turned their cattle into the forest and often burned over their woodlands for the sake of pasturage ...; under such treatment the forest, originally of moderate quality, grew steadily worse ...the condition of a large part of the forest was deplorable in the extreme" (as quoted by Pearson, op. cit. p.467).

This fundamental process of *cumulative causation* was recognised by Myrdal in situations of poverty, environmental degradation and under-development. Referring to this, Chambers wrote, "poor people in their struggle to survive are driven to doing environmental damage with long-term losses. Their herds overgraze; their shortening fallows on steep slopes and fragile soils induce erosion; their need for off-season incomes drives them to cut and sell firewood and to make and sell charcoal; they are forced to cultivate and degrade marginal and unstable land. Putting people first, and enabling them to meet their needs, can be, then, to reduce these pressures, to reduce degradation, and to maintain potentials for sustainable agriculture and sustainable development at higher levels of productivity. And this in turn means that more people in future can have adequate, secure, and decent, levels of living" (Chambers, as quoted by Barbier, 1998, p.4).

Initially , this vicious cycle of population, poverty and environmental deterioration was thought to be cases of localised collapses - encroachment on marginal lands, exhaustion of specific fisheries, and unsustainable shortening of fallow in regions still relying on slash-and-burn agriculture. However, in recent years there is growing recognition that ecological resources are inter-connected and biological diversity and genetic resources of international importance can be threatened by local destruction of habitat. Pearson notes that "deforestation directly or indirectly related to poverty, is significant for global warming. Inter-connectedness increases the international salience of what had for a time appeared to be localised incidences of unsustainable development" (Pearson, op cit. 467).

One most outstanding contribution to the modern thinking on sustainable development was made by Professor Kenneth, E. Boulding in 1966, when he wrote the paper, *The Economics of the Coming Spaceship Earth*. Boulding presented the contrasting models of an unsustainable 'cowboy' economy and the prospects of a 'spaceman' economy. Boulding wrote "the closed earth of the future requires economic principles which are somewhat different from those of the open earth of the past. For the sake of picturesqueness, I am tempted to call the open economy the 'cowboy economy', the cowboy being symbolic of the illimitable plains and also associated with reckless, exploitative, romantic and violent behavior, which is characteristic of open societies. The closed economy of the future might similarly be called the 'spaceman' economy, in which the earth has become a single spaceship, without unlimited reservoirs of anything, either for extraction or for pollution, and in which, therefore, man must find his place in a cyclical ecological system which is capable of continuous reproduction of material form even though it cannot escape having inputs of energy. The difference between the two types of economy becomes most apparent in the attitude towards consumption. In the cowboy economy, consumption is regarded as a good thing and production likewise; and the success of the economy is measured by the amount of the throughput from the 'factors of production', a part of which, at any rate, is extracted from the reservoirs of raw materials and non-economic objects, and other part of which is output into the reservoirs of pollution. If there are infinite reservoirs from which materials can be obtained and into which effluvia can be deposited, then the throughput is at least a plausible measure of the success of the economy. The gross national product is a rough measure of this total throughput. It should be possible, however, to distinguish that part of the GNP which is derived from exhaustible and that which is derived from reproducible resources, as well as that part of consumption which represents effluvia and that which represents input into the productive system again. Nobody, as far as I know, has ever attempted to break down the GNP in this way, although it would be an interesting and extremely important exercise...

By contrast, in the spaceman economy, throughput is by no means a desideratum, and is indeed to be regarded as something to be minimised rather than maximised. The essential measure of success of the economy is not production and consumption at all, but the nature, extent, quality, and complexity of the total capital stock, including in this the state of the human bodies and minds included in the system. In the spaceman economy, what we are primarily concerned with is stock maintenance, and any technological change which results in the maintenance of a given total stock with a lessened throughput (that is, less production and consumption) is clearly a gain. This idea that both production and consumption are bad things rather than good things is very strange things to economists, who have been obsessed with the income – flow concepts to the exclusion, almost, of capital – stock concepts" (Boulding, 1966, reprinted in Costanza, *et al.* 1997, pp.9-10).

Boulding also lamented that "there are problems here which the economics profession has neglected with astonishing single-mindedness. My own attempts to call attention to some of them, for instance, in two articles, as far as I can judge, produced no response whatever, and economists continue to think and act as if production, consumption, throughput, and the GNP were the sufficient and adequate measure of economic success" (ibid. p.11).

Another contribution to the sustainability debate in the last century was made by Garret Hardin in 1968. Hardin portrayed the unsustainability of the common property system of natural resource exploitation which ruins the commons. Hardin wrote: "The tragedy of the commons develops in this way. Picture a pasture open to all. It is to be expected that each herdsman will try to keep as many cattle as possible on the commons... As a rational being, each herdsman seeks to maximise his gain. Explicitly or implicitly, more or less consciously, he asks, 'what is the utility to me of adding one more animal to my herd?... the rational herdsman concludes that the only sensible course for him to pursue is to add another animal to his herd. And another ... But this is the conclusion reached by each and every rational herdsman sharing a commons. There in is the tragedy. Each man is locked into a system that compels him to increase his herd without limit – in a world that is limited. Ruin is the destination towards which all men rush, each pursuing his own best interests in a society that believes in the freedom of the commons. Freedom in a common brings ruin to all ... Likewise , the oceans of the world continue to suffer from the survival of the philosophy of the commons. Maritime nations still respond automatically to the shibboleth of the 'freedom of the seas'. Professing to believe in the 'inexhaustible resources of the oceans', they bring species after species of fish and whales closer to extinction" (Hardin, 1968, reprinted in Sankar, 2001, pp. 133-135).

A very pessimistic study which forecasted doom to the world economy was made by the Club of Rome in 1972. The report of the study entitled *Limits to Growth* was published by Meadows, *et al.* (Meadows, *et. al.* 1972). The report noted that "if the present growth trends in world population, industrialisation, pollution, food production, and resource depletion continue unchanged, the limits to growth on this planet will be reached sometime within the next 100 years. The most probable result will be a sudden and uncontrollable decline in the population and industrial capacity" (Meadows, *et al.* 1972, p.24).The main conclusions reached in this study, as summarised by Tietenberg are: "the first suggests that within a time span of less than100 years with no major change in the physical, economic, or social relationships that have traditionally governed world development, society will run out of the non-renewable resources on which the industrial base depends. When the resources have been depleted, a precipitous collapse of the economies will result, manifested in massive unemployment, decreased food production, and a decline in population as the death rate soars. There is no smooth transition, no gradual slowing down of activity; rather, the economic system consumes successively larger amounts of the depletable resources until suddenly they are gone. The characteristic behavior of the system is overshoot and collapse.

The second conclusion of the study is that piecemeal approaches to solving the individual problems will not be successful. To demonstrate this point, the authors arbitrarily double their estimates of the resource base and allow the model to trace out an alternative vision based on this new, higher level of resources. In this alternative vision the collapse still occurs, but this time it is caused by excessive pollution generated by the increased pace of industrialisation permitted by the greater availability of resources. The authors then suggest that if the depletable resources and pollution problems were some how jointly solved, population would grow unabated and the availability of food would become the binding constraint. In this model, the removal of one limit merely causes the system to bump subsequently into another one, usually with more dire consequences.

As its third and final conclusion, the study suggests that overshoot and collapse can be avoided only by an immediate limit on population and pollution, as well as a 'cessation of economic growth'. The portrait painted shows only two possible outcomes: the termination of growth by self-restraint and conscious policy – an approach that avoids the collapse – or the termination of growth by a collision with the natural limits, resulting in societal collapse. Thus, according to this study, one way or the other, 'growth will cease'. The only issue is whether the conditions under which it will cease will be congenial or hostile" (Tietenberg, 1984, p.5).

Commenting on this report, Pearson observes that "while the limits was severely criticised by economists for failing to incorporate market adjustments for adapting to increasing scarcity and for its idiosyncratic treatment of technological change, it did revitalise a dormant debate on physical limits to growth and did add a new limit, pollution, to the earlier concern for population, agriculture, and non-renewable resources. Its publication at the time of the first oil price shock added greatly to its impact on the public" (Pearson, op. cit. pp. 467-468).

A fundamental difference in the economist's approach to sustainability occurred with Daly recasting economics as *life science,* akin to biology and ecology, rather than a physical science like chemistry or physics (Daly 1968). It implied a fundamental change in the perception of the problems of resource allocation and how they should be addressed. More specifically it implied that the focus of analysis should be shifted from marketed resources in the economic systems to the biophysical basis of interdependent ecological and economic systems (Costanza, *et al.* 1997, p.62).

Daly further elaborated on this theme with his work on 'steady state economics' which acknowledged that the earth is materially finite and non-growing, and that the economy is a subset of this finite earth's ecosystem. Man is advised to adapt the pattern of this ecosystem for sustaining the economy. In Daly's own words, "the economy, in its physical dimensions, is a sub-system of the earth's ecosystem. The ecosystem is finite, non-growing and materially closed. In the earth's ecosystem solar energy enters and exists and it is this throughput of energy (itself finite and non-growing) that powers the material biogeochemical cycles on which life depends. Within the earth's ecosystem the economy exists as an open sub-system. That means that both matter and energy enter from the larger system. All physical processes of life and production are maintained by this metabolic flow-through (throughput) of matter –energy from and back to the environment. The economy lives off the environment in the same way that an animal does – by taking in useful (low-entropy) raw material and energy, and giving back waste (high-entropy) material and energy. The rest of the ecosystem, the part that is not within the economic sub-system (that is, natural capital), absorbs the emitted wastes, and through biogeochemical cycles powered by sun, reconstitutes much of the waste into reusable raw materials...

As the economic sub-system expands in its physical dimensions, it assimilates into itself a larger and larger proportion of the total matter – energy of the earth's ecosystem. More and more of total life space is converted into economic space–that is, living space for expanding populations and space taken over to provide sources of our raw materials and sinks for our waste materials. Consequently less and less life space remains outside the economy to provide the vital function of carrying out the biogeochemical cycles at the rates and through the pathways to which we are adapted...The planet earth develops without growing – that is, it evolves qualitatively without expanding quantitatively. The economy, as a sub-system of the earth, must at some scale adapt itself to this same pattern of 'development without growth' – which is what should be understood by the popular term 'sustainable development'. That is the paradigm or pre-analytic vision of steady state economics" (Daly, 1999, pp.635-636).

The 'steady state economics' as a model for sustainable development as prescribed by Daly, a World Bank economist has, however, raised doubts about the motives of the thinking: especially in the underdeveloped countries. As Opschoor, *et al.* put it, "it is absolutely a waste of time as well as morally backward to preach steady – state doctrines to under-developed countries before the over-developed countries have taken any measure to reduce either their own population growth or the growth of their per capita resource consumption. Therefore, the steady-state paradigm must first of all be adopted and applied in the over-developed countries" (Opschoor, *et al.* 1999, p.84).

These authors were, however, quick to add: "That does not mean, however, that the underdeveloped countries can be left out of consideration. For one thing, the underdeveloped countries are not ever going to develop…unless the overdeveloped countries moderate their demands on world resources and absorption capacities. One of the major forces necessary to push the over-developed countries toward a SSE will be Third World outrage at their over-consumption. In addition, underdeveloped countries will have to revise their expectations downward regarding their own growth. Although per-capita consumption levels are too low and must still grow, population size need not grow and must in fact, be significantly slowed down as a pre-condition for increasing the growth rate of per capita consumption. Investment can be used either to increase the standards of a given population or to increase the population at given standards. Under-developed countries must, regardless of the actions of over-developed countries, reduce their population growth" (ibid. pp.85-86).

The fundamental changes in the sustainable development debate in the seventies were summarised by Pearson thus: "Since the 1970s, the limits debate has focused more on ecological and environmental constraints than agriculture and commercialised natural resources. This shift reflects an easing of the energy crisis, considerably more rapid decline in population growth rates than had been anticipated, and an emerging view that securing adequate food supplies is more an income and distributional issue than an aggregate supply question. It also reflects the growing public awareness of the global environmental threats - green house gases, ozone depletion, loss of biodiversity, nuclear waste disposal - and a new appreciation for basic ecological functions of the environment.

The intellectual underpinning of environmental and ecological limits as opposed to raw material limits can be traced in part to the material balances approach introduced in the1970s, which utilises the first law of thermodynamics-where materials are extracted or harvested from nature, their mass is not significantly altered in production and 'consumption'… It follows that the throughput of an economic system is a flow of wastes, or residuals, disposed of in environmental media, and the capacity of the environment to absorb the wastes is at issue. Moreover, the second law of thermodynamics, which states that any conversion of energy to mechanical work increases entropy, has been invoked …Entropy is defined as a measure of dissipated or unavailable energy. In this fashion, entrophy, and particularly the limit it places on recycling materials, has become another limit to economic growth, although the practical significance is much debated ..." (Pearson, *op cit.* p.468).

Pearson also noted that "the concept of sustainable development is rooted in a longstanding debate concerning natural and environmental resource limits to economic growth. The terms of the debate have shifted over the years, with greater attention now paid to the residuals of economic activity and the effect those residuals have on the capacity of environmental resources to sustain a variety of life-support and economic functions. The constants in the debate are the degree to which society can rely on prices and markets for substitution as resources become progressively scarcer, and the degree to which technological improvements can push back the limits" (ibid, pp. 468-469).

The growing concern for sustainable development, or rather the unsustainability of the development path in the past had forced the United Nations to organise several international conferences and to establish international organisations to promote sustainable development on a global scale. These conferences, starting with the Lake Success conference at New York in 1949 on the subject of resource scarcity, extended to a range of subjects like population, settlements, water resources, desertification,the law of the sea, new and renewable resources of energy, environment and development, social development and world food supplies. Among these, the conferences on environment and development held at Stockholm and Rio de Janeiro in 1972 and 1992 respectively were most significant and comprehensive from the point of view of sustainable development. The latter (UNCED 1992) is discussed in the next section. The Stockholm Conference on the Human Environment (1972) declared that in accordance with international law, states have "the responsibility to ensure that activities within their jurisdiction or control do not cause damage to the environment of other states or areas beyond the limit of national jurisdiction" (as quoted by Pearson 2000, p.375).Referring to the Stockholm meeting, Cicin-Sain and Knecht observed that "the first effort to be comprehensive and indeed, even pro active, took place at a United Nations - sponsored conference on the environment held at Stockholm in 1972. The Conference, formally called the United Nations Conference on the Human Environment, was held at the peak of a wave of environmental concern triggered by incidents such as the January 1969 oil spill offshore from Santa Barbara, California, in the United States and by a growing realisation that environmental degradation was becoming a serious problem in many parts of the world.

The Stockholm conference was important in several respects. First, in preparation for the conference, many of the more than 100 nations attending prepared 'national reports' on environmental conditions in their countries. This exercise led to increased environmental awareness in these countries and might have contributed to the fact that a number of them went on to establish permanent environmental departments or ministries. One of the most significant actions of the conference was the creation of a new institution to coordinate environmental activities within the United Nations system – the United Nations Environment Programme (UNEP) and its governing council ...UNEP has been an important actor in the international arena since that time, organising such activities as the Regional Seas Programme and playing important role in ozone depletion and biodiversity issues, among others.

The Stockholm conference also acted as a catalyst in accelerating the adoption of several pending international agreements dealing with ocean dumping, vessel source pollution, and trade in endangered species. Moreover, the Stockholm declaration of principles and its accompanying 109-item action plan represented the first effort by the international community to deal with environmental problems on a comprehensive basis" (Cicin-Sain and Knecht, 1998, pp.72-73).

Several other relevant organisations also have sprung into being since then from private initiatives such as the Beijer International Institute of Ecological Economics and the International Institute for Environment and Development (Gilpin, 2000, p.71).

The last few decades of the last century had also witnessed the emergence and activation of several Non-Governmental Organisations (NGOs) and green parties through out the world which sought to promote sustainable development, focusing on natural resource conservation and social justice. The most prominent of these organisations are the World Conservation Union established in 1948, the World Wide Fund for Nature established in 1961, Green Peace and the Friends of the Earth established in 1971, the World Resources Institute set up in 1982 and the World Watch Institute founded in 1984.

In 1980, the World Conservation Strategy (WCS) was launched collectively by the World Conservation Union (WCU, formerly IUCN), the UN Environment Programme, and the World Wide Fund for Nature (WWF). It demonstrated that development can only be sustained by conserving the living resources on which that development depends, and by the integration of development and conservation policies. It urged every country to prepare its own national conservation strategy. The World Conservation Strategy emphasises "the maintenance of essential ecological processes and life support systems, the preservation of genetic diversity, and the sustainable utilisation of species and ecosystems with the over all aim of achieving sustainable development through the conservation of living resources" (as quoted by Barbier, 1998, p.1). A successor document, "Caring for the Earth: A Strategy for Sustainable Living' was published by these agencies in 1991. It included a wide range of recommendations for legal, institutional and administrative reform. The principles of a sustainable society as prescribed by the IUCN, UNEP and WWF are given in appendix 3.1.

The most significant event in the 1980s was the publication of the Brundtland Report, *Our Common Future*, by the World Commission on Environment and Development in 1987. The Report defined sustainable development as "development that meets the needs of the present without compromising the ability of future generations to meet their own needs". It recognises that any society setting itself the goal of sustainable development should therefore develop economically and socially in such a way that it minimises those activities the costs of which are borne by future generations, and, where such activities are unavoidable, due allowance is made for compensating future generations for those costs.

The Brundtland Report gave overriding priority for attending to the needs of the poor with in any society and in the world as a whole. It noted that sustainable development contains within it two key concepts: (1) the concept of 'needs', in particular the essential needs of the world's poor, to which overriding priority should be given (intra- generational equity) and (2) the idea of limitations imposed by the state of technology and social organisation on the environment's ability to meet present and future needs (intergenerational equity) (WCED, 1987, p.43).

The 'critical objectives' for sustainable development, proposed by the WCED are: 1. reviving growth, 2. changing the quality of growth, 3. meeting essential needs for jobs, food, energy, water and sanitation, 4. conserving and enhancing the resource base, 5. re-orienting technology and managing risk, and 6. merging environment and economics in decision–making. It called for a move from dealing with environmental effects, after their occurrence, to focusing on the 'policy sources' for preventive action. This is considered as a shift from a discussion of 'environment and development' to 'development and environment', making environment an integral part of development policy (Bartelmus,

1994, p.8). The report called for much more emphasis on conserving the natural resource base on which all development depends; and a greater regard for equity within society and between rich and poor nations, with a planning horizon that extends beyond the present generation. It also required an integration of economic, social and environmental considerations in decision-making at both government and enterprise level (Gilpin, 2000, pp. 90-91).

It is also noted that the intragenerational equity concern, that is, the distributional component of the Brundtland Commission's definition of sustainable development, has more recent and more political roots. Pearson observes that "environmental degradation entered the lexicon of international relations with the 1972 United Nations Conference on the Human Environment. In advance of that Conference, it was necessary to persuade developing countries that the environmental *problematique* was more than just industrial pollution, or the 'effluents of affluence'. The compromise struck in a preparatory meeting in Founex, Switzerland, was to redefine environmental degradation to include not only industrial pollution but the attributes of poverty-unsanitary water supplies, inadequate sewage disposal, urban slums, and over- exploitation of renewable resources...This broadening not only allowed developing countries to acknowledge an environmental problem, but, by placing poverty as the overarching problem, outlined the solution as rapid economic growth, preferably with the help of increased financial transfers from rich countries.

This idea of additionality in funding found its way 20 years later into the Frame Work Convention on Climate Change (FCCC) in the form of a commitment to pay full incremental costs, and was a central issue at the 1992 Rio Conference... In retrospect, the Founex compromise, while politically successful in attracting the involvement of poor countries, and while correctly highlighting the important relation between poverty and unsustainable resource use, had two negative consequences. First, by conflating poverty and environmental degradation, it promoted the simplistic idea that economic growth was a necessary and sufficient condition for environmental improvement. Second, it raised unrealistic expectations that additional aid from North to South would be forthcoming.

These expectations received a serious jolt with the abortive effort to create a New International Economic Order (NIEO) in the 1970s. Buoyed by the initial success of OPEC in pushing up oil prices in 1972 and by a belief that their position in natural-resources-based exports represented growing international market power – developing countries coalesed behind a broad programme to fundamentally alter the balance of international economic relations. The objectives were improved terms of trade through commodity agreements, improved market access for their exports, better terms for technology transfer, regulation of multinational corporations that was more favourable to host countries, and redistribution of income through financial transfers. By and large, the NIEO effort failed as the countries of the South over-estimated their market power and under-estimated the resistance from the industrial countries" (Pearson, *op cit.* pp. 469-470).

Commenting on the motive and working of the intragenerational equity principle, Pearson further observed that "it is fair to say that the intragenerational equity component of Brundtland's definition of sustainable development - meeting the needs of today's poor, to which overriding priority should be given - was included for the same reasons that the Founex compromise redefined the environmental *problematique* – to bring developing countries on board. And it seems to have met the same fate. Except for the Global Environmental Facility with its limited funds and mandate, the sustainable development debate has lost its intragenerational equity dimension. Indeed, among economists, sustainable development has been analysed almost exclusively from either an efficiency perspective or an intergenerational equity perspective ... Of course, this focus does rescue the subject of sustainability from merely an issue of poor countries, but it has very different emphasis than Brundtland" (ibid, p.471). The definition of sustainable development as given by WCED is considered to be vague. van Kooten and Bulte note that "definitions of sustainability typically lack rigour, as exemplified by the definition provided by the WCED. One can only conclude that attempts to define sustainable development need to be purposely vague if they are to be politically acceptable; ... but this is not helpful for scientists seeking to measure and debate sustainability" (van Kootan and Bulte, 2000, p.235).

Jones, *et al.* noted that "as befits a broad policy goal, the Brundtland definition was vague in a number of important respects ..."(Jones, *et al.* p.26). Pearson remarks that "at one level it is a clever term" and "if sustainable development is to serve as a spline to join economic and environmental strategies, it must take a more concrete and objective form"(Pearson, *op. cit.* p.461).

The underlying motive behind the globalisation of sustainable development is very clear. It has succeeded in placing the agenda of global economic growth in an unassailable position by arguing that growth is needed for meeting the needs of the poor (intragenerational equity), even at the cost of depleting natural capital with sufficient investment in reproducible capital (man-made capital) and technological assistance provided by developed countries as recommended by the neo-classical, neo-liberal economists. Suitable institutional changes at the global, regional, national, state and local levels were also suggested by this school. The WCED has in fact succeeded in pacifying the environmental (deep ecology) school and in bringing the ecological group and the economists and business favouring 'growth' to the negotiating table of international conventions in later years. In this way it has succeeded in keeping world business flourish, notwithstanding the token protests by radical environmental groups assisted by national and international NGOs funded by global funding agencies. In tune with this approach, it is found that "global commerce is increasingly governed by regional alliances and trade treaties aimed at increasing economic output in both rich and poor countries. Such agreements confer greater freedom and power on corporations and on international tribunals while restricting the authority of electorally accountable governments" (Rees, 1999, p.113). Global developments in the 1990s and thereafter very well prove this fact. It appears that the concept of sustainable development was strategically planned by meticulous calculations and designs of foresight by the industrial countries to maintain hegemony and control over global resources in the guise of the morally appealing principles of sustainable development. The fact that global economic policies have been tailor-made to suit this agenda of developed countries, aided by several international organisations, whether voluntary or official, democratic or coercive, very well establishes this point.

Among the several international organisations which assisted or influenced the design or working of the concept of sustainable development in recent decades are the OECD, World Bank, IMF, FAO, ILO and WTO . The OECD is credited for having prepared suitable guidelines and indications for sustainable environment and economic policies for member states. Some of the documents which contained these guidelines have been noted in the review of literature made in chapter two.

The World Bank and the IMF, though not directly involved in the sustainability debate of the earlier development decades, have now become major players influencing global development policies, especially financing policy. The role of World Bank and IMF in effecting sustainable development has been reviewed by Opschoor and Jongma. They wrote: "in the early 1970s, the World Bank was one of the very first international organisations to recognise the importance of environmental issues for the process of development...Since the early 1980s many WB projects have been criticised for their environmental and social aspects...Shortly after the WECD Conference on sustainable development in 1987, the rather small environmental unit of the World Bank was replaced by the Environmental Department...In 1993 attention to environmental issues was further institutionalised by establishing a Vice-Presidency for Environmentally Sustainable Development...Meanwhile, WB policy statements indicate that it wishes to adhere to – at least – weak sustainability. In general terms, the WB's environmental agenda consists of: (1) assisting countries in their environmental stewardship(through loans, assistance in policy development and institution building), (2) mitigating adverse environmental impacts of all bank financed projects, (3) developing human capital and promoting the efficient use of resources, and (4) addressing global environmental challenges. The WB analysis of environmental degradation hinges...on the recognition of environmentally relevant market imperfections and institutional weaknesses. The WB has developed a therapy for sustainable development which is composed of the following measures: (1) removal of price distortions and impediments for market forces, (2) clarifying property rights on environmental goods, (3) introduction of incentives for sustainable use of natural resources. Moreover, the World Bank displays a growing awareness of the environmental repercussions of macro-economic and sectoral policies. Not all economic reforms are claimed to benefit the environment, and economic growth without environmental policies may accelerate environmental damage. The WB proposes that such damages can be mitigated or compensated by *complementary policies...*" (Opschoor and Jongma, 1999, pp. 519-520).

It is also reported by these authors that "up till now economy-wide policy reforms designed to promote growth and liberalisation have been encouraged with little regard to their environmental consequences...due to the presumption that these effects could be ignored or could be dealt with separately ... The WB suggestion to develop complementary policies is one way of dealing with this. However, this would amount to an approach that can at best be characterised as 'retrofitting' economy-wide reforms where an integrated sustainability-oriented intervention might have long-run efficiency benefits"- (ibid, pp.520-521).

Referring to the working of World Bank assistance programmes, O'Riordan states: "Recent studies of World Bank aid, even those programmes which allegedly have a specific environmental component, indicate outcomes which are socially divisive and environmentally destructive" (O'Riordan, 1991, p.42).

Quoting Edward Goldsmith, this author makes further clear that "environmental degradation in third world is the inevitable consequence of present development policies, and third world people are poor, because they have been impoverished by previous development, because they have been robbed by developers of their means of sustenance, and are now condemned to scratching an ever more marginal existence from land that ever more closely resembles the surface of the moon" (ibid, p.42). Even while considering this view of Goldsmith as unsubstantiated rhetoric, O'Riordan reports that the World Bank ecologist Robert Goodland has admitted that "World Bank – financed major water projects have caused 'massive damage' and that there is an acute shortage of environmental specialists on the Bank staff" (ibid, p.42). The US Treasury is also believed to suspect "that the problems encountered in the environmental aspects of projects may be an instance of the over-emphasis of quantity rather than quality. If environmental considerations threaten expeditious project processing, the environment is assigned low priority and is left to be dealt with later" (ibid, pp.42-43). This corroborates the 'retrofitting' approach noted earlier, though diametrically opposed to the spirit of EIA and the precautionary approach.

Alan Gilpin reports that "the Bank has been accused of failing in its original role of reducing poverty and of disregarding in whole or part the environmental effects of major development projects. It has, it is claimed, financed roads for settlers who devastated the Amazon rain forest and financed dams that forced many thousands to be resettled in less satisfactory circumstances" (Gilpin, 2000, p.80). Some of these criticisms were confirmed by the Bank itself. Gilpin reports that "in its first report on the environment, the World Bank admitted that in the past it had financed projects that proved environmentally damaging. It singled out the Indira-Sagar-Sardar Sarovar Dam in India which would submerge 600,000 ha of land and displace 100,000 people, and the Carajas iron ore mine in Brazil, the development of which destroyed a large area of forest. The report also added that half of the loans made during the preceding year had included measures to protect the environment, and other loans had been made specifically for environmental improvements" (ibid, p.80).

Referring to the working of IMF in the context of promoting sustainable development, Opschoor and Jongma noted that "the IMF has not yet taken a position regarding the concept of sustainable development, but one may assume that at least it should intend not to induce (further) unsustainability as an impediment to international prosperity" (Opschoor and Jongma, *op. cit.* p.523).

The role of FAO, ILO and WTO in promoting sustainable development has been growing especially since the UNCED and the liberalisation of the world trading system. The impact of UNCED and the working of these institutions in the era of globalisation and their import for sustainable development are discussed in the next section.

### 3.3.5. Post-modern View

The post-modern view is attributed to the post-cold war period or the period after the *Perestroika* and the collapse of the former USSR. This period also witnessed the hastening of global economic reforms initiated since 1991. It also coincided with the period following the first US-Iraq war of 1991. The major event having maximum impact on global thinking on sustainability during this period was the United Nations Conference on Environment and Development (UNCED) held at Rio de Janeiro in 1992. The UNCED also known as the Earth Summit, was the largest international gathering ever held to discuss the global environmental issues.

Referring to the UNCED and the circumstances which led to it, Cicin-Sain and Knecht noted: "In the 1980s, several urgent new concerns were edging their way on to the international agenda, leading eventually to a decision to hold a second United Nations conference on the environment (and development in 1992), on the twentieth anniversary of the Stockholm meeting. The first of these concerns involved a growing awareness that a significant number of the world's ills were inexorably linked - that the abject poverty and soaring birth rates of much of the developing world, together with the unsustainable production and consumption of many developed nations, were contributing directly to worsening environmental despoliation - and that reversing the situation required a shift to sustainable use of the world's resources - that is, sustainable development on the part of all nations...

The second concern was related to the growing realisation that industrialised societies appeared capable of doing significant damage to the earth's climate and life support systems. First, there was a concern that compounds such as chlorofluorocarbons (CFCs) could destroy the earth's ozone shield, thus exposing the biosphere and its living populations (including humans) to harmful levels of solar ultraviolet radiation. Similarly, important groups of scientists had become convinced that increasing emissions of 'green house gases', especially carbon dioxide, were threatening to trigger climate changes on a global scale, including increases in temperature that could alter weather patterns and cause potentially dangerous rises in sea level...A second group of experts, under the leadership of the United Nations Environment Programme, was expressing grave concern over the increasing rate at which species were becoming extinct, signalling a serious decline in biological diversity worldwide ...

These growing concerns, important as they were, might not have been sufficient in themselves to cause an event of the scope and significance of UNCED to take place. Indeed, a 'window of opportunity' associated with a dramatic change in global politics allowed these issues to reach the top of the international agenda ... In the late 1980s, a political change of major consequence occurred with the collapse of the Soviet Union and the end of the cold war. This change was felt especially strongly in Europe, where it created an unprecedented opportunity for concerned governments (such as those of Germany, the United Kingdom and the Nordic countries) to shift their attention to global environmental problems in a new and more focused way. The availability of a coherent set of policy recommendations in the form of the 1987 report of WCED also helped set the stage for action in this policy area. European leaders at the highest levels became versed in the issue of climate change, bringing the matter to the agendas of the annual meetings of the world's industrialised democracies (the G.7 group) beginning with the Paris meeting in 1990.

Thus, the stage was set for these issues to be advanced to the top of the global agenda. The United Nations General Assembly adopted Resolution 44/228 at its eighty-fifth plenary meeting on December 22, 1989, formally deciding to convene the United Nations Conference on Environment and Development in Brazil in June 1992 ...The Resolution set forth the reasons prompting the decision to convene UNCED; ... affirmed (and reaffirmed) certain principles that should guide preparations for the conference; set out nine issues 'of major concern in maintaining the quality of the earth's environment and especially in achieving environmentally sound and sustainable development in all countries'; listed twenty-three objectives for the conference; and established a Preparatory Committee, authorising it to meet five times and charging with preparing a provisional agenda and draft decisions for the conference ..." (Cicin-Sain and Knecht, 1998, pp.73-75).

The major output of the UNCED were (1) the Rio Declaration on Environment and Development, (2) Agenda 21, (3) the Convention on Climate Change, (4) the Convention on Biological Diversity, and (5) the Statement of Forest Principles.

### 3.3.5.1.The Rio Declaration on Environment and Development

The Rio Declaration on Environment and Development, a set of twenty seven principles to guide national and international actions on environment, development and social issues, was approved by all nations attending the conference on June 14, 1992. Cicin-Sain and Knecht noted that "the Rio Declaration is clearly of a non-binding character; within the framework of international law, it can be considered as 'soft law'. As such, however, it can be seen as indicating the direction international law could take in the years ahead. Indeed, some of the principles might well find their way into legal instruments of one kind or another or, through common acceptance or acquiescence, ultimately become customary international law..." (ibid, pp.77-78).

The Rio principles, paraphrased and condensed by Cicin-Sain and Knecht into twenty principles and grouped into three categories – those that apply to development, those that apply to the environment and those relating to process – are given in table 3.1.

**Table 3.1.**

**Rio Principles on Environment and Development**

---

***On development***

1. Human beings are at the centre of concerns for sustainable development
2. States have the right to develop
3. Priority should be given to special needs of developing countries
4. States have a sovereign right to exploit resources but must ensure that their activities do not cause environmental damage to other jurisdictions

5. Nations have common but differentiated responsibilities for solving environmental problems
6. Unsustainable patterns of production and consumption must be reduced and eliminated
7. Appropriate demographic policies must be promoted.
8. A supportive and open international economic system must be promoted

***On environment***

1. Environmental protection must be an integral part of the development process
2. States shall enact effective environmental legislation (taking into account varying natural conditions)
3. States shall develop national law regarding liability and compensation for the victims of pollution and other environmental damage
4. States shall discourage or prevent the relocation and transfer to other states of environmentally harmful activities
5. States shall apply the precautionary approach
6. Polluters should bear the cost of pollution
7. States shall employ environmental impact assessment
8. States shall be responsible for international notification of natural disasters, emergencies, and other activities with negative transboundary consequences
9. States must consider the environmental rights of people under oppression
10. Peace, development, and environmental protection are interdependent and indivisible

***On process***

1. States need to promote the participation of all concerned citizens
2. States should be concerned with intergenerational equity and the rights of future generations

---

*Source:* Cicin-Sain and Knecht, 1998, p.78.

The full text of the Rio Declaration is given in appendix 3.2.

### 3.3.5.2.Agenda 21

Agenda 21 is a forty-chapter action plan intended to serve as a kind of road map pointing the direction toward sustainable development. As reported by Cicin-Sain and Knecht, "it represents an ambitious effort to provide recommendations across the entire spectrum of environment, development, and social issues confronting humankind today. In terms of social and economic issues, it addresses poverty, overconsumption and production, population, and human development problems.

In the areas of natural resources and environment, Agenda 21 deals with the atmosphere, land resources, deforestation, desertification and drought, mountain ecosystems, agriculture and rural development, biological diversity, biotechnology, oceans and coastal areas, freshwater resources, toxic chemicals, hazardous wastes, solid wastes, and radioactive wastes. It has chapters devoted to the roles of major groups, including women, children and youth, indigenous peoples, non-governmental organisations, local authorities, workers and trade unions, business and industry, the scientific and technological community, and farmers. Finally, concerning means of implementation, it discusses financial resources, transfer of technology, the roles of science, education, public awareness and training, capacity building, institutional arrangements, legal institutions, and information for decision making.

Like the Rio Declaration, Agenda 21 is a non-binding document. Yet in signing the document, governments indicated a willingness to be part of the international consensus seeking to move toward a more sustainable society along the lines set forth in Agenda 21" (ibid, pp.80-81).

### 3.3.5.3. The Convention on Climate Change

The overall objective of the Framework Convention on Climate Change adopted on May 9, 1992 was to achieve the "stabilisation of green house gas concentrations in the atmosphere at a level that would prevent dangerous anthropogenic interference with the climate system...within a time frame sufficient to allow ecosystems to adapt naturally to climate change, to ensure that food production is not threatened and to enable economic development to proceed in a sustainable manner..." The agreement includes two principles: that the parties "should protect the climate system for the benefit of present and future generations of humankind" ... and that "the specific needs and social circumstances of developing country parties ... should be given full consideration ..." (ibid. pp.78-79).

In ratifying the Convention on Climate Change, nations commit themselves to do the following:

1. Develop, periodically update, and publish national inventories on emissions by sources and removals by sinks
2. Formulate, implement, publish, and regularly update national programmes containing measures to mitigate climate change
3. Promote and cooperate in the development, application, and diffusion of practices and processes that could control, reduce, or prevent anthropogenic emissions of green house gases

Developed nations commit themselves to do the following:

1. Adopt national policies and take corresponding measure to mitigate climate change by limiting emissions
2. Communicate within six months of the convention's entry into force, detailed information on their policies and measures
3. Provide new and additional financial resources to meet the agreed full costs incurred by developing country parties ... (ibid. p.79).

### 3.3.5.4. The Convention on Biological Diversity

The objectives of the Convention on Biological Diversity signed on June 5, 1992 are (1) conservation of biological diversity, (2) sustainable use of its components, and (3) fair and equitable sharing of the benefits arising from the utilisation of genetic resources.

On ratifying this convention, each party commits itself to take the following actions:

1. Develop national strategies, plans, or programmes for the conservation and sustainable use of biological diversity
2. Integrate, as far as possible and appropriate, the conservation and sustainable use of biological diversity into relevant sectoral or cross-sectoral plans, programmes and policies
3. Identify components of biological diversity important for conservation and sustainable use
4. Monitor, through sampling and other techniques, the components of biological diversity, paying particular attention to those requiring urgent conservation measures and those offering greatest potential for sustainable use

5. Establish a system of protected areas or areas where special measures need to be taken to conserve biological diversity
6. Develop, where necessary, guidelines for selection, establishment, and management of protected areas
7. Promote the protection of ecosystems and natural habitats and the maintenance of viable populations of species in natural surroundings. Ratifying nations also commit themselves to a number of actions involving *ex situ* conservation, including the adoption of measures for recovery and rehabilitation of threatened species and reintroduction into their natural habitat under appropriate conditions. Developed country parties commit themselves to provide new and additional financial resources to enable developing country parties to meet the agreed full incremental costs of implementing measures (ibid. pp.79-80).

**3.3.5.5. Statement of Forest Principles**

The Statement of Principles for a global consensus on the management, conservation and sustainable development of all types of forests, a prelude to a possible future convention on forests was agreed to at the UNCED on June 13, 1992. As noted by Cicin-Sain and Knecht, "not surprisingly, the forest issue was one of the most intractable at the conference. Industrialised nations of the North see the expansive rain forests of the South as a necessary and valuable 'sink' for green house gas emissions. In contrast, nations of the South – Brazil and Malaysia are good examples – see the rain forests as entirely theirs to develop or conserve as they see fit. Broadening the discussion to include all forests rather than just tropical rain forests helped to move the dialogue in a positive direction, but it was impossible to reach agreement at UNCED on anything more than a set of principles. However, the agreed principles may be helpful in guiding post-UNCED discussions toward of a future convention on the protection of forests" (ibid. p.81).

**3.3.5.6. Post-UNCED Developments**

Following the UNCED (1992), the UN Commission on Sustainable Development was established in early 1993. It invited nations to report regularly to the Commission on their progress in the implementation of Agenda 21 and with respect to environmental management generally. The Commission is to review the finding and monitor the promised official assistance of 0.7 per cent of GDP due from the developed nations. It is also to review progress in respect of technology transfer and receive and analyse inputs from non-governmental organisations and bodies outside the UN. The implementation of UN conventions were also kept under the review of the Commission. The Commission meets annually for up to three weeks addressing various topics within Agenda 21 such as health, human settlements and freshwater, toxic chemicals and hazardous waste, land, desertification, forests and biodiversity, atmosphere, oceans and sustainable development.

At the Earth Summit II Conference in 1997, five years after the Earth Summit 1 was held in Rio de Janeiro, the Commission submitted a report warning world leaders that humanity is bound to face a global water crisis by 2025 caused by pollution and water overuse. The report contained the first UN warning about the risk of conflict caused by disputes over access to water. It also reported that the progress in human welfare was also disappointing. It further noted that the promised financial support from the developed countries had dwindled (Gilpin, 2000, pp.77-78).

In order to review the progress toward sustainable development after ten years, the World Summit on Sustainable Development was held at Johannesburg in 2002 ("Rio + 10"). The Summit focused on poverty and access to safe drinking water and sanitation. Among specific objectives, it agreed on (1) to reduce the number of people not connected to clean drinking water supplies from over 1 billion to 500 million by the year 2015, (2) to halve the number of people without proper sanitation to 1.2 billion and (3) to increase the use of sustainable energy sources and restore depleted fish stocks.

The venue of the summit witnessed protests by several environmental groups for the lack of progress in sustainable development since the Rio Summit in 1992. Politicians have reportedly pointed out that the Johannesburg meeting had moved on from issues like biodiversity and climate change to tackling poverty and poor living conditions.

Martin Khor, Director of Third World Network, reviewing the progress on sustainable development after ten years of UNCED, when national governments were preparing for the World Summit on Sustainable Development (Rio plus Ten) in Johannesburg in August 2002, observed that "unfortunately, almost a decade later, the process after Rio has largely failed. The Rio spirit seems to have faltered and been whittled down, if not away. The Rio plus five summit (UN General Assembly special session to review the implementation of the Rio agreement) concluded in June

1997 without a political statement because the divide between North and South countries was too wide to bridge. The ongoing negotiations for the Johannesburg World Summit on Sustainable Development (WSSD) – Rio Plus Ten – appear to be divided. A 'crisis of implementation' ..., is the diagnosis, among governments, UN officials and civil society organisations alike following the process.

The world's environment has continued to deteriorate. For example, forests continued to disappear or be degraded at a rate of 14 million hectares a year, greenhouse gases are still increasingly pumped into the atmosphere, but the US has rejected the Kyoto protocol and the present targets for emission reduction are clearly inadequate; there is a looming crisis of water shortages around the world; and new technologies such as genetic engineering pose new environmental and health threats.

Aid has fallen drastically even though UNCED promised new and additional financial resources from the North. The OECD countries' aid fell from US $61 billion in 1992 to US $ 56 billion in 1993, and 14 of 21 donors decreased the share of aid as a ratio of their Gross National Product (GNP). Since then, the situation has further worsened. The aid decline is inevitably seen as reflecting a lack of commitment and sincerity on the part of northern governments to implement the Rio agreements and has robbed the UNCED follow-up processes and institutions of their status and legitimacy.

There has been no tangible progress in the transfer of technology, either in general or in environmentally sound technology. Instead, since Rio, there has been much greater emphasis on increasing the rights of holders of intellectual property (mainly corporations of the North) and a corresponding downgrading of the rights of the public (and developing countries) in technology transfer and diffusion. This is mainly the result of the Uruguay Round's Agreement on Trade – Related Aspects of Intellectual Property Rights (TRIPS), which requires World Trade Organisation member states to tighten their national intellectual property right (IPR) regimes in favour of IPR holders, with detrimental effects on technology transfer or local development of technology. There is already evidence of how such patents regimes hinder transfer of environmental technology to the South" (Khor, 2002, pp.1-2).

Khor further noted that the failure of UNCED was due to four factors: (1) broken promises, (2) clash of paradigms, (3) failure to check the transnational corporations and (4) failure of political leadership. Referring to the first, he noted: "at the heart of the Rio 'compact' or core political agreement was the principle of common but differentiated responsibilities. This recognised that the global ecological crisis had to be solved in an equitable way, through partnership. It acknowledged that the North has historically and at present been more responsible for the despoliation of the global environment, has more resources due to the uneven nature of the world economy, and thus has a proportionately greater responsibility in resolving environmental problems. Unfortunately, almost a decade later the process after Rio has largely failed …" (ibid. p.3).

Referring to the second, Khor writes, "the reason for failure is not to be found in the sustainable development paradigm. Rather, the paradigm was not given the chance to be implemented. Instead, intense competition came from a rival: the countervailing paradigm of globalisation, driven by the industrialised North and its corporations, that has swept the world in recent years. This is perhaps the most basic factor behind the failure to realise the UNCED objectives ... The ... free market approach represents a very different paradigm. It advocated the reduction or removal of state regulations on the market, letting 'free market forces' reign, and a high degree of rights and 'freedoms' to the large corporations that dominate the market. The states should intervene only minimally, even in social services. On the environment, instead of public intervention or environmental controls, the market should be left free on the assumption that this would foster growth and the increased resources can be used for environmental protection. This approach also sidelines concerns of equity, or the negative results of market forces, such as poverty and non-fulfilment of basic needs. It assumes that market will solve all problems …

The free market paradigm represented by the Bretton Woods institutions has persisted in promoting structural adjustment programmes based on market liberalisation. The same paradigm ruled the GATT/WTO which was dominated by the Northern governments advocating the opening up of markets (especially of developing countries) to the exports and investments of corporations and financial institutions. The Uruguay Round of trade talks that ended in December 1993 heralded a new era where multilateral trade agreements and negotiations would subject countries to a great extent to the objectives of Northern governments advocating greater and wider 'market access' for their corporations. These were more powerful than the UNCED agreements and products of 1992 and the partnership approach that the latter promised.

In recent years Northern countries have also succeeded in downgrading the UN in social and economic affairs and policies, while enormously increasing the powers and influences of the Bretton Woods institutions and especially WTO in determining international economic and social policies. This shift in institutional location of authority has come about because the Bretton Woods /WTO institutions represent the paradigm advocated by the North who control these institutions in contrast to UN system where the South is better represented and where decision making processes are different.

With the higher status of the market paradigm, sustainable development concerns have been given lower priority. Governments of strong countries have become obsessed with competitiveness of their firms and countries; this has reduced the commitment to improve the environment and change production and consumption patterns. Deregulation has included the weakening of environmental policies (or their enforcement) in many countries. Interest in implementing the development components of UNCED ... has diminished" (ibid. pp.3-4).

Referring to the third factor, it is noted that "another major reason for the failure to implement the UNCED objectives is the absence of any kind of effective framework of accountability and disciplines for the behaviour and practices of big corporations. UNCED 1992 was itself responsible for this, as it did not propose any measures for regulating big corporations. These institutions are the main players responsible for generating much of the pollution and resource extraction in the world, as well as greatly contributing to the generation of unsustainable consumption patterns and a consumer culture. Instead of being regulated, their power and outreach have spread, facilitated by the implementation of the WTO's rules.

Not surprisingly, therefore, in the past few years, the power of big corporations has increased: they control even more of the world's resources and account for a greater share of production activities, distribution, finance and marketing. There has been no noticeable change in their production patterns. The 'business as usual' practice has resulted in the continuation or even intensification of environmental pollution and resource depletion. Through globalisation of media, their advertising and sales promotions of consumer products and tastes have had an even much greater impact in spreading the kinds of life styles and consumption patterns that are environmentally unsustainable.

Regulation of transnational corporations (TNCs) and business in general has worsened greatly, since the Rio summit. Efforts to finalise a code of conduct for TNCs were formally killed off in 1993 and the responsible agency, the UN Centre on Transnational Corporations was closed down. Many years of work and negotiations came to naught. Initiatives in the UN Conference on Trade and Development (UNCTAD), such as the Code of Conduct on Technology Transfer and the Set of Principles and Rules on Restrictive Business Practices, were also marginalised due to the reluctance of the developed countries to see their coming to effect.

Instead, there has been a strong opposite trend, which is now dominant to continuously reduce and remove regulations that governments have over corporations and to grant corporations increased rights and powers whilst removing the authority of states to impose controls over their behavior and operations.

The Uruguay Round has already granted far higher standards of intellectual property rights protection to the TNCs, thus facilitating further their monopolisation of technology and ability to earn huge rents through higher prices. There are now strong pressures from Northern governments at the WTO to grant foreign companies the right of entry, establishment and national treatment (treatment no less favourable than that accorded to their domestic counterparts) in all WTO member states. Other proposals on competition policy and government procurement would give them further rights of access to business in developing countries. The ability of governments to regulate the operations and effects of TNCs and companies in general is being severely curtailed.

It is most unlikely that businesses will voluntarily curb their own practices to be in line with sustainable development, especially with the current intensification of competition. Thus the removal of the rights of states to regulate business, especially TNCs, is a major and perhaps fatal blow in the international community's attempt to arrest environmental deterioration and promote sustainable development" (ibid. pp. 4-5).

Writing on the failure of political leadership, Khor notes that "there has also been a weakening of political leadership to address environmental, social or development issues. Northern political leadership has followed the imperatives of maintaining competitiveness in a globalising world, thereby placing environmental and social concerns much lower on the list of priorities. Instead, these governments are meeting the demands of their corporations to promote liberalisation and to champion their interests domestically and internationally.

Thus, at international negotiations, whether at the WTO or at the UN, Northern governments promote proposals that widen the rights of TNCs whilst blocking or diluting principles and points that are made on behalf of sustainable development.

In the international arena, Southern governments, individually and as a group, are generally inadequately prepared for negotiations, compared to the Northern governments. Despite the dramatic expansion of the importance of international organisations and processes in determining national policies, the political leadership and bureaucracy in most developing countries have not devoted adequate human and financial resources to preparations for international negotiations. Their resulting weak negotiating capacity sometimes makes them unable to effectively promote their points, and they have to agree to other points that are detrimental to their interests. Such a situation is particularly dangerous when the negotiations involve legally binding agreements, as in the WTO.

Many political leaders and bureaucrats may privately agree that the present state of affairs on environment and development is negative and requires drastic reforms. However, they go along with the big tide of liberalisation and cater to the demands and interests of the business elite. Many have declared that they are unable to change the situation, and that the forces of liberalisation and globalisation are too strong to counter" (ibid. p.5).

In the prevailing scenario, Khor raises the question "who, if not the political leaders, are going to take effective action to promote sustainable development" and declares that "while sustainable development is at a low ebb, there are also signs of its revival as a paradigm. The limitations and failures of globalisation have caused a major public backlash that may eventually result in some policy changes. Pro-sustainability forces within governments in developing countries are becoming more aware of their right or responsibility to try to rectify the present problems, including changing some of the rules in the WTO"(ibid. p.6).

Before concluding this section, it is noted that the role of FAO, like that of ILO and WTO, is to promote a global order in the realm of world food production and distribution and thereby to contribute to sustainable development. Since 1982, when the third Law of the Sea meeting was held by the UN and particularly after the UNCED in 1992, FAO has been playing an active role in propagating the message of sustainable development in world food production and consumption. The FAO's role in promoting sustainable development in fisheries is discussed in chapter four.

The ILO, while promoting global standards for working class, aims to promote sustainable development with equity and social justice, particularly in developing countries. It is however, now alleged that the ILO's global labour standards are being exploited by industrial nations to protect their vested interests and to prevent global competition from emerging developing countries.

The fundamental aim of WTO is to reduce or abolish barriers to trade and establish a 'just' trading system which is sustainable. The General Agreement on Tariff and Trade, the forerunner to the WTO, held the objective of promoting world trade through the progressive reduction of trade barriers. Through successive round of talks over many years, tariff reductions have been achieved to a great extent in many cases. However, the trade liberalisation policies of the WTO,as already noted, are promoting the interests of developed countries and transnational corporations. The trade policies of WTO are considered as inimical to sustainable development by environmentalists and others for the following reasons:

1. Trade liberalisation encourages economic growth and so damages the environment
2. By limiting national sovereignty, countries cannot apply any environmental measures they choose
3. GATT does not allow countries to keep out a product because of the way the product is produced or harvested.
4. GATT disapproves of the use of trade measures to influence environmental policies abroad as attempted by the EC and the US in the shrimp and turtle cases (Gilpin, 2000, pp.85-86)).

Referring to the absence of a pro-active role for the WTO in promoting sustainable development, especially since the Doha Round of negotiations, Mike Moore reports: "The relationship of the WTO to sustainable development remained ambiguous. Sustainable development is the only qualitative criterion for the work of the WTO that is identified in the preamble of the WTO agreement. The preambular section of the ministerial declaration is even more effusive in its adherence to sustainable development as a principle for the WTO. However, the phrase does not occur once in the operative sections of the Declaration. The Declaration is full of statements concerning development, and repeatedly expresses concern for developing and least developed countries. Indeed, some observers have declared that this was a 'development' Round - presumably in contrast to the Uruguay Round, which dealt primarily with matters of concern to developed countries. But the principal measures to operationalise the development dimension involve capacity building, a different task whose impact on economic development is largely unproven. Achieving a proper balance between environment, development and the economic policies that will be negotiated is a task that remains to be tackled" (Moore, 2004, p.16).

Some of the international dimensions of sustainable development has been highlighted by Pearson. Pearson noted that "sustainable development movement has had little apparent effect on changing the levels of international development assistance. In this respect, the intragenerational equity component of Brundtland's stricture has had minimal impact. But attention to sustainable development has reinforced a shift in World Bank funding for environmental protection and has encouraged the IMF to consider the environmental effects of its lending and macro-economic stabilisation advice. Sustainable development has also been popularised in an era characterised by accelerating economic integration through trade, foreign investment and technology flows and by increasing scrutiny of the trade-environment nexus, as well as heightened concern for international environmental degradation ... The most direct channel is, of course, international trade. The relevant feature of trade is that it separates production and consumption in a spatial sense. Hence consumption activity in one country can affect the environment in the country of production ...; this simply means that the exporting country should have adequate environmental protection measures in place. There is nothing inherently unsustainable in the trade relation ... But to realise these gains in a sustainable fashion requires the exporting country to internalise the full social costs of its production in the export price.

The same argument holds for foreign investment. While it is certainly possible for foreign investment to enter a country and despoil the environment, it is not a necessary consequence. Again, the principal responsibility rests with the host government in establishing adequate controls on the foreign investor. Both requirements may be difficult to accomplish in a poor country eager for export earnings and other benefits of foreign investment. Also, political and special-interest pressures opposed to full social cost pricing and strict controls on the environmental performance of multinational corporations (MNCs) may be difficult to resist … A country is unlikely to achieve sustainable development by selling its products in world markets at less than social costs or by inviting foreign investment to plunder its environment ... It is also possible that trade shifts the location of production towards countries less inclined to internalise international externalities, or countries with open-access natural resource regimes and excessive exploitation levels. For example, US restrictions on domestic logging, mining and oil extraction and development or Japan's domestic forest conservation practices may shift resource exploitation pressures to developing countries. This would be the raw material analogue of industrial relocation to pollution havens about which there has been much speculation. In general, however, the environmental costs of such shifts would be borne by the country of production ... When transnational pollution is present, however, one cannot rely on narrow national interest, and some control on relocating polluting activity through trade and foreign investment may be justified. Also governments are tempted toward policies that shift social costs onto future generations and under these circumstances trade and foreign investment can contribute to unsustainability…The long term implications for environmental stability from globalisation of trade and investment remains an open question…" (Pearson, op cit. pp.481-483). Some of the priorities for sustainable development in the post-UNCED era are noted in appendix 3.3.

The state of current global desperation about sustainable development is conveyed by Rees when he wrote: "There is a growing consensus that the current global economic development path is itself inherently unsustainable…Driven by both population growth and rampant consumerism, the world economy has expanded five-fold in half a century. Unfortunately, it is precisely continuous growth in the 'throughput' of energy and material required to feed aggregate human demand that causes the ecological crisis … Resource consumption already exceeds the productive capacity of certain critical biophysical systems on every continent. Waste production breaches the assimilative capacity of some ecosystems on every scale. As these trends continue, they have the potential to undermine the long-term stability and vital life-support functions of the ecosphere permanently.

There is no consensus on how to deal with this emerging reality. Many concerned humanists and techno-optimists remain dedicated to growth and global consumerism. They see freer markets and a new efficiency revolution as the only politically feasible solution to both global ecological decline and chronic Third World poverty. This approach would ostensibly decouple the economy from the environment. Other more ecocentric and community-oriented groups see growth-bound consumerism itself as the issue. They argue that beyond a certain point, there is no evident relationship between income and perceived well-being. Further growth may therefore be unnecessary. From this perspective, the solution lies more in changing consumer values and behaviour and in developing policies to ensure more equitable distribution of the world's present economic output. These actions would size the economy to the environment" (Rees, 1999, pp.102-103).

The fact, however, remains to be the opposite. As Rees reports "... the contemporary socio-cultural revolution seems perversely enigmatic. While the new science reveals a world of dynamic complexity and sudden surprise, the material philosophy of our globalising society assumes vapid simplicity and practical certainty. The past twenty years have witnessed the unprecedented homogenisation of the world's economic system. The most visible manifestation is the near-universal collapse of state socialism in all its historic forms and its rapid substitution by market-based economies. However, this shift represents more than the 'mere triumph of capitalism' over alternative approaches to production and consumption. It heralds an era in which simplistic economic considerations have come to override all other objectives in the arenas of public policy and international development ... Virtually all major governments, corporations and international institutions, particularly the UN, the World Bank and International Monetary Fund, the Organisation for Economic Cooperation and Development (OECD), and their offspring such as the World Trade Organisation (WTO), have made economic development their central preoccupation..." (ibid, 112).

It may be noted in concluding this section that in the post-UNCED era of globalisation, much of the environmental (ecological) and social dimensions of sustainability have become mere rhetorics and promotion of global business is the guiding principle. Achieving higher rates of growth by following a policy of privatisation, 'hire and fire' and technological change is the watch word and public policy is merely to facilitate the transition to privatisation and globalisation. Intragenerational and intergenerational equity concerns are now devalued and replaced by shibboleths like 'growth with a human face' 'social safety nets', etc. In achieving this transition, both national and international organisations are reformed and transformed with suitable personnel holding liberal perspectives appointed at the helm of affairs. 'Sustainable development' now seems to have become a mere synonym for 'sustainable growth' and it has lost its ethical dimensions of maintaining intragenerational and intergenerational equity as theorised earlier.

It is also noted here that the approach to sustainability has now lost its rigour with the complex issues of environment, ecology, economy, trade, technology, society, culture, etc. being looked at in isolation by specialists, making it less appealing for multidisciplinary studies and grappling the issues from the periphery rather than from the core. In spite of these developments, it is found that the contemporary literature on sustainable development has contributed significantly to the study of sustainability issues and the measurement of sustainable development. An attempt is made in the next section to have a brief look at the measurement issue.

### 3.4. Measurement of Sustainability

Measuring sustainability or sustainable development is important for practical purposes of planning, implementation and evaluation of sustainable development as a goal to be accomplished. Perman, *et al.* noted its significance thus: "if sustainable development is to be pursued, it is important that we have the ability to monitor the extent to which such a goal is being attained. This requires in turn, that a measure of sustainable development (SD) is available" (Perman, *et al.* 1996, p.64).

Goodstein defends the need for measurement from a slightly different, academic or scientific angle, saying that "economists are hands-on types, and if we can't measure something, we find it hard to talk about it. In concrete terms, how do we know if we are achieving sustainability or not?" (Goodstein, 2002, p.80). It is convincing reason for measuring sustainable development. It is, however, found that measuring sustainable development is a complex task owing to various reasons. As noted by Pearson, 'it is useful to reemphasise that with its multiple and often ambiguous definitions, sustainable development defies measure by a single index' (Pearson, 2000, p.485). What is apparent from this observation is that with the multiple, often confusing and conflicting, goals of sustainable development, formulating a single index of sustainable development is not in the realm of the possible. The existing literature on sustainable development is, however, found to offer certain criteria and indicators of sustainable development.

### 3.4.1. Criteria of Sustainable Development

Criteria are the reference points or norms or standards which the development process should fulfil in order to make it eligible to call itself as 'sustainable'. A number of criteria, depending on the goals and prescriptions for sustainable development, may be identified. Perman, *et al.* have identified five such criteria.

1. (*a*) A sustainable state is one in which utility is non-declining through time

   (*b*) A sustainable state is one in which consumption is non-declining through time

2. A sustainable state is one in which resources are managed so as to maintain production opportunities for the future.

3. A sustainable state is one in which the natural capital stock is non-declining through time.

4. A sustainable state is one in which resources are managed so as to maintain a sustainable yield of resource services.

5. A sustainable state is one which satisfies minimum conditions of ecosystem stability and resilience through time (Perman, op cit. pp. 56-57).

Taking a slightly different perspective, the various criteria of sustainable development may be classified as (*a*) neo-classical, (*b*) modern and (*c*) post-modern.

### 3.4.1.2. Neo-classical Criteria

The neo-classical (economic) criteria of sustainable development requires that the total (per capita) capital resources of the economy which consists of natural capital, human capital and physical capital (man-made or reproducible) should be kept constant (constant capital rule). It, however, permits substitution of natural capital (which is depletable) by human capital or reproducible capital, whose stock can be enhanced overtime as desired. This substitution possibility permits the present generation to compensate the future generation for its overuse of natural capital by saving and investing the rent earned on natural resources exhausted, thereby fulfilling the intergenerational equity requirement as enunciated in the Brundtland Report. It permits to overcome the 'limits to growth' by substitution of inputs and technological changes. It also ensures the efficiency criteria which is fundamental to the neo-classical thinking. It is, however, labelled as a 'weak sustainability' criteria, as it is quite 'soft' on its prescription for maintaining the stock of 'natural' capital, which is critical for the welfare of future generations. Accordingly it is a 'weak' guarantor of sustainable development.

### 3.4.1.3. Modern Criteria

The modern criteria are put forward by the ecological school which questions the neo-classical notion of substitution between man-made and natural capital, i.e. the 'weak sustainability hypothesis. It holds that sustainable development is possible only by maintaining the 'natural' capital in a 'steady', 'constant' or non-declining state. It considers that certain critical natural (capital) resources are essential for human well being (non-declining utility) and survival (air, water, etc.) and they should be maintained and are not substitutable as claimed by the neo-classical school. This is binding due to the 'uncertainty' of ecological processes and the 'irreversibility' of damages caused by human intervention. The 'uniqueness' of these resources also add to their non-substitutability (Pearce, 1997, p.392). The need to maintain critical natural capital in tact is hence fundamental to the modern view. The 'constant' natural capital rule is consistent with the intergenerational equity principle which requires that the present generation should leave the earth in a wholesome habitable and 'safe' form or without damaging its value to the next generation. This corresponds to the strong sustainability principle explained earlier in section 3.3.3.

### 3.4.1.4. The Post-modern Criteria

The post-modern criteria are attributable to the post-UNCED thinking, although their roots may be traced to the WCED (Brundtland) report. The Brundtland definition of sustainable development had popularised the need for meeting the needs of the present (intragenerational equity) without compromising the ability of the future generations to meet their own needs (intergenerational equity). The WCED perspectives (policy directions) for sustainable development are given in appendix 3.4. Following these premises, the UNCED recommendations (including the Rio-Declarations), institutionalised the basic objective of promoting development with due care to the environment. The post-UNCED literature is rampant with multiple goals (criteria) of development, all tuned to the 'music' of sustainability.

Barbier has categorised these (criteria) as relating to the following groups and sub-groups (Barbier, 1998, p.7).

1. Biological systems goals: genetic diversity – resilience - biological productivity.
2. Economic system goals: satisfying basic needs (reducing poverty) - equity enhancing -increasing useful goods and services.
3. Social system goals: cultural diversity - institutional sustainability - social justice - participation.

Barbier also notes that "the general objective of sustainable (economic) development, then, is to maximise the goals across all these systems through an adaptive process of trade offs ... it is not possible to maximise all these objectives all the time ... There may also be conflict among intra-system goals...Given these potential trade offs among goals, a choice must be made as to which objectives should receive priority, and thus greater weight, in the development strategy" (ibid. pp.7-8).

### 3.5. Indicators of Sustainable Development

Indicators are markers or pointers referring to which the state of the relevant parameters of the system can be studied and appropriate conclusions arrived at. Kuik and Gilbert note that "indicators are bits of information that highlight what is happening in the large system; they are small windows that provide a glimpse of the 'big picture'...The primary functions of indicators are simplification and communication. They are a compromise between scientific accuracy and the demand for concise information. The purpose of their use may be planning ... and/ or communication ..." (Kuik and Gilbert, 1999, p.722).

Indicators of sustainable development "should highlight or provide a glimpse of sustainable development" (ibid, p.722). They also "measure the gap between actual societal (including economic) development that may be called sustainable" (ibid p.724). As a matter of fact, it may be noted that the action programme of Agenda 21 had called for the development of indicators for sustainable development rather than for precise measurement. Agenda 21 noted that "indicators of sustainable development need to be developed to provide solid bases for decision making at all levels and to contribute to a self-regulating sustainability of integrated environment and development system" (UNCED, 1992, quoted by Kuik and Gilbert, 1999, p.722).

Nadia reports that "indicators are increasingly used to provide a convenient description of the current state or condition of a resource, as well as to gauge performance and predict responses. They need to be developed according to their perceived applications and this requires reliable statistics and raw data. Indicators are used to monitor and evaluate what is changing, the processes by which change is occurring and the sustainability of beneficial changes. Different types of indicators exist, depending on the scale (global, national, local) and the level of aggregations" (Nadia, 1998, p.52).

### 3.5.1. Neo-classical Indicator

The neo-classical indicator of sustainable development is a corrected measure of national economic activity calculated in terms of GDP, GNP, NI or NNP for environmental damages which lead to reduction in net welfare. It is known as net national welfare (NNW). Net National Welfare is defined as "the total annual output of both market and non-market goods and services minus the total externality costs associated with these products, minus the depreciation of capital, both natural and human-made, used up in production" (Goodstein, 2002, p. 81).

Goodstein represents it as NNW = Total output – Costs of Growth – Depreciation = GDP + Non-market output – Externality costs – Pollution abatement and clean-up costs – Depreciation of created capital – Depreciation of Natural capital. It is also noted that "the NNW must be adjusted to reflect changes in income distribution, since sustainability requires that the typical person be no worse off" (ibid, p.82). It favours intragenerational equity.

A 'weak' sustainability index is given by Pearce and Atkinson, which is considered to be complementary to the environmentally adjusted national accounts. To achieve weak sustainability, a country should keep its aggregate capital K (defined as the sum of man-made capital KM, human capital KH and natural capital KN) constant. The weak sustainability rule then is represented as

$$S(t) - d_M k_M - d_H k_H - d_N k_N \geq 0$$

where $S(t)$ represents aggregate savings at time '$t$' and $di$ ($i$ = K,H,N) is the depreciation rate for the relevant capital stock. If $d_H$ is assumed to equal zero, there is no depreciation of knowledge and skills. An economy is assumed sustainable if it saves more than the depreciation on its reproducible and natural capital. Depreciation of natural capital takes the form of depletion (e.g. extraction of a non-renewable resource) and degradation (e.g. air and water pollution). Dividing the above inequality by income 'm', we get the basic condition for 'weak' sustainability:

$$Z = \frac{S}{m} - \frac{d_M k_M}{m} - \frac{d_N k_N}{m} \geq 0$$

where Z is the weak sustainability index.

A strong sustainability criterion is obtained when $d_N k_N/m \leq 0$, i.e. when natural capital does not depreciate or is 'steady'. Pearce and Atkinson are reported to favour a combination of 'weak' and 'strong' sustainability rules to measure sustainable development (van Kooten and Bulte, 2000, p.260).

### 3.5.2. Modern Indicators

These are indicators proposed by the ecological school which considers the Net National Welfare (NNW) index as not quite useful and 'strongly' oppose the neo-classical 'weak' sustainability hypotheses of substitution of natural capital by man-made capital. This school favours the 'strong' sustainability hypothesis of preserving natural capital. The ecological school prefers such indictors as ecological footprints, carrying capacity relative to exploitation, and measures of resilience (biodiversity). The ecological footprint is considered as a measure of the natural capital requirements of an economy (van Kooten and Bulte, 2000, p.262). It is also defined as "the 'load' imposed by a given population on nature" and as "an accounting tool that enables us to estimate the resource consumption and waste assimilation requirements of a defined human population or economy in terms of a corresponding productive land area" (Wackernagal and Rees, 1996, 1997, quoted by van Kooten and Bulte, op. cit. p.262). It is measured by "the aggregate area of land and water in various ecological categories that is claimed by participants in an economy to produce all the resources they consume, and to absorb all the wastes they generate on a continuous basis, using the prevailing technology" (ibid, pp.262-263). The ecological footprint and carrying capacity of an economy are closely related. The ecological footprint indicates the extent of area (resources) being brought under utilisation while the carrying capacity shows the maximum potential resources up to which resources can be exploited. The ecological footprint as a proportion of the carrying capacity of an area, indicates the advancing shadow of human appropriation of natural resources and the approaching limits to growth of the region. Hence the ecological footprint can be used as a measure of the 'sustainability gap'. This measure is, however, criticised by many as it ignores the problem of aggregation, valuation, discounting and substitution of resources (ibid, pp.264-265).

Resilience and biodiversity are biophysical measures (index) of sustainability. Resilience or 'robustness' is considered as the "ability to 'bounce back' or absorb unexpected shocks and perturbations without collapsing" (Charles, 2001, p.224). It is fundamentally related to the complexity of the system, as well as the diversity inherent in it. Charles reports that diversity is helpful at each of the genetic, species and community levels since "a population with a wide range of genetic information among individuals is more likely to adapt successfully to changing environmental conditions than is a population with greatly reduced genetic diversity due to strong selection .... Similarly, a community composed of many species, some of which can fulfil the functional roles of other species is more likely to persist through periods of considerable environmental change" (ibid, p.224, quoting de Young, 1999). Resilience, backed by biodiversity indicators is expected to provide a good measure of sustainability.

### 3.5.3. Post-modern Indicators

The post-modern indicators are a composite of neo-classical, modern and emerging view points. They are numerous and apparently still growing in number. These indicators began to take shape since the WCED (Brundtland) Report of 1987 which highlighted the significance of intragenerational and intergenerational equity for sustainable development. The former aims at the "fairness between individuals and groups, within society, locally, regionally, nationally and globally" and the latter expects that "those living today should not compromise or restrict the opportunities open to future generations" (Gilpin, 2000, pp.96-97). They correspond to the 'weak' sustainability hypothesis of the neo-classical school and the 'strong' sustainability hypothesis of the modern (ecological) school respectively; the former permitting the downsizing of natural capital for current growth for meeting the needs of the present (intra-generational equity) and the latter demanding preservation of the natural capital for meeting the needs of the future (intergenerational equity). Hence, the WCED-UNCED indicators are a 'hybrid' or composite or compromise of neo-classical and modern indicators of sustainable development. Suitable indices of intragenerational equity can be prepared taking into account the ecological, economic, social, cultural and other relevant variables specifying the geographical stratum, highlighting the level of equality (equity) and sustainability of development over space at any point of time. The variables chosen may include population density, per capita income, quality of life index, asset holdings and other measures of social welfare. Standardising the value of the variables chosen over different socio-political-economy profiles may, however, be difficult.

Similar indices of intergenerational equity can also be made for different parameters at different points of time. The problems here, however, are primarily of assigning values using discount rates and making choice for future generations with out knowing their preferences. As noted by Barbier, "because the criteria underlying sustainable economic development differ so markedly from the conventional economic consensus, there is really need for a completely new analytical approach in that regard. Unfortunately, a rigorous exploration of such a new methodology has yet to be attempted ... There are many obstacles to be overcome. For one, the conceptual complexity of sustainable economic development makes precise measurement of its 'success' through quantitative indicators extremely difficult. The quantitative dimensions of sustainability (for example, increases in food, real income, life expectancy, and so on) can perhaps be captured by some 'basic needs' or 'physical quality of life' index. However, the more qualitative dimensions (for example, cultural diversity, social cohesion and stability, improvements in environmental quality, greater self-esteem, and so on) are virtually impossible to quantify" (Barbier, 1998, pp.6-7).

The post-WCED/UNCED literature presents several indicators of sustainable development, although most of them focus on selected dimensions of sustainability. Some of the indicators as reported by Nadia are: (1) Human development indicators, (2) Environmental indicators, (3) Performance indicators, (4) Interdependence indicators and (5) Pressure-response indicators (Nadia, 1998, p.52).

Human development indicators are proposed by the UNDP. The index combines factors such as longevity (associated with health and nutrition) and educational attainment with income. It takes into account basic human biophysical needs such as food, clothing and shelter, and satisfaction of basic socio-economic needs, such as access to essential goods and services (health, education) and equity in employment, income and wealth distribution. It also includes activities that have an impact on the environment or on other factors, and that are perceived as benefits (e.g. recreation opportunities, biological diversity or aesthetics), or costs or risks (e.g. exposure to, and magnitude of environmental contamination or hazards) (ibid, p.52).

The environmental indicators are developed by IUCN for conserving life support systems and biological diversity, ensuring the sustainable use of renewable resources, minimising the depletion of non-renewable resources and keeping within the carrying capacity of supporting eco-systems.

Performance indicators are being developed by OECD to measure changes in the capacity or the performance of groups, organisations or societies to work as effective systems and tools for performance reviews (ibid, pp.53-54).

Interdependence indicators seek to measure the degree of interdependence between human beings and the natural environment and the likelihood of the user (stake holder) conserving or destroying the environment. These indicators point to the sustainability or otherwise of the natural resource exploitation system. Nadia reports that the individual's 'dependence' on local resources is related to the degree of capital mobility. When capital is not mobile, tenants would tend to preserve the value of an environmental asset in time, and derive exclusive benefits of their work and investments. When capital is mobile, as in the globalised economy, and social constraints are lacking, the investor has little interest in preserving the ecosystem and the owner would tend, consciously to continue an unsustainable practice (i.e. maximising short-term yields) and then move on to another area to exploit (ibid, p.54).

The pressure-state-response indicators constitute "the most widely used framework for sustainability indicators at present" (ibid, p.54). The PSR framework provides a convenient representation of the linkages between the pressures exerted on natural resources by human activities, the changes in quality of the resource, and the responses of these changes as society attempts to release the pressure or to rehabilitate resources that have been degraded. The interchanges among these form a continuous feedback mechanism that can be monitored and used for assessment of natural resource quality (ibid, p.55). Nadia also reports that the Commission on Sustainable Development has produced a set of methodology sheets for using the PSR framework, following the call

made in Agenda 21 of the Earth Summit to develop and use indictors of sustainable development (ibid, p.56).

Loucks and Gladwell reported five main criteria indicators and sub-criteria indicators proposed by the Delft Hydraulics Laboratory in the Netherlands for project analysis. They correspond to the following with their sub-components.

1. Socio-economic aspects and impacts on growth, resilience and stability: effects on income distribution - effects on cultural heritage - feasibility in socio-economic structure
2. The use of natural and environmental resources including raw materials and discharge of wastes within the carrying capacity of natural systems: raw materials and energy - waste discharges (closing material cycles) - use of natural resources - effects on resilience and vulnerability of nature
3. Enhancement and conservation of natural and environmental resources and the improvement of the carrying capacity of natural and environmental resources: water conservation - accretion of land or coast - improvement and conservation of soil fertility - nature development and conservation of natural values
4. Public health, safety and well-being: effects on public health - effects on safety (risks) - effects on annoyance/hindrance (smell, dust, noise, crowding) - effect on living and working conditions.
5. Flexibility and sustainability of infrastructure works, management opportunities for multifunctional use and opportunities to adapt to changing circumstances: opportunities for a phased development - opportunities for multifunctional use and management and to respond to changing conditions - sustainable quality of structures (corrosion, wear) - opportunities for rehabilitation of the original situation (autonomous regeneration, active reconstruction and restoration)

While proposing this index, it is reported that each sub-criterion is given equal weightage. The sum of numerical values given to each sub-criterion is a sustainability index. The higher the index value, the greater the contribution of a project to sustainable development (ibid, pp.33-34).

Indicators of environmental crises and unsustainability have been reported by Bartelmus. The critical indicators noted by Bartelmus relate to the following: 1. Extinction of species, 2. Genetic impoverishment, 3. Climatic change, 4. Sea level increase, 5.Global warming, 6.Ozone layer depletion, 7.UV-B radiation, 8. Biodiversity loss, 9.Land degradation and desertification, 10. Environmental refugees, 11.Energy crises (Bartelmus, 1994, pp.14-15).

Agenda 21 of UNCED 1992 noted the need for building indicators of sustainable development with respect to the following parameters:

1. Social and economic dimensions: (*a*) accelerated sustainable development (*b*) poverty (*c*) consumption patterns (*d*) population (*e*) health (*f*) human settlement (*g*) integrated decision-making
2. Environmental concerns: (*a*) atmosphere (*b*) land (*c*) deforestation (*d*) fragile ecosystems (desertification, mountains) (*e*) sustainable agriculture (*f*) biodiversity and biotechnology (*g*) oceans (*h*) freshwater (*i*) wastes (toxic, hazardous, solid)
3. Major groups: (*a*) children and youth (*b*) indigenous people (*c*) NGOs (*d*) local authorities (*e*) workers (*f*) business (*g*) scientific community (*h*) farmers

Since 1995, the UN Commission on Sustainable Development (CSD) has promoted the development of indications for sustainable development and the FAO taking the initiative has prepared indictors for sustainable development of marine capture fisheries in 1999 (FAO 1999b and FAO 2000a, p.61). It (FAO) noted that "in general, indicators should reflect the state of the system and its outcomes in relation to societal goals and objectives, the long-term sustainability of the fishery, the eco-system supporting it and the generation of net benefits to fishery and society. Indicators of sustainability should reflect the well-being of (or the problems related to) the resource and human components of the system, as well as the progress (or lack of it) towards the objective of sustainable development ...The value of indicators must be interpreted in relation to target, limit or threshold reference values (or reference points) derived in various ways, even when there is a shortage of data. The target reference values define desirable states of the system and good performance. Limits indicate undesirable states of the system and bad performance. Thresholds identify situations in which action, possibly pre-arranged, should be taken. Together, these reference points give an indication of societal value judgments regarding the indicators. For example, an indicator of biomass below the limit level may be considered as illustrating a 'bad' situation. An indicator of biomass at the maximum sustainable level yield may be considered as good...A complete system of sustainable development indicators should include mechanisms for effective communication among (fisheries) stake holders, those responsible for governance and the general public" (FAO, 2000a, pp. 61-63).

A set of ecological, socio-economic/community and institutional sustainability indicators for assessing the sustainability of the fishery sector has been provided by Charles (2001). Appendix 3.5 presents the ecological, socio-economic/community and institutional sustainability indicators as outlined by Charles (Charles, 2001, pp.194-195).

Writing on the usual characteristics of indicators and the forces behind their development, Kuik and Gilbert noted: "The concept of sustainable development itself is to a large degree a political concept. The different approaches to indicator development reflect alternative political views ...

... Because of the political nature of much of the sustainable development debate, it is highly unlikely that a common and widely accepted set of indicators will be developed in the near future ... Therefore, different set of indicators of sustainable development and different approaches to indictors of sustainable development and different approaches to indicator development will in all likelihood, remain co-existing, reflecting the different societal concerns that underlie the concept of sustainable development" (Kuik and Gilbert, 1999, p.738).

### 3.6. Factors Behind Unsustainability

Mainstream economic thinking, notably the neo-classical economic thinking, has identified four major factors behind unsustainable development, or what is now essentially considered as development without recognising the environment as a 'source' of raw material for production and as a 'sink' for wastes of production and consumption. These factors form a cluster of four interrelated failures. They are (1) market failure, (2) government failure, (3) institution failure and (4) information failure.

#### 3.6.1. Market Failure

Market can fail for many reasons, such as when property rights are not complete, when information is not complete, when there are monopolies or monopsonies, when government policies distort prices or offer unfair advantages to certain economic actors (Kerr, *et al.* 1997, p.632).Much of the present constraints for sustained production and consumption in the economy are attributed to the failure of the 'market' system in giving proper signals to the economic agents. This is in contrast to what Adam Smith considered as the automatic working of the free market forces of supply and demand or the 'hidden hand'. The market fails in giving proper signals to the producers and consumers when the market prices do not reflect the real value of the goods to the community. This happens when many 'unpriced' factors of production are used in production without fully compensating them (female or child labour) or when 'unowned' common property resources are used without paying any rent for their use. In the latter case it leads to the over-exploitation of the natural resource base and the 'tragedy of the commons' as it is often called. In the former case it violates the criterion of intragenerational equity which is fundamental to sustainable development. The failure of the market in giving proper signals to the producers and consumers leads to 'free riding' and increased consumption in the present without making sufficient investment in man-made or 'natural capital' as compensation for the future as perceived by the neo-classical school. This in effect violates the criterion of intergenerational equity, a requirement for sustainable development.

### 3.6.2. Government Failure

Government failure or policy failure is considered as "the single most important cause of natural resource loss and ecosystem degradation. Policy failure is usually driven by the pursuit of short sighted economic gain and lack of awareness of the long term implications of non-intervention" (Nadia, 1998, p.14). It leads to a situation, when "policies do not respond to the actual or threatened degradation in the resource base or ecosystems, or do not take into account the public interest. It also leads to the weakening of local institutions needed to cope with the situation" (ibid, p.14).

Pearson notes thus: "it is now recognised that government policy itself is implicated in a good deal of environmental degradation. And when corrective policies addressing market failures are undertaken by government, the results often fall short of expectations or are unnecessarily costly" (Pearson, 2000, p.65). Pearson also reports the well known allegation that "policy makers and bureaucratic regulators often serve special interests or promote their own parochial objectives over the public interest ... Government failure *per se* occurs when the incentives of politicians and bureaucrats do not coincide with the public interest . Economics provides some insight into the sources of government failure, especially in the analysis of lobbying and rent-seeking, and in the public choice literature that identifies bureaucratic interests such as agency budget growth, and career-advancement opportunities in a revolving door system ... It is not surprising that unresponsive governments fail to seek, let alone obtain, maximum social welfare ..." (ibid, pp.65-66).

The failure or absence of a public policy relating to international trade affecting the environment is highlighted by Pearson. Pearson writes: "Traditionally, trade policy and environmental policy have been formulated by separate government agencies with little or no coordination between them. This is undesirable, as trade policy affects the use of environmental resources, and environmental policy affects international trade. These interactions may be described as trade-environment policy spill-overs, to distinguish them from physical pollution externalities. The policy coordination problem is relatively straight forward if there is only one trade distortion and one pollution externality distortion. Simultaneous trade policy reform and environmental policy reform using two instruments of, say, tariff/subsidies and pollution taxes, can be used jointly to improve welfare, although the extent to which each instrument is used depends on the extent to which the other is used. If only one policy is used, a simple second-best type problem emerges, and welfare improvement is no longer assured ... The policy coordination problem becomes more complex when multiple pollution externalities and multiple trade policy distortions exist and complete removal of all distortions is not feasible ... This is an important practical question, as many developing countries are liberalising trade and are concerned with the spill over to environmental resources and many countries are reforming environmental policies and are concerned with trade effects. Interestingly, the two policy reforms are not symmetrical. Trade policy reform generally consists of reducing trade restrictions and trade subsidies. Environmental policy reform generally consists of imposing pollution taxes or otherwise restricting pollution emissions ... A general conclusion from the theory of trade policy is that export and import bans and quantitative restraints are less efficient than tax/tariff measures. A general conclusion of environmental economics is similar: quantitative limits and bans on pollution are apt to be less efficient than tax or tradeable permit policies" (ibid, pp. 189-191).

Nadia reports that policy makers in poor countries "may take the view that their country is too poor to afford to conservation of renewable resources or ecosystems, and would opt for economic development even if it destroys some of the country's natural capital. The attitude may be different if policy makers are aware of the full economic value of the resource under threat and take account of the value of all the goods and environmental service it provides" (Nadia, 1998, p.15).

### 3.6.3. Institutional Failure

The institutional set up consisting of formal and informal rules, procedures and mechanisms greatly control the use of the natural environment and the social production and consumption of goods and services. This used to be the case with non- industrial economies where community management of common property resources continued for several centuries. However, as industrialisation progressed and trade expanded, the institutional mechanisms prevailing in these societies failed to regulate and protect the environment leading to overexploitation of the natural resource base and unsustainable development. Costanza, *et al.* noted, "as trade expands, it creates new problems and challenges the communication systems of existing groups. Existing commons institutions become obsolete as the geographic scope of effects beyond the market that they managed expands beyond their existing boundaries. Thus, communities that have some autonomy, that are not constantly being challenged by strong external forces but rather are evolving largely through internal dynamics, are more likely to develop and sustain viable institutions to encourage individuals to transfer appropriate levels of assets. Such autonomy has not been a characteristic of the past few centuries of globalisaltion. Thus there is good reason to be concerned that the rise of trade and geograhic expansion of economic activity has broken down the institutions of many separate communities which facilitated asset transfer. This globalisation has also worsened the conditions for new institutions to arise as the expanding number of people who must come to terms geometrically increases the cost of coming to a new agreement..." (Costanza, *et al.* 1997, pp.166-167)

Many environmentalists and ecologists now believe that much of the natural resource destruction in the world is due to the warped view on man and nature held by the western society. Tietenberg, paraphrasing Lynn White Jr. a historian, states that "the environmental crisis is due to the teachings of Judaism and Christianity which in Western culture have created a warped view of the proper relationship between humans and their environment..."(Tietenberg, 1988, p.58). Based on the passage in the Old Testament, White suggested that "it is God's will that man exploit nature for his proper ends" and "this is a rather unique view of the human/environment relationship" (ibid, p.58). Jones, *et al.* also reported this Christian tradition stating thus: "Because God had created the Earth for human use – essentially human dominion – then humans were free to do with it as they liked ...the established medieval position was firmly in favour of absolute dominion"(Jones, *et al.* 2000, p.53). It seems that the 'economic man' based on this rationality has now become the global player with no scrouples for destroying the environment, wherever it suits the self-interest.

### 3.6.4. Information Failure

It may be noted that one of the basic reasons for the failure of markets and governments and other institutions is the absence of proper information. The fundamental cause of market failure and it giving wrong signals is imperfect knowledge of the market conditions as is reported to be the case with monopoly and monopolistic competition. Government (public) policy also fails unless based on sound information and knowledge. Social institutions become docile or defunct without proper communication net-works. Information failure is a serious constraint in developing countries for natural resource management. Nadia reports: "Frequently in developing countries, information is lacking, especially in such areas as renewable resources and, more particularly, on the status of renewable resources (especially fisheries), natural resource dynamics, land-use and tenure patterns, institutional, social and cultural conditions, and levels of investment in coastal areas. Similarly, environmental monitoring, for example of water quality, is often scant" (Nadia,1998, p.15). It is only natural that common property natural resources are abused and the environment spoiled as is the situation now in poor countries where markets, governments and social institutions fail to respond to changing global economic developments.

## 3.7. Policy for Sustainable Development

It is not the intention here to give a comprehensive picture of sustainable development strategy. Many of the components of that strategy may be found in the WCED-UNCED Reports and the action programmes of the UN, following the UNCED. A good summary of international institutions and economic instruments available for sustainable environmental policy at the global level has been given by Gilpin (Gilpin,

2000). The OECD Council on the Use of Economic Instruments in Environmental Policy recommended, *inter alia,* that the member states should:

- make greater and more consistent use of economic instruments as a complement to or as a substitute for other policy instruments such as regulations, taking into account national socio-economic conditions,
- work towards improving the allocation and efficient use of natural and environmental resources by means of economic instruments so as to better reflect the social costs of using those resources,
- make efforts to reach further agreements at an international level on the use of environmental policy instruments with respect to solving regional and global environmental problems as well as ensuring sustainable development,
- develop better modelling, forecasting and monitoring techniques to provide information on the environmental consequences of alternative policies and their economic effects (as quoted by Gilpin, 2000, p.142).

Pearson outlines the policy initiatives needed for sustainable development thus:

"A first step is to reform government policies that contribute to inefficient use of resources. Of these, subsidies are the most prevalent and the most pernicious. These include subsidies for irrigation, industrial, and household water use; subsidised waste water treatment, pesticide, herbicide, and insecticide subsidies; land subsidies, especially for ill-conceived ranching and agricultural colonisation schemes; mining subsidies; energy subsidies, especially fossil fuels; and many others. The removal of these subsidies, some of which support other legitimate social objectives, is not easy and will encounter resistance from vested interests.

At a broader level, whole sectors of the economy may be 'subsidised', or artificially promoted by industrial and trade policy. If these sectors are characterised by unregulated externalities or place unwarranted pressure on natural resources, the result is either unsustainable or wasteful use of these resources ... In short, a sustainable development strategy should not stop at the removal of specific subsidies, but must consider the environmental implications of sector policy.

A further step toward sustainable development is for government to establish, clarify, or enforce private property rights, or to strengthen communal property regimes that effectively regulate access. This is particularly important with regard to land. Without secure property rights, farmers have little incentive for land conservation and improvement through terracing, erosion control, rotation of crops, and other sustainable practices. And without secure tenure, they have greater difficulty in securing loans for conservation. In the forestry sector, long-term concessions are a necessary condition for conservation and replanting ... Again, the tools for government to improve property rights and their enforcement are well known – granting secure land tenure, zoning, liability regulations, environmental bonding schemes, establishing tradeable quota rights for fisheries, and so forth.

A third step for government is to correct for obvious market failures, and in particular externalities and the provision of public goods" (Pearson, 2000, pp.479-480).

Pearson, however, cautions that "implementing these steps requires a thorough integration of economic and environmental analyses at the project, sector, and macro-economic levels. The most practical and important legacy of introducing the concept of sustainable development may be stronger efforts at integrating economic-environmental analysis and policy. Having said this, internalising externalities will not be easy, as industry will point to loss of profits, production, and jobs in the short run" (ibid, pp.480-481).

Costanza, *et al.* have suggested a simple framework of these policy instruments to achieve sustainability as conceived by the neo-classical school. They are:

1. a broad Natural Capital Depletion (NCD) tax to assure that resource inputs from the environment to the economy are sustainable, while giving strong incentives to develop new technologies and processes to minimise impacts…
2. application of the precautionary polluter pays principle (4P)to assure that the full cost of outputs from the economy to the environment are charged to the polluter in a way that adequately deals with the huge uncertainty about the impacts of pollution and encourages technological innovations…
3. a system of ecological tariffs as one way (short of global agreements that are difficult to negotiate and enforce) to allow

countries to implement the first two proposals without putting themselves at an undue disadvantage (at least on the import side) relative to countries that have not yet implemented them (Costanza, *et al.* 1997, p.207).

It may be noted that much of the policy prescriptions cited above are derivatives of the neo-classical economic thinking focusing on natural capital depletion and the threat of failure to meet the criterion of intergenerational equity for sustainable development. These prescriptions are almost silent on the policies for meeting intragenerational equity questions which is predominantly a problem of the Southern, less developed countries, but having implications in the North as well. This is notwithstanding the exhortations for intragenerational equity as a criterion for sustainable development put forward by both the WCED and the UNCED. The implication is that the developing countries have to design new models of sustainable development taking into account the supply and demand for natural, human and physical capital and the ecological, economic and social constraints for sustainable development. The concept of sustainable development as reviewed in this chapter should, however, help in understanding the sustainability issues of contemporary societies and in devising policies for sustainable development of the economy in general or of any specific sector.

### 3.8. Summary

The myriad of definitions and observations on sustainable development made in this chapter pointed to the failure of (1) ecological systems in providing inputs and services ('source' and 'sink') for production and consumption on a steady basis, (2) the economic system in providing optimum condition for sustained production and consumption for want of proper signals and incentives from the market and (3) the social systems in meeting the requirements of intragenerational and intergenerational equity. The basic approach to sustainability indicated in most definitions was to modify the producing and consuming systems with suitable changes in technology and social/ institutional set up.

A review of development of the concept of sustainable development traced its origin and growth through the classical, Marxian, neo-classical, modern and post-modern thoughts. The classical economists, notably Smith, Malthus, Ricardo and Mill anticipated the emergence of the 'stationary state' arising from scarcity of land, growth in population and diminishing returns in production. Improvements in the art of production (technological change) and extension of markets (including colonies) for raw material and products were considered as possible solutions. The Marxian school viewed the capitalist mode of production as quite unsustainable due to capitalist exploitation of labour, changing organic composition of capital, the resulting disproportionality crisis (falling demand), class struggle, etc. The capitalists try to impart sustainability through technological improvements and colonial trade.

The neo-classical writers of the early twentieth century had recognised the sustainability issues and the economy slipping to crises of unemployment and secular stagnation. Later neo-classical writers were optimists who considered that the natural resource constraint can be overcome by the substitution of scarce resources by abundant ones and by man-made capital.

The modern view on sustainable development which had its beginning with the 'Conservation Movement' in the USA in the beginning of the last century also had its flowering in the last decades of the last century, with the World Conservation Union and many ecologists highlighting the threat to natural resources and global environment. The implications for global sustainability was made clear by the ecological school which underscored the role of environment as a 'source' of raw material and as a 'sink' for wastes of production and consumption. This school established the 'limits' to growth and called for saving 'critical' natural resources and environment and making sufficient investments in natural capital for conservation and sustainable development.

The post-modern view which is predominantly a post-cold war, post-UNCED development focused initially on creating a just and equitable society where there is harmony between rich and poor nations, between North and South and between developed and developing countries. It, while upholding the principles of intra- generational and intergenerational equity as popularised by the WCED and Rio Declarations has sought to reform global economic relations, policies and institutions to achieve the goal of sustainable development. However, with the rising tide of liberalisation, privatisation and globalisation of the world economy, it appears that sustainable development as a moral principle has lost its appeal as conveyed in the Brundtland Report. This is evident from the growing conflicts of interests of the rich and poor nations at the global trade negotiating fora and the visible 'business--as-usual' attitude of world business, which is having scant regard for environmental protection or for fulfilling the criterion of intragenerational equity.

This chapter further recognised the need for measuring sustainable development and noted the criteria and indicators for sustainable development. They were discussed under three categories: neo-classical, modern and post-modern.

This chapter also noted the major factors behind unsustainable development. They included market failure, government failure, institutional failure and information failure.

Some of the policy recommendations for sustainable development made outside the UN-fold, notably by OECD and other scholars were also cited. These prescriptions were, however, found to be predominantly pro-advanced countries, based on neo-classical economic thinking. The conclusion thus emerging from these theoretical positions is that the developing countries have to rework and redesign these models, taking into account the supply and demand for natural, human and physical resources and the prevailing ecological, economic, social, political, institutional and technological constraints for sustainable development, world-wide.

# 4

# SUSTAINABILITY ISSUES IN GLOBAL FISHERIES

## 4.1. Introduction

This chapter outlines the major sustainability issues of global fisheries and the factors leading to unsustainability. Many of these issues are also measures or indicators of unsustainability. These issues are discussed under five major categories, as corresponding to (1) ecological (2) economic (3) social/institutional (4) technological and (5) other versions. The following sections give an account of these issues. A final section notes the summary of issues discussed in this chapter.

## 4.2. Ecological issues

Much of the threats to the sustainability of global fisheries is emanating from the damages caused to the ecosystem by human induced changes. They have adversely affected the natural resource base and the continued operation of the industry. This has been made explicit by the UNCED (1992), FAO (1995b,1997a,b,c, 1999a,b, 2000a, 2002, 2004, etc.), Symes (1997), Nadia (1998), Pullen, *et al.* (1999), Charles (2001), Sinclair and Valdimarsson (2003a) and many others.

The UNCED *Agenda 21* highlighted the state of unsustainable development in the fisheries of the world when it noted that "fisheries in many areas under national jurisdiction face mounting problems, including local overfishing, unauthorised incursions by foreign fleets, ecosystem degradation, overcapitalisation and excessive fleet sizes, undervaluation of catch, insufficiently selective gear, unreliable data bases, and increasing competition between artisanal and large-scale fishing, and between fishing and other types of activities" (UNCED 1992, quoted in Caddy and Griffiths, 1995, p.161).

Sinclair and Valdimarsson observed that "in many respects, the context for management has improved a great deal over recent years. Overfishing has been recognised, widely and formally, as a fact and as a problem calling for solutions ...In addition, the broader biodiversity and habitat considerations are being addressed and the need to protect the ecosystem is broadly accepted as both an ethical principle and a fundamental need" (Sinclair and Valdimarsson, 2003a, pp. 16-17).

Referring to the degradation of the fishery environment, the International Conference on the Sustainable Contribution of Fisheries to Food Security (1995) noted that "in most coastal countries and in a number of countries with large inland waters, the productivity of fisheries is adversely affected by an increasing demand for coastal space and resources. More often than not, this competition is reflected in the degradation of the marine environment. The changes which take place may be generated either within the fisheries sector itself or, more frequently and usually with a large impact, outside the sector" (FAO and Government of Japan, 1995, p.13).

The major ecological issues threatening the sustainability of global fisheries are (1) biological overfishing, (2) environmental pollution, (3) habitat loss, (4) biodiversity loss and (5) climate change. A brief outline of these issues is given in the following sub-sections.

### 4.2.1. Biological Overfishing

The overfishing problem has been the basis for the classical biological theory of fisheries management, which considers unlimited increase in fishing effort as leading to overexploitation of the stock beyond maximum sustainable yield (MSY) levels and the eventual collapse of the fishery under unmanaged conditions (Korakandy, 1996, pp.15-17). The ACMRR has defined overfishing simply as "fishing harder ... than some desirable level" (ACMRR, 1980). Lawson observes that "biological overfishing may create situations in which the fishing mortality reduces the biomass to a level where recruitment and/or growth are adversely affected ... Growth overfishing occurs when fishing mortality (F) is greater than the rate of fishing mortality at which the average catch pert recruit is at a maximum (F max.). Recruitment overfishing is defined as a situation in which the spawning stock has been reduced to a level at which the average recruitment of the stock is significantly reduced" (Lawson, 1984, p.268).

Caddy and Griffiths put it as "catching such a high proportion of one or all age classes in a fishery as to reduce the stock's biomass, spawning potential and future catches, to below safe levels" (Caddy and Griffiths, 1995, p.124). These authors further point out that, "intensive fishing modifies the abundance, age structure, species composition and potential for reproduction of fish stocks. Moderate levels of exploitation remove old, slow-growing individuals and reduce the abundance of large predators thereby increasing the productivity, hence the sustainable yield, of the remaining stocks. High levels of exploitation may reduce to 'commercial extinction' the abundance of older mature age classes and of large slow growing species in general. Although very few cases of actual species extinction by fishing alone have been documented, intensive fishing reduces genetic diversity of the species concerned.

The fact that fishing gear and methods of fishing are generally aimed at a marketable size of fish, in some fisheries (it) has not prevented capture and discard of considerable quantities of species and sizes that, with further development, could be marketed as a valuable source of protein. In recent years public concern about the so-called 'by-catch problem' has been directed particularly towards intentional or incidental capture or entanglement of marine mammals, birds and turtles by operative fishing gear, or its accidental capture by lost or discarded fishing gear; so-called 'ghost' fishing" (ibid, p.55; word in parentheses added). It is also noted that "trawling and dredging can affect the marine environment by, for instance, destroying organisms of the sea bed or sea-grass meadows by mechanical disturbance and siltation. Illegal fishing techniques such as the use of dynamite or chemicals to capture reef fish also damage the habitat ... However, fishing by trawling, drift netting and seining, even when carried out with improved gear in a responsible fashion, will inevitably capture non-target species in small numbers ..." (ibid, p.55).

The overfishing problem in recent times has been emphasised by FAO on many occasions. The FAO report of 1993, *Marine Fisheries and the Law of the Sea: A Decade of Change* noted thus:

"By far the most significant environmental change related to fisheries is that resulting from the overfishing of stocks. It was estimated more than 20 years ago that an additional 20 million tonnes of catch could be achieved by rehabilitating overfished stocks ... Although there are a few instances where rehabilitation has occurred, such gains have been more than counter-balanced by the increased depletion of other stocks.

With limited supplies and rising demand, there is an increase in the pressure on fish stocks. Where there is no control over access to the stocks, individual fishermen have the incentive to intercept stocks at earlier stages in their life cycles which generally occur close to shore and when fish are smaller. Furthermore, the gear used in this competitive race is generally less selective and takes greater quantities of by-catch" (FAO 1993a, p.29). The same report also noted that "the 1989 marine catch of 85 million tonnes had a gross value at the fisherman's level of about US $70,000 million. If management measures were implemented to allow stock rehabilitation, the 20 million tonnes of increased catch that could eventually occur would add more than US $ 16,000 million to the gross revenue, *ceteris paribus*. This estimated foregone loss, however, is only a portion of the economic waste in global fisheries, since total world catch could be taken with considerably lower amounts of fishing effort and considerably lower total costs.

Depletion of stocks occurs not only because of the overfishing of target stocks but also because of the large by-catches of other species. With a few minor exceptions (e.g. harpoons), all types of fishing gear take other species in addition to those intended ... Bottom trawls (particularly for shrimp but also for ground fish in general in coastal areas) are perhaps the most in need of improvement for environmental reasons. In the tropical waters of developing countries, the shrimp taken in trawls may be only 10 to 20 per cent of the total haul, with the rest made up of other aquatic species. Most of this is trash fish, which may be thrown overboard or sold for fish meal, for processing into fish paste or as feed for aquacultural operations. Some is sold to low-income consumers. Much of this by-catch is made up of juveniles of species, which could be sold at high prices as adults.

Increased intensity in shrimp trawling in the past two decades has led to increases in the proportion of by-catch. Although real prices of shrimp have declined in the past two or three years because of increased production from aquaculture, this has not necessarily led to a decreased intensity in trawling, since there has been a rise in demand for trash fish for use as food in aquaculture. In fact, in some countries, shrimp farmers are now investing in trawls with small mesh nets to target trash fish. This is considered a form of 'biomass fishing'.

Another development in recent years has been the move to areas far from land. Certain species have been fished in the high seas for many years, including tuna, salmon and squid. In the last decade, however, some distant water fleets, facing declining stocks and increasing difficulties and costs in gaining access to EEZs, have increased their efforts in areas beyond 200 miles from shore. Squid and tuna remain major targets but high sea fishing for pollock and horse mackerel is also taking place. The amounts and associated by-catches are sufficient to raise issues concerning the management of these high sea resources" (ibid, p.30).

The FAO-Government of Japan collaboration report noted that "overfishing is a long established feature of many of the oldest fishing grounds of the northern hemisphere, for example in the North sea, where it was identified in the early 1900s, the north Pacific and north Atlantic. It often reaches serious levels in coastal areas where there are high population densities and scare alternative employment opportunities. This is the case in many of the coastal areas of Asia, for example in India; in some African countries, e.g. Ghana, Kenya, Tanzania and Senegal; in parts of Latin America, such as, Costa Rica and Mexico; and in many small island developing states. In addition, over- fishing by local fishers has often been aggravated by long-range fishing fleets from industrialised countries within the Exclusive Economic Zones of many developing countries, mainly under fishing agreements" (FAO-Government of Japan, 1995, p.11).

It also observed that "there is a considerable danger that overfishing will continue and worsen. In many developing countries population pressure and few alternative employment opportunities, when coupled with the absence of effective fisheries management, will increase the attraction of fisheries as the employment of last resort.

Existing levels of overfishing are being worsened in many areas by a continuing increase in the number and capacity of vessels, although the rate of increase of new constructions has diminished since 1990. In this connection, it appears that many of the vessels taken out of the former USSR and East European countries' fleets as a result of their rationalisation, and many of the vessels withdrawn from the distant-water fleets of some other countries are continuing to fish under new ownership. In addition, some countries, for example China, are continuing to expand their distant-water fishing operations.

An important factor contributing to the continuing increase in fishing effort is that the rate of improvements in storage and catching technology (such as monofilament nets, sounders, satellite navigation systems and improved engines and deck equipment in larger vessels, etc.) has been accelerating. These technological innovations have had the result that the same number of vessels can exert a much higher fishing mortality than previously. These changes apply particularly in industrial and semi-industrial fisheries but also in many artisanal fisheries where dramatic increases in fishing power can be obtained with very little investment. These changes are compounding the effect of the increasing number of vessels" (ibid, p.11).

Nadia observes that "biological overexploitation implies that increases in effort decreases the size of the fish stock to the point where its long term productivity declines' (Nadia, 1998, p.156). She also notes that increasing levels of exploitation tend to be associated with a number of undesirable features which include:

1. the number of fish year-class tends to decline, leading to year to year variability of stock size,
2. the average size of fish tends to fall, resulting in less consumer satisfaction and lower returns since larger fish command higher prices,
3. the environmental 'niche' of the overexploited species may become occupied by less attractive species,
4. competitive innovation is likely to occur among fishers, but it will give low overall returns under conditions of open access,
5. the fishing season often becomes shorter, decreasing consumer satisfaction where fresh fish is sought, and increasing processing costs since the high capacity required during the peak season will lie practically idle for the rest of the year (ibid, p.156).

*The State of World Fisheries and Aquaculture* 2000 published by FAO in 2000 observed thus:

> "Globally, between 1974 and 1999, there appears to have been an increase in the proportion of stocks classified as 'exploited beyond the MSY limit', i.e. overfished, depleted or slowly recovering. When the information is stratified by large oceanic regions, the North Atlantic and North Pacific show a continuous worsening of the situation until the 1980s or early 1990s with a possible stabilisation afterwards - particularly, in the North Atlantic. In the tropical and southern regions of these oceans the situation seems still to be deteriorating, with the possible exception of the tropical Atlantic, where stabilisation might have started" (FAO, 2000a, p.101).

The report made it further clear that "in 1999, four per cent of the stocks appeared to be underexploited, 21 per cent were moderately exploited, 47 per cent fully exploited, 18 per cent overexploited, nine per cent depleted and one percent recovering" (ibid, p.100).

Garcia and Moreno after a detailed review of global marine fisheries and the related studies observe that "more recent papers ... argue that overfishing is the main cause of degradation of the state of world stocks, above pollution and all other forms of human intervention ... The high pressure exerted on stocks has ecological effects, which have been stressed repeatedly and are demonstrated by the change in quality (species composition, size, commercial value, trophic level) observed in the landings, largely reflecting changes in the resource base ...Few resources could support higher fishing pressure, and these tend to be prey species for which an increase in exploitation may lead to questionable ecological consequences, including for predator stocks that society would like to see rehabilitated. There is practically no other fishing area or resource of significance to be discovered. The world's oceans are exploited from the poles to the tropics, the littoral to the open sea, and the surface to the deep bottom. Deep-sea resources on slopes and sea mounts are already under heavy pressure (and possibly overfished in many areas) and their low natural productivity and resilience put them in serious danger. There is hardly anywhere else to go to employ existing excess fishing capacity' (Garcia and Moreno, 2003, p.20).

*The State of World Fisheries and Aquaculture 2004* published by the FAO in 2004 gives the most extensive review of the overfishing problem. It stated: "The current global situation follows the general trend observed in previous years. It is estimated that in 2003 about one-quarter of the stocks monitored were underexploited or moderately exploited (3 per cent and 21 per cent respectively) and could perhaps produce more. About half of the stocks (52 per cent) were fully exploited and therefore producing catches that were close to their maximum sustainable limits while approximately one quarter were overexploited, depleted or recovering from depletion (16 per cent, seven per cent and one per cent respectively) and needed rebuilding. From 1974 to 2003 there was a constant downward trend in the proportions of stocks offering potential for expansion. At the same time there was an increasing trend in the proportion of overexploited and depleted stocks, from about 10 per cent in the mid- 1970s to close to 25 per cent in the early 2000s ..." (FAO, 2004, p.32).

The above Report also gave a picture of the state of over-exploitation of major stocks of fish. It reported thus: "Of the top ten species that account in total for about 30 per cent of the world capture fisheries production in terms of quantity ..., seven correspond to stocks that are considered to be fully exploited or overexploited (Anchoveta, Chilean jack mackerel, Alaska pollock, Japanese anchovy, blue whiting, capelin and Atlantic herring)" (ibid, pp.32-33).

This report further speaks of the major areas subjected to overexploitation and the prevailing circumstances in those fisheries. It noted: "The percentage of stocks exploited at or beyond their maximum sustainable levels varies greatly by area. In the Eastern Central Pacific, only 33 per cent of the stocks for which assessment information is available are recorded as fully exploited, with the remainder being either underexploited or moderately exploited, whereas in the Western Central and Northeast Atlantic and the Western Indian Ocean, all the stocks for which information is available are reported as being fully exploited (73 per cent, 59 per cent and 75 per cent respectively) or as being exploited beyond this level ... In 12 of the 16 FAO statistical regions at least 70 per cent of stocks are already fully exploited or overexploited suggesting that the maximum fishing potential has been reached and that more cautious and restrictive management measures are needed. This conclusion is also supported by analysis of the trend in fisheries production of the regions. Four of the 16 regions are at their maximum historical level of production, while in 12 regions production has declined slightly and in four the declines have been sharper, including the Northwest Atlantic (50 per cent decline from a peak in 1968), Southeast Atlantic (47 per cent decline from a peak in 1978) and Southeast Pacific (31 per cent decline from a peak in 1994). In most cases overfishing has been a major contributory factor and in some cases this has been associated with adverse or highly variable environmental conditions. All the information available tends to confirm the estimates made by FAO in the early 1970s that the global potential for marine capture fisheries is about 100 million tonnes, of which only 80 million tonnes are probably achievable. It also confirms that, despite total differences, overall, this limit has been reached. These conclusions lend support to the call for more rigorous stock recovery plans to rebuild stocks that have been depleted by overfishing and to prevent the decline of those being exploited at or close to their maximum potential" (ibid, pp.33-34).

Referring to the situation in the inland fisheries of the world, *The State of World Fisheries and Aquaculture 2000*, noted that "inland aquatic resources continue to be under pressure from loss or degradation of habitat and overfishing. Fresh water species are reported to be the most threatened group of vertebrates harvested by humans; however, accurate data are difficult to collect. In areas where studies have been carried out, about 20 per cent of freshwater species are threatened, endangered or extinct" (FAO, 2000a, p.11).

*The State of World Fisheries and Aquaculture 2004*, notes that "inland fishery resources are undervalued and under threat from habitat alteration, degradation and unsustainable fishing activities. This trend unfortunately appears to be continuing...a recent symposium on managing the fisheries of large rivers noted that the availability of global information on river fisheries is poor, that over 50 per cent of inland species occur in rivers and that rivers contain a higher proportion of organisms classed as endangered or threatened than do most other ecosystems. Many river basins especially in developing countries, support intensive fisheries and in many cases catches have increased, although changes in their species composition have occurred as catches of large and late-maturing species have declined. River fisheries continue to provide substantial catches in developing countries, even in the face of intensive exploitation. However, in the Mekong River, for the first time, there is evidence that stocks are being overfished. Numerous lake fisheries are also showing signs of overexploitation. In Lake Victoria, for example, the Nile perch fishery decreased from a record catch of 371526 tonnes in 1990 to 241130 tonnes in 2002. Sturgeon fisheries in the countries surrounding the Capsian Sea have also decreased from approximately 20000 tonnes in 1988 to less than 1400 tonnes in 2002, owing to a combination of illegal fishing, over fishing and habitat degradation. Inland fishes in general have been characterised as the most threatened group of vertebrates used by humans" (FAO, 2004, pp.35-36).

A very recent note of alarm on the unsustainability of global fisheries has been raised by the UNEP in its report, *Global Environmental Outlook* (GEO). The agency reported that "rising demand for seafood and other marine produce will lead to a collapse of today's commercial fish stocks by 2050 unless better management is introduced, exemplifying the challenges facing Governments in a globalised world" (Seafood Export Journal, 2007a, p.15).

### 4.2.2. Environmental Pollution

The GESAMP defined pollution as "the introduction by man, directly or indirectly, of substances or energy into the marine environment (including estuaries) resulting in such deleterious effects as harm to living resources, hazards to human health, hindrance to marine activities including fishing, impairment of quality for use of sea water, and reduction of amenities" (quoted in Caddy and Griffiths, 1995, p.65).

Environmental degradation, notably aquatic pollution, is causing a serious threat to the sustainability of global fisheries. It has adversely affected the biological productivity of the stock base and its survival. Referring to this critical issue, the FAO observed as early as 1993 thus:

"Another pervasive and damaging change in the marine environment has been the increasing severe degradation of the coastal zone. It has been estimated that two thirds of marine fish production comes from stocks which pass the first and most vulnerable stages of their life cycles in coastal areas.

Coastal zone damage is particularly acute in developing tropical countries where both natural and economic conditions contribute to the high vulnerability of these areas. In these countries, the growth in population and migration to coastal cities and regions are leading to increases in municipal and industrial discharges and landfill, mangrove clearing, coral mining and other construction-related damages. In some countries, situation is becoming severe as a result of deforestation, the construction of lumber roads and land clearing. Intensified agriculture is contributing increasing amounts of pesticides and herbicides to coastal waters.

Intensive forms of aquaculture are themselves a source of pollution. The release of excess feeds and faeces in semi-enclosed environments has already generated eutrophication problems and oxygen deficiencies, which are directly detrimental to farming enterprises. In shrimp farming, the clearing of mangroves, the extensive harvesting of wild larvae and the indiscriminate use of antibiotics to control diseases are negatively affecting other important commercial marine fish stocks.

In addition, certain fishing practices are having severe environmental effects. Such practices include the use of dynamite and poisons as well as techniques in which fish are driven into nets by swimmers pounding the coral reefs with rocks, for example the *'muro ami'* fishing in the Philippines. Local populations resort to these highly destructive techniques when faced by increasingly scare resources and a lack of alternative opportunities for employment.

In the past two decades, the degradation of the marine environment has increased significantly, mainly through exacerbated overfishing and coastal zone pollution. The trend is highly disturbing, since fish are one of the major sources of animal protein and are of critical importance to the increasing populations in developing countries" (FAO, 1993a, p.30).

The FAO also noted that: "more immediately apparent are the several kinds of changes taking place in the coastal aquatic ecosystems. One is the increase in nutrient rich wastes coming from municipalities and farms. In some cases, such nutrient discharges may enhance fishery production but, more generally, they may have damaging effects, such as oxygen depletion (resulting in fish larvae kills) or blooms of phytoplankton species. The latter is often a cause of 'red tides' and can produce paralytic shellfish poisoning (PSP).

The growing amounts of soil erosion and freshwater run-off resulting from deforestation and certain agricultural practices are leading to increased siltation and changes in water temperatures, salinity levels and transparency, with consequent damages to coral reefs and aquatic vegetation.

Chemical pollutants may enter the coastal zone: when discharged directly into water from industrial operations that are not governed by international conventions or in cases of accidents; as pesticide and herbicide run-off from farms; or as fall out from the atmosphere. Changes are also occurring through the extraction of sand and gravel and the mining of coral as well as through land reclamation activities, including the clearing of mangroves, often for the purpose of shrimp farming" (ibid, p.43).

It further reported that "pressures on the coastal zone ecosystem will increase in the future. It is estimated that, by the year 2000, 60 per cent of the three billion people living in urban areas will be concentrated in settlements less than 50 miles from the sea, while many more will be in settlements along rivers, sufficiently close to carry pollutants into the sea. Developing countries will be at a particular disadvantage in attempting to cope with the pressures because the immediate and manifest needs for food, living space and employment are likely to outweigh the less direct and visible need to avoid damage to the coastal zone. For example, dichlorodiphenyltrichloroethane (DDT) is commonly used and sometimes subsidised in developing countries even though the downstream damages are such that it has been banned in many developed countries.

It is estimated that 80 per cent of marine pollution comes from land-based sources whereas the preponderance of the harm is felt by marine fisheries and aquaculture. There is therefore an asymetry between those who cause environmental harm and those who bear the costs" (ibid, p.43).

The impact of environmental pollution on the fishery system has been noted by Caddy and Griffiths. They point out that "the unrestrained use of rivers and estuaries for the discharge of nutrients and toxic compounds leads to significantly adverse impacts on critical marine habitats, but water extraction and, more generally, the regulation of rivers for navigation and flood prevention often have adverse effects on riverine fish ... and diadromous species such as salmon, eels, and shad .." (Caddy and Griffiths, 1995, pp.11-12). These authors also note that "soil erosion due to the removal of plant cover (e.g. deforestation) in watersheds, increases sediment loading of rivers and changes the seasonal cycle and amount of freshwater run-off to coastal seas, as well as the levels of siltation...High riverine sediment loads adversely affect anadromous species such as Salmon and Sturgeon, and estuarine organisms such as oysters. It also has a serious negative impact on coastal coral reefs...and on aquatic vegetation which is often of key importance as fish habitat" (ibid, p.12).

Referring to the role of contaminants in affecting the marine ecosystems, these authors quoted the GESAMP, which stated "the major causes of immediate concern ...are coastal development and the attendant contamination of seafood, fouling of the seas by plastic litter, continued build-up of chlorinated hydrocarbons, especially in the tropics and subtropics, and accumulation of tar on beaches" (ibid, p.13).

The GESAMP report of 1990 also noted that "although the open ocean was still relatively clean, some contamination was occurring, with atmospheric routes for contaminant transmission being of primary importance. Also of considerable concern is the widespread occurrence through out the world oceans of floating plastic debris which may impede (by entanglement, etc.) movement, and interfere with the feeding of birds, mammals and fish species living in or off the surface layers of the oceans" (ibid, p.41).

Caddy and Griffiths note that "chemical pollution may influence fish production in numerous ways: reduction of stock by mass mortalities; gradual decline, or changes in composition, of populations or entire ecosystems; increased occurrence of diseases; deterioration of fish food quality; lowered growth rates. The seas, and land-locked water bodies, receive a significant proportion of pollutant chemicals via the atmosphere, so that effects distant from the source cannot be discounted" (ibid, p.66). These authors also noted that "the problems of contamination of the inland and coastal environments and, consequently of aquatic products by pathogenic bacteria and viruses contained in water contaminated with sewage and in uncontrolled domestic runoff from urban areas, are growing world wide ... Nutrients from the same sources also encourage blooms of toxic dinoflagellates and red tides that may contaminate fish and shellfish, whether wild or cultured; this type of contamination is paralleled in some tropical areas by the increasing prevalence of ciguatere ... Other forms of fish toxicity and algal booms induce fish kills in the tropics...In the areas of oil exploitation, catches and fishing gears may have to be discarded because of tainting" (ibid, pp.66-67).

The impacts of other coastal activities like coastal construction, coastal industry, coastal mining, tourism, aquaculture, shipping, etc. have also been pointed out by Caddy and Griffiths. They noted that "coastal human populations are still growing in many countries; construction has increased accordingly, in the form of human residences and hotels, ports, marinas, and the associated infrastructure (sewage treatment plants and rubbish dumps, shops, banks, post offices, hospitals, and so on), as well as industrial installations ... Not only does human settlement bring with it problems of contamination ... but it also threatens the habitat of many species of marine life: fish, turtles, birds, mammals and other organisms that habitually live in the coastal zone, in the sea or on the land nearby. Uncontrolled cutting of mangroves, whether to facilitate coastal construction for shrimp ponds, or to use mangrove wood ... may, in excess, also be examples of environmental degradation that have adverse effects on coastal marine resources ...

Coastal construction significantly impacts the local marine ecosystems and often forces fishers to change their gears/methods and target species...

Industries are established in coastal zones mainly because of the need for a place (the sea) to dump waste, or the use of the sea as a source of cooling water (i.e. to dump heat). Most industries also have to dispose of chemical waste from manufacturing processes (e.g. mercury compounds/fungicides from paper-pulp production), and sometimes physical waste such as sludges (e.g. from the processing of aluminum or titanium oxide ores). Desalination plants, by definition, are sited at the coast; and besides heat, they may discharge hot brines.

Not only can coastal industries degrade the local marine environment where they discharge, but they also occupy terrestrial environment in their vicinity at the expense of other biologically important critical habitats for marine and costal species. To the extent that disruption and contamination depress the quality and abundance of the marine fauna, local fisheries are adversely affected by coastal industry; and in the long term, the sum of all coastal industrial discharges not fully absorbed by the sea has the potential to adversely affect coastal marine fisheries in general … On the whole, coastal industry (even including industrial scale fish farming) has the potential to be prejudicial to coastal fishery interests … Marine mining … adversely affects benthic organisms by destroying habitats and damaging spawning grounds of demersal and other fishes; it also interferes with trawling and other bottom-fishing methods …

To 'force-feed' cultured species by the addition of food to the natural environment may, in certain circumstances, lead to abnormal discharge of wastes to the local coastal sea, leading to local eutrophication … perhaps causing harmful plankton blooms…

Busy commercial shipping routes are not easily compatible with commercial fishing. Apart from the risk of oil spills, oil tankers, besides being generally very large and not easily maneuverable near shore, may wash out their oil tanks (albeit illegally) thus giving rise to a form of oil pollution that may be unfavourable to fishers (degradation of the marine environment, tainting of fish flesh, oiling of fishing gear, especially nets, etc) … Inappropriate agricultural practices in the hinterland of the coast have the potential to pose a serious problem to coastal fishermen both with respect to pesticide and fertilizer loss.

Pesticides, which may be over-applied, can be washed by rain from the cultivated land surface directly into the sea, or indirectly via rivers debouching into the sea, with potentially adverse effects on the coastal fauna and species of fishery interest. There is also a substantial transport of agricultural pesticides by the atmosphere …, they may reach the sea, but over a wide area (regional, if not global) so that although the effects on the coastal sea are not easily quantifiable, distant ecosystems, such as those in the Antarctic, may accumulate detectable levels of industrial chemicals …

The effects of fertilisers washed or discharged via rivers into the sea … are potentially very important, often adversely in the vicinity of point sources, perhaps more positively farther away after dispersion has taken place…" (ibid. pp.65-70).

Highlighting the environmental pollution impacts, the FAO-Government of Japan collaboration report noted: "In most coastal countries and in a number of countries with large inland waters, the productivity of fisheries is adversely affected by an increasing demand for coastal space and resources. More often than not, this competition is reflected in the degradation of the marine environment. The changes which take place may be generated either within the fisheries sector itself or, more frequently and usually with a larger impact, outside the sector.

With regard to the first of these factors, the damage to fish habitat caused by the fisheries sector can be significant. Among the principal causes are: trawling, which may adversely affect certain habitats from bottom fauna; the use of dynamite and some destructive fishing techniques (e.g. *muro ami* fishing); the destruction of coastal wetland and mangrove areas by aquaculture pond construction; aquatic pollution caused by intensive coastal aquaculture; and others.

Looking at the second of the sources of marine environmental degradation, the use of resources outside the sector may have a major impact on fish abundance. Fish habitats are being rapidly degraded in many parts of the world by industrial, urban and agricultural pollution, landfill, damming and diversion of rivers, clearance of mangroves, sedimentation, resource mining, marine based pollution, deforestation in the hinterland, etc. In some areas, the destruction of fish habitat has become the prime cause of the reduction of fish abundance. This is particularly so in, but not confined to, a number of marine areas dependent on the harvesting of shellfish. Such degradation results in the loss, or reduction of the economic value of the goods and services provided by the affected ecosystems and a loss of biodiversity and genetic resources" (FAO-Government of Japan, 1995, p.13).

Referring to the issue of coastal pollution, Clark notes that "coastally discharging rivers gather and carry large amounts of pollutants to the coast with their rampaging flood waters...Consequently, a large share of the world's pollution ends up in coastal lagoons, estuaries, wetlands, submerged grass beds, and coral reefs...Contaminants are transported from land to sea by rivers, direct run-off, or point discharges. They are partly retained in the water and sediments of estuaries, bays, beaches or open coastal waters, and partly transported through these boundary areas to the open ocean. The disposal of domestic sewage and industrial effluents from population and industrial centers located along the coastline extends coastal pollution beyond the estuaries. Moreover, coastal waters are not only more polluted than the open ocean, they also offer significantly more opportunities for exposure through contamination of the world's most important fisheries and recreation areas ...

The persistence of pesticides and other toxic chemicals and heavy metals is of great concern to maintenance of biodiversity and on the suitability of seafood for the human diet ...

Pollution is often at its worst in the harbours of large coastal cities and industrial ports where sewage and toxic industrial wastes combine to damage coastal environments and resources as well as to jeopardise human health...

The most dramatic threat to the estuarine ecosystem is a catastrophic spill of oil, or release of other hazardous materials. The large volume of petroleum and chemical products transported through the estuarine zone by ships, barges, pipelines and railroads present a continuing potential for accidental bulk spills of oil or chemicals. Oil pollution may originate during exploration, production and transportation phases of the oil industry ..." (Clark, 1996, pp.383-385).

Quoting a United Nations' source, Clark further reported that "the major causes of immediate concern" in the global marine environment upon entering the decade of the 1990s were "coastal development and the attendant destruction of habitats, eutrophication, microbial contamination of seafood and beaches, fouling of the seas by plastic litter, progressive build up of chlorinated hydrocarbons, especially in the tropics and subtropics, and accumulation of tar on beaches" (ibid, p.385).

It is also noted by Clark that "not all pollution comes from pipes or other specific points. Sources of 'diffuse' (or 'non-point') pollution that affect coastal areas are septic tanks, dumps, landfills, concentrations of boats, and particularly, storm water run off from adjacent watersheds. These sources may cause serious eutrophication or toxicity where pollutants concentrate in confined lagoons or estuaries ...

Among the most important causes of non-point source pollution are land alteration activities, principally those associated with site preparation for development and for crop land, as well as shoreline and water basin alterations ..." (ibid, p.385).

Referring to the other major source of coastal pollution, Clark states that the "major disturbance of coastal ecosystems from development in the hinterlands includes drainage water pollution, alteration of the run off water cycle, and loss of coastal wetlands. Sedimentation, nutrient enrichment, and inflow of toxic substances – the principal pollutants -

are caused by soil fertilizers, animal wastes, biocides and waste oil carried into tidal waters with surface runoff and stream flow from coastal watersheds from watersheds that drain to the coast. Soil erosion is often the leading problem" (ibid, p.465).

Clark further pointed out that "uncontrolled development activity can destroy critical coastal natural habitat and create sources of water pollution. A major source of degradation of shallow littoral basins is their continued use as pollutant discharge areas. Aside from outright fish kills and other dramatic effects, pollution causes a general decline in the natural carrying capacity of the system. Lagoons are particularly vulnerable because they have restricted circulation.

Effects of pollution are evidenced by the gradual disappearance of fish or shellfish, or a general decline in the natural carrying capacity of the system. The most likely sources of pollution are agricultural and industrial chemicals and organic wastes. One major source of lagoon/ estuary degradation is their continued usage as pollutant discharge areas. Aside from outright fish kills and other dramatic effects, pollution causes pervasive and continuous degradation. Such contaminants in high concentrations create a hostile environment that drives away fish, prevents shellfish from reproducing, and/or undermines the food chain" (ibid, p.341).

The seriousness and magnitude of this problem have been highlighted by Nadia as well. Nadia reports that "coastal waters are the ultimate recipient for pollutants coming from land, rivers, air and the sea. Coastal lagoons, estuaries, semi-enclosed seas and shallow littoral waters of the open coast seem to be the areas where most damage is concentrated ... Most aquatic pollution in coastal areas originates from land-based sources, the rest coming from shipping waste dumping, oil production and offshore mining. Land-based pollution can be transported in a variety of ways (eg. rivers, freshwater runoff, the atmosphere). Pollution may significantly decrease marine environmental quality. Population growth in coastal areas which leads to urban development and changes in land and other resource uses, also induces various forms of pollution. A major factor is increased waste water discharge into the sea leading to nutrient and organic enrichment and ecosystem disruption, including adverse consequences of eutrophication and reduction of freshwater inflow caused by irrigation and urban uses.

Another common source of pollution is agricultural waste such as toxic compounds from pesticides. Many such compounds have long half-lives and consequently tend to have long-term effects. Industrial waste also comprises many toxic substances including heavy metals, radioactive elements, acids and industrial chemicals. Oil spills are another common source of acute pollution.

Aquatic pollution, even at low levels, may influence fish production in numerous ways: reduction of stocks by mass mortality (particularly of larval and juvenile fish); gradual decline or changes in species composition of fish populations or entire ecosystems; increased occurrence of diseases; slower growth rates; and deterioration of the food quality of fish. Long-term effects of aquatic pollution on fish should not be underestimated. Species may be disadvantaged through chronic effects such as tissue damage, impaired reproduction or abnormal larval development.

Pollution can have especially severe effects on shellfish. In Canada, for example, over 2,00,000 ha of near-shore waters are closed for shellfish harvesting because of pollution; in the United States, one third of shellfish beds have been closed. On a larger scale, the crash of the entire fisheries economy of the Black Sea area as a result of pollution, over-fishing and the introduction of aquatic species that feed on fish larvae is estimated to cost some US $ 1 billion per year …

Both capture fisheries and aquaculture are affected by land-based pollution. The problem is at once world-wide yet highly specific to different geographic, ecological, social, and economic situations …" (Nadia, 1998, pp.161-164).

Nadia also noted that "many of these problems may be aggravated, if not actually caused by, coastal tourism. Tourism leads to increased sewage (much of which is left untreated), resource depletion and conflict (e.g. between recreational and commercial fishers). Such problems are likely to be especially severe in the case of islands …" (ibid, p.164).

### 4.2.3. Habitat Loss

Along with environmental pollution, habitat loss /destruction is posing a major threat to the sustainability of global fisheries. Referring to this problem, Clark observes that "ecologically, impacts from any uncontrolled development activity anywhere near coastal areas – in watersheds, flood plains, wetlands, tidelands, or water basins – have the potential to deplete fisheries and coastal resources … The most serious threat is habitat destruction. This destruction takes many forms: (*a*) the replacement of entire habitats by settlements, harbours, and other human constructions, by cropland, grazing land, and plantations, and by mines and quarries; (*b*) the effects of dams (blocking spawning migrations, drowning habitats, and altering chemical or thermal conditions); (*c*) drainage, channelisation, and flood control; (*d*) pollution and solid waste disposal (from domestic, agricultural, industrial, and mining sources); (*e*) overuse of ground water aquifers (for domestic, agricultural, and industrial purposes); (*f*) removal of materials (such as vegetation, gravel, and stones) for timber, fuel, construction, etc.; (*g*) dredging and dumping; and (*h*) erosion and siltation" (Clark, 1996, pp.3-4).

Clark also noted that "the most serious adverse impacts of human activities on the coastal zone are water pollution and habitat destruction ... Pollutants can enter marine ecosystems from direct discharge, runoff from land, or atmospheric deposition. Direct discharges include pipeline discharges ('point sources') of municipal and industrial wastes into marine environments, discharge into rivers which then flow into marine environments, and discharge from vessels. Runoff (often called 'non-point' sources pollution) from agricultural and forest lands and from urban areas of coastal buildings may be the greatest threat to marine ecosystems, as well as most difficult one to stop. Nutrients, such as phosphate and nitrogen – applied in large quantities in agriculture as fertilizers – can cause eutrophication in coastal ecosystems by stimulating photoplankton, algae, and submerged vegetation, which rapidly grow and then die giving rise to anaerobic conditions.

Toxic substances form another category. They include heavy metals, pesticides and hydrocarbons which are harmful to marine species and to humans. The effects of these substances may be lethal or chronic, including maladies as tumors, skeletal deformations, and shell diseases. 'Bioaccumulation' often results in threats to human health, when toxic substances become concentrated in tissues of marketable fish and shellfish ... Increased loads of suspended sediment from land erosion and dredge spoils also cause pollution. They cloud waters, reducing the penetration of sunlight, thereby reducing normal levels of photosynthesis. Excessive sedimentation may smother benthic ecosystems, including coral reefs: for example, 70 per cent of the coral reefs of the Philippines are said to have been degraded by sediments in the near shore waters. Suspended sediments may be contaminated with toxic substances ...

Habitat destruction has been a monumental problem in coastal wetlands, which are filled, dredged, chananelised, flooded, and paved over. Because they are based upon a fragile physical structure, coral reef ecosystems are also highly vulnerable to habitat destruction. Direct habitat destruction has been less severe in other marine ecosystem, but there is reason for concern. Dredging and dredge disposal activities have destroyed habitat in many estuaries and more recently in off-shore environments. Proposals for seabed disposal of waste and sea bed mining for mineral poses threats to deep-water benthic eco-systems. Large spills of hazardous substances, such as oil, can cause instantaneous habitat destruction with a long recovery period. Habitat destruction can also occur indirectly, as a result of the cumulative effects of severe water pollution and water diversion ... Some types of fishing are also destructive of habitat such as: dynamite, '*muri-ami*', '*kayaka*', and otter trawling near coral reefs and other sensitive areas" (ibid, pp.323-326).

Some of the factors which impact on the coast and lead to habitat loss as noted by DuBois and reported by Clark (ibid, p.323) are listed below: 1. Loss of mangrove forests, 2. Coral reef destruction, 3. Congestion and intensive use of coastal resources, 4. Depletion of wild life species, 5. Pollution of coastal waters, 6.Beach and coastal line erosion, 7. Swamp land filling, 8. Upland deforestation, 9. Overfishing, 10. Saltwater intrusion

Looking broadly at the state of global inland fish resources, *The State of World Fisheries and Aquaculture 1998* noted that "neither the present state of nor the short-term outlook for inland aquatic resources is encouraging. An increase in the loss and degradation of land and forest resources and of biodiversity and habitat as well as the growing scarcity and pollution of freshwater can be observed in Africa, Asia and the Pacific, Latin America and the Caribbean and West Asia. Europe and the CIS and the Baltic states are also experiencing increasing biodiversity loss and habitat degradation ..." (FAO 1999a, p.10).

Referring to the inland fisheries particularly, it was noted that "the greatest threat to the sustainability of inland fisheries resources is not overexploitation, but degradation of the environment ... The global situation regarding inland aquatic resources is not encouraging, mainly owing to land and forest degradation, loss of biodiversity, the scarcity and pollution of freshwater and hence the degradation and loss of habitats. Another measure of the state of the inland aquatic environment has been provided by the analysis of the stress exerted in 145 large watersheds around the world...Stresses were found to be especially severe in watersheds that were already substantially modified or degraded. In particular, China, India and southeast Asia stood out as areas where pressures on wetlands are intensifying. This is a cause of concern, as they are the world's most important areas for inland fish production. Other major watersheds such as the Amazon and the Congo are less degraded. Nonetheless, these are also beginning to experience rapid change.

A world-wide study has been carried out on river basins that support a high level of aquatic biodiversity. The study concluded that 30 per cent of the basins should be managed very carefully because they have a rich diversity of fish species but are highly vulnerable to future pressures. Of these river basins, 39 per cent (by total area) are in Africa, 35 per cent in Asia, 26 per cent in Latin America...In conclusion, it is apparent that most freshwater fish faunas of the world are in serious decline and in need of immediate protection. Among the heavily fished faunas, fish losses appear to be highest in: (1) industrialised countries: (2) in regions with arid or Mediterranean climates; (3) in tropical regions with large human populations; and (4) in big rivers" (ibid, pp.60-61).

Nadia writes that "civil engineering works (e.g. road construction, dams, ports) may place further stress on coastal ecosystems as a result of soil run off and degradation of critical habitats. Similarly, agriculture and forestry activities, through their impact on soil stability, may affect coastal sedimentation. Because of their importance for the productivity of marine communities and because of their particular location in the coastal area, a number of critical habitats must be considered specifically as growing pressures on them may have significant consequences for the fisheries sector. These include mangroves, sea grass, lagoons and estuaries...

The common feature of these habitats is that they provide valuable services that are difficult to observe and are unpriced. Because they are difficult to observe, there is a tendency to ignore them, for example fishers themselves may trawl through sea grass meadows despite the impact that this may have on their own future welfare. In many cases the value of such resources is grossly underestimated, pointing to an urgent need for studies and research to demonstrate their value..." (Nadia, 1998, p.164). Some of the threats and drivers that lead to ecological crisis in marine ecosystem are given in appendix 4.1.

### 4.2.4. Biodiversity Loss

Biodiversity refers to the total richness and variety of life on earth. It designates the variety of life in all its forms, levels and combinations and includes ecosystem, species and genetic diversity. Biodiversity loss is a major threat to the sustainability of global fisheries. Biodiversity is being lost from nearly all aquatic ecosystems at an ever increasing rate, due mainly to the rising human population and anthropogenic changes in the environment. McConnell notes that "damming rivers has interrupted fish spawning runs..., wet lands have been drained, introduced alien species have ousted native ones, in addition to pollution and overfishing" (McConnell, 1999, p.31).

A report on the status of the earth's 'living' resources, including aquatic resources, prepared for the Rio Summit showed that "about 20 per cent of commercial freshwater fish species are now extinct or imperiled; the main threats being habitat degradation, introduction of alien species, over harvesting, pollution and competition for water" (ibid, p.30).

McAllister noted that "glimpses of what is happening to freshwater biodiversity can be provided by examining three of the better known taxonomic groups...734 species of fishes are critically endangered, endangered or vulnerable. Another 93 are extinct or extinct in the wild, i.e. 8.1 per cent of freshwater fishes are 'threatened' or extinct, at least in the wild. Of course there are many species whose status has not yet been evaluated. Estimates of all freshwater fishes which are threatened or extinct range from 20 per cent to 35 per cent, while 59 per cent of freshwater mammals and 43 per cent of crocodilians are threatened. Freshwater invertebrates are less well studied, but three quarters of the freshwater mussel species in the USA are at risk. All this suggests that a high proportion of freshwater species is at risk. Commercial species are at risk too. The number of wild salmon returning to the Columbia River in the U.S. is now less than 10 per cent of what it was before dams were built" (McAllister, 1999, pp.25-26).

It is further reported by McAllister that "until 1996, when the World Wildlife Fund and the IUCN held a workshop in London, only a handful of marine fish species was considered threatened. The workshop helped raise the number of threatened species of marine fishes in the 1996 IUCN Red List ... to 117 exclusively marine species. This demonstrated that it was chiefly the lack of evaluation and resources which had limited the listing of marine fish species ...

A few statistics demonstrate the extent of the assault on marine ecosystem by humans: 58 per cent of the world's reefs are potentially threatened ..., 50 per cent of the mangrove forests of the world have been lost; at least eight per cent of the continental shelf has been damaged by trawling and 16 per cent of that habitat has been fragmented..., and there has been a 14 per cent reduction in the Arctic sea ice habitat between 1978 and 1994. A first approximation suggests that eight per cent of sea grass beds of the world are lost or heavily degraded. The largest marine ecosystem area-wise, the neuston (tiny or small biota living on, at or just under the water's surface) is being affected by oil slicks (10 per cent of the total sea area is affected), increased UV radiation, persistent toxic chemicals, and flotsam ... The neuston is the ocean's main biotic nursery. Eggs, embryos and larvae normally thrive here because of abundant sunshine, oxygen, phyto and zooplankton. A stress on the neuston means an inevitable stress on ocean ecosystems, from the surface to the deep-sea. High productivity in the surface layers feeds the whole water column even to the deep-sea benthos, where falling plankton 'snow' from upper waters is an important energy source" (ibid, p.27).

The primary causes of aquatic biodiversity loss noted by McAllister are:

1. Growth in population and per capita consumption
2. The increased power of and control by transnational corporations over the policies and programmes of democratically elected governments, with some exceptions
3. International organisations, like the World Trade Organisation and International Monetary Fund and legal instruments, like the North American Free Trade Agreement and the draft Multilateral Agreement on Investment, undermine environmental agreements, e.g. the Convention on Biological Diversity
4. Militarism consumes billions of dollars and wastes the talents of drafted young people, harming the environment and diminishing assets that could be used for the environment (ibid, p.27).

McNeely of the IUCN gives some further evidences and causes of aquatic biodiversity loss thus: "... one of the largest skates in the Northwest Atlantic, the barndoor skate (*Raja laevis)* is close to extinction, at least partly because of directed fishery for the skate initiated off the coast of Newfoundland and Nova Scotia that began in 1994. Several marine mammals have been driven to commercial extinction by overharvesting and two, Stellar's sea cow and the West Indian monk seal, have become extinct in the past 400 years ...In the Black Sea, 21 of 26 major fish species have become 'commercially extinct', i.e. too few remain to be worth chasing. Already menaced by a string of ecological disasters around the Capsian Sea, the sturgeons that are exploited for caviar are rapidly becoming the latest victims of the collapse of the Soviet Union. In the early 1990s, four independent states and two autonomous regions appeared around the Capsian, which contains more than 90 per cent of the world's sturgeon stocks. As a result, the tightly regulated caviar cartel formed by the USSR and Iran has collapsed, leading to a free-for-all in which poachers, organised crime bosses and bureaucrats muscle their way into this lucrative business ... Experts believe that, within three or four years, sturgeon stocks will be completely depleted" (McNeely, 1999, p.34).

McNeely further observed that "commercial fishing can also seriously reduce the genetic diversity of wild fish. As just one example, the organge roughy (*Hoplostethus atlanticus*) is a medium-sized fish living in deepwaters off the continental shelf of Australia and New Zealand, spawning around ancient sea mounts, where it forms enormous aggregations...Today, the catch is around 38,000 tonnes and the total biomass of orange roughy in the New Zealand fishing grounds has been reduced by 60 to 70 per cent probably including the oldest and most genetically diverse portion of the population. This species has also the distinction being one of best documented examples of a loss in genetic diversity through fishing ...

Modern biotechnology may pose a threat at the genetic level. Scientific research laboratories in China, Japan, Singapore and Malaysia are working on transgenic fish, often in association with companies that expect to commercialise the genetically modified fish that grow faster than their wild or traditionally-bred aquaculture siblings. One problem is that transgenic fish are often created from eggs hatched from collections in the wild, so they are capable of mating with wild fish; this leads to concerns that the transgenic fish could escape to rivers or coastal areas where they could mate with wild fish and threaten the diversity of the wild population gene pool. They could also disrupt aquatic ecosystem by preying on and out-competing native species showing how genetic factors can have ecosystem effects.

Overfishing can also have significant ecosystem effects. The impact of fisheries on other species is well known in the literature as 'incidental take', involving impacts on dolphins, marine turtles, whales, seabirds, and so forth; this is one reason why the CBD focuses sustainable use on whole ecosystems rather than on individual species. Fishing also changes the trophic composition of fish communities for example by selectively harvesting predators...reflecting a gradual transition in landings from long lived, high-trophic level, piscivorus demersal fish toward short-lived, low trophic level of invertebrates and planktivorous pelagic fish.. This effect, also found to be occurring in inland fisheries, is most pronounced in the northern hemisphere. Fishing at lower trophic levels leads at first to increasing catches, then to stagnating or declining caches, indicating that present exploitation patterns are unsustainable" (ibid, pp.34-35).

McNeely further noted that "sea urchins eat kelp and other seaweeds and with the decline of cod, a major predator on sea urchins in the North Atlantic, sea weeds have been so heavily grazed by sea urchins that they have been replaced by encrusting pink algae and a rocky bottom. This significantly reduces the habitat available to other species, thereby reducing the overall productivity of the habitat. Similarly, the reduction of sea otters in the North Pacific has allowed sea urchins to expand greatly their impact on kelp ....

Aquaculture also has some negative impacts on fisheries. For example, in 1995, prawn production in Thailand brought in about $2 billion in export earnings, 40 per cent of the world market and the country's fifth largest source of foreign revenue. On the downside, prawn farming has helped to clear about two-thirds of Thailand's 388,500 ha of coastal mangrove forests, essential nurseries for Thai fisheries.

Biodiversity in freshwaters is seriously threatened in many parts of the world, and indeed is probably where the threat of extinction is most grave. A survey in Malaysia found fewer than half of the 266 fish species previously known from the country ...In the south eastern United States, ... one-third of natural freshwater fish species are extinct or endangered to some degree ...Over the past century, North American freshwater environments lost 21 of 297 mussel and clam species and 40 of the country's approximately 950 species of fish...

Global transport can also cause biodiversity loss and threaten sustainable use. Many ocean going ships carry ballast in the form of seawater that is taken on in port and released at subsequent ports of call. Transport of entire coastal planktonic assemblages across oceanic barriers to similar habitats renders bays, estuaries, and inland waters among the most threatened ecosystems in the world...

In fisheries and aquaculture, the introduction and transfer of alien organisms has helped some local economies but sometimes at the expense of ecological stability" (ibid, pp.35-36). There is also currently a "concern that genetically modified organisms (GMOs) will either have an adverse impact on local biodiversity through increased predatory or competitive ability, or that they will breed with related species and disrupt the local genetic diversity" (FAO, 2002, p.74).

Long reported that "modern industrial fishing practices are thought to kill and waste between 18 and 40 million tonnes of unwanted fish, birds, turtles, dolphins and other marine wild life each year" (Long, 1999, p.146). Their impact on biodiversity is obvious.

**4.2.5. Climate Change**

Changes in weather or climate is now considered as a major parameter affecting the sustainability of global fisheries. It, along with other environmental parameters influence the reproduction, growth and availability of the stock for commercial exploitation by the fishermen. The significance of this factor has been recognised by the FAO when it noted "the influence of natural climatic change is particularly strong for shoaling pelagic species which are caught in extraordinarily large quantities; the Peruvian anchoveta and the Japanese, South American and South African pilchard, for example. In these situations, it is difficult to separate the effects of environmental degradation and intensive fishing from those of natural climatic fluctuations.

Thus, there are not only uncertainties with regard to the degree to which global warming may occur but also in terms of the effects it may have on fisheries. Certainly, if there is a large rise in sea level, the devastating effects on coastal cities and communities will make the effects on fisheries pale into significance. But a moderate rise in global temperatures still deserves attention. It is unlikely that total marine fish production will change very much, although changes in the composition of species that make up the catch can certainly be expected, as can changes in areas of high productivity. The highly fertile tropical upwelling zones may move closer to the poles. Changes in rainfall patterns could lead to increased erosion on formerly dry land areas, with associated increases in coastal siltation and to decreased run-off from river basins, with associated declines in nutrients" (FAO, 1993a, p.42).

Caddy and Griffiths also highlighted the influence of this factor. They noted that "short-term (seasonal) and long-term (inter-annual to decadal) environmental variations, producing comparable variations in abundance of sardines and other species...preceded the influence of man ... They must, nevertheless, be taken into account to achieve sustainable-and optimal-development.

Long-term variations in the marine environment due to climate change have been documented and changes in fish abundance have been correlated with them. For example, it is known from fish scales in cores of bottom sediments that different species replaced each other even prior to man's influence on marine ecosystems...Also, the 'little ice-age', in the Northern hemisphere during the early Middle Ages, apparently caused by abnormalities in the sunspot cycle, was a period during which cod populations off Greenland declined and were replaced by seals and other fully Arctic species ...

... Changes in rainfall patterns, river run-off and sea-level rise will especially affect life in enclosed and semi-enclosed seas, coastal wetlands, estuaries, lagoons, mangroves and other important coastal nursery areas. Land erosion may increase, leading to coastal siltation, reduction of the marine photic zone and further degradation of coral reefs and sea-grass beds..." (Caddy and Griffiths, 1995, p.51).

These authors further point out that "some of the variations in the conditions under which marine ecosystems exist now, and in the future, are likely to be due to 'global climate change'... Such changes will add to the natural variations all ecosystems have always been subject to ...

Preparatory studies suggest that carbon dioxide (a 'greenhouse' gas) in the atmosphere is likely to double by 2025-2050 on a 'business as usual' basis leading to a probable increase in the global mean temperature of 1.5°C to 4.5°C... This may cause a rise in mean sea level of about 20 cm by 2030, and of about 65 cm by 2100, and to an increase in sea-surface temperature of between 0.2°C and 2.5°C.

The global climate changes mentioned above are not expected to have an adverse effect on fish production, as on terrestrial, lacustrine and riverine ecosystems, although particular stocks may be adversely affected and changes in rainfall and river run-off will particularly affect life in semi-enclosed seas and coastal nursery areas. Coastal aquaculture will also be affected. Tropical upwelling zones, which produce large amounts of fish resources, may shift polewards and increase in intensity. The year-to-year-variability of the resources they support may increase: however, increased phytoplankton productivity may reduce oxygen levels and lead locally to anoxic situations..." (ibid, pp. 71-72).

The FAO-Government of Japan collaboration report notes that "changes in oceanic conditions on a global time scale, as well as being responsible for changes in supply due to large-scale variations in stocks, can have an adverse effect on sustainability. They aggravate the mismatch between the level of investment and the availability of fishery resources, as investment made in response to a period of high abundance of fish is excessive in the following period of relatively low abundance.

Another consequence of climate change is the many coral reefs affected by 'bleaching' due to sea level rise and associated rising seawater temperature. In turn, this change in the reefs results in their loss as fish habitat..." (FAO-Government of Japan, 1995, p.14). Natural hazards such as cyclones, floods, typhoons, sea surges, tidal waves, earth quakes and landslides are also reported to have devastating effects on the fishing community and their economy. The tsunami of December 26, 2004 which struck the coasts of South East Asia had severe impacts on the economy of the fisher folk as it depressed the natural resources base , employment and market for the product.

The catastrophic effect of natural phenomenon like the El Nino current on the tropical and sub-tropical fisheries during the 1990s is presented in appendix 4.2.

Clark, while referring to the impact of global warming stated: "Global warming may bring more hurricanes (cyclones) each year to coasts like the Atlantic coast of the United States. It will also increase beach erosion and flooding of coastal communities by elevating sea level (sea water expansion and melting of the South polar ice cap). Sea level has risen by six inches on the USA Atlantic coast in the last half century ... Sea life will be affected by the green house effect in the following ways ... (1) Rainfall patterns will shift and freshwater flows alter, leading to shifts in environmental conditions, particularly of lagoons, estuaries and bays, (2) New hydrological regimes could force an ecological transition with more impact than human development, pollution, and resource depletion.

Thus mega-changes are predicted for coastal ecosystems with extremely complex rebalancing of physical, chemical, and biological parameters. Some changes will benefit fisheries and sea life in general, others will jeopardise them, and most will induce some amount of stress, temporary or permanent ...

... While the most dramatic effects may be seen in polar seas, even tropical reefs will experience major impacts. In fact, the world-record hot year 1987 produced the first serious outbreak of "coral bleaching", a stress reaction in which various corals turn pale and go into a prolonged state of shock when the water temperature exceeds 86°F (31°C).

The specter of an ocean too warm and warm for coral reefs is disturbing because so many tropical countries depend heavily on their reefs for food, jobs and hard currency earnings from tourism. Equally serious are the prospects that sea level may increase too fast for the reef-building coral organisms to adjust.

Rising sea temperatures (as high as 2.5°C for some parts of the sea) will convert some temperate water bodies (like the northern Gulf of Mexico, USA) into tropical seas and shift most species northward. This will include fishes and other aquatic species like seals, alligators and pelicans.

To understand the future global climate change, scientists have been looking for past events, like the El Nino of 1982-83 during which a large area of the Pacific Ocean surface was heated by 7°F, an extreme change in ecological terms. (El Ninos are rapid ocean warmings along the Pacific Equator caused by global climatic shifts). The change translated to a 2-3°C increase in water temperature off the coasts of California and Oregon (USA) – enough to have had a major impact on fish" (Clark, 1996, pp.320-321).

Quoting Fluharty, another author, Clark also reported that "the salmons were more dispersed along the coast, their growth was slower and, judging from the lower rate of return to the streams for spawning, their survival was poorer" (ibid, p.321). Fluharty also noted the unusual occurrence of squids, leatherback turtles, and brown pelicans off the north Pacific coast (ibid, p.321).

Nadia summarises the effects of climate change (global warming) thus: "The potential effects of global warming would presumably affect many coastal areas through sea-level rise, water temperature increase, deviations from present patterns of precipitation, wind and water circulation. Estuaries would experience loss of habitat, intrusion of marine waters and associated organisms, changes in circulation patterns that effect retention of some indigenous species, and increased hypoxia and storm surges…"(Nadia, 1998, p.171).

FAO makes the further observation that "the fact that long-term climatic changes could determine major epochal increases in fish production from some stocks in some areas, and equivalent declines from other stocks and areas, merits serious consideration because the impact at the local and regional levels are bound to be far larger. For instance, at present, large international market flows come from developing areas into developed ones (i.e. from the tropics to the North), but the oscillations in production between the North Atlantic and the Pacific Ocean are likely to result in changes to these trade flows. Such changes would have significant impacts on national and regional markets, even though the total supply could remain stable. Changes in investments and fleet movements (and fishing agreements) are also expected to be greater than suggested by the world accumulated total landing figures ...; available data suggest that there is a link between fish production and climate, the need to include the effects of global warming in possible projections is clear. The results reported suggest that shifts in climate could have noticeable positive or negative effects on some, if not most, major commercial fish stocks" (FAO, 2002, p.91).

Peter Barret, the Director of Victoria University's Antarctic Research Centre expressed the worst fear of mankind's extinction within another 100 years due to climate change (The New Indian Express, 19.11.04).

### 4.3 Economic Issues

Global fisheries, as an economic activity, are beset with a number of economic issues which also adversely affect their sustainability. These issues, to a certain extent, measure and indicate the level of unsustainability of the industry. The major economic issues outlined in this section, are: (1) decline/stagnation in production, (2) stagnation in consumption, (3) overcapitalisation, (4) uneconomic operation, (5) declining employment and productivity, (6) poverty and (7) barriers to trade.

#### 4.3.1 Decline/Stagnation in Production

Global fish production since 2000 has been showing an unsteady trend indicating the unsustainability of output at higher levels. Table 4.1 shows the trend in global fish production from 1998 to 2003.

Global total fish production, which stood at 118.2 million tonnes in 1998, increased to 131.0 million tonnes in 2000, decreased to 130.7 million tonnes in 2001, and rose to 133.0 million tonnes in 2002 but fell again to 132.2 million tonnes in 2003, indicating the unsustainability of output at higher levels.

The unsustainability of production is glaring in the case of capture fisheries, where the output decreased from 95.5 million tonnes in 2000 to 90.3 million tonnes in 2003. The fall in the output of capture fisheries is entirely due to the fall in the output of marine capture fisheries, where the output fell from 86.8 million tonnes in 2000 to 81.3 million tonnes in 2003.

**Table 4.1**

**Trend in global fish production from 1998 to 2003**

(in million tonnes)

| *Production* | *1998* | *1999* | *2000* | *2001* | *2002* | *2003* |
|---|---|---|---|---|---|---|
| *Inland* | | | | | | |
| Capture | 8.1 | 8.5 | 8.7 | 8.7 | 8.7 | 9.0 |
| Aquaculture | 18.5 | 20.2 | 21.3 | 22.5 | 23.9 | 25.2 |
| Total inland | 26.6 | 28.7 | 30.0 | 31.2 | 32.6 | 34.2 |
| *Marine* | | | | | | |
| Capture | 79.6 | 85.2 | 86.8 | 84.2 | 84.5 | 81.3 |
| Aquaculture | 12.0 | 13.3 | 14.2 | 15.2 | 15.9 | 16.7 |
| Total marine | 91.6 | 98.5 | 101.0 | 99.4 | 100.4 | 98.0 |
| Total capture | 87.7 | 93.8 | 95.5 | 92.9 | 93.2 | 90.3 |
| Total aquaculture | 30.6 | 33.4 | 35.5 | 37.8 | 39.8 | 41.9 |
| *Total world fisheries* | 118.2 | 127.2 | 131.0 | 130.7 | 133.0 | 132.2 |

*Source:* FAO, 2004, p.3

It is worth recalling here that "increasing coefficients of output variation ... are prima facie evidence of declining resilience and hence declining sustainability" (Pearce, 1998, p.47).

Global aquaculture production is, however, found to be steadily rising during this entire period, both in the case of inland aquaculture and marine aquaculture. Total aquaculture production increased from 30.6 million tonnes in 1998 to 41.9 million tonnes in 2003.

The unsustainability of output at higher levels is found to be a critical issue for many countries. This is highlighted in table 4.2, which gives details of capture production of fish by principal producers during 1998-2003.

It is apparent from table 4.2 that out of the 20 countries, which produced more than one million tonnes of fish in 2003, only 10 had succeeded in maintaining or increasing their annual production from 1998 to 2003. They are USA, Indonesia, Philippines, Vietnam, Mexico, Myanmar, Malaysia, Bangladesh, Taiwan (China) and Canada. All the rest, including mainland China, Peru, Japan, India, etc. had failed to increase or sustain their output at higher levels.

**Table 4.2**
**Details of capture production of fish by principal producers during 1998-2003***

(in million tonnes)

| *Sl. No.* | *Country* | *1998* | *1999* | *2000* | *2001* | *2002* | *2003* |
|---|---|---|---|---|---|---|---|
| 1. | China | 17.22 | 17.24 | 16.99 | 16.53 | 16.55 | 16.76 |
| 2. | Peru | 4.33 | 8.42 | 10.66 | 7.98 | 8.76 | 6.09 |
| 3. | USA | 4.71 | 4.75 | 4.72 | 4.94 | 4.94 | 4.94 |
| 4. | Indonesia | 3.96 | 4.04 | 4.12 | 4.27 | 4.34 | 4.68 |
| 5. | Japan | 5.30 | 5.19 | 4.99 | 4.71 | 4.36 | 4.60 |
| 6. | India | 3.37 | 3.47 | 3.67 | 3.78 | 3.74 | 3.69 |
| 7. | Chile | 3.27 | 5.05 | 4.30 | 3.80 | 4.27 | 3.62 |
| 8. | Russia | 4.45 | 4.14 | 3.97 | 3.63 | 3.23 | 3.28 |
| 9 | Thailand | 2.93 | 2.95 | 3.00 | 2.83 | 2.84 | 2.82 |
| 10. | Norway | 2.86 | 2.63 | 2.70 | 2.69 | 2.74 | 2.55 |
| 11. | Philippines | 1.83 | 1.87 | 1.90 | 1.95 | 2.03 | 2.17 |
| 12. | Iceland | 1.68 | 1.74 | 1.98 | 1.98 | 2.13 | 1.98 |
| 13. | Viet Nam | 1.30 | 1.39 | 1.45 | 1.49 | 1.51 | 1.67 |
| 14. | Korea Republic | 2.03 | 2.12 | 1.82 | 2.00 | 1.67 | 1.65 |
| 15. | Mexico | 1.18 | 1.21 | 1.32 | 1.40 | 1.45 | 1.45 |
| 16. | Myanmar | 0.83 | 0.92 | 1.07 | 1.17 | 1.31 | 1.35 |
| 17. | Malaysia | 1.15 | 1.25 | 1.29 | 1.23 | 1.28 | 1.29 |
| 18. | Bangladesh | 0.84 | 0.96 | 1.00 | 1.07 | 1.10 | 1.14 |
| 19. | China, Taiwan | 1.09 | 1.10 | 1.09 | 1.01 | 1.04 | 1.13 |
| 20. | Canada | 1.00 | 1.02 | 1.00 | 1.04 | 1.06 | 1.08 |

*Includes only those countries, which produced more than one million tonnes of fish in 2003.

*Source:* FAO, 2005a, p.38.

At the fishing area (ocean) level, the decline in output was found to be perceptible in the Pacific and the Atlantic ocean regions. Table 4.3 gives the trend in the output of marine capture fisheries of major fishing areas (oceans) from 1997 to 2003.

**Table 4.3**
**Trend in the output of capture fisheries of major fishing areas (oceans) from 1997 to 2003**

(in million tonnes)

| *Fishing areas* | *1997* | *1998* | *1999* | *2000* | *2001* | *2002* | *2003* | *% change in 2003 over 1997* |
|---|---|---|---|---|---|---|---|---|
| Atlantic Ocean | 24.82 | 23.83 | 23.73 | 24.04 | 24.53 | 23.85 | 23.89 | -3.74 |
| Indian Ocean | 8.43 | 8.49 | 8.70 | 8.77 | 8.83 | 9.40 | 9.60 | 13.87 |
| Pacific Ocean | 53.36 | 47.15 | 52.68 | 53.80 | 50.60 | 50.88 | 48.65 | -8.82 |
| Southern Ocean | 0.89 | 1.04 | 1.16 | 1.37 | 1.21 | 1.47 | 1.40 | 57.30 |

*Source:* FAO, 2005a, p.37.

The trend in the output of marine capture fisheries was quite unsteady and generally declining in the Pacific and Atlantic regions where the output in 2003 declined by 8.82 per cent and 3.74 per cent respectively over their 1997 level of output. In the Indian Ocean region and the Southern Ocean area, the output registered notable rates of growth. However, these areas accounted for only 13.53 per cent of the total marine capture fisheries production in 2003.

Among the principal species of fish caught by capture fisheries, during the period from 1999 to 2003, the unsustainability issue was found to be severe in the case of *anchoveta* (Peruvian anchovy), where the output decreased from 11.28 million tonnes in 2000 to 6.2 million tonnes in 2003. In the case of Alaska Pollock (Walleye poll), the catch decreased from 3.28 million tonnes in 1999 to 2.89 million tonnes in 2003. Atlantic herring and Chub mackerel also registered decreases in the output. In the case of the former, the output decreased from 2.41 million tonnes to 1.96 million tonnes and in the case of the latter it decreased from 1.95 million tonnes to 1.85 million tonnes during the same period. The output of California pilchard decreased from 1.09 million tonnes in 1999 to 0.85 million tonnes in 2003. Several other species with less than one million tonnes of output have witnessed varying levels of decline in their output during this period. (FAO,1999a, p.41). Appendix 4.3 gives details of catch of principal capture fisheries of the world from 1999 to 2003.

A corresponding problem which is also usually highlighted in the sustainability debate is the issue of 'by catch and discards'. Referring to this problem the *State of World Fisheries and Aquaculture 1998* noted: "The discarding of by-catch has been recognised as wasteful, although inevitable by the nature of fishing. It constitutes a loss of valuable food, has negative consequences for the environment and biodiversity and can be aesthetically offensive. By-catch was propelled to the forefront of public debate in reaction to the incidental capture of dolphins in tuna purse seine nets, turtles in shrimp trawls and marine mammals, birds, turtles and fish in high seas squid drift nets. The outcome for all the fisheries concerned was dramatic, and not always perceived as rational from the view point of fisheries interests.

An order of magnitude of the quantities of fish discarded was provided for the first time in an assessment published by FAO in 1994. Annual discards from the world's fisheries were estimated to range from 17.9 million to 39.5 million tonnes. A subsequent re-evaluation of these estimates together with adjustments allowing for subsequent reductions in discarding, indicates that current levels are at the lower end of the range. The most recent FAO estimate of 20 million tonnes, if correct, is equivalent to 25 per cent of the reported annual production from marine capture fisheries, which are those from which most of the discards derive ...

... In most respects, the decision by fishers to discard components of their catch is driven by economic factors. In an unregulated fishery, fishers have an incentive to discard if the expected net price, i.e. the real price less landing costs, is negative and if the resultant costs incurred in landing are greater than those incurred by discarding. Furthermore, there is an incentive to discard if the boat has a limited holding capacity. In such cases, fishers tend to discard the low-value components and retain those of higher values, a practice that is often referred as high-grading" (FAO, 1999a, 51).

### 4.3.2. Stagnation in Consumption

Stagnation in global consumption of fish is partly a consequence of the general decline or stagnation in fish production, as noted above. At the micro-level, per capita availability of fish is influenced by aggregate supply of edible (food) fish, changes in population size, etc. To the extent per capita consumption (availability) of fish is determined by the level of fish supplies, changes in consumption levels indicate the state of health and sustainability of the industry.

With global fish production not keeping pace with the growing world population, the per capita availability and consumption of fish is found to stagnate over the years. Table 4.4 shows the trend in global per capita food fish supply and aggregate human consumption of fish from 1998 to 2003.

**Table 4.4**

**Global per capita food fish supply and aggregate human consumption of fish from 1998 to 2003**

| *Item* | *1998* | *1999* | *2000* | *2001* | *2002* | *2003* |
|---|---|---|---|---|---|---|
| Global per capita food fish supply (kg) | 15.8 | 15.9 | 15.9 | 16.2 | 16.2 | 16.3 |
| Global per capita food fish supply (kg) (excluding China) | 13.3 | 13.2 | 13.2 | 13.4 | 13.2 | 13.3 |
| Global aggregate human consumption (million tonnes) | 93.6 | 95.4 | 96.8 | 99.5 | 100.7 | 103.0 |
| Global aggregate human consumption (million tonnes) (excluding China) | 62.3 | 62.9 | 63.7 | 65.6 | 65.5 | 66.8 |

*Source:* FAO, 2004, pp.3-4.

Global per capita food fish consumption is found to stagnate between 15.8 kg and 16.3 kg during 1998-2003. The per capita consumption is, however, found to be less and fluctuating between 13.2 kg and 13.4 kg when China, the major producer and consumer of fish is excluded from the calculations.

The unsustainability of global fish consumption is manifest from the regional and country profile, where there are marked differences in the availability and consumption. Highlighting this difference, FAO noted: "The role of fish in nutrition shows marked continental, regional and national differences as well as income-related variations...For example, world wide, 100 million tonnes were available for consumption in 2001, but only 6.3 million tonnes were consumed in Africa (7.8 kg per capita); two-thirds of the total were consumed in Asia, of which 34.8 million tonnes were consumed outside China (14.1 kg per capita) and 32.3 million tonnes in China alone (25.6 kg per capita). Per capita consumption in Oceania was 23.0 kg, in North America 21.6 kg, in Europe 19.8 kg, in Central America and the Caribbean 9.3 kg and in South America 8.7 kg" (FAO, 2004, p.40-41). Table 4.5 shows the total and per capita food fish supply by continent and economic groupings in 2001.

**Table 4.5**

**Total and per capita food fish supply by continent and economic groupings in 2001**

| *Area* | *Total food fish supply (million tonnes live weight equivalent)* | *Per capita food fish supply (kg)* |
|---|---|---|
| World | 100.2 | 16.3 |
| World excluding China | 67.9 | 13.9 |
| Africa | 6.3 | 7.8 |
| North and Central America | 8.5 | 17.3 |
| South America | 3.1 | 8.8 |
| China | 32.3 | 25.6 |
| Asia (excluding China) | 34.8 | 14.1 |
| Europe | 14.4 | 19.8 |
| Oceania | 0.7 | 23.0 |
| Industrialised countries | 26.0 | 28.6 |
| Economies in transition | 4.7 | 11.4 |
| Low income food deficit countries (LIFDCs) (excluding China) | 22.5 | 8.5 |
| Developing countries excluding LIFDCs | 14.9 | 14.8 |

*Source:* FAO, 2004, p.39.

It is apparent from table 4.5 that the bulk of the food fish produced is consumed by Asia (including China) and by industrialised countries. They together consumed 93.1 million tonnes of food fish in 2001. Per capita fish consumption is found to be the highest in industrialised countries (28.6 kg).

The global disparity in fish availability and consumption is further illustrated by the trend in the per capita consumption of fish in country groupings as shown in table 4.6.

**Table 4.6**
**Per capita consumption of fish in country groupings for selected years ( in kg)**

| *Country groupings* | *1986* | *1990* | *1994* |
|---|---|---|---|
| Association of South East Asian Nations | 18.7 | 19.5 | 21.9 |
| Caribbean Community and Common Market | 12.7 | 11.1 | 11.4 |
| Common Wealth of Independent States | — | — | 7.3 |
| Economic Community of West African States | 9.9 | 12.8 | 8.7 |
| European Community | 20.2 | 21.9 | 22.4 |
| Latin American Economic System | 9.0 | 9.3 | 9.0 |
| League of Arab States | 5.4 | 5.5 | 6.0 |
| North American Free Trade Agreement | 17.3 | 19.3 | 20.3 |
| South Asian Association of Regional Cooperation | 3.7 | 4.1 | 4.6 |
| Southern African Development Community | 10.0 | 9.9 | 6.3 |
| South Pacific Forum | 20.6 | 21.0 | 20.1 |

*Source:* FAO, 2000a, pp.119-141.

Table 4.6 reveals that per capita consumption levels were the highest in the European Community area (Austria, Belgium, Denmark, Finland, France, Germany, Greece, Ireland, Italy, Luxembourg, the Netherlands, Portugal, Spain, Sweden and the United Kingdom) followed by South Pacific Forum (Australia, Cook Islands, Federated States of Micronesia, Fiji, Kiribati, Marshall Islands, Nauru, New Zealand, Niue, Palau, Papua New Guinea, Samoa, Solomon Islands, Tonga, Tuvalu and Vanuatu), Association of South East Asian Nations (Brunei Darussalam, Cambodia, Indonesia, the Lao Peoples Democratic Republic, Malaysia, Myanmar, the Philippines, Singapore, Thailand and Vietnam) and North American Free Trade Agreement zone (Canada, Mexico and the United States). Per capita consumption was moderate in the Caribbean Community and Common Market Area (Antigua and Barbuda, Bahamas, Barbados, Belize, Dominica, Grenada, Guyana, Haiti, Jamaica, Montserrat, Saint Lucia, Saint Kitts and Nevis, Saint Vincent and the Grenadines, Suriname and Trinidad and Tobago), in the Economic Community of West African States (Benin, Burkina Faso, Cape Verde, Cote d'Ivoire, the Gambia, Ghana, Guinea, Guinea-Bissau, Liberia, Mali, Mauritania, the Niger, Nigeria, Senegal, Sierra Leone and Togo), in the Southern African Development Community

(Angola, Botswana, the Democratic Republic of the Congo, Lesotho, Malawi, Mauritius, Mozambique, Namibia, Seychelles, South Africa, Swaziland, and the United Republic of Tanzania, Zambia and Zimbabwe) and in the Latin American Economic System (Argentina, the Bahamas, Barbados, Belize, Bolivia, Brazil, Chile Colombia, Costa Rica, Cuba, the Dominican Republic, Ecuador, El Salvador, Grenada, Guatemala, Guyana, Haiti, Honduras, Jamaica, Mexico, Nicaragua, Panama, Paraguay, Peru, Suriname, Trinidad and Tobago, Uruguay and Venezuela).

Per capita food fish consumption was quite low in the Common Wealth of Independent States (Armenia, Azerbaijan, Belarus, Georgia, Kazakhstan, Kyrgystan, the Republic of Moldova, the Russian Federation, Tajikistan, Turkmenistan, Ukraine, and Uzbekistan), in the League of Arab States (Algeria, Bahrain, the Comoros, Djibouti, Egypt, Iraq, Jordan, Kuwait, Lebanon, the Libyan Arab Jamahiriya, Mauritania, Morocco, Oman, Palestine, Qatar, Saudi Arabia, Somalia, the Sudan, the Syrian Arab Republic., Tunisia, the United Arab Emirates and Yemen) and in the South Asian Association for Regional Cooperation (Bangladesh, Bhutan, India, Maldives, Nepal, Pakistan and Sri Lanka).It is worth noting here that some individual countries in the country groupings may be having high or low per capita consumption levels due to their unique geographic position, income or population levels.

The sharp difference in per capita consumption of food fish world wide between nations has been explained by FAO thus: "Fish consumption is distributed unevenly around the globe; there are significant differences among countries, with per capita apparent consumption ranging from less than one kg per capita to more than 100 kg. Geographical differences are also evident within countries, with consumption usually being higher in coastal areas. Dietary consumption patterns are influenced by complex interactions of several factors such as availability, income, prices, tradition and tastes, as well as demographic and lifestyle trends. Over the last few years, the consumption of fish and fishery products has been strongly influenced by improvements in transportation, in marketing and in food science and technology, which have led to significant improvements in efficiency, lower costs, wider choice and safer and improved products. The extent and range of these changes have varied among regions …" (FAO, 2004, p.41).

### 4.3.3. Over Capitalisation

Ward, *et al* define over capitalisation thus: "in its simplest form, over capitalisation can be considered to exist if the fleet size is greater than that required to harvest a particular yield" (Ward, *et al.* 2004, p.1). Overcapitalisation or overinvestment is yet another problem plaguing global fisheries. Traditionally, it was considered to be a problem of the catching sector, where under common property systems with unlimited access to the resources, additional investments were made by profit seeking enterprises till the industry suffered total collapse as a result of the ensuing stock depletion due to overfishing. Presently, overcapitalisation is a problem affecting all the branches of the industry, viz. the catching, culture, processing and marketing branches. The processing branch is universally known for building up excess capacity to cope with seasonal abundance in fish landings and this capacity becoming redundant during the rest of the seasons.

Referring to the issue in the catching branch (harvesting sector) Ward, *et al.* further noted that "excessive levels of harvesting capacity are a serious problem facing fishery managers in the new millennium" (ibid, p.1). Quoting Mace, these authors also reported over capacity as "the single most important factor threatening the long-term viability of exploited fish stocks and the fisheries that depend on them" (ibid, p.1). They also cited the findings of Garcia and Newton, two FAO scientists, that "world fishing capacity would need to be reduced by 25 per cent for revenues to cover operating costs and by 53 per cent for revenues to cover total costs" (ibid, p.1).

Outlining the situation and the factors that lead to it, FAO notes: "where this condition exists, fleet size (and capital investment) will tend to be greater than that required to take optimum yields from the stocks. Open access provides an incentive to over-capitalise…Although, with the extension of limits (200 mile EEZ), foreign fishermen no longer have free and open access, overcapitalisation may still be significant because access fees are generally paid by governments rather than by the fishermen. Fishermen therefore have no incentive to reduce their fleets.

Overcapitalisation is exacerbated by the ease of entry into fisheries and the difficulties of exit. When prices rise or stocks are abundant, new vessels are built, but when prices or yields drop and there are no alternative opportunities for employment of the vessels, they remain in the fisheries as long as they are able to cover their direct operating costs. When the owners can no longer cover such costs, they often sell their vessels to fishermen in other fisheries or in other countries. The scrapping of fishing vessels tends to be delayed well beyond the time of scrapping in most other maritime industries; that is generally not until refit costs approach the costs of a new vessel.

This situation may be particularly significant for the large vessels of many distant-water fleets. These fleets have been sufficiently mobile to move from one ocean region to another as the abundance of the stocks has changed because of overfishing or natural variations. Yet, such alternative opportunities for the employment of the fleets have become increasingly restricted as overfishing has become more pervasive" (FAO, 1993a, pp.20-21).

Another factor which led to considerable excess capacity or overcapitalisation in global fishing fleets is the encouragement given to the industry by states in the form of various subsidies and other support. In many instances, the industry was able to cover the revenue gap (deficit) with the subsidy provided by the governments. The FAO reported in 1993 that "massive subsidies supported the former USSR fleet as well as the fleet of East European countries. These subsidies account for only a portion of the total deficit when capital costs are included, however. In Japan, the Japan Fisheries Association noted that the current credit balance extended to fisheries from both the commercial and government sectors is about US $19,000 million ...; in order to support business entities in financial difficulties, the government financing system will assume their liabilities. The amount of liability taken over by the government has been substantial in recent years due to the severe economic status of the fisheries industry.

European Community fisheries also receive substantial support. Between 1983 and 1990, EEC support rose from US $ 80 million to US $ 580 million, about 20 per cent of which was for the construction of new vessels and modernisation of old ones ... This amount does not include substantial subsidies provided by the national governments. Elsewhere in Europe, Norway also provides significant fisheries support, which amounted to about US $ 150 million per year during the second half of 1980s.

Fisheries are directly or indirectly subsidised in a variety of ways. Traditional kinds of subsidy are: import restrictions and tariffs (including limits on landings of foreign vessels); export support; price control systems; fuel subsidies; and low-cost loans or outright grants for the construction of vessels or the purchase of gear; the construction of ports, marketing facilities and other infrastructure.

In addition, there are fishery specific subsidies such as the payments made by governments to coastal states for access to their zones and the waiving of payments by domestic fishermen for access to their national zones. Free access to a natural resource constitutes a subsidy to the users since no payments are being made for the resource ...

The reasons for granting such subsidies are as manifold as the type of support schemes. In many cases, financial help is given to the fishing sector – and less frequently to the post-harvest sector-for social reasons; for example, to sustain employment in sometimes sparsely inhabited coastal districts. Subsidies might also be given for general policy reasons, since the competing agricultural sector enjoys similar support on a large scale. In other cases, particularly in the former centralised economies of Eastern Europe, food policies were designed to ensure an adequate supply of fish to the population and fish was calculated to be cheaper than other animal protein if produced domestically. Even larger, vertically integrated corporate enterprises, whether privately or state-owned have often accepted losses in the fishing sector because such losses were compensated by profits in processing and marketing operations" (ibid, pp.21-24).

Garcia, *et al.* noted that "overcapacity, its dynamics and control (and reduction) are among the most pressing economic issues and have broad implications for all the other issues ... Subsidised public investment in port and market infrastructure, budget support for public fisheries corporations,. subsidised credit and investment incentive policies are among the factors that lead to overfishing ..." (Garcia, *et al.* 1999, p.379).

The FAO Technical Guidelines for Responsible Fisheries (No.4) noted that "without proper management mechanisms, fishers tend to have insufficient incentives and information to take into account the effects their activities have on others in the short and long term. This produces a pervasive tendency for over expansion of fishing effort beyond the point of maximum economic yield. Economic overfishing manifests itself in excessive input allocation to the fishery, inducing particularly in industrial fisheries, overcapitalisation and frequently excess fishing capacity as stocks are progressively depleted. Eventually, in most fisheries a point will be reached where the cost of fishing exceeds the value of the catch. In addition, this typically occurs in a context where fluctuations in fish abundance, market prices and operating costs are continuous and induces cycles of investment and stock depletion" (FAO, 1997b, pp, 16-

17). In this context, it also advised that "states should therefore strive to prevent or, where necessary, eliminate excess fishing capacity, thereby maintaining fishing effort at levels appropriate to the productivity of the resource or resources" (ibid, p.17).

A later report of the FAO, while highlighting this issue noted that "several of the world's most important fisheries are subject to excess capacity, and this a cause of growing concern. Excess capacity means that in many of the world's fisheries fleets are not only larger than they need to be to catch and land (at the lowest cost) the volumes of fish currently available, but they would also exceed the requirements for fishing in the event of stocks being permitted to recover in size. Not only does this threaten the sustainability of the fish stocks being exploited but it also constitutes a potential threat to other stocks. This situation has resulted from investors purchasing additional vessels to generate more returns even when the fleet size is optimal from a general socio-economic point of view. Excess fishing capacity is thus caused by a lack of control over fishers' access to fish stocks. Additionally, in some countries, it is also brought about by public funding of investments in new vessels and/ or the rehabilitation of old ones ...

Over capacity is generally caused by excessive investments and an indiscriminate use of fishing inputs. Two manifestations of excess capacity are poor economic performance or inefficiency, and biological overfishing. Overcapitalisation in capture fisheries wastes investment capital and therefore leads to high fishing costs. Similarly, overexploitation of stocks wastes fish resources...

A fundamental problem for many countries is the lack of reliable data on the numbers and characteristics of craft and gear. Also important is the extent to which the vessels may be moved between fisheries, as action taken to reduce capacity in one fishery may be the direct cause of over capacity in another, owing to the rapid relocation of the excess capacity. Unfortunately, this has been a common outcome in countries that have sought to reduce capacity solely on a fishery-by-fishery basis. The problem has been recognised in some countries, for example New Zealand, and country groupings, such as the EC, which have chosen to reduce capacity concurrently in each fishery as well as globally at aggregated fleet levels ...

From a broader view, efforts made by some developed countries to reduce fishing capacity have led to the relocation of vessels in the fisheries of other (usually developing and least developed) countries. On a global scale, this does not constitute a reduction in capacity. Furthermore, there are several reasons why these relocations might be detrimental to many of the importing countries. For instance, the vessels are usually purchased at a low price, and hence can be operated profitably (at least temporarily) even when fish stocks are depleted – a situation that is conducive to the further depletion of stocks. There have been many cases of local conflicts arising over the fact that such imported vessels, which are usually of an industrial type, operate in direct competition with artisanal fleets.

Fishing capacity is in excess in most regions of the world. For example, with increasing fishing pressure in South Asia, many coastal pelagic and demersal fish stocks in the Bay of Bengal, the Gulf of Thailand and the South China Sea are fully exploited or overfished. This is evident, *inter alia*, in the increasing proportion of low-value species being caught ..." (FAO, 1999a, pp.41-45).

The FAO report, *The State of World Fisheries and Aquaculture 2004,* however, notes that "after years of expansion of the world fishing fleet until the late 1980s and early 1990s, the number of decked vessels world wide has remained fairly stable at around 1.3 million. In addition, the word fleet engaged in marine and inland waters comprised about 2.8 million un-decked vessels, 65 per cent of which were not powered. About 85 per cent of total decked vessels, 50 per cent of powered un-decked vessels, and 83 per cent of total non-powered boats were concentrated in Asia. The remaining 15 per cent of the world's total decked fishing vessels were accounted for by Europe (8.9 per cent), North and Central America (4.5 per cent), Africa (1.0 per cent), South America (0.6 per cent) and Oceania (0.2 per cent) ... Countries in North and Central America had 21 per cent of the open fishing vessels with engines; Africa had 16 per cent, South America six per cent, and Oceania three per cent.

The aggregate gross tonnage (GT) of large marine fishing vessels (considered to be those abaove 100 gross tonnes) increased to a peak of 15.6 million GT in 1992 (24074 vessels) and has subsequently declined. However, the number of these vessels increased gradually until 2001 and has remained relatively stable, at around 24000 vessels in recent years ... In 2002, the number of large vessels increased slightly to 24406 vessels and has fluctuated around that number until 2004. However, since 1992 the total tonnage of this fleet has contracted as many countries began to adopt programmes of capacity containment ..." (FAO, 2004, p.24).

The nature of excess capacity, and the major source of it prevailing in the catching branch (harvesting sector) can be partly understood from the following observation of FAO. It noted: "in 1997 there were four countries with more than 1000 vessels reported to Lloyd's Register: Japan, the Republic of Korea, Spain and the United States. The countries of CIS and the Baltic States, when taken together, also fall into this category ... The increase in the Republic of Korea's fleet since 1994 is believed to be due to vessels that were previously flagged under open registers being reflagged under their national flag.

Contrary to the development of these five fleets, those of some major fish producers among the developing countries have been expanding. This is true of several countries in Latin America, for India, Indonesia, Morocco and the Philippines...In many cases, a substantial part of the build up has been due to older vessels being bought from developed countries.

Several European countries had fleets of between 100 and 600 vessels above 100 GRT in 1997...The United Kingdom's fleet was also augmented by vessels owned in Spain and the Netherlands being reflagged to the United Kingdom as part of the so-called 'quota hopping' exercise.

The fleets of the main Latin American fishing countries continued to increase, with Mexico being the main exception...

The number of vessels flagged under open registers or "flags of convenience' has continued to increase, albeit at a slower rate than in the early 1990s. Although the number of vessels registered in Panama and Honduras has decreased, there has been a continued increase in registration in Belize (158 in 1997), Cyprus (32), St. Vincent and the Grenadines (139) and Vanuatu (35) ..." (FAO, 1999a, pp.74-75).

*The State of World Fisheries and Aquaculture 2004,* however, reported that "in 2003, several of the major fishing nations appeared to be substantially reducing their numbers of vessels of 100 GT and above by flagging out...Japan was foremost, with a total reduction of 140 vessels. Iceland, the Netherlands, Norway, and the United States all flagged out more than they have flagged in. The United Kingdom has substantially reduced its fleet by scrapping older vessels and flagging out. Spain on the other hand, has substantially increased its fleet by building new vessels. Vessels flagging out to the 'unknown' category account for more than 25 per cent of those reflagging.

The Lloyd's Register records 1213 'unknown' flag vessels over 100 gross tons and considered to be still in operation in 2003 (records before 1970 excluded) . Of the vessels for which records of the previous flag exists, 51 per cent were flagged in one of the following countries: Belize, Equatorial Guinea, Honduras, Panama, Saint Vincent and the Grenadines, and Vanuatu, and 56 per cent of these vessels were constructed either in Japan or Taiwan province of China" (FAO, 2004, p.28).

Referring to the increase in decked fishing vessels in China, *The State of World Fisheries and Aquaculture 1998*, noted that "had it not been for the increase in the fleet of decked fishing vessels in China ..., the number of decked fishing vessels in the world fleet would have remained stable between 1980 and 1995....In line with Chinese policy to develop offshore and distant water fisheries, the average tonnage of decked vessels has increased. In fact, the proportion of Chinese vessels of more than 24 m in length increased from about 1.5 per cent in the late 1980s to about 3 per cent in 1996, which is three times the world average. China's fishing fleet, totalled about 6 million GT (in 1996), is now by far the largest in the world. It is followed by the fleet of the Russian Federation, with a tonnage of about 3 million GT" (FAO, 1999a, pp.67-69).

Recent FAO studies have indicated the prevalence of "overcapacity in the world's industrial tuna fishing fleets" (FAO, 2004, p.27). It appears that the problem of excess capacity (overcapitalisation) in other branches of the industry, especially in the processing sector is now recognised by the FAO. *The State of World Fisheries and Aquaculture 2004* noted that "overcapacity develops in the form of over expanded harvesting (and processing) capacity" (FAO, 2004, p.118). It also reiterated that "the problems of over capacity and capacity management have become key issues for fisheries management in the new millennium. Over capacity and over fishing are really symptoms of the same underlying management problem – the absence of well-defined property or user rights. If fishers enjoyed exclusive and more secure rights, they would be able to adjust their harvesting capacity to the quantity of fish available and not be stimulated to invest in excessive capacity to catch the fish before some one else does" (ibid, p.118).

The rationale of overcapitalistion has been summed up by Collet thus: "the rationality of the predator's behaviour leads to a high value being placed on the immediate harvesting of the resource. Under conditions of '*res nullius*', or a freely available resource, it is logical for a fisherman to increase his capital investment in order to harvest more fish more quickly, because there is no guarantee of more fish tomorrow. This logic of maximising the utility (value) of the resource leads to over capitalisation and the eventual dissipation of the rent from the resource" (Collet, 2000, p.122; parentheses added).

### 4.3.4. Uneconomic Operation

The uneconomic nature of fishing or poor economic viability of operations has been reported as a major threat to the sustainability of global fishing industry. The issue was raised to the centre of the sustainability debate by the FAO in the early 1990s when it reported the massive loss being suffered by the global fishing industry. It reported that "the total annual operating costs of the global fishing fleet for 1989 is US $92,000 million, without including returns to capital or allowances for debt servicing...Based on 1989 gross revenue of around US $ 70,000 million...the annual operating deficit is estimated to be approximately US $ 22,000 million without considering the cost of capital. While some debt servicing costs can be at preferentially low rates, particularly those provided through international finance institutions and bilateral assistance, in most cases the debt servicing charges are at least equal to commercial rates, and have been high.

With a replacement value of US $ 3,20,000 million, the return to capital would at least have to equal opportunity costs, which, since there are limited opportunities for converting fishing vessels to other uses, may be lower than other maritime practices and can be set at 10 per cent for this exercise. The resulting costs for the fleet would increase by US $ 32,000 million for a deficit of about US $ 54,000 million ..." (FAO, 1993a, pp.17-18).

It (FAO) also noted that "a comparison of estimated gross revenues of marine catch with the estimated costs of the global fishing fleet produces a remarkable conclusion. These calculations indicate that the annual operating costs of the global marine fishing fleet in 1989 were in the order of US $ 22,000 million greater than the total revenue, with no account being taken of capital costs. Although the calculations are tentative, they still suggest that global marine fisheries may be incurring very significant losses" (ibid, p.20). When the capital costs of US $ 32,000 million were also added, the loss had increased to US $ 54,000 million in 1989 as already noted. In the prevailing circumstances the industry was reportedly sustained with the help of governmental subsidy and other support in most fishing nations (ibid, pp 20-23). Since the publication of the above findings in 1993, the FAO has managed to collect new details of costs and earnings of "world's major fisheries" and the summary of the findings has been given by the FAO in *The State of World Fisheries and Aquaculture 2000.* These details give a generally satisfactory picture of profitability of fishing vessels operating from selected countries in the four continents of Africa, Asia, Latin America and Europe. Curiously, it did not give any picture of profitability of vessels operating from North America (US and Canada) and Oceania (Australia, New Zealand, etc.). In the section on 'over-view and comparison by continent' it noted: "in spite of heavily and sometimes overexploited fisheries resources, marine capture fisheries are still an economically and financially viable undertaking. In most cases, they generate sufficient revenue to cover the cost of depreciation and the opportunity cost of capital, thus generating funds for reinvestment. Marine capture fisheries are an important source of income and generate employment and foreign exchange earnings, particularly in developing countries" (FAO 2000a, p.92). The following details have been given in summary form.

With respect to Africa, it noted: "the following practices in Ghana and Senegal were studied: small-scale hook and line fisheries, drift netting, bottom set gill netting, beach seining, purse seining, small scale multipurpose fishing operations, medium-and large-scale fish and shrimp trawling, and pole and line fishing. Only small-scale gill netters in Senegal generated negative cash flow. All the others generated a positive net surplus" (ibid, p.92).

Referring to Latin America, it stated: "All of the various types of trawlers and purse seiners studied in Peru and Argentina generated a positive net surplus (ibid, p.92).

For Asia, it noted: "All of the fishing fleet units studied in the Republic of Korea, Taiwan province of China and Malaysia generated a positive net surplus, as did five of the seven typical medium-and large scale fishing units in Indonesia. The fishing units that generated positive net returns include purse seiners, bottom and mid water trawlers and pair trawlers, jiggers, stow netters, set netters, seiners, tuna and other long liners, and pole and line vessels. Negative net results were recorded for small-scale gill netters in Indonesia and small bottom pair trawlers and stow netters in China. In India, three types of medium-and large-scale fishing units – tuna longliners, purse seiners and trawlers – generated a positive net surplus, while two of the three small scale fishing units studied – seiners and handliners – scarcely broke even or had a negative cash flow" (ibid, p.92).

In the case of Europe, it reported: "of the 27 types of small-medium- and large-scale fishing vessels studied in France, Spain and Germany, only two types of deep-sea trawlers operating in France had negative net results. The other 25 types – including hand liners, gill netters, seiners, pole and line vessels, longliners and inshore and offshore trawlers – all generated positive net surpluses" (ibid, p.92).

Commenting on economic viability and sustainability outlook, the report noted thus: "the findings of the study suggest that, with the exception of some small-scale fishing units in Indonesia, India and Senegal, some of the large-scale industrial trawlers in France and one type of pair-trawler and a stow-netter in China, marine capture fisheries in the Latin American, African, European and Asian countries studied usually generate sufficient revenues to cover their operating costs and also supply funds for reinvestment" (ibid. pp. 96-97).

The above findings are in sharp contrast with the previous (1993) findings of the FAO (FAO 1993a). Referring to this contradictory situation, FAO noted thus:

> "The findings of this study seem to contradict earlier FAO studies that concluded that when all the world's fishing vessels are considered as one fleet, that fleet is losing money. There are two plausible explanations for this discrepancy. The first concerns active versus non-active vessels. In the earlier global studies, all vessels - whether active or not - were included, while the more recent study includes only active vessels. The second factor is related to subsidies or 'financial transfers'. The global studies included proforma estimates of income and costs, developed by FAO on the basis of the average known costs of the major factors of production and the longevity of physical assets. They therefore did not include any country-specific financial transfers from government to fisheries sectors. The more recent study uses a different approach. The costs and incomes derived for the various fleets are based on expenditures and income over time, and do not consider individual financial transfers. The present study includes (all) financial transfers, while the global studies excluded most of them.
>
> The degree to which either of these factors can explain the difference between the two studies is difficult to assess, although those familiar

with both studies regard the first factor as being particularly significant" (FAO, 2000a, p.97; word in parentheses added).

A bit apologetically and probably in support of the present finding, the FAO also observed that "the more recent study also shows that marine capture fisheries provide employment and income, as well as contributing much needed export earnings in many developing countries. They also play important roles in meeting the nutritional needs of the population and in food security, particularly in developing countries" (ibid. p.97).

Taking a holistic position and giving a note of caution, the FAO also stated thus: "However, the generally positive economic performance of marine capture fisheries is being achieved in an environment where fisheries resources are fully exploited, and in many cases over exploited; so how long can it last?" (ibid. p.97).

In the same breath, though as a platitude, the FAO adds that "the fishing industry, both small - and large-scale, and the general public have a vital interest in safeguarding and sustaining the beneficial economic and nutritional role of fisheries. If sustainability and viability are to be ensured, there is an urgent need to strengthen and put in place efficient measures to limit fishing effort and rehabilitate coastal areas and aquatic resources. In order to be successful, these measures must be designed and implemented in close cooperation with fishers and fisheries industry associations.

The impact of fisheries management measures on the economic performance of the fisheries industry and its various sectors needs to be closely monitored through studies similar to the one described...so that benefits can be maximised and negative impacts minimised. Another important area for monitoring in the future is the impact of subsidies, economic incentives and fiscal policies and measures on the profitability and sustainability of fishing operations.

In order to safeguard the important economic and social role of the small-scale fisheries sector as a provider of employment, income and food, particularly in rural areas of developing countries, special efforts are needed to protect the sector" (ibid, pp.97-98).

Curiously, but apparently clinching the earlier findings, the FAO report notes in the course of the above observations that "the findings of the study suggest that the sector's economic performance has already been negatively affected by the overexploitation of costal fisheries resources and competition with more 'catch-efficient' commercial fishing vessels, such as purse seiners and trawlers" (ibid, p.98).

Pursuing this position, it suggested that "government and private sector support to the fishing industry, both small-and large-scale in the form of technical advice and guidance, training and investment and credit support, is essential for successful adaptation to the changes accompanying the introduction of responsible and sustainable fishing practices and related management measures and regulations" (ibid, p.98).

### 4.3.5. Declining Employment and Productivity

Declining employment in the industry is now considered to be a problem affecting the economic and social sustainability of fisheries, world wide. Fall in employment is a problem in all branches of the industry, though it is considered to be more severe in the catching (capture) branch. Although information on the state of employment in the fisheries sector, is incomplete, *The State of World Fisheries and Aquaculture 1998*, noted that "while the number of people employed in fishing and aquaculture has been growing steadily in most low and middle income countries, in industrialised economies the numbers of fishers have been declining or are stationary. In Japan and Norway the numbers of fishers were halved between 1970 and 1990" (FAO, 1999a, p.65).

Highlighting the trend in global employment in capture fisheries and aquaculture, *The State of World Fisheries and Aquaculture 2004* noted thus: "Although the national statistics available to FAO are often too irregular and lacking in detail to permit a more in-depth analysis of the employment structure at world level, it is apparent that, in most important fishing nations that systematically provide this information, the share of employment in capture fisheries is stagnating and increased opportunities are being provided by aquaculture.

In China, where the combined numbers of fishers and fish farmers (12.3 million) represent nearly one-third of the world total, in 2002, 8.4 million people worked in capture fisheries and 3.9 million in aquaculture. However, existing fleet-size reduction programmes in China, aimed at reducing overfishing, are reducing the number of full-time and part-time fishers. The latter have decreased by almost two per cent from two years before and there are plans to move four per cent of the total number of fishers to other jobs by 2007 ...

In many industrialised countries, notably Japan and European countries, employment in fishing – and as a consequence, in associated land-based professions – has been declining for several years. This is the result of several factors combined, including lower catches, programmes to reduce fishing capacity and the increased productivity brought about by technical progress. In the European Union (EU-15) the decline in the number of fishers in recent years averaged about two per cent per year.

In Norway, employment in fishing has been decreasing for several years...In 2002, about 18650 people were employed in fishing (excluding fish farming), representing a decline of eight per cent compared with 2000 and almost 20 per cent compared with five years before. The largest decline has occurred in fishing as a main occupation, which accounts for more than 75 per cent of the total. In Iceland, average employment in fisheries was fairly stable in the five years to 2002, although there were seasonal variations; however, the share of fishing and fish processing – where the majority of workers are women – as a source of employment, dropped to eight per cent in 2002 from 10 per cent five years earlier. In Japan, the number of marine fishery workers has been falling yearly since 1991, reaching a low of 243,320 people in 2002" (FAO, 2004, pp.20-22).

Table 4.7 gives details of fishers and fish farmers in selected countries for selected years from 1990 to 2002.

*The State of World Fisheries and Aquaculture 2004,* also reported that "the fishing work force in most developed economies is advancing in age, mainly because of the profession's decreasing attractiveness to younger generations. For instance, in Japan, 95750 male fishers (or 47.2 per cent of the total) were 60 years of age or older in 2002. The share of this age class has recently been increasing at a rate of one per cent per year and in 2002 was nearly 25 per cent above the figure of 20 years previously. By comparison, the younger group of workers (under 40 years of age), which represented one–quarter of the total number of marine fishery workers in 1982, had decreased to 12.1 per cent of the 243320 people engaged in marine fishery by 2002" (ibid, p.22).

Table 4.8 gives details of fishers and fish farmers, continent-wise, for selected years from 1990 to 2002.

**Table 4.7**

**Details of fishers and fish farmers in selected countries for selected years from 1990 to 2002**

(in lakhs)

| *World/Country* | *Fishery* | *1990* | *1995* | *2000* | *2001* | *2002* |
|---|---|---|---|---|---|---|
| World | FI+AQ | 278.35 | 333.14 | 357.97 | 365.34 | 377.95 |
| | | (78) | (93) | (100) | (102) | (106) |
| | FI | - | - | 269.74 | 274.94 | 279.80 |
| | | (-) | (-) | (100) | (102) | (104) |
| | AQ | - | - | 88.23 | 90.40 | 98.15 |
| | | (-) | (-) | (100) | (102) | (111) |
| China | FI+AQ | 90.93 | 114.29 | 122.33 | 129.44 | 123.38 |
| | | (74) | (93) | (100) | (106) | (101) |
| | FI | 73.53 | 87.59 | 85.11 | 90.97 | 83.77 |
| | | (86) | (103) | (100) | (107) | (98) |
| | AQ | 17.40 | 26.69 | 37.22 | 38.47 | 39.61 |
| | | (47) | (72) | (100) | (103) | (106) |
| Indonesia | FI+AQ | 36.18 | 45.68 | 52.48 | 54.77 | 56.63 |
| | | (69) | (87) | (100) | (104) | (108) |
| | FI | 19.95 | 24.63 | 31.05 | 32.87 | 33.93 |
| | | (64) | (79) | (100) | (106) | (109) |
| | AQ | 16.22 | 21.05 | 21.43 | 21.90 | 22.70 |
| | | (76) | (98) | (100) | (102) | (106) |
| Japan | FI+AQ | 3.71 | 3.01 | 2.60 | 2.52 | 2.43 |
| | | (142) | (116) | (100) | (97) | (94) |
| Peru* | FI+AQ | 0.44 | 0.63 | 0.66 | 0.66 | 0.67 |
| | | (66) | (95) | (100) | (100) | (100) |
| Norway | AI+AQ | 0.28 | 0.28 | 0.24 | 0.23 | 0.22 |
| | | (116) | (119) | (100) | (95) | (93) |
| | FI | 0.28 | 0.24 | 0.20 | 0.19 | 0.19 |
| | | (137) | (118) | (100) | (94) | (94) |
| | AQ | - | 0.05 | 0.04 | 0.04 | 0.03 |
| | | (-) | (127) | (100) | (100) | (95) |
| Iceland | FI+AQ | 0.07 | 0.07 | 0.06 | 0.06 | 0.06 |
| | | (114) | (115) | (100) | (98) | (98) |

*Note:* FI = Fishing, AQ = Aquaculture; Figures limited to two decimals (figures in parentheses show index value with index for 2000 = 100).

*Data for Peru exclude inland fishers and fish farmers

*Source:* FAO, 2004, p.23.

**Table 4.8**
**Details of fishers and fish farmers, continent-wise, for selected years from 1990 to 2002**

(in '000)

| *Continents* | *1990* | *1995* | *2000* | *2001* | *2002* |
|---|---|---|---|---|---|
| *Fishers and fish farmers (total)* | | | | | |
| Africa | 1917 | 2238 | 2585 | 2640 | 2615 |
| North and Central America | 767 | 770 | 751 | 765 | 762 |
| South America | 769 | 814 | 784 | 760 | 770 |
| Asia | 23654 | 28552 | 30770 | 31493 | 32821 |
| Europe | 654 | 864 | 821 | 796 | 746 |
| Oceania | 74 | 76 | 86 | 80 | 81 |
| World | 27835 | 33314 | 35797 | 36534 | 37795 |
| *Fish farmers only* | | | | | |
| Africa | - | 105 | 112 | 115 | 111 |
| North and Central America | 53 | 74 | 74 | 69 | 65 |
| South America | 16 | 88 | 92 | 92 | 93 |
| Asia | 3698 | 6003 | 8503 | 8720 | 9502 |
| Europe | 11 | 36 | 37 | 39 | 39 |
| Oceania | Negligible | 1 | 5 | 5 | 5 |
| World | 3778 | 6307 | 8823 | 9040 | 9815 |

*Source:* FAO, 2004, p.22.

It is apparent from table 4.8 that the number of fishers and fish farmers were either decreasing or stagnating in all the continents, except Asia during the period from 1990 to 2002.

A hidden threat to the sustainability of global fisheries along with the decline in employment is the prevailing low and declining output per fisherman. Table 4.9 presents details of average output per fisherman for selected years in six continents.

It appears from table 4.9 that the average output per fisherman at the global level was quite low and it decreased from 4.97 tonnes in 1970 to 3.47 tonnes in 1990, marking a decrease of 30.18 per cent. The prevailing low output per fisherman at the global level is largely influenced by the low output per fisherman in Asia, Africa and Oceania. Referring to the situation in Asia, *The State of World Fisheries and Aquaculture 1998* noted that "the downward trend there is a result of diminishing yields for capture fishers, the growing share of part-time fishers and an expansion of aquaculture production and employment …

**Table 4.9**

**Details of average output per fisherman for selected years in six continents**

(tonnes per year)

| *Continent* | *1970* | *1980* | *1990* | *Change in 1990 over 1970 (%)* |
|---|---|---|---|---|
| Africa | 2.71 | 2.72 | 2.76 | 1.85 |
| Asia | 2.23 | 2.28 | 1.90 | -14.79 |
| North America | 11.59 | 12.69 | 11.35 | -2.07 |
| Latin America | 28.47 | 15.19 | 18.40 | -35.37 |
| Europe | 26.61 | 33.59 | 29.35 | 10.30 |
| Oceania | 4.42 | 1.86 | 5.20 | 17.65 |
| Global Total | 4.97 | 4.36 | 3.47 | -30.18 |

*Source:* FAO, 1999a, p.66

Among countries in Asia, there are of course wide variations in fishery labour productivity; partly as a consequence of differences in the amount of capital available to each fisher. There are highly industrialised and often capital intensive fisheries in the region, particularly in Japan and the Republic of Korea, resulting in a high tonnage per person employed. There are also fisheries that produce less than one tonne per fisher per year" (FAO, 1999a, p.66).

Among continents, Europe is found to show the highest productivity. It is, however , reported that there are noticeable differences in productivity across Europe. For instance, "in 1995 each of Iceland's 5000 fishers produced an average of 280 tonnes of fish whereas an annual rate of six tonnes or less per fisher is true for the fishers of all Mediterranean countries other than France and Italy. Part of the difference is explained by the importance of high-volume, low-value fisheries for small pelagics that provide raw material for fish meal industries in Iceland" (ibid. p.66). The declining productivity in Latin America is largely a reflection of the crisis in the Peruvian anchovy fisheries.

### 4.3.6. Poverty

Poverty in the fishing community, as in other traditional societies, is a major threat to the economic sustainability of the fishing industry. It is against the principle of intra-generational equity which is a fundamental principle and criterion of sustainable development. The issue of poverty has been specially noted and discussed by the FAO in its *State of World Fisheries and Aquaculture 2002*. It stated that "the continued levels of poverty in small-scale fishing communities, and in the world as a whole, require that all those concerned take fresh look at the problem.

It is increasingly acknowledged that poverty is a very complex, multidimensional concept that has many determinants and is concerned with far more than low earnings, i.e. income poverty …

Poverty in small-scale fishing communities, as in other sectors, is difficult to measure. While there are many studies of poverty in farming communities and among the urban poor, few empirical studies have focused on fisheries. Those that have often concentrate exclusively on income and on the fishers themselves, rather than on a broader concept of poverty in fishing households and communities. There is now an acceptance that poor fishers and their dependents are not a homogenous, unchanging group of people. The levels of absolute and relative poverty, within and among small- scale fishing communities, vary considerably by area, country and region.

Although there are poverty traps in fishing communities, over time community members can sometimes become less, rather than more, poor. Fishing communities are often relatively cash-rich compared with farming communities, mainly because fishers sell a larger proportion of their production, more frequently and consistently than do most farmers. They remain vulnerable to sudden variations in earnings, however, making fishing communities often more vulnerable than are communities that rely exclusively on farming. In fact, the issue of vulnerability may be as important as poverty is. It should be recognised however, that some factors may be important determinants of poverty but not of vulnerability and vice versa" (FAO, 2002, p.69).

Highlighting the vulnerability issue it noted: "small-scale fishing communities are vulnerable to many events, the outcome of which may be poverty. Examples include: climate/natural events such as yearly and seasonal fluctuations in stock abundance, poor catches, bad weather and such natural disasters as cyclones and hurricanes; economic factors such as market price fluctuations and variable access to markets; and the dangers of working at sea. People in small-scale fishing communities may also be vulnerable to poor health and other wider determinants of poverty ...; studies suggest that vulnerability appears to be increasing among the poor in small-scale fishing communities.

In developing countries, many millions of people live in small-scale fishing communities. While it is now acknowledged that not all small-scale fishers can be assumed to be poor, a large proportion of them are, and remain so, despite the efforts of donor agencies, national and local governments, non-governmental organisations (NGOs) and the communities themselves. Reasons for continued poverty include factors from within and outside the fisheries sector: vulnerability ...; insecure access to resources; tendency to resource depletion; the remoteness of many fishing communities; the agro-ecological characteristics of nearby land; low socio-economic, cultural and political status; a lack of political and financial support (often as a result of an emphasis on semi-industrial and industrial fishing); and competition and conflict with industrial vessels and other economic sectors in coastal areas" (ibid. pp.69-70.).

Some 'crude estimates' of the number of 'income-poor' fishers have been given by FAO. Table 4.10 gives details of poverty in small-scale fisheries sector during 1998.

**Table 4.10**

**Details of poverty in small-scale fisheries sector in 1998**

| *Type of fishers* | *Africa* | *South America* | *Asia* | *Oceania* | *Former USSR* | *Total* |
|---|---|---|---|---|---|---|
| Inland | 279598 | 2583 | 514023 | 0 | 0 | 796204 |
| Marine (coastal) | 112119 | 10148 | 95837 | 458 | 1331 | 219893 |
| Marine (other) | 112875 | 43867 | 551133 | 13515 | 0 | 721390 |
| Unspecified | 320733 | 40716 | 3660428 | 0 | 0 | 4021877 |
| Total | 825325 | 97314 | 4821421 | 13973 | 1331 | 5759364 |
| Number of related income-poor jobs | 2475974 | 291940 | 14464262 | 41916 | 3993 | 17278085 |
| Total income-poor | 3301299 | 389254 | 19285683 | 55889 | 5324 | 23037449 |

*Note:* Only fishers having an income of <US $ 1, a day are included.
*Source:* FAO, 2002, p.73.

Table 4.10 shows that about 5.76 million fishers constituting 20 per cent of the world's 29 million fishers were earning less than one US $

per day. Of these, 4.82 million were in Asia and 0.83 million in Africa. The number of income-poor in related upstream and downstream activities such as boat building, marketing and processing, is estimated to be about 17.3 million. The overall estimate of total income-poor in the small-scale fisheries sector was 23 million.

### 4.3.7. Barriers to Trade

The sustainability of global fisheries which is very much dependent on international trade is now threatened by the ever growing number of barriers to trade. Much of the development in world fisheries during the second half of the last century is attributed to export-led growth. Highlighting the significance of this development, FAO observed:

"Fish production and trade have grown significantly in the last decades, assisted by improvements in technology, transportation and communications and by sustained demand. A large share of fish production enters international marketing channels, with about 37 per cent exported in 2000 (live weight equivalent) in various food and feed product forms. LIFDCs play an active part in this trade and at present account for almost 20 per cent of the value of fishery exports. In 2000, developing countries as a whole supplied slightly more than 50 per cent of total exports in value terms. Although there is an important trade of fish and fishery products among the more developed economies, trade tends to flow from the less developed to the more developed countries. About 76 per cent of the import value is concentrated in three main areas: Japan, the EC and the United States. Although trade among developing countries is increasing, it is still not very substantial and accounted for about 20 percent of those countries' total exports in 1998-2000 ...

Fish products traded among industrialised countries are mostly from demersal species, which are traded in fresh, frozen whole and fillet form; lower-value pelagic species such as herring and mackerel, which are traded in fresh and frozen form; and fresh and frozen salmon. Developing countries' exports concern mainly tuna, small pelagics, shrimps, prawns, rock lobsters and cephalopods (octopus, squids and cuttlefishes). In the past, developing countries were involved primarily in exports of raw material for the processing industries of developed countries, but in recent years they have been increasingly involved in adding value to their products, prior to export. In addition, a large part of the world's trade in fishmeal originates from developing countries in Latin America. Developing countries' imports concern mainly frozen small pelagics and cured, dried and smoked fish. There are also some imports of raw material (e.g. frozen tuna) for further processing (eg. canned tuna)and re-export. Emerging markets (Hong Kong Special Administrative Region, Taiwan Province of China, the Republic of Korea, Malaysia and Singapore) are increasingly importing high-value commodities (rock lobster, squid, etc.) for domestic consumption" (FAO, 2002, pp.39-40).

Referring to the recent trends in world fish trade and its sustainability, the FAO noted that "in 2002, total world fish trade of fish and fish products increased to US $ 58.2 billion (export value), representing a five per cent increase relative to 2000 and a 45 per cent increase since 1992...In terms of quantity, exports were reported to be 50 million tonnes (live weight equivalent), having grown by 40.7 per cent since 1992, but showing a slight decline (one per cent) compared with 2000 levels. The quantity of fish traded has remained stagnant over the last few years following decades of strong increases. Many of the economic factors responsible for the high growth in world fishery trade in the previous decade have now diminished in importance or are not strong enough to sustain past performance levels. While preliminary estimates for 2003 indicate a slight increase in the value of fishery exports, it is unlikely that the trends of pre-2000 years will be repeated in the short term, especially given set backs resulting from geopolitical tensions" (FAO, 2004, p.43).

It is emphasised here that apart from the constraints on global fish production arising from ecological and other economic issues, the sustainability of world trade in fish and fishery products is affected by the many artificial barriers to trade imposed by developed and developing nations for various reasons.

The major barriers to trade may be broadly grouped into two categories: (1) tariff barriers and (2) non-tariff barriers. Tariff barriers are erected by trading nations in the form of customs duty on imports and exports. By raising or lowering these tariffs, nations can influence trade flows between nations. A higher tariff on imports can limit the inflow of goods to a country while a similar tariff on export can constrain the outflow to other countries. Tariffs remove the comparative advantage of the exporting country and thereby restrict trade to a considerable extent depending upon the levels of the tariff. However, since the evolution of the GATT rules and the WTO formulae, tariff barriers are generally on the wane but new measures of trade restrictions in the form of non-tariff barriers are finding overt and covert acceptance by leading trading nations.

Non-tariff barriers take several forms. As applied to global trade and investments, they are introduced in the form of measures such as quantitative restrictions on imports and exports (quota system), voluntary export restrictions (VER) or voluntary restraint-agreements (VRA), government procurement provisions (public distribution), domestic content provisions, restrictions on service trade, administrative (selective) controls by customs, exchange-rate controls, exchange rationing, advance deposit requirement for imports, additional domestic policy to protect health and environment and to promote food safely (HACCP, SPS, eco-labelling), trade related aspects of intellectual property rights (TRIP), trade related investment measures (TRIM) and subsidies, including managerial (personnel) training, infrastructure, and other spill-over benefits. Many of these measures, including HACCP, SPS, eco-labelling, etc. are known as Technical Barriers to Trade (TBT). Application of these measures help the states to alter the comparative cost advantages of other states and to make these work as effective barriers to trade, protecting the domestic industry and curbing free trade, which is expected to promote global economic development (Appleyard and Field, Jr., 1998, pp.249-263).

Among the several non-tariff barriers noted above, the one that is profoundly projected and sought to be removed by the FAO, the WTO and many developed countries is subsidies which are believed to be one of the major factors behind overcapitalisation and overfishing in world fisheries. Highlighting the prevailing subsidy system in global fisheries, the FAO, noted: "Fisheries are directly or indirectly subsidised in a variety of ways. Traditional kinds of subsidy are: import restrictions and tariffs (including limits on landings of foreign vessels); export support; price control systems; fuel subsidies; and low-cost loans or outright grants for the construction of vessels or the purchase of gear; the construction of ports, marketing facilities and other infrastructure.

In addition, there are fishery - specific subsidies such as the payments made by governments to coastal states for access to their zones and the waiving of payments by domestic fishermen for access to their national zones. Free access to a natural resource constitutes a subsidy to the users since no payments are being made for the resource. Under a system of controlled access, economic rents are captured by the government through tax or licence fees.

The reasons for granting such subsidies are as manifold as the types of support schemes. In many cases, financial help is given to the fishing sector – and less frequently to the post-harvest sector – for social reasons; for example to sustain employment in sometimes sparsely inhabited coastal districts. Subsidies might also be given for general policy reasons, since the competing agricultural sector enjoys similar support on a large-scale. In other cases, particularly in the former centralised economies in Eastern Europe, food policies were designed to ensure an adequate supply of fish to the population and fish was calculated to be cheaper than other animal protein if produced domestically. Even larger, vertically integrated corporate enterprises, whether privately or state-owned have often accepted losses in the fishing sector because such losses were compensated by profits in processing and marketing operations" (FAO, 1993a, pp.23-24).

The global concern about fishery subsidies and their impact on sustainability has been growing during the last one decade. Referring to this concern the FAO reports: "interest in fishery subsidies has grown during the last dozen years, with such intergovernmental agencies as the World Bank, the Organisation for Economic Cooperation and Development (OECD), the United Nations Environment Programme (UNEP) and the FAO focusing on fishery subsidies and publishing documents to bring the problem to the attention of the public. The Fourth Ministerial meeting of the WTO, held in Doha in 2001, resulted in an explicit directive to the negotiators in the subsequent round of international trade talks to improve WTO discipline to control fishery subsidies. The Plan of Implementation of the 2002 World Summit on Sustainable Development, held at Johannesburg, re-emphasised the Doha Declaration's call for the WTO to act with respect to fishery subsidies" (FAO, 2004, p.128).

Highlighting the complexity in the management of the subsidy system and the difficulty in its definition, the FAO noted: "Regardless of the definition used, subsidies can alter the actions of firms in ways that interfere with international trade and affect fishing effort and, ultimately, the sustainability of the fish stock. They are introduced for presumably socially beneficial reasons and are not inherently evil. Those that violate the conditions of the International Agreement on Subsidies and Countervailing Measures are clearly actionable under current WTO rules and are inherently in violation of international standards. But not all subsidies fall into this class. The problems of non-actionable subsidies arise when the context in which they were implemented has changed to the extent that they become a threat to stock sustainability. For instance, with the extension of fisheries jurisdiction to the 200 mile limit, a coastal state might have wanted to replace a foreign distant-water fleet with a domestic fleet which, among other things, it would find easier to control for purposes of fishery management. Society might view favorably a subsidy with that objective. Over time, however, the subsidy might become so embedded in the thinking of the operators of fishing enterprises that it becomes difficult to eliminate it once the goal, in this case the development of domestic fleet, has been reached. Pursuing the example a little further, because the subsidy encourages the building of domestic vessels, it is not removed at the appropriate time, boat building will embed excess capacity in the industry and the existence of that excess capacity will lead to overfishing" (ibid. p.128).

It is interesting to note here that the subsidy (bounty) system prevailing in England in the 18th century was criticised by Adam Smith when he wrote that "the usual effect of such bounties is to encourage rash undertakers to adventure in a business which they do not understand and what they loss by their own negligence and ignorance more than compensate all that they can gain by the utmost liberality of government..." (Adam Smith, 1937, p.488).

Outlining the justification for fishery subsidies, the FAO noted: "there are at least three potential justification for subsidies. First, there is the infant industry concept wherein the government must provide seed capital if a domestic industry is to take hold in the face of existing foreign competition. Second, a large and important firm may encounter temporary financial difficulties, which, if the firm went out of business, could spill over and damage other, healthy aspects of the economy. By temporarily offering subsidy protection, the government might protect the entire economy. Third, subsidies can be used to encourage firms to behave in environmentally friendly ways.

Forty years ago, subsidies were generally seen as being socially useful, largely under the infant industry argument. With the passage of years, and changing views of the role of government in the economy, subsidies are less often seen as socially useful – although many find the environmental justification of subsidies to be compelling" (FAO, 2004, p.129).

The political economy of the present debate and the global position with regard to subsidy is summarised by the FAO thus:

"There has been great frustration with the apparent inability of existing international arrangements to control overfishing. Because of the existence of strong enforcement procedures under the WTO, there has been interest by a number of nations to find a legitimate way for the WTO to become involved in sustainability issues. As early as 1999, five nations presented a submission to the WTO's Committee on Trade and the Environment urging governments to pursue work with the WTO to achieve the gradual elimination of environment-damaging and trade-distorting fishery subsidies. These discussions continued until the Doha Declaration in 2001 intensified the urgency of the matter. The issue subsequently came under the purview of the WTO's Negotiating Group on Rules. Eight Nations – Australia, Chile, Equador, Iceland, New Zealand, Peru, the Philippines and the United States – made a submission that started by noting that commercial fisheries are often exploited or potentially exploited by more than one nation. As a result, the argument continued, fishery subsidies have implications for trade far beyond the distortion of competitive relationships. In most industries, subsidies that encourage production impinge on trade only at the market level; they have no effect on the trading partner's ability to produce the goods. With shared fishery resources, a trading partner's ability to produce fish products may be hindered if one country subsidises the fishery to the extent that the resource is diminished. Thus, the eight countries supported the Doha Declaration's appeal for strengthening the WTO's disciplines with regard to fisheries.

Opposition to the proposal came from countries that, among other arguments, suggested that the new UN Fish Stocks Agreement should be given time to see if it will prove effective. This agreement was intended to solve exactly the problems that the eight nations raised. From October 2002 to July 2003 there was a second flurry of correspondence addressed to the WTO's Negotiating Group on Rules. The United States proposed a 'traffic light' system whereby a certain category of subsidies would face a red light (i.e. they would be forbidden) and a second category of subsidies would face an amber light (where the subsidy would be considered as presumptively harmful). The European Communities presented an alternative proposal, which stressed a simple dichotomy of subsidies into 'prohibited' and 'permitted' classes. The discussion is continuing via correspondence, so far, from Argentina, Chile, Iceland, Japan, the Republic of Korea, New Zealand, Norway and Peru. In addition, a group of 'small vulnerable coastal states' has sought differential treatment on such matters as access fees, development assistance, fiscal incentives to domestication and fisheries development, and artisanal fisheries. Only time will tell whether or not WTO 'disciplines' will be adapted to the special problems of fisheries" (FAO, 2004, pp.130-131).

Outlining the relationship between subsidies and excess capacity in the industry, Garcia, *et al.* noted that "subsidised public investment in port and market infrastructure, budget support for public fisheries corporations, subsidised credit and investment incentives, and trade and investment policies are among the factors that lead to over fishing. Such development support measures, if introduced at all, should be minimised over time, and accompanied by effective management of fishing effort. This does not usually happen ..." (Garcia, *et al.* 1999, p.379).

In a final comment on the issue of subsidies, Shrank observed that "the international trade implications of this situation (subsidy) as apparently conceived by the eight nations (noted above) are minor compared to the sustainability implications. If the WTO were used as a framework for solving the problem, there are likely to be future implications for a range of other industries" (Shrank, 2003, p.47, words in parentheses added).

Some of the other major non-tariff barriers currently applied by developed countries to protect domestic interests, but circumventing free-trade and affecting the sustainability of global fisheries are quantitative restrictions (import quota), exchange rate controls, rigorous environment and health standards (EU labelling, SPS, HACCP, etc.), advance deposit requirements for import, TRIP, TRIM, etc. Referring to these and related issues, the FAO observed:

"During recent years, international trade in fishery products has faced the following major issues: the change in quality control measures in the main importing countries towards a preventive Hazard Analysis and Critical Control Point (HACCP) – based strategy; the concept of risk assessment; general public concern regarding over exploitation of the resource; environmental concerns regarding aquaculture; and the discussion of traceability and labelling. The EC and the United States made HACCP plans mandatory for all plants producing fish products for their markets. While the United States enforces these measures through importers in the United States, the EC controls the competent authorities in the exporting countries. Risk assessment (i.e. analysis of the risk of consumers falling sick after consuming fish) is still being developed in many countries. The sustainable trade of fish – from either the wild or aquaculture – is of concern to consumers, especially in the developed world. Information about dangerous antibiotics in cultured fish species, or about overfished resources, scares consumers away from fish products. Mangrove depletion through shrimp aquaculture has also received negative press coverage recently. On 1 January 2002, the EC enforced a law on the traceability of fish, which obliges producers to indicate the following on product labels: the commercial name of the species and the Latin name; whether the fish comes from the wild or from aquaculture; the country of origin for freshwater, wild and cultured fish; and the ocean of origin for wild marine species. A range of types of labelling such as eco-labelling or organic product labelling, are being developed and used for fishery products, and this is creating confusion among consumers" (FAO, 2002, p.40).

Referring to eco-labelling as a non-tariff regulatory measure, Wessells, *et al.* noted that "the WTO agreement that directly addresses eco-labelling is the Agreement on Technical Barriers to Trade (TBT). WTO members negotiated the TBT Agreement to ensure that members do not use technical regulations or standards as disguised measures to protect domestic industries from foreign competition. The TBT is also intended to reduce the extent to which technical regulations and standards operate as barriers to market access, primarily by encouraging the development of international standards. International standards are expected to reduce the obstacles to international trade that can be created by the proliferation of numerous, different standards and regulations in various countries" (Wessells, *et al.* 2001, pp.59-60).

Highlighting on the functioning of eco-labelling, Wessells, et al. reported that "there are already several national, international, industry-sponsored, NGO-led and consumer-supplier partnership certification and standards schemes under development in the fisheries sector. The range of possible labels is broad. The focus of claims can range from 'not over-fished, to no marine mammal by-catch and not over-fished, to no by-catch of any sort and not over-fished, to ecosystem friendly where the entire ecosystem with its complicated food chain is not harmed.

The number of institutions and the diversity of their interests guarantee conflicts in the definition of what constitutes sustainable use of fisheries. This is all the more true since criteria for sustainability of fisheries are complex. Moreover, labels may be labelling entirely different things. For example, a standard indicating that a management system for sustainable fisheries is in place is not the same as certifying that a given consignment of fisheries products was sustainably produced, but both may appear on labels. The risk is that competing claims or conflicting labels will confuse consumers, causing them to lose confidence in the scheme and thus depriving the approach of its value" (ibid, p.5).

Reporting on the trade-restricting and other adverse aspects of eco-labelling, Wessels, *et al.* noted "... some governments, producers and civil society groups have expressed various concerns about eco-labelling.

First, an overriding complaint is of lack of transparency and opportunities for participation in the development of product standards such as those that might play a role in assessments of sustainability. This is of particular concern in the fisheries sector where governments have primary management responsibility for fisheries within national exclusive economic zones and, moreover, are obliged under international law to co-operate with governments of other countries in the management of shared fish stocks and fish stocks on the high seas ...

Second, there are concerns among some governments and industry groups, particularly from countries with strong fish export interests, that eco-labelling schemes could a) disguise underlying intentions to protect domestic industries, b) restrict market access and c) erode national competitiveness for those less able to meet or afford foreign labelling and certification standards.

Possible discriminatory effects of national and regional eco-labelling schemes can be attributed to a number of factors, including: (1) eco-labelling tends to be based on domestic environmental priorities and technologies in the importing country and may overlook acceptable products and manufacturing processes in the country of production; (2) the definition of product categories, and the determination of criteria and limit values may favour domestic over foreign producers; (3) eco-labelling may require foreign producers to meet criteria which are not relevant in the country of production; (4) environmental infrastructures may differ widely across countries; and (5) certain parameters used for calculating the environmental effects of products throughout their life-cycle may be based on information collected in the importing country or countries with comparable conditions, and may overestimate the environmental impacts in the actual country of production. Furthermore, given the influence of the voluntary purchasing decisions of large wholesale, retail and restaurant chains that control large market shares in large fish consuming and importing regions, particularly in Europe and North America, these schemes could effectively lead to reductions in the capacity of non-eco-labelled products to be exported to or simply sold within those markets.

Third, there are fears that the costs of bringing fisheries management practices into compliance with the criteria and principles of transnational or foreign eco-labelling schemes, going through the certification process, and maintaining certifiable status could be prohibitive. One challenge is that the quantity and quality of fisheries data is often low in developing countries and this factor may be a constraint to certification. Also, the burden of complying with foreign product standards may fall disproportionately on small suppliers to the market for whom the cost of acquiring information about, and achieving, certifiable status and standards is relatively higher. There have been complaints that the lack of auditing/certification/eco-labelling infrastructure in developing countries will leave them dependent on expensive foreign consultants. As a result, developing countries have emphasised their need for greater financial and technical assistance for the improvement of fisheries management systems. The challenge of obtaining sustainability is not at all unique to developing countries. Many fisheries in developed countries are depleted and unlikely to achieve certification in the near future.

In developing countries, there are many fisheries that are less developed/depleted and for which certification might be more easily achieved. Therefore, in terms of the state of a fish stock, some certification programmes may in fact favour fisheries in developing countries over those in some developed countries.

Fourth, the voluntary nature of eco-labelling can raise challenges. While voluntary schemes need not result in explicit restrictions as some mandatory schemes might, they may indirectly affect trade due to institutional factors in producing countries. Institutional factors could include difficulties faced by producers in some countries in obtaining adequate supplies of materials, environmentally friendly technologies and other materials, which are acceptable for use in, or necessary to comply with standards for, eco-labelled products. Other institutional constraints could be inadequate and unequal financial and technical capacity within domestic regulatory agencies to facilitate sustainable fisheries management. Without the support of governments, many private industries cannot reasonably be expected to become sufficiently organised to independently institute effective management schemes and achieve certifiable status. In cases where governments either fail to act (or act inappropriately) to manage fisheries, the fishing industry may be penalised due to lower sales prices in the absence of certification.

Finally, it can be argued that even if participation in eco-labelling schemes is voluntary, the definition of criteria for certification could clearly influence the impact of the schemes on countries with varied environmental and socio-economic conditions and interests. In the absence of some common international understanding, governments could be required to try to monitor, intervene or improve each individual scheme that arises to ensure the interests of their countries are not compromised. Internationally agreed guidelines on eco-labelling could reduce this potential burden of monitoring. Otherwise, there is the possibility that promoters of voluntary competing eco-labelling schemes, for example, at the national level, are likely to seek to discredit the schemes of competitors" (ibid, pp.55-58).

Yet another problem prevalent in global fisheries and acting as a barrier to free trade is the difficulties in fish species and fish product identification. Highlighting this issue, *The State of World Fisheries and Aquaculture 2004* noted: "Seafood companies and exporting countries are increasingly seeking to sell their products using commercial names with established international repute so as to derive maximum value and recognition. The matter is exacerbated by the fact that different species may have the same common name in different countries (or even regions of the same country). On the other hand, sometimes the same species has different names in the same language in different locations within the same country ....

On the other side, food companies, trade associations and even entire countries can be protective of market niches for given fish species and products. They consider that establishing such market niches often requires significant investment in research and development, publicity, promotion and consumer sensitisation towards the claimed attributes of the specific product they are trying to protect. Therefore, the successful companies or countries are unwilling to accept that other similar products may use the same commercial denominations and compete in the same market niches. Such occurrences may be a source of trade disputes between countries.

Recent examples of international trade disputes (scallop muscles, canned sardines – arbitrated by the WTO) show that the implications of fish species identification represent a recurrent and world-wide issue. Although such disputes generally involve a limited number of countries, they have a direct impact on international fish trade" (FAO, 2004, p.82).

What is apparent from the above various observations is that many of the tariff and non-tariff (technical) barriers to trade imposed by developed countries in the guise of protecting the environment, human health, etc. are intended to protect the domestic (national) or regional markets of those countries, rather than promoting the global sustainability of fisheries. Barriers to trade prevent the equitable sharing of the gains from trade and thus violate the criterion of intragenerational equity which is a must for sustainable development.

### 4.4. Social/Institutional Issues

The sustainability of global fisheries is further threatened by serious social issues, which are both the cause and consequence of some of the ecological and economic issues, discussed earlier. The major social issues affecting the sustainability of global fisheries, particularly, the harvesting sector, may be grouped under the following categories: (1) institutional crisis, (2) socio-economic conflicts (intrause and interuse conflicts), and (3) occupational hazards.

#### 4.4.1. Institutional Crisis

Traditional fishing communities, world-wide are facing the crisis of collapse of their indigenous community organisations, customs and rules leading to chaos, conflict and lack of social cohesion. In the wake of industrialisation, modernisation and now globalisation, these communities find that their indigenous social organisations have become rather defunct or superfluous and no more binding and valid for governing the society. The indigenous community organisations, where they exist, are non-functional and their authority is very much challenged. The traditional knowledge systems and the community based co-management institutions are no longer respected and their utility is lost.

A major consequence of the above development is the loss of 'social capital', which is vital for the sustainability of the fishery system. Like the loss of 'natural' capital (natural resource), the loss of social capital can also endanger the sustainability of the industry. As pointed out by Throsby, "an overarching principle of sustainability is the proposition that no part of any system exists independently of other parts. In this respect it can be suggested that cultural capital makes a contribution to long-term sustainability, which is similar in principle to that of natural capital.

It is now well understood that natural ecosystems are essential to supporting the real economy and the neglect of natural capital through overuse of exhaustible resources or unsustainable exploitation of renewable capital stocks may cause such systems to breakdown, with consequent loss of welfare and economic output. A parallel proposition can be put in regard to cultural capital …; it is becoming clearer that cultural 'ecosystems' underpin the operations of the real economy, affecting the way people behave and the choices they make. Neglect of cultural capital, by allowing heritage to deteriorate, by failing to sustain the cultural values that provide people with a sense of identity and by not undertaking the investment needed to maintain and increase the stock of both tangible and intangible cultural capital, will likewise place cultural systems in jeopardy and may cause them to breakdown, with consequent loss of welfare and economic output. Thus this final principle, in essence draws together the entire concept of sustainability when applied to cultural capital, providing an overall framework within which the more specific principles can be seen to operate" (Throsby, 2001, pp. 57-58).

Referring to the prevailing cultural conflict and the loss of social capital in the fishing community, world-wide, McGoodwin noted: "when such peoples are drawn into conflicts regarding their rights to utilise and manage the resources, they will perceive these not only as threats to their economic well-being, but to the sustainability of their cultures as well.

Where native and long-resident traditional community-based fishers have come into conflict with new, more competitive culture or sub-cultures for important fishery resources, they have often been the losers – as a result of social, political and economic marginalisation, or resource depletions, or both. Examples can be found in various fisheries around the world – in the Gulf of Thailand, …or around the North Atlantic rim. Only where powerful countervailing cultural pressures have been successfully launched have these tragedies been averted – in Japan, for example, which long ago developed cultural institutions to protect its small-scale coastal fishing cultures, and more recently in New Zealand, northern Norway and among certain Arctic dwelling native peoples of Alaska, United States. Where there is pervasive cultural disregard for these matters – in cultures where financial concerns are the pre-eminent values and where other developmental opportunities promise greater profitability – conflicts in the fisheries may become both persistent and acute …" (McGoodwin, 1995, pp.2-3).

Explaining the breakdown of traditional fishing cultures, McGoodwin noted: "A tragic by-product of the commercialisation and modernisation of small-scale fishers is often the breakdown of their traditional fishing cultures, as well as their systematic dehumanisation, as they struggle to remain competitive in a world that is increasingly dominated by modern industrial institutions and their corresponding ethos regarding the utilisation of fishery resources" (ibid, p.6).

The breakup of traditional community organisations in the wake of modernisation has led to the violation of indigenous code of conduct for the fishermen and the 'ethics of the sea', resulting in overexploitation of the resource base and ecological and economic unsustainability of fishing operations. Accelerated by global pressures, the sustainability of the industry is now at great stake. The global fishing industry is further threatened by the growing tide of socio-economic conflicts.

### 4.4.2. Socio-economic Conflicts

Socio-economic conflicts are now rampant in the fishing community as the coastal zones are witnessing quick economic expansion with multiple economic activities developing in the region and the fisheries sector itself expanding. These conflicts may be broadly classified as (1) intrause conflicts and (2) interuse conflicts. Intrause conflicts are conflicts within the broad generic community of fishermen for using the same natural resource base (environment) for fulfilling their diverse, but conflicting interests. The common examples of this conflict are the conflict between traditional (small-scale) and modern (industrial) fishermen using different craft-gear combinations over the same space-time contours. This type of conflict also prevails between subsistence, commercial and recreational fishermen in advanced and developing fisheries in different degrees. Intrause conflict between local and migrant fishermen and between domestic and foreign fishermen is also well known in the global literature. Interuse conflicts are conflicts between different industries (activities) using the same natural environment for producing different goods or providing different services. The predominant interuse conflicts reported in the coastal zone affecting the sustainability of global fisheries are the conflicts between fishing and activities such as agriculture, aquaculture, defence, forestry, mining, port, power production, shipping, transport, tourism, urban development, waste dumping, etc.

Caddy and Griffiths noted variables/activities such as marine pollution, coastal construction, coastal shipping, and agriculture, to produce negative impacts to conflict with fisheries interests (Caddy and Griffiths, 1995, pp. 65-70)

Referring to the socio-economic and culture-based conflicts in global fisheries, McGoodwin further noted: "The world's fisheries and fishing peoples also find themselves caught up in this conflict-laden, transitional era, as various groups, nations, cultures and sub-cultures contend to see their ideas concerning the best use of living marine resources prevail. Especially for the world's small-scale fishing peoples, who comprise more than 90 per cent of all people involved in fishing world-wide, it is extremely important to resolve or mitigate culturally based conflicts over living marine resources, since they may threaten these groups' food security, and in many cases their cultural survival as well. Obviously, many of these conflicts will be solved over time as the weight of societal public and political opinion eventually tilts decisively in one direction or another. But for now, culturally based conflicts regarding the use of living marine resources are perhaps at their peak" (McGoodwin, 1995,p.3).

The culture based conflicts in the fisheries sector which are essentially intrause and interuse conflicts, have been elaborated by McGooodwin in the report of the International Conference on Sustainable Contribution of Fisheries to Food Security, held at Kyoto, Japan, during 4-9 December 1995.

The major conflicts discussed by McGoodwin are(1) conflicts between fishers having different cultural orientations, (2) conflicts between fishers and non-fishing groups concerned about various marine species (e.g. marine mammals, sea-turtles, etc.), (3) conflicts between fishers and aquaculture and mariculture enterprises, (4) conflicts between fishers and travel, tourism and recreational interests, and (5) conflicts between fishers and other competitors for marine resources (e.g. agriculture, industrial users, polluters, etc.).

Included in the first category are (1) internal conflicts, (2) conflicts regarding native fishers, (3) conflicts involving traditional community based small scale fishers, (4) international and intranational fishery conflicts, (5) fishers in conflict with fisheries management sub-cultures, and (6) fishers in conflict with fisheries development sub-culture. In the second category come (1) conflicts regarding marine mammals, (2) conflicts regarding seals, sea lions and sea otters, (3) conflicts regarding whales, (4) conflicts regarding porpoises or dolphins, (5) conflicts regarding sea turtles, and (6) conflicts regarding other species (bald eagles). Placed in the third category are conflicts between fishers and aquaculture and mariculture enterprises as noted above. The fourth category deals with conflicts between fishers and travel, tourism and recreational interests as already specified. Found in the last category are (1) conflicts regarding agriculture, (2) industrial and other sources of pollution prompting conflicts in fisheries, (3) conflicts engendered by petroleum industries, (4) conflicts regarding the timber industry, and (5) conflicts entailing a coalition of usual antagonists (ibid, pp.4-48).

Among the most widespread and outstanding conflicts noted above are international and intranational fishery conflicts. Elaborating these conflicts, McGoodwin noted:

"Because so many fisheries are located in waters that have been regarded as part of the 'global commons', or because weaker nations often have valuable fisheries close to their shores which they cannot protect against incursions by stronger nations, or because coastal fishers are vulnerable to incursions by more powerful groups coming from within their own countries, fisheries have long been the reason for conflicts among nations, as well as within nations.

Conflicts among nations can entail competition regarding a particular fishery as well as migratory resources, which spend parts of their life cycles in various national domains. Conflicts in some fisheries are sometimes only aspects of more general conflicts between nations. Thus, sea faring fishers may become pawns in conflicts between nations, or at least see their fishing activities greatly curtailed during serious conflicts between nations, such as occurred during the 1967 Arab-Israeli war, which disrupted the passage of fishing vessels to Port Saint Gaza and through the Suez Canal" (ibid. p.16).

McGoodwin further pointed out: "Conflicts surrounding the imposition of colonialist regimes were problematic in many fisheries from the 16$^{th}$ through the 19$^{th}$ centuries. In the 20$^{th}$ century, nationalist movements have enabled many countries to throw off long-standing colonial regimes, although in many of them colonial-type relationships have persisted in the form of neo-colonialism and internal colonialism ...

For regulating conflicts between nations, various treaties, multilateral agreements and laws of the sea have long been important. However, because of the increasing social, economic, political and technological changes that have occurred since the Industrial Revolution, a stable or certain *status quo* in fisheries have never been achieved.

International conflicts have increased steadily during this century, corresponding to the collapse of important fisheries targeting cod, haddock, flounder, salmon and tuna, as well as smaller fisheries for such species as blue-fin tuna, red snapper, sword fish and sharks...Thus, in the modern era, nations are inevitably thrust into conflicts with one another over the exploitation of marine fisheries.

Neo-colonialism must also be recognised as an important aspect underlying these conflicts. In essence, neo-colonialism is the process whereby a more modern and industrialised nation strives to exploit a less developed nation politically and economically, at the same time acculturating it to certain of its important cultural institutions ... it entails 'the ability to get actions faourable to one's position, or the probability of being able to carry out one's own will despite resistance from others.'

Today, the modern industrial nations collectively constitute an articulated, grand-scale , world culture in which the individual nations may be conceived of as its sub-cultures-each nation having certain sub-cultural distinctiveness deriving from its distinct culture history, as well as differential amount of social, economic and political power in the overall global scheme. However, this is not to say that all international conflicts in fisheries are an aspect of neo-colonialism since it is also sometimes the case that two comparatively strong countries clash these days ...

Nowadays, conflicts also arise with increasing frequency as a result of the volatility of social, economic and political change within various nations - that is, as international conflict, much of which is prompted by internal colonialism.

Internal colonialism entails processes in which institutionalised social, political and economic power enables powerful members of a national society – the power elite, consisting mainly of urbanites who control the nation's political and economic high ground - to exploit less powerful groups ...

One good example of internal colonialism concerns ... how powerful economic interests within the US broke down traditional and regional salmon markets, reorienting these to serving US and global luxury seafood markets.

Another good example of internal colonialism, this from a developing country, concerns the comparatively recent ascendancy to political and economic dominance of outside investors in the traditional and highly productive raft fisheries of South Sulawesi Province, Indonesia. Investors from outside the region, many of whom had considerable business experience, but no prior knowledge of the fisheries, recently took control of the region's main fish market, with important implications for production as well.

The result has been increasingly heated conflict between the traditional participants in the fishery and the new investors ..." (ibid, pp.17-18).

McGoodwin also warns that "both processes, neo-colonialism and internal colonialism alike, can be considered world-wide problems with tremendous potential for disrupting traditional societies and drawing them into desperate conflict to sustain their cultural survival. At the same time, the potential of these two colonial 'isms' for bringing about environmental and other resource problems should not be under-estimated" (ibid, p.19).

One factor which is explicitly contributing to international and intranational conflicts is globalisation and the resulting 'fluid sovereignty' of third world states. Focusing on the 'economic vulnerability' of third world states and their loss of sovereignty, Miller observed thus: "Economic actors and processes have a more significant impact on Third World states than on the major industrialised states because of the structural inequality that characterises the world system. This structural trait is illustrated by political inequality, an unequal distribution of wealth and asymmetrical economic dependence. These states' vulnerability is exacerbated by the neo liberal policies that drive institutions such as the International Monetary Fund and the World Trade Organisation.

Increasingly, the global economy is rendering the concept of national economy meaningless. Buyers, sellers, and investors can ignore national policies and undermine a country's capacity to ensure a particular social and economic order ...For example, a state's use of the interest rate as a policy tool is rendered difficult because of the rise of global financial markets that enable funds to pour in and out of individual economies at will. Electronic activity has functioned to move greater segments of the economy outside of the control of states. For example, transaction speed and volume in the foreign currency market have left most central banks incapable of influencing exchange rates. The recent crises in Asia and Latin America have demonstrated that the central banks of Third World states are more vulnerable than those of major industrialised states such as the United States and Germany.

Transnational corporations also effectively reduce states' control. Since transnational corporations control the bulk of world trade and investments, they retain effective means of reducing Third World state's options in policy areas such as industry and environment …They wield the economic power and political influence needed to encourage or impose corporate-friendly policies.

International organisations, such as the World Trade Organisation, the International Monetary Fund, and the World Bank also undercut state's authority and control, but the Third World states are particularly vulnerable. These organisations reflect the structural advantages of the industrialised states, and they provide avenues for intrusion into the economic life of developing countries as decisions at the international level diminish states' control over their economies and decrease their development options" (Miller, 2000, pp.239-240). The devious ways in which third world sovereignty is usurped by developed countries and trading partners, often with the collusion of ruling coalitions is exemplified in the Indian context by the reported move of the Central Government to send IAS officers to American Universities for training if they are to become eligible for promotion after 26-28 years of service. This move has been, no doubt, criticised by the left parties in the country, which think that it could open the doors and windows to 'US penetration in the administration' and it is 'detrimental to national sovereignty' (Jacob, 2007). It is only common knowledge that many a foreign collaboration programmes in the country in the past were 'tied' and influenced by donor participation interests. The above observations while exposing the way global capitalism is working also convey the negative implications for sustainability as they prevent the fulfillment of intragenerational and intergenerational equity criteria of sustainable development.

Highlighting the growing social conflicts and the overall unsustainability of global fisheries, the FAO noted in 1998 that "about 34 per cent of the world's coast are at a high potential risk of degradation and another 17 per cent are at moderate risk. As an estimated 90 per cent of the world's marine capture fisheries production is dependent on coastal habitats, the relevance to fisheries is obvious. Moreover, coastal fishing communities are typically characterised by intense competition for scarce resources (e.g. for access to and use of fishing grounds, water or land), which is often associated with unregulated access to these resources.

The known consequences of habitat damage include a loss or lowering of productivity and the associated threat to local food security; contaminated aquatic food products; reduced economic viability; increased levels of conflict involving fishers; sometimes physical displacement of communities; increased unemployment; and the loss of trade opportunities. Heightened anxieties within the communities affected lead to frequent disputes and in extreme cases physical violence. While fisheries is the sector that is most frequently disadvantaged, it is also a contributor to environmental damage and to the exacerbation of conflict. The use of bottom trawls, dredges and explosives and the careless anchoring of craft are examples of fisheries practices that have a negative impact on aquatic habitats. They may negatively affect bottom fauna such as sea grass beds and coral reefs. Likewise, some aquatic practices have caused negative environmental effects, such as the physical destruction of ecologically sensitive habitat, excessive nutrient and organic enrichment of seabed owing to the release of wastes from cage and pond farms, and the introduction of harmful alien species.

Conflicts over coastal fisheries resources occur between groups of fishers. A frequently occurring example is conflict over the use of shrimp trawlers in the near shore areas frequented by artisanal fishermen using traditional methods. Apart from reduced catches, the artisanal fishers risk damage to their gear. In such cases, their response may not always be rational, as when they intensify their exploitation of juvenile fish in nursery areas or employ destructive fishing methods to maintain their livelihoods.

Often, the fisheries sector and its institutions do not have the necessary economic and institutional clout needed to guide and coordinate management. Many instances exist where government agencies have insufficient expertise to undertake the necessary integrative evaluations and planning. There may even be a lack of basic knowledge about the fisheries in question.

However, as other economic sectors expand in the coastal zone, the relative economic importance of fisheries declines, a process that may be speeded up as a result of damage to habitat and spatial competition. Naturally, this acts to weaken further the influence of the fisheries agencies in determining policy" (FAO, 1999a, pp.37-40).

Garcia, *et al.* reported, "such conflicts are now growing between artisanal and industrial operators, between national and foreign fishermen, operating under fishing agreements or illegally; and conflicts between policy measures aiming respectively at enhancing exports and improving food security" (Garcia, *et al.* 1999, p.380).

It is apparent that the social conflicts in global fisheries are primarily the consequences of the evolving ecological and economic crises in the industry, although the fisheries sector (fishers) also contributes to these crises.

### 4.4.3. Occupational Hazards

Occupational hazards and the corresponding risk to life is a major factor affecting the availability of manpower in the fishing industry and having implications for the sustainability of the industry. The declining percentage of younger fishermen in the work force as noted earlier (in section 4.3.5.) is indicative of the occupational hazards and the reluctance on the part of the younger generation to join the ranks of fishing crew in many countries. Fishing, as reported by Garcia and Moreno, seems to be still "one of the most dangerous types of employment on earth with more than 25,000 fatalities each year" (Garcia and Moreno, 2003, p.11). Probably in view of this, it is also considered as the 'occupation of last resort' (FAO 1999a, p.66).

Highlighting the issues of occupational hazards and fishers' safety, FAO noted thus:

> "Fishing at sea is the most dangerous occupation in the world. The data gathered from countries that keep accurate records show that occupational fatalities in those countries' fishing industries far exceed the overall national averages. For example, in the United States the fatality rate among fishers is 25 to 30 times the national average; in Italy it is more than 21 times the national average; and in Australia it is 143 per 1,00,000, compared with the average of 8.1 per 1,00,000"(FAO, 2000a, p.41).

Continuing its observation in this regard, FAO further reported that "it seems plausible that the fatality rate in countries for which information is not available might be higher than it is in those that do keep records. Thus, the International Labour Organisation's (ILO) estimate of 24,000 fatalities world wide, per year, may be considerably lower than the true figure.

Of the 36 million people engaged in fishing and fish farming, FAO estimates that roughly 15 million fishers are employed aboard decked or undecked fishing vessels operating in marine capture fisheries, and that more than 90 per cent of these fishers are working on vessels that are less than 24 m in length" (ibid. p.41).

Citing the social consequences and the circumstances which drive to this situation, the FAO noted: "The consequences of loss of life fall heavily on dependants. In developing countries, the consequences can be devastating: widows have a low social standing; there is no welfare state to support bereaved families; and, lacking an alternative source of income, widows and children may face destitution.

Of particular concern are the reports from fishing administrations and fishers' organisations indicating that fatality rates are increasing in the artisanal sector of developing countries. In most cases, the increase in fatalities can be traced back to changes in the basic nature of fishing operations: over exploitation of coastal resources; advances in vessel and fishing technologies, including motorisation and new types of fishing gear; lack of training, experience and skills; commercial pressure; and new fisheries management regimes.

Where inshore resources have been over exploited, fishers are often opting to work farther away from shore, sometimes for extended periods, in fishing craft that are based on designs for inshore fishing, which is limited to daily operations. Such vessels are often built by untrained builders who copy traditional and imported craft, and cost- cutting practices and the builders' lack of experience result in vessels that are unsound. Frequently, they do not comply with national regulations. Furthermore, older generations have no experience of fishing offshore, so there is a lack of traditional knowledge for today's crew about such essential issues as navigation, weather forecasting, communications, living habits during extended periods at sea (several days instead of only one) and the vital culture of safety at sea. The problem is compounded by fishing being a potential source of income for casual workers and the landless or urban unemployed; the fishing industry frequently provides employment for those who have no hope of an alternative source of income ...

In the absence of an international instrument, fishers must often rely on national legislation to ensure the safety of their catch, particularly when the vessel owner does not participate as a crew member. While most countries have regulations concerning the design, construction and equipment of vessels, in developing countries these are sometimes outdated, inappropriate and inadequately enforced. In developed countries, the application of more stringent regulations has not always led to any significant decrease in fatalities; it seems that, as vessels are made safer, operators take greater risks in their ever-increasing search for good catches" (ibid, pp. 41-43).

A substantial report entitled Safety and Health in the Fishing Industries, prepared by the International Labour Organisation as the basis for discussions at the Tripartite Meeting on Safety and Health in the Fishing Industry, held in Geneva in December 1999, noted that "the fishing industry has changed considerably as a result of new management regimes, technology advances and overcapacity, resulting in fishing operations and employment arrangements that create an incentive to work long hours and minimise the number of crew members. This, in turn, results in more frequent accidents... the international standards and training related to safety and health may not be reaching the majority of the world's fishers" (ibid, pp. 44-45).

While recognising the failure and difficulties in mitigating the occupational risks, the FAO noted that "the global fleet is aging – with consequent effects on the occupational safety and health of crews. The existing ILO fishing labour standards that apply to persons working on board fishing vessels are the conventions on minimum age, medical examination, articles of agreement, accommodation and competency certificates, and the recommendations on vocational training and hours of work. Two of the existing labour standards - competency certificates and accommodation of crews - also explicitly exclude small-scale fishing vessels from their scope. In practical terms, the scope of the existing labour standards in fishing, in general, does not include people who work on artisanal and small-scale fishing vessels. New issues that are not covered by existing instruments include identity documents, repatriation, recruitment, medical care at sea, occupational safety and health, social security protection, and compliance and enforcement.

Although it is almost 40 years since the last ILO fishing labour standard was adopted, the ratification levels of these conventions have been very low. Moreover, these instruments are no longer fully relevant and need to be updated to reflect the changing nature of fishing operations in today's world. The ILO is therefore in the process revising them in order to update and strengthen the organisation's standard-setting system to reflect the changes in the sector" (FAO, 2004, pp. 74-75).

In the prevailing circumstances, it is felt that occupational hazards constitute a major challenge to the sustainability of global fishing industry.

### 4.5. Technological Issues

Much of the historical developments in global fisheries is the contribution of new technology or technological changes. These changes, which include changes in the design, construction and operation of fishing vessels, fishing harbour facilities, fish finding and navigational aids, aquaculture, processing and marketing, etc. have contributed progressively to enhance production and consumption of fish, world-wide. The technological changes, particularly in fishing craft and gear, have been instrumental in tapping almost every species of fish to its maximum potential (MSY) or even beyond that leading to the present crisis of unsustainability. This unmistakably points to a situation where the neo-classical solution of infinite substitution of one factor for the other (here capital and know-how for biomass or natural capital) has failed. The fact that industrial fishing techniques like trawling has led to biological or ecosystem over-fishing has been pointed out in section 4.2.1 on biological overfishing.

The adverse effects of technology on environment and their implication for the sustainability of fisheries have been indicated by Valdimarsson and Suuronen (2003). Highlighting on the issue, these authors wrote:

"The removal of non-target organisms has been a cause of concern for fisheries management for many years. For instance, the extensive capture of juvenile and young fish of commercially important species frequently has been regarded as a threat to recruitment of stocks. Many fisheries harvest individuals of the target species before they reach their optimal size in terms of future yield ... A more recent concern, beginning in the 1970s, was the unintended capture and killing of animals, such as marine mammals, sea birds and turtles, by commercial fisheries. In particular, the incidental capture and mortality of endangered or threatened species that are long lived and have low reproductive rates has aroused growing conflict. The unseen mortality due to ghost fishing by lost gear has also attracted much attention recently.

Such trends in public concern have provoked environmental groups to question the fishing practices currently in use ... During the last two decades, there has been increasing concern over the effects of bottom-fishing activities on the benthic ecosystems in all regions where commercial fishing is practised. The evidence that fishing gear may injure benthic organisms, reduce habitat complexities and reduce biodiversity has appeared in various media, with increasing frequency ...Many experimental studies have shown that it is possible to detect local changes in the physical structure of the sea bed and the benthic community in response to fishing disturbances ... Species that show the greatest decline tend to be slow growing and physically vulnerable to damage by contact with fishing gear" (Valdimarsson and Suuronen, 2003, pp.322-323).

The specific damage that the predominant gears (techniques) cause to the ecosystem communities have been pointed out by these authors. With respect to trawling, they noted: "An inherent disadvantage of trawl gear is that in addition to the target species, trawls often encounter and capture organisms that for various reasons should have been avoided, such as under-sized individuals of the target species, endangered species, low value fish and aesthetically appealing species like sea turtles and marine mammals" (ibid, p.323).

Referring to purse seining it was noted thus: "Purse seining is a widely used technology, whereby a detected school of fish is encircled and captured . It is generally known as a non-selective fishing method. The incidental capture of dolphins and porpoises in tuna purse seine fisheries was a major cause of concern in the 1960s. It was actually the first case of environmental and conservation organisations forcing a by-catch issue to the top of international fisheries management agenda. The pressure from these groups was so strong that authorities and the fishing industry were forced to find practical solutions that could substantially reduce the incidental killing of dolphins in the tuna purse-seining fishery. A major reason for the problem was the practice of encircling groups of dolphins that were associated with the tuna. In the early years of this fishery, the incidental mortality of dolphins using this method was high (an average of 350,000 dolphins, annually during the 1960s) which was believed to have caused significant declines in populations of dolphins...There have been increasing concerns recently over the discard of small fish, sharks, rays and some other species captured as by-catch in tuna purse seines when fishing near or under floating objects and fish aggregating devices (FADs). These unwanted organisms are associated with such floating objects and therefore it is difficult to avoid their capture when targeting tunas swimming near them. This type of fishery is regarded as a non-sustainable practice for which a solution is urgently needed" (ibid, pp.328-329).

In the case of gillnetting, they noted that "a specific problem in many coastal areas is that during certain seasons gillnets may catch substantial numbers of seabirds that become entangled in gillnets while diving for prey ... There is also growing concern about the impacts of ghost fishing by lost gillnets. Lost gillnets may continue to fish for several weeks, months or even years, depending on the depth and prevailing environmental conditions (light levels, temperature and current speed)" (ibid, p.329).

With respect to long lining also it was noted that "baited lines can be hazardous to seabirds when they try to eat bait on the hooks while these are floating on or near the surface behind the vessel. The incidental catch of seabirds occurs in most areas where long lining is done, but the problem is greatest in higher latitudes in both hemispheres, where seabirds are most numerous and where long line fisheries are common ...The incidental capture of sea turtles on long line hooks is also a problem but, unlike seabird- longline interactions, technical solutions have not yet been found. Research is therefore needed to produce hooks and baits that reduce incidental capture of sea turtles, and facilitate their release" (ibid, p.330).

The problem with trap fishing, another popular method of fishing, is that "large numbers of traps are lost at sea and may continue to catch fish or other organisms (ghost fishing)" (ibid, p.331).

Valdimarsson and Suuronen made the further observation that "of the commonly employed fishing techniques, bottom trawls and dredges have been characterised as having the most potential to damage marine habitats ...It is notable that, in recent years, bottom trawling has been expanding into areas that are likely to be more vulnerable" (ibid, pp.331-332).

The impact of trawling on benthic habitats and communities had been briefly reviewed and reported by the FAO in 2004. It noted that "the effects of fishing and other anthropogenic activities on the marine environment have always been a source of great concern to fishers. Over the last two decades this concern has increased, with interest mainly focusing on the impacts of towed fishing gears such as trawls and dredges on benthic habitats and organisms ...

The most serious effects of ottertrawling have been demonstrated for hard, bottom habitats with vertical structures. In such habitats, the abundance of large sessile organisms such as sponges, anthozoans and corals has been shown to decrease considerably as a result of the passage as ground gear. Habitats dominated by large sessile fauna may thus be severely affected by trawling.

A few studies have been conducted to determine the impacts of experimental trawling on sandy-bottom (offshore) fishing grounds. These studies showed declines in the abundance of some benthic species. However, they seemed to recover within a year or less. They also indicated that trawling does not produce large changes in the benthic communities studied. The habitats, however, showed considerable temporal and spatial variability in the numbers of species and individuals ...

Although changes in several benthic species were observed during the course of the research, few consistent and unambiguous effects could be attributed to trawling disturbance. However, these soft-bottom habitats showed pronounced temporal changes in many benthic species as a result of natural variability; changes caused by trawling may be masked by this variability and therefore difficult to demonstrate.

The relatively few studies carried out to determine impacts of beam trawling were conducted mainly in the North Sea and the Irish Sea, where certain areas of the sea-bed have been intensively trawled for many decades. These studies demonstrated a considerable decrease in abundance of several benthic species (sometimes by as much as 50 per cent). Also, clear evidence of short-term effects of intensive beam trawling was demonstrated. The long-term effects were not studied owing to the lack of undisturbed areas suitable for use as control sites.

Studies on scallop dredging are far more numerous than those on beam trawling. The effects of scallop dredging seem to be similar to those for beam trawling, with a considerable decrease in abundance of several benthic species..."(FAO, 2004, pp.115-117).

Similar problems with respect to technology in aquaculture, posing threat to the sustainability of fisheries have been reported by FAO. *The State of World Fisheries and Aquaculture 2004* noted that "a number of important issues have yet to be resolved relating to the impacts on third parties of management practices that are environmentally questionable – especially the use of wild seed and the use of raw fish as feed" (FAO, 2004, p.69).

The presence of antibiotic residues in aquaculture products is another threat to the industry. *The State of World Fisheries and Aquaculture 2002* reported that "antibiotics have not always been used in a responsible manner in aquaculture and, in a number of reported situations, control of the use of antibiotics has not provided a proper assurance of the prevention of risks to humans ... During the last year, the detection of chloramphenicol in internationally traded shrimp products has caused much concern. The substance has been found in cultured products, resulting in a slow down in imports, causing economic loss among the concerned producers and reflecting negatively on all shrimp and on aquaculture overall" (FAO, 2002, p.75).

An even more serious technological problem with aquaculture is relating to genetically modified organisms (GMO). *The State of World Fisheries and Aquaculture 2000* reported that "there is concern in aquaculture as in other food producing sectors that transgenic technology poses new risks and must therefore be carefully monitored and regulated to ensure that the environment and human health are not endangered" (FAO, 2000a, p.71).

The problems with genetically modified organisms (fish) as reported by the FAO are many and they relate to environment, human health, trade, intellectual property rights, labelling, ethics and public perception. "The environmental issues center on the import and release into the environment of GMOs. GMOs may either be introduced into the environment on purpose, as in stock enhancement programmes, or accidentally through escape from aquaculture...There is currently concern that GMO will either have an adverse impact on local biodiversity through increased predatory or competitive ability, or that they will breed with related species and disrupt the local genetic diversity" (ibid. p.74).

From the human health perspective, "one area of potential concern is the future development of disease resistance. A theoretical possibility is that, if a GMO is more disease-resistant, it may become a host for new pathogens, some of which may be transmissible or pathogenic to humans" (ibid, p.74).

With respect to trade, it is pointed out that "although no aquatic GMOs are traded, genetically modified soybean is an ingredient of shrimp and other animal feeds that are traded globally. The EC and Japan have labelling requirements for this feed, and the feed industry is studying the world wide reaction to the labelling and many look for soybean replacements for feeds" (ibid, p.74).

The problem with intellectual property rights noted by FAO is that "world-wide patenting laws are extremely complex and sometimes even contradictory; WTO and some countries allow the patenting of living organisms, but the EC does not. Many groups have moral objections to the patenting of life...and innovations that are contrary to public morality cannot be patented" (ibid. p.75).

The conflict with regard to labelling is clear from the position that "Europe and the United States are in conflict over the labelling of genetically modified crops. Some countries maintain that labelling is impractical and would, in any case, be ambiguous while others think that it is necessary for informed consumer choice and to prevent a public relations disaster. A major issue in labelling is that of 'substantially equivalent' which means that, if the GMO or product is equivalent to the non-GMO counterpart, no extra labelling is needed. How to assess equivalence, how much information should go on to a label and how the authenticity of labels can be established will be difficult matter to resolve" (ibid. p.75).

Ethical questions with regard to aquatic GMOs usually focus on "whether humans have the right to modify natural creations ...Other ethical dimensions include autonomy and the right to information" (ibid, p.75). It is further pointed out that "from the crop sector, it appears that a main cause of concern are multinational agribusinesses, which are seen as taking control away from farmers and withholding information from consumers" (ibid. p.75).

These issues are, however, considered as less important in fisheries, as no genetically modified edible fish is supplied, at present. It might still impact on the ornamental fisheries sector where genetic modifications are reportedly taking place.

Referring to public perception, FAO noted that "although no genetically modified fish, shellfish or seaweed are available to consumers, the issue permeates the popular media and is a topic of discussion in nearly every general meeting on aquaculture development. This is because the public perceives that there is a problem, and policy-makers and NGOs strive to address the issues their publics find important. Because this is such an emotive issue, much of the news and research reports are presented by special interest groups in ways that suit their particular agendas; industry claims that the technology has been carefully tested and is safe, while opponents forecast environmental and health disasters" (ibid, p.75).

The fundamental problem with the fish processing technology and industry is the high cost of technology and the resulting failure by many firms especially from the developing countries to meet the global demand for high standards of quality and food safety in the era of globalisation. Referring to this situation, *The State of World Fisheries and Aquaculture 2000* noted: "Over the last ten years, both the fishing industry and the fish and food inspection services in many developing countries have made a very determined effort to adapt processing and inspection methodologies that satisfy HACCP requirements. Many countries have been successful ...

However, not all developing countries were able to make the necessary initial investments. Some times credit for this purpose was scarce or non-existent and, as a result, some countries suffered a drastic reduction in the number of establishments authorised to export to EC markets" (ibid. p.49).

The issue is further highlighted by *The State of World Fisheries and Aquaculture 2004* when it noted that "globalisation and further liberalisation of the world trade, while offering many benefits and opportunities, also present new safety and quality challenges. Fish safety regulators have been applying a host of control measures, from mandating the use of the Hazard Analysis and Critical Control Point (HACCP) system to increasing testing, with varying degrees of success ...

Progress in this area will require enhanced international co-operation in promoting scientific collaboration, harmonisation, equivalency schemes and standard-setting mechanisms that are based on scientific principles. The World Trade Organisation's Agreements on Sanitary and Phyto-Sanitary Measures and Technical Barriers to Trade, together with the benchmarking role of the Codex Alimentarius Commission, provide an international platform in this respect. Meeting these challenges will be of the utmost importance for fish trade, both in developed and developing countries, particularly as the latter contribute more than 50 per cent (in value) of international fish trade" (FAO, 2004, p.47).

### 4.6. Other Versions

A different version of sustainability issues in global fisheries was given in the report of the International Workshop on the Implementation of International Fisheries Instruments and Factors of Unsustainability and Overexploitation in Fisheries, held at Mauritius during 3-7 February 2003. This report reiterated the findings of the earlier international workshop on the same subject held at Bangkok during 4-8 February 2002. The following six factors where identified as contributing to unsustainable development of fisheries: (1) lack of good governance, (2) inappropriate incentives, (3) high demand for limited resource, (4) poverty and lack of alternatives, (5) complexity and lack of knowledge, and (6) interactions of the fisheries sector with other sectors and environment (Swan and Greboval, 2004, p.7).

## 4.7. Summary

The major sustainability issues discussed in this chapter were grouped under five categories: (1) ecological, (2) economic, (3) social/institutional, (4) technological and (5) other versions. The major ecological issues threatening the sustainability of global fisheries are biological overfishing, environmental pollution, habitat loss, biodiversity loss, and climate change. The economic issues outlined are decline/stagnation in production, stagnation in consumption, overcapitalisation, uneconomic operation, decline in employment and productivity, poverty and barriers to trade. The social and institutional issues identified included institutional crisis involving the collapse of indigenous community organisations, socio-economic conflicts (intrause and interuse conflicts) and occupational hazards. The social/institutional issues are considered as both the cause and consequences of ecological and economic issues. Many of the technological changes that took place in the catching, culture, processing and marketing branches of the industry are also noticed to cause problems for the sustainability of the industry. This casts doubt on the technological solution for unsustainability.

A different version of sustainability issues reported included lack of good governance, inappropriate incentives, high demand for limited resources, poverty and lack of alternatives, complexity and lack of knowledge, and interactions of the fisheries sector with other sectors and environment.

# 5

# FISHERIES DEVELOPMENT IN INDIA— AN INVENTORY OF RESOURCES

## 5.1. Introduction

Sustainable development of fisheries in India demands an understanding of the resource base as the basis for planning and decision-making. The present chapter intends to look at these resources from an empirical point of view. The resources are classified and discussed under four categories: (1) natural resources, (2) physical resources, (3) human resources and (4) social/institutional capital. These capital endowments are discussed in different sections. The public sector (government) investments made in the industry during the various plan periods are also discussed in one of the sections. A final section presents the summary of main points discussed in the various sections.

## 5.2. Natural Resources

Natural resources in the form of the aquatic environment and the living resources they sustain constitute the 'natural' capital, or the raw material basis for all production activity in the sector. These resources my be classified as corresponding to marine fisheries and inland fisheries respectively.

### 5.2.1. Marine Fisheries

The natural resources of the marine fisheries sector consist of the marine ecosystem and its living resources spread over the coastal zone and the continental shelf of the country. The country has a coastal length of 8118 km spread over nine coastal states and four Union territories. The exclusive economic zone (EEZ) of India extending up to 200 nautical miles has an extent of 2.02 million sq. km. of which 0.86 million sq. km. are on the west coast, 0.56 million sq. km. on the east coast, and 0.60 million sq. km. around the Andaman and Nicobar Islands (Yadava, 2004, p.80). The continental shelf of India has a spread of approximately 0.53 million sq. km (Dept. of Animal Husbandry, Dairying and Fisheries,

2005, p.1). Table 5.1 gives details of approximate length of coastline, continental shelf, number of landing centres and number of fishing villages of India.

**Table 5.1**

**Length of coastline, continental shelf, number of landing centres and fishing villages of India**

| *Sl. No.* | *State/UT* | *Approximate length of coast line (Km)* | *Continental shelf ('000 sq. km.)* | *Number of landing centres* | *Number of fishing villages* |
|---|---|---|---|---|---|
| 1. | Andhra Pradesh | 974 | 33 | 508 | 508 |
| 2. | Goa | 104 | 10 | 88 | 72 |
| 3. | Gujarat | 1600 | 184 | 286 | 851 |
| 4. | Karnataka | 300 | 27 | 29 | 221 |
| 5. | Kerala | 590 | 40 | 226 | 222 |
| 6. | Maharashtra | 720 | 112 | 184 | 395 |
| 7. | Orissa | 480 | 26 | 63 | 329 |
| 8. | Tamil Nadu | 1076 | 41 | 362 | 446 |
| 9. | West Bengal | 158 | 17 | 65 | 652 |
| 10. | A & N Islands | 1912 | 35 | 57 | 45 |
| 11. | Daman & Diu | 27 | - | 7 | 31 |
| 12. | Lakshadweep | 132 | 4 | 11 | 10 |
| 10. | Pondicherry | 45 | 1 | 28 | 45 |
| | Total | 8118 | 530 | 1914 | 3827 |

*Source:* Department of Animal Husbandry, Dairying and Fisheries, 2005, p.97.

The total coastline of the country which is approximately 8118 km is predominantly spread over the states of Gujarat, Tamil Nadu and Andhra Pradesh and the Union territory of Andaman and Nicobar Islands. The continental shelf areas of the country which is approximately 0.53 million sq. km is largely concentrated off the coasts of Gujarat and Maharashtra.

The number of fishing villages in the country is about 3827, the bulk of which is spread over the states of Gujarat, West Bengal, Andhra Pradesh,. Tamil Nadu, Maharashtra,. Orissa, Kerala and Karnataka, in that order. The number of fish landing centres are reported to be about

1914, and predominantly distributed over the coasts of Andhra Pradesh, Tamil Nadu, Gujarat, Kerala and Maharashtra.

The harvestable potential of the marine fishery resources (fish stock) of the exclusive economic zone of India has been worked out at about 3.92 million tonnes (Department of Animal Husbandry, Dairying and Fisheries, 2005, p.99). Table 5.2 gives details of potential yield of fishery resources of the exclusive economic zone of India.

**Table 5.2**

**Potential yield of fishery resources of the EEZ of India**

(million tonnes)

| *Depth Zone* | *Depth range (m)* | | | *Oceanic* | *Total* |
|---|---|---|---|---|---|
| | *0-50* | *50-200* | *200-500* | | |
| Demersal | 1.28 | 0.62 | 0.03 | - | 1.93 |
| Neretic pelagic | 1.00 | 0.74 | - | - | 1.74 |
| Oceanic pelagic | - | - | - | 0.25 | 0.25 |
| Total | 2.28 | 1.36 | 0.03 | 0.25 | 3.92 |
| Percentage of total | 58.15 | 34.86 | 0.71 | 6.27 | 100.00 |

*Source:* Department of Animal Husbandry, Dairying and Fisheries, 2005, p. 99.

Table 5.2 shows that about 58 percent of the resources are available in the 0-50 metre depth zone, 35 per cent in the 50-200 metre depth zone, and seven per cent in areas having depth beyond 200 metres. This distribution more or less indicates the extent of availability of resources in the inshore, offshore and deep sea (oceanic) areas of the EEZ of India.

The coast-wise distribution of these resources is shown in table 5.3.

**Table 5.3**

**Coast-wise distribution of the fishery resources of India**

(million tonnes)

| *Depth zone* | *West coast* | *East coast* | *Laksha-dweep* | *A & N Islands* | *Total* |
|---|---|---|---|---|---|
| Demersal | 1.25 | 0.66 | - | 0.02 | 1.93 |
| Pelagic | 1.11 | 0.43 | 0.06 | 0.14 | 1.74 |
| Oceanic | - | - | - | 0.25 | 0.25 |
| Total | 2.36 | 1.09 | 0.06 | 0.41 | 3.92 |
| Percentage of total | 60.17 | 27.83 | 1.61 | 10.39 | 100.00 |

*Source:* Department of Animal Husbandry, Dairying and Fisheries, 2005, p. 99.

It is clear from table 5.3 that the bulk of the resources of the EEZ of India are located along the west coast of the country and the rest along the east coast and the Andamans. There is a more or less equal distribution of resources between the 'demersal' and the 'oceanic-pelagic' zones as two distinct depth zones. The estimated potential yield of the marine fishery resources of the EEZ of India is given in appendix 5.1.

The estimated potential yield of major pelagic fishery resources of the EEZ of India is given in table 5.4.

**Table 5.4**
**Estimated potential yield of major pelagic fishery resources of the EEZ of India ***

(in tonnes)

| *Sl. No.* | *Group/species* | *Estimates* | *Percentage of total* |
|---|---|---|---|
| 1. | Wolf herring | 16492 | 0.99 |
| 2. | Oil sardine | 294869 | 17.62 |
| 3. | Other sardines | 101490 | 6.06 |
| 4. | Hilsa shad | 26029 | 1.56 |
| 5. | Other shads | 14690 | 0.88 |
| 6. | Bombay duck | 116227 | 6.94 |
| 7. | Anchovies | 141817 | 8.47 |
| 8. | Other clupeoids | 78932 | 4.72 |
| 9. | Ribbon fish | 193670 | 11.57 |
| 10. | Carangids | 238148 | 14.23 |
| 11. | Mackerel | 295040 | 17.63 |
| 12. | Seer fish | 61719 | 3.69 |
| 13. | Coastal tunas | 65472 | 3.91 |
| 14. | Barracuda | 20849 | 1.25 |
| 15. | Mullet | 8101 | 0.48 |
| | Total | 1673545 | 100.00 |

*Excluding oceanic resources
*Source:* Silas, 2000, table 6

It is apparent from table 5.4 that oil sardine, mackerel, ribbon fish, anchovies, Bombay duck, other sardines, etc. constituted the major pelagic resources of the EEZ of India.

Table 5.5 presents the estimated potential yield of major demersal fishery resources of the EEZ of India.

Table 5.5 shows that shrimps, croakers, bivalves, mantis shrimp, perches, cephalopods, elasmobranchs, cat fishes, silver bellies, pomfrets, flat fishes, etc. formed the major group/species among the demersal fishery resources of the EEZ of India.

Table 5.6 gives the details of the estimated potential of oceanic resources of the EEZ of India.

**Table 5.5**

**Estimated potential yield of major demersal fishery resources of the EEZ of India***

(in '000 tonnes)

| *Sl. No.* | *Group/species* | *Estimates* | | *Group total as percentage of total* |
|---|---|---|---|---|
| | | *Group total* | *Sub Total* | |
| 1. | Elasmobranchs | 71407 | — | 3.54 |
| | (*a*) Shark | | 43064 | |
| | (*b*) Skate | | 3686 | |
| | (*c*) Rays | | 22658 | |
| 2. | Perches | 226793 | | 11.24 |
| | (*a*) Grouper | | 15748 | |
| | (*b*) Pig face bream | | 9184 | |
| | (*c*) Red snapper | | 10945 | |
| | (*d*) Threadfin breams | | 128458 | |
| | (*e*) Bull's eye | | 28416 | |
| | (*f*) Other perches | | 34042 | |
| 3. | Catfishes | 51255 | 51255 | 2.54 |
| 4. | Eel | 9081 | 9081 | 0.45 |
| 5. | Croakers | 273027 | 273027 | 13.54 |
| 6. | White fish | 17474 | 17474 | 0.87 |
| 7. | Threadfins | 9342 | 9342 | 0.46 |
| 8. | Silverbellies | 67247 | 67247 | 3.33 |
| 9. | Indian driftfish | 7947 | 7947 | 0.39 |
| 10. | Goat fishes | 19572 | 19572 | 0.97 |
| 11. | Lizard fishes | 27568 | 27568 | 1.37 |
| 12. | Flat fishes | 47304 | 47304 | 2.35 |

| Sl. No. | Group/species | Estimates | | Group total as percentage of total |
|---|---|---|---|---|
| | | Group total | Sub Total | |
| 13. | Moon fish | 256 | 256 | 0.01 |
| 14. | Pomfret | 46088 | | 2.28 |
| | (*a*) Silver pomfret | | 29958 | |
| | (*b*) Chinese pomfret | | 922 | |
| | (*c*) Black pomfret | | 15209 | |
| 15. | Kingfish | 727 | 727 | 0.04 |
| 16. | Tiger fish | 9073 | 9073 | 0.45 |
| 17. | Black ruff | 27176 | 27176 | 1.35 |
| 18. | Deep sea shark | 543 | 543 | 0.03 |
| 19. | Green eye | 4696 | 4696 | 0.23 |
| 20. | Other deep sea fishes | 65526 | 65526 | 3.25 |
| 21. | Other fishes | 218422 | 218422 | 10.83 |
| 22. | Shrimps | 334811 | | 16.59 |
| | (*a*) Penaeid shrimps | | 194192 | |
| | (*b*) Non-penaeid shrimps | | 138711 | |
| | (*c*) Deep sea shrimps | | 1908 | |
| 23. | Crabs | 31980 | 31980 | 1.59 |
| 24. | Mantis shrimp | 120351 | 120351 | 5.97 |
| 25. | Rock lobster | 2727 | 2727 | 0.14 |
| 26. | Deep sea lobsters | 1147 | 1147 | 0.06 |
| 27. | Cephalopods | 101259 | | 5.02 |
| | (*a*) Squids | | 49821 | |
| | (*b*) Cuttle fishes | | 49989 | |
| | (*c*) Octopus | | 1449 | |
| 28. | Bivalves | 201601 | | 9.99 |
| | (*a*) Oysters | | 37090 | |
| | (*b*) Clams and cockles | | 126988 | |
| | (*c*) Mussels | | 24114 | |
| | (*d*) Window pane oyster | | 13409 | |
| 29. | Chank & other gastropods | 22672 | | 1.12 |
| | (*a*) Chanks | | 6225 | |
| | (*b*) Other gastropods | | 16447 | |
| | Total | 2017072 | 2017072 | 100.00 |

*Excluding oceanic resources

*Source:* Silas, 2000, table 5.

**Table 5.6**

**Estimated potential of oceanic resources of the EEZ of India**

(in tonnes)

| *Sl. No.* | *Group/species* | *Estimates* |
|---|---|---|
| 1. | Yellow fin tuna | 114800 |
| 2. | Big eye tuna | 12500 |
| 3. | Skip jack tuna | 85200 |
| 4. | Bill fishes | 5100 |
| 5. | Pelagic shark | 26200 |
| | Total | 243800 |

*Source:* Silas, 2000, table 7.

Among the oceanic resources of the EEZ of India, yellow fin tuna, skipjack tuna and pelagic shark are the ones having higher potential.

### 5.2.2. Inland Fisheries

The inland fishery resources of the country consist of the water bodies, their environment and the living resources therein. The water bodies of the country include the rivers and canals, reservoirs, tanks and ponds, floodplain lakes and derelict water bodies (oxbow lakes) and brackish water areas. Table 5.7 gives details of inland water bodies of India.

Table 5.7 shows that the country as a whole has a river length (including canals) of 1,95,210 km, reservoirs of 29.07lakh ha, tanks and ponds of 24.14 lakh ha, flood plain lakes and derelict water bodies of 7.98 lakh ha, and brackish water areas of 12.40 lakh ha. A major part of the river stretches and canals are concentrated in the states of Uttar Pradesh, Jammu and Kashmir, Madhya Pradesh, Maharashtra, Andhra Pradesh, Karnataka and Tamil Nadu. Much of the resevoir areas falls in the states of Tamil Nadu, Karnataka, Maharashtra, Orissa, Gujarat, Andhra Pradesh, Madhya Pradesh, Uttar Pradesh and Rajasthan. Tanks and ponds are concentrated in the states of Andhra Pradesh, Karnataka, West Bengal, Arunachal Pradesh, Rajasthan and Orissa. A large part of the area under flood plain lakes and derelict water bodies is found in Kerala, Orissa, Uttar Pradesh and Assam. Brackish water areas are concentrated in the maritime states of Orissa, Kerala, West Bengal, Gujarat, Goa, Andhra Pradesh and Tamil Nadu and in the Union territory of Andman and

Nicobar islands. Total area under water bodies (excluding rivers and canals) is found to be maximum in Orissa, followed by Andhra Pradesh, Karnataka, Tamil Nadu, West Bengal, Kerala, Uttar Pradesh, Gujarat, Maharashtra, Rajasthan, Madhya Pradesh, etc. in that order.

**Table 5.7**

**Inland water bodies of India**

| Sl No. | State/UT | Rivers & Canals (km) | Reservoirs (lakh ha) | Tanks & ponds (lakh ha) | Flood plain lakes & derelict water bodies (lakh ha) | Brackish water areas (lakh ha) | Total water bodies (lakh ha)* |
|---|---|---|---|---|---|---|---|
| 1. | Andhra Pradesh | 11514 | 2.34 | 5.17 | - | 0.60 | 8.11 |
| 2. | Arunachal Pradesh | 2000 | - | 2.76 | 0.42 | - | 3.18 |
| 3. | Assam | 4820 | 0.02 | 0.23 | 1.10 | - | 1.35 |
| 4. | Bihar | 3200 | 0.60 | 0.95 | 0.05 | - | 1.60 |
| 5. | Goa | 250 | 0.03 | 0.03 | - | neg. | 0.06 |
| 6. | Gujarat | 3865 | 2.43 | 0.71 | 0.12 | 1.00 | 4.26 |
| 7. | Haryana | 5000 | neg. | 0.10 | 0.10 | - | 0.20 |
| 8. | Himachal Pradesh | 3000 | 0.42 | 0.01 | - | - | 0.43 |
| 9. | Jammu & Kashmir | 27781 | 0.07 | 0.17 | 0.06 | - | 0.30 |
| 10. | Karnataka | 9000 | 4.40 | 2.90 | - | 0.10 | 7.40 |
| 11. | Kerala | 3092 | 0.30 | 0.30 | 2.43 | 2.40 | 5.43 |
| 12. | Madhya Pradesh | 17088 | 2.27 | 0.60 | - | - | 2.87 |
| 13. | Maharashtra | 16000 | 2.79 | 0.59 | - | 0.10 | 3.48 |
| 14. | Manipur | 3360 | 0.01 | 0.05 | 0.04 | - | 0.10 |
| 15. | Meghalaya | 5600 | 0.08 | 0.02 | neg. | - | 0.10 |
| 16. | Mizoram | 1395 | - | 0.02 | - | - | 0.02 |
| 17. | Nagaland | 1600 | 0.17 | 0.50 | neg. | - | 0.67 |
| 18. | Orissa | 4500 | 2.56 | 1.14 | 1.80 | 4.30 | 9.80 |
| 19. | Punjab | 15270 | neg. | 0.07 | - | - | 0.07 |
| 20. | Rajasthan | 5290 | 1.20 | 1.80 | - | - | 3.00 |
| 21. | Sikkim | 900 | - | - | 0.03 | - | 0.03 |

| Sl No. | State/UT | Rivers & Canals (km) | Reser-voirs (lakh ha) | Tanks & ponds (lakh ha) | Flood plain lakes & derelict water bodies (lakh ha) | Brackish water areas (lakh ha) | Total water bodies (lakh ha)* |
|---|---|---|---|---|---|---|---|
| 22 | Tamil Nadu | 7420 | 5.70 | 0.56 | 0.07 | 0.60 | 6.93 |
| 23 | Tripura | 1200 | 0.05 | 0.13 | - | - | 0.18 |
| 24 | Uttar Pradesh | 28500 | 1.38 | 1.61 | 1.33 | - | 4.32 |
| 25 | West Bengal | 2526 | 0.17 | 2.76 | 0.42 | 2.10 | 5.45 |
| 26 | A & N Islands | 115 | 0.01 | 0.03 | - | 1.20 | 1.24 |
| 27 | Chandigarh | 2 | - | neg. | neg. | - | 0.00 |
| 28 | Dadra & Nagar Haveli | 54 | 0.05 |  | - | - | 0.05 |
| 29 | Daman & Diu | 12 | - | neg. | - | neg. | 0.00 |
| 30 | Delhi | 150 | 0.04 | - | - | - | 0.04 |
| 31 | Lakshadweep | - | - | - | - | - | 0.00 |
| 32 | Pondicherry | 247 | - | neg. | 0.01 | neg. | 0.01 |
| 33 | Chattisgarh | 3573 | 0.84 | 0.63 | - | - | 1.47 |
| 34 | Uttranchal | 2686 | 0.20 | 0.01 | 0.00 | - | 0.21 |
| 35 | Jharkhand | 4200 | 0.94 | 0.29 | - | - | 1.23 |
|  | Total | 195210 | 29.07 | 24.14 | 7.98 | 12.40 | 73.59 |

*Not including river length; neg = negligible.
*Source:* Department of Animal Husbandry, Dairying and Fisheries, 2005, p.98.

Referring to the inland fishery resources of India, Sugunan and Sinha noted thus: "India is blessed with a bounty of natural resources in the form of rivers, ponds, lakes, reservoirs and flood plain wetlands. Fish production systems in India can be classified into the capture fisheries of the rivers and estuaries, various forms of intensive aquaculture in ponds and the culture based fisheries of reservoirs, lakes and flood plain wet lands" (Sugunan and Sinha, 2001, p.44).

Table 5.8 gives details of open water fishery resources of India.

**Table 5.8**

**Open water fishery resources of India**

| *Resources* | *Resource potential* | *Mode of management* |
|---|---|---|
| Rivers (km) | 29000 | Capture fisheries |
| Mangroves (ha) | 356000 | Subsistence |
| Estuaries (ha) | 300000 | Capture fisheries |
| Estuarine wet lands/ *bheries* (ha) | 39600 | Aquaculture |
| Backwaters/lagoons (ha) | 190500 | Capture fisheries |
| Large & medium reservoirs (ha) | 1667809 | Enhancement (stock and species) |
| Small reservoirs (ha) | 1485557 | Capture based fisheries |
| Flood plain wetlands (ha) | 202213 | Culture based fisheries |
| Upland lakes (ha) | 720000 | Not known |

*Source:* Sugunan and Sinha, 2001, p.45.

It appears from table 5.8 that large and medium reservoirs constituted the most important resource base for inland fisheries, followed by small reservoirs, upland lakes, flood plain wet lands, mangroves, estuaries and backwaters/lagoons, in that order. The aggregate fish production potential of the inland water resources of the country has been estimated at 4.5 million tonnes (Department of Animal Husbandry, Dairying and Fisheries, 2005, p.1).

Details of major rivers of India, their length and distribution over states are given in table 5.9.

**Table 5.9**

**Length of major rivers of India**

| *Sl.No.* | *River* | *Total length (km)* | *Distribution over states* | *Length (km)* |
|---|---|---|---|---|
| 1. | Ganga | 2525 | (*a*) Uttar Pradesh | 1450 |
| | | | (*b*) Bihar | 445 |
| | | | (*c*) West Bengal | 520 |
| | | | (*d*) Boundary of Bihar and U.P. | 110 |
| 2. | Brahmaputra | 916 | (*a*) Arunachal Pradesh | 218 |
| | | | (*b*) Assam | 698 |
| 3. | Indus | 1114 | Jammu & Kashmir | 1114 |

| Sl.No. | River | Total length (km) | Distribution over states | Length (km) |
|---|---|---|---|---|
| 4 | Brahmani | 799 | (a) Orissa | 541 |
| | | | (b) Bihar | 258 |
| 5. | Krishna | 1401 | (a) Maharashtra | 640 |
| | | | (b) Andhra Pradesh | 386 |
| | | | (c) Karnataka | 375 |
| 6. | Mahanadi | 851 | (a) Madhya Pradesh | 357 |
| | | | (b) Orissa | 494 |
| 7. | Sabarmati | 371 | (c) Rajasthan | 48 |
| | | | (d) Gujarat | 323 |
| 8. | Narmada | 1312 | (a) Madhya Pradesh | 1079 |
| | | | (b) Gujarat | 159 |
| | | | (c) Boundary of M.P. and Gujarat | 39 |
| | | | (d) Boundary of M.P. and Maharashtra | 35 |
| 9. | Mahi | 583 | (a) Madhya Pradesh | 167 |
| | | | (b) Rajasthan | 174 |
| | | | (c) Gujarat | 242 |
| 10. | Tapi | 724 | (a) Madhya Pradesh | 228 |
| | | | (b) Maharashtra | 228 |
| | | | (c) Gujarat | 214 |
| | | | (d) Boundary of M.P. and Maharasthra | 54 |
| 11. | Godavari | 1465 | (a) Andhra Pradesh | 771 |
| | | | (b) Maharashtra | 694 |
| 12. | Pennar | 597 | (a) Karnataka | 61 |
| | | | (b) Andhra Pradesh | 536 |
| 13 | Cauveri | 800 | (a) Karnataka | 320 |
| | | | (b) Tamil Nadu | 416 |
| | | | (c) Boundary of Karnataka and Tamil Nadu | 64 |
| 14 | Subarnarekha | 395 | (a) Bihar | 269 |
| | | | (b) West Bengal | 64 |
| | | | (c) Orissa | 62 |

*Source:* Department of Animal Husbandry and Dairying, 2001, p.123.

As is apparent from table 5.9, much of the Ganga flows through Uttar Pradesh, Bahmaputra through Assam, Indus through Jammu and Kashmir, Brahmini through Orissa, Krishna through Maharashtra, Mahanadi through Orissa, Sabarmati through Gujarat, Narmada through Madhya Pradesh, Mahi through Gujarat, Tapi evenly through Madhya

Pradesh, Maharashtra and Gujarat, Godavari through Andhra Pradesh and Maharashtra, Pennar through Andhra Pradesh, Cauveri through Tamil Nadu and Karnataka and Subarnarekha predominantly through Bihar.

Referring to the rivers and the riverine fishery resources of India, the National Commission on Agriculture noted: "The rivers of India are broadly classified into the Himalayan and the peninsular rivers. The former comprise the Indus, the Ganga and the Brahmaputra systems. The peninsular rivers are further divisible into coastal streams (as many as 600 on the west coast and a few on the east coast) and the inland rivers which comprise the Narbada and the Tapti flowing westwards and the Mahanadi, the Godavari, the Krishna and the Cauvery, flowing eastwards.... The three Himalayan rivers together with their tributaries have their origin in the glaciers of the Himalayas and are perennial since they are fed by the melting of the snow in spring and summer months and are rain fed during monsoon. The peninsular rivers, on the other hand, are only rain fed, and since the monsoon is limited to about four months, these rivers are in very low flowing during the pre-monsoon months; they even tend to dry up during this period, particularly in the upper and middle reaches. It would be natural to expect more flourishing fisheries in rivers having a perennial flow pattern. The riverine systems in the plains are characterised by the occurrence of warm water fisheries and those in the high altitude by cold water fisheries" (Ministry of Agriculture and Irrigation, 1976, mimeo, p.6).

Writing on the warm water fisheries, it noted that "the bulk of the riverine fish production comes from the warm water fisheries. The catch mainly comprise carps, catfishes, feather backs, murrels and Hilsa or Indian shad, Hilsa ilisha. The Indian major carps viz., catla, rohu and mrigal are considered to be the most favoured freshwater fishes and have, therefore special importance in the production aspect from all types of freshwater resources, whether capture or culture. There is a significant difference between the warm water fisheries of the Himalayan and peninsular rivers. There is a great abundance of major carps in the former, whereas the major carp fishery in the latter is either poor or absent" (ibid, pp.6-7).

Referring to the cold water fisheries, the Commission observed that "fisheries in streams and lakes, situated in high altitude regions of the country comprise indigenous fishes, chiefly the mahseer, the snow-trout, and the exotic species, mainly trout. Until recently, the developmental work in cold water fisheries was directed towards establishing trout fishery which is the most popular sport fish in the world. There has, however, been growing realisation for developing indigenous cold water fisheries. The production from cold water fisheries is, however, not of much significance in the total inland fish production of the country" (ibid, pp.12-13).

Highlighting the riverine fishery resources of the country, Sugunan and Sinha noted that "the river systems of the country comprise 14 major rivers (catchment of >20000 km$^2$), 144 medium rivers (catchment of 2000 km$^2$ to 20000 km$^2$)and innumerable small rivers and desert streams that have drainage of less than 2000 km$^2$. Different river systems of the country having a combined length of 29,000 km provide one of the richest fish genetic resouces in the world. Their highly diverse natural fish fauna characterises Indian rivers. The Gangetic system alone harbours not less than 265 species of fish. Similarly, 126 species belonging to 26 families have been recorded from Brahmaputra system. The peninsular rivers have been reported to bear at least 76 fish species ....Based on the information collected by CIFRI on selected stretches of the rivers Ganga, Brahmaputra, Narmada, Tapti, Godavari and Krishna, fish yield from these rivers vary from 0.64 to 1.64 ton per km, with an average of one ton per km" (Sugunan and Sinha, 2001, p.46).

Referring to the reservoirs of India, the National Commission on Agriculture noted: "Considerable importance has been given in the Five Year Plans to the construction of reservoirs which are impoundments on rivers so as to form artificial lakes. These reservoirs are primarily meant for irrigation and the generation of electricity but along with these the stored water has been put to various other uses – domestic and industrial. These man-made lakes constitute new and extensive areas for inland fishery development. It has been estimated that nearly 3.0 million hectares of water spread area are available in this way" (Ministry of Agriculture and Irrigation, 1976, p.18).

Sugunan and Sinha noted that reservoirs constituted "the single largest inland fisheries resource in terms of resource size and production potential" (Sugunan and Sinha, op. cit. p.51). These authors further reported that India has 19,134 small reservoirs with a total water surface area of 14,85,557 ha, 180 medium reservoirs with 15,27,541 ha, and 56 large reservoirs with 11,40,268 ha (ibid, pp.51-52).

Writing on the estuarine fisheries of India, the National Commission on Agriculture stated that "under the term estuarine fisheries is included the fishery output from the mouth of rivers, the large brackish water lakes, the innumerable tidal creeks and backwaters along the coast and the coastal canal system" (Ministry of Agriculture and Irrigation, *op. cit.* p.30). The major estuarine systems noted by the National Commission on Agriculture are (1) Hooghly-Matlah, (2) Mahanadi, (3) Godavari, (4) Chilka, (5) Pulicat and (6) Vembanad (ibid, .30-35).

Table 5.10 gives details of major estuaries and associated backwaters of India as reported by Sugunan and Sinha (2001).

**Table 5.10**

**Major estuaries and associated backwaters of India**

| *Estuary/Backwaters* | *Area (ha) (tonnes)* | *Annual production* | *Major fisheries* |
|---|---|---|---|
| Hoogly-Matlah estuary | 234000 | 20000-26000 | Tanualosa ilisha, Harpodan nehereus, Setipinna phasa Trichiurus sp. Lates calcarifer, Prawns |
| Godavari estuary | 18000 | 5000 | Mullets, Prawns |
| Mahanadi estuary | 30,000 | 550 | Mullets, Lates calcarifer, Sciaenids, Prawns |
| Narmada estuary | - | 4000 | Hilsa, Mullets, Prawns |
| Peninsular estuaries | - | 2000 | Mullets, Prawns, Clupeids, Crabs |
| Chilka lagoon | 103600 | 4000 | Prawns, Mullets, Cat fishes, Clupeids, Perches, Thread fins, Sciaenids |
| Pulicat lake | 36900 | 760-1370- | Prawns, Mullets, Perches, Crabs, Clupeids |
| Vembanad lake* & other backwaters of Kerala | 50000 | 14000-17000 | Prawns, Mullets, Lates calcarifer, Etroplus suratensis, Chanos chanos |
| Estuarine wetlands (*bherries*) | 42600 | 37500 | Prawns, Mullets, Tilapia, Lates calcarifer |
| Mangroves | 356500 | — | — |

*Area of Vembanad reported earlier was 26,000 ha.

*Source:* Sugunan and Sinha, 2001, p.50.

It appears from table 5.10 that among the estuaries, the Hoogly-Matlah estuarine system is the largest in terms of area, followed by Chilka, Pulicat and Mahanadi estuaries. Mangroves, though apparently the largest in terms of total area reported, are subject to maximum encroachment and destruction, in the wake of other developments in the coastal zones of the country. The deterioration of the inland fishery resources of the country and its impact on sustainable development will be discussed in the next chapter.

Describing the flood plain wetlands and the derelict water bodies, the National Commission on Agriculture, noted: "The freshwater fishery resources, which have progressively gone into dereliction, comprise the ox-bow lakes, locally known as *mans* in Bihar, *beels* in West Bengal and Assam and *jheels* in Uttar Pradesh. These are long, narrow and bent courses of water spreads which were formerly beds of rivers or streams which have changed their courses. Most of these waters have connecting channels with nearby flowing rivers or streams allowing entry of adult fishes and seed fish, including major carps during floods. They also receive rain water from the surrounding catchment areas. Some of the ox-bow lakes, which have no link with steams, receive water, fish and seed fish through extensive low lying areas nearby which get inundated during floods...These swamps, varying in depth up to 10 meters in the central zone with shallower margins of considerable extent have adequate water for several months during the year. These derelict waters, therefore, offer excellent opportunities for the construction of small ponds, providing occupation to several fish farmers. The possibility of constructing similar freshwater fish farming ponds exist in the larger type of swampy areas, i.e. the lake like '*beels*' which are wide and shallow areas of low lying extensive water spreads having inadequate drainage..." (Ministry of Agriculture and Irrigation, op. cit. pp.27-28).

The Ramsar Convention defined the wetlands as "areas of marsh, fen, peat land or water, whether natural or artificial, permanent or temporary, with water which is static or flowing, fresh, brackish or salt including areas of marine waters, the depth of which at low tide does not exceed nine meters" (Sugunan and Sinha, 2001, p.59), Sugunan and Sinha point out that "the *beels*, or flood plain wetlands usually represent the lentic component of flood plains, viz. ox-bow lakes, sloughs, meander scroll depressions, residual channels and the back swamps and excludes the lotic component (the main river channels, the levee region and the flats). They are either shallow depressions or dead riverbeds generally connected to the principal rivers and/or receive back flow water from the rivers during floods or from the huge catchment area following monsoon rains" (ibid, p.59).

Referring to the flood plain wetlands of the country, Sugunan and Sinha observed: "Floodplain wetlands form an important fishery resource in Assam, West Bengal and Bihar, where thousands of poor fishermen are dependent on these water bodies for their livelihood" (ibid, p.59).

Distribution of floodplain wetlands of India is shown in table 5.11.

**Table 5.11**

**Distribution of floodplain wetlands in India**

| *State* | *Distribution over districts* | *River basin* | *Local name* | *Area (ha)* |
|---|---|---|---|---|
| Arunachal Pradesh | East Kameng, Lower Subansiri, East Siang, Dobang valley, Lohit, Changlang and Tirap | Kameng, Subansiri, Libang, Lohik Dihing and Tirap | Beel | 2500 |
| Assam | Brahmaputra and Barak valley | Brahmaputra and Barak | Beel | 100000 |
| Bihar | Savan, Champaran, Saharsa, Muzaffarpur, Dharbhanga, Monghyr and Turnea | Gandak and Kosi | Maun, Chaure Dhar | 40000 |
| Manipur | Imphal, Thoubal and Bhishnupur | Iral, Imphal and Thoubal | Pat | 16500 |
| Meghalaya | West Khasi hills and West Garo hills | Someswari and Jingiram | Beel | 213 |
| Tripura | North, South and West Tripura | Gumti | Beel | 500 |
| West Bengal | 24-Parganas - North and South, Hoogly, Nadia, Murshidabad, Meldah, Cooch Behar, Burdwan, North and South Dinajpore and Midnapore | Hoogly, Ichhamati, Bhagirathi, Churri, Kalindi, Dharub, Dharala, Pagla, Jalangi, Behula, Torsa and Mahananda | Beel charha and Baor | 42500 |
| Total | | | | 202213 |

*Source:* Sugunan and Sinha, 2001, p.59.

Table 5.11 reveals that among the seven north-eastern states, Assam is having the maximum area under flood plain wetlands, followed by West Bengal and Bihar.

With respect to Assam, Sugunan and Sinha noted that: "the state of Assam has the maximum number, and water area, under flood plain wetlands, mainly associated with the rivers Brahmaputra and Barak.The state has 1392 *beels* spread over more than 100000 ha. A unique feature of the flood plain wetlands of Brahmaputra basin is the rich growth of marginal and submerged vegetation, which often tends to replace the plankton community. Progressive replacement of plankton community with macrophytes as the main primary producer hastens the pace of eutrophication. However, this process can be reversed through effective management. Closed *beels* are mostly chocked with floating (water hyacinth), submerged (*Najes,* Vallisnaria, Hydrilla and *Chara*) and marginal (Typha) vegetation affecting productivity" (ibid. p.60).

Writing on the floodplain wetlands of West Bengal, Sugunan and Sinha reported: "Gangetic West Bengal represents the deltaic reaches of river Ganga, its tributaries and distributaries, where the river course passes through alluvial plains of a very low gradient, resulting in extensive changes in floodplain configuration. The state has more than 150 *beels* covering an area of 42000 hectares and constituting 22 per cent of the total freshwater area of the state. Thus, the *beels* are an important natural resource playing vital role in the fisheries, rural economy and environment of the state" (ibid, p.61).

Referring to the upland lakes, Sugunan and Sinha write: "Natural lakes situated in the colder upland regions of India are estimated to cover an area of 720000 ha ... But, these lakes have not been studied for their fishery potential. On account of their limnological characteristics, they are suitable for developing coldwater fisheries. These lakes support a lucrative indigenous and exotic fish fauna comprising *Schizothoracids*, mahseers, trouts, tench, Crucian carps and the minor carp...The catches in most of these lakes are dominated by *C.carpio* with sizeable contribution to *Schizothoracids* and mahseers in northern lakes and *Oreochromis mossambicus* in Deccan lakes" (ibid p.67).

The issues of management and sustainability of inland fishery resources are discussed in chapters six and seven.

### 5.3. Physical Capital

The physical or material investments made in the industry form the physical capital/ resources. These are sometimes called as 'man-made' capital. Man-made capital constitute the material means of production, in the form of tools, machineries and other infrastructure.

These investments assist in enhancing production and productivity in the industry. New vintages of such capital also carry or embody new technology which improve the art of production. It was the policy of the Government of India to encourage the adoption of better means of production (new technology) and better organisation of production for promoting balanced development of the industry. Accordingly, it had encouraged greater investments in the hardware of production and the software of new knowledge (R & D) and new organisations (institutions).

The major physical (capital) investments made in the industry are discussed under the following heads: (1) fishing vessels (craft and gear), (2) fishing harbours, (3) fish farming infrastructure, (4) fish processing plants, (5) fish marketing infrastructure and (6) ancillary services.

### 5.3.1. Fishing Vessels (craft and gear)

Fishing vessels constituted the major capital investments in the industry, particularly in the marine fisheries sector. The marine fisheries sector uses a variety of crafts and gear depending on the coast and the fisheries. In the inland fisheries sector, the use of craft is minimum and predominantly depends on traditional crafts (small canoes/rafts) and indigenous gears like cast nets, traps and pots.

The major craft types used in the marine fisheries sector of the country are trawlers, gill netters, dol netters, purse-seiners and 'other' crafts in the mechanised sector and plank-built boats, dugout canoes, catamarans and 'others' in the non-mechanised (motorised/non-motorised) sector.

The predominant gear types used are trawl nets. purse-seines, drift/gill nets, boat-seines, fixed bag nets (stake nets), hook and lines, shore-seines, *(rampons),* traps, scoop-nets, and 'others'.

Table 5.12 gives details of fishing crafts in the marine fisheries sector of India during 1985 and 1995.

It appears from table 5.12 that in 1995, the country had 190857 artisanal fishing units, of which 39303 were motorised and 151554 non-motorised. During the same year, the country had 37901 mechanised fishing units of which 24099 were trawlers, 464 purse-seiners and 13338 other types. The bulk of the artisanal crafts were found to concentrate in the states of Andhra Pradesh, Tamil Nadu and Kerala. Similarly, the majority of the mechanised crafts were concentrated in the states of Maharashtra, Gujarat, Kerala, Tamil Nadu and Andhra Pradesh.

Table 5.13 presents details of fishing crafts in coastal states and Union territories of India during 1999.

**Table 5.12**

**Details of fishing crafts in India during 1985 and 1995**

| Maritime states/UT | Year | Artisanal sector | | | Mechanised sector | | | |
|---|---|---|---|---|---|---|---|---|
| | | Non-motorised | Motorised | Total | Trawlers | Purse-seiners | Other | Total |
| Gujarat | 1985 | 7749 | 1566 | 9315 | 1835 | - | 2722 | 4557 |
| | 1995 | 8745 | 3575 | 12320 | 3456 | - | 2839 | 6295 |
| Maharashtra | 1985 | 12685 | - | 12685 | 2792 | 40 | 2753 | 5585 |
| | 1995 | 7336 | 11005 | 18341 | 4079 | 20 | 2699 | 6798 |
| Goa | 1985 | 2454 | 25 | 2479 | 700 | 58 | 64 | 822 |
| | 1995 | 1759 | 754 | 2513 | 723 | 60 | 67 | 850 |
| Karnataka | 1985 | 9401 | - | 9401 | 1814 | 390 | 663 | 2867 |
| | 1995 | 12523 | 321 | 12844 | 2065 | 374 | 2155 | 4594 |
| Kerala | 1985 | 25353 | 5337 | 30690 | 3224 | 90 | 726 | 4042 |
| | 1995 | 13633 | 13634 | 27267 | 4181 | 10 | 1050 | 5241 |
| Tamil Nadu | 1985 | 41656 | - | 41656 | 2495 | - | 1069 | 3564 |
| | 1995 | 33456 | 5904 | 39360 | 3412 | - | 1463 | 4875 |
| Pondicherry | 1985 | 3522 | - | 3522 | 313 | - | 55 | 368 |
| | 1995 | 5582 | 420 | 6002 | 511 | - | 60 | 571 |
| Andhra Pradesh | 1985 | 43173 | - | 43173 | 1981 | - | 350 | 2331 |
| | 1995 | 50547 | 2660 | 53197 | 3767 | - | 665 | 4432 |
| Orissa | 1985 | 11759 | - | 11759 | 962 | - | 170 | 1132 |
| | 1995 | 13873 | 730 | 14603 | 1700 | - | 500 | 2200 |
| West Bengal | 1985 | 4211 | - | 4211 | 73 | - | 1394 | 1467 |
| | 1995 | 4100 | 300 | 4400 | 205 | - | 1840 | 2045 |
| Total | 1985 | 161963 | 6928 | 168891 | 16189 | 578 | 9966 | 26733 |
| | 1995 | 151554 | 39303 | 190857 | 24099 | 464 | 13338 | 37901 |

*Source:* Devaraj, 1998, p.53.

Table 5.13 shows that out of a total of 280491 fishing crafts, 81284 were traditional crafts, 44578 motorised traditional crafts and 53684 mechanised boats. Taking the total number of crafts in each state, Andhra Pradesh is found to have the maximum number of crafts, followed by Tamil Nadu, Kerala, Gujarat, Karnataka, Maharashtra, etc. in that order.

However, when the mechanised boats alone are taken, the lead is taken by Gujarat, followed by Tamil Nadu, Maharashtra, Andhra Pradesh, Kerala, West Bengal, etc. in that order. Traditional motorised crafts are the maximum in Kerala, followed by Tamil Nadu, Gujarat, Andhra Pradesh, Karnataka, etc. in that order. The pure traditional crafts are the maximum in Andhra Pradesh, followed by Tamil Nadu, Kerala, Karnataka, Orissa, Maharashtra, Gujarat, etc. in that order.

**Table 5.13**
**Fishing crafts in coastal states and Union territories of India during 1999**

| *Sl. No.* | *State/U.T.* | *Traditional crafts* | *Motorised traditional crafts* | *Mechanised boats* | *Total** |
|---|---|---|---|---|---|
| 1. | Andhra Pradesh | 53853 | 4164 | 8642 | 66659 |
| 2. | Goa | 1094 | 1100 | 1092 | 3286 |
| 3. | Gujarat | 9222 | 5391 | 11372 | 25985 |
| 4. | Karnataka | 19292 | 3452 | 2866 | 25610 |
| 5. | Kerala | 28456 | 17362 | 4206 | 50024 |
| 6. | Maharashtra | 10256 | 286 | 8899 | 19441 |
| 7. | Orissa | 10993 | 2640 | 1276 | 15854 |
| 8. | Tamil Nadu | 33945 | 8592 | 9896 | 52433 |
| 9. | West Bengal | 8450 | 270 | 3362 | 8482 |
| 10. | A & N Islands | 1180 | 160 | 230 | 1570 |
| 11. | Daman & Diu | 252 | 350 | 805 | 1407 |
| 12. | Lakshadweep | 594 | 306 | 478 | 1378 |
| 13. | Pondicherry | 7927 | 505 | 560 | 8362 |
| | Total | 81284 | 44578 | 53684 | 280491 |

*Total includes 810 FRP catamarans and 135 beach landing crafts of Orissa.
*Source:* Department of Animal Husbandry, Dairying and Fisheries, 2005, p.142.

Based on a 'rapid' census of fishing crafts and gear, the CMFRI has estimated the following distribution of crafts in India: 30979 trawlers, 9968 gill netters, 5538 *dol* netters and 81033 other craft (Modayil and Jayaprakash, 2003, p.3).

A different estimate of fishing crafts made by Sathiadhas and Biradar for 1996-97 is given in table 5.14.

**Table 5.14**

**Estimate of fishing crafts in India during 1996-97**

| *Type of craft* | *Number of crafts* |
|---|---|
| *Mechanised* | |
| Trawlers | 37574 |
| Gill netters | 6373 |
| Dol netters | 1219 |
| Purse seiners | 1118 |
| Others | 716 |
| Sub-total | 47000 |
| *Traditional (non-motorised)* | |
| Plank-built boats | 36921 |
| Dugout canoes | 17270 |
| Catamarans | 94427 |
| Others | 11382 |
| Sub-total | 160000 |
| *Motorised* | |
| Ring-seines | 3141 |
| Plank-built boats | 9423 |
| Dug out canoes | 6283 |
| Catamarans | 10639 |
| Plywood boats | 2514 |
| Sub-total | 32000 |
| Deep sea vessels | 180 |

*Source:* Sathiadhas and Biradar, 2000, p.11

This estimate, though different from other estimates gives further details of the craft-gear combinations in use in India. Among mechanised crafts, trawlers, constitute the bulk while catamarans form the most numerous craft in both the motorised and the non-motorised sector. Somvanshi noted a decrease in the number of tuna long liners operated in the country from 58 in 1990 to 17 in 1994 (Somvanshi, 2003, p.116).

### 5.3.2. Fishing Harbours

Fishing harbours constituted the second most important capital investment in the catching sector. Provision of fishing harbour facilities at selected ports and landing centres was a major component of fisheries development planning in India. Referring to this initiative, Korakandy noted: "The need for providing landing and berthing facilities for small mechanised boats in the country had become quite pressing by the turn of the sixties. Initially the small boats were using the shallow waters of the coast or the river mouths or lakes as their anchorge. This had, however, proved to be disastrous because the boats had begun to congregate at or near the commercial ports of the country, where facilities for landing, berthing, fuel, water, ice and other accessories are available. This also created problems of navigational hazards and hygiene. The need for providing separate full-fledged fishing harbour with all essential facilities like landing jetties, auction halls, berthing quays, slipways, dredging machines, fuel bunks, water supply, ice and cold-storage, processing halls, transport, repair and maintenance, etc. were felt very important. This was also thought to be the 'logical step' for the industrial concentration of fishing to major ports with modern amenities for commercial fishing, processing and marketing. It was also the considered opinion of the Government that the proper exploitation of the distant water fishery resources of the country needed a network of major and minor fishing harbours in the country ,..." (Korakandy, 1994, p.175).

Highlighting on the public policy of the Government of India in this regard, the Ministry of Agriculture, noted that "in order to meet the infrastructure requirement of fishery sector, the Ministry of Agriculture, Government of India introduced a centrally sponsored scheme in 1964 with the objective of providing infrastructure facilities for safe landing and berthing of mechanised fishing vessels, traditional fishing craft and deep sea fishing vessels. The facilities being created under the scheme are fishing harbours and fish landing centres which include breakwater, wharf, jetty, dredging, reclamation, quay, auction hall, slipway, workshop, net mending shed and other ancillary facilities.

Since inception of the scheme, six major fishing harbours, 153 minor fishing harbours and 188 fish landing centres have been taken up for implementation. Out of which, six major fishing harbours, 38 minor fishing harbours and 142 fish landing centres have been completed and put to use. The remaining 15 minor fishing harbours and 46 fish landing centres are at various stages of construction at present" (Department of Animal Husbandry, Dairying and Fisheries, 2005, p.163).

Table 5.15 gives details of major fishing harbours in India during 2004.

**Table 5.15**

**Details of major fishing harbours in India during 2004**

| *Harbour* | *Cost (Rs lakhs)* | *Year of sanction* | *Status* | *Designed capacity* | | | |
|---|---|---|---|---|---|---|---|
| | | | | *DSV (No.)* | *MFV (No.)* | *Draft (m)* | *TL (m)* |
| Visakhapatnam | 955.50 | 1975 | C | 90 | 300 | 4.5 | 1938 |
| Stage I | 955.50 | 1975 | C | 90 | 300 | 4.5 | 1938 |
| Stage II | 1099.20 | 1978 | C | Details not available | | | |
| Stage III | 454.30 | 1988 | C | " | | | |
| Stage IV | 354.00 | 2001 | C | " | | | |
| Madras (Chennai) | | | | | | | |
| Stage I | 1334.00 | 1973 | C | 50 | 500 | 3 | 1220 |
| Stage II | 850.00 | 1994 | UC | No change in capacity – Stage II for additional facilities | | | |
| Cochin | | | | | | | |
| Stage I | 494.00 | 1971 | C | 57 | 450 | 6 | 560 |
| Stage II | 77.00 (100.00)* | 1993 | UC | No change in capacity – Stage II for additional facilities | | | |
| Calcutta (Kolkata) Roy Chowk | 370.00 | 1971 | C | 15 | - | 6 | 120 |
| Paradip | 2834.00 (3807)* | 1990 | C | 50 | 500 | 6 | 2335 |
| Mumbai (Sassoon Dock) | 825 (1099)* | 1977 | UC | - | 700 | 3 | 1153 |

*Figures in brackets indicate the revised cost
C – completed/commissioned
UC – under construction
DSV – deep sea vesselsMFV – mechanised fishing vessels
TL – total length of landing, berthing, outfitting and repair quay/wharf.
*Source:* Department of Animal Husbandry, Dairying and Fisheries, 2005, p.74.

Table 5.16 presents details of minor fishing harbours and fish landing centres commissioned and under construction in India during 2004.

Table 5.16 indicates that by 2004, a total number of 38 minor fishing harbours were commissioned and 15 were under construction. It is also clear that a total of 142 fish landing centres were commissioned and another 46 under construction. Appendix 5.2 and 5.3 give the location and cost of minor fishing harbours and landing centres constructed/ commissioned in India by 2004 and those under construction, respectively.

### 5.3.3. Fish Farming Infrastructure

Development of inland fisheries, which now constitute the dominant component of Indian fisheries has been given a major priority in the

**Table 5.16**

**Details of minor fishing harbours and landing centres commissioned and under construction in India during 2004**

| Sl. No. | State/UT | Minor fishing harbours | | Fish landing centres | |
|---|---|---|---|---|---|
| | | Commissioned | Under construction | Commissioned | Under construction |
| 1. | Andhra Pradesh | 3 | 1 | 2 | 15 |
| 2. | Goa | - | - | 2 | 2 |
| 3. | Gujarat | 4 | 2 | 20 | 2 |
| 4. | Karnataka | 6 | 3 | 10 | 3 |
| 5. | Kerala | 8 | 5 | 23 | 5 |
| 6. | Maharashtra | 1 | 1 | 35 | 1 |
| 7. | Orissa | 3 | 2 | 21 | 7 |
| 8. | Tamil Nadu | 7 | - | 11 | 10 |
| 9. | West Bengal | 4 | 1 | 12 | - |
| 10. | A & N Islands | 1 | - | - | 1 |
| 11. | Daman & Diu | - | - | 2 | - |
| 12. | Lakshadweep | - | - | 3 | - |
| 13. | Pondicherry | 1 | - | 1 | - |
| | Total | 38 | 15 | 142 | 46 |

*Source:* Department of Animal Husbandry, Dairying and Fisheries, 2005, p. 75.

fisheries development plans of the country. Aquaculture, which is now considered as a 'sunrise' industry and which contributes to the bulk of inland fish production has been developed with considerable advancements in the fields of induced breeding, seed production, transportation of seed, composite fish culture and management of large scale fish culture practices. Suggesting these developments, Silas reported that "researches and developmental programmes towards wide application of induced breeding techniques, establishment of modern hatcheries and seed banks, increased production of fish from reservoirs and lakes, conversion of small farms into viable larger units, intensive cultivation employing composite fish culture techniques and successful implementation of Fish Farmers Development Agencies will not only enhance inland fish production but also provide gainful employment to large number of fishermen and fish farmers" (Silas,1977, pp.79-80).

Highlighting on the main programmes for inland fisheries development in India during the Seventh Five Year Plan, the Planning Commission noted: "The main emphasis will be on intensive fish farming in tanks and ponds through the Fish Farmers Development Agencies and to introduce prawn farming in brackish water areas by establishing 'Area Development' prawn farming estates. Those culturable resources will be the only source of additional inland fish production during the seventh plan period. This approach will also create a 'cadre' of trained fish farmers in the country to undertake scientific fish farming and provide self-employment for them in rural areas. Minor and modern irrigation reservoirs will be developed for culture-cum-capture fisheries through cooperative societies for fishermen. Judicious stocking and management of the reservoirs will be undertaken by the cooperatives/corporations to raise the level of fish production from reservoirs. Further, sewage fish culture, air breathing fish culture and reclamation of *bheels* and *mans* for fish culture will also get attention during the plan period.

Fish seed is the basic input for fish farming in tanks and ponds, and culture-cum-capture fisheries in reservoirs ...The National Fish Seed Programme will be strengthened to support the State Governments in this effort" (Planning Commission, 1985, p.35).

Writing on the recent initiatives for the development of freshwater aquaculture in India, the Department of Animal Husbandry, Dairying and Fisheries, Government of India, noted: "Development of freshwater aquaculture is one of the most important production oriented programmes of the Government of India being implemented by the States/UTs as a centrally sponsored scheme through the network of 429 Fish Farmers Development Agencies (FFDAs) from 1973-74 onwards. The main objectives of the scheme are to popularise fish farming, create employment opportunities, diversify aquaculture practices and provide assistance to fish farmers with a view to create a cadre of trained and well organised fish farmers fully engaged in aquaculture. During 2002-03, additional area brought under fish culture was about 23,032 hectare. About 27,250 fishers were trained in improved practices during the same period and the scheme has benefited about 37,260 persons involved directly or indirectly in the fisheries related activities. During 2003-04, additional area of 30,000 ha and training of 20000 fishers has been the tentative target under the programme. Due to introduction of improved technology of fish farming and the efforts of FFDAS, the national average productivity of ponds and tanks covered under the programme is about 2270 kg/ha/annum. Since inception of the scheme, till 2002-03, these agencies have brought about 6.49 lakhs ha water area under scientific fish culture and trained 7.61 lakh fish farmers/fishermen in improved practices of fish farming. The number of beneficiaries covered under the programme is about 11.25 lakh over the same period" (Department of Animal Husbandry, Dairying and Fisheries, 2005, p.159).

With regard to the development of brackish water aquaculture it noted: "With a view to provide technical, financial and extension support to shrimp farmers in the small-scale sector, 39 Brackish Water Fish Farmers Development Agencies (FFDAs) have been sanctioned to all the coastal sates, and the Union territories of Andaman and Nicobar Islands. During 2002-03, the additional area brought under shrimp culture was about 570 hectare. About 340 fishers were trained in improved practices of shrimp culture during the same period" (ibid, pp.159-160).

Table 5.17 gives details of achievements of Fish Farmers Development Agencies (FFDAs) in various states/UT of India till 2003-04.

Table 5.17 shows the presence of 429 Fish Farmers Development Agencies spread over 28 states and one Union territory. A good number of these FFDAs were distributed in states like Uttar Pradesh, Madhya Pradesh, Bihar, Orissa and Maharashtra, where large water bodies are expected to contribute to increased fish production through aquaculture. The FFDAs in the country were designed to work as catalyst for promoting real investment in infrastructure for aquaculture development. Table 5.17 also reveals that the total water area brought under aquaculture as about 6.50 lakh hectares with approximately 7.6 lakh fish farmers having got training and 11.25 lakh persons benefited from the scheme. The average productivity of the water area was found to be 2216 kg/ha/year. Appendix 5.4 shows the location of FFDAs in the states and Union territories of India.

Another major programme intended to promote investment and growth in coastal aquaculture was the establishment of Brackish Water Fish Farmers Development Agencies.

Table 5.18 shows the details of Brackish Water Fish Farmers Development Agencies working in India during 2004.

**Table 5.17**

**Details of achievements of Fish Farmers Development Agencies (FFDAs) in various states/UTs of India till 2003-04**

| *Sl. No.* | *State/UT* | *No. of FEDAs* | *Water area covered (ha)* | *Fish Farmers trained (No.)* | *No. of benefi-ciaries* | *Average production (Kg/ha/Yr)* |
|---|---|---|---|---|---|---|
| 1. | Andhra Pradesh | 22 | 4120 | 11927 | 5805 | 3500** |
| 2. | Arunachal Pradesh | 2 | 824 | 3500 | 4907 | 1000-1200 |
| 3. | Assam | 23 | 4522 | 22882 | 13190 | 1750 |
| 4. | Bihar | 33 | 25290 | 30459 | 33773 | 2180 |
| 5. | Goa | 1 | - | - | - | - |
| 6. | Gujarat | 21 | 61322 | 25886 | 17583 | 1040 |
| 7. | Haryana | 18 | 13948 | 16055 | 17547 | 3730 |
| 8. | Himachal Pradesh | 2 | 573 | 5560 | 2523 | 2800 |
| 9. | J & K | 2 | 9162 | 4443 | 4614 | 3000 |
| 10. | Karnataka | 18 | 54564 | 15875 | 11161 | 3417 |
| 11. | Kerala | 14 | 28177 | 25052 | 83458 | 1465 |
| 12. | Madhya Pradesh | 38 | 81773 | 40461 | 91984 | 1360 |
| 13. | Maharashtra | 29 | 27487 | 17076 | 61618 | 1135 |
| 14. | Manipur | 8 | 2909 | 4853 | 8773 | 2400 |
| 15. | Meghalaya | 2 | 798 | 2067 | 2067 | 1500 |
| 16. | Mizoram | 5 | 1310 | 7326 | 5327 | 3000 |
| 17. | Nagaland | 8 | 2998 | 3915 | 16931 | 1800 |
| 18. | Orissa | 30 | 37326 | 48552 | 134721 | 2390 |
| 19. | Punjab | 17 | 17515 | 22982 | 14493 | 6094 |
| 20. | Rajasthan | 15 | 7637 | 11604 | 7537 | 1447 |
| 21. | Sikkim | 1 | 181 | 1345 | 1634 | 3500 |
| 22. | Tamil Nadu | 17 | 23255 | 7792 | 13690 | 1000 |
| 23. | Tripura | 4 | 10023 | 102678 | 48951 | 2200 |
| 24. | Uttar Pradesh | 53 | 111265 | 113986 | 107751 | 2550 |
| 25. | West Bengal | 18 | 116483 | 205225 | 383640 | 2685 |
| 26. | Pondicherry | 2 | 242 | 701 | 994 | 1410 |
| 27. | Uttaranchal | 3 | 134 | 1050 | 1394 | 2240 |
| 28. | Jharkhand | 16 | 537 | 5759 | 19895 | 1200 |
| 29. | Chattisgarh | 7 | 5083 | 2767 | 9405 | 2373 |
| | Total | 429 | 649458 | 761778 | 1125366 | 2216 |

**Figures of 2002-03

*Source:* Department of Animal Husbandry, Dairying and Fisheries, 2005, p. 147.

**Table 5.18**

**Details of Brackish Water Fish Farmers Development Agencies (BFDAs) working in India during 2004**

| *Sl. No.* | *State/UT* | *No.of BFDAs* | *Location (District)* |
|---|---|---|---|
| 1. | Andhra Pradesh | 6 | Krishna, Nellore, Srikakulam, East Godavari, West Godavari, Prakasam. |
| 2. | Gujarat | 3 | Valsad, Surat, Bhroach. |
| 3. | Karnataka | 2 | Uttar Kannada, Dakshin Kannada. |
| 4. | Kerala | 7 | Ernakulam, Quilon, Cannanore, Thrissur, Alappuzha, Kozhikode, Kasargode. |
| 5 | Maharashtra | 4 | Thana, Ratnagiri, Raigad, Sindhudurg. |
| 6 | Orissa | 7 | Kendrapara, Ganjam, Khurda, Puri, Jagat Singhpur, Balasore, Bhadrak. |
| 7 | West Bengal | 3 | North 24 Parganas, South 24 Parganas, Midnapore. |
| 8 | Tamil Nadu | 5 | South Arcot, Thanjavur, Chidambranar, Chengal Anna, Ramnad. |
| 9 | Goa | 1 | South and North Goa. |
| 10 | A & N Islands | 1 | Port Blair. |
| | Total | 39 | — |

*Source:* Department of Animal Husbandry, Dairying and Fisheries, 2005, p. 151.

Table 5.18 indicates the wide distribution of BFDAs in 39 of the costal districts of the country spread over nine coastal states and one Union territory.

Another major investment in infrastructure (physical capital) for the development of aquaculture made in the country since the inception of planning was the setting up of fish seed hatcheries

As on 31st August 1995, there were 911 fish seed hatcheries in India, of which 334 were in the public (government) sector and 577 in the private sector. Table 5.19 gives details of fish seed hatcheries in the public sector and private sector in India.

**Table 5.19**

**Details of fish seed hatcheries in public sector and private sector in India in 1995 (capacity in million fry)**

| *Sl. No.* | *State/UT* | *Public sector* | | *Private sector* | |
|---|---|---|---|---|---|
| | | *No. of Hatchery* | *Capacity* | *No. of Hatchery* | *Capacity* |
| 1. | Andhra Pradesh | 92 | 180 | 80 | 400 |
| 2. | Arunachal Pradesh | 4 | 20 | - | - |
| 3. | Assam | 13 | NA | 48 | NA |
| 4. | Bihar | 5 | 208 | 4 | 225 |
| 5. | Goa | - | - | - | - |
| 6. | Gujarat | 10 | 1020 | - | - |
| 7. | Haryana | 21 | 40 | - | - |
| 8. | Himachal Pradesh | 8 | 15 | - | - |
| 9. | Jammu & Kashmir | - | - | - | - |
| 10. | Karnataka | 25 | 220 | 4 | 24 |
| 11. | Kerala | 3 | 6 | 1 | 6 |
| 12. | Madhya Pradesh | 35 | 313 | 9 | 200 |
| 13. | Maharashtra | 18 | NA | - | - |
| 14. | Manipur | 3 | NA | - | - |
| 15. | Meghalaya | 2 | ·1 | - | - |
| 16. | Mizoram | - | - | - | - |
| 17. | Nagaland | - | - | - | - |
| 18. | Orissa | 34 | 384 | 10 | 11 |
| 19. | Punjab | 2 | 9 | 3 | 15 |
| 20. | Rajasthan | 13 | 70 | 3 | 10 |
| 21. | Sikkim | - | - | - | - |
| 22. | Tamil Nadu | 20 | NA | 26 | NA |
| 23. | Tripura | 2 | Neg. | 2 | 1 |
| 24. | Uttar Pradesh | 16 | 255 | 25 | 75 |
| 25. | West Bengal | 7 | 300 | 3602 | 11300 |
| 26. | A & N Islands | - | - | - | - |
| 27. | Chandigarh | 1 | Neg. | - | - |
| | Total | 334 | 3041 | 577 | 12287 |

NA – Not available: Neg. – Negligible

*Source:* Department of Agriculture and Cooperation, 1996, p.142.

Table 5.19 shows that a major chunk of the physical infrastructure for seed production was concentrated in the private sector in West Bengal. Moderate facility (capacity) for seed production is seen in states like Bihar, Uttar Pradesh, Madhya Pradesh, Andhra Pradesh, Orissa and Karnataka.

Establishment of fish seed hatcheries in the country was made with central support under centrally sponsored schemes. Table 5.20 gives details of fish seed hatcheries set up with central assistance.

**Table 5.20**

**Details of fish seed farms set up with central assistance**

| *State* | *Location (district) of fish seed farm/hatchery* | *Production capacity (million fry)* |
|---|---|---|
| Andhra Pradesh | Pochmpad (Nizamabad) | 20 |
| | Somasita (Nellore) | 20 |
| | Brahmagari (Cuddappa) | 20 |
| Assam | Jolukoni (Jorhat) | 20 |
| | Borjamuguri (Darrang) | 20 |
| Bihar | Bhausala Danapur (Patna) | 20 |
| | Raghopur Bhakri (Sitamarhi) | 20 |
| | Mahinathpur (Madhubani) | 20 |
| Gujarat | Bhadaranja (Kheda) | 20 |
| | Kosamada (Surat) | 20 |
| Haryana | Jyotisar (Kurukshetra) | 20 |
| | Lahli Banyani (Rohtak) | 20 |
| | Hissar (Hissar) | 20 |
| Himachal Pradesh | Milwan (Kangra) | 20 |
| Jammu & Kashmir | Check Desa Singh (Kathua) | 20 |
| | Manasbal (Manasbal) | 20 |
| Karnataka | Bhadr Reservoir (Shimoga) | 20 |
| Kerala | Polachira (Pathanamthitta) | 20 |
| | Malampuzha (Palghat) | 20 |
| Madhya Pradesh | Demar (Raipur) | 54 |
| | Salud (Durg) | 20 |
| Maharashtra | Upper Wardha (Amravati) | 20 |
| | Upper Painganga (Yavatmal) | 20 |
| Orissa | Saramanga (Balasore) | 30 |
| | Binika (Bolangir) | 28 |
| | Chiplima (Sambalpur) | 54 |
| | Bhanjagar (Ganjam) | 54 |
| | Bayasagar (Kalahandi) | 20 |

| *State* | *Location (district) of fish seed farm/hatchery* | *Production capacity (million fry)* |
|---|---|---|
| Punjab | Banga (Jalandhar) | 20 |
| | Phagan Majra(Patiala) | 20 |
| Rajasthan | Kasimpura (Kota) | 20 |
| | Bhimpura (Banswara) | 20 |
| Tripura | Mahuripur (S.Tripura) | 20 |
| | Serma (S.Tripura) | 20 |
| Tamil Nadu | Bhavanisagar (Amravathy) | 20 |
| | Manimuthar (Tirunelveli) | 20 |
| Uttar Pradesh | Gomtinagar (Lucknow) | 20 |
| | Seoranpatti (Allahabad) | 20 |
| | Paglabhari (Faizabad) | 20 |
| | Amethi (Sultanpur) | 20 |
| | Chhapra (Gorakhpur) | 20 |
| West Bengal | Jamunadigri (Burdwan) | 54 |
| | Pacamatti Mohalla (Murshidabad) | 13 |
| | Manikpara (Midnapore) | 20 |
| State Farms Corporation | Bugulia (Baharaich) | 20 |
| of India | Kuliaguri (Baharaich) | 20 |
| | Kokilabari (Barpeta) | 20 |
| Total | | 1059 |

*Source:* Department of Agriculture and Cooperation, 1996, pp.140-141.

Table 5.20 makes it clear that 47 fish seed farms were set up with central assistance and they are spread over 18 states and having a capacity to produce approximately 1059 million fry per annum.

With the growth in infrastructure for fish seed production, seed production in the country has grown significantly. Table 5.21 presents the trend in fish seed production in India for selected years.

Table 5.21 shows the significant increase in fish seed production, particularly after the completion of the sixth plan. Appendix 5.5 shows the trend in fish seed production in states and Union territories of India.

**Table 5.21**

**Trend in fish seed production in India for selected years**

| *Year* | *Seed production (million fry)* |
|---|---|
| 1973-74 (end of IV Plan) | 409 |
| 1978-79 (end of V Plan) | 912 |
| 1984-85 (end of VI Plan) | 5639 |
| 1985-86 | 6322 |
| 1986-87 | 7601 |
| 1987-88 | 8608 |
| 1988-89 | 9325 |
| 1988-90 | 9691 |
| 1990-91 | 10332 |
| 1991-92 | 12203 |
| 1992-93 | 12500 |
| 1993-94 | 14239 |
| 1994-95 | 14544 |
| 1995-96 (provisional) | 15007 |
| 1996-97 (target) | 16500 |

*Source:* Department of Agriculture and Cooperation, 1996, p.149.

### 5.3.4. Fish Processing Plants

Another area, where in major physical capital investments were made by both the public sector and the private sector was the fish processing sector. As noted earlier, it was the policy of the Government of India to encourage greater investments in the sector for balanced growth of the industry. Side by side with the growth in investment in the catching and culture branches of the industry, investments in the fish processing sector was also envisioned and planned by the Government. Investments in the fish processing sector by the private sector was encouraged through a policy of providing infrastructure, financial support and subsidies. The infrastructure provided by the Governments (Central and State) consisted of facilities for storage and transportation of fish by establishing ice plants and cold storages at selected fish landing centres (harbours) in the country, introduction of refrigerated rail van services, R & D support for product development, quality assurance, etc. The financial support and subsidy programmes consisted of providing liberal loans at concessional rates of interest and investment subsidies for 100 per cent export-oriented units. Accordingly, it is significant to note that the physical investments (infrastructure) in the processing sector of the country has increased considerably.

Table 5.22 gives details of infrastructure available for fish processing in India during June 2006.

Table 5.22 shows the presence of 369 freezing plants with a daily capacity of 10730.6 tonnes, eight canning plants with a capacity 28.5 tonnes, 215 ice plants with a capacity of 4243 tonnes,16 fish meal plants with a capacity of 783 tonnes, 495 cold storages with a capacity of 144421 tonnes, 138 other storages with a capacity of 10974.5 tonnes, 500 peeling sheds with a capacity of 4907 tonnes and three accelerated freeze drying (ADF) plants with a capacity of 3.5 tonnes. It is also observed that the bulk of the freezing plants and capacity are located in the states of Gujarat, Andhra Pradesh and Maharashtra. The few canning plants present are in Goa, Kerala and in Gujarat. Ice plants are distributed in all the coastal states, but the daily production capacity is found to be the maximum in Gujarat. Infrastructure for fish meal production is maximum in Andhra Pradesh followed by Karnataka. Cold storage facilities are found in all states, but their concentration is significant in Gujarat, Kerala, Maharashtra, Andhra Pradesh and Tamil Nadu. 'Other' storage facilities are more in Andhra Pradesh, Karnataka, Gujarath, Maharashtra and Tamil Nadu. Peeling sheds are present in all coastal states, but the daily handling capacity is highest in Kerala. Accelerated freeze drying (AFD) plants are found only in Kerala and Karnataka with a total daily capacity of 3.5 tonnes.

With improvements in technology and changes in global demand for fishery products, the fish processing sector, particularly the freezing units, have diversified their production base and capacity. Table 5.23 shows the regional/sub-regional distribution of different types of freezers and their capacity in June 2006.

It is apparent from table 5.23 that the predominant type of freezer in use is the 90 minute (quick) freezer with a total number of 807 units and a daily capacity of 4964.36 tonnes .A good many of these units are located in the Veraval, Cochin,Vizag and Bombay regions. The next important type of freezers in use is blast/tunnel freezer, with a total strength of 387 units and capacity of 4115.95 tonnes per day. A good number of these units are operating in the Veraval, Bombay and Cochin

**Table 5.22**

**Details of infrastructure for fish processing in India during June 2006**

(capacity tonnes per day)

| State | Freezing plant | | Canning plant | | Ice plant | | Fish meal plant | | Cold storage | | Other storage | | Peeling shed | | AFD* plant | |
|---|---|---|---|---|---|---|---|---|---|---|---|---|---|---|---|---|
| | No | Capacity | No | Capacity | No | Capacity | No | Capacity | No | Capacity | No | Capacity | No | Capacity | No | Capacity |
| Gujarat | 57 | 2965.2 | 2 | 4.0 | 53 | 1750.0 | 2 | 23.0 | 59 | 36042.0 | 23 | 2240.0 | 62 | 650.8 | 0 | 0.0 |
| Maharashtra | 36 | 2027.0 | 0 | 0.0 | 11 | 423.0 | 4 | 73.0 | 42 | 29118.0 | 21 | 1655.0 | 51 | 733.6 | 0 | 0.0 |
| Goa | 5 | 263.5 | 2 | 13.0 | 7 | 278.5 | 0 | 0.0 | 6 | 2300.0 | 0 | 0.0 | 6 | 72.0 | 0 | 0.0 |
| Karnataka | 11 | 310.9 | 0 | 0.0 | 26 | 514.5 | 4 | 299.0 | 13 | 4225.0 | 9 | 2342.0 | 16 | 167.2 | 1 | 0.4 |
| Kerala | 108 | 2225.2 | 3 | 11.5 | 59 | 187.0 | 0 | 0.0 | 169 | 32807.1 | 3 | 27.0 | 198 | 2584.2 | 2 | 3.1 |
| Tamil Nadu | 45 | 832.3 | 0 | 0.0 | 30 | 511.0 | 4 | 73.0 | 98 | 13795.0 | 65 | 1196.0 | 49 | 83.5 | 0 | 0.0 |
| Andhra Pradesh | 56 | 1263.0 | 1 | 0.0 | 9 | 91.0 | 2 | 315.0 | 56 | 14820.0 | 6 | 3316.0 | 65 | 354.9 | 0 | 0.0 |
| Orissa | 19 | 375.0 | 0 | 0.0 | 16 | 406.0 | 0 | 0.0 | 19 | 4895.0 | 9 | 202.0 | 18 | 120.4 | 0 | 0.0 |
| West Bengal | 32 | 468.6 | 0 | 0.0 | 4 | 81.5 | 0 | 0.0 | 32 | 6404.0 | 2 | 14.5 | 35 | 140.5 | 0 | 0.0 |
| Delhi | 0 | 0.0 | 0 | 0.0 | 0 | 0.0 | 0 | 0.0 | 1 | 15.0 | 0 | 0.0 | 0 | 0 | 0 | 0.0 |
| Total | 369 | 10730.6 | 8 | 28.5 | 215 | 4243.0 | 16 | 783.0 | 495.0 | 144421.1 | 138 | 10974.5 | 500 | 4907.2 | 3 | 3.5 |

*AFD - Accelerated Freeze Drying.

*Source:* MPEDA. Fact sheet, 3.8.2006, p.1.

## Table 5.23

**Details of regional/sub-regional distribution of different types of freezers and their capacity**

(capacity - tonnes per day)

| Region sub region | Traditional plate freezers | | 90 minute freezer | | IQF freezer | | Blast tunnel freezer | | Surimi plant | | Total | |
|---|---|---|---|---|---|---|---|---|---|---|---|---|
| | No | Capacity | No | Capacity | No | Capacity | No | Capacity | No | Capacity | No | Capacity |
| Veraval region | 0 | 0 | 163 | 1290.20 | 18 | 118.75 | 142 | 1556.20 | 3 | 127.00 | 326 | 3092.15 |
| Bombay region | 0 | 0 | 77 | 597.00 | 18 | 157.00 | 73 | 991.30 | 18 | 244.00 | 188 | 2000.30 |
| Goa sub-region | 0 | 0 | 9 | 75.50 | 0 | 0 | 15 | 206.00 | 0 | 0 | 24 | 283.50 |
| Mangalore sub-region | 0 | 0 | 18 | 136.32 | 14 | 192.74 | 9 | 77 | 1 | 34.00 | 42 | 440.06 |
| Cochin region | 15 | 123.83 | 145 | 810.69 | 35 | 267.80 | 69 | 634.80 | 0 | 0 | 269 | 1885.68 |
| Quilon sub-region | 0 | 0 | 29 | 171.00 | 7 | 82.60 | 11 | 107.00 | 0 | 0 | 47 | 360.60 |
| Tuticorin sub-region | 0 | 0 | 50 | 298.80 | 2 | 22.00 | 17 | 140.00 | 0 | 0 | 69 | 460.80 |
| Madras region | 5 | 14.50 | 61 | 258.25 | 7 | 54.20 | 9 | 66.50 | 0 | 0 | 82 | 393.45 |
| Visakhapatnam region | 0 | 0 | 162 | 809.00 | 33 | 323.00 | 21 | 124.00 | 0 | 0 | 216 | 1256.00 |
| Bhubaneswar region | 8 | 69.00 | 29 | 147.50 | 5 | 52.00 | 12 | 106.50 | 0 | 0 | 54 | 375.00 |
| Calcuta region | 8 | 16.50 | 64 | 370.10 | 2 | 17.00 | 9 | 104.00 | 0 | 0 | 83 | 507.60 |
| Total | 36 | 223.83 | 807 | 4964.36 | 141 | 1287.10 | 387 | 4115.30 | 22 | 405.00 | 1400 | 11055.14 |

*Source:* MPEDA, Fact sheet, 3.8.2006, p.1.

regions. IQF units number about 141 with a daily capacity of 1287 tonnes, the bulk of which are concentrated at Visakhapatanam, Cochin, Bombay and Veraval regions and the Mangalore sub-region. Traditional plate freezers number only 36 with a daily capacity of 223.83 tonnes, and most of these are found in the Cochin and Bhubaneswar regions. Surimi plants number only 22 with a daily capacity of 405 tonnes. Most of these units are in the Bombay region.

Highlighting on the processing (post-harvest) infrastructure development programmes under the Tenth Five Year Plan, the Department of Animal Husbandry, Dairying and Fisheries noted: "The programme under this component for the Tenth Five Year Plan consists of two sub-components, i.e. (1) developing fish preservation and storage infrastructure and (2) developing marketing infrastructure such as retail vending Kiosks, aqua-shops, insulated/refrigerated vehicles, ice-box, fish display cabinets, visi coolers, etc. This programme is implemented through self-help groups of fisherwomen, NGOs, cooperatives, joint sectors, Government undertakings and corporations in a location specific manner. The funding pattern under the component is (1) 100 per cent grant (limited to Rs.1.00 crore) to Government undertakings/ Corporations/ Federations; (2) 75 per cent grant (limited to Rs.0.75 crore) to NGOs/Cooperatives/Joint sector/ Group of fisher-women in North Eastern Region/Hilly/Tribal areas and 50 per cent grant (limited to Rs.0.50 crore) in general areas; and (3) 50 per cent grant (limited to Rs.0.40 crore) to Assisted/Private sector in north Eastern region/Hilly/Tribal areas and 25 per cent grant (limited to Rs.0.25 crore) in general areas" (Department of Animal Husbandry, Dairying and Fisheries, 2005, pp.163-164).

### 5.3.5. Fish Marketing Infrastructure

Considerable investments have been made by the Government to provide the infrastructure for fish marketing. Basically, these consisted of providing facilities for storage and transportation of fish from producing centres to consuming centres. Reviewing the progress in this area prior to the Fourth Five Year Plan, the Working Group on Fisheries for the Fifth Five Year Plan (1974-79) noted: "prior to the five year plans, the range of movement of inland fish was mostly limited to the vicinity of the centres of fishing. In regard to marine fish, as the production in most cases far exceeded the local demand, the surplus fish was cured, the less priced fish being merely dried on the open beach, while fish of better quality was salted and dried... Refrigeration facilities were practically non-existent before the commencement of the First Plan. The few plants in the fisheries sector were located in the Crawford Market, Bombay, Connemara Market, Trivandrum and a few cold storages in Goa, Daman and Diu.

During the first three plans, special stress was laid in increasing the refrigeration facilities in the field of fisheries. In fact, next to potato cold storages, the largest number of cold storages set up were for storage of fish. Side by side with the provision of cold storage facilities, plants were also erected for the supply of ice, freezing of fish and storage of frozen fish" (Department of Agriculture, 1973, p.14).

Table 5.24 gives details of infrastructure for storage of fish established in India prior to 1972.

**Table 5.24**
**Details of infrastructure for storage of fish established in India prior to 1972**

(capacity-tonnes per day)

| Sl. No. | Plan period | Ice plant | | Cold storage | | Freezing plant | | Frozen storage | |
|---|---|---|---|---|---|---|---|---|---|
| | | No | Capacity | No | Capacity | No | Capacity | No | Capacity |
| 1. | Pre-Plan | - | - | 1 | 42 | 1 | 0.75 | 1 | 10 |
| 2. | First Plan (1951-56) | 6 | 39.00 | 8 | 300 | 2 | 14.00 | 4 | 460 |
| 3. | Second Plan (1956-61) | 13 | 74.50 | 21 | 735 | 3 | 21.00 | 3 | 169 |
| 4. | Third Plan (1961-66) | 33 | 170.75 | 31 | 686 | 4 | 20.50 | 3 | 805 |
| 5. | Annual Plan (1966-67) | 4 | 10.50 | 2 | 20 | - | - | - | - |
| 6. | Annual Plan (1967-68) | 5 | 19.00 | 9 | 126 | 3 | 9.00 | 3 | 65 |
| 7. | Annual Plan (1968-69) | 14 | 88.50 | 21 | 494 | 2 | 14.50 | 2 | 100 |
| 8. | Fourth Plan (1969-74) | | | | | | | | |
| 8a. | 1969-70 | 12 | 105.00 | 14 | 516 | 5 | 50.00 | 5 | 700 |
| 8b. | 1970-71 | 3 | 33.00 | 2 | 265 | - | - | - | - |
| 8c. | 1971-72 | 2 | 15.00 | 2 | 65 | 1 | 2.50 | 1 | 50 |
| | Total | 92 | 555.25 | 111 | 3248 | 21 | 132.25 | 22 | 2359 |

*Source:* Department of Agriculture, 1973, p.126.

Table 5.24 shows the progressive additions made to the infrastructure for storage of fish in India between1951 and 1972. The number of ice plants increased from zero in the pre-plan period to 92 by1971-72. The number of cold storages increased from one to 111, freezing plants from one to 21, and frozen storage from one to 22. Their capacity also increased correspondingly during this period.

Table 5.25 shows the distribution of infrastructure for storage of fish in states and Union territories of India during 1972.

Table 5.25 indicates that much of the infrastructure for storage during this period was concentrated in states like Kerala, Maharashtra, Mysore (Karnataka), Tamil Nadu and Orissa.

Referring to the development of infrastructure for fish transport prior to the Fourth Plan, the Working Group reported: "During the second five year plan, the TCM of U.S. supplied insulated road vans and equipment for the construction of refrigerated rail vans. The road vans were operated by the states, while the refrigeration equipment was handed over to the Railways which commissioned by 1960-61 six refrigerated rail vans on major routes like Calcutta-Madras, Palasa-Howrah and Bombay-Delhi. During 1965, 26 refrigerated road vans were imported from Hungary and distributed among the various state governments for transport of fish by road. Five refrigerated road vans were also constructed indigenously with imported refrigeration units. Currently the Railways have started using indigenously manufactured refrigeration units and an Indian firm has also taken up manufacture of refrigerated road vans with indigenous components. The industry has also, in the mean while, become more or less fully self-sufficient in the matter of refrigeration equipment, controls and insulation" (ibid, p.35).

Reviewing the progress in the infrastructure for storage and processing during the Fourth Plan Period, the Working Group noted: "By the beginning of the Fourth Plan, considerable interest had already been generated in the private sector in providing refrigeration facilities. Under Government sector programmes, 10 composite refrigeration plants, 73 ice plants and cold storages and 20 refrigerated rail vans were taken up. These targets are likely to be achieved except in regard to introduction of additional refrigerated rail vans" (ibid, p.29).

Referring to the progress in transportation facility, the Working Group reported: "At present 10 refrigerated rail vans are in operation. Besides two meter gauge refrigerated rail vans are nearing completion in Railway Workshops and orders for the construction of six broad gauge vans have been placed with the Ministry of Railways.

**Table 5.25**

**Distribution of infrastructure for storage of fish in states and Union territories of India during 1972**

(Capacity in tonnes/day)

| Sl. No | State/UT | Ice plant | | Cold storage | | Freezing plant | | Frozen storage | |
|---|---|---|---|---|---|---|---|---|---|
| | | No | Capacity | No. | Capacity | No | Capacity | No. | Capacity |
| 1. | Andhra Pradesh | 9 | 56.00 | 9 | 271.00 | - | - | - | - |
| 2. | Assam | 1 | 0.50 | 1 | 3.00 | - | - | - | - |
| 3. | Andamans | 1 | 5.00 | 1 | 15.00 | - | - | - | - |
| 4. | Bihar | 3 | 3.50 | 1 | 6.00 | - | - | - | - |
| 5. | Gujarat | 6 | 44.00 | 6 | 260.00 | - | - | - | - |
| 6. | Goa | 2 | 12.00 | 3 | 170.00 | 1 | 1 | 1 | 75.00 |
| 7. | Haryana | - | - | 1 | 4.00 | - | - | - | - |
| 8. | Kerala | 18 | 173.00 | 23 | 1272.00 | 10 | 68.25 | 11 | 1065.00 |
| 9. | Laccadives | 1 | 5.00 | 1 | 20.00 | - | - | - | - |
| 10. | Mysore | 12 | 61.00 | 12 | 250.00 | 4 | 34.00 | 4 | 640.00 |
| 11. | Maharashtra | 10 | 98.00 | 11 | 549.00 | 3 | 18.00 | 3 | 474.00 |
| 12. | Madhya Pradesh | 3 | 9.00 | 3 | 5.00 | - | - | - | - |
| 13. | Orissa | 3 | 12.00 | 3 | 35.00 | 1 | 0.50 | 1 | 5.00 |
| 14. | Punjab | - | - | 4 | 16.00 | - | - | - | - |
| 15. | Pondicherry | 1 | 2.00 | 2 | 7.00 | - | - | - | - |
| 16. | Tamil Nadu | 20 | 61.25 | 28 | 165.00 | 2 | 10.5 | 2 | 100.00 |
| 17. | West Bengal | 2 | 13.00 | 2 | 180.00 | - | - | - | - |
| | Total | 92 | 555.25 | 111 | 3248.00 | 21 | 132.25 | 22 | 2359.00 |

*Source:* Department of Agriculture, 1973, p.127.

In all, 18 vans are likely to be available by the end of the Fourth Plan, operating on the following routes:

(1) Palasa-Howrah-6 vans (broad gauge), existing; (2) Calicut-Madras-2 vans (broad gauge), existing; (3) Veraval-Delhi-1 van (meter gauge), existing; (4) Masana-Delhi-1 van (meter gauge), existing; (5) Rameswaram-Coimbatore-2 vans (broad gauge), to be introduced; (6) Delhi-Howrah-6 vans (broad gauge) to be introduced.

Refrigerated road vans are used for movement of frozen cargo. However, many state governments have not found adequate use of these vans. Open trucks are used for movement of ice and iced fish for which insulated trucks would have been more suitable" (ibid, p.30).

Reporting on the approach to the provision of infrastructure for storage under the Fifth Five Year Plan, the Working Group noted: "In order to ensure maximum use of fish in fresh condition, ice and cold storage facilities should be further extended. Review of the utilisation of the existing ice plants and cold storages in the Government sector has revealed that it would be uneconomical to run small plants. The approach proposed for the fifth plan is to establish large ice plants in important consuming and distribution centres and to link the small fishing villages by using insulated road transport, preferably by trailer units which can also be used as stationary cold storage units.

A few fish meal plants and oil extraction plants are likely to be put up towards the end of the fifth plan consequent to location of large resources of anchovies, sardine and mackerel as a result of the current pelagic fisheries investigations" (ibid, p.57).

Commenting on the utilisation of the infrastructure for transport of fish, the Working Group noted: "The operation of the refrigerated rail van scheme has been reviewed in consultation with the Ministry of Railways, and it has been found that while the traffic on the Palasa-Howrah route is quite satisfactory, the capacity has not been adequately utilised on other routes even though the routes selected connect some of the best producing and consuming centres. The reasons for the inadequate utilisation have been broadly assessed as absence of daily service, existence of surcharge, unsuitable train timings, limited loading facilities enroute and the practice of returning the vans empty on return journey. These deficiencies are proposed to be remedied in the fifth plan by providing daily services on all routes selected and introducing insulated vans which will require lower maintenance expenditure.

A new line of development envisaged during the fifth five year plan is to provide frozen fish storages at important production and consuming centres and linking them up with necessary refrigerated rail vans maintaining a temperature of minus 20°C. In the past it was emphasised that the refrigerated rail vans should be hauled by fast trains. While this helped in the quick movement of fish, it had the disadvantage that many of the wayside stations could not avail of the refrigerated rail van service as the Railways offer facilities for loading and unloading only at important junctions and that too for a limited period" (ibid. pp.57-58).

During the Fifth Five Year Plan, to develop the infrastructure for processing and marketing, a scheme to demonstrate improved methods of fish handling, salting, dehydration, etc. was included in the central sector under 'Marine Fisheries – Pilot Scheme'. In the state sector, three schemes – (*a*) fish sausage and ham plants for trash fish utilisation, (*b*) establishment of large ice plants and (*c*) establishment of fish meal and oil extraction plants - were initiated.

With regard to the development of infrastructure for transport of fish, the Working Group noted: "During the Fifth Plan all routes so far taken up for refrigerated transport will be provided with daily services, for which 15 insulated rain vans and eight insulated barges will be required. The existing fleet of 18 refrigerated vans maintaining a temperature of 0°C, including vans pending delivery will be used for movement of chilled fish, taking over 20 hours for the journey. For movement of frozen fish, 20 refrigerated rail vans will be introduced ...Provision has separately been made for construction of motorable roads to fish landing centres for the movement of insulated trucks/trailers. The insulated trucks/trailers will also serve as stationary cold storages as no appreciable heat leakage is expected and blocks of ice will be maintainable without significant loss up to about seven days" (ibid, p.121).

Table 5.26 gives details of processing and storage facilities available and proposed at selected processing and marketing centres in India during Fifth Five Year Plan (1974-79).

**Table 5.26**

**Details of processing and storage facilities available and proposed at selected processing and marketing centres during the fifth five year plan (1974-79)**

(Capacity in tonnes)

| *Centre/ Location* | *Ice plant* | | *Cold storage* | | *Freezing plant* | | *Frozen storage* | |
|---|---|---|---|---|---|---|---|---|
| | *Existing* | *Addition* | *Existing* | *Addition* | *Existing* | *Addition* | *Existing* | *Addition* |
| **A. Processing Centre** | | | | | | | | |
| Cochin | >200 | Nil | 14000 | Nil | >100 | 5(BF) | Nil | 1000 |
| Bombay | 100 | Nil | 800 | Nil | >25 | 5(PF) | >300 | 1000 |
| Veraval | 62 | 10 | 200 | 200 | 20 | 5 (BF) | 400 | 1000 |
| Mangalore | 22 | Nil | 45 | Nil | 8 | Nil | 150 | 1000 |
| **B. Marketing Centre** | | | | | | | | |
| Calcutta | >2000 | 10 | 160 | 500 | Nil | 5 (BF) | Nil | 2000 |
| Delhi | 1000 | 10 | Nil | 200 | Nil | Nil | Nil | 1000 |
| Bangalore | Nil | 5 | Nil | 100 | Nil | Nil | Nil | 500 |
| Coimbatore | Nil | 5 | Nil | 100 | Nil | Nil | Nil | 500 |
| Kanpur | 100 | 5 | Nil | 100 | Nil | Nil | Nil | 500 |
| Durgapur | Nil | 5 | Nil | 100 | Nil | Nil | Nil | 500 |

BF = Block Freezing; PF = Plate Freezing

*Source:* Department of Agriculture, 1973, p.136.

Table 5.26 indicates the presence of moderate facilities for manufacture of ice, cold storage, freezing and frozen storage at all processing centres. It also shows the provision for providing ice, cold storage and frozen storage facilities in the marketing centres during the Fifth Plan period.

The Sixth Five Year Plan reiterated that a "cold-chain scheme linking major production centres and internal market points would be taken up through public sector and private sector enterprises" (Planning Commission, 1981, p.135).

The Seventh Five Year Plan noted that "product development for domestic and export markets from unconventional fish of low value, landed by mechanised boats and trawlers will be taken up. In addition, handling and processing facilities will be strengthened to save the quality of fish landed in large quantities during the good fishing season ... Emphasis will also be given to set up hygienic markets for sale of fish through an integrated cold chain of wholesale and retail outlets preferably under the corporate (fisheries corporation) or cooperative sector" (Planning Commission, 1985, p.35. words in parentheses, added).

The Eighth Five Year Plan observed that "suitable infrastructure for processing of (this)fish would also be developed. This would require new post-harvest techniques for product development and value addition... Other important schemes include setting up of 'cold chain' scheme ..." (Planning Commission, 1992, p.22; parentheses, added).

Table 5.27 gives details of central assistance (investment) for setting up of fish marketing units during the eighth and ninth plan.

Table 5.27 shows a high level of assistance for the setting up of marketing infrastructure in Uttar Pradesh, Madhya Pradesh, Kerala, Orissa, West Bengal, Jammu and Kashmir, Maharashtra, Karnataka and Haryana.

Table 5.28 shows the details of central assistance (investment) for the setting up of fish marketing units during the tenth plan.

The partial data on central assistance for the setting up of marketing units as shown in table 5.28 still highlights the significance attached to the development of infrastructure for marketing.

**Table 5.27**

**Details of central assistance for the setting up of fish marketing units during the eighth and ninth five year plans**

| *Sl. No.* | *State/UT* | *No. of Units* | *Amount (Rs lakhs)* |
|---|---|---|---|
| 1. | Andhra Pradesh | 1 | 89.00 |
| 2. | Bihar | 1 | 49.00 |
| 3. | Gujarat | 3 | 103.00 |
| 4. | Haryana | 2 | 137.40 |
| 5. | Himachal Pradesh | 1 | 49.00 |
| 6. | Jammu & Kashmir | 3 | 172.00 |
| 7. | Karnataka | 3 | 139.00 |
| 8. | Kerala | 4 | 196.00 |
| 9. | Madhya Pradesh | 3 | 252.00 |
| 10. | Manipur | 1 | 45.00 |
| 11. | Maharashtra | 2 | 148.00 |
| 12. | Mizoram | 1 | 49.00 |
| 13. | Nagaland | 1 | 46.00 |
| 14. | Orissa | 2 | 184.25 |
| 15. | Punjab | 2 | 91.32 |
| 16. | Rajasthan | 2 | 98.00 |
| 17. | Tamil Nadu | 1 | 48.24 |
| 18. | Uttar Pradesh | 6 | 431.00 |
| 19. | West Bengal | 2 | 172.00 |
| | Total | 41 | 2499.21 |

*Source:* Department of Animal Husbandry, Dairying and Fisheries, 2005, p. 152.

**Table 5.28**

**Details of central assistance for the setting up of fish marketing units during the tenth plan**

| *Sl. No.* | *State/UT* | *No. of Units* | *Location* | *Amount released (Rs lakhs)* |
|---|---|---|---|---|
| 1. | Andhra Pradesh | 1 | Vijayawada | 35.00 |
| 2. | Arunachal Pradesh | 1 | Iranagar | 50.00 |
| 3. | Karnataka | 1 | Malpe | 24.00 |
| | | 1 | Mangalore | 50.00 |
| 4. | Madhya Pradesh | 1 | Bhopal | 100.00 |
| 5. | Tripura | 1 | Agartala | 50.00 |
| | Total | 6 | | 309.00 |

*Source:* Department of Animal Husbandry, Dairying and Fisheries, 2005, p. 152.

### 5.3.6. Ancillary Industries

With the planned development of the main industry (catching, culture, processing and marketing branches), considerable investments (improvements) were made in the ancillary industries which provide inputs to the main industry. Such improvements are to be found predominantly in the boat-building, net-making, manufacturing of other accessories for the capture, culture, processing and marketing branches and in the provision of electronic devices, etc.

Referring to the developments in the boat building sector, the National Commission on Agriculture noted in 1976 that "India has progressively developed both skills and facilities in fabricating coastal cargo boats, traditional fishing craft and, in the last twenty five years, mechanised fishing boats. There are about 69 wooden boat-building yards in the country ...Besides these, fabrication of small traditional craft by the side of several fishing villages is a common scene" (Ministry of Agriculture and Irrigation, 1976, p.206).

Table 5.29 shows the state-wise distribution of wooden boat-building yards in India during 1974.

**Table 5.29**
**State-wise distribution of wooden boat-building yards in India during 1974**

| *State/UT* | *No. of yards under* | | | | *Total* |
|---|---|---|---|---|---|
| | *Government* | *Corporations* | *Cooperatives* | *Private sector* | |
| Gujarat | - | - | 5 | 4 | 9 |
| Maharashtra | - | - | 2 | 5 | 7 |
| Goa | - | - | - | - | - |
| Karnataka | 2 | - | 3 | 4 | 9 |
| Kerala | 1 | 4 | 1 | 20 | 26 |
| Lakshadweep | 1 | - | - | - | 1 |
| Tamil Nadu | 4 | - | 1 | 2 | 7 |
| Andhra Pradesh | 1 | - | - | - | 1 |
| Orissa | - | 1 | 1 | 2 | 4 |
| West Bengal | 1 | - | - | 1 | 2 |
| Punjab | - | - | 1 | 2 | 3 |
| Total | 10 | 5 | 14 | 40 | 69 |

*Source:* Ministry of Agriculture and Cooperation, 1976, p.297.

Table 5.29 indicates the presence of 69 boat-building yards during 1974, of which 26 were in Kerala, nine each in Gujarat and Karnataka, seven in Tamil Nadu, four in Orissa, three in Punjab and one each in Andhra Pradesh and Lakshadweep. The majority of the boat-building yards were in the private sector. It is noted here that some of the major shipyards in the country are now offering their service for building larger commercial fishing vessels of steel. Many new firms are also reported to be in the service of fabricating ferro-cement, fibreglass reinforced plastic (FRP) and fibreglass vessels of small and medium sizes for the fishing industry.

Referring to the boat building facility in India during the 1970s, Silas reported that "besides the numerous small unregistered boat yards constructing different indigenous crafts and small boats, there are 69 registered wooden boat-building yards, 16 ship yards where trawlers are constructed, and three yards where FRP boats are constructed. Recognition of eight additional yards where fishing vessels are proposed to be constructed is under consideration. The country has adequate material, expertise and suitable designs for the construction of wooden and steel vessels up to 30 m long" (Silas, 1977, p.73).

There were about nine marine diesel engine manufacturing firms in India during 1977. Table 5.30 gives details of marine diesel engine manufacturers in India during 1977.

**Table 5.30**

**Details of marine diesel engine manufacturers in India, during 1977**

| *Sl. No.* | *Name of manufacturer* | *Name of engine* | *Horse power* | *Annual licensed capacity* |
|---|---|---|---|---|
| 1. | Veegal Engineers Ltd., Calcutta | Veegal outboard | 5 | NA |
| 2. | Lynx Machinery Ltd., Calcutta | NA | 9-18 | 900 |
| 3. | Lakshmi-Narathan Engg. Works Ltd. | Lister | 18-42 | 142 |
| 4. | Ruston & Hornsby (India) Ltd., Poona | Ruston | 25-75 | 720 |
| 5. | Premier Automobiles | Meadows | 44-700 | 3000 |
| 6. | Ashok Leyland | Leyland | 70-130 | NA |
| 7. | Kirloskar-Cummins Ltd., Poona | Kirloskar | 120-372 | NA |
| 8. | Kirloskar Oil Engines Ltd., Poona | Kirloskar | 300-600 | 600 |
| 9. | Garden Reach Workshop (Marine Engine Division), Ranchi | NA | 800-10000 | NA |

*Source:* Silas, 1977, p.73.

In addition to boat building facilities, boat repair and servicing facilities were also developed at selected major fish landing centres/fishsing harbours in the country. Such facilities were reported to be present at Veraval, Porbandar and Bulsar in Gujarat; Satpati, Bassein, Bombay, Ratnagiri and Alibag in Maharashtra; Marmagoa in Goa; Karwar, Malpe and Mangalore in Karnataka; Cannanore, Cochin and Quilon in Kerala; Cuddalore, Nagapatinam, Colachel, Rameswaram, Mandapam and Madras in Tamil Nadu and Kakinada and Visakhapatnam in Andhra Pradesh. Dry-docking and slipway facilities for underwater maintenance of vessels are available at Bombay, Goa, Cochin, Mandapam, Madras, Visakhapatnam and Calcutta (ibid. p.73).

For the manufacture of fishing nets, four net making plants were set up in the public sector, with a capacity to manufacture over 400 tonnes of twine from nylon yarn per year. Besides, there were also four small units and four large licensed firms producing nylon for nets for the fishing industry (ibid, p.73). It is also reported that the "various fishing vessel components such as reverse-reduction gear, stern gear, power take-off clutches, auxillary engines and machinery, trawl winches and other equipments such as radio telephone, cold-storage and refrigeration equipment and life-saving appliances like life-buoys and life-rafts required by the fishing industry, are manufactured in the country" (ibid, p.73).

### 5.4. Human Resources

Human resources are the moving and motivating factor behind all production and consumption activities in the economy. They provide the 'energy' and 'urge' to work and sustain the economic system. The human resources available to the fishery sector of India are diverse consisting of active fishermen (marine and inland), fish farmers (aquaculturists) , workers engaged in the fish processing industry, people engaged in storage, transportation and distribution (marketing) of fish, workers engaged in ancillary industries, personnel involved in research and development ( R & D) activities in the fisheries sector, personnel involved in fisheries education and training and personnel engaged in fisheries administration and governance (management).

The total number of active (working) fishermen in India in 1991 was reported to be 5.62 million of which 1.87 million were full-time, 1.33 million part-time, and 2.42 million occasional fishermen (Department of Agriculture and Cooperation, 1996, p.135). These figures have increased to 5.79 million, 1.98 million, 1.38 million and 2.45 million respectively by 1992 (ibid, p.135).. Table 5.31 gives the distribution of active fishermen in states and Union territories of India during 1991 and 1992.

**Table 5.31**

**Distribution of active fishermen in states and Union territories in India during 1991 and 1992**

| *Sl. No.* | *States/UT* | *Year* | *Full-time* | *Part-time* | *Occasional* | *Total* |
|---|---|---|---|---|---|---|
| 1. | Andhra Pradesh | 1991 | 115820 | 89173 | 579133 | 784126 |
| | | 1992 | 115820 | 89173 | 579133 | 784126 |
| 2. | Arunachal Pradesh | 1991 | - | 4509 | 856 | 5365 |
| | | 1992 | - | 4509 | 856 | 5365 |
| 3. | Assam | 1991 | 362819 | 72413 | 39728 | 474960 |
| | | 1992 | 362819 | 72413 | 39728 | 474960 |
| 4. | Bihar | 1991 | 274859 | 454143 | 307480 | 1036582 |
| | | 1992 | 281834 | 465495 | 315168 | 1062497 |
| 5. | Goa | 1991 | 15709 | 2439 | 688 | 18836 |
| | | 1992 | 15709 | 2439 | 688 | 18836 |
| 6. | Gujarat | 1991 | 51699 | 16355 | 47211 | 115265 |
| | | 1992 | 51699 | 16355 | 47211 | 115265 |
| 7. | Haryana | 1991 | 6187 | 6150 | 2700 | 15037 |
| | | 1992 | 6187 | 6150 | 2700 | 15037 |
| 8. | Himachal Pradesh | 1991 | 3151 | 4950 | 4394 | 12495 |
| | | 1992 | 3284 | 5777 | 3406 | 12467 |
| 9. | Jammu & Kashmir | 1991 | 8100 | 2400 | 2100 | 12600 |
| | | 1992 | 8302 | 2449 | 2249 | 13000 |
| 10. | Karnataka | 1991 | 20688 | 9849 | 779931 | 810468 |
| | | 1992 | 20688 | 9849 | 779931 | 810468 |
| 11. | Kerala | 1991 | 222300 | 66700 | 93880 | 382880 |
| | | 1992 | 282658 | 87722 | 116962 | 487342 |
| 12. | Madhya Pradesh | 1991 | 18920 | 80660 | - | 99580 |
| | | 1992 | 19881 | 84754 | - | 104635 |
| 13. | Maharashtra | 1991 | 73319 | 25623 | 380564 | 479506 |
| | | 1992 | 73319 | 25623 | 380564 | 479506 |

| Sl. No. | States/UT | Year | Full-time | Part-time | Occasional | Total |
|---|---|---|---|---|---|---|
| 14. | Manipur | 1991 | 18400 | 7800 | 5142 | 31342 |
| | | 1992 | 18400 | 7800 | 5142 | 31342 |
| 15. | Meghalaya | 1991 | 2164 | 3472 | 4310 | 9946 |
| | | 1992 | 2260 | 4105 | 4416 | 10781 |
| 16. | Mizoram | 1991 | - | - | 625 | 625 |
| | | 1992 | - | - | 600 | 600 |
| 17. | Nagaland | 1991 | - | 20149 | 47013 | 67162 |
| | | 1992 | - | 25280 | 50020 | 75300 |
| 18. | Orissa | 1991 | 131580 | 57000 | 30745 | 219325 |
| | | 1992 | 134146 | 58111 | 31345 | 223602 |
| 19. | Punjab | 1991 | 950 | 1800 | 850 | 3600 |
| | | 1992 | 1000 | 1900 | 900 | 3800 |
| 20. | Rajasthan | 1991 | 5589 | 3761 | 3003 | 12343 |
| | | 1992 | 6576 | 4853 | 1654 | 13083 |
| 21. | Sikkim | 1991 | - | 300 | 250 | 550 |
| | | 1992 | - | 300 | 250 | 550 |
| 22. | Tamil Nadu | 1991 | 144000 | - | - | 144000 |
| | | 1992 | 164000 | - | - | 164000 |
| 23. | Tripura | 1991 | 17605 | 15984 | 13785 | 47374 |
| | | 1992 | 18020 | 16361 | 14110 | 48491 |
| 24. | Uttar Pradesh | 1991 | 30042 | 71089 | 59692 | 160823 |
| | | 1992 | 30042 | 71089 | 59692 | 160823 |
| 25. | West Bengal | 1991 | 298590 | 298590 | - | 597180 |
| | | 1992 | 298590 | 298590 | - | 597180 |
| 26. | A& N Islands | 1991 | 2800 | 500 | 200 | 3600 |
| | | 1992 | 2900 | 500 | 200 | 3600 |
| 27. | Chandigarh | 1991 | 200 | - | 50 | 250 |
| | | 1992 | 200 | - | 50 | 250 |
| 28. | Dadra & Nagar Haveli | 1991 | 120 | 10 | - | 130 |
| | | 1992 | 120 | 10 | - | 130 |
| 29. | Daman & Diu | 1991 | 14200 | 3000 | 12800 | 30000 |
| | | 1992 | 14300 | 3150 | 12850 | 30300 |

| *Sl. No.* | *States/UT* | *Year* | *Full-time* | *Part-time* | *Occasional* | *Total* |
|---|---|---|---|---|---|---|
| 30. | Delhi | 1991 | 550 | 480 | - | 1030 |
| | | 1992 | 560 | 490 | - | 1050 |
| 31. | Lakshadweep | 1991 | 3500 | 725 | 1075 | 5300 |
| | | 1992 | 3600 | 735 | 1215 | 5550 |
| 32. | Pondicherry | 1991 | 28532 | 10425 | 718 | 39675 |
| | | 1992 | 28532 | 10425 | 718 | 39675 |
| | Total | 1991 | 1872483 | 1330449 | 2418923 | 5621855 |
| | | 1992 | 1965446 | 1376407 | 2451758 | 5793611 |

*Source:* Department of Agriculture and Cooperation, 1996, pp.134-135.

Table 5.31 shows the presence of maximum number of active fishermen (1.06 million) in Bihar state during 1992,of which, 2.82 lakhs are full-time, 4.65 lakh part-time and 3.15 lakh occasional fishermen . The total number of active fishermen are found to be quite large in Andhra Pradesh, West Bengal, Kerala, Maharashtra, Assam and Orissa.

The total number of active fishermen in India is reported to have increased to 5.95 million in 1994, of which, 2.39 million are full-time, 1.44 million part-time, and 2.12 million occasional fishermen (Department of Agriculture and Cooperation, 1996, p.137).

Appendix 5.6 gives the distribution of active fishermen in states and Union territories of India during 1993 and 1994. It is, however, noted in this context that the figures given for certain states are found to be constant, while there is significant increase in the figures for certain other states and this naturally raises some doubt about the reliability of this data in general.

Referring to the manpower employed in the fisheries sector of India, Sathiadhas and Biradar noted: "Marine fisheries provide substantial employment to human resource both in the production and post-harvest sectors. The manpower employed in India in active fishing alone is currently estimated at 10.3 lakhs in marine fisheries ... the pre-harvest and post-harvest operations in marine fisheries including the internal and external marketing provide employment to another 12 lakh people.

The manpower employed in active fishing in the mechanised sector is estimated at 2.0 lakh people, of which 1.5 lakh fishermen are engaged in trawl fisheries alone and the remaining 0.5 lakh in gill-netters, *dol*-netters, purse-seines and deep sea vessels. The motorised sector employs 1.7 lakh people in active fishing, where 66 per cent are engaged in the operation of ring seiners, mini trawlers and gill-netters and the rest 58,000 persons are employed in the motorised dug-out canoes, catamarans and plywood boats. The non-mechanised sector provides the maximum employment to 6.6 lakh people where the majority of 2.7 lakh are engaged in catamarans, another 2.0 lakh in plank-built boats and the rest in dug-out canoes, *musula* boats and others. The pre-harvest operations of marine fisheries provide job opportunities to about 1.0 lakh people. The activities such as boat-building and repairing, net mending, supply and repair of engines, suppliers of diesel, kerosene and other essential items at the landing centres are coming under this category... About 25 per cent of those employed in the pre-harvest operations are women mostly engaged in net making. Export and internal marketing including transportation, processing, packing and selling at different stages provide employment to 12 lakh people; 2.0 lakh in export marketing and 10 lakh in internal marketing. The innumerable auctioneers at landing and wholesale centres, persons involved in transportation, loading, unloading and packing and distributors of ice, commission agents, wholesalers and retailers come under the post-harvest sector. The people involved in the wholesale and retail marketing is estimated at 5.0 lakh in which 50 per cent are women.

Even though women are not involved in active fishing in marine fisheries, they contribute substantially in the pre and post-harvest operations. About 25 per cent of the labour force in the pre-harvest activities, 60 per cent in the export marketing and 40 per cent in the internal marketing are women. Altogether about 5 lakh women are employed in pre and post-harvest operations in the marine fisheries sector, out of the total work force of 12 lakh persons ...

In case of inland fisheries, there are about 1.4 million active fishers and about 2.0 million part-time and occasional fishers, involved in aquaculture and capture fisheries" (Sathiadhas and Biradar, 2000, pp.9-10).

According to the 17th All India Live Stock Census held in 2003, the fishermen population in the country is reported to be 14.49 million. Table 5.33 gives details of fishermen population and fishermen engaged in different activities in India during 2003.

**Table 5.32**

**Details of fishermen population and fishermen engaged in different activities in India during 2003***

| *Category* | *Number* |
|---|---|
| Fishermen Population (total) | 14,485,354 |
| Males | 4,696,158 |
| Females | 4,033,963 |
| Children | 5,755,233 |
| Fishermen engaged in fishing (total) | 2,005,203 |
| Full-time | 933,124 |
| Part-time | 1,072,079 |
| Fishermen engaged in related activities (total) | 1,017,000 |
| Marketing of fish | 391,000 |
| Repair of fishing nets | 245,100 |
| Processing of fish | 46,200 |
| Other activities | 334,700 |

*As per 17th All India Live Stock Census, 2003.

*Source:* Department of Animal Husbandry, Dairying and Fisheries, 2005, p.2.

Table 5.32 indicates that the total fishermen population in the country during 2003 was about 14.49 million, of which 4.70 million were males, 4.03 million females and 5.76 million children below 14 years of age. The total number of fishermen engaged in the actual operation of fishing was about 2.01 million of whom 0.93 million were full-time fishermen and 1.07 million part-time fishermen. The table makes no mention of occasional fishermen as a class. The total number of fishermen engaged in the related activities of marketing of fish, repairing of nets, and processing of fish, and 'other' non-fishery activities came to about 1.02 million.

### 5.4.1. Investment in Human Resources

The importance of investing in human capital for enhancing production and productivity of labour was recognised by the Government of India much earlier and programmes were initiated for training fishermen in the new methods of handling and operation of fishing vessels through institutions like the Central Institute of Fisheries Technology, the Central Institute of Fishery Nautical and Engineering Training (formerly the Central Institute of Fisheries Operatives) and the Integrated Fisheries Project (Korakandy, 1994, p.70).

Table 5.33 shows details of manpower trained for fishing vessels at the Central Institute of Fisheries Nautical and Engineering Training (CIFNET).

**Table 5.33**

**Details of manpower trained for fishing vessels at the CIFNET**

(Number as on 31.10.2003).

| *Sl. No.* | *State/UT* | *Fishing mate* | *Engine driver* |
|---|---|---|---|
| 1. | Andhra Pradesh | 60 | 51 |
| 2. | Assam | 1 | - |
| 3. | Bihar | 21 | 14 |
| 4. | Goa | 6 | 15 |
| 5. | Gujarat | 31 | 37 |
| 6. | Karnataka | 75 | 55 |
| 7. | Kerala | 136 | 119 |
| 8. | Maharashtra | 26 | 34 |
| 9. | Manipur | 1 | - |
| 10. | Orissa | 38 | 22 |
| 11. | Punjab | - | 1 |
| 12. | Rajasthan | - | 2 |
| 13. | Tamil Nadu | 45 | 37 |
| 14. | Uttar Pradesh | 4 | 5 |
| 15. | West Bengal | 8 | 9 |
| 16. | A & N Islands | 23 | 28 |
| 17. | Lakshadweep | 55 | 41 |
| 18. | Pondicherry | 118 | 149 |
| 19. | Private industry | 41 | 43 |
| 20. | Private candidates | 1203 | 1229 |
| 21. | ICAR candidates | 1 | - |
| 22. | Overseas candidates | 5 | - |
| | Total | 1896 | 1891 |

*Source:* Department of Animal Husbandry, Dairying and Fisheries, 2005, p. 81.

It is apparent from table 5.33 that a total number of 1896 candidates were trained as fishing mates and 1891 candidates as engine drivers by the CIFNET. Excluding private candidates which constituted the majority of candidates trained, maximum candidates were from Kerala, Pondicherry, Karnataka and Andhra Pradesh.

Table 5.34 presents details of manpower trained for ancillary services at the CIFNET.

**Table 5.34**

**Details of manpower trained for ancillary services at the CIFNET**

(Number as on 31.10.2003)

| Sl.No. | State/UT | ADFGTC | EDME | RTOC | GTC | BBFC | SMC | TTC |
|---|---|---|---|---|---|---|---|---|
| 1 | Andhra Pradesh | 1 | - | 7 | 7 | - | 2 | - |
| 2 | Assam | - | - | - | 0 | 1 | - | - |
| 3 | Gujarat | - | - | 2 | 12 | 7 | 1 | - |
| 4 | Goa | - | - | 2 | 1 | - | 3 | - |
| 5 | Jammu & Kashmir | 2 | - | - | - | - | - | - |
| 6 | Karnataka | 1 | 1 | 13 | 8 | 2 | 14 | - |
| 7 | Kerala | - | - | 20 | 22 | 29 | 15 | 12 |
| 8 | Madhya Pradesh | - | - | - | 1 | - | - | - |
| 9 | Maharashtra | - | - | 1 | 4 | 2 | 14 | - |
| 10 | Manipur | 2 | - | - | - | - | - | - |
| 11 | Orissa | - | - | 2 | 6 | 2 | 4 | 6 |
| 12 | Tamil Nadu | 1 | 1 | 9 | 17 | 5 | 6 | 7 |
| 13 | Uttar Pradesh | - | 1 | - | 4 | - | - | - |
| 14 | West Bengal | 2 | - | - | 7 | 2 | 14 | 4 |
| 15 | A & N Islands | - | - | - | 5 | 3 | 4 | 2 |
| 16 | Lakshadweep | - | - | 13 | 1 | 3 | 73 | 1 |
| 17 | Pondicherry | - | 1 | - | 4 | 1 | 36 | - |
| 18 | Private industry | - | 16 | 47 | 9 | 6 | 19 | - |
| 19 | Private candidates | - | - | 101 | 26 | 35 | 64 | - |
| 20 | ICAR candidates | - | - | 1 | - | - | - | - |
| 21 | Overseas candidates | 11 | - | 1 | 10 | 1 | 7 | - |
| | Total | 20 | 20 | 219 | 144 | 99 | 276 | 32 |

Abbreviations: ADFGTC = Advance Diploma in Fishing Gear Technology Course; EDME = Engineering (Fishing Vessel) Course for Diploma Holders in Mechanical Engineering; RTOC = Radio Telephone Operators' Course; GTC = Gear Technician Course; BBFC = Boat Building Foreman Course; SMC = Shore Mechanic Course; TTC = Teachers' Training Course.

*Source:* Department of Animal Husbandry, Dairying and Fisheries, 2005, p.82.

Table 5.34 makes it clear that the CIFNET offered training to candidates for ancillary services as gear technicians, vessel engineers, radio telephone operators, boat building foreman, and shore mechanics and as teachers for fishermen training centres. A good many of these candidates were from Kerala, Karnataka, Tamil Nadu, Lakshadweep and Pondicherry and 'private candidates' and from 'private sector'.

To encourage the development of human resources for fisheries development in the country, a new programme for fishermen awareness and training was initiated by the Central Government since the late 1990s. Table 5.35 shows the number and location of fishermen awareness centres and training centres sanctioned from 1997-98 to 2004-05.

**Table 5.35**

**Number and location of fishermen awareness centres and training centres sanctioned from 1997-98 to 2004-05.**

| *Sl. No.* | *State/UT* | *Awareness Centre* | | *Training Centre* | |
|---|---|---|---|---|---|
| | | *No.* | *Location* | *No.* | *Location* |
| 1 | Andhra Pradesh | 1 | Hyderabad | 3 | Hyderabad<br>Kurnool<br>Kadium |
| 2 | Arunachal Pradesh | | | 1 | Emchi |
| 3 | Bihar | | | 2 | Mithapur<br>Madhubani |
| 4 | Goa | | | 1 | Ela Dhamji |
| 5 | Haryana | 1 | Gurgaon | | |
| 6 | Himachal Pradesh | | | 1 | Pattrikhuki |
| 7 | Jammu & Kashmir | 1 | Baagh-e-Bhu | 1 | Manasbai |
| 8 | Karnataka | 1 | Mangalore | 3 | Bellary |
| 9 | Kerala | 1 | Kannur | 1 | NA |
| 10 | Madhya Pradesh | | | 2 | Nowgang<br>Bhopal |
| 11 | Maharashtra | 1 | Ratnagiri | | |
| 12 | Manipur | | | 1 | Lamphel |
| 13 | Meghalaya | | | 1 | Tura |
| 14 | Nagaland | 1 | Dimapur | 4 | Kohima<br>Tuensang<br>Mokokchung<br>Wokha |

| *Sl. No.* | *State/UT* | *Awareness Centre* | | *Training Centre* | |
|---|---|---|---|---|---|
| | | *No.* | *Location* | *No.* | *Location* |
| 15 | Orissa | | | 2 | Balugam<br>Bomalel |
| 16 | Punjab | 1 | Katli (Ropar) | 3 | Kapurthala<br>Faridkot |
| 17 | Rajasthan | 1 | Jaipur | | Charabahi |
| 18 | Tamil Nadu | 1 | Neelankaral | 4 | Santhanur Dam<br>Vaniachavadi<br>Killai<br>Maniumthar Dam |
| 19 | Tripura | 2 | Agarthala<br>Udaipur | 3 | Agarthala<br>Tripura<br>Tripura |
| 20 | Uttar Pradesh | 2 | Lucknow<br>Jhansi | 3 | Lucknow<br>Mitali<br>S.K.Nagar |
| 21 | West Bengal | 1 | Kolkatta | 1 | Kulia |
| 22 | Chattisgarh | 1 | Raipur | 3 | Bilaspur<br>Ambikapur<br>Korba |
| 23 | Uttaranchal | | | 1 | Hardwar |
| 24 | Jharkhand | | | 1 | Ranchi |
| | Total | 16 | | 42 | |

*Source:* Department of Animal Husbandry, Dairying and Fisheries, 2005, pp. 153-154.

Table 5.35 shows that 16 fishermen awareness centres and 42 training centres were sanctioned during the period from 1997-98 to 2004-05. A good number of these centres are found located in the interior states, indicating the growing interest and importance of fisheries in these areas.

It is further noted in this context that the manpower in the fisheries sector is also trained by a variety of other sources like the Department of Fisheries of the various states, Colleges of Fisheries, University Departments, CIFE and other ICAR institutions, (Abidi and Biradar, 2001, pp.300-303).

## 5.5. Social / Institutional Capital

The social capital consists of the community's inherited culture, traditions and values, and the social organisations which promote and protect its economic, social and cultural interests. The social or 'cultural capital' as noted by Throsby "can provide a means of representing culture which enables both tangible and intangible manifestations of culture to be articulated as long lasting stores of value and providers of benefits for individuals and groups" (Throsby, 2001, p.44).

The social capital of the fishermen community in India may be broadly categorised as (1) those associated with the traditional social organisations of production (institutions) and (2) those associated with modern social relations of production. In the traditional social relations of production, the mode of production is controlled by community decisions and ethical code of conduct for social behaviour. The country is believed to have a plurality of such codes which are applicable to different communities in different regions. Some of the well known social institutions of fishermen in the country which are still alive, though waning include the 'kadakodis' of North Kerala and indigenous community organisations of fishermen.

The modern social organisations are mainly the creations of state powers or governments to promote fisheries development and to enhance their contribution to the economy. These organisations include the Department of Fisheries of the Central and State Governments and the cooperative organisations of fishemen which are semi-governmental or controlled by the 'state'. In addition to these, there are several non-govenmental organisations (NGOs) and trade-related bodies to promote the cause of the fisheries sector in India.

The notable departments / ministries of the Central Government which exercise powers to promote/regulate the working of the fisheries sector are (1) Ministry of Agriculture, (2) Ministry of Food Processing Industries, (3) Ministry of Commerce and Industry, (4) Ministry of Surface Transport, (5) Ministry of Finance, (6) Ministry of Environment and Forests and (7) Ministry of Science and Technology. Most State/ UT Governments have Department of Fisheries to cater to the needs of the fisheries sector in the respective areas.

The major national institutions which promote fisheries development in India with education, training, and research and development (R & D) support are (1) Central Marine Fisheries Research Institute, Cochin; (2) Central Institute of Fisheries Technology, Cochin; (3) Central Institute for Inland Capture Fisheries, Barackpore; (4) Central Institute of Brackish Water Aquaculture, Madras; (5) Central Institute of Freshwater Aquaculture, Bhubaneswar; (6) National Bureau of Fish Genetic Resources, Allahabad; (7) National Research Centre on Coldwater

Fisheries, Dehra Dun; (8) Fisheries Survey of India, Bombay, (9) Integrated Fisheries, Project, Cochin; (10) Central Institute of Coastal Engineering for Fisheries, Bangalore; (11) Central Institute of Fisheries Nautical and Engineering Training, Cochin; (12) The Marine Product Export Development Authority, Cochin; (13) National Institute of Oceanography, Goa and (14) The Bay of Bengal Programme, Madras. A good many of these institutions are the research wing of the Indian Council of Agricultural Research (ICAR).

It is significant to note here that one of the social institutions promoted by the state machinery, even prior to independence and further strengthened in the era of planning was fishermen cooperatives. Fishermen cooperatives were established at primary (village), central (district) and apex (state) levels to promote savings (credit), production, processing and marketing of fish and for management of fisheries in the country. Indeed, the programmes for mechanisation of craft, modernisation of gear, better handling, storage, transportation and distribution (marketing) of fish were all organised through cooperatives as a form of people's organisation to eliminate the middlemen and to improve the socio-economic condition of the fishermen and for their cultural advancement.

Table 5.36 shows the structure of fisheries cooperatives in India during 2004.

**Table 5.36**

**Structure of fisheries cooperatives in India during 2004**

| *Sl. No.* | *State/UT* | *State Federation* | *Central Societies* | *Primary Societies* | *Membership (No.)* |
|---|---|---|---|---|---|
| 1. | Andhra Pradesh | 1 | 10 | 3646 | 359021 |
| 2. | Arunachal Pradesh | - | - | 4 | 300 |
| 3. | Assam | 1 | - | 456 | 3909 |
| 4. | Bihar | 1 | 5 | 532 | 40000 |
| 5. | Delhi | - | - | 2 | 239 |
| 6. | Goa | 1 | - | 10 | 1000 |
| 7. | Gujarat | 1 | 4 | 385 | 80000 |
| 8. | Haryana | - | - | 59 | 1005 |
| 9. | Himachal Pradesh | - | 1 | 28 | 7096 |
| 10. | Jammu & Kashmir | - | - | - | - |

| *Sl. No.State/UT* | *State Federation* | *Central Societies* | *Primary Societies* | *Membership (No.)* |
|---|---|---|---|---|
| 11. Karnataka | 1 | 3 | 296 | 76136 |
| 12. Kerala | 1 | 16 | 292 | 200000 |
| 13. Madhya Pradesh | 1 | 7 | 1001 | 62571 |
| 14. Maharashtra | 1 | 21 | 2024 | 208273 |
| 15. Manipur | 1 | - | 181 | 9182 |
| 16. Meghalaya | - | - | 58 | 2569 |
| 17. Mizoram | - | - | 36 | 808 |
| 18. Nagaland | - | - | 168 | 4285 |
| 19. Orissa | 1 | 4 | 482 | 120000 |
| 20. Punjab | - | - | 4 | 60 |
| 21. Rajasthan | 1 | - | 107 | 4624 |
| 22. Sikkim | - | - | - | - |
| 23. Tamil Nadu | 1 | 10 | 675 | 444866 |
| 24 Tripura | 1 | - | 129 | 14225 |
| 25 Uttar Pradesh | 1 | 5 | 110 | 41000 |
| 26 West Bengal | 1 | 20 | 1072 | 160000 |
| 27 A & N Islands | - | - | 45 | 3812 |
| 28 Chandigarh | - | - | 1 | - |
| 29 Dadra & Nagar Haveli | - | - | - | - |
| 30 Daman & Diu | - | - | 6 | 2993 |
| 31 Lakshadweep | - | - | 2 | - |
| 32 Pondicherry | 1 | 2 | 36 | 28754 |
| 33 Chattisgarh | - | - | - | 31427 |
| 34 Jharkhand | - | - | - | 9150 |
| Total | 17 | 108 | 11847 | 1917305 |

*Source:* Department of Animal husbandry, Dairying and Fisheries, 2005, p. 148.

Table 5.36 makes it clear that there were 17 apex societies (state federations), 108 central (district level) societies, and 11847 primary (village level) societies with a membership of 1.92 million fishermen and related workers. Membership was found to be the highest in Tamil Nadu, followed by Andhra Pradesh, Maharasthra, Kerala, West Bengal, Orissa, etc. in that order.

It is also worth noting here that the National Federation of Fishermen's Cooperatives, Ltd. (FISHCOPFED) with headquarters at New Delhi is coordinating the welfare programmes for the fishermen and international schemes for cooperative education and transfer of 'appropriate' technology through cooperatives. The National Cooperative Development Corperation (NCDC) also assists fisheries cooperatives in the country.

Another major institutional set up made by the Government was the establishment of a number of State Fisheries Development Corporations to promote fisheries development in the country. These institutions, conceived as public sector undertakings, predominantly in the 1960s, were to promote investments in fisheries and to enhance production, processing and marketing of fish in the country and export. They were also expected to work as models and catalysts for promoting technological changes in the catching , culture, processing and marketing branches of the industry. Fisheries Corporations were established in Gujarat, Maharashtra, Karnataka, Kerala, Tamil Nadu, Andhra Pradesh, Orissa, West Bengal, Bihar, Madhya Pradesh, Uttar Pradesh and Assam. In Kerala, it was later liquidated and became part of the present Kerala State Cooperative Federation for Fisheries Development (MATSYAFED).

There are also several voluntary, social, charitable, academic, trade and industrial organisations which assist in promoting the cause of fisheries sector in India. Among the charitable organisations (societies) are South Indian Federation of Fishermen Societies, Coastal Poor Development Action Network India, Programme for Community Organisations, International Collective in Support of Fishermen's Union, World Fishermen's Forum, etc. Among the academic bodies which support the cause of fisheries development in India are Asian Fisheries Society (Indian Chapter), Aquaculture Foundation of India, Indian Fisheries Association, Forum of Fisheries Professionals, Indian Fisheries Association, Inland Fisheries Society of India, Society of Fisheries Technologists, Marine Biological Association, etc. Industry-trade related bodies include Association of Indian Fisheries Industries, Seafood Exporters' Association of India and Aquarist Society of Karnataka (Dixitulu and Paparao, 1994, pp. 379-385).

Besides the national institutions, there are international organisations like the Food and Agriculture Organisation (FAO), International Bank for Reconstruction and Development (World Bank), Interntional Labour Organisation (ILO), European Economic Community (now European Community), Danish International Development Agency (DANIDA), Canadian International Development Agency (CIDA), Japanese Overseas Development Agency (ODA), etc. which extend financial, technical and organisational support for fisheries development in India.

### 5.6. Public Sector Investment in Indian Fisheries

Much of the fisheries development in India, as in most developing countries and even in many advanced nations, was financed by state (public sector) investment in strategic sectors of the industry. Investment in fisheries by the private sector was encouraged by the state (government) policy of providing liberal credit and subsidy support to the industry under various plan schemes. Direct investment by state (public sector) was made in strategic sectors of the industry like infrastructure for development of capture, culture, processing and marketing of fish, research and development (R & D) in the industry, fisheries education and training, technological changes in all branches of the industry and in institution building for fisheries development. Successive five-year plans have progressively increased the provision for fisheries development in India under central, centrally sponsored and state schemes.

Table 5.37 gives details of outlay and expenditure for fisheries development in India over the five year plans.

Table 5.37 shows that the outlay and expenditure for fisheries which stood at Rs 5.13 crore and Rs 2.78 crore respectively during the first plan increased to Rs 2069.70 crores and Rs 1414.41 crores respectively during the ninth plan, marking an increase of 402 times in outlay and 508 times in expenditure. The table also shows an absolute and relative increase in the expenditure under central and centrally sponsored schemes during the later plans. Appendixes 5.8, 5.9, 5.10, 5.11 and 5.12 give details of central and centrally sponsored schemes for fisheries development in India during the fifth plan, annual plans (1978-79 and 1979-80), sixth plan, seventh plan and eighth plan, respectively.

Table 5.38 presents details of expenditure for fisheries development by states and Union territories during the fifth, sixth, seventh, eighth and ninth five year plans.

**Table 5.37**

**Details of outlay and expenditure for fisheries development in India over the five year plans**

(Rs. in crores)

| *Plan period* | *Central scheme* | | *Centrally sponsored scheme* | | *State scheme* | | *Total* | |
|---|---|---|---|---|---|---|---|---|
| | *Outlay* | *Expenditure*** | *Outlay* | *Expenditure*** | *Outlay* | *Expenditure*** | *Outlay* | *Expenditure*** |
| First Plan | 1.00 | 0.38 | @ | @ | 4.13 | 2.40 | 5.13 | 2.78 |
| 1951-56 | | (13.66) | | | | (86.33) | | (100.00) |
| Second Plan | 3.73 | 1.80 | @ | @ | 8.53 | 7.26 | 12.26 | 9.06 |
| 1956-61 | | (19.87) | | | | (80.13) | | (100.00) |
| Third Plan | 5.72 | 3.03 | @ | @ | 21.55 | 20.29 | 28.27 | 23.32 |
| 1961-66 | | (13.00) | | | | (87.00) | | (100.00) |
| Annual Plans | 15.30 | 9.04 | @ | @ | 26.91 | 23.63 | 42.21 | 32.67 |
| 1966-69 | | (27.67) | | | | (72.33) | | (100.00) |
| Fourth Plan | 28.00 | 8.11 | 6.00 | 5.17 | 48.68 | 40.83 | 82.68 | 54.11 |
| 1969-74 | | (14.99) | | (9.55) | | (75.45) | | (100.00) |
| Fifth Plan | 51.05 | 39.93 | 17.00 | 4.07 | 83.19 | 71.11 | 151.20 | 115.10 |
| 1974-79 | | (34.69) | | (3.54) | | (61.78) | | (100.00) |
| Sixth Plan | 137.10 | 75.54 | 36.62 | 28.8 | 197.40 | 182.60 | 371.10 | 287.00 |
| 1980-85 | | (26.33) | | (10.04) | | (63.64) | | (100.00) |

| *Plan period* | *Central scheme* | | *Centrally sponsored scheme* | | *State scheme* | | *Total* | |
|---|---|---|---|---|---|---|---|---|
| | *Outlay* | *Expenditure*** | *Outlay* | *Expenditure*** | *Outlay* | *Expenditure*** | *Outlay* | *Expenditure*** |
| Seventh Plan | 156.58 | 116.93 | 60.75 | 53.26 | 329.19 | 307.40 | 546.52 | 477.59 |
| 1985-90 | | (24.48) | | (11.50) | | (64.36) | | (100.00) |
| Annual Plans | 25.45 | 16.48 | 55.16 | 43.73 | 212.10 | 211.90 | 292.74 | 272.11 |
| 1990-92 | | (6.06) | | (16.07) | | (77.87) | | (100.00) |
| Eighth Plan | 139.00 | 161.01 | 300.00 | 268.02 | 766.39 | 689.43 | 1205.39 | 118.46 |
| 1992-97 | | (14.39) | | (23.96) | | (61.64) | | (100.00) |
| Ninth Plan | 240.00 | 124.97 | 560.00 | 273.18 | 1269.78 | 1016.26 | 2069.70 | 1414.41 |
| 1997-02 | | (8.84) | | (19.31) | | (71.85) | | (100.00) |
| Tenth Plan* | 175.00 | 112.18 | 565.00 | 180.55 | 1321.24 | - | 2060.54 | - |
| 2002-07 | | | | | | | | |

*data relate to only the first three years
@ included under Central scheme
**figures in parentheses show percentage of total
*Source:* Department of Animal Husbandry, Dairying and Fisheries, 2005, p.89.

**Table 5.38**

**Details of expenditure for fisheries development by states and Union territories during the fifth, sixth, seventh, eighth and ninth five year plans**

(Rs. in lakhs)

| Sl. No. | State UT | Fifth Plan | | Sixth Plan | | Seventh Plan | | Eighth Plan | | Ninth Plan | |
|---|---|---|---|---|---|---|---|---|---|---|---|
| | | Expenditure | % of total | Expenditure | % of total | Expenditure | % of total | Expenditure | % of total | Expenditure | % of total |
| (1) | (2) | (3) | (4) | (5) | (6) | (7) | (8) | (9) | (10) | (11) | (12) |
| 1 | Andhra Pradesh | 444.00 | 6.24 | 1554.62 | 8.51 | 2377.56 | 7.73 | 1620.00 | 2.35 | 1986.00 | 1.95 |
| 2 | Arunachal Pradesh | 36.90 | 0.52 | 120.65 | 0.66 | 247.93 | 0.81 | 735.00 | 1.09 | 950.00 | 0.94 |
| 3 | Assam | 283.00 | 3.98 | 570.31 | 3.12 | 1717.42 | 5.59 | 2789.00 | 4.05 | 5534.00 | 5.45 |
| 4 | Bihar | 213.00 | 3.00 | 630.39 | 3.45 | 1050.73 | 3.42 | 725.00 | 1.05 | 672.00 | 0.66 |
| 5 | Goa | 181.80 | 2.56 | 317.41 | 1.74 | 444.05 | 1.44 | 644.00 | 0.93 | 686.00 | 0.68 |
| 6 | Gujarat | 779.00 | 10.95 | 1914.90 | 10.49 | 2108.37 | 6.86 | 3626.00 | 5.26 | 6367.00 | 6.27 |
| 7 | Haryana | 51.00 | 0.72 | 378.23 | 2.07 | 679.34 | 2.21 | 1277.00 | 1.85 | 2354.00 | 2.32 |
| 8 | Himachal Pradesh | 32.00 | 0.45 | 151.00 | 0.83 | 329.67 | 1.07 | 1058.00 | 1.53 | 1370.00 | 1.35 |
| 9 | Jammu & Kashmir | 37.00 | 0.52 | 242.28 | 1.33 | 534.17 | 1.74 | 1155.00 | 1.68 | 2354.00 | 2.32 |
| 10 | Karnataka | 439.00 | 6.17 | 1145.07 | 6.27 | 1470.46 | 4.78 | 8098.00 | 11.75 | 5215.00 | 5.13 |
| 11 | Kerala | 1150.00 | 16.17 | 2079.19 | 11.39 | 3294.41 | 10.72 | 11337.00 | 16.44 | 14984.00 | 14.74 |

| (1) | (2) | (3) | (4) | (5) | (6) | (7) | (8) | (9) | (10) | (11) | (12) |
|---|---|---|---|---|---|---|---|---|---|---|---|
| 12 | Madhya Pradesh | 228.00 | 3.21 | 592.15 | 3.24 | 909.64 | 2.96 | 2028.00 | 2.94 | 2995.00 | 2.95 |
| 13 | Maharashtra | 399.00 | 5.61 | 1471.54 | 8.06 | 1783.90 | 5.80 | 2736.00 | 3.97 | 5138.00 | 5.06 |
| 14 | Manipur | 126.00 | 1.77 | 270.17 | 1.48 | 504.89 | 1.64 | 956.00 | 1.39 | 922.00 | 0.91 |
| 15 | Meghalaya | 49.00 | 0.69 | 110.09 | 0.60 | 201.49 | 0.66 | 413.00 | 0.60 | 521.00 | 0.51 |
| 16 | Mizoram | 24.30 | 0.34 | 76.27 | 0.42 | 174.10 | 0.57 | 334.00 | 0.48 | 586.00 | 0.58 |
| 17 | Nagaland | 39.00 | 0.55 | 108.94 | 0.60 | 351.79 | 1.44 | 571.00 | 0.83 | 715.00 | 0.70 |
| 18 | Orissa | 307.00 | 4.32 | 944.57 | 5.17 | 2670.53 | 8.69 | 5263.00 | 7.63 | 6955.00 | 6.84 |
| 19 | Punjab | 80.00 | 1.12 | 210.27 | 1.15 | 536.76 | 1.75 | 1048.00 | 1.52 | 1049.00 | 1.03 |
| 20 | Rajasthan | 102.00 | 1.43 | 185.14 | 1.01 | 274.99 | 0.89 | 590.00 | 0.86 | 376.00 | 0.37 |
| 21 | Sikkim | 27.00 | 0.38 | 71.35 | 0.39 | 79.95 | 0.26 | 150.00 | 0.22 | 178.00 | 0.18 |
| 22 | Tamil Nadu | 755.00 | 10.62 | 1042.43 | 5.71 | 1467.94 | 4.78 | 7817.00 | 11.34 | 11178.00 | 11.00 |
| 23 | Tripura | 104.00 | 1.46 | 419.52 | 2.30 | 1149.86 | 3.74 | 1883.00 | 2.73 | 1635.00 | 1.61 |
| 24 | Uttar Pradesh | 82.00 | 1.15 | 953.00 | 5.22 | 1239.74 | 4.03 | 2380.00 | 3.45 | 3023.00 | 2.97 |
| 25 | West Bengal | 863.00 | 12.14 | 2012.34 | 11.02 | 3917.40 | 12.74 | 6164.00 | 8.94 | 18214.00 | 17.92 |
| 26 | A & N Islands | 49.80 | 0.70 | 126.41 | 0.69 | 150.98 | 0.49 | 1387.30 | 2.01 | 1829.00 | 1.80 |
| 27 | Chandigarh | 1.10 | 0.02 | 9.25 | 0.05 | 17.17 | 0.06 | 16.88 | 0.24 | 19.00 | 0.02 |

| (1) | (2) | (3) | (4) | (5) | (6) | (7) | (8) | (9) | (10) | (11) | (12) |
|---|---|---|---|---|---|---|---|---|---|---|---|
| 28 | Dadra & Nagar Haveli | 0.20 | 0.00 | 0.00 | 0.00 | 3.08 | 0.01 | 5.26 | 0.00 | 3.04 | 0.00 |
| 29 | Daman & Diu | | | included in Goa | | 136.55 | 0.44 | 203.29 | 0.29 | 316.00 | 0.31 |
| 30 | Delhi | 31.80 | 0.45 | 57.32 | 0.31 | 49.34 | 0.16 | 73.10 | 0.11 | 92.00 | 0.09 |
| 31 | Lakshadweep | 79.00 | 1.11 | 154.72 | 0.85 | 327.15 | 1.06 | 817.31 | 1.19 | 1094.00 | 1.08 |
| 32 | Pondicherry | 117.40 | 1.65 | 341.25 | 1.87 | 538.95 | 1.75 | 1042.63 | 1.51 | 1403.00 | 1.38 |
| 33 | Chattisgarh | - | - | - | - | - | - | - | - | 454.00 | 0.45 |
| 34 | Uttaranchal | - | - | - | - | - | - | - | - | 143.00 | 0.14 |
| 35 | Jharkhand | - | - | - | - | - | - | - | - | 312.00 | 0.31 |
| | Total | 7111.30 | 100.00 | 18260.78 | 100.00 | 30740.31 | 100.00 | 68942.76 | 100.00 | 101626.04 | 100.00 |

*Source:* Department of Animal Husbandry, Dairying and Fisheries, 2005, p.90.

Table 5.38 shows that the expenditure for fisheries development in India by states and Union territories increased from Rs 71.11 crores during fifth plan to Rs 182.60 crores during sixth plan, Rs 307.40 crores during seventh plan, Rs 689.42 crores during eighth plan and Rs 1016.26 crores during ninth plan. Among states, the fifth plan expenditure was the highest in Kerala (Rs 11.50 crores; 16.17 per cent), followed by West Bengal (8.63 crores; 12.14 per cent), Gujarat (Rs 7.79 crores; 10.95 per cent), Tamil Nadu (Rs 7.55 crores; 10.62 per cent), Andhra Pradesh (Rs 4.44 crores; 6.24 per cent), Karnataka (Rs 4.39 crores; 6.17 per cent), etc. During the sixth plan, expenditure was the highest, again in Kerala (Rs 20.79 crores; 11.39 per cent) followed by West Bengal (Rs 20.12 crores; 11.02 per cent), Gujarat (Rs 19.14 crores; 10.49 per cent), Andhra Pradesh (Rs 15.54 crores 8.51 per cent), Maharashtra (Rs 14.71 crores; 8.06 per cent), Karnataka (Rs 11.45 crores; 6.27 per cent) etc. During the seventh plan, expenditure was the highest in West Bengal (Rs 39.17 crores; 12.74 per cent) followed by Kerala (Rs 32.94 crores; 10.72 per cent), Orissa (Rs 26.70 crores; 8.69 per cent), Andhra Pradesh (Rs 23.77 crores; 7.73 per cent), Gujarat (Rs 21.08 crores; 6.87 per cent), Maharashtra (Rs 17.83 crores; 5.80 per cent), etc. Expenditure during the eighth plan was the highest in Kerala (Rs 113.37 crores; 16.44 per cent), followed by Karnataka (Rs 80.98 crores; 11.75 per cent), Tamil Nadu (Rs 78.17 crores; 11.34 per cent), West Bengal (Rs 61.64 crores; 8.94 per cent), Orissa (Rs 52.63 crores; 7.63 per cent), Gujarat (Rs 36.26 crores; 5.26 per cent), Assam (Rs 27.89 crores; 4.05 per cent), etc,. Expenditure during the ninth plan was highest in West Bengal (Rs 182.14 crores; 17.92 per cent), followed by Kerala (Rs 149.84 crores; 14.74 per cent), Tamil Nadu (Rs 111.78 crores; 11.00 per cent), Orissa (Rs 69.55 crores; 6.84 per cent), Gujarat (Rs 63.67 crores; 6.27 per cent), Assam (Rs 55.34 crores; 5.45 per cent), etc. The consistently high investments (expenditure) by Kerala, West Bengal, Tamil Nadu, Andhra Pradesh, Gujarat, Maharashtra, Karnataka and Orissa indicate the high priority given to fisheries development in these coastal states for sustaining their contribution to the regional economy.

Table 5.39 gives the outlay for fisheries development under state schemes during the tenth five year plan.

Table 5.39 indicates the high priority given to fisheries development in Tamil Nadu, West Bengal, Kerala, Maharashtra, Karnataka and Gujarat among maritime states and Assam and Uttar Pradesh among interior states.

**Table 5.39**

**Outlay for fisheries development under state schemes during the tenth five-year plan (2002-07)**

(Rs in lakhs)

| Sl. No. | States/UT | Outlay |
|---|---|---|
| 1 | Andhra Pradesh | 1270 |
| 2 | Arunachal Pradesh | 2394 |
| 3 | Assam | 6829 |
| 4 | Bihar | 1895 |
| 5 | Goa | 780 |
| 6 | Gujarat | 6639 |
| 7 | Haryana | 3720 |
| 8 | Himachal Pradesh | 1574 |
| 9 | Jammu & Kashmir | 4537 |
| 10 | Karnataka | 6765 |
| 11 | Kerala | 17500 |
| 12 | Madhya Pradesh | 2989 |
| 13 | Maharashtra | 7020 |
| 14 | Manipur | 1375 |
| 15 | Meghalaya | 700 |
| 16 | Mizoram | 607 |
| 17 | Nagaland | 950 |
| 18 | Orissa | 3445 |
| 19 | Punjab | 694 |
| 20 | Rajasthan | 302 |
| 21 | Sikkim | 200 |
| 22 | Tamil Nadu | 20400 |
| 23 | Tripura | 2603 |
| 24 | Uttar Pradesh | 5000 |
| 25 | West Bengal | 17560 |
| 26 | A & N Islands | 2725 |
| 27 | Chandigarh | 100 |
| 28 | Dadra & Nagar Haveli | - |
| 29 | Daman & Diu | 223 |
| 30 | Delhi | 50 |

| Sl. No. | States/UT | Outlay |
|---|---|---|
| 31 | Lakshadweep | 5989 |
| 32 | Pondicherry | 1280 |
| 33 | Chatisgarh | 1884 |
| 34 | Uttaranchal | - |
| 35 | Jharkhand | 2075 |
| | Total | 132054 |

*Source:* Department of Animal Husbandry, Dairying and Fisheries, 2005, p. 92.

Table 5.40 shows the expenditure for major and minor fishing harbours during different plan periods

**Table 5.40**

**Expenditure for major and minor fishing harbours during different plan periods**

(Rs. In lakhs)

| *Plan period* | *Major harbours* | *Minor harbours*** |
|---|---|---|
| Third plan (1961-66) | 17.00 | - |
| Three Annual Plan (1966-67 to 1968-69) | 3.00 | 157.00 |
| Fourth plan (1969-74) | 158.00 | 485.00 |
| Fifth plan (1974-79)† | 1210.00 | 321.00 |
| Annual plan (1978-79) | 308.00 | 394.00 |
| Annual plan (1979-80) | 206.00 | 1.00 |
| Sixth plan (1980-85) | 1320.00 | 1795.00 |
| Seventh plan (1985-90) | 1684.00 | 2169.00 |
| Annual plan (1990-91) | 492.00 | 432.00 |
| Annual plan (1991-92) | 545.00 | 600.00 |
| Eighth plan (1992-97) | 4575.00 | 4903.00 |
| Ninth plan (1997-2002)* | 6144.96 | - |
| Total | 16662.96 | 11257.00 |

*includes major and minor ports

†fifth five year plan terminated in March 1978

**includes fish landing centres as well.

*Source:* Department of Animal Husbandry, Dairying and Fisheries, 2005, p. 73.

Table 5.42 again illustrates the high priority attached to survey of fishery resources, development of infrastructure for harvest and post-harvest operations in marine fisheries, development of inland fisheries and aquaculture, welfare of fishermen, etc. in the plan. This is evident from the plan allocation for 2002-07 and the annual expenditure up to 2004-05. Appendix 5.13 shows the developmental thrust and expenditure for fisheries during the various five-year plans.

## 5.7. Summary

This chapter identified and discussed the major resources for fisheries development in India. It took note of the natural, human, physical and social capital available to the industry. The natural resources (capital) available to the industry consisted of the marine ecosystem and the living resources spread over the coastal zone and the continental shelf of the country and the inland water ecosystems of the rivers, reservoirs, canals, tanks, ponds, flood plain lakes and derelict water bodies and brackish water areas.

The physical (man-made) capital investments in the industry consisted of investments in fishing vessels, fishing harbours, fish farming infrastructure, fish processing plants, fish marketing infrastructure and ancillary industries.

The human resources available to the fishery sector consisted of the active fishermen, fish farmers, workers engaged in the fish processing industry, people engaged in storage, transportation and distribution (marketing) of fish, workers engaged in ancillary industries, personnel involved in research and development (R & D) activities in the industry, personnel involved in fisheries education and training and personnel engaged in fisheries administration and governance (management).

The social / institutional capital for fisheries development in India included the traditional community organisations and the modern multiple functional organisations created by state (government) machinery and other voluntary, national and international organisations.

This chapter also noted the significant investments made by the state (public) sector for fisheries development in India during the plan periods. Notable public sector investments were made in strategic fields like infrastructure for the development of capture, culture, processing and marketing branches of the industry, research and development (R & D) in the industry, fisheries education and training, technological changes in all branches of the industry and in institution-building for fisheries development in India.

**Table 5.42**

**Profile of central plan schemes and expenditure for fisheries development in India during the tenth five year plan (2002-07)**

(Rs in lakhs)

| *Sl. No.* | *Scheme* | *Allocation for 2002-07* | *2002-03* | | *2003-04* | | *2004-05* | | *2005-06* |
|---|---|---|---|---|---|---|---|---|---|
| | | | *Budget estimate* | *Expenditure* | *Budget estimate* | *Expenditure* | *Budget estimate* | *Expenditure* | *Budget estimate* |
| 1 | Central Institute of Fisheries Nautical & Engineering Training (CIFNET) | 3885 | 206 | 207 | 61 | 127 | 206 | 275 | 859 |
| 2 | Central Institute of Coastal Engineering for Fisheries (CICEF) | 55 | 30 | 30 | 10 | 25 | 10 | 0 | 5 |
| 3 | Integrated Fisheries Project (IFP) | 560 | 191 | 55 | 71 | 50 | 83 | 60 | 114 |
| 4 | Fisheries Survey of India (FSI) | 13000 | 4073 | 2940 | 4158 | 2775 | 4201 | 3967 | 4548 |
| 5 | Fisheries training & extension | 1500 | 100 | 169 | 100 | 92 | 150 | 127 | 150 |
| 6 | Strengthening of data base and information | 2450 | 100 | 50 | 200 | 138 | 1500 | 499 | 510 |
| 7 | Development of marine fisheries, infrastructure and post-harvest operations | 25000 | 1500 | 997 | 1250 | 795 | 4600 | 5584 | 5750 |
| 8 | Development of inland fisheries and aquaculture | 13500 | 1900 | 1112 | 1600 | 1005 | 2750 | 2112 | 2500 |
| 9 | National scheme for welfare of fishermen | 12000 | 1900 | 1697 | 2000 | 1882 | 2500 | 2427 | 2500 |
| | Total | 71950 | 10000 | 7277 | 9450 | 6889 | 16000 | 15051 | 16936 |

*Source:* Department of Animal Husbandry, Dairying and Fisheries, 2005, p.94.

It is apparent from table 5.40 that a total investment of approximately Rs 166.63 crores was made for the development of major fishing harbours and Rs 112.57 crores for the development of minor fishing harbours during the period from 1961-62 to 2001-02.

Table 5.41 gives the profile of central plan schemes and expenditure for fisheries development in India during the ninth five year plan (1997-2002)

**Table 5.41**

**Profile of central plan schemes and expenditure for fisheries development in India during the ninth five year plan (1997-2002)**

| *Sl. No.* | *Scheme* | *Expenditure (Rs. in lakhs)* |
|---|---|---|
| 1 | Central Institute of Fisheries Nautical & Engineering Training (CIFNET) | 1323 |
| 2 | Central Institute of Coastal Engineering for Fisheries (CICEF) | 187 |
| 3 | Integrated Fisheries Project (IFP) | 1111 |
| 4 | Fishery Survey of India (FSI) | 7366 |
| 5 | Fisheries training and extension | 485 |
| 6 | Development of inland fisheries statistics | 441 |
| 7 | Acquisition of dredger with Japanese assistance | 209 |
| 8 | Central Project Unit for World Bank assisted project for shrimp and fish culture | 883 |
| 9 | Fishing harbours at major and minor ports | 6144 |
| 10 | Development of freshwater aquaculture | 5522 |
| 11 | Integrated brackish water fish farm development | 787 |
| 12 | Development of coastal marine fisheries | 5400 |
| 13 | Welfare of fishermen | 8978 |
| 14 | Assistance for strengthening inland fish marketing | 339 |
| 15 | Assistance to Coast Guard | 153 |
| 16 | Development of aquaculture in hilly regions | 400 |
| 17 | Development of inland capture fisheries resources | 87 |
| | Total | 39815 |

*Source:* Department of Animal Husbandry, Dairying and Fisheries, 2005, p. 93.

Table 5.41 shows the high priority attached to several schemes like welfare of fishermen, survey of fishery resources, fishing harbour development, development of freshwater aquaculture, and development of coastal marine fisheries.

Table 5.42 presents the profile of central plan schemes for fisheries development during the tenth plan.

# FISHERIES DEVELOPMENT IN INDIA

# FISHERIES DEVELOPMENT IN INDIA

## The Political Economy of Unsustainable Development

(In Two Volumes)

(Volume–2)

Dr. Ramakrishnan Korakandy

PUBLICATIONS

KALPAZ PUBLICATIONS

DELHI-110052

Fisheries Development in India : The Political Economy of Unsustainable Development

Rs. 1800 (Set)



ISBN: 81-7835-632-5 (Set)
ISBN: 81-7835-634-1 (Vol. 2)



Published in 2008 in India by
Kalpaz Publications
C-30, Satyawati Nagar,
Delhi-110052
E-mail: kalpaz@hotmail.com
Phone : 9212729499

*Laser type setting by* Quick Media, Delhi
*Printed at* Vishal Kaushik Printers, Delhi

# DEDICATION

This book is dedicated to the loving memory of the late Professor N.K. Velankar, who was Consultant to establish the School of Industrial Fisheries during 1976-78, the late Professor (Dr.) P.G.K. Panikkar, former Director, Centre for Development Studies, Thiruvananthapuram, and Padmasree Professor (Dr.) M.V. Pylee, former Vice-Chancellor, Cochin University of Science and Technology, for their kind gesture in giving me an academic chair at the School of Industrial Fisheries in 1978 which sustained me all these years.

# CONTENTS

# LIST OF TABLES

# LIST OF APPENDICES

# 6

# FISHERIES DEVELOPMENT IN INDIA— SUSTAINABILITY ISSUES AND INDICATORS

## 6.1. Introduction

Planning for sustainable development of fisheries in India requires a clear understanding of the sustainability issues and a realistic measurement of the extent of unsustainability prevailing in the industry. This in other words means the need to identify the diverse threats to the sustainability of the industry and a meaningful estimate of unsustainability characteristics. The unsustainability situation in the industry can be understood with the help of indicators or indices which show the magnitude of the problem. As noted by the FAO, "indicators assist in the process of assessing the performance of fisheries policies and management at global, regional, national and sub-national levels. They provide a readily understood tool for describing the state of fisheries resources and fisheries activity and for assessing trends regarding sustainable development objectives. In the process of measuring progress towards sustainable development, a set of indicators should also stimulate action to achieve sustainable development" (FAO, 1999b, p.12).

The present chapter seeks to present the sustainability issues of Indian fisheries with the help of suitable indicators of (un)sustainability. The sustainability issues represent the negative impacts (externalities) of development in the fisheries sector as well as other sectors of the economy. They work to impede the continued operation of the industry in the future. The sustainability issues are discussed under five main categories, focusing on the ecological, economic, social/institutional, technological and other versions (dimensions) of unsustainable development. This is in tune with the criteria and indicators of sustainable development of fisheries as formulated by the FAO and other sources (ibid, p.17). The different dimensions and criteria (indictors) of sustainable development of fisheries as put forward by the FAO are presented in appendix 6.1. A final section in this chapter gives the summary of points discussed in the various sections.

### 6.2. Ecological Issues

As pointed by the FAO, "an ecosystem based view of sustainable development focuses on maintenance of the stability and resilience of the ecosystem. Sustainable development recognises the interdependencies of human economies with their environment and highlights the need for scientific understanding of ecosystem functioning and change" (ibid. p. 9). The main ecological issues discussed in this section are: (1) biological overfishing, (2) environmental pollution, (3) habitat destruction, (4) biodiversity loss, and (5) climate change.

#### 6.2.1. Biological Overfishing

This corresponds to a situation where more biomass weight of fish is taken from a population than that is added by way of recruitment and growth of individual fishes in the stock. This indicates fishing beyond the so-called MSY levels of catch. The two components of biological overfishing are, as noted by Pauly, 'growth overfishing' and 'recruitment overfishing', the first referring to such levels and kind of fishing effort which does not allow individual fishes to reach the stage of maturity and first breeding and the second referring to reductions in recruitment due to fishery related and other factors (Clark, 1996, p. 313). How far these phenomena are working in Indian fisheries and their impact on sustainability are not quite well understood. However, indicative information may be traced to throw some light on the sustainability situation.

The possibility of biological overfishing in the coastal waters of Kerala for small pelagic fishes in the late 1950s and 1960s was indicated by the Expert Committee on Marine Fisheries of Kerala, when it noted that "there is some reason to believe that the reduction in effort at around 35 to 45 million man-hours in the pre-1969 period was prompted by a realisation by the traditional fishermen that they have overfished the resources during the 1956-59 period with much more effort ...and got in to problems of diminishing returns" (Expert Committee, 1985, p. 210).

Similar possibility of overfishing in the inshore waters of Kerala had been reported by the Expert Committee on Marine Fisheries Management in Kerala, appointed by the Government of Kerala in 1989. It noted "if size overfishing is allowed beyond limits, such as catching all before they reach the size at first maturity so as not to give them a chance to spawn at least once, then recruitment over fishing will set in and there will not be a fishery resource worth mentioning for immediate exploitation" (Nair, 1989, p. 4).

Making an appraisal of the exploited marine fishery resources of India, Srinath noted that "the marine fisheries sector of India has witnessed a phenomenal growth during the last five decades both quantitatively and qualitatively. This phenomenal growth also brought in imbalances in the exploitation across the regions and among the resources. Besides, with production levels for most of the commercially important resources showing signs of approaching saturation levels, intersectoral conflicts increased due to competition to exploit the common resource ..." (Srinath, 2003, p.1).

A closer look at the estimated potential yields, current production and the historical maximum landings of the commercially important species/groups of marine fishes would indicate the possibility of biological overfishing taking place or approaching it.

Table 6.1 gives the estimated potential yield, current yield and maximum landings of commercially important pelagic resources of India.

**Table 6.1**

**Estimated potential yield, current yield and maximum landings of commercially important pelagic resources of India**

(in '000 tonnes)

| *Resources* | *Potential yield (2000)** | *Current yield (2001)* | *Maximum landings *** |
|---|---|---|---|
| Oil sardine | 295 | 268 | 367 (2000) |
| Other sardines | 101 | 76 | 128 (1995) |
| White baits | 142 | 45 | 101 (1988) |
| Other clupeids | 136 | 144 | 195 (1998) |
| Bombay-duck | 116 | 86 | 138 (1981) |
| Ribbon fishes | 194 | 176 | 183 (2001) |
| Carangids | 238 | 118 | 197 (1995) |
| Indian mackerel | 295 | 90 | 291 (1989) |
| Seer fishes | 62 | 43 | 55 (1998) |
| Tunas | 65 | 48 | 52 (1990) |
| Barracudas | 21 | 19 | 22 (1998) |

*as revalidated by the Working Group for Revalidating the Potential of Fishery Resources in the EEZ of India in 2000.

**figures in parentheses denote the year of maximum landings.

*Source:* Srinath and Balan, 2003, p.287.

The fact that the maximum yield of several species have exceeded the potential yield, particularly in recent years give credence to the fear of biological overfishing taking place in the sector. This will be further evident from the fact that the current yield in many cases do not leave a biological minimum balance of 50 per cent of the potential yield for reproduction as prescribed by global agencies (FAO, 1996a, p.17).

The same trend is visible in the case of demersal fisheries. Table 6.2 shows the estimated potential yield, current yield and maximum landings of commercially important demersal resources of India.

**Table 6.2**

**Estimated potential yield, current yield and maximum landings of commercially important demersal resources of India**

(in '000 tonnes)

| *Resources* | *Potential yield (2000)** | *Current yield (2001)* | *Maximum landings*** |
|---|---|---|---|
| Elasmobranchs | 72 | - | |
| Sharks | 45 | 35 | 48 (2000) |
| Skates | 4 | 2 | 4 (1983) |
| Rays | 23 | 20 | 27(1997) |
| Eels | 9 | 8 | 13(1977) |
| Cat fishes | 51 | 50 | 68(1982) |
| Lizard fishes | 28 | 24 | 34(1995) |
| Perches | 227 | 203 | - |
| Rock cods | 16 | 26 | 26 (2001) |
| Red snapper | 11 | 4 | 6 (1999) |
| Pig face bream | 9 | 13 | 14 (1997) |
| Thread fin bream | 128 | 114 | 117 (2000) |
| Other perches | 63 | 46 | 57 (2000) |
| Goat fishes | 20 | 10 | 33 (1991) |
| Thread fins | 9 | 7 | 11 (1995) |
| Croakers | 273 | 121 | 200 (1998) |
| Silver bellies | 67 | 52 | 92 (1983) |
| Big jawed jumper | 17 | 5 | 25 (1985) |
| Pomfrets | 46 | 39 | 54 (1983) |
| Silver pomfret | 30 | 25 | 42 (1983) |
| Chinese pomfret | 1 | 1 | 1 (2001) |
| Black pomfret | 15 | 13 | 20 (1995) |
| Flat fishes | 47 | 39 | 63 (1992) |

* As revalidated by the Working Group for Revalidating the Potential of Fishery Resources in the EEZ of India in 2000

**Figures in parentheses denote the year of maximum landings.

*Source:* Srinath and Balan, 2003, p.288.

What is apparent from table 6.2 is the fact that the current yield is below the potential yield as well as maximum landings in the case of several species, especially sharks, skates, rays, threadfin breams, other perches, croakers, etc. It is indicative of the possibility of the fishery facing biological overfishing over a period of time which led to the fall in their current yield.

The possibility of biological overfishing is indicated in the case of crustacean and molluscan fisheries as well. Table 6.3 presents the estimated potential yield, current yield and maximum landings of commercially important crustcean and molluscan resources of India.

**Table 6.3**

**Estimated potential yield, current yield and maximum landings of commercially important crustacean resources of India**

(in '000 tonnes)

| *Resources* | *Potential yield (2000)** | *Current yield (2001)* | *Maximum landings*** |
|---|---|---|---|
| Penaeid prawns | 194 | 177 | 225 (1994) |
| Non-Penaeid prawns | 139 | 145 | 174 (1998) |
| Crabs | 32 | 30 | 48 (2000) |
| Lobsters | 4 | 1.4 | 4.1 (1985) |
| Stomatopods | 120 | 35 | 100 (1987) |
| Bivalves | 202 | marginal | 3 (1990) |
| Gastropods | 23 | marginal | 3 (1996) |
| Cephalopods | 101 | 101 | 117 (1995) |

*As revalidated by the Working Group for Revalidating the Potential of Fishery Resources in the EEZ of India in 2000.

**Figures in parentheses denote the year of maximum landings.

*Source:* Srinath and Balan, 2003, p.288-289.

As is clear from table 6.3, the fall in the current yield after realising higher landings in the case of penaeid prawns, non-penaeid prawns, crabs, lobsters and cephalopods indicates the possibility of their stock slumping due to high pressure in the limited fishing zones.

The possibility of 'growth overfishing' and 'recruitment overfishing' taking place in the case of several species in the Indian waters is indicated as in most tropical, non-selective, fishing operations. Writing on the sardine fisheries of India, Pillai, *et al.* noted: "In the ring-seines operated along the Kerala coast, a significant portion of the catch during the May-July period is composed of young fishes of size 50-90 mm which occur along with spawners in the inshore fishing grounds. The estimated landings of young fish (<150 mm) in this gear during May-July 2000 period along the Kerala coast was 11,138 tonnes which formed nearly 38 per cent (in weight) of the total sardine catch of the period, the rest being constituted mainly by 'virgin' spawners ...Off Mangalore along the Karnataka coast, bull- trawlers operated during September-November period have been reported to land young sardines of 45-77 mm size during the nineties. Considerable quantities of spawners also occur in purse-seine catches here during April-June which could have an adverse effect on the fishery in the ensuing season" (Pillai, *et al.,* 2003, p.21).

Referring to the biological overfishing of seer fishes, Muthiah, *et al.* noted: "The king seer is exposed to higher fishing pressure along both coasts of India by all gears except by gill net in Gujarat ... The spotted seer is exposed to higher fishing pressure by trawl at Mangalore and Kakinada and by gillnets at Chennai and Kakinada. The stock size of king seer is considerably reduced over a period of time due to continuous increase in exploitation by different gears and that of spotted seer is also reduced but not as critical as the king seer.

Gillnets and multi-day trawls at present heavily exploit seer fish stocks and there is need to reduce the effort of these gears. Since the capital investment of these units is on the higher side, it is natural that the fishermen target quality finfishes and shellfishes for easy and quick returns. Therefore, they would be quite unmindful to scale down the effort in the near future unless harsh measures are adopted. The other alternative is to increase the minimum size at first capture by increasing the mesh size. Presently, the gillnets of 65-170 mm exploit king seer and spotted seer below the optimum size and minimum size at first maturity ...

The gillnets of smaller mesh types like 'podivalai' (70-100 mm) along the Tuticorin coast and the trawlers along both the coasts land exclusively small sized king seer resulting in recruitment overfishing, which is detrimental to the recoupment of the stock and therefore should be discouraged" (Muttiah, *et al.,* 2003, p.49).

Highlighting the position with regard to tuna resources of the EEZ of India, Pillai and Gopakumar observed: "Based on the population parameters and stock estimates, the coastal tunas have been found to be exploited at or above the optimum levels. Along the coastal waters, the exploitation rate of *E. affinis* vary in different states (Kerala 0.86; Karnataka 0.86; Gujarat 0.77 and Tamil Nadu 0.75) whereas the optimum exploitation rate of *E. affinis* was estimated at 0.4 only. This indicates that the exploitation of this species in the current fishing grounds is relatively high. The exploitation rates of *A. thazard, T. tonggol* and *T. albacore* were 0.72, 0.35 and 0.81 respectively whereas the otimum exploitation rates were at 0.40, 0.42 and 0.37 indicating that there is further scope for increasing the exploitation of *T. tonggol* while the other species are exploited relatively at high rates in recent years in the coastal waters" (Pillai and Gopakumar, 2003, p.57).

These authors, however, remarked that the "stock estimates made on tunas have several limitations. Except for the pole and line fishing at Lakshadweep, there is no aimed fishery for tunas in the coastal seas along the mainland. The gears in which tunas (are) caught are not operated exclusively for tunas. The highly migratory and straddling nature of tunas and the occurrence of multiple fisheries which are seasonal and very short at different localities make it difficult to arrive at realistic conclusions on their stock positions. Hence any decline in the catch rate with time and size cannot be attributed unambiguously to fishing pressure as opposed to migration" (ibid, p.57).

Referring to the 'growth overfishing' prevailing in the mackerel fisheries of India, Yohannan and Sivadas noted: "The important factor that limits the yield from the mackerel stock is the large scale exploitation of the juveniles along the west coast. Fishes below the size of 15 cm form almost 42 per cent of the catch from the west coast. Increasing the size at first capture from 140 mm to 160 mm by controlling exploitation during the recruitment or increasing the mesh size of the large seines to a minimum of 35 mm can solve both these problems. The peak recruitment to the mackerel population of the west coast takes place during July-September period. The non-selective large seines operated during the period heavily exploit the early juveniles" (Yohannan and Sivadas, 2003, p.64).

Reporting on the carangid fisheries of the country, Kasim noted that "out of the eleven species studied, only five are over fished and that too in a restricted area" (Kasim, 2003, p.75). The species overfished are *Megalaspis cordyla* at Veraval and south west coast, *Decapterus russelli* in the east coast and Kakinada in particular, *Alepes kalla* in south west coast and *Alepes djedaba* and *Atule mate* in Kerala (ibid. p.72).

Highlighting on the levels of exploitation of the ribbon fishes of India, Radhakrishnan Nair and Prakasan observed: "The exploitation rates (E) indicated that the stock was being slightly overfished. The occurrence of large quantities of juveniles and pre-adults in the landings along the east coast also supports this view ... the export market has paved the way for targeted fishing of this resource recently leading to certain degree of overexploitation in major centres, especially along the east coast" (Radhakrishnan Nair and Prakasan, 2003, p.86).

Referring to the nature of exploitation in the Bombay-duck fishery, Kurian noted: "The Bombay-duck has been exploited with a mixture of success and failure in the past. Large scale landings of indeterminate and immature fish have been a source of concern since long" (Kurian, 2003, p.91).

The probability of biological over fishing was noted in the case of elasmobranchs (sharks, skates and rays) in Kerala and Karnataka, where the catch rates were considerably higher than the MSY estimates. The average catch of these species in the two states in recent years stood at 6034 tonnes and 1940 tonnes while their estimated MSY stood at 4239 tonnes and 1429 tonnes respectively indicating biological overfishing (Raja and Joshi, 2003, p.100).

Referring to the exploitation of cat fishes, Menon noted: "The region-wise production data clearly show that the higher input of mechanisation (trawling and purse-seining) was responsible for sudden increase in landings in 1970-85 periods. Simultlaneously this fishing has also caused damages to shoaling species like *T. tenuispinis* and *T. dussumieri* by way of growth over fishing (trawl net impact) and recruitment over fishing (purse-seine impact). As the spawning stock migrations are pronounced in the south west region, the effect of over fishing is felt at an alarming magnitude mainly in this area" (Menon, 2003, p.117).

Writing on the state of the pomfret fisheries of India, Sivakami, *et al.* noted that "pomfrets are one of the most delicious food fish available along the Indian coast...This endearing resource caught in trawl, gillnet and *dol* net of late is under threat of overexploitation and hence warrants measures of conservation" (Sivakami, *et al.,* 2003, p.147). Heavy fishing pressure is reported in Kerala, Karnataka and Gujarat (ibid, p.152).

Highlighting the possibility of overexploitation in the case of goat fishes, Vivekanandan, *et al.* noted: "Stock estimates for *U. taeniopterus* off Chennai for the years 1997-2000 indicated a total stock of 1,215 tonnes and MSY of 952 tonnes against the yield of 711 tonnes. The exploitation rate was 0.48. Stock estimates for *U. Vittatus* off Visakhapatnam for the years 1994-99 indicted very high exploitation rate of 0.79, suggesting overexploitation of the stock" (Vivekanandan, *et al.*, 2003, p.163).

Explaining the state of exploitation of flatfishes, Vivekanandan, *et al.* wrote: "Stock assessment studies indicate that the exploitation rate is high (0.7) for the Malabar sole off Calicut and Mangalore. Increase in effort may yield better catches but the increase in the cost of fishing may not fetch the required quantum of additional catch" (Vivekanandan, *et al.*, 2003, p.169).

Indicating the possibility of biological overfishing of white fish, *Lactarius lactarius,* Vivekanandan, *et al.,* noted: "The length at first maturity of the species is 135 mm. The mean length in the trawl fishery (138 mm off Mangalore during 1998-99) is very close to the length at first maturity, suggesting exploitation of large number of juveniles. In terms of number, 34.6 per cent of the individuals in the fishery at Mangalore were juveniles during 2000-01. In terms of biomass, the juveniles contributed 23 per cent to the total landings of the white fish" (Vivekanandan, *et al.,* 2003, p.173).

Describing the state of deep sea prawn fishing in Kerala and its impact on stock, Rajan *et al.* noted: "The deep sea prawn stock cannot withstand more fishing pressure in future and yield the same returns as registered in the recent operations and the catch rate is bound to come down in the ensuing fishing season. The deep sea prawn fishery was characterised by absence of juvenile populations and heavy dominance of berried, impregnated or mature females in almost all species ...it will be prudent on the part of the industry not to enhance the fishing pressure on this fragile stock ..." (Rajan, *et al.,* 2001, p.11).

Writing on the state of exploitation of penaeid prawn resources of India, Nandakumar and Maheswarudu stated: "The study showed that average annual yield of all commercial species such as *P. indicus, P. semisulcatus, M. dobsoni, M. monoceros,* and *P. stylifera* had reached MSY. The yield per recruit analysis further confirmed that there may not be any significant improvement in the yield with increase in fishing effort" (Nandakumar and Maheswarudu, 2003, p.180).

Highlighting the state of overfishing for lobsters, Radhkrishnan and Manisseri wrote: "On the north west, available scientific information clearly indicates that the resources of the spiny lobster *P. polyphagus* and the sand lobster *T. orientalis* are overexploited. The current landings of lobsters in India constitutes only 58 per cent of the peak catch once obtained in 1985 and consists of smaller specimens, which bring lesser value. In Mumbai, average landings during 1996-2000 has come down by 57 per cent compared to production during 1986-90. The situation is similar at Veraval and other major fishing centers along the south west and south east coasts. At Tuticorin, nearly 43 per cent of the lobster landings are by trawlers and a situation similar to the north east prevails here also ...With the beginning of the live lobster exports, exploitation of juveniles and under sized lobsters has been on the increase. The overseas demand is higher for smaller sizes. India exports undersized lobsters also while other countries have enforced strict regulations on size of these shellfishes fished and exported. This situation has affected the lobster resources of the country to a great extent" (Radhakrishnan and Manisseri, 2003, p.201).

Referring to the overexploitation of marine bivalves, Kripa and Appukuttan noted: "indiscriminate exploitation of seed clams is prevalent in Kerala and Andhra Pradesh. In Vembanad lake, the black clam and in Ashtamudi lake, *P. malabarica*, *V. cyprinoides* and *M. casta* seed clams targeted for shell industry are fished and they form 40 to 50 per cent of the total landings. In Kakinada bay, the intensity of blood clam fishery has increased and in 1991 small sized clams formed 43.4 per cent of the total landings. In the mussel fishery of Kerala, destruction of seed mussel has been observed as the fishers discard the seed mussel after they are fished from the natural bed" (Kripa and Appukuttan, 2003, p.216).

It is apparent from the above review and excerpts from CMFRI scientific studies that nearly 17 of the major exploited marine fishery resources of the country are facing threat of biological overfishing. No serious threat of biological over fishing was reported in the case of 13 other species of fishes reviewed by CMFRI during 2003 (Modayil and Jayaprkash ,2003).

Writing on the loss of marine turtles in India, Rajagopalan and Vijayakumaran noted:

> "Large scale mortalities (as high as 50,000 in the past five years), of Olive Ridleys by drowning in trawl nets on Orissa coast have

been reported by *Operation Kachhappa*. Incidental capture of turtles in the trawl nets are likely elsewhere also but certainly not in such magnitude as in Orissa coast, where world's second largest rookery for Olive Ridley is located". *Operation Kachhappa* is a collaborative effort of the Orissa Forest Department and two NGOs, viz. Wildlife Protection Society of India, New Delhi and Wildlife Society of Orissa, Cuttack. (Rajagopalan and Vijayakumaran, 2001, p.15).

The magnitude of the overfishing problem (both growth overfishing and recruitment overfishing) in the marine fisheries of India was indicated by Luther and Sastry as well. They observed:

> "It is now common knowledge that the average life span of the majority of the species comprising the tropical marine fisheries resources is short being around 2-3 years. The fisheries for most of our resources are supported to a large extent by juvenile fish whose average life span is about one year. This means that the majority of individuals born at a time do not have the chance to spawn at least once in their lifetime. If this situation is allowed to go beyond a limit, the stock position is bound to go down leading to diminishing returns. This decreasing trend in the stock may be vitiated further if the spawners too are exposed to higher fishing pressure" (Luther and Sastry, 1993, p.1).

These authors also specified the seasons when juveniles formed the bulk of the catches of selected centres as follows: "The available information shows that juveniles form dominant catches during September-January and May off Veraval; November-December off Bombay; September-December and April off Karwar; January and October off Mangalore; September-November off Calicut; June-September off Cochin; July-November off Vizhinjam; April-September off Tuticorin; May-June and October off Mandapam; July-October off Kakinada and February and September off Visakhapatnam" (ibid. p.2).

Luther and Sastry further stated that the "present study has indicated that fisheries for some of the major fishery resources at some centres are largely supported by juvenile fish. They are mentioned in the order of their magnitude as well as the localities where such a situation has existed in the recent past; *Caranx kalla* off Calicut; *Sardinella fimbriata* at Karwar, *Megalaspis cordyla* at Calicut; *Eupleurogramnius muticus* at Kakinada, *Tachysurus thalassinus* at Visakhapatnam, *Harpadon nehereus* at Veraval and Bombay, *S. fimbriata* at Vizhinjam, *Oratosquilla nepa* at Mangalore-Malpe, *Trichiurus lepturus* at Kakinada, *Metapenaeus affinis* at Cochin, *Leiognathus bindus* at Kakinada, *Rastrelliger kanagurta* at Cochin, *S. gibbosa* and *S. albella* at Mandapam, *S. Longiceps* at Karwar, *Rastrelliger kanagurta* in Andamans, *Leiognathus jonesi* and *T. Lepturus* at Mandapam, *S. longiceps* at Calicut and *Nemipterus japonicus* at Cochin. The fact that the greatest bulk of the landings of *Lactarius lactarius* landed at Visakhapatnam in the past comprised juveniles and that the fish itself now being rare in the same locality clearly indicates the damage done to the resource of the species in the past. This should sound a note of caution to reduce fishing pressure on the juveniles so as to allow them to grow and reach at least the size at first maturity. In respect of the young fish landing also, *Lactarius lactarius* at Visakhapatnam received the highest rank, followed by *Megalaspsis cordyla* at Calicut, *Trichiurus lepturus* at Vizhinjam, *leiognathus bindus* at Calicut, *Rastrelliger kanagurta* in Andamans, *Harpodon nehereus* at Veraval, *Oratosquilla nepa* at Mangalore and *Sardinella gibbosa* at Mandapam" (ibid. p.8).

Increased exploitation of juvenile fish population by bull-trawlers during the early post-monsoon fishing season along the South Kanara Coast in Karnataka in 1992 was reported by Rohit, *et al.* They pointed out that "one of the striking features of the bull-trawl fishery of the season was the incidence of several commercially important fishes. Out of the total catch of 800.7 tonnes, juvenile fishes formed 184.5 tonnes, constituting 23 per cent of the total catch" (Rohit, *et al.,* 1993, p.9).

Table 6.4 conveys the details of estimated catch, length range, modal size groups, percentage contribution of juveniles and their normal length distribution in the commercial fishery of Mangalore and Malpe.

Table 6.4 shows that among the different groups of juvenile fishes landed, those belonging to *Chorinemus spp., Decapterus spp., Caranx kalla, Sardinella longiceps.* and *Leiognathus spp.,* formed the bulk. Most notable is the fact that the entire catch of *Chorinemus spp., S. longiceps, Tachysurus thalasimus, T. tenuispinus* and seer fish was constituted by juveniles. The relative share in other species varied between10 to 20 per cent. It is also noteworthy that the size groups of juveniles of all species landed were smaller compared to the normal size groups of commercial landings of these species.

**Table 6.4**

**Estimated catch, length range, modal size groups, percentage contribution of juveniles and their normal length distribution in the commercial fishery of the bull-trawlers during September-November 1992 at Mangalore and Malpe**

| *Species* | *Catch* (Kg.) | *Length range* (mm) | *Modal size* (mm) | *Percentage of juveniles* (%) | *Normal length distribution in commercial fishery* (mm) |
|---|---|---|---|---|---|
| *Chorinemus spp.* | 61247 | 115-200 | 145-155 | 100 | 300-400 |
| *Sardinella longiceps* | 11636 | 45-75 | 55 | 100 | 130-160 |
| *Tachysurus thalasimus* | 4679 | 105-190 | 120 | 100 | 300-500 |
| *T. tenuispinus* | 4679 | 155-195 | - | 100 | 220-250 |
| Seer fish | 3654 | 200-300 | - | 100 | 750-1000 |
| *Decapterus spp.* | 43113 | 95-120 | 105 | 20 | 170-200 |
| *Caranx Kalla* | 25774 | 40-65 | - | 20 | 125-145 |
| *Leiognathus* | 15189 | 40-60 | - | 20 | 70-100 |
| *Megalaspis cordyla* | 597 | 150-180 | - | 10 | 200-300 |
| Sciaenids | 4533 | 55-75 | - | 10 | 150-200 |
| Soles | 1698 | 40-50 | - | 10 | 130-150 |
| Pomfrets | 2538 | 80-120 | - | 10 | 170-200 |
| *Thryssa sp.* | 5143 | 80-100 | - | 10 | 150-180 |

*Source:* Rohit, *et al.*, 1993, p.11.

Srinath and Pillai further reported that "from the resource monitoring programmes of CMFRI, it is observed that there is a general decline in resource availability as evidenced by decline in catches and catch rates and incidence of a large proportion of juveniles and young fish in the landings and decrease in the average length at capture. It is also reported that there is a considerable volume of discards and non-target resources by the multi-day trawlers. Stock assessment studies have also revealed that most of the stocks are over fished, especially the demersal stocks mainly exploited by the mechanised sector. The stocks of shrimps in regions of exploitation along the entire Indian coast, Bombay duck and pomfrets along Maharashtra and Gujarat, sharks, catfishes, mackerel, croakers, pomfrets, squids and cuttlefish in the south west and south east are heavily exploited and their catches and catch rates are fast declining. Studies have also revealed that there is an increasing tendency to fish down the marine food web, which is threatening the resource balance in the marine food chain. Excessive trawling was also found to adversely affect the biodiversity and ecosystem productivity which would negatively impact the fish production" (Srinath and Pillai, 2006, p.17).

Overexploitation and decline in the catches of inland fisheries have been reported by Sugunan and Sinha. Referring to the situation in the Ganga river system, Sugunan and Sinha noted: "The catch statistics over the years indicate some disturbing trends in the riverine fisheries, especially the Ganga. The biologically and economically desirable species have started giving way to the low value species, exhibiting an alarming swing in the population structure of the Gangetic carps. A sharp decline in fish production from five stretches of the Ganga, viz. Kanpur, Allahabad, Buxar, Patna and Bhagalpur is testimony to the deleterious effects of environmental changes on fish output" (Sugunan and Sinha, 2001, p.46).

Table 6.5 shows the trend in the catch and catch composition of Ganges at Allahabad, Patna and Bhaglpur.

**Table 6.5**

**Trend in the catch and catch-composition of Ganges at Allahabad, Patna and Bhgalpore**

(In tonnes)

| *Centre Catch* | *1958-59 to 1965-66 (average)* | *%* | *1973-74 to 1985-86 (average)* | *%* | *1989-90 to 1994-95 (average)* | *%* | *1996-97* | *%* |
|---|---|---|---|---|---|---|---|---|
| **Allahabad** | | | | | | | | |
| Major carps | 91.35 | 44.5 | 40.44 | 28.7 | 11.04 | 11.5 | 4.94 | 8.3 |
| Catfish | 46.66 | 22.7 | 30.82 | 21.9 | 21.50 | 22.5 | 14.28 | 24.1 |
| Hilsa | 19.94 | 9.7 | 0.87 | 0.6 | 0.92 | 1.0 | 2.47 | 4.2 |
| Miscellaneous | 47.48 | 23.1 | 68.79 | 48.8 | 62.10 | 65.0 | 37.61 | 63.4 |
| Total | 205.43 | 100 | 140.92 | 100 | 95.56 | 100 | 59.30 | 100 |
| **Bhagalpur** | | | | | | | | |
| Major carps | 16.62 | 18.2 | 10.06* | 10.8 | - | - | 7.31 | 20.4 |
| Catfish | 19.43 | 21.4 | 25.21* | 27.1 | - | - | 14.91 | 41.7 |
| Hilsa | 4.08 | 4.5 | 0.87* | 0.9 | - | - | 0.38 | 1.1 |
| Miscellaneous | 50.82 | 55.9 | 56.96* | 61.2 | - | - | 13.20 | 36.8 |
| Total | 90.95 | 100 | 93.10* | 100 | - | - | 35.80 | 100 |
| **Patna** | - | - | 57.73** | 100 | 37.70*** | 100 | 18.00 | 100 |

* for the period 1973-74 to 1983-84

** for the period 1986-89

*** for the period 1990-93

*Source:* Sugunan and Sinha, 2001, p.47

Table 6.5 reveals that the average total catch from Allahabad, which was 205 tonnes between1958-59 and 1965-66 has decreased to 59 tonnes during 1996-97. The catch of major carps collapsed from 91.35 tonnes to 4.94 tonnes during the same period. The share of major carps fell from 44.5 per cent to 8.3 per cent during this period. Similar changes in quantity and variety were noted in the catches of Bhagalpur and Patna.

Another glaring feature of the catch structure, which is indicative of overfishing, as noted by Sugunan and Sinha is "the increasing domination of lower age groups in the commercial catches. During the 1960s, two year age groups in respect of *Cirrhinus mrigala*, two – three year in respect of *Catla catla* and three year in respect of *Labeo rohita* dominated the fishery. The once lucrative hilsa fishery above the Farraka barrage collapsed due to the obstruction of the fish's migratory path" (ibid. p.47).

The likelihood of biological overfishing in the Brahmaputra is indicated from the declining catch rates (kg/day) of major carps and other species from the river. Table 6.6 gives the details of catch rates and catch structure in Brahmaputra during 1970s and 1999s.

Table 6.6 shows that the average catch/day of most groups decreased drastically during 1996-98 in comparison with the catches of 1973-79. The table further reveals the fall in the relative share of all species, except feather backs and other miscellaneous groups. There was a 30 per cent fall in the catches of all groups put together. Sugunan and Sinha also reported a large scale destruction of brood fishes and juveniles in the Brahmaputra (ibid. p.47).

**Table 6.6**

**Details of catch rate and catch-structure in Brahmaputra during 1970s and 1990s**

| *Group* | *1973-79 average catch (kg/day)* | *Percentage of total* | *1996-98 average catch (kg/day)* | *Percentage of total* | *Change (%)* |
|---|---|---|---|---|---|
| Major carps | 38.2 | 19.4 | 18.7 | 13.6 | –51 |
| Minor carps | 27.8 | 14.1 | 9.6 | 7.0 | –65 |
| Catfishes | 46.8 | 23.8 | 19.5 | 14.2 | –58 |
| Feather backs | 7.1 | 3.6 | 8.0 | 5.8 | 13 |
| Hilsa | 22.1 | 11.2 | 2.9 | 2.1 | –87 |
| Prawn | 9.8 | 5.0 | 2.9 | 2.1 | –70 |
| Other (miscellaneous) | 45.1 | 22.9 | 75.8 | 55.2 | 68 |
| Total | 196.9 | 100 | 137.3 | 100 | –30 |

*Source:* Sugunan and Sinha, 2001, p.48.

The issue of overfishing in the Chilka lake has been highlighted by Jhingran when he wrote "the problem of overfishing and depletion of Chilka stocks will assume ominous overtones if their intensive exploitation is undertaken in coastal waters.

Fishes like *H. ilisha*, which depend on the river for breeding, however, face the problem of depletion in a more ominous manner under conditions where recruitment is related to stock density. For these fishes, which move into and return from rivers through estuaries/lagoons, fishing intensity beyond certain level at estuaries/lagoons may prove critical. This is very much the case in regard to Chilka Hilsa" (Jhingran, 1991, p.256).

Indicating the over fishing problem in the cold water fisheries of India, Singh and Lakra observed: "In hill streams, the present trend of decline of coldwater fish is primarily due to overexploitation, and other anthropogenic factors in the upper catchment areas of the streams..." (Singh and Lakra, 2000, p.22).

### 6.2.2. Environmental Pollution

Environmental pollution acting as a major threat to the sustainability of global fisheries has been pointed out in chapter four. Referring to the issue of coastal pollution, Clark reported quoting from the UN report of 1990 that the "major causes of immediate concern" in the global marine environment upon entering the decade of the 1990s were "coastal development and the attendant destruction of habitat, eutrophication, microbial contamination of seafood and beaches, fouling of the seas by plastic litter, progressive build up of chlorinated hydrocarbons, especially in the tropics and sub tropics, and accumulation of tar on beaches" (Clark, 1996, p.385).

Clarifying the nature of this pollution further, Clark noted that being at "sea level elevation, the coast is the eventual receiving basin for all land run off water and the wastes it carries. Coastally discharging rivers gather and carry large amounts of pollutants to the coast with their rampaging flood waters ... Consequently, a large share of the world's pollution ends up in coastal lagoons, estuaries, wetlands, submerged grass beds, and coral reefs ... contaminants are transported from land to sea by rivers, direct run off, or point discharges. They are partly retained in the water and sediments of estuaries, bays, beaches or open coastal waters, and partly transported through these boundary areas to the open ocean. The disposal of domestic sewage and industrial effluents from population and industrial centers located along the coastlines extends coastal pollution beyond the estuaries. Moreover, coastal waters are not only, more polluted than the open ocean, they also offer significantly more opportunities for exposure through contamination of the world's most important fisheries and recreation areas ..." (ibid. p.383).

Though no national or regional study on the extent of damage caused to fisheries by environmental pollution (marine or inland) is available at present, indicative observations have been made by many sources at various points of time. Writing on the state of coastal pollution in Kerala in 1985, the Expert Committee on Marine Fisheries in Kerala noted that "with increasing industrialisation, urbanisation and exploitation of natural resources, there is not only increasing deterioration of environmental quality and depletion of exploitable resources, but also human health hazards through consumption of contaminated food. Environmental pollution or alterations in Kerala that affect harvestable fisheries resources from the sea, rivers and estuaries including the backwaters and lagoons owe largely to industrial effluents, domestic sewage, pesticides and also land reclamation" (Expert Committee, 1985, p.340).

The Committee also observed that "in Kerala there are about 175 large and medium scale industries discharging such effluents. There are also more than 8000 small-scale industrial units out of which at least 2000 contribute to the pollution load. It is estimated that 6.5 lakh $m^3$ of trade effluents are being dumped into the rivers and tidal waters every day. Of this, 45 per cent of the wastes are from chemical industries containing chemical pollutants and another 45 per cent from industries with organic pollutants. The balance represent wastes from engineering industries and other categories" (ibid. p.340).

Highlighting on the state of water pollution of the rivers of the state, the Expert Committee noted that "there are 44 rivers in the state of which 41 are west-flowing and three east- flowing. Out of the 41 west flowing rivers, 10 are major ones. These are Chandragiri, Valapattanam, Chaliyar, Chalakudy, Bhrathapuzha, Periyar, Pamba, Achenkoil, Muvattupuzha and Kallada. These 10 rivers carry nearly 45,100M.$m^3$ (million cubic meters) of water per year. The other 31 west flowing rivers carry only 91,200 M $m^3$ of water per year. About 71.5 per cent of the utilisable yield is contributed by these 10 major rivers. The stretches of five out of the ten major rivers, namely Chaliyar, Chalakudy, Periyar, Pamba and Kallada and certain portions of the backwaters like Vembanad and Ashtamudi are subjected to pollution due to waste discharges. Lower reaches of all these rivers are tidal and tidal reaches receive most of the chemical wastes of the state. Similarly, organic effluents contaminate the freshwater stretches of these major rivers.

The river Periyar receives the maximum quantity of effluents, of which a major portion is from the chemical industry. A cluster of chemical and metallurgical industries, which is about 25 per cent of the industry of the state, is located within a short stretch of one km on the banks of this river in the Udyogamandal area. This lower reach of Periyar below Udyogamandal is heavily polluted. The discharge of wastes containing mercury from the major chlor-alkali industry, viz. M/s Travancore Cochin Chemicals, the likely presenence of radioactive materials from the discharges of M/s Indian Rare Earths Ltd., and the DDT and other insecticides from the Hindustan Insecticides Ltd., combined with polluting chemicals from the industries make the pollution problem in this river serious, which warrants urgent control measures and strict enforcement of the standards. The water in the Chaliyar river downstream of the two factories of the Gwalior Rayons is polluted heavily due to their effluent discharges. Stretches of river Chalakudy are polluted due to the discharges from industrial establishments like Ms Madura Coats, Polson's Distillery, Tapioca Starch Products and Kerala Chemicals and Proteins Limited.

River Pamba receives waste discharge from M/s Travancore Sugars and Chemicals and stretches of river Kallada are heavily polluted due to the discharge from the Punalur Paper Mills. Bharathapuzha river is under the risk of pollution hazards due to discharges from Vanjinad Leathers" (ibid. pp.343-344).

Reporting on the extent of pollution in the backwaters, the Committee noted that "a comparative study between six polluted (sewage and particulate matter) stations and one unpolluted or clean station in the Cochin backwaters between Aroor and the bar-mouth revealed high biological oxygen demand of up to 420.6 ppm, low and fluctuating dissolved oxygen values from less than 0.05 to 3.81 ml per litre, and total sulphide up to 4.92 ppm...; the extent of occurrence of pathogenic bacteria like *Eccherina Coli* and *Salmonella faecelis* in the Cochin backwaters warrants thorough bacteriological quality control of the seafood marketed ...The main source of faecal pollution of the Cochin backwaters is the latrines from about one million households which opens directly in to the backwaters, while the remaining four million households have latrines opening in the septic tanks. Retting of coconut husk is another cause for water quality deterioration in Kerala backwaters .... Environmental degradation in the Cochin backwaters has evidently been so high that out of the 22 species of bryozoans that flourished here during 1963-67, only four species which are the hardiest remained in 1983-84. Extensive infestations of Kerala backwaters by the water hyacinth locally known as the *African payal (Salvinia moleste)* has reduced the biological productivity potential of this otherwise high productive ecosystem considerably. Decaying water hyacinth contributes extensively to the biological pollution of Cochin backwaters ..." (ibid, p.351).

Depicting the marine (nearshore) pollution in the Kerala Coast, the Committee noted that "a decrease in inter-tidal and sub-tidal sea life in the polluted near shore environment of Travancore Titanium Plant, Trivandrum has been reported ... Everyday, this plant discharged about 4000 $m^3$ of effluents, characterised by very high temperature (at discharge point) of 45°C to 50°C, sulphuric acid content of 10-40 g/litre ..." (ibid. p.351).

Baba *et al.* noted that "the water bodies in the costal zone are susceptible to pollution mainly due to effluents discharged from industries, domestic and community sewage. Drainage from agricultural lands (containing fertilisers, pesticides, fungicides, etc.), coconut husk retting areas and spillage of oil and kerosene in the vicinity of major commercial fishing harbours also contribute to pollution of water bodies. Some of the major industries that discharge waste materials into the coastal zone are Western India Plywood, Mavoor Rayons, FACT, Cochin Refineries, Lakshmi Starch Factory, Hindustan Instictides, Indian Rare Earths and Travancore Titanium Products. Long-term monitoring of the pollution of coastal waters is being carried out under COMAP Project in which Kerala coastal zone is studied by CESS and NIO. This study indicates that the threshold values exceeded nowhere in Kerala. However, if precautions are not taken, pollution can reach dangerous levels at several locations" (Baba, *et al.*,1995, p.20).

Heavy metal pollution in the costal waters has been reported by Nanda and Mohopatra at Saurashtra Coast, Bombay Harbour Bay, Mandovi-Zuary Estuary (Goa), Kali Estuary (Karwar), Cochin Backwaters, Vellar Estuary (Tamil Nadu), Ennore Creek (Madras), Porto Novo (Tamil Nadu), Cuddalore Coast (Tamil Nadu), Point Calimare (Tamil Nadu), etc. (Nanda and Mohapatra, 1995, pp.21-23).

Writing on coastal pollution in Cochin, Devaraj, et al. observed that "the backwaters are used for transport of oil, chemicals, toxic materials by barges, pipes, etc., public transport, mining, waste disposal, mariculture, recreation, reclamation for agriculture, and residential development. Domestic and industrial effluents discharged from the urban habitations and industries have led to instances of fish kills, degradation of benthic biota and a general decline in the natural capacity of the system....the industrial effluents (ammonia, ammoniac nitrogen, fluorides, mercury, DDT, acidic chemicals, and suspended solids) discharged from the Eloor-Edayar industrial belt into the Periyar river (which joins the Cochin backwaters), is estimated to be over 200 million litres/day" (Devaraj, *et al.,* 1999, pp.10-12).

They further pointed out that "many locations in the middle and upper stretches of the estuaries serve as retting grounds, where extremely poor environmental conditions prevail resulting in low diversity index for zooplankton and benthos. There are over 200 medium and large scale industries and about 2000 small scale industries discharging their effluents into the estuaries, besides a discharge of about 650 tonnes of organic matter per day from14 municipal bodies. Hotspots of industrial pollution have been identified and demarcated in the estuaries of Calicut, Cochin and Trivandrum. The heavy traffic of mechanised and motorised fishing vessels and cargo ships also contributes significantly to marine pollution which is very intense in the Azhikode to Alleppey, and Quilon to Kollengode belts" (ibid. p.10).

These writers also noted that "a recent report on the status of pollution in the Periyar river has quantified the annual load of mercury (2000 kg), zinc (10,095 kg), copper (327 kg), fluorides (250 t) and iron (30 t) dumped into the river ..." (ibid. p.12).

They further pointed out that "mass mortality of fish due to industrial pollution has been reported from the upper reaches of Cochin backwaters at Chitrapuzha and Champakara. Ammonia load of 432 to 560 ppm along with acids and the suspended solids has been found to be deleterious to fish in this backwater lake. Mecury concentration ranged from 0.15 to 1.10 ppm in the monsoon season in the sediment while at the effluent discharge point, it recorded 5.5 to 11.5 ppm. Indiscriminate application of about 10 types of pesticides to the tune of 480 t/year in the Periyar catchment area has led to the occurrence of DDT in clams and organochlorine in the black clams and fishes in the Cochin backwaters. High concentration of coliform bacteria has been detected in fish and bivalves from Cochin backwaters. About 40 ha of saline mudflat within the Cochin backwaters is being used for coconut husk retting. This has resulted in anoxia conditions and hydrogen sulphide accumulations rendering the area unsuitable for almost any type of life. An EIA study conducted in the Cochin backwaters during 1994-95 has revealed low benthic populations in the Udyogamandal canal and a general decline in fish production" (ibid. p.12).

The severity of the pollution problem and its impact on fisheries was further highlighted by the Expert Committee for Fisheries Management Studies, Kerala, in 2000. It noted that "the inland water bodies of Kerala are subjected to various types of pollution hazards mainly from industrial effluents, pesticides, chemical fertilisers and sewage" (Expert Committee, 2000, p.51). Giving the details of this problem, it stated that "there are over 200 medium scale industries and about 2000 small-scale industries discharging effluents into the inland water bodies. Discharge of heavy metals such as copper, mercury, zinc and cadmium above the permitted levels lead to serious pollution problems. High concentration of zinc, copper, iron, manganese and mercury were observed in the water, sediments and sedentary populations inhabiting the Cochin backwaters. Frequent incidence of mass mortality of fishes is a usual affair in the major rivers such as the Periyar (Chitrapuzha), Chaliyar, Kallada and the lakes, viz. Vembanad, Ashtamudi, etc.

The fishes inhabiting these water bodies are facing reproductive hazards, growth retardation and morphological abnormalities, apart from total destruction of eggs and larvae. Fish mortality due to industrial affluent carrying heavy load of ammonia at the rate of 432-560 ppm pouring into the area together with many pollutants such as acids, suspended solids, alkalis, fluorides, radio active materials, etc. could change the water quality to extreme toxic conditions and result in heavy fish mortality. Fish shoals entering the polluted zone could not tolerate the cumulative effects of pollution and results in their sudden mortality. The Eloor-Varapuzha regions of Cochin backwaters are getting transformed into barren contaminated cess pools.

Indiscriminate application of pesticides has been noticed in the paddy fields of Kuttanad, which eventually get washed off and reach the down stream region. According to the data compiled by the KWBSP, 10 types of pesticides with total quantity of 490 tonnes, are used in Kuttanad annually of which 370 tonnes are applied for *Punja* cultivation and 120 tonnes for *Viruppu* cultivation. High levels of DDT have been detected in water, sediment and clams collected from lower Kuttanad region in April. Similarly, significant concentration of organochloride pesticides is also detected in the samples of black clam and fishes analysed from this part of the lake.

In the absence of adequate facilities for the disposal of sewage and sullage from human settlements, they are directly discharged into the inland water bodies. Hung latrines visible all along the backwaters are the major source of faecal contamination. Sewage discharge cause detrimental environment to fish life. In the canals of Alappuzha, the cell number of *E. coli* varied from 500-5000, while in the stagnant channels it reached up to 13000 faecal coli per 100 ml sample. High concentrations of *coli* form bacteria were detected in fishes collected from the Cochin backwater. Very high concentrations of pathogenic bacteria *Vibrio parahaemolyticus* from the shellfishes of Cochin backwaters have also been recorded.

The backwaters of Kerala are also used for the retting of coconut husk. Fishes used to desert such areas due to the presence of noxious gases such as $H_2S_1$, methane and high BOD, turbidity, etc. In the Vembanad lake alone around 245 ha are used for husk retting" (Expert Committee, 2000, pp. 51-52; parentheses added).

Two other industries which pollute the coastal waters on a large scale are aquaculture and fish processing. The former, apart from polluting the water bodies lead to the destruction of mangroves, wetlands and biodiversity. Both these activities which form part of the fisheries sector create externalities which are detrimental to the sustainability of the sector itself.

Highlighting the scale of aquatic pollution caused by aquaculture, Shiva and Karir noted that "the large scale pumping of seawater into the shrimp farms is one of the most serious environmental impacts of shrimp farming. The massive extraction of freshwater from underground aquifers for salinity control in the ponds poses a serious threat to the salinity control of the coastal ecosystem" (Shiva and Karir, 1997, p.39). They further pointed out that "prawn culture activity requires the pumping of seawater into ponds, since the majority are marine prawn species which require a salinity between 25-30 parts per trillion (ppt). The growing period for prawn is between120-150 days, meaning water is also on the land for this period of time which is sufficient to allow salt water to seep into the neighbouring agricultural farm areas and as well into the water table.

Destruction of mangrove forests also leads to increased salinity as there is an increase in flood area thereby allowing further intrusion of salt water onto land. The massive extraction of freshwater from underground aquifers for salinity control in the ponds also intensifies the problem of salinity. Estimates show that roughly 6600 $m^3$ of freshwater are needed to dilute seawater on a one hectare pond at one meter water depth over a cropping period of four months. Emptied aquifers are subject to saltwater intrusion. Seepage from the tanks also increases salinisation of ground water" (ibid. pp.39-40).)

The potential for aquaculture to pollute the water base is further indicted by these authors. They pointed out that "shrimp farms flush their effluents and waters directly into the sea and neighbouring mangrove and agricultural lands. The water quality of prawn farms is maintained by the regular refilling of ponds with fresh sea water. The out-flowing pond water contaminated with heavy concentrations of pesticides and antibiotics, is discharged either back to the sea or to rivers and canals. Further pollution occurs, as a result of the use of organic waste and commercially produced food pellets, instead of natural feed. The use of various chemicals in the feed, some 32 ingredients, accumulate at the 'surface bottom' of the pond causing deposits of algae and bacteria which affect the oxygen balance of the water ... The prawn industry utilises feed and fertilisers to help maintain the production of the shrimp. A fair amount of the fertilisers and feed gets collected at the bottom of the pond ... intensive shrimp farming is based on dense stocking rate and over-crowding, which induces stress problems and increases susceptibility to diseases. Over-crowding leads to poor water quality due to increased oxygen demand, high accumulated metabolic products and excreta, rapid growth and transmission of noxious parasites, micro organisms and pathogens" (ibid. pp.41-43).

Another major source of aquatic pollution in the coastal regions, along with agriculture, aquaculture and other industries is the fish processing industry. Indeed, this industry was included in the list of prohibited activities in the 'coastal zones' as per the CRZ notification of the Government of India in 1991. The concentration of a large number of fish processing plants in the coastal/backwater stretches of the country is believed to cause large-scale aquatic pollution in the vicinity of those plants. Table 6.7 gives a picture of the comparative levels of pollution caused by fish processing plants, shrimp farms and domestic sewage.

**Table 6.7**

**Comparative levels of pollution caused by fish processing plants, shrimp farms and domestic sewage**

| *Sl. No.* | *Parameter mg/l* | *Effluent from* | | | | | |
|---|---|---|---|---|---|---|---|
| | | *Shrimp farm* | *Harvest effluent* | *Domestic sewage* | | | *Fish processing plant* |
| | | | | *Untreated* | *Primary* | *Bio-logical* | |
| 1. | BOD | 4.0-10.2 | - | 300 | 200 | 30 | 10000-18000 |
| 2. | Total nitrogen | 0.03-1.24 | 5.25-14.8 | 75 | 60 | 40 | 700-4530 |
| 3. | Total phosphorus | 0.001-2.02 | 0.03-0.08 | 20 | 15 | 12 | 120-298 |
| 4. | Suspended solids | 119-225 | 60-243 | 500 | - | 15 | 1880-7475 |

*Source:* Raghu, 2002, p.226.

Table 6.7 reveals that the pollution levels are higher in the effluents discharged from processing plants and domestic sewage.

Highlighting the impact of environmental pollution on the sustainability of fisheries, Nair stated: "Growing human settlement on the coastal fringe of continents is the single most important pressure on coastal marine ecosystem. Consequent activities result in changes in the structure and community dynamics of marine ecosystems leading to habitat loss, increasing pollution levels and effects of excessive fishing mortality. It is true that over fishing has caused enormous quantity of biomass flips, wherein a dominant species rapidly drops to a low level to be succeeded by another species generating cascading effects among other components of the ecosystem. Also biomass yields are being influenced by multiple, but different, driving forces in marine ecosystems, a major one being effect of environmental perturbations and pollution on living marine resources" (Nair, 2004, p.434).

This author also reported the presence of 308 industrial units in the coast generating 1.35 million cubic meters of liquid effluents and about 34,500 tonnes of solid wastes every day (ibid. p.434). Table 6.8 gives details of coastal industries and waste generation in India.

**Table 6.8**

**Coastal industries (large and medium) and waste generation in India**

| *Item* | *East coast* | *West coast* | *Total* |
|---|---|---|---|
| Industries (no.) | 75 | 233 | 308 |
| Aquaculture farms (no.) | 138 | - | 138 |
| Industrial effluents (in million m3/day | 0.50 | 0.85 | 1.35 |
| Aquaculture farm waste (in million m3/day | 2.37 | - | 2.37 |
| Industrial solid waste (tonnes/day) | 19,834 | 14,642 | 34,476 |

*Source:* Nair, 2004, p.435.

It is apparent from table 6.8 that aquaculture farms numbering 138, all located in the East coast generated more liquid waste than that produced by industrial establishments.

Pointing out the biological impact of pollution on the fishery in general, Nair noted:

> "Anthropogenic perturbations affect fisheries in different ways. In general, protection of any living marine resource can be accomplished only by maintaining the stability/equilibrium between tropic levels. Imbalance in productivity at lower levels, namely, primary productivity, secondary productivity and benthic productivity can interfere with the fishery potential of an ecosystem as many fishes directly feed on plankton and benthos. Although fishes are able to swim away from polluted areas, the larval stages being planktonic, drift with tides and currents. The offshore industrial/sewage outfall can often adversely affect the health of the larvae leading to deformities of notochord, eye and head ... Fish and shrimp nurseries

are often placed in shallow estuarine or costal areas where pollution exerts its major effects. Uncontrolled and poorly planned dredging/ reclamation activities tend to aggravate the environmental problems for the nursery ground and the environment as a whole" (ibid. p.442).

Highlighting the effects of oil spills on the fishery, Nair points out: "Petroleum hydrocarbons in a marine environment can cause wide variety of short and long term effects in fishes depending on their bio-availability and persistence and the ability of the organism to metabolise them. Fish often shows avoidance reaction even at low concentrations of oil in water. Moreover, the fish possess an enzyme system which can deal with petroleum hydrocarbons in tissues. Hence fish kills due to oil pollution are rare. No conspicuous decline in fisheries of accidental oil spill areas are observed though some changes in the composition of catch and total population are reported. Large spills in enclosed areas can make the habitat unsuitable for fishing and render the fish commercially unacceptable due to tainting. However, the greatest threat of oil pollution is to benthic fish and spawning/breeding grounds of fish. Concentration over one mg/litre of petroleum in water can cause lethal effects on fish eggs and larvae ..." (ibid. p.442).

Referring to the environmental impact of fish culture, Nair reports: "There is a growing concern about the environmental implications of aquaculture development comprising the adverse effects of aquaculture operations on the environment as well as the consequences of increasing aquatic pollution affecting feasibility and sustainable development ... In general, some 85 per cent of phosphorus, 80-88 per cent of carbon and 52-95 per cent of nitrogen put into a marine fish culture system as feed may be lost into the environment as waste ... Problems caused by high organic and nutrient-loadings conflict with other uses of the coastal zone. The use of chemicals and the introduction of pathogens and new genetic strains have also raised environmental concerns.

Results of various studies show that some 23 per cent of carbon, 21 per cent of nitrogen and 53 per cent of phosphorus of feed input into the culture system is getting accumulated in the bottom sediment affecting significantly an area confined within one kilometer of the farm. This can lead to high sediment oxygen demand, anoxic sediment, production of toxic gases and a decrease in benthic diversity" (ibid. p.443).

Referring to the various environmental impacts caused by other sectors on Indian fisheries, Sampath stated: "Soil erosion is one of the greatest man-made disasters which has resulted in siltation not only of the river basins, backwaters and estuaries, but also in a considerable depletion of fishery resources. It is estimated that in India, roughly 16 tonnes per ha of soil is being eroded every year, resulting in a loss of about 5.37 – 8.4 million tonnes of major nutrients (nitrogen, phosphorus and potash) and the Indian Ocean receives annually 34 x $10^8$ tonnes suspended sediments, of which 16 x $10^8$ tonnes come from rivers flowing through the sub-continent. Due to the increasing human intervention such as mining, clearance of land for agriculture, urbanisation, industrialisation, etc. the quantity of suspended sediments is increasing day by day. Most of the silt settles near the river mouths and in the coastal areas, decreasing their productivity and thus depleting their fishery resources.

Increased suspended sediments and sedimentation caused by deforestation and consequent erosion have had a serious impact on biodiversity. The sediment, which settles on or penetrates into the stream-bed, is more deleterious than the suspended sediment, as it would have a long-term effect on the fish and invertebrate population. Increased turbidity also leads to a reduction in the algal growth and consequent further reduction in the diversity of plants. Sediment deposition, particularly through its influence on the mortality of eggs and larvae in the spawning species, is the most significant cause of the decline in the fish population ...

During the monsoon months, the inshore waters of the Palk Bay become very turbid, leading to silting up of the coral reefs, causing mortality to many coral colonies. Apart from this, the destruction of corals in this region also damages the reef-associated organisms. The region of Kavaratti reef in the Lakshadweep, and the reefs found in the major parts of the Greater Nicobar Islands have also disappeared because of the withdrawal of coral debris and the use of coral debris and corals as a raw material for the cement industry, while the others have been exterminated due to their constant exposure to pollution, particularly oil.

Coastal pollution has seriously affected the living and non-living exploitable resources of the marine waters. Major pollution sources include: discharge of raw or partially treated industrial and urban wastes, harbour activities, including fish landing, cargo handling, dumping of ship washings, spilling of oil, ores, oil slicks, land run off, etc..

Untreated urban and municipal wastes from the coastal cities and towns are thrown directly into the sea along the east and west coasts, resulting in eutrophication and hypoxia. If such wastes are discharged in the vicinity of the sea grass beds, their productivity is lowered. It also affects the epiphytic algae, crustaceans and molluscs which use sea grass beds as a substrate and as a major detrital food. Such an instance has been reported from the Gulf of Mannar region where eleven species of sea grasses occur. The thermal discharge from the thermal power plant and the excessive brine run off from the salt pans around Tuticorin have also affected the sea grass beds and the flora and fauna associated with them in the near shore waters.

River run offs, mechanised and chemical weathering of the rocks, and all industrial plants are the major sources of metallic pollution in the coastal and estuarine waters. Cadmium, copper, lead, mercury, nickel and zinc are the heavy metals found in the coastal waters. The sources of these are chlor-alkali factories, industrial solvent water discharge, municipal waste water, dredging and dumping of sediments from the harbours, use of anti-fouling paints, etc.

Oil pollution results from the transport, storage and refining of crude oil, leakage from the ships / fishing trawlers, production of petrochemicals, etc. Other sources of oil pollution in the marine environment are tanker accidents (38 per cent), river run off (29 per cent), natural seepage (18 per cent), coastal municipal wastes and non-petroleum industries (8 per cent),urban run off (5 per cent), offshore exploration and production (1.5 per cent) and coastal refineries (0.5 per cent). In India, the total crude oil production from the offshore area is 20-25 million tonnes per annum ... The ecosystems worst affected by oil pollution would be the coral reefs in Andaman-Nicobar and Lakshadweep groups of islands.

In the river run off, pesticides, lindane, endosulfan and DDT are the major pesticides which are washed into the coastal environment. While the lindane levels increase in the water, endosulfan increases in the sediments and DDT in the biota, particularly in the plankton. High concentration of DDT has been observed in the plankton organisms, edible oysters, clams, mullets, catfishes, etc. along the east coast" (Sampath, 1998, pp.75-77).

A detailed review of studies of instances of water pollution in the major river systems causing damage to the inland fisheries of the country has been provided by Jhingran (Jhingran, 1991,pp.112-121). Table 6.9 gives details of major river systems, hotspots, and industries/activities causing water pollution and threat to fisheries in India.

**Table 6.9**

**Major river systems, hotspots and industries/activities causing water pollution and threat to fisheries in India**

| *Sl. No.* | *River systems* | *Hotspots in the sub-systems* | *Industries/activities causing pollution* | *Effect on fisheries* |
|---|---|---|---|---|
| 1 | The Ganga | | | |
| | (a) | River Yamuna at Delhi | City sewage, DDT factory | Not known |
| | (b) | River Ganga at Kanpur, U.P. | Tannaries, textiles<br><br>and other species | Destroys spawning grounds of carps |
| | (c) | River Kali near Aligarh, U.P. | Sugar mill, distillery, tin, glycerine, paints and soap works; spinning, rayon, silk and yam mills | Loss of 300 quintals of fish reported in a stretch of 160 km zone |
| | (d) | River Dajora at Bareilly, U.P. | Synthetic rubber manufacturing units | Not known |
| | (e) | River Suvaon (tributary of Rebti) at Balarampur, U.P. | Sugar factory | Fish mortality reported in three km. stretch |
| | (f) | River Gomati at Lucknow | Pulp and paper factory, distillery and sewage | Not known |
| | (g) | River Rend at Rihand | Chlorine discharged from Kanoria Chemical industry, various units manufacturing caustic soda, bleaching powder and gammayane | Heavy fish mortality reported, *M. aor*, *Clupisoma, garua*, *C. catla* and a number of wild fishes subjected to severe mortality |
| | (h) | River Son at Dehri-on-Son, Bihar | Paper, chemicals, sugar, cement, caustic soda and chlorine plants | Heavy fish mortality reported |
| | (i) | River Daha at Siwan, Bihar | Sugar factory, distillery | Heavy fish mortality reported |

| | | | |
|---|---|---|---|
| (j) | River Damodar in Bihar and West Bengal | Sindri unit of Fertiliser Corporation of India, Bihar Government's Super Phosphate Factory, The Associated Cement Company, Coal Washeries between Bhokaro and Sindri, Bhokaro Thermal Power Plant, etc. | Adversely affecting spawning of fish in the entire belt of Asansol-Durgapur industrial belt on Lower Damodar Valley |
| (k) | River Hooghly at Calcutta | Paper and pulp, distillery, heavy chemicals, textiles, shellac industries and domestic outfalls | Spawning grounds destroyed |
| (l) | River Kulta near Calcutta | City sewage and many industrial units | Fishes, except *Pangasius* virtully eliminated |
| 2. | The Mahanadi | | |
| | River Ib at Brajarajnagar, Orissa | Orient Paper Mill | Riverine fishery affected for about 24 km down stream |
| 3. | The Krishna | | |
| | River Bhadra at Bhadravathi, Mysore | Steal industry, pulp and paper mill | 18 out of 36 commercially important species reported as lost. Spawning migration affected and mortality reported when digester washings were let out. |
| 4. | Other Rivers of Peninsular India | | |
| (a) | River Godavari at Rajamundry, Andhra Pradesh | Andhra Paper Mill at Rajamundry | Fishery in the area considerably dwindled |
| (b) | River Cauvery at Mettur Dam, Tamil Nadu | Mettur Chemicals and Industrial Corporation, Mettur Dam. | Carps and catfishes suffered mortality |
| (c) | River Cooum at Madras | Washings from slums, cattle yards, over flow from sewage pumping stations, waste from automobile workshops and factories | River has become devoid of fish life |

| | | | |
|---|---|---|---|
| (d) | River Chaliyar at Mavoor, Calicut, Kerala | Gwalior Rayon Factory at Mavoor | Large scale fish mortality reported |
| (e) | River Kalu in Bombay | Nearly 100 industries, notably Amar Dye and Chemical Company, Indian Dyes, Century Rayon, National Rayon, Central Chemicals, Paper and Caustic soda | Hilsa, which was once prolific, stopped ascending with the acidic barrier in the river. Presence of mercury in the flesh of thirty species reported |

*Source:* Jhingran, 1991, p.113-120

Table 6.9, though cursory in its coverage of instances of water pollution and its impact on the inland fisheries, is still indicative of the ubiquitous nature of the problem. Jhingran further reported that "there has been a large number of cases of fish mortality in ponds and lakes, arising out of use of pesticides, in all parts of India" (ibid. p.121). Lakshmanan *et al.*, however, reported that the average concentration of all (toxic/trace) metals were significantly lower in the edible parts of all the fish/shell fish analysed meant for export from Cochin, Quilon, Mangalore and Mumbai regions (Lakshmanan, *et al.* 2001, p.42).

### 6.2.3. Habitat Destruction

Habitat destruction is another major threat to the sustainability of Indian fisheries. This is the consequence of many negative externalities caused by the over all economic development of the marine, coastal, and inland water environment, which impacts on the fishery adversely through landfills, waste dumping, pollution and other harmful effects on the resource base. It is also partly a consequence of adverse technological processes like trawling and developments in aquaculture, which lead to water pollution and environmental degradation. The extent of the damage caused to the sustainability of Indian fisheries through habitat destruction is not known precisely at present. Indicative references are, however, available to some extent. Writing about the habitat destruction in the inland water areas of Kerala, the Expert Committee for Fisheries Management Studies, Kerala, noted that "the inland water bodies are prone to various types of man-made stresses which have essentially resulted in the loss or impairment of the natural habitat of many fishes and shellfishes" (Expert Committee for Fisheries Management Studies, Kerala, 2000, p.40). Some of the facts which ultimately led to the loss of habitat and the resulting fall in fish catches noted by the Committee are, (*a*) construction of bunds, barriers, anicuts, weirs, dams, etc., (*b*) shrinkage in the extent of inland water bodies, (c) fall in the depth of inland water bodies and (*d*) deforestation of mangroves (Korakandy, 2005, p.329).

Referring to the destruction of mangroves in Kerala, the Committee noted that "in Kerala, a century ago there were bout 70,000 ha of mangroves. However, in recent years it has been reduced to isolated patches less than 70 ha. Available reports suggest that penaeid prawns and fishes such as pearl spot, mullets and sea bass used to take shelter in these mangrove sanctuaries and the destruction of these vegetation occurring in the fringes of backwaters might have adversely affected the fisheries resources of the state" (Expert Committee for Fisheries Management Studies, Kerala, 2000, p.51).

A newspaper report by Karunakaran from Cochin in 2001 stated that "Kerala's mangrove ecosystems which once dotted the entire coastline, withstanding ravages of severe storms and changing tides for many millinia have been disappearing at an accelerating rate with little public empathy, remorse on the part of authorities, or even the environmentalists" (Karunakaran, 2001).

An earlier newspaper report from Kannur in 1997 by Mohammed Nazeer stated that the "process of destruction of mangroves continue in the district despite protests from environmentalists. In a latest instance of reclaiming the wetland for construction in the mangrove rich areas in the district, hundreds of mangroves on a plot adjoining the Valapatanam river at Pappinisseri near here were destroyed allegedly by the land owner..." (Nazeer, 1997). Nazeer also reported that "a state convention on protection of wetlands held here recently had highlighted the large-scale destruction of mangroves in Kannur which has 755 hectares of mangrove forests, the largest in the state, scattered in Payyannur, Thalassery, and Pappinisseri. Conversion of vast areas of wetland into aquaculture ponds has caused irreparable damage to mangroves, which constitute a rich ecosystem ..." (ibid).

The damage to the fish habitat caused by trawling off Kerala coast has been pointed out by the Fisheries Expert Committee on Ban on Monsoon Trawling in Kerala during 1989. It noted that "indiscriminate bottom trawling during the recent past has caused serious disturbance of living animal communities of the benthos. The excessive pressure exerted on the sea bottom through intensive bottom trawling will naturally affect recoupment and regeneration. Another disturbing factor is that great quantities of eggs and young ones of bottom living fishes are hauled up by the trawl nets particularly during the monsoon season. The Conmmittee is of the view that during the monsoon months total ban on mechanised fishing efforts violently disturbing the sea bottom is necessary in the interest of conservation of resources" (Nair, 1991, p. 93).

Devaraj, *et al.* also noted that "the coastal waters of Kerala are subjected to high fishing pressure by the mechanised (46 per cent of total catch) and motorised (50 per cent of total catch) sectors, mostly in the depths of 0-50 metres covering an area of 12,560 km$^2$ which is only 7 percent of the all India area within 0-50 metre depth... Bottom trawling is estimated to destroy about 13,000 tonnes of benthic organisms per year in Kerala, causing thereby great loss to the benthic biodiversity and habitat degradation" (Devaraj, *et al.* 1999, p.5).

The damage to the habitat caused by wetland reclamation has been noted by these writers. They noted that "reclamation for various purposes has reduced the Kerala brackish waters area from 4,226 km$^2$ to 652 km$^2$ at present" (ibid, pp.9-10). They also reported that "there is a total area of 1278 ha of mangroves, either discontinuous or patchy, distributed in the lower reaches of the estuaries in Cannanore (755 ha), Calicut (263 ha) and Ernakulam (260 ha) districts. This habitat which is nursery for many shell fishes (mainly shrimps and prawns) and finfishes is vulnerable to over fishing" (ibid. p.10).

Some of the natural and man-made factors which impede the sustainable development of the coast as identified by the International Ocean Institute (India) and reported by these authors and having close bearing with habitat destruction are (1) coastal erosion, (2) sewage ingress, (3) global warming and sea level rise, (4) natural disaster from floods, storms, hurricanes and cyclones, (5) outbreak of diseases, (6) sedimentation, (7) population pressure and urbanisation, (8) land-use changes including reclamation and construction, (9) shore protection works such as seawalls, groins and bulkheads, (10) overfishing and inshore aquaculture, (11) destruction of habitats and biodiversity including mangroves, coral reefs and benthos, (12) mining, (13) impact of ports and marine transport, (14) uncontrolled tourism, (15) manufacturing and processing industries, (16) domestic, industrial and agricultural discharge (ibid, p.15). The first six are natural processes while the rest are anthropogenic in nature and all posing threat to the natural habitat of fish.

Writing on the damage to some of the sensitive coastal habitats of the country, viz. coral reefs, sea grass meadows, mangrove forests, coastal beaches and estuaries, Devaraj, *et al.,* noted: "Besides natural processes like global warming, cyclones, erosion, siltation, diseases, pests (boring sponges and bivalves), algal blooms (*Noctiluca, Trichodesmium, Alexandrium*, etc.), indiscriminate exploitation of corals and the associated flora and fauna, dredging, reclamation and pollution have further threatened the reef ecosystem. Recent rise in sea surface temperature by 2-3°C has caused bleaching of corals (30 to 80 per cent) in different parts of the world ...

... There are altogether 14 species (seven genera) of sea grasses in the Gulf of Mannar, Palk Bay, Mandovi estuary, Lakshadweep island lagoons and the Andaman and Nicobar islands. High-energy storms, grazing, predation, pests, diseases and human activities cause destruction of sea grass meadows. Studies conducted on the Indian sea grass habitats reveal considerable habitat loss and degradation at many places. Five to ten kilogram of sea grass and seaweeds per boat per day are removed from the Palk Bay while fishing for *Penaeus semisulcatus*...

About 45 species of mangroves are available in India. In the peninsular India, mangroves occupy only a limited 380 km long coast covering an area of about 3,55,500 ha, of which 82 per cent is along the east coast and the Andaman and Nicobar islands and 18 per cent along the west. Large stretches of mangrove vegetation have been removed and the land reclaimed for housing, agriculture, aquaculture and industrial activities ...

The beaches constitute the interface between the land and the sea, where the natural physical processes are dynamic and intense; the shorelines are in a state of flux and seasonally subjected to erosion and accretion. Long sandy beaches with dunes are found along the east coast, whereas the west coast presents sandy pockets, rocky clefts and sprites, creek, bays and headland. The seasonal and annual longshore and onshore-offshore sediment transport modifies the beach profile. Natural processes and human activities increasingly stress the beaches ...

The estuaries occupy an area of 1.25 million ha along the Indian coast spread over nine maritime states and the Andaman and Nicobar islands. About 52 per cent of total backwaters are in Orissa and West Bengal and 19.7 per cent in Kerala. Problems posed by industrial growth along the banks of estuaries and upstream impoundment (e.g., Thanneermukkom bund in Vembanad Lake in Kerala) can be addressed through an integrated approach to coastal zone management" (ibid. pp.15-16).

One frequently noted factor responsible for large scale destruction of habitat is wetland reclamation. Referring to this anomaly, the Expert Committee for Fisheries Management Studies, Kerala, observed that "in recent years a substantial reduction in the total extent of water bodies could be discernible due to indiscriminate reclamation being carried out, especially in the backwaters of Kerala for the purpose of agriculture, urbanisation, housing, aquaculture, etc. The reclamation is done either as part of various developmental scheme of the central or state governments or undertaken by private parties illegally. These activities could result in the reduction of the nursery ground of shrimps, besides also considerably altering the physical features of the estuary such as the tidal flow, water circulation, current flow, etc, which together adversely affect the fishery wealth. The available reports suggest that the total area of the Vembanad lake which was 44,000 ha in the beginning of the 19th century has now been reduced to 21,000 ha as a result of reclamation for the purpose of agriculture, prawn farming, urbanisation, housing, harbour development, etc." (Expert Committee for Fisheries Management Studies, Kerala, 2000, p.50).

The threat to the Vembanad lake ecology posed by the proposed project to interlink the Pamba and the Achenkoil rivers with the Vaipar river in Tamil Nadu, will be quite serious. The lake will soon become a marsh devoid of water flow and a 'biological desert loosing its biodiversity' attracting land developers and real estate business. The fisheries of the lake will be the first casualty to suffer the major negative externality of the new development (Korakandy, 2005a, p.333).

The damage caused by trawling to the habitat of white fish resources of the country has been pointed out by Vivekanandan, *et al.* They noted that "irrational bottom trawling is known to severely affect the benthic habitat. Degradation of the benthic habitat and the consequent non-availability of the preferred food items would also have affected the white fish stock particularly along the southeast coast ..." (Vivekanandan, *et al.*, 1998, pp.174-175). Trawling has been found to disturb the habitat of the Cephalopod resources as well. Meiyappan and Mohammed noted that "indiscriminate bottom trawling severely disturbs the habitat that facilitates the Cephalopods to lay their egg masses. It also affects their food availability ..." (Meiyappan and Mohammed, 1998, p.227). The loss of habitat is reported to affect the stock of marine mammals like sea cow. Rajagopalan and Menon reported that "the sea cow *Dugong dugon* ... feed exclusively on sea grass and weeds ... the degradation and denudation of its unique feeding habitat has further compounded the devastation process and forced dugongs to seek similar pristine habitat elsewhere" (Rajagopalan and Menon, 2003, p.244).

Referring to the damage caused to habitat by developments in aquaculture, Sampath wrote:

"Reports reveal that due to prolonged water logging in the confined prawn farming farms along the periphery of the Chilka lake, anaerobic conditions have surfaced in the ponds. The pond soils have become low in nitrogen, phosphorus and iron content and the pond water has become appreciably high in acidity and the total alkalinity has become low. This indicates poor buffering capacity of the food ecosystem, which might restrict productivity to certain levels. It has been suggested that, without improving pond conditions, if fertilisation of the ponds and heavy stocking are continued, it would result in further environmental degradation. These ponds are of 0.2 ha to 0.5 ha in size. While the large ponds are more amenable to improved management practices, smaller static or confined ponds are showing adverse conditions for higher inputs and self-purification problems. Increased use of snail meat in the ponds could also lead to reduction in the population of snails in the area.

The expansion in coastal aquaculture also saw the increased demand for quality shrimp feed which has to be imported at high cost ... The absence of any cheap and acceptable pelletised shrimp feed has resulted in a number of shrimp farms resorting to compounding their own feeds, using buffalo meat and other high fibre content materials, snail to clam meat, etc., particularly in Andhra Pradesh. The BOBP/ODA Post-harvest Fisheries Project study on shrimp feed trials at Kakinada (1990-91) has revealed that when the shrimps were fed with local feed of dough balls, the pond bottom was found to have been spoiled by decaying and unconsumed feed particles, as was evident from the distinctly black colour of the pond bottom compared to the clean, muddy bottom observed in the ponds fed with pelletised feed.

In the deltaic Sunderbans area of West Bengal, clusters of extensive shrimp farms and semi-intensive farms, extending to more than 100 ha each, are coming up. It is estimated that Hooghly-Matla estuary, which criss-crosses the Sunderbans area, brings with it over 360 gallons of organic and industrial wastes per day from Greater Calcutta, degrading the entire ecosystem. Bioaccumulation of heavy metals and pesticides in the fish/shellfish population in the area could find a way into the cultured shrimps, if the affected fish/shellfish are used as feed.

.... In Tuticorin (Tamil Nadu) immediately after the1992 floods, all the semi-intensive shrimp farms in that area were affected by diseases and they had to be closed down for culture operations for more than four months. This is one area in Tamil Nadu where cluster of shrimp farms has come up. During 1994-95, the disease out-break in Andhra Pradesh and Tamil Nadu assumed great proportions and an over 22,000 ha area was affected resulting in loss of crop and revenue for the shrimp culturists ...

The other adverse impact of clustering of shrimp farms in the same area is eutrophication of the ponds due to concentration of the pond water containing heavy organic load for want of adequate tidal flow. While the integrated farms, adopting high levels of technology and management, could survive the possible adverse effects of the expansion of aquaculture, the medium-level entrepreneurs and small farmers, who have no access to such types of management skills and technology, might be the worst suffers from such adverse environmental conditions" (Sampath, 1998, pp.74-75).

### 6.2.4. Biodiversity Loss

Loss of biodiversity acting as a major threat to the sustainability of global fisheries has been noted in chapter four. As noted by Mc Connell in the global context, "biodiversity is being lost from nearly all aquatic ecosystems at an ever increasing rate, due mainly to the rising human population and anthropogenic changes to the environment: damming rivers has interrupted fish spawning runs (though opening up opportunities for new evolution), wetlands have been drained, introduced alien species have ousted native ones, in addition to pollution and over harvesting" (McConnell, 1999, p.31).

Some of the causative factors leading to biodiversity loss as reported by Clark are (1) pollution and other environmental damages that stress a population, causing differential mortality, extinction, or both, (2) fishing pressure that favours one genotype over another, (3) artificial selection and domestication, which can result in conscious or unconscious inbreeding and genetic impoverishment and (4) introduction of exotic species and diseases (Clark, 1996, p.314).

The extent to which these factors are working as constraints on the sustainability of Indian fisheries is not well documented. There are, however, scattered evidences and references to show that the sustainability of Indian Fisheries is being threatened by the loss of biodiversity.

While writing on the coastal zone governance in Kerala, especially relating to the 'rocky outcrops, islands and coral patches', Devaraj, *et al.* noted: "owing to their rich biodiversity and importance as nursery grounds, some of the rich biodivesity pockets along the rocky habitats off Kovalam, Varkala and Tellicherry covering an area of about 20 $km^2$, and another 35 $km^2$ of patchy reaf areas off Thangassery may be treated as sensistive ..." (Devaraj, *et al.* 1999, p.8).

These authors further pointed out that "the estuaries in Kerala maintain exceptionally high levels of biological productivity. They play such important ecological roles as (a) nutrient and organic material transport through tidal circulation, (b) fishing grounds, (c) nursery grounds for many species of marine shrimps, crabs and fishes and (d) breeding grounds for the freshwater caridian prawns. The berried population of the freshwater prawns (*Macro brachium rosenbergii*) migrates downstream the Cochin backwaters during September-December for hatching and the completion of larval metamorphosis. Out of the downstream migrating berried population, only 30.2 per cent reaches the spawning grounds while the remaining 69.8 per cent is lost due to fishing ... The Cochin backwater popularly known as the Vembanad lake extends across the Alleppey and Ernakulam districts with two seasonal openings and one permanent opening into the Arabian sea. Six rivers discharge into this backwater lake. Fishing takes place in this lake round the year. Due to reclamation, the lake area of 36,500 ha as estimated in 1834 has reduced to 12,700 ha in 1983. The lake is inhabited by 150 species of fin fishes, seven species of penaeid prawns, six species of palaemonidae and two species of clams, and is characterised by very high primary, secondary and benthic production. The estimated annual fisheries production is around 7200 tonnes (penaeid prawns, 48.6 per cent; fin fishes, 45.8 per cent; crabs, 3.8 per cent, and palaemonid prawns, 1.8 per cent) while the black clam production is more than 7000 tonnes per year.

Species diversity index (H) for polychaetes and crustaceans in the Cochin backwaters determined in 1978 revealed a gradual reduction from the bar mouth towards the higher gradients, where the stress due to pollution was very high. The species diversity of bryozoans ranged from 0.42 during the monsoon season of oligohaline conditions to 1.82 during the pre-monsoon season for a station within a radius of one km from the bar mouth. The upper reaches of the estuary indicted low diversity. This reduced diversity index could be due to the changes that have taken place in the water quality of the Cochin backwaters. The bryozoans are excellent indicators of aquatic pollution" (ibid. pp.11-12).

Writing on the extent and value of coastal biodiversity of India, Devaraj, *et al.* noted that the "coastal biodiversity occupies different habitats ranging from sandy, rocky, coral or mudflat intertidal to the shelf edge, each with characteristic flora and fauna. The uses and applications of biodiversity knowledge are ethical, aesthetic, direct economic and indirect economic. Several coastal plants and animals contribute to our food, many constitute the food of other marine organisms and birds, some of them yield valuable drugs, a few others form the raw material for industrial extraction, about 50 species are cultivable at present, a wide spectrum of coastal biota are used as marine curios, many of them are candidates for marine aquaria, while the general marine ecosystem itself together with its fascinating biodiversity, is a magnificent object of recreation.

Although the fisheries resources are exploited for human consumption, a large number of species get destroyed in the process of exploitation. The biodiversity of sensitive coastal ecosystems (beaches, mangroves, estuaries, coral reefs, sea grass beds, and spawning and nursery grounds) face many anthropogenic threats. The most common man-made threats include the land use changes, conversion of natural areas, overexploitation of food species, destruction of non-target biota, habitat degradation and destruction, domestic and industrial discharges, oil spills, waste dumping, coastal mining, etc." (Devaraj, *et al.,* 1999, pp.16-17).

Referring to the loss of biodiversity in the inland waters of Kerala, the Expert Committee for Fisheries Management Studies, Kerala noted: "Overexploitation of the fish resources coupled with habitat destruction result in the shrinkage of fish populations. Due to these factors a number of fishes in some conventional fishing grounds are declining rapidly and some have become endangered. Recently in the CAMP workshop held at the National Bureau of Fish Genetic Resources (NBFGR), Lucknow, the status of some 90 species of freshwater fishes of Kerala were assessed as per IUCN red list criteria. Of these, 18 species were listed as critically endangered, of which 12 are facing serious risks of extinction in the wild ... due to alarming population decline, habitat destruction and deterioration. Among them,13 are endemic to Kerala. Thirty one species have the status of endangered species which are also facing high risk of extinction (in the world) ... of which 12 are also endemic to Kerala.. Under vulnerable category there are 18 species, which are also facing high risk of extinction ... Among them two are endemic to Kerala waters. Under threatened species of lower risk, there are 13 species, while there are five species under risk of least concern category. The status of five species could not be ascertained due to insufficient data base" (Expert Committee, 2000, pp. 53-54; parentheses added).

Other factors like clandestine introduction of exotic fish species and fish diseases also have negative impacts on the species diversity of the state. The Expert Committee observed that "the exotic varieties of fishes such as *Oreochromis mossambicus, Cyprinus carpio*, silver carp, grass carp, *Gambusia* and the African catfish *Clarius quariepinus* are likely to have interaction with indigenous fish species. Instances of extermination of indigenous species by the exotic species have already been reported in different parts of the country.

Likewise, *Oreochromis mossambicus* has established itself in the backwaters of Kerala and has resulted in the partial replacement of the native species such as *Etroplus suratensis* and *E. maculatus*. The indigenous fishes are under threat due to the clandestine introduction of the predatory and carnivorous African catfish *Clarius quariepinus* which is being bred in controlled systems in Kerala. Though the Union Agriculture Ministry ... ordered ... to destroy the existing stock, it is understood that ... this species is still available in some of the hatcheries of Kerala and grow outs in Alappuzha, Kottayam, Thrissur and Ernakulam" (ibid. p.54).

The impact of fish diseases has also been noted by the Committee. It found that "among the various diseases caused by bacteria, fungi, viruses, etc., the most virulent and menacingly threatening many species is the Epizotic Ulceration Syndrome (EUS). The outbreak of EUS was first noticed in Kuttanad in Kerala in June 1991 and its recurrence in varied intensities could be registered in the past several years in different parts of the state. The species mainly affected by EUS are mullets, *thooli,* barbs, pearl spots, etc. As a result of the outbreak of this disease, the economy of the state has been adversely affected and has thrown around 25000 full-time and 7000 other persons engaged in fishery related activities out of employment" (ibid. p.54).

Reporting on the biodiversity loss of the fish fauna of the Muriyad wetlands of Thrissur Kole lands, Subash Babu, *et al.* noted that "one significant feature observed in the present study is that there is the absence of *Wallago attu* and *Heteropensustus fossilis* in the present collections ...; it is said that *Wallago* of about six feet in length was not rare from certain parts (Kokrachal area) of the wetland. A sudden decline in the availability of two economically important species required detailed investigation and urgent attention. It is relevant to note that both these species are bottom feeders and hence accumulation of aquatic pollutants like pesticides in the bottom sediments affecting the normal physiology of the fish species cannot be ruled out ..." (Subash Babu, *et al.*, 2002, p.62).

The possibility of environmental damages in the upstreams of India causing threat to the ecology and biodiversity of the Bay of Bengal has been indicated by the Mc Allister, who noted that "three billion metric tonnes of eroded soil are carried annually by the Ganges and Brahmaputra rivers to benthic habitats in the Bay of Bengal" (Mc Allister, 1999, p.25).

Threats to the biodiversity of freshwater fishes of India like Mahseer have been indicated by Sugunan and Sinha. They noted: "Mahseers, once plentiful in the upstream stretches of rivers, are already under threat of extinction" (Sugunan and Sinha, 2001, p.47). They further observed that, "decline of fish populations in rivers is universal phenomenon due to a variety of factors including destruction of habitat, effluent discharge and cascading effects of dams and other obstructions ... the decline of major carps in rivers has also been attributed to the flood control measures and large scale water abstraction for irrigation purpose. In the Ganga basin, 33.5 billion $m^3$ of water is presently held in storage reservoirs behind the weirs and barrages apart from 18 major canal net works diverting water to irrigate 7 m ha of agricultural land. Indian carps are known to undertake short breeding migrations to the limpid shallow areas during monsoon. Water abstractions and impoundments of water behind weirs have destroyed a good amount of these breeding grounds resulting in recruitment failure. Flood plains are cut off from the river often converting them into virtual fish traps.

Riverine fishes, by nature, are extremely sensitive to change in flood regime because of their dependence on seasonal floods, which inundate the grounds needed for feeding and reproduction. Thus, any change in the form and dimension of the flood curve in the rivers is bound to affect the community structure.

Collapse of hilsa fisheries in the Ganga above Farakka ... is one of the classical examples of physiological strain and breeding failure that can be caused by the dams and barrages to the migratory fishes. Catadromous migrants like eels, freshwater prawns and the non-predatory catfish, *Pangasius pangasius* have also been affected by the barrage. Heavy siltation from catchment areas cuts off oxbow lakes and deep pools during summer. Major carps are known to retreat to these areas during dry season and get destroyed either due to drying of the area or due to indiscriminate exploitation. Studies conducted at CIFRI and elsewhere have shown that aquatic community, as a whole is highly vulnerable to toxic chemicals and pesticides" (ibid. pp. 48-49).

Large scale collection of shrimp seed for culture from wild sources and the incidental capture and destruction of unwanted species are also reported to affect the biodiversity of the region (ibid. p.147). Development of aquaculture in the country, by clearing the mangroves, is considered to cause significant loss of biodiversity and affect the long-term sustainability of fisheries in the country. The flipside of this is the low index of biodiversity utilisation for aquaculture (BUA) as noted by Kutty (Kutty, 2001, p.197).

Sampath reported that "popularisation of shrimp farming for earning huge profits within a short span of time has increased the demand for shrimp seed, substantially in recent years ...; the gap between the demand and supply of shrimp seed has put tremendous pressure on natural shrimp seed resources ...; some of the *bheries* in West Bengal have resorted to collection of *Penaeus monodon* post-larvae from the wild for stocking so as to enhance shrimp production. This has led to large scale lifting of *P. monodon* seeds from the Sunderbans estuarine system and the prawn seed trade has thus, come into being. It has been estimated by the Central Institute of Brackish Water Aquaculture (CIBA) Madras, that, for every single *P. monodon* larva collected, about 18 post-larvae of other species of shrimp and several of finfish species are being sacrificed. The study has further revealed that in West Bengal alone the total harvest of wild prawn seed is around 400 million per annum, which results in the destruction of nearly 20 billion fry or juveniles of unwanted species. It is also reported that the known seed grounds in Orissa and Andhra Pradesh are also being heavily exploited to meet shrimp seed requirements.

Although many of the organisms destroyed may be of no use to a shrimp farmer, it may, in the long run affect the fishery of a number of economic finfish species and also degrade the artisanal and commercial capture fishery in the area" (Sampath, 1998, p.73).

Writing on the biodiversity degradation of the Chilka lake, Kadekodi and Nayampalli noted: "Like many wetland areas of the world over, Chilka lake is also subjected to a multiplicity of pressures and impacts, ranging from local to global in geographical scale, over short to very long periods, with an ultimate effect on the socio-economic conditions of the region. All these are partly driven by market forces and partly due to socio-political situations and compulsions" (Kadekodi and Nayampalli, 2005, p.527).

Depletion of the standing stock and biodiversity have been reported in the case of sea weeds in India. Kaladharan and Jayasankar noted that "sea weeds are exploited for commercial purposes only from south east coast of India, especially from Vedaranyam to Kanyakumari coast which resulted in the depletion of standing stock and species diversity ... Despite rich resources of the sea weeds, the exploitation is not uniform in many centres, as a result of which overexploitation is actually felt in the Gulf of Mannar ..." (Kaladharan and Jayasankar, 2003, p. 230). They also reported that the number of species of marine algae in Krusadi island in Tamil Nadu has decreased from 134 in 1955 to 77 in 1992 (ibid. p.230).

Das, *et al.* reported that out of 694 species, 106 species are under the threat of extinction in West Bengal. Of these, 12 species are critically endangered, 34 endangered, 36 vulnerable and 13 near vulnerable (Das, *et al.*, 2004, p.74).

Referring to the loss of marine biodiversity in general, Sinha noted: "Biodiversity loss in marine areas could be faster as the response times to environmental perturbations are relatively short. Losses of marine biodiversity, although, are highest in coastal areas ...The consequences of heavy fishing pressure on commercial species is that the size distribution changes, which in turn leads to loss of genetic diversity (e.g., Orange Roughy). Also changes in fish species combination have dramatic effects on other species dependent on fish, such as seabirds and mammals. Overexploitation of these resources can lead to local or regional species extinction. Also, local extinction of fish can occur where estuaries are made unfit for spawning. Trawling for bottom living fishes is having major effect on the habitat for species other than target species. The threats to marine biodiversity are mainly by ocean dumping; UV-B radiation; human population and demographic trends in coastal areas;

habitat degradation, fragmentation and destruction; global climate change; over- exploitation and other effects of fishing; pollution; eutrophication; species introduction or invasions; watershed alteration; physical alteration of coasts; tourism; marine litter and ... little perception of the oceans and their marine life. The threats frequently are inter-linked. Most critical threat, of course, is habitat loss" (Sinha, 2004, pp.449-450).

Table 6.10 gives details of marine hotspots in India, which has implications for sustainability of Indian fisheries.

**Table 6.10**

**Marine hot spots in India**

| *Sl. No.* | *Resources* | *Locations* |
|---|---|---|
| 1 | Phytoplankton | South West Coast, North Bay of Bengal, Andaman and Nicobar Islands, Lakshadweep Islands |
| 2 | Zooplankton | South West Coast (Bombay, Cochin and Goa to Mangalore), East Coast (Visakhapatnam to Chennai), West Bay of Bengal, and off Ratnagiri, Konkan, Quilon, North East Bay of Bengal |
| 3 | Sea weed and sea grass | Off Tamil Nadu, Gujarat, Maharashtra, Lakshadweep Islands, Andaman and Nicobar Islands |
| 4 | Mangroves | East Coast, Sunderbans, Koringa, Mahanadi – Godavari delta, Gulf of Kutch, Andaman and Nicobar Islands |
| 5 | Coral reefs | Palk Bay, Gulf of Mannar, Gulf of Kutch, Malvin, Lakshadweep Islands, Andaman and Nicobar Islands |
| 6 | Marine fishes | West coast |
| 7 | Benthos (sub-tidal)<br>(*a*) Macrofauna<br>(*b*) Meio fauna | North West Arabian Sea, North Bay of Bengal, North West and South West Arabian Sea, North Bay of Bengal, Off Goa and Andaman Sea |
| 8 | Marine molluscs | Off Maharashtra Coast, Goa, Kakinada Bay, Tamil Nadu, Gulf of Kutch, Gulf of Mannar, Kerala |
| 9 | Marine crustaceans | Kerala, Gulf of Mannar, Colachal to Kanyakumari |
| 10 | Marine sponges | Off Lakshadweep Islands, Gulf of Mannar, Palk Bay |

| *Sl. No.* | *Resources* | *Locations* |
|---|---|---|
| 11 | Holothurians | South East Coast, Palk Bay, Gulf of Mannar, Gulf of Kutch, Lakshadweep Islands, Andaman & Nicobar Islands |
| 12 | Marine birds | Andaman Sea |
| 13 | Marine crocodiles | East Coast, Andaman Sea |
| 14 | Prawns and shrimps | South West Coast, Off Maharashtra, Kerala, Lakshadweep |
| 15 | Tuna | North and South Arabian Sea, Lakshadweep Islands |
| 16 | Sharks | East Coast |
| 17 | Marine turtles | South Calcutta, Gulf of Mannar, Palk Bay, Andaman Sea, Orissa Coast (Bhitarkanika and Gahirmata) |
| 18 | Whales | Southern Indian ocean |
| 19 | Dolphins | Cochin, Quilon, Bombay, Calicut, Vizhinjam Zone of Kerala Coast, Mangalore-Calicut Area |
| 20 | Dugongs | Lakshadweep Island, Andaman & Nicobar Islands |

*Source:* Sinha, 2004, pp.468-469.

Some of these resources are reported as facing serious crisis of overexploitation and bio- diversity loss.

Referring to mangroves, Sinha noted: "Mangrove forest cover in India has reduced drastically from 14 lakh ha to 7 lakh ha till late 1980s. Recently Forest Survey of India has come up with the actual figure of 3.54 lakh ha which is quite alarming. Deforestation, reclamation for land and aquaculture, and marine pollution are major causes of destruction of this unique habitat. Use of mangrove foliage for grazing live stock has severely damaged mangrove forests in the northern coastal areas of India; so has been the logging for mangrove timber and wood chips …" (ibid. p.459).

Recently Kaladharan, *et al.* noted: "In Kerala and West Bengal, human interventions and transformation of topography/morphology and overexploitation of resources resulted not only in the shrinking of the mangroves, but also deteriorated the general environment considerably which are evidenced by the disappearance or rare occurrence of certain commercially important species of flora and fauna with very low population" (Kaladharan, *et al.*, 2005, pp.11-12).

Writing on other species, Sinha noted: "Box tortoise, *Batagur baska*, ... are generally found along the coast of West Bengal near Calcutta. They are now severely depleted. Marine crocodiles are popularly represented by *Crocodylus porosus*, the carnivores inhabiting mangrove swamps of Eastern India and Andaman sea. They are fastly approaching extinction ...

The average landings of deep-sea shrimps have declined to nine tonnes in 1991 from 23-25 tonnes prior to 1985 ...

Yellow fin tuna fishery being done in Western Indian Ocean presently may fall in the range of moderate to above 'maximum sustainable yield' (MSY) level ... Uncertainty exists regarding the stock of big-eye tuna also. The skipjack tuna stock has been declared fully exploited in 1994 by FAO. Blue fin tuna is also over fished and heavily depleted ...

Gulf of Mannar (between Pamban and Kanyakumari) and Palk Bay (between Rameswaram and Mimisal) are places of regular fishery of green turtles. Their population is also dwindling in the Andaman Sea. The primarily carnivorous hawks bill or tortoise shell turtle (*Eretmochelys imbricata*) nests exclusively on island beaches. It is seriously depleted throughout its island habitats, including the Andaman and Nicobar islands. Predominantly carnivorous leatherback turtle (*Dermochelys coriacea*), the largest of all turtles, are found around Great Nicobar island and Little Andaman island. In 1979, there were only 150 of them left in the Indian waters ..." (ibid. pp. 459-465).

An approximate idea of the damage caused to the ecosystem and biodiversity by trawling is given by Jagadish, *et al.,* when they wrote: "Although mechanised bottom trawling is targeted at shrimp or cephalopods, the fishing has invariably trampled the bottom habitat often affecting other components in the ecosystem through by-catch, physical damage or through food chain effects. The non-edible biological components that are being destroyed or dislocated by trawling are very basic and important for the eco-balance and recruitment. These bottom trawl literally sweep the sea bottom while fishing and causes habitat alteration, degradation and loss of feeding grounds of many benthic fishes" (Jagadish, *et al.* 2004, p.608). The major non-edible biota displaced reported by these authors included crab (non-edible stomatopods, molluscs, echinoderms, jellyfish, sea pen, gorgonids, antipatharians, sponges, ascidians, and sea plants (ibid, p.623).

The bycatch of the deep sea shrimp fishery along the North East Coast of India is estimated to be 26000 tonnes per annum, which is discarded at sea, causing serious damage to the biodiversity and sustainability of the industry (Rao, 2004, p.679).

Referring to the deforestation of mangroves of India, Kaladharan, *et al.,* wrote: "Deforestation and overexploitation of the mangrove resources have resulted into the formation of open marshyland of approximately 1,00,000 ha. The coastal areas like Gulf of Kutch (Gujarat), Mumbai (Maharashtra) and Cochin (Kerala) are the glaring examples of deforestation, reclamation, conversion and pollution due to population pressure ... mangroves south of Cochin are in highly degraded condition both in the case of topography/morphology and biodiversity ... the over exploitation of fishery resources, especially the seeds of fin-fishes and shell-fish for aquaculture have affected the capture fishery resources of coastal West Bengal... the extensive anthropogenic activities resulted in the dwindling of Sunderban mangrove resources and shrinking of this important wetland ecosystem" (Kaladharan, *et. al.,* 2005, pp.8-9).

### 6.2.5. Climate Change

Some of the implications and effects of climate change on global fisheries and sustainability have been noted in chapter four. Global warming, sea level rise and other phenomena like floods, typhoons and tsunami were found to affect the fisheries adversely. Although the effect of global warming and sea level rise on the sustainability of Indian fisheries are not immediate and pronounced at present, other adverse natural processes like floods, typhoons and tsunami have caused noteworthy damages to the fishery sector of India. The information in this regard is, however, not well documented. The limited information may be nevertheless, noted.

Singh and Raje had reported about the squally weather disrupting fishing activity along the Maharashtra coast in September 1988. They noted that "the fishing activities along the Maharashtra coast were severely disrupted when sudden fury of the sea caught several fishermen in the sea with wind speeds up to 55 kmph on September 23, 1988, off many fishing villages of Greater Bombay, Bassein, Satpati and Arnala.

... One fisherman off Worli died when his *thoni* overturned in the sea off Napean Sea Road. Three other bodies, possibly of fishermen from Gujarat were washed ashore off Carter Road, Bandra on 26th September. A fisherman and his three sons suffered injuries when their boat was buffeted in the rough seas off Worli. Two other fishermen of Koliwada village were drifted three km away when their *thoni* overturned but were washed ashore near Sea Rock Hotel.

Naval personnel responding to distress call rescued at least 30 people from the sea and a helicopter made several sorties in search and rescue operation. Four fishermen were rescued by another vessel from the sunken boat *Mahamanorama*" (Singh and Raje, 1989, p.15).

Referring to the loss of property, they reported: "the estimated loss of property was about rupees one crore. At least six boats sank and many were badly damaged. Some boats returned safely but lost their gear.

Prominent among the sunken boat was the trawler, *Mahamanorama,* which was operating from Sassoon Dock. It sank 25 km off Nuvud. Three boats sank near Mudh resulting in heavy financial losses. A customs boat *Angohsia* sank near Vasai Creek. The trawler *Dnyaneshwari Prasad* also sank" (ibid. p.15).

Dey and Dan reported that "a severe cyclonic storm with a velocity of 250 km/hr swept through the coastal districts of 24 Parganas and Midanpur in the midnight of 29$^{th}$ November 1988 which caused extensive damage to public and private properties ... The loss of crops, livestock and fisheries amounted to Rs 8,00,000. Three mechanised boats along with 37 crew members were missing from Kalisthan" (Dey and Dan, 1989, p.17). These authors further noted that "fishermen who got advances from traders usually repay during the fishing season but due to cyclone and the consequent dislocations they were not able to do this in 1989. Besides these fishermen had taken advances for repairing their boats and huts which also they could not return (repay) ... Affected fishermen were given money and material in the form of craft and gear. Bamboo and *hogla* were supplied to them for the construction of their huts. Essentials like *dothies*, blankets and food were supplied by Amarabati Gramapanchayat" (ibid, p.17; word in parenthesis is added).

Table 6.11 gives details of damage to fishing centres due to cyclone in West Bengal in November 1988.

Table 6.11 reveals the widespread damage caused to the fisheries sector in terms of fishermen missing, boats and nets damaged or lost, fishermen's sheds destroyed and dry fish lost.

Dey and Dan further reported that "generally the fisheries sector is one of the worst affected by the cyclone, especially in the districts of

24 Parghanas. Fishing villages most affected were Gasaba, Basanthi, Canning, Raydighi, Bakkhali, Kalisthan, Zamboo and Gangasagar. About 2000 huts were blown away by the wind exposing dry fish stock worth Rs 400,000.Loss of life and property and boat in the district of Midnapore by this cyclone was comparatively less" (ibid, p.19).

Purandhara reported on the set back to the fishing sector of Dakshina Kannada, Karnataka, due to the cyclone during November 1992. Purandhara stated:

"Cyclone which are common along the east coast of India during October-December period rarely occur along the west coast. However, the recent cyclone which hit the west coast in the third week of November, 1992 left a trail of damages and destructions to the fishing craft along the Dakshina Kannada coast of Karnataka ...

On 14.11.1992, a country craft (plank-built boat, 10.8 m long and 1.8 m broad) with 25 people on board on a routine fishing trip (*Kairampani* operation) hit against the sand dunes due to the high waves off Suratkal and was broken to pieces. The fishing crew, however, escaped unhurt. The total loss was estimated to be Rs 80,000.

One trawler of overall length of 10.8 m and breadth 3.3 m fitted with 88 BHP engine was caught in the high waves and it hit against the sand bar of the bar mouth at Mangalore and sank on 16.11.1992. Two of the five crew in the boat who were seriously injured had died. The fishermen in the vicinity rescued the other three persons on board.

Besides human life, the financial loss on the vessel, gear and fish catch was estimated at about seven lakhs. On the same day at Polipu, a fishing village about 50 km north of Mangalore, another trawler of the same type hit against rocks due to high waves and was broken to pieces. The loss in this case was about Rs 5 lakhs.

A total loss due to loss of fishing craft, gear and fish catch and due to non-fishing during the short period of four days along the Dakshina Kannada coast was estimated to be about Rs 25 lakhs" (Purandhara, 1993, pp.15-16).

Arumugham, *et al.* reported the impact of cyclone along the Tuticorin coasts during November 1992. The report said: "A severe cyclonic storm with a wind velocity of 100-130 km per hour swept through the coastal villages of Chidambaranar district of Tamil Nadu on the afternoon of 13.11.1992 leaving behind a trail of destruction along its path ...

## Table 6.11
### Details of damage to fishing centres due to cyclone in West Bengal during November 1988

| Sl. No. | Name of Place | No. of persons affected | No. of persons missing (fishermen) | Nets damaged | | Boats damaged | | | | Dry fish lost | | Boats missing (mech. & non-mech.) | | Nets lost | | Fishermen's sheds destroyed | | Total worth |
|---|---|---|---|---|---|---|---|---|---|---|---|---|---|---|---|---|---|---|
| | | | | | | Mech. | | Non-mech. | | | | | | | | | | |
| | | | | No. | Worth (Rs) | No. | Worth (Rs.) | No. | Worth (Rs.) | Kg. | Worth (Rs.) | No. | Worth (Rs.) | No. | Worth (Rs.) | No. | Worth (Rs.) | (Rs.) |
| 1 | Bakkhali (Canal) | 30 | - | 1GN | 250 | 1 | 800 | - | - | 400 | 2,000 | - | - | - | - | 10 | 5,000 | 8,050 |
| 2 | Bakkhali (Stand) | - | - | - | - | - | - | - | - | - | - | - | - | - | - | - | - | - |
| 3 | Frazergunj | 200 | 600 | 4GN | 1,200 | - | - | 1 | 300 | 2,000 | 10,000 | - | - | - | - | 25 | 30,000 | 42,100 |
| | | | | 38BN | 600 | - | - | - | - | - | - | - | - | - | - | - | - | - |
| 4 | Kalisthan | 300 | 20 | 8BN | 1,600 | - | - | 4 | 1,200 | 4,000 | 20,000 | 2 mech | 60,000 | 4 | 8,000 | 40 | 80,000 | 1,70,800 |
| 5 | Kaylaghata | - | - | - | - | - | - | - | - | - | - | - | - | - | - | - | - | - |
| 6 | Namkhana | - | - | - | - | - | - | - | - | - | - | - | - | - | - | - | - | - |
| 7 | Kakdwip | - | 4 | - | - | - | - | - | - | - | - | - | - | - | - | - | - | - |
| 8 | Beguakhali | 250 | - | 7BN | 1,400 | - | - | 6 | 1,800 | 3,000 | 15,000 | - | - | - | - | 30 | 45,000 | 63,200 |
| 9 | Zamboo | 400 | 25 | 15BN | 4,500 | 5 | 5,000 | - | - | 9,000 | 45,000 | 2 mech | 80,000 | 3 | 6,000 | 50 | 10,000 | 1,50,500 |
| 10 | Raydighi | - | 2 | 1GN | 3,000 | 1 | 8,000 | - | - | - | - | - | - | - | - | - | - | 11,000 |
| 11 | Diamond Harbour | - | - | - | - | - | - | - | - | - | - | - | - | - | - | - | - | - |
| 12 | Junput | 400 | - | 20BN | 4,000 | 1 | 3,000 | 4 | 800 | 2,000 | 10,000 | - | - | - | - | 40 | 8,000 | 25,800 |
| 13 | Digha Mohana | 250 | - | 10GN | 3,000 | 30 | 15,000 | - | - | - | - | - | - | - | - | 20 | 40,000 | 50,000 |
| 14 | Digha | 500 | - | 4GN | 12,000 | 60 | 18,000 | - | - | 4,000 | 20,000 | - | - | - | - | 45 | 90,000 | 1,40,000 |
| 15 | Jaldah | - | - | 63 (small BN) | 6,300 | 7 | 21,000 | 22 | 4,400 | 1,200 | 6,000 | - | - | - | - | - | - | 39,700 |
| | | - | - | 10 BN | 2,000 | - | - | - | - | - | - | - | - | - | - | - | - | - |
| | Total | 2,330 | 51 | 85 | 39.850 | 104 | 70,800 | 37 | 8.500 | 25,600 | 1,28,000 | 4 | 1,40,000 | 7 | 14,000 | 260 | 3,08,000 | 7,09,150 |

GN: Gill net; BN: Big Bag net: Figures do not tally with the total loss (worth) as complete details are not given in the source.
*Source:* Dey and Dan, 1989, p.18.

The cyclone lashed the coast for a period of 3-4 hours accompanied by ghastly winds, heavy rains and huge tidal waves thereby causing untold havoc to life and property involving an overall loss of Rs 35-54 crores due to damage to crops, livestock, fishing boats, private and public properties ...

In the fisheries sector, the worst affected were the traditional fishermen. Altogether, nineteen villages were affected by this cyclone. Among them, ... Theraspuram (Tuticorin North), Punnakkayal and Tharuvaikulam were the worst affected. The loss suffered by the fisher-folk was estimated at Rs 1.1 crores ...

... Loss incurred were due to damages caused to *Valloms*, Catamarans and nets ... About 350 victims incurred loss. Damages of the magnitude of about Rs 11 lakhs were caused to *Valloms*, Rs 20,000 to Catamarans and Rs 3 lakhs to nets (*Podivalai, Paruvalai* and *Vala valai*" (Arumugham, *et al.*, 1993, pp.25-26).

Referring to the cyclone of November 1996, which struck the Andhra coast, FAO reported, "on the night of 6 November1996, during a severe cyclone, approximately 1435 fishers perished in the state of Andhra Pradesh on the east coast of India. Of these fishers, 569 were lost while fishing in mechanised boats at sea and 830 were lost while carrying out shrimp seed collection and other shore based activities in areas remote from the villages. The causes of death differed between the two groups; the former were lost at sea in conditions of high winds and heavy seas, and the latter were lost on land, largely as a result of the storm surge.

The 569 fishers who were reported lost at sea were working in 110 trawlers, which foundered in when struck by the cyclone. They had departed from Kakinada port several days before the cyclone struck and were fishing in an area south east of Kakinada, along the coast of the Godavari delta. These trawlers were typically 11 to 15 m long and engaged in fishing trips of 10 to15 days duration. They were poorly designed and built, ... Few, if any of the vessels were equipped with safety equipment or even simple transistor radios. Thus, despite the media's transmission of cyclone warnings, the fishers were unaware of the intensity of the approaching cyclone and of its speed of advance" (FAO, 2000a, p.42).

Referring to the impact of the cyclone of November 1996 on the life and economy of marine fishing communities of Andhra Pradesh, Subba Rao wrote that "approximately 1,435 fisher- folk were reported dead ... Of the total estimated loss of Rs 14.66 crores to the marine fishery sector, 70 per cent was at Kakinada fishing harbour and about 27 percent at Bhairavavanipalem and adjacent fishing villages and this was due to loss of houses as well as damages to fishing trawlers, traditional fishing craft and gear, dried fish and so on ..." (Subba Rao, 2004, p.27).

Ammini, Khambadkar and Burman reported the impact of the cyclone of April-May 2002 in West Bengal. They noted that "during the cyclone of April-May 2002, the landing centers of Ramaganga and Gangasagar were totally devastated and at the end of the year, Ramaganga fishermen were forced to unload their catch at Raidighi and Kakdwip. In Midnapore, an important landing centre, Sankarpur, was closed. Boats could not enter the nearby canal to unload their catches as the canal was full of sand.

Cyclone storm hit 24 Parganas on 12$^{th}$ November 2002 at a speed of 100-120 km/hour; 12 gill netters along with 73 fishermen were reported missing. Besides this, so many *doba behundi* nets and *vasa behundi* nets along with good quantities of dried and semi dried fishes and their shelters were damaged. Beguakhali, Gangasagar west, Baliara, Jambudip and Kalisthan were mostly affected. Estimated loss due to destruction worked out to be Rs 1.47 crores" (Ammini, Khambadkar and Burman, 2004, p.10)

One of the most well known natural calamity in recent times that caused maximum damage to the fisheries sector of India was the tsunami of 26.12.2004 which struck the coasts of South India and the Andaman & Nicobar islands. The World Fish Centre tsunami update of 21.1.2005 noted that "the tsunami caused extensive damage in southern regions of India and Andaman & Nicobar islands affecting a total of 2,260 km of coast line. The waves were reported to be as high as 3-10 metres in southern India and penetrated from 300 m to 3 km inland. The worst affected regions were the states of Tamil Nadu and the Andaman and Nicobar archipelago. The states of Pondicherry, Andhra Pradesh and Kerala were affected to a lesser extent" (http://www .worldfishcentre.org/ news...india.pds). The update noted that 10,714 people have been killed, 5669 missing and 6,47,521 displaced.

Referring to the damage to the fisheries sector of India, it noted: "The fisheries sector in Tamil Nadu, Andhra Pradesh and Andaman & Nicobar islands has suffered major damages ... the worst hit places like Nagapattinam have been closed ... fearing epidemics ... many fishers are unable to work due to loss of boats and gear, or due to fear of the sea. Fishers in some areas are beginning to return to sea. However, the market for seafood has plummeted due to public fear of disease and contamination from bodies. This issue persists despite resounding dismissal by health authorities throughout the region, further complicating the lives of those fishers still able to work" (ibid).

The state-wise details of the damage gave the following picture. Referring to Tamil Nadu, it noted: "Tamil Nadu was the worst affected state with around 8000 people killed. All thirteen coastal districts were affected but the worst losses occurred in Nagapattinam district where more than 6000 people were killed. An estimated 85 per cent of people affected by the tsunami in Tamil Nadu are believed to be from the fishing community ...The fisheries sector has suffered major damage in terms of lives, boats, gear and ... infrastructure such as harbours and fish landing centers" (ibid.)

Referring to Andhra Pradesh, the update stated: "Fishers were affected along 1000 km of coastline with Krishna and Prakasam districts the most serious, and damage also to Guntur, Nellore, West Godavari, East Godavari and Visakhapatnam. Approximately 2000 fishing boats and 47,370 nets were lost. At Visakhapatnam there was damages to trawlers, fishing equipment and fish stored for export. Nearly 3,00,000 have been rendered jobless and they are estimated to be losing Rs 50 million a day" (ibid).

Referring to Kerala it noted: "Fishers were affected along 250 km of coastline. Those who have not lost their fishing crafts and implements have resumed fishing in Kollam, Alappuzha and Ernakulam districts. Other traditional fishermen and boat owners have not resumed fishing activities due to boat/gear damage" (ibid).

In Pondicherry "25 km of coastline was affected by the tsunami with penetration ranging from 300 m to 3 km affecting 26 villages" (ibid).

In Andaman and Nicobar, "30 of the 38 inhabited islands of the Nicobars were affected, with the worst being Car Nicobar, Great Nicobar and the Nan Cowrie group. The total population of the affected islands is about 60,000. Seven islands were fully evacuated including Trinket, Kondul, Pilomillow, Little Nicobar, Bambooka, Chowra and Tilanchang ...

Port Blair was damaged but four of the six jetties are now functional. There are 49 jetties in Andaman and Nicobar islands of which 29 are now operational including 11 jetties in Andaman district. All small harbours and jetties in the Nicobar islands have been damaged ..." (ibid).

Table 6.12 presents the details of damage/loss caused to fishing villages by the tsunami of 26.12.2004.

As already noted, the damage/loss was the highest in Tamil Nadu. The above update also gave a review of the damage to coastal aquaculture. It noted: "Many hatchery facilities in the southern India regions were severely affected. While the second harvest had been completed, farm infrastructure has been badly damaged and this is likely to impact on future production. In the Kovalam, Marakanam, and Pondy belt, most of the shrimp hatcheries have lost their pump houses, fencing, etc. Shrimp farms at Cuddalore, Chidambaram and Sirkali were severely affected with collapsed bunds and damaged pumps; shrimp farms in the Vellar estuaries (Chidambaram and Sirkali) were heavily damaged from seawater inundation. Sea-based farms in Tharangampadi, Vedaranyam, Nagapattinam and Velankanni had their bunds and equipment including motors and pumps destroyed. Broodstock availability is likely to decline due to damage to fishing vessels, further reducing the likelihood of having a crop in the next season" (ibid).

Total loss in Kerala is estimated around Rs 14,900,000. At least 14 shrimp hatcheries have been affected covering four districts (Kollam, Alleppey, Ernakulam and Kannur).

Total loss in Tamil Nadu is estimated at around Rs 62,700,000. It includes the loss suffered by 120 ha of small scale shrimp farms in Nagapattinam and 11 hatcheries.

In Andhra Pradesh, official sources reported damage to 400 fish tanks. Un-official estimates of loss are about Rs 500 million. Aquaculture farms over 400 acres were reported as damaged. Seabass hatcheries in Thirumullaivassal were reported as badly affected with one farm totally submerged (ibid).

**Table 6.12**

**Details of damage caused to fishing villages by the tsunami of 26.12.2004**

| State U.T. | Districts affected | Village | | | Landing centres damaged[2] | Number of fishers affected | Human beings lost and missing[3] | Fishing vessels | |
|---|---|---|---|---|---|---|---|---|---|
| | | Total | Fishing village | Villages and people affected[1] | | | | Damaged | Lost |
| A & N Islands | 2 | 38 inhabited islands | - | 30 islands | 49 (20) | - | 1899 (5554) | - | - |
| Tamil Nadu | 13 | 13182 | 591 | 362 (890885) | 362 | 698268 | 7983 (383) | 45920 | 10000 |
| Pondicherry | 2 | - | - | 33 (43432) | - | - | 591 (75) | 6678 | |
| Andhra Pradesh | 7 | - | - | 301 (196320) | - | - | 105 (11) | 1362 | 2000 |
| Kerala | 3 | - | - | 187 (130000) | - | - | 171 | 10065 | - |
| Total | 27 | - | - | 30 Islands (883) | - | - | 9675 (6490) | - | - |

[1]Number of people affected in parentheses
[2]Number of landing centres damaged in parentheses
[3]Number of human beings missing in parentheses
*Source:* (http://www.worldfishcentre.org/news...india.pds)

Another natural phenomenon which is also having serious impact on the sustainability of coastal fisheries, as in Kerala, is beach erosion, particularly during the monsoons. Referring to this phenomenon, The Kerala State Gazetteer noted: "The problem is of serious magnitude along the Kerala coast line. Kerala has a coastline of about 590 km. Of this, about 320 km is subject to erosion, especially during the monsoon. Annually about two to five metres of land is lost on an average. In one place near Cochin about two km width of land has been eroded since 1850. During the southwest monsoon from June to September waves measuring about four metres in height pour the coast from the south west direction and erosion is very severe during this time" (Kerala Gazetteers Department, 1989, pp.322-323).

The Expert Committee on Marine Fisheries in Kerala also noted that "a characteristic of the 590 km long coast line of Kerala is that almost 25 per cent of it is subjected to varying degrees of erosion, especially during the monsoon season. The shoreline between Trivandrum and Alleppey, a track of several kilometers north and south of Cochin, the shoreline between Calicut and Cannanore and in the coastal area of Manassery, Thottapally and Purakkad, are prone to severe sea erosion. Though no direct correlation between erosion and fisheries is on record, the socio-economic impact of this environmental phenomenon on the fishermen community through considerable reduction in the traditional shore landing facilities is quite alarming" (Expert Committee, 1985, pp.351-352).

## 6.3. Economic Issues

The major economic issues affecting the sustainability of Indian fisheries discussed in this section are: (1) stagnation in production, (2) overcapitalisation, (3) uneconomic operations, (4) declining employment, (5) static or declining consumption, (6) unstable global market for fish and barriers to trade and (7) meagre contribution to the GDP.

### 6.3.1. Stagnation in Production

A major indicator of the threat to the sustainability of fisheries in India from the economic point of view is the emerging stagnation in fish production in the country especially in marine fish production in recent years. Table 6.13 shows the trend in fish production in India from 1991-92 to 2003-04.

**Table 6.13**

**Trend in total fish production in India from 1991-92 to 2003-04**

(in million tonnes)

| *Year* | *Marine* | *Inland* | *Total* |
|---|---|---|---|
| 1991-92 | 2.45 | 1.71 | 4.16 |
| 1992-93 | 2.58 | 1.79 | 4.37 |
| 1993-94 | 2.65 | 2.00 | 4.65 |
| 1994-95 | 2.69 | 2.10 | 4.79 |
| 1995-96 | 2.71 | 2.24 | 4.95 |
| *Average* | 2.62 | 1.97 | 4.58 |
| 1996-97 | 2.97 | 2.38 | 5.35 |
| 1997-98 | 2.95 | 2.44 | 5.39 |
| 1998-99 | 2.70 | 2.60 | 5.30 |
| 1999-00 | 2.85 | 2.82 | 5.67 |
| 2000-01 | 2.81 | 2.85 | 5.66 |
| *Average** | 2.86 | 2.62 | 5.47 |
| | (1.83) | (6.6) | (3.89) |
| 2001-02 | 2.83 | 3.13 | 5.96 |
| 2002-03 | 2.99 | 3.21 | 6.20 |
| 2003-04 | 2.94 | 3.46 | 6.40 |
| *Average** | 2.92 | 3.27 | 6.19 |
| | (0.7) | (8.27) | (4.39) |

*Figures in parentheses show the average annual growth rate over the previous period.

*Source:* Department of Animal Husbandry Dairying and Fisheries, 2005, p.5.

It is quite apparent from table 6.13 that the average annual fish production in the country which stood at 4.58 million tonnes between 1991-92 and 1995-96 increased to 5.47 million tonnes between 1996-97 and 2000-01 and to 6.19 million tonnes between 2001-02 and 2003-04 showing an annual increase (growth rate) of 3.89 per cent during the second period over the first and 4.39 per cent during the third period over the second period. The slightly higher average annual growth rate during the third period cannot be considered as indicative of the sustainability of high levels of natural production since much of the increase in output is from inland source which is sustained by aquaculture, where the annual average growth rate is high at 8.27 per cent during the third period i.e. between 2001-02 and 2003-04. As is further clear from the table, the average annual growth rate of marine fish production in the country has decreased from 1.83 per cent during the second period to 0.7 per cent during the third period. The average output of marine fisheries stagnated at around 2.92 million tonnes during this period (i.e. from 2001-02 to 2003-04) varying only marginally between 2.83 million tonnes and 2.99 million tonnes.

It is to be emphasised here that the observed marginal increase in total fish production in the country in recent years is largely the contribution of aquaculture, where the output has increased significantly. Table 6.14 shows the trend in aquaculture production in India between 1994 and 2003.

**Table 6.14**

**Trend in acquaculture production in India between 1994 and 2003**

| *Year Aquaculture* | *Aquaculture production* | | |
|---|---|---|---|
| | *Quantity (tonnes)* | *Value (US $ '000)* | *production as % of total** |
| 1994 | 1519528 | 13394363 | 31.73 |
| 1995 | 1658807 | 15703878 | 33.54 |
| 1996 | 1758739 | 18272012 | 32.9 |
| *Average* | 1645691 | 15790084 | 32.8 |
| 1997 | 1864322 | 20356070 | 34.51 |
| 1998 | 1908485 | 21559305 | 36.03 |
| 1999 | 2134814 | 22631659 | 37.57 |
| 2000 | 1942204 | 24317140 | 34.28 |
| *Average*** | 1962456 (4.7) | 22216044 (10.12) | 35.57 |
| 2001 | 2119839 | 26445691 | 35.57 |
| 2002 | 2187189 | 28824296 | 35.32 |
| 2003 | 2215590 | 31440632 | 34.69 |
| *Average*** | 2174206 (3.57) | 28903540 (10.06) | 35.06 |

* Based on total for financial year from source 2 below.

** Figures in parentheses show the average annual growth rate over the previous period.

*Source:* 1. FAO, 2005 b, p.42

2. Department of Animal Husbandry Dairying and Fisheries, 2005, p. 5.

**Table 6.15**

**Trend in total fish production in states and Union territories of India between 1991-92 and 2003-04**

(in '000 tonnes)

| Sl. No. | States/UT | 1991-92 | 1992-93 | 1993-94 | 1994-95 | 1995-96 | Average of 91-92 to 95-96 | 1996-97 | 1997-98 | 1998-99 | 1999-00 | 2000-01 | Average of 96-97 to 00-01 | 2001-02 | 2002-03 | 2003-04 | Average of 01-02 to 03-04 | Average annual growth rate* Per. (2) over Per.(1) | Per (3) over Per (2) |
|---|---|---|---|---|---|---|---|---|---|---|---|---|---|---|---|---|---|---|---|
| (1) | (2) | (3) | (4) | (5) | (6) | (7) | (8) | (9) | (10) | (11) | (12) | (13) | (14) | (15) | (16) | (17) | (18) | (19) | (20) |
| 1 | Andhra Pradesh | 264.67 | 264.55 | 321.37 | 345.39 | 355.96 | 310.39 | 359.36 | 372.86 | 410.82 | 547.06 | 589.69 | 455.96 | 676.11 | 827.9 | 944.64 | 816.22 | 9.38 | 26.34 |
| 2 | Arunachal Pradesh | 1.49 | 1.60 | 1.70 | 1.80 | 1.85 | 1.69 | 1.85 | 2.13 | 2.30 | 2.40 | 2.50 | 2.24 | 2.60 | 2.60 | 2.65 | 2.62 | 6.51 | 5.65 |
| 3 | Assam | 130.00 | 140.00 | 151.65 | 153.06 | 155.00 | 145.96 | 154.61 | 155.13 | 155.71 | 159.77 | 158.62 | 156.77 | 161.45 | 165.52 | 181.00 | 169.32 | 1.48 | 2.67 |
| 4 | Bihar | 184.97 | 164.07 | 200.71 | 195.37 | 239.58 | 196.94 | 249.78 | 208.54 | 237.98 | 254.74 | 222.16 | 234.64 | 240.40 | 261.00 | 266.49 | 255.96 | 3.83 | 3.03 |
| 5 | Goa | 49.55 | 104.26 | 105.44 | 101.90 | 87.82 | 89.79 | 97.06 | 92.05 | 69.02 | 65.62 | 71.57 | 79.06 | 69.92 | 76.53 | 87.36 | 77.94 | -2.39 | -0.51 |
| 6 | Gujarat | 556.95 | 638.00 | 684.86 | 715.36 | 66.00 | 651.03 | 725.35 | 816.50 | 630.00 | 741.28 | 660.74 | 714.77 | 701.60 | 777.91 | 654.62 | 711.38 | 1.96 | -0.16 |
| 7 | Haryana | 24.30 | 20.15 | 22.58 | 24.13 | 28.01 | 23.83 | 30.00 | 32.05 | 32.52 | 30.00 | 33.04 | 31.52 | 34.57 | 35.18 | 39.13 | 36.29 | 6.45 | 5.04 |
| 8 | Himachal Pradesh | 6.02 | 6.39 | 6.63 | 5.29 | 5.94 | 6.05 | 6.27 | 6.69 | 6.79 | 7.00 | 7.02 | 6.75 | 7.22 | 7.24 | 6.63 | 7.00 | 2.31 | 1.23 |
| 9 | Jammu & Kashmir | 14.05 | 14.30 | 14.50 | 16.10 | 16.52 | 15.09 | 17.80 | 18.53 | 18.85 | 19.01 | 17.51 | 18.34 | 18.85 | 19.75 | 19.75 | 19.45 | 4.31 | 2.02 |
| 10 | Karnataka | 295.75 | 299.89 | 279.15 | 274.04 | 334.87 | 296.74 | 354.43 | 315.13 | 285.61 | 322.30 | 333.37 | 322.17 | 249.61 | 266.42 | 257.00 | 257.68 | 1.71 | 6.89 |
| 11 | Kerala | 565.13 | 534.40 | 604.69 | 596.56 | 582.14 | 576.58 | 631.03 | 583.86 | 649.22 | 667.85 | 651.81 | 636.75 | 671.82 | 678.32 | 684.30 | 678.27 | 2.09 | 2.17 |

| (1) | (2) | (3) | (4) | (5) | (6) | (7) | (8) | (9) | (10) | (11) | (12) | (13) | (14) | (15) | (16) | (17) | (18) | (19) | (20) |
|---|---|---|---|---|---|---|---|---|---|---|---|---|---|---|---|---|---|---|---|
| 12 | Madhya Pradesh | 40.68 | 55.71 | 54.53 | 80.18 | 91.28 | 64.48 | 110.53 | 115.16 | 119.59 | 127.43 | 48.84 | 104.31 | 47.46 | 42.17 | 50.82 | 46.82 | 12.35 | -18.37 |
| 13 | Maharashtra | 455.39 | 464.74 | 433.62 | 446.88 | 464.00 | 452.93 | 590.00 | 580.00 | 520.38 | 533.29 | 526.10 | 549.94 | 537.05 | 514.10 | 545.13 | 532.09 | 4.28 | -1.08 |
| 14 | Manipur | 9.95 | 11.20 | 11.51 | 12.01 | 12.50 | 11.43 | 12.70 | 13.70 | 15.31 | 15.51 | 16.05 | 14.65 | 16.45 | 16.60 | 17.60 | 16.88 | 5.63 | 5.07 |
| 15 | Meghalaya | 3.31 | 3.56 | 3.98 | 3.96 | 3.58 | 3.68 | 3.58 | 3.09 | 4.53 | 4.68 | 6.18 | 4.41 | 4.97 | 5.37 | 5.15 | 5.16 | 3.97 | 5.67 |
| 16 | Mizoram | 3.14 | 3.38 | 2.50 | 2.00 | 2.50 | 2.70 | 2.55 | 2.70 | 2.78 | 2.89 | 2.86 | 2.76 | 3.15 | 3.25 | 3.38 | 3.26 | 0.44 | 6.04 |
| 17 | Nagaland | 1.50 | 1.50 | 1.82 | 2.50 | 3.00 | 2.06 | 4.00 | 3.70 | 4.50 | 5.00 | 5.50 | 4.54 | 5.20 | 5.50 | 5.56 | 5.42 | 24.08 | 6.46 |
| 18 | Orissa | 182.91 | 213.14 | 232.28 | 257.66 | 258.04 | 228.81 | 276.96 | 309.51 | 284.23 | 261.24 | 259.64 | 278.33 | 281.95 | 287.53 | 306.9 | 292.13 | 4.33 | 1.65 |
| 19 | Punjab | 17.00 | 16.00 | 19.00 | 24.00 | 26.00 | 20.40 | 32.00 | 36.00 | 44.50 | 47.18 | 52.00 | 42.34 | 58.00 | 66.00 | 83.65 | 69.22 | 21.51 | 21.16 |
| 20 | Rajasthan | 8.36 | 10.92 | 12.22 | 13.97 | 12.40 | 11.57 | 14.30 | 15.10 | 12.00 | 12.97 | 12.12 | 13.30 | 14.27 | 25.60 | 14.30 | 18.06 | 2.99 | 11.93 |
| 21 | Sikkim | 0.09 | 0.09 | 0.10 | 0.10 | 0.15 | 0.11 | 0.15 | 0.14 | 0.14 | 0.14 | 0.14 | 0.14 | 0.14 | 0.14 | 0.14 | 0.14 | 5.45 | 0.00 |
| 22 | Tamil Nadu | 385.00 | 406.00 | 424.92 | 438.50 | 448.00 | 420.48 | 459.79 | 464.60 | 469.75 | 475.00 | 481.42 | 470.11 | 485.00 | 473.50 | 474.14 | 477.55 | 2.36 | 0.53 |
| 23 | Tripura | 23.24 | 23.37 | 24.50 | 25.10 | 25.71 | 24.38 | 27.47 | 27.91 | 28.41 | 29.34 | 29.42 | 28.51 | 29.45 | 29.52 | 17.98 | 25.65 | 3.39 | -3.34 |
| 24 | Uttar Pradesh | 113.31 | 121.43 | 132.37 | 139.90 | 145.70 | 130.54 | 149.43 | 160.02 | 183.03 | 192.71 | 208.29 | 178.78 | 225.37 | 249.84 | 267.00 | 247.40 | 7.39 | 12.79 |
| 25 | West Bengal | 734.00 | 757.00 | 806.00 | 820.42 | 893.00 | 802.08 | 937.00 | 950.02 | 995.00 | 1045.70 | 1060.23 | 997.59 | 1100.60 | 1120.00 | 1169.60 | 1129.90 | 4.88 | 4.42 |
| 26 | A & N Islands | 25.28 | 24.27 | 25.13 | 26.17 | 25.73 | 25.32 | 26.44 | 27.27 | 27.44 | 28.20 | 27.68 | 27.41 | 27.08 | 28.30 | 31.15 | 28.84 | 1.65 | 1.74 |
| 27 | Chandigarh | 0.09 | 0.05 | 0.16 | 0.08 | 0.09 | 0.09 | 0.08 | 0.00 | 0.00 | 0.03 | 0.08 | 0.04 | 0.04 | 0.08 | 0.08 | 0.07 | -11.11 | 22.22 |
| 28 | Dadra & Nagar Haveli | - | 0.02 | 0.09 | 0.08 | 0.04 | 0.06 | 0.04 | 0.02 | 0.02 | 0.03 | 0.04 | 0.03 | 0.05 | 0.05 | 0.05 | 0.05 | -18.00 | 22.22 |
| 29 | Daman & Diu | 15.94 | 13.43 | 11.53 | 11.54 | 15.28 | 13.54 | 15.28 | 18.81 | 26.85 | 15.95 | 16.38 | 18.65 | 21.52 | 11.26 | 13.77 | 15.52 | 7.55 | -5.59 |

| (1) | (2) | (3) | (4) | (5) | (6) | (7) | (8) | (9) | (10) | (11) | (12) | (13) | (14) | (15) | (16) | (17) | (18) | (19) | (20) |
|---|---|---|---|---|---|---|---|---|---|---|---|---|---|---|---|---|---|---|---|
| 30 | Delhi | 3.40 | 3.60 | 3.80 | 3.90 | 4.00 | 3.74 | 4.00 | 4.20 | 4.42 | 4.30 | 3.98 | 4.18 | 3.20 | 2.25 | 2.10 | 2.52 | 2.35 | -13.24 |
| 31 | Lakshadweep | 5.81 | 9.73 | 9.41 | 9.75 | 9.82 | 8.90 | 11.75 | 10.55 | 13.54 | 13.60 | 12.00 | 12.29 | 13.65 | 7.50 | 10.03 | 10.39 | 7.62 | -5.15 |
| 32 | Pondicherry | 35.83 | 38.55 | 41.61 | 40.93 | 40.82 | 39.55 | 42.65 | 42.52 | 42.70 | 42.83 | 43.30 | 42.80 | 44.50 | 45.02 | 48.00 | 45.84 | 1.64 | 2.37 |
| 33 | Chattisgarh | - | - | - | - | - | - | - | - | - | - | 43.39 | 43.39 | 95.76 | 99.80 | 111.05 | 102.20 | - | 45.18 |
| 34 | Uttaranchal | - | - | - | - | - | - | - | - | - | - | 9.07 | 9.07 | 6.42 | 2.55 | 3.83 | 2.56 | - | -19.26 |
| 35 | Jharkhand | - | - | - | - | - | - | - | - | - | - | 42.60 | 42.60 | 101.10 | 45.38 | 75.38 | 73.92 | - | 24.51 |
| | India | 4156.61 | 4365.30 | 4644.36 | 4788.57 | 4949.39 | 4580.85 | 5348.24 | 5388.49 | 5297.94 | 5675.03 | 5655.34 | 5473.00 | 5955.93 | 6199.68 | 6399.39 | 6185.00 | 3.90 | 4.34 |

*Period 1 = 1991-92 to 1995-96; Period 2 = 1996-97 to 2000-01; Period 3 = 2001-02 to 2003-04.

*Source:* Department of Animal Husbandry, Dairying and Fisheries, 2005, pp.8-9.

It is quite evident from table 6.14 that the average annual output of aquaculture increased from 1.65 million tonnes during 1994-96 to 1.96 million tonnes during 1997-2000, and to 2.17 million tonnes during 2000-03. This amounted to an increase of 4.70 per cent per annum during 1997-2000 over the 1994-96 level of output and 3.57 per cent increase during 2001-2003 over the 1997-2000 level of output.

The growth rate in value was, however, higher at around 10 per cent per annum during both periods. The significant point to note here is that the share of aquaculture to total fish production in India has increased from 32.80 per cent during 1994-1996 to 35.57 per cent during 1997-2000, although it has shown a slight decrease during 2001-03 to reach 35.06 per cent. In all these cases, it shows the unsustainability of higher levels of production and growth in capture fisheries, both in the marine and the inland sector.

It may be interesting to look at the trend in the output of fisheries in the states and Union territories of India and their implication for sustainability at the state/regional level. Table 6.15 gives the trend in total fish production in the states and Union territories of India between 1991-92 and 2003-04.

It is apparent from table 6.15 that the total fish production has gone up significantly in most of the states during the period from 1991-92 to 2003-04. However, taking note of the recent trends in the output of different states/Union territories, it is found that many of the states were not able to maintain their growth rates and have experienced either a fall in the growth rates or negative growth rates, leading to a decline in their total production. Among states, Goa, Gujarat, Karnataka, Madhya Pradesh, Maharashtra, Tripura and Uttaranchal have witnessed negative growth rates during recent years as revealed from their falling average annual output for the period from 2001-01 to 2003-04. The fall in the output and growth rate of Madhya Pradesh was, however, due to the bifurcation of the state to form the new state of Chattisgarh. Among Union territories, Daman and Diu, Delhi and Lakshadweep witnessed negative growth rates. States such as Arunachal Pradesh, Bihar, Haryana, Himachal Pradesh, Jammu and Kashmir, Manipur, Nagaland, Orissa, Punjab, Sikkim, Tamil Nadu and West Bengal experienced a decline in their growth rates which are still positive. It may be noted that some of these states, viz. West Bengal, Tamil Nadu, Maharashtra, Gujarat, Karnataka, Orissa and Bihar are leading producers of fish in the country and the negative or declining growth rates as noted in these states have implications for the sustainability of fisheries in India.

**Table 6.16**

**Trend in marine fish production in coastal states and Union territories of India from 1991-1992 to 2003-2004**

(in '000 tonnes)

| Sl. No. | States/UT | 1991-92 | 1992-93 | 1993-94 | 1994-95 | 1995-96 | Average of 91-92 to 95-96 | 1996-97 | 1997-98 | 1998-99 | 1999-00 | 2000-01 | Average of 96-97 to 00-01 | 2001-02 | 2002-03 | 2003-04 | Average of 01-02 to 03-04 | Average annual growth rate* Per. (2) over Per.(1) | Average annual growth rate* Per (3) over Per (2) |
|---|---|---|---|---|---|---|---|---|---|---|---|---|---|---|---|---|---|---|---|
| 1 | Andhra Pradesh | 125.79 | 113.07 | 154.32 | 150.26 | 151.99 | 139.09 | 152.05 | 146.55 | 150.00 | 166.48 | 182.50 | 159.52 | 204.94 | 248.50 | 263.93 | 239.12 | 2.94 | 16.63 |
| 2 | Goa | 47.11 | 101.49 | 102.11 | 98.46 | 84.21 | 86.68 | 93.76 | 88.81 | 65.84 | 62.11 | 67.33 | 75.57 | 66.55 | 72.29 | 83.76 | 74.20 | -2.56 | -0.60 |
| 3 | Gujarat | 516.85 | 589.00 | 619.84 | 645.26 | 600.00 | 594.19 | 660.07 | 745.71 | 550.00 | 670.95 | 620.47 | 649.44 | 650.83 | 743.64 | 609.14 | 667.87 | 1.86 | 0.95 |
| 4 | Karnataka | 231.41 | 234.19 | 204.52 | 203.75 | 247.51 | 224.28 | 252.78 | 219.86 | 190.61 | 195.63 | 205.90 | 212.96 | 128.42 | 180.16 | 187.00 | 165.19 | -1.01 | -7.48 |
| 5 | Kerala | 524.76 | 496.24 | 559.20 | 548.37 | 532.55 | 532.22 | 578.92 | 526.34 | 583.36 | 593.72 | 566.57 | 569.78 | 593.78 | 603.29 | 608.52 | 601.86 | 1.41 | 1.88 |
| 6 | Maharashtra | 390.86 | 387.55 | 350.40 | 357.00 | 387.00 | 374.56 | 481.00 | 453.10 | 394.88 | 397.90 | 402.84 | 425.92 | 414.27 | 386.86 | 420.01 | 407.05 | 2.74 | -1.48 |
| 7 | Orissa | 87.88 | 119.38 | 103.93 | 122.89 | 123.20 | 111.46 | 133.46 | 156.08 | 124.33 | 125.94 | 121.09 | 132.18 | 113.89 | 115.01 | 116.88 | 115.26 | 3.72 | -4.27 |
| 8 | Tamil Nadu | 301.00 | 308.00 | 317.72 | 330.50 | 340.00 | 319.44 | 350.79 | 355.10 | 359.55 | 363.00 | 367.86 | 359.26 | 371.00 | 371.50 | 373.00 | 371.83 | 2.49 | 1.17 |
| 9 | West Bengal | 142.00 | 145.00 | 153.00 | 151.20 | 153.00 | 148.84 | 172.00 | 164.00 | 171.50 | 180.00 | 181.00 | 173.70 | 184.30 | 181.50 | 181.60 | 182.47 | 3.34 | 1.68 |
| 10 | A & N Islands | 25.19 | 24.17 | 25.08 | 26.12 | 25.68 | 25.25 | 26.40 | 27.23 | 27.40 | 28.15 | 27.62 | 27.36 | 27.02 | 28.23 | 31.06 | 28.77 | 1.67 | 1.72 |
| 11 | Daman & Diu | 15.94 | 13.43 | 11.53 | 11.50 | 15.28 | 13.54 | 15.28 | 18.81 | 26.85 | 15.95 | 16.38 | 18.65 | 21.52 | 11.26 | 13.77 | 15.52 | 7.55 | -5.59 |
| 12 | Lakshadweep | 5.81 | 9.73 | 9.41 | 9.75 | 9.82 | 8.90 | 11.75 | 10.55 | 13.54 | 13.60 | 12.00 | 12.29 | 13.65 | 7.50 | 10.03 | 10.39 | 7.62 | -5.15 |
| 13 | Pondicherry | 32.68 | 35.00 | 37.78 | 36.75 | 36.82 | 35.81 | 38.55 | 38.42 | 38.60 | 38.62 | 38.95 | 38.63 | 39.60 | 40.11 | 42.80 | 40.84 | 1.57 | 1.91 |
| | India | 2447.26 | 2576.25 | 2648.84 | 2691.81 | 2707.06 | 2614.25 | 2967.81 | 2950.46 | 2696.46 | 2852.05 | 2810.57 | 2855.26 | 2829.77 | 2989.05 | 2941.50 | 2920.37 | 1.84 | 0.76 |

*Period 1 = 1991-92 to 1995-96, Period 2 = 1996-97 to 2000-01, Period 3 = 2001-02 to 2003-04

*Source:* Department of Animal Husbandry, Dairying and Fisheries, 2005, pp.10-11.

It may be noted here that states like Andhra Pradesh, Assam, Kerala, Meghalaya, Mizoram, Rajasthan and Uttar Pradesh and Union territories such as Andaman & Nicobar Islands and Pondicherry were able to maintain positive and steady growth rates as reflected in their rising average annual output for both the periods, viz. from 1996-97 to 2000-01 and from 2001-02 to 2003-04.

The positive and higher growth rates observed at the national level for both the periods, i.e. from 1996-97 to 2000-01 and from 2001-02 to 2003-04 are largely the contribution of expansion in aquaculture production as already noted. It may thus appear that the apparent sustainability of fish production in India is now predominantly dependent on aquaculture.

It may be interesting at this juncture to look at the trend in marine fish production in the coastal states and Union territories and their implications for sustainability. Table 6.16 shows the trend in marine fish production in coastal states and Union territories of India from 1991-92 to 2003-04.

It is clear from table 6.16 that the average annual output of marine fisheries sector has increased continuously only in Andhra Pradesh, Gujarat, Kerala, Tamil Nadu, West Bengal, Andaman & Nicobar Islands and Pondicherry, where positive growth rates were noted in the average output of the period from 1996-97 to 2000-01 and from 2001-02 to 2003-04. In some of these states (Gujarat and West Bengal), the growth rates although positive, were declining during the last period. The growth rates were negative in Goa, Karnataka, Maharashtra, Orissa, Daman and Diu and Lakshadweep during the period from 2001-02 to 2003-04. In Goa and Karnataka, the growth rates were negative during the earlier period, i.e. from 1996-97 to 2000-01 as well. The implications of the negative or declining growth rate in output for sustainability is obvious. Evidently, the total output of the marine fisheries sector of the country as a whole could register only 0.76 per cent growth rate in the last period, i.e. from 2000-01 to 2003-04.

An attempt may be made at this stage to look at the trend in the landings of different species of marine fishes in India and their implication for sustainability. Table 6.17 presents the trend in the landings of different species of marine fishes in India from 1994 to 2003.

**Table 6.17**

**Trend in the landings of different species of marine fishes in India from 1994 to 2003**

(in tonnes)

| *Sl. No.* | *Species* | *Period -1* | | | | | *Average of 1994-98* | *Period -2* | | | | *Average of 2000-03* | *Average annual growth rate in period 2 over period 1 (%)* |
|---|---|---|---|---|---|---|---|---|---|---|---|---|---|
| | | *1994* | *1995* | *1996* | *1997* | *1998* | | *2000* | *2001* | *2002* | *2003* | | |
| (1) | (2) | (3) | (4) | (5) | (6) | (7) | (8) | (9) | (10) | (11) | (12) | (13) | (14) |
| 1 | *Hilsa illisha* (Tenualosa) | 39383 | 43266 | 52289 | 51158 | 51377 | 47495 | 47500 | 42783 | 49341 | 40954 | 45145 | -1.24 |
| 2 | Flat fish | 31127 | 24681 | 24197 | 29252 | 23928 | 26637 | 18554 | 13552 | 20063 | 20412 | 18145 | -7.97 |
| 3 | *Bregmaceros* | 905 | 931 | 975 | 984 | 1147 | 988 | 1282 | 2127 | 2282 | 2239 | 1983 | 25.18 |
| 4 | *Harpodon nehereus* | 138280 | 159271 | 185112 | 213116 | 179773 | 175110 | 134197 | 144011 | 135684 | 139901 | 138448 | -5.23 |
| 5 | Sea catfishes | 85877 | 74301 | 73125 | 78150 | 71794 | 76649 | 80816 | 95466 | 87087 | 77715 | 85271 | 2.81 |
| 6 | Lizard fishes | 20528 | 23989 | 19670 | 13528 | 13829 | 18309 | 39574 | 37746 | 5509 | 5860 | 22172 | 5.27 |
| 7 | *Muraenssox spp.* (Eels) | 10428 | 8696 | 10611 | 11519 | 10739 | 10399 | 10984 | 11104 | 8545 | 8697 | 9833 | -1.36 |
| 8 | *Lactarius* (Parava) | 6310 | 7087 | 6930 | 7942 | 9591 | 7572 | 6061 | 7283 | 6852 | 6587 | 6696 | -2.89 |
| 9 | *Leiognathus* (Silver Bellies) | 60986 | 63394 | 68582 | 67369 | 53376 | 62741 | 49279 | 51791 | 56563 | 54479 | 53028 | -3.87 |
| 10 | *Sciaenidae* (Croakers) | 308466 | 287403 | 296287 | 312466 | 271544 | 295233 | 267861 | 245844 | 273934 | 259918 | 261889 | -2.82 |

| (1) | (2) | (3) | (4) | (5) | (6) | (7) | (8) | (9) | (10) | (11) | (12) | (13) | (14) |
|---|---|---|---|---|---|---|---|---|---|---|---|---|---|
| 11 | *Upeneus spp.* (Goat fish) | 19981 | 18869 | 18129 | 15769 | 15434 | 17636 | 10536 | 16736 | 18545 | 18485 | 16076 | -2.21 |
| 12 | *Lates sp. Lutjanus* (Perches) | 41012 | 37983 | 115879 | 87710 | 80380 | 72593 | 94560 | 80354 | 82326 | 70162 | 81851 | 3.19 |
| 13 | *Hemiramphus spp.* (Half beaks) | 3617 | 8674 | 6568 | 5574 | 4470 | 5781 | 7643 | 6170 | 8110 | 7889 | 7453 | 7.23 |
| 14 | *Exocoetus* (Flying fish) | 2836 | 2345 | 1886 | 2094 | 653 | 1963 | 2711 | 2446 | 2783 | 2764 | 2676 | 9.08 |
| 15 | *Sphyraena spp.* (Barracudas) | 7653 | 9070 | 8873 | 7827 | 13163 | 9317 | 4162 | 4864 | 8073 | 7310 | 6102 | -8.63 |
| 16 | *Mugilidae* (Mullets)) | 15134 | 12046 | 14413 | 17558 | 15553 | 14941 | 17642 | 17347 | 16457 | 15988 | 16859 | 3.21 |
| 17 | *Polynemidae* (Indian Salmon) | 11124 | 9647 | 6585 | 6679 | 6883 | 8184 | 5710 | 6116 | 6227 | 5811 | 5966 | -6.78 |
| 18 | *Caranx spp.* (Kata Banguda) | 60109 | 21439 | 67879 | 50833 | 65375 | 53127 | 39571 | 46840 | 40074 | 43823 | 42577 | -4.96 |
| 19 | *Trachinotus spp.* | 4692 | 8897 | 6784 | 3697 | 2342 | 5279 | 12 | 11 | 12 | 15 | 13 | -24.94 |
| 20 | *Carangidae* (Bangada) | 19223 | 22489 | 34225 | 32752 | 24712 | 26680 | 11130 | 13091 | 31563 | 45742 | 25382 | -1.22 |
| 21 | *Stromatidae* (Butter fish) | 62923 | 57978 | 37496 | 36731 | 34517 | 45929 | 25391 | 23757 | 35535 | 28360 | 28261 | -9.62 |
| 22 | *Sardinella* –( Indian oil sardine) | 96315 | 105916 | 136713 | 227192 | 223849 | 157997 | 327425 | 341667 | 267811 | 271168 | 302018 | 22.79 |
| 23 | *Engraulidae* (Anchovies) | 59156 | 60979 | 80694 | 81221 | 76196 | 71649 | 68608 | 71517 | 69777 | 93091 | 75748 | 1.43 |
| 24 | Other Clupeids | 54489 | 59041 | 76640 | 81023 | 89257 | 72090 | 63883 | 58873 | 70176 | 65739 | 64668 | -257 |
| 25 | *Chirocentrus spp.* | 21975 | 20472 | 19510 | 19788 | 16122 | 19573 | 16074 | 18726 | 21871 | 16084 | 18189 | -1.77 |
| 26 | Wahoo | - | - | - | - | - | - | - | - | - | - | - | - |
| 27 | Spanish mackerels | 10294 | 7836 | 3525 | 3943 | 3561 | 5832 | 16660 | 1899 | 16386 | 15965 | 12728 | 29.56 |
| 28 | King mackerel (Indo-Pacific) | 55057 | 50317 | 3050 | 3488 | 3050 | 22992 | 34651 | 43819 | 44434 | 54735 | 44410 | 23.29 |
| 29 | *Thazard cirrus* (Streaked seer fish) | 3561 | 7389 | 15454 | 13131 | 11532 | 10213 | 381 | 381 | 431 | 431 | 406 | -24.00 |
| 30 | *Scomberomorus spp.* (seer fish) | 38184 | 37214 | 36426 | 30529 | 29723 | 34415 | 42277 | 43559 | 48919 | 41569 | 44081 | 7.02 |

| (1) | (2) | (3) | (4) | (5) | (6) | (7) | (8) | (9) | (10) | (11) | (12) | (13) | (14) |
|---|---|---|---|---|---|---|---|---|---|---|---|---|---|
| 31 | *Auxis Thazard* (Frigate bullet tuna) | 2382 | 10781 | 8941 | 6685 | 4450 | 6648 | 8743 | 7031 | 9407 | 8210 | 8348 | 6.39 |
| 32 | *Euthynnus affinis* (Kawa Kawa) | 1711 | 1592 | 19391 | 17123 | 6174 | 9198 | 5999 | 5983 | 6913 | 6496 | 6348 | -7.75 |
| 33 | *Katsuwonus pelamis* (Skipjack tuna) | 6976 | 7779 | 7138 | 6243 | 9066 | 7440 | 23360 | 21789 | 6134 | 6134 | 14354 | 23.23 |
| 34 | *Thunnus tonggon* (Long-tail tuna) | 237 | 301 | 2388 | 3492 | 4741 | 2232 | 4377 | 541 | 13146 | 13862 | 7982 | 64.40 |
| 35 | *Istiophoridae* (Marlin sail fish) | 39 | 56 | 36 | 67 | 80 | 56 | 117 | 42 | 132 | 1132 | 106 | 22.32 |
| 36 | *Scombridae* (Tuna like fishes) | 5419 | 6335 | 96510 | 84904 | 38263 | 46286 | 1518 | 1166 | 940 | 1111 | 4735 | -22.44 |
| 37 | *Trichiuridae* (Hairtails) | 65467 | 50582 | 53941 | 67350 | 44080 | 56284 | 120596 | 144474 | 133547 | 111479 | 127524 | 31.64 |
| 38 | *Rastrelliger kanagurta* (Indian mackerel) | 206322 | 197233 | 293526 | 211759 | 185170 | 218802 | 78821 | 58905 | 52860 | 51568 | 60539 | -18.08 |
| 39 | *Elasmobranchs* (Sharks, Rays and Skates) | 83689 | 77078 | 132160 | 131362 | 123946 | 109647 | 76057 | 72568 | 66923 | 63266 | 69704 | -9.11 |
| 40 | Other marine fishes | 204267 | 206899 | 137977 | 191710 | 153848 | 178940 | 310344 | 281860 | 228482 | 253131 | 268454 | 12.51 |
| 41 | Penaeid prawns | 219635 | 176289 | 150593 | 146111 | 158373 | 170200 | 204587 | 195356 | 167798 | 202327 | 192517 | 3.28 |
| 42 | Non-penaeid prawns | 91825 | 84016 | 118494 | 92613 | 107186 | 98827 | 112119 | 106790 | 119965 | 87722 | 106649 | 1.98 |
| 43 | Other crust crab | 36871 | 16705 | 1547 | 2237 | 2375 | 11947 | 23651 | 25044 | 19984 | 20059 | 22185 | 21.42 |
| 44 | Natanian decapods | 27469 | 21984 | 23501 | 24343 | 15233 | 22506 | 445 | 3496 | 18351 | 15642 | 9484 | -14.47 |
| 45 | Marine crust crab | 29717 | 23685 | 28047 | 24339 | 26163 | 26390 | 14750 | 11504 | 11119 | 12491 | 12466 | -13.19 |
| 46 | Squid and cuttlefish | 95109 | 103739 | 85120 | 117624 | 94358 | 99190 | 96408 | 114680 | 87344 | 87350 | 96446 | -0.69 |
| 47 | Other molluscs | 1792 | 2452 | 15299 | 4750 | 2718 | 5402 | 1796 | 1469 | 1240 | 607 | 1278 | -19.08 |
| 48 | Miscellaneous* | 369290 | 454310 | 317725 | 279589 | 260844 | 336352 | 259171 | 285248 | 581330 | 548221 | 418493 | 6.11 |
| | Total | 2737842 | 2693744 | 2920791 | 2926314 | 2641478 | 2784034 | 2787993 | 2787827 | 2960984 | 2911701 | 2862126 | 0.70 |

*include deep sea catches, yellow-fin tuna, big-eye tuna, etc.

*Source:* 1. Department of Animal Husbandry and Dairying, 2001, pp.20-39.

2. Department of Animal Husbandry, Dairying and Fisheries, 2005, pp.16-31.

It is apparent from table 6.17 that out of the 48 species groups listed, 25 species were showing negative growth rates in the average annual landings during the period from 2000 to 2003. These included important species like *Hilsa illisha, Harpodon nehereus, Leiognathus (*silver bellies), *Sciaenidae* (croakers), *Upeneus spp.* (goat fishes), *Caranx spp.* (Kata Bangada), *Carangidae* (Bangada), *Stromatidae* (Butter fish), other clupeids, *Chirrocentrus spp. Rastrelliger kanagurta* (Indian mackerel), *Elasmobranchs* (sharks, rays and skates), marine crust crab, and squid and cuttlefish. Positive growth rates were noted in the case of major species like catfishes, lizard fishes, perches, mullets, Indian sardines, anchovies, Spanish mackerel, King mackerel, seer fish, skipjack tuna, *Trichiuridae* (Hair tails), other marine fishes, penaeid prawns, non-penaeid prawns, other crust crab and miscellaneous groups. The species showing positive growth rates altogether contributed to approximately 65 per cent of average annual output of the marine fisheries sector during 2000-2003. The species showing negative growth rates accounted for the remaining 35 per cent of the total marine fish production. The threat to the sustainability of fish production in the country is obvious from this position.

The trend in the landings of different species of inland fishes may also be looked at for identifying their vulnerability to unsustainable levels of production. Table 6.18 shows the trend in the production of different species of inland fishes in India from 1994 to 2003.

Table 6.18 makes it clear that the average annual growth rate was quite high in the case of all species groups except 'other freshwater fishes', where the growth rate was negative. Major carps like catla, rohu, mrigal and calbasu together have an average annual growth rate of 10.20 per cent during 2000-2003 over their average annual production of 1994-1998. Minor carps registered 15.11 per cent annual growth rate during this period. Exotic carps had a growth rate of 7.16 per cent during the same period. Production of murrels grew at only 0.37 per cent per annum. Production of catfishes had an average annual growth rate of 11.77 per cent. The average annual growth rate was the highest for 'other' species (18.08 per cent), which includes shrimp, and scampi. State-wise details of production of shrimp and scampi during the period from 2002-03 to 2005-06 are given in appendix 6.2. As already noted, the production of 'other freshwater fishes' registered a negative growth rate of 4.0 per cent when the average annual output declined from 3.72 lakh tonnes during 1994-1998 to 3.13 lakh tonnes during 2000-2003.

**Table 6.18**

**Trend in the production of different species of inland fishes in India from 1994 to 2003**

(in tonnes)

| Sl. No. | Species | Period -1 | | | | | Average of 1994-98 | Period -2 | | | | Average of 2000-03 | Average annual growth rate in period 2 over period 1 (%) |
|---|---|---|---|---|---|---|---|---|---|---|---|---|---|
| | | 1994 | 1995 | 1996 | 1997 | 1998 | | 2000 | 2001 | 2002 | 2003 | | |
| 1 | Major carps (Catla, Rohu, Mrigal & Calbasu) | 1120166 | 1200197 | 1348119 | 1395090 | 1511578 | 1315030 | 1609630 | 1781238 | 1992840 | 2022721 | 1851607 | 10.20 |
| 2 | Minor carps | 64364 | 109429 | 97603 | 101273 | 138999 | 102334 | 133839 | 155773 | 178362 | 188781 | 164189 | 15.11 |
| 3 | Exotic carps (common, silver & grass carp) | 197689 | 214836 | 238067 | 261535 | 226080 | 227641 | 264943 | 349412 | 283473 | 292244 | 297518 | 7.67 |
| 4 | Murrels (*Ophiocephalus spp.)* | 90762 | 93933 | 94944 | 105496 | 109686 | 98964 | 139409 | 122851 | 66392 | 73011 | 100416 | 0.37 |
| 5 | Cat fishes *(Wallago attu, Pangasius, bagarius)* | 15498 | 52848 | 85127 | 91163 | 97380 | 68403 | 116239 | 78367 | 101488 | 106282 | 100594 | 11.77 |
| 6 | Other fresh water fishes | 416903 | 391695 | 342840 | 354119 | 356289 | 372369 | 300710 | 401018 | 270115 | 279225 | 312767 | -4.00 |
| 7 | Others | 124541 | 152603 | 133344 | 147614 | 160214 | 143663 | 263336 | 195588 | 273256 | 258143 | 247581 | 18.08 |
| | Total | 2029923 | 2215541 | 2340044 | 2456290 | 2600226 | 2328405 | 2828106 | 3084247 | 3165927 | 3220407 | 3074672 | 8.01 |

*Source:* 1. Department of Animal Husbandry and Dairying, 2001, pp.40-49.
2. Department of Animal Husbandry, Dairying and Fisheries, 2005, pp.32-39.

The average annual growth rate for the inland fisheries sector as a whole during this period was 8.01 percent. This indeed has helped in preventing the fisheries sector of India from succumbing to the impending stagnation as noted in the case of marine fisheries.

### 6.3.2. Overcapitalisation

A major indicator of the creeping unsustainability in the fisheries sector is the over- capitalisaltion or overinvestment problem in the different branches of the industry. This has been a critical problem in global fisheries and it has been pointed out in chapter four. Over -capitalisation and the resulting economic inefficiency or wastage has indeed been at the root of the neo-classical economic theory of commercial fishing which called for optimisation by regulation of fishing by limiting entry.

An attempt is made in this section to look at the extent of overcapitalisation in the catching and processing branches of the fisheries sector of India. This attempt is, however, thwarted by the paucity of information on capital investments in the industry and the actual and potential value of output of the different branches.

As early as 1985, the Expert Committee on Marine Fisheries in Kerala had noted the existence of overcapitalisation in the fishing fleet of Kerala, particularly in the shrimp trawling sector. It noted: "there are about 2500 shrimp trawlers in Kerala ... of which 1145 trawlers, considered to be the optimum number will be engaged in shrimp trawling in areas beyond the 20 m depth line. The remaining 1355 trawlers, considered excess for the shrimp fishery, may be deployed in other fisheries ..." (Expert Committee, 1985, p.97). It is significant to point out here that the number of all crafts (mechanised and motorised) in the state have increased since then and with further technological advancements and capital inputs in the industry overcapitalisation issue is likely to be of greater concern, not withstanding some extension of fishing to outer seas.

The prevalence of excess capacity (overcapitalisation) in the marine fishing industry of India has been noted by Sathiadhas and Biradar. They observed: "The dwindling catch per unit of operation of different types of fishing techniques over the years in spite of the overall increase in total landings clearly indicates that there is excess capacity of fishing fleets. The introduction of technologically advanced and capital-intensive fishing implements made the existing older units less economical and non-operational thereby creating substantial excess capacity of fishing fleets and rampant underemployment of the labour force ...

...The estimated number of units effectively operated are 25840 as against the existing fleet size of 47,000 in the mechanised sector, 13,270 in the motorised sector as against the existing fleet of 32,000, and 20,930 in the non-mechanised sector as against the existing fleet size of 1.8 lakh. In terms of percentage, it (fleet capacity utilised) is 55%, 41% and 12% respectively. Thus, the excess fleet works out (at ) 45 per cent in mechanised, 59 per cent in motorised and 88 per cent in non-mechanised sector. In fact, the stiff competition to harvest the resources with excessive fishing fleets in each sector results in less number of fishing days and high level of under-employment among the labour force in Indian marine fisheries" (Sathiadhas and Biradar, 2000, pp.11-12, words in parentheses added).

In the absence of any concrete measure of capital invested in the industry and their non-homogenous nature, the nominal fishing effort (boat days) put in by different classes of vessels may be taken as a rough index of human and physical capital input in the industry at any point of time and the resulting catch (output) and catch per unit of effort, as an indicator of the performance of capital expended at that point of time, keeping all other factors as constant. An increase in fishing effort not followed by an increase in catch or catch per unit of effort is presumed to be a measure of economic wastage or wastage of capital (over-capitalisation).

Table 6.19 gives an estimate of catch, effort and catch per unit of effort of major craft types in the maritime states of India during 1985 and 1995.

Table 6.19 shows that an increase in fishing effort during 1995 as compared to 1985 in the case of trawlers in Orissa and Maharashtra, purseseiners in Goa, and mechanised gillnetters in Orissa, Tamil Nadu and Pondicherry are followed by decreases in the catch per unit effort of these crafts, indicating overcapitalisation and wastage of economic inputs. The relative fall (negative growth) in the catch per unit effort of trawlers in Goa, puseseiners in Goa and Karnataka, and gill-netters in Kerala even when fishing effort decreased in these cases also points to non-optimum conditions in the industry. The observed reduction in the fishing effort during 1995 as compared with 1985 in the case of non-motorised artisanal crafts in many states must be due to the motorisation

**Table 6.19**

**Estimates of catch, effort and catch per unit effort of major craft types in the maritime states of India during 1985 and 1995**

| State/UT | Catch (tonnes) | | | Effort (boat days) | | | Catch per unit effort (kg/boat/day) | | |
|---|---|---|---|---|---|---|---|---|---|
| | 1985 | 1995 | Change in 1995 over 1985 (%) | 1985 | 1995 | Change in 1995 over 1985 (%) | 1985 | 1995 | Change in 1995 over 1985 (%) |
| **Artisanal-non-motorised Crafts** | | | | | | | | | |
| West Bengal | 2785 | 10840 | 289.22 | 47902 | 67138 | 40.16 | 58 | 161 | 177.58 |
| Orissa | 17589 | 6339 | -63.96 | 1010987 | 224330 | -77.81 | 17 | 28 | 64.71 |
| Andhra Pradesh | 85263 | 51619 | -39.45 | 2190970 | 1350738 | -38.35 | 39 | 38 | -2.56 |
| Tamil Nadu | 105002 | 89552 | -14.71 | 3681440 | 2270703 | -38.32 | 29 | 39 | 34.48 |
| Pondicherry | 11147 | 6469 | -41.97 | 377427 | 210684 | -44.18 | 30 | 31 | 3.33 |
| Kerala | 77125 | 19374 | -74.88 | 1808204 | 957857 | -47.03 | 43 | 20 | -53.49 |
| Karnataka | 13200 | 3877 | -70.63 | 300394 | 112453 | -62.56 | 44 | 34 | -22.73 |
| Goa | 5952 | 1600 | -73.12 | 39472 | 18829 | -52.30 | 151 | 85 | -43.71 |
| Maharashtra | 10897 | 2823 | -74.09 | 177222 | 62269 | -64.86 | 61 | 45 | -26.23 |
| Gujarat | 60205 | 90460 | 50.25 | 582941 | 952211 | 63.35 | 103 | 95 | -7.77 |

| | (1) | (2) | (3) | (4) | (5) | (6) | (7) | (8) | (9) |
|---|---|---|---|---|---|---|---|---|---|
| **Artisanal-motorised crafts** | | | | | | | | | |
| West Bengal | - | - | - | - | - | - | - | - | - |
| Andhra Pradesh | - | 21616 | - | - | 346883 | - | - | - | - |
| Tamil Nadu | - | 6080 | - | - | 105384 | - | - | - | - |
| Pondicherry | - | 3361 | - | - | 62757 | - | - | 54 | - |
| Kerala | 127469 | 290421 | 127.84 | 705285 | 1295235 | 83.65 | 181 | 224 | 23.76 |
| Karnataka | - | 16708 | - | - | 105955 | - | - | 158 | - |
| Goa | 159 | 4057 | 2451.57 | 2880 | 73075 | 2437.32 | 55 | 56 | 1.82 |
| Maharashtra | - | 304 | - | - | 18403 | - | - | 17 | - |
| Gujarat | - | 49810 | - | - | 408541 | - | - | 122 | - |
| **Mechanised crafts** | | | | | | | | | |
| **Trawlers** | | | | | | | | | |
| West Bengal | 47 | 15184 | 32206.38 | 124 | 18210 | 14585.48 | 379 | 834 | 120.05 |
| Orissa | 26694 | 24509 | -8.19 | 68083 | 75878 | 11.45 | 392 | 323 | 17.60 |
| Andhra Pradesh | 33224 | 62123 | 87.01 | 105630 | 93985 | 11.02 | 315 | 661 | 109.84 |
| Tamil Nadu | 90120 | 251232 | 268.66 | 384616 | 571544 | 48.6 | 234 | 440 | 88.03 |
| Pondicherry | 4981 | 2312 | -53.58 | 27290 | 9040 | 66.87 | 183 | 256 | 39.89 |
| Kerala | 97037 | 215287 | 121.86 | 370176 | 508853 | 37.46 | 262 | 423 | 61.45 |
| Karnataka | 26011 | 78863 | 203.19 | 138875 | 173892 | 25.21 | 187 | 454 | 142.78 |

| | (1) | (2) | (3) | (4) | (5) | (6) | (7) | (8) | (9) |
|---|---|---|---|---|---|---|---|---|---|
| Goa | 27541 | 11344 | -58.81 | 83047 | 51102 | 38.47 | 332 | 222 | 33.13 |
| Maharashtra | 117728 | 213435 | -81.30 | 176635 | 361099 | 104.43 | 667 | 591 | 11.39 |
| Gujarat | 132888 | 255088 | 91.96 | 90128 | 140872 | 56.30 | 1474 | 1811 | 22.86 |
| **Purseseiners** | | | | | | | | | |
| Kerala | 11482 | 4228 | -63.18 | 4707 | 1643 | 65.09 | 2439 | 2573 | 5.49 |
| Karnataka | 76941 | 49081 | -36.21 | 40015 | 33302 | 16.78 | 1923 | 1474 | 23.35 |
| Goa | 13363 | 13368 | 0.04 | 9721 | 21883 | 125.11 | 1375 | 611 | 55.56 |
| Maharashtra | 1312 | 1678 | 27.90 | 51028 | 14639 | 71.31 | 26 | 115 | 342.31 |
| **Gillnetters** | | | | | | | | | |
| West Bengal | 4716 | 27633 | 485.94 | 43864 | 79438 | 81.10 | 108 | 348 | 222.22 |
| Orissa | 2257 | 9184 | 306.91 | 28075 | 118485 | 322.03 | 80 | 78 | -2.05 |
| Andhra Pradesh | 54 | 6109 | 11212.96 | 626 | 51201 | 8079.07 | 86 | 119 | 38.37 |
| Tamil Nadu | 4861 | 62918 | 1194.34 | 70993 | 1136206 | 1500.45 | 68 | 55 | -19.12 |
| Pondicherry | 351 | 1420 | 304.56 | 3198 | 18466 | 477.42 | 90 | 77 | -14.44 |
| Kerala | 12361 | 1380 | -82.81 | 84343 | 10755 | -87.25 | 147 | 128 | -12.93 |
| Karnataka | 2499 | 412 | -83.51 | 20658 | 3233 | -84.35 | 121 | 127 | 4.96 |
| Goa | 510 | 606 | 18.82 | 5970 | 6795 | 13.82 | 85 | 89 | 4.71 |
| Maharashtra | 22341 | 15474 | -30.74 | 191855 | 109041 | -43.17 | 116 | 142 | 22.41 |
| Gujarat | 50648 | 22552 | -55.47 | 298896 | 94891 | -68.25 | 190 | 238 | 25.26 |

*Source:* Devaraj, 1998, pp.51-52.

of these crafts as reflected in the fishing effort under motorised crafts during 1995, which was not seen in many states during 1985. It should also be noted here that a fall in the fishing effort of any particular class of vessel in any particular year may not be salvaging itself of the overcapitalisation problem since the sunk capital is a dead investment and it cannot be put for alternative uses to recover the cost. Hence, the observed reduction in fishing effort in the case of mechanised crafts in many states may indeed be reflecting the malaise of overcapitalisation and the resulting economic crisis in the industry rather than a solution to the problem.

A broad, segment-wise, picture of overcapitalisation in the marine fishing industry of India can be obtained from the catch per unit effort of different craft-gear types operating in the country. Table 6.20 gives the catch, effort, and catch per unit effort of different craft-gear combinations operating in India between1991 and 1996.

Table 6.20 highlights a situation where the average catch per unit effort for 1994-96 showed a decrease over the average catch per unit effort of 1991-93 in the mechanised purseseiners, mechanised gillnetters, mechanised bagnetters, motorised boatseiners, and motorised gillnetters indicating wastage of capital investments in the fleet or prevalence of over- exploitation. The fact that the decrease in the catch per unit effort of mechanised purseseiners and bagnetters and of motorised ringseiners and non-motorised crafts was in spite of notable reductions in the fishing effort of these crafts also indicate the superfluousness of much of the capital investments in these crafts. The table further shows that the mechanised gill netters and motorised gill netters and boatseiners had increased their fishing effort adding to the overcapitalisation problem and leading to decreases in the catch per unit effort of these crafts.

Sathiadhas, *et al.* reported excess capacity, to the tune of 47.86 per cent in the mechanised sector, 50.75 per cent in the motorised sector and 82.41 per cent in the non-motorised sector (Sathiadhas, *et al.*, 1999, p.55).

The prevalence of significant excess capacity (overcapitalisation) in the fishing fleet of India is indicated by Somvanshi, when the author gave an estimate of optimum fleet size for the country, based on 1998 data from CMFRI. Table 6.21 shows details of estimated optimum fleet size for India in 1998.

**Table 6.20**

**Estimates of catch, effort and catch per unit effort of different craft-gear combinations operating in India during 1991-93 and 1994-96**

*(Average)*

| Sl. No. | Craft -gear combination | Catch (tonnes) 1991-93 | Catch (tonnes) 1994-96 | Catch: Change in 1994-96 over 1991-93 (%) | Effort (boat days) 1991-93 | Effort (boat days) 1994-96 | Effort: Change in 1994-96 over 1991-93 (%) | Catch per unit effort (Kg/boat/day 1991-93 | Catch per unit effort (Kg/boat/day 1994-96 | Change in 1994-96 over 1991-93 (%) |
|---|---|---|---|---|---|---|---|---|---|---|
| 1 | Mechanised trawler | 1030017 | 1202234 | 16.72 | 1901928 | 2016386 | 6.02 | 542 | 598 | 10.33 |
| 2 | Mechanised purseseiner | 173917 | 127570 | -26.65 | 96518 | 79975 | -17.14 | 1805 | 1613 | -10.64 |
| 3 | Mechanised gillnetter | 113320 | 121731 | 7.42 | 739206 | 1093105 | 47.88 | 155 | 120 | -22.58 |
| 4 | Mechanised bagnetter | 165082 | 127747 | -22.62 | 259685 | 234503 | -9.70 | 644 | 567 | -11.96 |
| 5 | Motorised boat seiner | 19721 | 22265 | 12.90 | 50828 | 66898 | 31.62 | 408 | 315 | -22.79 |
| 6 | Motorised gillnetter | 107046 | 142342 | 32.97 | 1300687 | 2014653 | 54.89 | 83 | 73 | -12.05 |
| 7 | Motorised ringseiner | 197387 | 187685 | -4.92 | 275549 | 224499 | -18.53 | 717 | 846 | 17.99 |
| 8 | Non-motorised craft | 346547 | 289711 | -16.40 | 6974514 | 5293992 | -25.00 | 50 | 55 | 10.00 |

*Source:* Kurup and Devaraj, 2000, pp. 3-4.

**Table 6.21**

**Estimated optimum fleet size for India in 1998**

| *Fleet segment* | *Optimum fleet size in 1998* | *Actual fleet size in 1995* | *Excess fleet size* | *Excess as % of actual* |
|---|---|---|---|---|
| A. *Mechanised crafts* | 20928 | 37901 | 16973 | 44.78 |
| 1. Trawlers | 12245 | 24099 | 11854 | 49.18 |
| 2. Purseseiners | 835 | 464 | -371 | - |
| 3. Gill netters | 3972 | 13338 | 5490 | 41.16 |
| 4. Bagnetters | 2193 | | | |
| 5. Other | 1683 | | | |
| B. *Motorised crafts* | 15998 | 39303 | 23305 | 59.30 |
| 1. Bagnetter | 326 | | | |
| 2. Gillnetters | 10746 | | | |
| 3. Ring seiners | 1302 | | | |
| 4. Dolnetters | 159 | | | |
| 5. Other | 3465 | | | |
| C. *Non-motorised crafts* | 31058 | 151554 | 120496 | 79.51 |

*Source:* Somvanshi, 2003, pp.115,117.

Table 6.21 shows an excess fleet of 16973 mechanised crafts consisting of 11854 trawlers and 5490 other crafts including gillnetters and bagnetters. The number of purseseiners were found to be less than the optmum worked out at 835. The number of motorised crafts were found to be more than the optimum by 23305 crafts. The fleet size of non-motorised crafts were in excess by 120496 units. The above estimates are, however, unlikely to be based on the very many uncertainties, variations and interactions prevalent in multispecies fisheries like the Indian marine fisheries. Accordingly, these estimates have only general indicative value.

The prevalence of excess capacity in the ring seine fishery for oil sardines in Kerala is indicated by Pillai, et al. when they noted that "currently (1992), about 2259 ring seine units are in operation against an optimum fleet of 1178 units with bigger units being added to this fleet every year" (Pillai, *et al.,* 2003, p.21).

Based on their 2002 study, Unnithan, *et al.* reported that "only 55 per cent of the fishing capacity was actually utilised during the year under study ... the vessels remain only for a few days at sea in lean fishing season or remain idle in jetties during certain other times due to uneconomic fishing and hence the reduction in the utilised fishing capacity" (Unnithan, *et al.,* 2005, p.81).

The overcapitalisation problem in the fish processing sector had been recognised as early as 1981. Iyer, et al. reported the prevalence of idle capacity in the freezing plants of India, in the west coast in 1981 and in the east coast in 1982. Table 6.22 gives the details of installed capacity and idle capacity in the freezing plants of coastal states of India during 1978 and 1979.

It is clear from table 6.22 that the extent of idle capacity ranged from 69.4 per cent in Tamil Nadu to 85.3 per cent in Karnataka during 1978 and 63.6 per cent in Goa and 84 per cent in West Bengal during 1979. The extent of idle capacity was slightly lower in the east coast during both 1978 and 1979. Compared to 1978, there was some decrease in excess capacity during 1979 in all states except West Bengal. In absolute terms, the extent of idle capacity was the highest in Kerala in both the years, viz., 84 thousand tonnes in 1978 and 83 thousand tonnes in 1979.

**Table 6.22**

**Details of installed capacity and idle capacity in the freezing plants of India during 1978 and 1979**

*(in '000 tonnes)*

| | | *1978** | | | *1979** | | |
|---|---|---|---|---|---|---|---|
| *Sl. No.* | *States* | *Installed capacity* | *Idle capacity* | *% of idle capacity* | *Installed capacity* | *Idle capacity* | *% of idle capacity* |
| 1 | Kerala | 112.1 | 84.0 | 74.9 | 112.1 | 83.0 | 74.0 |
| 2 | Karnataka | 28.0 | 23.9 | 85.3 | 28.0 | 22.3 | 79.7 |
| 3 | Goa | 7.3 | 5.9 | 79.9 | 7.3 | 4.7 | 63.6 |
| 4 | Maharashtra | 55.5 | 41.0 | 73.8 | 55.5 | 37.8 | 68.2 |
| 5 | Gujarat | 17.8 | 14.5 | 81.9 | 17.8 | 13.6 | 76.9 |
| | West Coast (total) | 220.7 | 169.7 | 76.9 | 220.7 | 161.4 | 73.2 |
| 6 | Tamil Nadu | 39.4 | 27.4 | 69.4 | 38.5 | 24.8 | 64.5 |
| 7 | Andhra Pradesh | 12.6 | 9.7 | 77.0 | 12.6 | 8.8 | 70.1 |
| 8 | West Bengal | 31.9 | 26.6 | 83.5 | 29.2 | 24.5 | 84.0 |
| | East Coast (total) | 83.9 | 63.7 | 75.9 | 80.3 | 58.2 | 72.5 |

*Working on two shifts for 250 days

*Source:* Iyer, *et al.*, 1981, p. 112 and Iyer, *et al.*, 1982, p.11.

The extent of capacity utilisation in the fish processing plants in Kerala in the last decade was reported by Unnithan, et al., in 1998. Table 6.23 presents details of capacity utilisation in fish processing plants in Kerala during 1996.

**Table 6.23**

**Details of capacity utilisation in fish processing plants in Kerala during 1996**

| *Plant size (capacity in tonnes)* | *Number of plants* | *Annual installed capacity (000 tonnes*)* | *Estimated annual production (tonnes)* | *% of capacity utilisation** |
|---|---|---|---|---|
| 1-10 | 78 | 194.4 | 32060 | 29.7 |
| 10-15 | 24 | 128.5 | 17400 | 24.4 |
| 15-30 | 25 | 245.9 | 39086 | 28.6 |
| All | 127 | 568.8 | 88540 | 28.0 |

*Based on two shifts, working for 300 days in a year

*Source:* Unnithan, *et al.,* 1998, p.123.

Table 6.23 shows that in the 1-10 tonnes capacity plants, the extent of capacity utilisation was 29.7 per cent while it was 24.4 per cent and 28.6 per cent respectively in plants of 10-15 and 15-30 tonnes capacity and assuming these plants work for 300 days in two shifts. The over - all capacity utilisation was 28 per cent implying approximately 72 per cent excess capacity which is quite an economic waste.

It is, however, necessary to note here the viewpoint in the industry circles that since the fish landings in the industry are seasonal, it is essential for the processing sector to have additional captive capacity to absorb peak landings and this captive holding capacity cannot be strictly considered as excess capacity. This view, however, does not take into account of the opportunity cost of capital and the implicit wastage of investments in a truly competitive market economy situation and their implication for the long term sustainability of the industry.

Unnithan, *et al.* further reported that "non-availability of raw material was the main reason for low capacity utilisation. Unhealthy competition for purchase of raw material, unsteady increase in raw material prices, huge investments required for upgradation of plants, financial constraints, insufficient and unsteady power supply, high cost of production, unsteady export markets, non-judicious licensing to new processing units and shortage of potable water were other major factors responsible for the underutilisation of plants" (Unnithan, *et al.* 1998, p.125.). Tharakan reported that the capacity utilisation in the industry in relation to the installed capacity was only14 per cent (Tharakan, 1998, p.6).

### 6.3.3. Uneconomic Operations

The declining profitability and uneconomic nature of operations have been pointed out as a major threat to the sustainability of global fishing industry in chapter four. The FAO which probed the economic viability of fishing operations world-wide in the early1990s and late 1990s had come out with rather contradictory evidences indicating heavy economic loss in the former study and economic viability in the latter study. The second study reported that in India "three types of medium and large scale fishing units – tuna long liners, purse seiners and trawlers – generated a positive net surplus, while two of the three small-scale fishing units studied – seiners and handliners – scarcely broke even or had a negative cash flow" (FAO, 2000a, p.92). An attempt is made here to look at some of the domestic studies to see the nature and extent of viability in the marine fishing industry of India and their implication for sustainability.

Panikkar, *et al.* reported satisfactory returns for gill-netters, trawlers and purse seiners operating from Cochin during 1982-86 (Panikkar, *et al.*, 1990). The comparative profitability of different types of fishing units studied by Devaraj (1998) during 1985 and 1995 is given in table 6.24.

It appears from table 6.24 that all types of fishing units studied were earning profits in both 1985 and 1995. The profit earned was found to be the highest for purseseiners in Karnataka, followed by purseseiners in Goa and Maharashtra during 1995. Mechanised gillnetters in all states had satisfactory returns. Artisanal and motorised crafts in all states also had moderate profits in both the years. The table, however, does not make clear whether the study did take note of all expenses of production including those of 'owned' inputs and 'unpaid' services to reflect 'true' viability.

Senthilathiban, *et al.* reported an average net profit of Rs 2402 per trip for trawlers fitted with 105 HP engines operating from Tuticorin in Tamil Nadu during 1992-93 (Senthilathiban, *et al.*, 1997, p.34).

Table 6.25 gives details of costs and earnings and comparative profitability of different types of artisanal fishing units in the marine fishing sector of India during 1993-94.

**Table 6.24**

**Comparative profitability (net profit) of different types of fishing units during 1985 and 1995**

*(Rs. In lakhs)*

| *Maritime state/UT* | *Artisanal craft* | | *Motorised craft* | | *Mechanised trawlers* | | *Purseseiners* | | *Mechanised gillnetters* | |
|---|---|---|---|---|---|---|---|---|---|---|
| | 1985 | 1995 | 1985 | 1995 | 1985 | 1995 | 1985 | 1995 | 1985 | 1995 |
| Gujarat | 0.08 | 0.12 | 0.01 | 0.15 | 0.65 | 0.82 | - | - | 0.65 | 0.95 |
| Maharashtra | 0.10 | 0.07 | - | 0.12 | 0.26 | 1.50 | 0.80 | 1.50 | 0.50 | 0.80 |
| Goa | 0.06 | 0.05 | 0.12 | 0.17 | 0.68 | 0.71 | 0.90 | 2.38 | 0.44 | 0.65 |
| Karnataka | 0.08 | 0.07 | 0.12 | 0.50 | 0.93 | 0.84 | 1.10 | 3.14 | 0.40 | 0.60 |
| Tamil Nadu | 0.02 | 0.05 | - | 0.10 | 0.65 | 0.72 | - | - | 0.50 | 0.75 |
| Pondicherry | 0.04 | 0.05 | - | 0.10 | 0.65 | 0.72 | - | - | 0.50 | 0.75 |
| Andhra Pradesh | 0.03 | 0.05 | - | 0.07 | 0.70 | 0.89 | - | - | 0.65 | 0.80 |
| Orissa | 0.05 | 0.06 | - | 0.09 | 0.75 | 0.86 | - | - | 0.45 | 0.75 |
| West Bengal | 0.08 | 0.10 | - | 0.10 | 0.75 | 0.86 | - | - | 0.70 | 0.90 |

Source: Devaraj, 1998, p.54.

**Table 6.25**

**Costs and earnings and comparative profitability of different types of artisanal fishing units in the marine fishing sector of India during 1993-94**

| *Sl. No.* | *Parameter* | *Catamaran and Hook and Line (Tamil Nadu)* | *Catamaran and Gillnet (Tamil Nadu)* | *Canoe and Boatseine (Tamil Nadu)* | *Canoe and Gillnet (Kerala)* | *Canoe and Hook and Line (Kerala)* |
|---|---|---|---|---|---|---|
| 1 | Initial investment (Rs lakhs) | 0.17 | 0.32 | 0.85 | 0.65 | 0.40 |
| 2 | Annual catch (tonnes) | 7.50 | 13.00 | 51.00 | 17.50 | 11.00 |
| 3 | Value (Rs lakhs) | 0.45 | 0.55 | 1.28 | 0.71 | 0.75 |
| 4 | Operating cost (Rs lakhs) | 0.36 | 0.42 | 0.98 | 0.46 | 0.58 |
| 5 | Fixed cost (Rs lakhs) | 0.04 | 0.08 | 0.20 | 0.19 | 0.12 |
| 6 | Total cost (Rs lakhs) | 0.40 | 0.50 | 1.18 | 0.65 | 0.70 |
| 7 | Net operating income (Rs lakhs) | 0.09 | 0.13 | 0.30 | 0.25 | 0.17 |
| 8 | Net income (Rs lakhs) | 0.05 | 0.05 | 0.10 | 0.06 | 0.05 |
| 9 | Rate of return (%) | 44.00 | 31.00 | 27.00 | 24.00 | 28.00 |
| 10 | Pay back period (years) | 2.50 | 3.90 | 4.60 | 5.2 | 4.40 |
| 11 | Value realised per Kg of fish (Rs) | 6.00 | 4.23 | 2.51 | 4.06 | 6.47 |
| 12 | Average total cost per Kg of fish (Rs) | 5.33 | 3.85 | 2.31 | 3.71 | 6.03 |
| 13 | Average operating cost per Kg of fish (Rs) | 4.80 | 3.23 | 1.92 | 2.63 | 5.00 |

*Source:* Sathiadhas, *et al.*, 1995, pp.10-11.

**Table 6.26**

**Costs and earnings and comparative profitability of different types of motorised fishing units operating in the marine fishing sector of India during 1993-94**

| Sl. No. | Parameter | Catamaran and Hook and Line (Tamil Nadu) | Catamaran and Gillnet (Tamil Nadu) | Canoe and Ringseine (Kerala) | Canoe and Gillnet (Kerala) | Canoe and Hook and Line (Kerala) | Canoe and Gillnet (Gujarat) |
|---|---|---|---|---|---|---|---|
| 1 | Initial investment (Rs lakhs) | 0.35 | 0.50 | 5.00 | 1.00 | 0.75 | 1.20 |
| 2 | Annual catch (tonnes) | 14.50 | 16.20 | 220.00 | 21.00 | 18.4 | 16.95 |
| 3 | Value (Rs lakhs) | 0.82 | 0.76 | 6.43 | 1.08 | 1.50 | 1.50 |
| 4 | Operating cost (Rs lakhs) | 0.65 | 0.54 | 3.98 | 0.69 | 1.09 | 1.15 |
| 5 | Fixed cost (Rs lakhs) | 0.09 | 0.13 | 1.47 | 0.26 | 0.25 | 0.20 |
| 6 | Total cost (Rs lakhs) | 0.74 | 0.67 | 5.45 | 0.95 | 1.34 | 1.35 |
| 7 | Net operating income (Rs lakhs) | 0.17 | 0.22 | 2.45 | 0.39 | 0.41 | 0.35 |
| 8 | Net income (Rs lakhs) | 0.08 | 0.09 | 0.98 | 0.13 | 0.16 | 0.15 |
| 9 | Rate of return (%) | 38.00 | 33.00 | 35.00 | 28.00 | 36.00 | 28.00 |
| 10 | Pay back period (years) | 3.00 | 3.60 | 3.40 | 4.40 | 3.20 | 4.10 |
| 11 | Value realised per Kg of fish (Rs) | 5.66 | 4.69 | 2.92 | 5.14 | 8.15 | 8.85 |
| 12 | Average total cost per Kg of fish (Rs) | 5.10 | 4.14 | 2.48 | 4.52 | 7.28 | 7.96 |
| 13 | Average operting cost per Kg of fish (Rs) | 4.48 | 3.33 | 1.81 | 3.29 | 5.92 | 6.78 |

*Source:* Sathiadhas, *et al.*, 1995, pp.13-14.

Table 6.25 shows that all the five different types of artisanal crafts operating from Kerala and Tamil Nadu during 1993-94 were earning profits ranging from Rs 0.05 lakh to Rs 0.10 lakh after meeting the total (fixed and variable) costs of operation. The rate of return is found to be the highest for the catamarans operating hook and lines from Tamil Nadu.

Table 6.26 presents details of costs and earning, and comparative profitability of different types of motorised fishing units operating in the marine fishing sector of India during 1993-94.

It is clear from table 6.26 that all the motorised crafts operating from Tamil Nadu, Kerala and Gujarat during 1993-94 were earning profits ranging from Rs 0.08 lakhs to Rs 0.98 lakhs. The rate of return was the highest for catamarans operating hook and line from Tamil Nadu.

Table 6.27 gives details of costs and earnings and comparative profitability of small trawlers (32′- 36′) operating from different maritime states of India during 1993-94.

It is apparent from table 6.27 that the small trawlers operating from all the maritime states were earning net income (profit) ranging from Rs 0.71 lakh to Rs 1.05 lakh, the highest profit being in Maharashtra and the lowest in Tamil Nadu. The rate of return was the highest in West Bengal.

Table 6.28 shows the details of costs and earnings and comparative profitability of 'other' types of mechanised boats operating from selected coastal states of India during 1993-94.

Table 6.28 makes it clear that all 'other' types of mechanised crafts operating in the country were showing profits ranging from Rs 0.34 lakh to Rs 3.14 lakh, the highest being in the case of purseseiners in Kerala and the lowest for gill netters in Maharashtra. The rate of return was also found to be the highest for purseseiners in Kerala.

Table 6.29 presents the details of costs and earnings and comparative profitability of different types of off-shore fishing vessels of India during 1989-92 (average).

**Table 6.27**

**Costs and earnings and comparative profitability of small trawlers (32' - 36') operating from different maritime states of India during 1993-94**

| *Sl.* | *Parameter* | *Gujarat* | *Maharashtra* | *Goa* | *Karnataka* | *Kerala* | *Tamil Nadu* | *Andhra Pradesh* | *Orissa* | *West Bengal* |
|---|---|---|---|---|---|---|---|---|---|---|
| 1. | Initial investment* (Rs lakhs) | 5.25 | 6.00 | 5.50 | 5.20 | 5.60 | 5.20 | 4.85 | 4.50 | 4.20 |
| 2. | Annual catch (tonnes) | 68.00 | 57.00 | 43.50 | 72.00 | 89.00 | 99.60 | 51.00 | 40.00 | 34.00 |
| 3. | Value (Rs lakhs) | 9.25 | 9.34 | 7.22 | 9.04 | 11.24 | 10.71 | 9.10 | 6.78 | 6.01 |
| 4. | Operating cost (Rs lakhs) | 6.85 | 6.49 | 5.13 | 6.58 | 8.72 | 8.39 | 6.75 | 4.57 | 3.90 |
| 5. | Fixed cost (Rs lakhs) | 1.58 | 1.80 | 1.38 | 1.56 | 1.68 | 1.56 | 1.46 | 1.35 | 1.26 |
| 6. | Total cost (Rs lakhs) | 8.43 | 8.29 | 6.51 | 8.14 | 10.40 | 9.95 | 8.21 | 5.92 | 5.16 |
| 7. | Net operating income (Rs lakhs) | 2.40 | 2.85 | 2.09 | 2.46 | 2.52 | 2.32 | 2.35 | 2.21 | 2.10 |
| 8. | Net income (Rs lakhs) | 0.82 | 1.05 | 0.71 | 0.90 | 0.84 | 0.76 | 0.89 | 0.86 | 0.85 |
| 9. | Rate of return (%) | 33.60 | 35.50 | 30.90 | 35.38 | 33.00 | 32.60 | 36.40 | 37.11 | 38.20 |
| 10. | Pay back period (years) | 3.62 | 3.39 | 4.01 | 3.41 | 3.70 | 3.75 | 3.29 | 3.21 | 3.11 |
| 11. | Value realised per Kg of fish (Rs) | 13.60 | 16.39 | 16.60 | 12.55 | 12.60 | 10.75 | 17.84 | 16.95 | 17.70 |
| 12. | Average total cost per Kg of fish (Rs) | 12.40 | 14.54 | 14.97 | 11.31 | 11.69 | 9.98 | 16.10 | 14.80 | 15.18 |
| 13. | Average operating cost per Kg of fish (Rs) | 10.07 | 11.39 | 11.79 | 9.10 | 9.80 | 8.42 | 13.20 | 11.43 | 11.47 |

*The new additions to the trawler fleet along the Indian coasts are reported to be mostly of 55' size costing about Rs 14 lakhs in 1995

*Source:* Sathiadhas, *et al.*, 1995, pp.18-19.

**Table 6.28**
**Costs and earnings and comparative profitability of 'other' types of mechanised crafts operating in selelcted maritime states of India during 1993-94**

| Sl. No. | Parameter | *Gillnetters* *Maharashtra* | *Gillnetters* *Tamil Nadu* | Purseseiners *Kerala* | *Dol* netters *Maharashtra* | *Dol* netters *Gujarat* | Pair trawlers *Tamil Nadu* | Sona boat *Orissa* |
|---|---|---|---|---|---|---|---|---|
| 1. | Initial investment* (Rs lakhs) | 3.30 | 3.50 | 10.00 | 3.20 | 3.75 | 9.00 | 11.00 |
| 2. | Annual catch (tonnes) | 22.00 | 23.00 | 280.00 | 51.00 | 52.00 | 150.00 | 22.00 |
| 3. | Value (Rs lakhs) | 3.36 | 4.38 | 12.00 | 4.54 | 5.25 | 13.00 | 20.00 |
| 4. | Operating cost (Rs lakhs) | 2.02 | 2.63 | 5.80 | 2.95 | 3.00 | 8.80 | 15.00 |
| 5. | Fixed cost (Rs lakhs) | 1.00 | 1.05 | 3.06 | 0.96 | 1.13 | 2.25 | 2.75 |
| 6. | Total cost (Rs lakhs) | 3.02 | 3.68 | 8.86 | 3.91 | 4.13 | 11.05 | 17.75 |
| 7. | Net operating income (Rs lakhs) | 1.34 | 1.75 | 6.20 | 1.59 | 2.25 | 4.20 | 5.00 |
| 8. | Net income (Rs lakhs) | 0.34 | 0.70 | 3.14 | 0.63 | 1.12 | 1.95 | 2.25 |
| 9. | Rate of return (%) | 28.30 | 38.00 | 46.00 | 37.69 | 34.10 | 37.00 | 35.00 |
| 10. | Pay back period (years) | 4.48 | 3.13 | 2.40 | 3.20 | 3.34 | 3.20 | 3.30 |
| 11. | Value realised per Kg of fish (Rs) | 15.26 | 19.64 | 4.29 | 8.90 | 10.10 | 8.67 | 90.91 |
| 12. | Average total cost per Kg of fish (Rs) | 13.73 | 16.00 | 3.16 | 7.60 | 7.94 | 7.37 | 80.68 |
| 13. | Average operating cost per Kg of fish (Rs) | 9.80 | 11.43 | 2.07 | 5.78 | 5.76 | 5.87 | 68.18 |

*The new additions to the purseseine fleet along the Indian coast are mostly of 55' size costing about Rs 15 lakh in 1995

*Source:* Sathiadhas, *et al.*, 1995, p.21.

**Table 6.29**

**Costs and earnings and comparative profitability of different types of off-shore fishing vessels of india during 1989-92**

**(average)**

| *Sl. No.* | *Parameter* | *Deep sea trawler (25 m OAL)* | *Deep sea multipurpose vessel 26 m OAL* | *Tuna longliner (30 m OAL)* |
|---|---|---|---|---|
| 1 | Initial investment (Rs lakhs) | 160.00 | 150.00 | 164.00 |
| 2 | Annual catch (tonnes) | 46.00 | 76.00* | 910.00 |
| 3 | Value (Rs lakhs) | 78.20 | 68.30 | 101.00 |
| 4 | Operating cost (Rs lakhs) | 33.00 | 26.00 | 41.00 |
| 5 | Fixed costs (Rs lakhs) | 28.00 | 30.00 | 40.00 |
| 6 | Total costs (Rs lakhs) | 61.00 | 56.00 | 81.00 |
| 7 | Net operating income (Rs lakhs) | 45.20 | 42.30 | 60.00 |
| 8 | Net income (Rs lakhs) | 17.20 | 12.30 | 20.00 |
| 9 | Rate of return (%) | 26.00 | 24.00 | 27.00 |
| 10 | Pay back period (years) | 7.60 | 7.60 | 4.70 |
| 11 | Value realised per Kg of fish (Rs) | 170.00 | 90.00 | 11.00 |
| 12 | Average total cost per Kg of fish (Rs) | 133.00 | 74.00 | 9.00 |
| 13 | Average operating cost per Kg of fish (Rs) | 72.00 | 40.00 | 4.50 |

*includes 36 tonnes prawns and 40 tonnes fish

*Source:* Sathiadhas, *et al.*, 1995, p.23.

Table 6.29 reveals that all the three types of offshore fishing vessels had earned net incomes ranging from Rs 12.30 lakhs to Rs 20.00 lakhs, the former by multipurpose vessels and the latter by tuna longliners. It is, however, reported that many of these crafts (trawlers) have since then ceased operations as they found it very difficult to earn the break-even revenue (Sathiadhas, *et al.*, 1995, p.22). This finding in the case of deep sea fishing vessels have special significance in the context of sustainable development of the sector.

Table 6.30 gives details of costs and earning and comparative profitability of traditional, motorised and mechanised fishing units operating from Tamil Nadu coast during 1997.

**Table 6.30**

**Costs and earnings and comparative profitability of traditional, motorised and mechanised fishing units operating from Tamil Nadu coast during 1997**

| *Sl. No.* | *Parameter* | *Traditional crafts* | *Motorised crafts* | *Mechanised crafts* |
|---|---|---|---|---|
| 1 | Initial investment (Rs) | 37711 | 175630 | 452279 |
| 2 | Fixed cost (Rs) | 13858 | 65924 | 148420 |
| 3 | Operating cost (Rs) | 48533 | 291767 | 558748 |
| 4 | Total cost (Rs) | 62411 | 357691 | 707168 |
| 5 | Catch (Kg) | 2308 | 15386 | 56326 |
| 6 | Value of catch (Rs) | 59796 | 362125 | 791159 |
| 7 | Net operating income (Rs) | 12243 | 70358 | 232411 |
| 8 | Net income (Rs) | - 2615 | 4434 | 83991 |

*Source:* Narayankumar, *et al.*, 2000, p.87.

It is apparent from table 6.30 that both the motorised crafts and the mechanised crafts were earning surplus revenues (net income) during 1997 while the traditional crafts were incurring losses to the tune of Rs 2615 per annum.

The operations of pole and line fishing for tuna in Minicoy (Lakshadweep) island was reported to be quite profitable by Sivadas (Sivadas , 2004, pp.684-686).

Table 6.31 presents the details of costs and earnings and comparative profitability of stern trawlers, tuna longliners and purseseiners operating along the coasts of India, studied by FAO during 1997-98.

**Table 6.31**

**Costs and earnings and comparative profitability of stern trawlers, tuna long liners and purse- seiners operating along the coasts of India during 1997-98.**

**(Value in US $)**

| *Sl. No.* | *Parameter* | *Stern trawlers (14.6 m)* | *Tuna long liners (36.0 m)* | *Purse seiners (13.0 m)* |
|---|---|---|---|---|
| 1 | Initial investment | 53460 | 841270 | 47680 |
| 2 | Running costs | 20710 | 139450 | 4160 |
| 3 | Labour charges | 18970 | 279970 | 8240 |
| 4 | Vessel costs | 6380 | 34600 | 7870 |
| 5 | Fixed costs | 8070 | 125030 | 7570 |
| 6 | Total costs | 54130 | 579050 | 27840 |
| 7 | Total earnings | 66950 | 751730 | 35560 |
| 8 | Net cash flow | 12820 | 172680 | 7720 |
| 9 | Return on investment (%) | 24.00 | 20.50 | 16.20 |

*Source:* Lery, *et al.*, 1999, pp. 45-47.

Table 6.31 shows that all the three types of boats studied by FAO were showing good returns. This finding incidentally matches with the FAO's global findings on viability of commercial fishing in general.

Somvanshi reported good economic prospects and profitability for operating 36 m tuna longliners from Indian coasts (Somvanshi, 2001, p.84)

Table 6.32 presents details of costs, earnings and profitability of an 18 m steel trawler operating along the Kerala coast during 2001-03.

**Table 6.32**

**Costs, earnings and profitability of an 18 m steel trawler operating along the Kerala coast during 2001-03.**

| *Sl. No.* | *Parameter* | *2001-02* | *2002-03* |
|---|---|---|---|
| 1 | Initial investment (Rs) | 2500000 | 2500000 |
| 2 | Total revenue (Rs) | 2222068 | 1873813 |
| 3 | Total operating cost (Rs) | 1435252 | 1340195 |
| 4 | Total variable cost (Rs)[1] | 1715752 | 1530430 |
| 5 | Gross cash flow (Rs)[2] | 506316 | 343383 |
| 6 | Total fixed costs (Rs) | 293100 | 286350 |
| 7 | Total costs (Rs) | 2008852 | 1816780 |
| 8 | Net profit (Rs)[3] | 213216 | 57033 |
| 9 | Operating profit (Rs)[4] | 786816 | 533618 |
| 10 | Return on investment (%)[5] | 8.53 | 2.28 |

1. Total variable cost includes total operating costs, crew share and bonus
2. Gross cash flow = total revenue – total variable costs
3. Net profit = total revenue – total costs
4. Operating profit = total revenue – total operating costs
5. Return on investment = (Net profit ÷ initial investment) x 100

*Source:* Unnithan, *et al.*, 2004, pp.75-76.

It appears from table 6.32 that the vessel was earning profit in both the years, although profitability was quite low in the second year. The return on investment was only 2.28 per cent in 2002-03.

Referring to the working of the 18 m steel trawler off Kerala coast during 2001-03, Unnithan, *et al.* noted that out of the 76 fishing trips made during this period, 72 per cent were profit-making and the rest 28 per cent were incurring loss (Unnithan, *et al.,* 2004, p.74).

It is also significant to note in this context that Unnithan, *et al.*, while reviewing the fuel consumption pattern by the mechanised fishing sector in Kerala, reported that "the small crafts below 40' were observed to be slowly vanishing from the fishing activities as a result of poor economic returns" (Unnithan, *et al.*, 2005, p.79). They also noted: "Considering the fact that the fuel cost is the major component in the operational cost of the mechanised vessels, a substantial rise in the fuel cost will adversely affect the economic viability of fishing vessels and hence there is an urgency of attaining fuel efficiency by suitable means" (ibid. p.81).

It is worth recalling here the observations made by the Expert Committee on Marine Fisheries in Kerala in 1985. The Committee noted then: "The deterioration in the economic performance of the trawler fleet became particularly evident since the beginning of 1980 synchronising with an abrupt and sharp increase in the diesel price ...; between June 1980 and July 1981 alone, the price of diesel was hiked three times, as a result of which, there was a doubling of price within a period of one year. The diesel bill doubled from Rs 50,000 to Rs 100,000 a year per trawler ...

The main sufferers of a diesel price hike are the mechanised fishermen who have little say in the price of shrimps and cuttle fishes in the international markets, where the price of these commodities, although seemingly attractive, does not seem to increase in real terms in relation to the periodic fossil fuel price hike by the OPEC ...

Thus in view of the overcapitalised fleet and stagnant shrimp yield, the maintenance of at least the status quo in respect of mechanised shrimping would depend critically on stable oil prices" (Expert Committee on Marine Fisheries in Kerala, 1985, pp. 29-31).

It is significant to note here that the domestic fishing industry in India had to be supported by concessional supply of oil and certain tax exemptions to make it sustainable. The impact of globalisation and economic reforms which affect the sustainability of Indian fisheries will be reviewed in section 6.3.6.

A brief look at the economic viability of the aquaculture sector is made here. Table 6.33 gives the costs and earnings of freshwater aquaculture systems in Andhra Pradesh during 1992-93 and 1998-99.

**Table 6.33**

**Costs and earnings of freshwater aquaculture systems in Andhra Pradesh during 1992-93 and 1998-99**

*(Figures in Rs./ha/crop)*

| *Sl. No.* | *Parameter* | *1992-93* | *1998-99* | *Change in 1998-99 over 1992-93 (%)* |
|---|---|---|---|---|
| A. | ***Variable Costs*** | | | |
| 1 | Seed | 2912 | 10000 | 243.41 |
| 2 | Fertilisers (organic & inorganic) | 6459 | 7000 | 8.38 |
| 3 | Feed | 15632 | 32000 | 104.71 |
| 4 | Pest and disease control | 626 | 1000 | 59.74 |
| 5 | Fuel and electricity charges | 1492 | 4000 | 168.10 |
| 6 | Hired labour | 821 | 2800 | 241.05 |
| 7 | Pond preparation costs | 1050 | 5000 | 376.19 |
| 8 | Interest on working capital | 3654 | 10080 | 175.86 |
| 9 | Family labour | 2821 | - | - |
| | Total | 35467 | 71880 | 102.66 |
| B. | ***Fixed Costs*** | | | |
| 1 | Supervision and watch and ward | 1582 | 7200 | 355.12 |
| 2 | Insurance charges | 692 | 750 | 8.38 |
| 3 | Depreciation | 864 | 2000 | 131.48 |
| 4 | Lease cost of the land | - | 14000 | - |
| 5 | Annuity value for pond | 1761 | 7142 | 305.57 |
| 6 | Interest on fixed capital | 848 | 5000 | 489.62 |
| | Total | 5747 | 36092 | 528.01 |
| C. | ***Total Costs (A+B)*** | 41214 | 133972 | 225.06 |
| D. | ***Total Returns*** | 82881 | 168000 | 102.70 |
| E. | ***Gross profit (D - A)*** | 47414 | 70120 | 47.88 |
| F. | ***Net profit (D -C)*** | 41667 | 34028 | -18.33 |

*Source:* Bhatta, 2001, p.187.

Table 6.33 shows that there was net profit in both the years, although it has come down by 18 per cent during 1998-99 as compared to 1992-93.

Table 6.34 presents the costs and earnings of brackish water prawn farming in Uttar Kannada district of Karnataka state during 1997-98.

**Table 6.34**

**Costs and earnings of brackish water prawn farming in Uttar Kannada district of Karnataka state during 1997-98**

*(Rs./ha)*

| *Sl. No.* | *Parameter* | *Traditional farming* | *% of total cost/ revenue* | *Scientific farming* | *% of total cost/revenue* |
|---|---|---|---|---|---|
| A. | Costs | | | | |
| 1 | Leasing charge | 20860 | 51.90 | 34953 | 8.67 |
| 2 | Feed | - | - | 172042 | 42.69 |
| 3 | Prawn seed (fingerlings) | - | - | 58000 | 14.39 |
| 4 | Labour | 4835 | 12.03 | 37285 | 9.25 |
| 5 | Depreciation of equipments and maintenance of pond | 2963 | 7.37 | 13864 | 3.44 |
| 6 | Lime, fertiliser and manure | - | - | 32573 | 8.08 |
| 7 | Fuel and lubricants | - | - | 12027 | 2.98 |
| 8 | Harvest expenses | 6864 | 17.08 | 13886 | 3.45 |
| 9 | Miscellaneous expenditure including depreciation and interest on loans | 4667 | 11.61 | 28341 | 7.03 |
| | Total | 40189 | 100.00 | 402971 | 100.00 |
| B. | Earnings | | | | |
| 1 | Value of prawns sold | 85300 | 98.01 | 880944 | 99.85 |
| 2 | Value of fish, crabs and other items | 1728 | 1.99 | 1296 | 0.15 |
| | Total | 87028 | 100.00 | 882240 | 100.00 |
| C. | Net earnings (B-A) | 46839 | - | 481629 | - |
| D | Benefit/Cost ratio | 2.17 | - | 2.20 | - |

*Source:* Naik, *et al.*, 2000, p.113.

**Table 6.35**

**Costs and earnings of different freshwater aquaculture systems in India during 2001-02**

*(Rs/ha)*

| Sl. No. | Parameter | Carp culture | | | Sewage-fed | | Weed based | Integrated | | | | Pen culture | Air breathing | Prawn culture | Carp/ prawn culture |
|---|---|---|---|---|---|---|---|---|---|---|---|---|---|---|---|
| | | Low input | Medium input | High input | Without feed | With feed | | Duck | Poultry | Pig | Paddy | | | | |
| 1 | Total cost | 41925 | 120400 | 306375 | 53212 | 90837 | 52137 | 61382 | 104812 | 59662 | 43537 | 101050 | 172000 | 161250 | 118250 |
| 2 | Total earnings | 75000 | 180000 | 375000 | 90000 | 150000 | 90000 | 110000 | 148000 | 96400 | 60000 | 120000 | 240000 | 300000 | 190000 |
| 3 | Profit | 33075 | 59600 | 68625 | 36788 | 59163 | 37863 | 48618 | 43188 | 36738 | 16463 | 18950 | 68000 | 138750 | 71750 |
| 4 | B:C ratio | 1.79 | 1.5 | 1.22 | 1.69 | 1.65 | 1.73 | 1.79 | 1.41 | 1.62 | 1.38 | 1.19 | 1.40 | 1.86 | 1.61 |

NCAP, 2004, pp. 18-19.

Table 6.34 shows remarkable profitability for both traditional and scientific shrimp farming in the Uttar Kannada (North Kanara) district of Karnataka. The benefit-cost ratios were high at 2.17 and 2.20 respectively for the two types of farming indicating more than 100 per cent return on total cost.

Dey, *et al.,* reported an average rate of return of 138.39 per cent over variable costs to carp fish cultivators in India during 2000 (Dey, *et al.*, 2001, p.38).

Table 6.35 gives the costs and earnings of different freshwater aquaculture systems in India during 2001-02.

Table 6.35 shows that all forms of aquaculture studied produced satisfactory levels of profit, with prawn culture showing the maximum level of profit of Rs 1.38 lakh/ha$^{-1}$. The benefit-cost ratios ranged between 1.19 for pen culture and 1.86 for prawn culture.

Table 6.36 gives the costs and earnings of inland capture fisheries in India during 2001-02.

**Table 6.36**

**Costs and earnings of inland capture fisheries in India during 2001-02**

| *Sl. No.* | *Parameter* | *Property right regime* | | |
|---|---|---|---|---|
| | | *Common property* | *Private property* | *Cooperatives* |
| A. | Costs | | | |
| 1 | Fixed costs per year (Rs) | 2907 | 3017 | 1451 |
| 2 | Variable costs per year (Rs) | 1712 | 1737 | 285 |
| 3 | Total cost (Rs) | 4619 | 4754 | 1736 |
| B | Earnings | | | |
| 4 | Gross earnings per year (Rs) | 34490 | 14656 | 13108 |
| 5 | Net earnings per year (Rs) | 29871 | 9902 | 11372 |
| 6 | Net returns (Rs/Kg) | 21 | 13 | 30 |
| 7 | Input-output ratio | 7.49 | 3.00 | 7.55 |

*Source:* NCAP, 2004, p.21

Table 6.36 indicates the viability of capture fisheries in inland waters of the country. The net returns were the highest under common property

The economic viability of the marketing sector also may be looked at for understanding the sustainability of the sector. Published information on the viability of the sector in recent times is, however, quite scanty.

Gopal, *et al* reported the prevalence of large marketing margins and price spreads during peak landing periods for major varieties of fishes in Kerala and Gujarat, making it possible for the marketing channels to earn good returns indicating economic viability (Gopal, *et al.*, 2001, pp.131-132).

Patnaik reported profitability in production and marketing of value-added dry fish products in Orissa (Patnaik, 2000, p.54).

The National Centre for Agricultural Economics and Policy Research, New Delhi reported on the viability of fish marketing. Table 6.37 presents the costs and earnings of inland fish merchants in India during 2003.

**Table 6.37**

**Costs and earnings of inland fish merchants in India during 2003**

*(Rs./tonne)*

| *Sl.No.* | *Parameter* | *Wholesaler* | *Retailer* |
|---|---|---|---|
| **A.** | ***Fixed Cost*** | | |
| 1 | Rent | 15 | 6 |
| 2 | Electricity | 2 | 3 |
| 3 | Family labour | 162 | 643 |
| 4 | Labour cost | 304 | 511 |
| | Total | 481 | 1163 |
| **B.** | ***Variable Cost*** | | |
| 1 | Fish purchased | 19881 | 23444 |
| 2 | Transportation | 2333 | 823 |
| 3 | Ice | 1433 | 594 |
| 4 | Packaging | 466 | 151 |
| 5 | Handling loss | 1313 | 350 |
| | Total | 25426 | 25362 |
| **C.** | ***Total Cost (A + B)*** | 25907 | 26525 |
| **D.** | ***Total revenue*** | 36375 | 39209 |
| **E.** | ***Net revenue (D - C)*** | 10468 | 12684 |
| **F.** | ***Benefit-cost ratio (total revenue/total cost)*** | 1.40 | 1.48 |

*Source:* NCAP, 2004, p.68.

Table 6.37 shows that the main marketing channels, viz. wholesalers and retailers were earning satisfactory returns on their operation. The benefit-cost ratios for the first group was 1.40 and for the second 1.48.

### 6.3.4. Declining Employment

The global trend of declining employment in the fishing sector and the rising proportion of aging work force in the sector have been reported by FAO and noted in chapter four. Comparable information is, however, lacking on the fishery sector of India. An attempt is, nevertheless, made in this section to work out the (work) participation rate in the fishermen community in India. This is accomplished by taking note of the total fishermen population in the country and subtracting the number of active (working) fishermen (male and female) engaged in different activities including fishing (full time and part time) and other related activities of marketing of fish, repairing of nets, processing of fish, etc. and, the resulting figures considered to indicate the non-active members of the fishermen population which include children and the aged. This in fact gives the dependent population of fishermen showing the economic burden on the community and the industry, having implications for the sustainable development of the industry. Table 6.38 gives the estimate of non-working fishermen population in states and Union territories of India during 2003.

It is clear from Table 6.38 that the percentage of the fishermen population (including children and the aged) not engaged in any work is considerably higher at 76.60 per cent at the national level with the majority of states including interior states like Bihar, Chattisgarh, Jharkhand, Madhya Pradesh, Nagaland and Sikkim showing higher percentages of non-working population. This is in addition to the fear that the estimates of total fishermen population in states like Bihar, Madhya Pradesh, Jharkhand and Chhattisgarh are apparently inflated ones.

A partial picture of the unemployment problem in the coastal (marine) fishing community of Kerala can be obtained from table 6.39.

**Table 6.38**

**Estimate of non-working fishermen population in states and Union territories of India during 2003**

| *Sl. No.* | *State/U.T.* | *Total fishermen population* | *Working population* | *Non-working population* | *Non-workingas as % of total* |
|---|---|---|---|---|---|
| 1. | Andhra Pradesh | 893365 | 573088 | 320277 | 35.85 |
| 2. | Arunachal Pradesh | 4399 | 1942 | 2457 | 55.85 |
| 3. | Assam | 390380 | 233206 | 157174 | 40.26 |
| 4. | Bihar | 4959516 | 142070 | 4817446 | 97.13 |
| 5. | Chattisgarh | 1911368 | 84664 | 1826704 | 95.57 |
| 6. | Goa | 13970 | 4121 | 9849 | 70.50 |
| 7. | Gujarat | 493255 | 172359 | 320896 | 65.06 |
| 8. | Haryana | 16491 | 10158 | 6333 | 38.40 |
| 9. | Himachal Pradesh | 5622 | 1760 | 3862 | 68.69 |
| 10. | Jammu & Kashmir | 30453 | 10516 | 19937 | 65.46 |
| 11. | Jharkhand | 1930920 | 48959 | 1881961 | 97.46 |
| 12. | Karnataka | 158952 | 79030 | 79913 | 50..27 |
| 13. | Kerala | 747837 | 223110 | 524727 | 70.17 |
| 14. | Madhya Pradesh | 716974 | 34339 | 682635 | 95.21 |
| 15. | Maharashtra | 171830 | 118413 | 53417 | 31.09 |
| 16. | Manipur | 70468 | 12242 | 58226 | 82.63 |
| 17. | Meghalaya | 2383 | 498 | 1885 | 79.10 |
| 18. | Mizoram | 17907 | 3099 | 14808 | 82.69 |
| 19. | Nagaland | 14862 | 43 | 14819 | 99.71 |
| 20. | Orissa | 180026 | 135456 | 44570 | 24.75 |
| 21. | Punjab | 9085 | 6559 | 2526 | 27.80 |
| 22. | Rajasthan | 7316 | 2833 | 4483 | 61.27 |
| 23. | Sikkim | 26814 | 1621 | 25193 | 93.95 |
| 24. | Tamil Nadu | 476618 | 195624 | 280994 | 58.96 |
| 25. | Tripura | 46733 | 17692 | 29041 | 62.14 |
| 26. | Uttar Pradesh | 179064 | 47647 | 131417 | 73.39 |
| 27 | Uttaranchal | 90 | - | - | - |
| 28. | West Bengal | 911622 | 167457 | 744165 | 81.63 |
| 29. | Andaman & Nicobar | 17552 | 10996 | 6556 | 37.35 |
| 30. | Chandigarh | 479 | - | - | |
| 31. | Dadra & Nagar Haveli | 0 | 0 | 0 | 0 |
| 32. | Daman & Diu | 25485 | 7134 | 18351 | 72.00 |
| 33. | Delhi | 2515 | 787 | 1808 | 71.89 |
| 34. | Lakshadweep | 13029 | 9508 | 3521 | 27.02 |
| 35. | Pondicherry | 37974 | 15306 | 22668 | 59.69 |
| | Total | 14485354 | 3389685 | 11095669 | 76.60 |

*Source:* Department of Animal Husbandry, Dairying and Fisheries, 2005, p.141.

**Table 6.39**

**Non-working fishermen (marine) in the coastal districts of Kerala in 1999-2000**

| *Sl. No.* | *Districts* | *Fishermen population** | *Active fishermen* | *Non-active fishermen* | *Non-active as % of fishermen population* | *Non-active (%) excluding < 15 and > 60 age group*** |
|---|---|---|---|---|---|---|
| 1 | Thiruvananthapuram | 170135 | 51488 | 118647 | 69.73 | 30.95 |
| 2 | Kollam | 95752 | 20531 | 75221 | 78.55 | 39.77 |
| 3 | Alappuzha | 113647 | 30435 | 83212 | 73.21 | 34.43 |
| 4 | Ernakulam | 73981 | 15157 | 58824 | 79.51 | 40.73 |
| 5 | Thrissur | 71183 | 9694 | 61489 | 86.38 | 47.60 |
| 6 | Malappuram | 81641 | 23131 | 58510 | 71.66 | 32.88 |
| 7 | Kozhikode | 100754 | 18312 | 82442 | 81.82 | 43.04 |
| 8 | Kannur | 56909 | 5404 | 51505 | 90.50 | 51.72 |
| 9 | Kasargode | 44636 | 10697 | 33939 | 76.03 | 37.25 |
| | Total | 808638 | 184849 | 623789 | 74.14 | 38.36 |

* Figures are at variance with that in table 6.38 as the sources are different

** The <15 and >60 age group constituted 38.78 per cent of the population of the state. This percentage is deducted from the figures of the previous column to get an estimate of the 'workable' population remaining unemployed.

*Source:* Korakandy, 2005 b, p.341.

Table 6.39 shows that out of the total marine fishermen population of 8.08 lakhs in 1999-00, only 1.84 lakhs were active, leaving 6.23 lakhs as non-active (non-working). The non-working population constituted 77.14 per cent of the population. Excluding the normal non-working population in the age group of below 15 and above 60 (38.78 per cent for total population of the state), the percentage of the non-working population among fishermen can be estimated at 38.36 per cent which is still quite significant. At the district level, this percentage is found to vary between 30.95 per cent in Thiruvananthapuram and 51.72 per cent in Kannur indicating high levels of unemployment among the coastal marine fishermen of the state. A similar picture of unemployment among inland fishermen of Kerala is indicated in table 6.40.

**Table 6.40**

**Non-working fishermen (inland) in Kerala in 1999-2000**

| *Sl. No.* | *Districts* | *Fishermen population* | *Active fishermen* | *Non-active fishermen* | *Non-active as per cent of fishermen population* | *Non-active (%) excluding < 15 and > 60 age group** |
|---|---|---|---|---|---|---|
| 1 | Thiruvanthapuram | 1357 | 350 | 1001 | 74.09 | 35.31 |
| 2 | Kollam | 34323 | 8080 | 26243 | 76.45 | 37.67 |
| 3 | Pathanamthitta | 1450 | 466 | 984 | 67.86 | 28.78 |
| 4 | Alappuzha | 62388 | 10140 | 52248 | 83.74 | 44.96 |
| 5 | Kottaym | 24985 | 6664 | 18321 | 73.32 | 34.54 |
| 6 | Idukki | 52 | 30 | 22 | 42.30 | 3.52 |
| 7 | Ernakulam | 64482 | 16118 | 48362 | 75.00 | 36.22 |
| 8. | Thrissur | 19947 | 4832 | 15115 | 75.77 | 36.99 |
| 9 | Palakkad | 1041 | 495 | 546 | 52.44 | 13.66 |
| 10 | Malappuram | 4387 | 1227 | 3160 | 72.03 | 33.25 |
| 11 | Kozhikode | 12124 | 2814 | 9310 | 76.78 | 38.00 |
| 12 | Wayanad | 1039 | 254 | 785 | 75.55 | 36.77 |
| 13 | Kannur | 1548 | 920 | 628 | 40.56 | 1.78 |
| 14 | Kasargode | 953 | 285 | 668 | 70.09 | 31.31 |
| | Total | 230070 | 52675 | 177395 | 77.10 | 38.32 |

* The <15 and>60 age group constituted 38.78 per cent of the population of the state. This percentage is deducted from the figures of the previous column to get an estimate of the 'workable' population remaining unemployed.

*Source:* Korakandy, 2005 b, p.342.

Table 6.40 indicates that out of a total inland fishermen population of 230070, only 52675 were active, leaving 177395 as non-active (non-working). The non-working group constituted 77.10 per cent of the inland fishermen population. Excluding the below 15 and above 60 age group, the non-working population formed 38.32 per cent of the population, again marking a large contingent of unemployed persons. One of the frequently pointed out reasons for the rise in unemployment in the fisheries sector, apart from the growth in population is the negative impacts of modernisation leading to social displacement of fishermen in the catching, culture, processing and marketing branches of the industry.

An adverse situation developing as a result of developments in shrimp farming leading to the displacement of labour has been reported by Nandakumar and Muraleekrishna in 1998. They noted that on an average, labour displacement takes place at 1:5 ratio, *i.e.,* a modern shrimp farm employs one person whereas traditional systems would have five workers. In a state like Kerala, where the population is high and more so in poverty-ridden primary sector, this labour displacement has far-reaching consequences. This labour displacement, weighed against mere foreign exchange earning for a few and the social costs created, exerts an imbalance, accentuating social inequality" (Nandakumar and Muraleekrishna, 1998, p.64-65).

Sathiadhas, et al. reported that "currently unemployment is the greatest problem faced by the marine fisheries sector. Excess fleet size and less number of actual fishing days are mainly responsible for the under employment in active fishing. The labour intensive fishing techniques such as *Rampani* (shoreseine) operations have almost vanished ...; on an average with the entire fleet strength, the mechanised and motorized boats could operate about 100 days while the non-mechanised boats would operate only less than 50 days in a year" (Sathiadhas, et al., 1999, p.55). The introduction purseseines reportedly had adverse effect on employment. Kurup and Devaraj noted that "purse seine in Kerala effectively replaces 4.8 out-board boat seines, 32.2 out-board gillnets, 2.5 out-board ring seines and 73.5 non-motorised units and so on. The socio-economic implications of such replacement schedule, as has been happening in the south west coast of India, is quite formidable and alarming" (Kurup and Devaraj, 2000, p.11).

Selvam, *et al.*, noted displacement of labour in shrimp farming. They observed that "one of the negative consequences of shrimp culture is displacement of labour... Average labour requirement for paddy cultivation in one hectare of land was estimated to be 183.1 man days. In the case of shrimp farming, it created an average 90 days per year per hectare. Under existing conditions this shows that labour requirement of crop cultivation was two times higher than that in shrimp farming. The other important fact is that bulk of the labour requirement in the crop cultural activities is mainly from the family in the case of small and tenant farmers. In the case of shrimp culture, the labour is mostly hired. So, the shrimp farming is showing adverse impacts on employment of small farmers and agricultural labourers.

Woman play a major role in rice production, post-harvest processing and marketing. Much of the women labour in rice cultivation is hired female labour. But shrimp production does not hire any women labour at the production level" (Selvam, et al., 2000, p.306).

The NCAP team reported that "capture fisheries is not likely to provide increasing source of employment at any significant scale in the coming years. There is disguised unemployment in the sector ..." (NCAP, 2004, p.xix).

Krishna also reported that "women in traditional fishing villages lost access to post-harvest operations as motorisation (mechanisation) necessitated centralised landings and a shift in job opportunities. Automation displaced a large number of women from net making, an area once entirely dominated by them. Unemployment and underemployment forced some youths to migrate to other states and countries in search of livelihood" (Krishna, 1997, p.17, word in parentheses added).

Seasonal unemployment of fishermen has also been reported. Krishna, et al. reported that "unemployment levels of the trawler workers were high during the (trawl) ban period in two of the major fishing centres (of Kerala) studied, viz; Munambam and Ponnani" (Krishna, et al., 2002, words in parentheses added). Occupational displacement of fishermen of Chilka lake in Orissa has been reported by Samal (Samal, 2002, p.1714).

### 6.3.5. Static or Declining Consumption

The stagnation that is prevailing in global per capita fish consumption has been noted in chapter four. Per capita consumption of fish in India is found to stagnate over the years. Table 6.41 shows the trend in per capita consumption of fish in India between 1981 and 1995.

**Table 6.41**

**Trend in per capita consumption of fish in India between 1981 and 1995**

| *Year* | *Per capita consumption (Kg)* |
|---|---|
| 1981 | 3.1 |
| 1982 | 3.0 |
| 1983 | 3.1 |
| 1984 | 3.4 |
| 1985 | 3.3 |
| 1986 | 3.3 |
| 1987 | 3.2 |
| 1988 | 3.4 |
| 1989 | 3.8 |
| 1990 | 3.9 |
| 1991 | 4.0 |
| 1992 | 4.1 |
| 1993 | 4.2 |
| 1994 | 4.3 |
| 1995 | 4.3 |
| 1996 | 4.6 |
| 1997 | 4.7 |
| 1998 | 4.7 |
| 1999 | 4.8 |
| 2000 | 4.7 |
| 2001 | 4.9 |

*Source:* http://apps.fao.org/Food Balance Sheet of Fish and Fishery Products, p.168.

Table 6.41 presents the tardy growth in the per capita consumption of fish in India and the near static position after 1997. Dey, et al. reported the changes in per capita consumption of major groups of fishes in India between 1980 and 1998. Table 6.42 presents the trend in the per capita consumption of major groups of fish in India during 1980, 1990 and 1998.

**Table 6.42**

**Trend in the per capita consumption of major groups of fish in India during 1980, 1990 and 1998.**

| *Major species groups* | *Per capita consumtion (Kg)* | | |
|---|---|---|---|
| | 1980 | 1990 | 1998 |
| All species | 3.1 | 3.8 | 4.6 |
| Freshwater species | 1.3 | 1.9 | 2.5 |
| Demersal species | 0.6 | 0.7 | 0.9 |
| Pelagic species | 0.7 | 0.7 | 0.6 |
| Other marine fishes | 0.2 | 0.3 | 0.4 |
| Crustaceans | 0.3 | 0.2 | 0.2 |
| Cephalopods | 0.0 | 0.0 | 0.0 |
| Molluscs | 0.0 | 0.0 | 0.0 |

*Source:* Dey, et al., 2001, p.41

Table 6.42 shows that the per capita consumptions of all species in India increased from 3.1 Kg in 1980 to 3.8 Kg in 1990 and 4.6 Kg in 1998 which is quite insignificant taking into account the long period of 18 years. Freshwater species constituted the major component of this increase The low per capita consumption of fish in India may be attributed to the non-availability of fish to the vast majority of the population of the interior states where inland fish production is seasonal and in short supply and where marine fish supplies are not accessible. As noted by NCAP "the share of fish in the animal origin food was about 12 per cent. Only 35 per cent population in India was estimated to be fish eater; 46 per cent in coastal states and 27 percent in non-coastal states. The share of fish in the total non-vegetarian food in non-coastal states declined from 57 per cent in 1983 to 51 percent in 1999" (NCAP, 2004, p.71). Table 6.43 shows the distribution of fish eating households and their consumption pattern.

**Table 6.43**

**Distribution of fish eating households and consumption pattern**

| Year | *Fish eating households* | | |
|---|---|---|---|
| | *Share of fish eating population in total (%)* | *share of fish in food expenditure (%)* | *Share of fish in total meat fish & eggs (%)* |
| ***Non-maritime states*** | | | |
| 1983-84 | 23.2 | 5.71 | 57.10 |
| 1987-88 | 26.2 | 6.39 | 53.80 |
| 1993-94 | 28.2 | 7.10 | 50.00 |
| 1999-00 | 27.3 | 5.54 | 50.90 |
| ***Maritime states*** | | | |
| 1983-84 | 45.70 | 5.61 | 59.20 |
| 1987-88 | 46.70 | 6.81 | 62.00 |
| 1993-94 | 48.20 | 7.50 | 56.40 |
| 1999-00 | 45.60 | 7.16 | 62.60 |
| ***All India*** | | | |
| 1983-84 | 33.80 | 5.65 | 58.40 |
| 1987-88 | 35.40 | 6.64 | 58.00 |
| 1993-94 | 37.10 | 7.34 | 53.80 |
| 1999-00 | 35.20 | 6.49 | 57.90 |

*Source:* NCAP, 2004, p.72

Table 6.43 makes it clear that although the share of the fish eating population in the non-maritime states has increased from 23.2 per cent in 1983-84 to 27.3 per cent in 1999-00, the share of fish in food expenditure has decreased from 5.71 per cent to 5.54 per cent during the same period. As already noted, the share of fish among the non-vegetarian items also has shown similar decrease from 57.1 per cent to 50.9 per cent in these states during this period. This probably indicates the negative substitution taking place against fish perhaps due to non-availability of the item as a cheap substitute for other goods.

The share (percentage) of fish eating population shows slight decrease over the years in the maritime states, although the percentages of expenditure on fish within the food basket and the share of fish among non-vegetarian items show some increase.

At the national level, the percentage of the fish eating population has increased from 33.80 per cent in 1983-84 to 35.20 per cent in 1999-00. The share of fish in total food expenditure also has increased from 5.65 per cent to 6.49 per cent during this period. Notwithstanding this, the share of fish in the non-vegetarian mix is found to fall slightly from 58.40 per cent to 57.90 per cent over the same period indicating some possible substitution by other products. As noted by NCAP "the real prices of fish, in general, have increased over the past 20 years. The relative prices of fish have also soared up compared to the steeply declining meat and grain prices over the same period. It is feared that the poor who used to take small quantities of animal protein through fish eating are likely to substitute it with milk and meat as these have become relatively cheaper" (ibid. p.xvii). It is significant to note here that such developments have implications for the economic and social sustainability of fisheries sector in India.

As is well known, regional, rural, urban and income-class variation in consumption of fish is noted in the country. Table 6.44 shows the regional, rural, urban and income-class variation in the consumption of fish in India between 1983-84 and 1999-00.

Table 6.44 shows growth in per capita consumption of fish both in rural and urban areas between 1983-84 and 1999-00. Per capita consumption was however, relatively low in rural areas.

Among non-maritime states, per capita consumption was comparatively high and growing in the eastern and north eastern states. Among the fish-eating sample households of maritime states, it was high in southern and western states. Looking at the economic groups (classes) of maritime and non-maritime states, it is found that the 'rich' and the 'non-poor' households have higher levels of consumption which is quite natural and the 'poor' and 'very poor' households show only lower levels of consumption. Expectedly, consumers of maritime states of all classes have an edge over consumers of all classes in non-maritime states.

Table 6.45 presents details of monthly per capita consumption of fish (quantity and value) in states and Union territories of India during 1999-2000.

**Table 6.44**

**Regional, rural/urban and income-class variation in the consumption of fish in India between 1983-84 and 1999-00**

**(Per capita/kg/year)**

| *Region/class* | *Fish eating sample households* | | | | *All sample households* | | | |
|---|---|---|---|---|---|---|---|---|
| | *1983-84* | *1987-88* | *1993-94* | *1999-00* | *1983-84* | *1987-88* | *1993-94* | *1999-00* |
| *(1)* | *(2)* | *(3)* | *(4)* | *(5)* | *(6)* | *(7)* | *(8)* | *(9)* |
| Rural | 6.97 | 7.54 | 7.23 | 9.12 | 2.39 | 2.73 | 2.77 | 3.35 |
| Urban | 8.01 | 8.57 | 9.18 | 11.05 | 3.87 | 4.38 | 4.81 | 5.48 |
| All-India | 7.30 | 7.86 | 7.90 | 9.79 | 2.45 | 2.78 | 2.93 | 3.45 |
| Non-maritime states (regions) | | | | | | | | |
| East | 5.63 | 5.35 | 4.97 | 5.72 | 2.66 | 2.90 | 2.75 | 3.39 |
| West | 3.86 | 3.62 | 3.40 | 3.45 | 0.46 | 0.37 | 0.43 | 0.37 |
| North | 5.25 | 4.25 | 3.83 | 4.68 | 0.50 | 0.30 | 0.29 | 0.46 |
| Hills | 4.12 | 3.59 | 4.04 | 7.44 | 0.30 | 0.34 | 0.25 | 0.20 |
| North-East States | 5.85 | 6.13 | 6.77 | 13.56 | 3.75 | 4.46 | 4.95 | 8.94 |
| All states | 5.37 | 5.30 | 5.37 | 7.78 | 1.25 | 1.39 | 1.52 | 2.13 |
| Maritime states (regions) | | | | | | | | |
| East | 6.93 | 8.62 | 7.92 | 8.58 | 5.41 | 7.27 | 6.98 | 7.47 |
| West | 6.49 | 7.60 | 8.10 | 9.44 | 1.48 | 1.84 | 1.96 | 2.04 |
| South | 10.52 | 11.44 | 12.31 | 15.04 | 4.55 | 4.75 | 5.13 | 5.97 |
| All states | 8.45 | 9.64 | 9.72 | 11.37 | 3.87 | 4.50 | 4.68 | 5.18 |

| (1) | (2) | (3) | (4) | 5) | (6) | (7) | (8) | (9) |
|---|---|---|---|---|---|---|---|---|
| Non-maritime states (Sample households by income-class) | | | | | | | | |
| Very poor | 3.60 | 3.45 | 3.28 | 3.57 | 0.64 | 0.71 | 0.69 | 0.98 |
| Poor | 4.69 | 4.04 | 3.81 | 5.70 | 1.13 | 1.04 | 1.10 | 1.74 |
| Non-poor | 5.05 | 4.72 | 4.93 | 7.64 | 1.34 | 1.32 | 1.52 | 2.26 |
| Rich | 7.43 | 6.99 | 7.23 | 9.53 | 1.69 | 1.89 | 2.02 | 2.35 |
| Maritime states (Sample households by income-class) | | | | | | | | |
| Very poor | 5.03 | 4.86 | 4.44 | 4.10 | 2.08 | 1.84 | 1.73 | 1.71 |
| Poor | 6.41 | 6.68 | 5.80 | 6.12 | 2.98 | 3.16 | 2.79 | 2.80 |
| Non-poor | 8.21 | 8.75 | 8.26 | 9.06 | 3.85 | 4.16 | 4.09 | 4.24 |
| Rich | 12.77 | 13.90 | 13.96 | 14.97 | 6.08 | 6.77 | 6.98 | 6.79 |

*Source*: NCAP, 2004, p.73

Table 6.45 shows that the monthly per capita consumption of fish (quantity) at the national level was almost equal in both rural and urban areas, the quantities being 0.21 kg and 0.22 kg respectively. Per capita consumption and expenditure were comparatively more in both rural and urban areas of Arunachal Pradesh, Assam, Goa, Kerala, Manipur, Tripura, West Bengal, Andaman & Nicobar, Daman & Diu and Lakshadweep. They were correspondingly low in most other states and Union territories.

The number of households reporting consumption of fish at the national level was only 33.66 percent in rural areas and 28.5 per cent in urban areas. Appendix 6.3 gives the number of households per 1000 households reporting consumption of fish in rural and urban areas of states and Union territories of India during 1999-2000. In 18 out of the 32 states and Union territories, the number of households reporting consumption of fish is less than 50 per cent.

The central point emerging from the above discussion is that consumption of fish is not yet quite widespread and not showing any significant growth in the country which has implications for its sustainability. The limiting factors may be non-availability, non-accessibility, low income, high prices, etc.

### 6.3.6. Unstable Global Market for Fish and Barriers to Trade

A major threat to the sustainability of fisheries sector in India is its heavy dependence on the global market for fish, which is quite unstable and subject to a variety of international political, economic, environmental and diplomatic bargains and manoeuvreings. As is well known, most technological advancements in Indian fisheries since independence and particularly in recent times have been impelled by the prospects of earning foreign exchange for the country by exporting selected 'highpriced' varieties of fish to international markets. This has helped the country in earning more foreign exchange and improving its balance of payments position. The export of marine products from the country has increased from 15732 tonnes valued at Rs 3.92 crores during 1961-62 to 412017 tonnes valued at Rs 6091.95 crores during 2003-04, at current prices, marking an increase of 26 times in quantity and 1554 times in value. The unit value (Rs/tonne) realised during this period increased from Rs 2491.74 to Rs 147857 showing an increase of 59 times. (Department of Animal Husbandry, Dairying and Fisheries, 2005, p.65). Appendix 6.4 shows the trend in the export of marine products from India between 1961-62 and 2003-04.

**Table 6.45**

**Monthly per capita consumption of fish (quantity and value) in states and Union territories of India during 1999-2000**

| *Sl No.* | *States/Union territories* | *Per capita consumption* | | | |
|---|---|---|---|---|---|
| | | *Rural* | | *Urban* | |
| | | *Quantity (kg)* | *Value (Rs)* | *Quantity (kg)* | *Value (Rs)* |
| *(1)* | *(2)* | *(3)* | *(4)* | *(5)* | *(6)* |
| 1 | Andhra Pradesh | 0.18 | 2.45 | 0.08 | 2.40 |
| 2 | Arunachal Pradesh | 2.18 | 16.45 | 1.19 | 25.70 |
| 3 | Assam | 0.52 | 19.24 | 0.79 | 42.55 |
| 4 | Bihar | 0.15 | 4.96 | 0.16 | 6.02 |
| 5 | Goa | 2.26 | 58.62 | 1.90 | 71.73 |
| 6 | Gujarat | 0.03 | 0.89 | 0.03 | 0.98 |
| 7 | Haryana* | - | 2.77 | - | 7.31 |
| 8 | Himachal Pradesh* | - | 8.77 | 0.01 | 0.56 |
| 9 | Jammu & Kashmir* | - | 25.38 | 0.01 | 0.55 |
| 10 | Karnataka | 0.13 | 2.74 | 0.12 | 3.25 |
| 11 | Kerala | 1.75 | 43.50 | 1.88 | 47.68 |
| 12 | Madhya Pradesh | 0.05 | 1.58 | 0.05 | 2.29 |
| 13 | Maharashtra | 0.10 | 3.02 | 0.15 | 6.48 |
| 14 | Manipur | 1.01 | 15.06 | 0.71 | 25.92 |
| 15 | Meghalaya | 0.26 | 14.19 | 0.41 | 19.30 |

| (1) | (2) | (3) | (4) | (5) | (6) |
|---|---|---|---|---|---|
| 16 | Mizoram | 0.20 | 14.18 | 0.14 | 10.22 |
| 17 | Nagaland | 0.32 | 15.38 | 0.44 | 25.46 |
| 18 | Orissa | 0.31 | 7.77 | 0.35 | 12.68 |
| 19 | Punjab* | - | 5.64 | - | 9.37 |
| 20 | Rajasthan* | - | 4.66 | - | 9.89 |
| 21 | Sikkim | 0.03 | 1.72 | 0.16 | 9.14 |
| 22 | Tamil Nadu | 0.17 | 5.65 | 0.18 | 6.94 |
| 23 | Tripura | 0.85 | 36.09 | 0.95 | 60.48 |
| 24 | Uttar Pradesh | 0.06 | 1.86 | 0.03 | 0.88 |
| 25 | West Bengal | 0.59 | 21.48 | 0.86 | 38.84 |
| 26 | A & N Islands | 1.24 | 31.56 | 1.14 | 34.71 |
| 27 | Chandigarh* | 0.04 | 1.69 | - | 14.83 |
| 28 | Dadra & Nagar Haveli | 0.08 | 3.08 | 0.09 | 4.89 |
| 29 | Daman & Diu | 0.54 | 16.13 | 1.19 | 30.84 |
| 30 | Delhi* | - | 7.96 | 0.12 | 3.00 |
| 31 | Lakshadweep | 2.39 | 79.56 | 4.04 | 112.30 |
| 32 | Pondicherry | 0.44 | 18.06 | 0.43 | 17.52 |
| | All India | 0.21 | 6.22 | 0.22 | 8.08 |

*includes meat and egg

*Source*: Department of Animal Husbandry, Dairying and Fisheries, 2005, pp.144-145.

It is significant to note here that the growth in the export of marine products from the country has not been quite steady and was showing considerable fluctuations in quantity and value over the years and especially in recent times coinciding with the era of globalisation. Table 6.46 shows the trend in the quantity, value and unit-value of export of marine products from India between 1991-92 and 2003-04.

**Table 6.46**

**Trend in the quantity, value and unit-value of export of marine products from India between 1991-92 and 2003-04.**

| *Year* | *Quantity (tonnes)* | *Annual growth rate (%)* | *Value (Rs crore)* | *Annual growth rate (%)* | *Unit-value (Rs/tonne)* | *Annual growth rate (%)* |
|---|---|---|---|---|---|---|
| 1991-92 | 171820 | - | 1375.89 | - | 80077.41 | - |
| 1992-93 | 209025 | 21.65 | 1768.56 | 28.54 | 84609.97 | 5.66 |
| 1993-94 | 243960 | 16.71 | 2503.62 | 41.56 | 102624.20 | 21.29 |
| 1994-95 | 307337 | 25.98 | 3575.27 | 42.80 | 116330.61 | 13.36 |
| 1995-96 | 296277 | -3.73 | 3501.11 | -2.07 | 118170.16 | 1.58 |
| 1996-97 | 378199 | 27.65 | 4121.36 | 17.72 | 108973.32 | -7.78 |
| 1997-98 | 385818 | 2.01 | 4697.48 | 13.98 | 121753.78 | 11.73 |
| 1998-99 | 302934 | -21.48 | 4626.87 | -1.50 | 152735.25 | 25.45 |
| 1999-00 | 343031 | 13.24 | 5116.67 | 10.56 | 149160.57 | -2.34 |
| 2000-01 | 440473 | 28.41 | 6443.79 | 25.94 | 146294.78 | -1.92 |
| 2001-02 | 424470 | -3.63 | 5957.05 | -7.56 | 140340.90 | -4.07 |
| 2002-03 | 467297 | 10.09 | 6881.31 | 15.52 | 147257.74 | 4.93 |
| 2003-04 | 412017 | -11.83 | 6091.95 | -11.47 | 147856.76 | 0.41 |

*Source:* Department of Animal Husbandry, Dairying and Fisheries, 2005, p.65.

It is quite clear from table 6.46 that there was significant fluctuations in the quantity, value and unit-value of marine products exported from the country since 1991-92, coinciding with the period of globalislation or global trade reform. The ups and downs in the quantity, value and unit-value of marine products exported from the country were primarily due to the strategic buying pattern of the major buyers of marine products from India as reflected in the trend in the export of marine products to these countries. Table 6.47 presents the trend in the export of marine products from India to major markets from 1996-97 to 2003-04.

## Table 6.47

### Trend in the export of marine products from India to major markets from 1996-97 to 2003-04

| Markets | Q/V/UV* | 1996-97 | % of total | 1997-98 | % of total | 1998-99 | % of total | 1999-00 | % of total | 2000-01 | % of total | 2001-02 | % of total | 2002-03 | % of total | 2003-04 | % of total |
|---|---|---|---|---|---|---|---|---|---|---|---|---|---|---|---|---|---|
| Japan | Q | 64656 | 17.10 | 70955 | 18.39 | 67277 | 22.21 | 66990 | 19.53 | 68983 | 15.66 | 64905 | 15.29 | 54916 | 11.75 | 50020 | 12.10 |
| | V | 1886.04 | 45.76 | 2326.09 | 49.52 | 2295.48 | 49.61 | 2272.78 | 44.42 | 2560.39 | 39.73 | 1820.69 | 30.56 | 1534.76 | 22.30 | 1163.69 | 19.10 |
| | UV | 291704 | | 327826 | | 341198 | | 339272 | | 371162 | | 280516 | | 279474 | | 232645 | |
| USA | Q | 29792 | 7.88 | 32914 | 8.53 | 34472 | 11.38 | 36645 | 10.68 | 41747 | 9.48 | 49041 | 11.55 | 61703 | 13.20 | 53153 | 12.90 |
| | V | 436.05 | 10.58 | 583.75 | 12.43 | 617.32 | 13.34 | 775.35 | 15.15 | 1164.40 | 18.07 | 1421.38 | 23.86 | 2051.12 | 29.81 | 1682.06 | 27.61 |
| | UV | 146365 | | 177356 | | 179079 | | 211584 | | 278918 | | 289835 | | 332418 | | 316456 | |
| European Union | Q | 71192 | 18.82 | 34875 | 9.04 | 54261 | 17.91 | 65402 | 19.07 | 68827 | 15.63 | 82895 | 19.53 | 94541 | 20.23 | 96284 | 23.37 |
| | V | 790.11 | 19.17 | 412.53 | 8.78 | 684.62 | 14.80 | 905.56 | 17.70 | 1025.26 | 15.91 | 1150.07 | 19.31 | 1388.47 | 20.18 | 1470.99 | 24.15 |
| | UV | 110983 | | 118288 | | 126172 | | 138461 | | 148962 | | 138738 | | 146864 | | 152776 | |
| South East Asia including China | Q | 189456 | 50.09 | 218263 | 56.57 | 116610 | 38.49 | 147749 | 43.09 | 223519 | 50.75 | 187191 | 44.10 | 214908 | 45.99 | 174408 | 42.33 |
| | V | 854.44 | 20.73 | 1139.09 | 24.25 | 766.06 | 16.56 | 914.79 | 17.88 | 1290.39 | 20.03 | 1135.98 | 19.07 | 1404.86 | 20.42 | 1222.23 | 20.00 |
| | UV | 45100 | | 52189 | | 65694 | | 61915 | | 57731 | | 60686 | | 65370 | | 70079 | |
| Middle East | Q | 9672 | 2.56 | 17618 | 4.57 | 17274 | 5.70 | 13274 | 3.87 | 17236 | 3.91 | 19159 | 4.51 | 19668 | 4.21 | 14711 | 3.57 |
| | V | 63.56 | 1.54 | 144.66 | 3.08 | 147.97 | 3.20 | 115.09 | 2.25 | 188.32 | 2.92 | 181.06 | 3.04 | 204.74 | 2.98 | 201.52 | 3.31 |
| | UV | 65715 | | 82109 | | 85661 | | 86703 | | 109260 | | 94504 | | 104098 | | 136986 | |
| Others | Q | 13431 | 3.55 | 11193 | 2.9 | 13040 | 4.30 | 12970 | 3.78 | 20161 | 4.58 | 21279 | 5.01 | 21561 | 4.61 | 23441 | 5.60 |
| | V | 91.16 | 2.21 | 91.36 | 1.94 | 115.42 | 2.49 | 133.10 | 2.60 | 215.03 | 3.34 | 247.87 | 4.16 | 297.36 | 4.32 | 351.46 | 5.70 |
| | UV | 67873 | | 81622 | | 88512 | | 102621 | | 106656 | | 116486 | | 137916 | | 149934 | |
| Total | Q | 378199 | 100 | 385818 | 100 | 302934 | 100 | 343030 | 100 | 440473 | 100 | 424470 | 100 | 467297 | 100 | 412017 | 100 |
| | V | 4122.36 | 100 | 4697.48 | 100 | 4626.87 | 100 | 5116.67 | 100 | 6443.79 | 100 | 5957.05 | 100 | 6881.31 | 100 | 6091.95 | 100 |
| | UV | 109000 | | 121754 | | 152735 | | 149162 | | 146293 | | 140341 | | 147258 | | 147857 | |

*Q = Quantity in tonnes; V = Value in Rs Crores; UV = Unit value in Rs/tonne

*Source:* Department of Animal Husbandry, Dairying and Fisheries, 2005, p.58.

The most outstanding feature emerging from table 6.47, from the point of view of sustainability of the seafood industry, is the instability in the quantity and value of marine products exported from the country. This instability is visible in all the major markets, viz. Japan, USA, European Union, South East Asia including China, Middle East and 'others'. Japan which bought 22.21 per cent of the quantity exported by India during 1998-99 and contributed to 49.61 per cent of the value during that year bought only12.10 per cent of the exports during 2003-04 and subscribed to only 19.10 per cent of the value of export for that year. There were year-to-year fluctuations during the entire period noted in the table indicating the fluctuating demand and changing bargains of the trade.

The USA, which contributed to the largest share of value (27.61 per cent) of marine products exported from India during 2003-04 bought only 12.90 per cent of the quantity during that year. But both quantity and value were less than the previous year's magnitudes. The unit-value was also less than that for 2002-03. All these indicates the instability of the market.

The European Union which contributed to the second highest share of value of exports (24.15 per cent) during 2003-04, bought 23.37 per cent of the quantity of exports of that year, the unit value realised being much less than what was paid by Japan and the USA. There were significant fluctuations in the quantity and value of marine products bought by the countries of the European Union during the period noted. The South East Asian countries (including China) which bought the bulk of the product during the entire period, contributed to only 20 per cent of the value during most of the years noted in the table and exhibited wide fluctuations in quantity, reflecting the ambivalence of the market. The unit-value realised in this market was the lowest.

The Middle East and 'other' markets, which together contributed to less than 10 per cent of the quantity and value of marine products exported from the country during most of the years, also exhibited annual variations in the purchase of fish and fishery products from India.

What is apparent from the above observations is the instability of the export market for fish and the unstable demand for fish from India. Instability in the export market for marine products from India has been studied by Salim and Palanisami. Table 6.48 presents the indices of instability (market-wise) of marine products exports from India as worked out by Salim and Palanisami.

**Table 6.48**

**Indices of instability of marine products exports from India (marketwise)***

| *Market* | *Parameter* | *Pre-liberalisation period (1979-1990)* | *Post-liberalisation period (1991-2002)* |
|---|---|---|---|
| Japan | Quantity (tonnes) | 7.43 | 18.04 |
| | Value (Rs) | 16.43 | 24.02 |
| | Unit-value (Rs) | 13.73 | 11.06 |
| USA | Quantity (tonnes) | 27.81 | 17.96 |
| | Value (Rs) | 36.84 | 29.73 |
| | Unit-value (Rs) | 9.79 | 13.78 |
| European Union | Quantity (tonnes) | 36.30 | 21.09 |
| | Valaue (Rs) | 34.84 | 22.22 |
| | Unit-value (Rs) | 12.79 | 5.89 |
| South East Asia | Quantity (tonnes) | 18.53 | 33.35 |
| | Value (Rs) | 28..21 | 46.71 |
| | Unit-value (Rs) | 1.06 | 22.27 |
| Middle East | Quantity (tonnes) | 24.32 | 36.93 |
| | Value (Rs) | 36.52 | 98.61 |
| | Unit-value (Rs) | 17.52 | 58.59 |
| Others | Quantity (tonnes) | 54.38 | 60.47 |
| | Value (Rs) | 51.02 | 75.51 |
| | Unit-value (Rs) | 32.90 | 20.30 |
| Total | Quantity (tonnes) | 12.57 | 23.40 |
| | Value (Rs) | 16.28 | 17.75 |
| | Unit-value (Rs) | 10.23 | 16.29 |

*See Source for methodology of working out the index

*Source:* Salim and Palanisami, 2006, p.17-18.

Table 6.48 indicates higher levels of instability in all markets, although, the degree of instability has come down to some extent in the European and the US markets during the period of liberalisation. The instability of unit value has, however, increased in the USA during this period.

Table 6.49 shows the indices of instability (product-wise) of marine products exports from India.

**Table 6.49**

**Indices of instability of marine products exports from India (product-wise)***

| *Product* | *Parameter* | *Pre-liberalisation period (1979-1990)* | *Post-liberalisation period (1991-2002)* |
|---|---|---|---|
| Frozen shrimp | Quantity (tonnes) | 17.28 | 11.60 |
| | Value (Rs) | 17.51 | 23.67 |
| | Unit-value (Rs) | 12.11 | 15.81 |
| Frozen Lobster | Quantity (tonnes) | 128.80 | 14.18 |
| | Value (Rs) | 39.90 | 40.15 |
| | Unit-value (Rs) | 22.54 | 27.93 |
| Frozen Squid | Quantity (tonnes) | 63.24 | 19.30 |
| | Value (Rs) | 63.00 | 74.30 |
| | Unit-value (Rs) | 127.80 | 69.64 |
| Frozen Cuttle fish | Quantity (tonnes) | 37.39 | 15.40 |
| | Value (Rs) | 62.96 | 33.56 |
| | Unit-value (Rs) | 58.28 | 21.77 |
| Fresh & frozen fish | Quantity (tonnes) | 61.19 | 31.64 |
| | Value (Rs) | 37.15 | 35.30 |
| | Unit-value (Rs) | 27.57 | 16.91 |
| Others | Quantity (tonnes) | 42.17 | 48.33 |
| | Value (Rs) | 157.09 | 235.57 |
| | Unit-value (Rs) | 77.60 | 154.61 |
| Total | Quantity (tonnes) | 12.57 | 23.40 |
| | Value (Rs) | 16.28 | 27.94 |
| | Unit-value (Rs) | 10.23 | 16.29 |

*See the source for methodology of working out the index

*Source:* Salim and Palanisamy, 2006, p.17.

Table 6.49 conveys a high degree of instability for frozen shrimp, frozen lobster and 'others' and a lesser degree of instability for frozen squid, frozen cuttle fish, and fresh and frozen fish in the era of liberalisation. Overall, the indices of instability are higher for 'all' products in the era of globalisation (liberalisation).

The observed phenomenon of instability in marine products exports from the country, especially in the era of globalisation, draws our attention to the existing barriers to trade in the global market. Several (tariff and non-tariff) barriers to trade in fish and fishery products of India in the international market have been reported. Most of these barriers have their origin in the existing and evolving WTO arrangements, which are reportedly 'abused' and 'misused' by developed importing countries, much against the interests of developing countries and the principles of sustainable development.

The major barriers to free trade in the global market for fish fall in the categories of tariff and non-tariff barriers. Referring to the tariff barriers on fish and fishery products export of India, Venkatesan noted that "...fish and fishery products, especially processed or value added items are still subjected to tariff peaks (apply to specific types of fish) and tariff escalation (duties that are increased depending upon how much processing a commodity receives). EU, which reduced the tariffs for certain primary processed items, retained high tariff for processed/ value added items to protect its domestic industry" (Venkatesan, 2005, pp.4-5). Table 6.50 presents the tariff levels for processed fish in selected importing countries.

**Table 6.50**

**Tariff levels for processed fish in selected importing countries**

*(Percentage of value)*

| *Product* | *Japan* | *EU* | *China* | *Korea* |
|---|---|---|---|---|
| Live fish | 1.7 | 8.0 | 28.8 | 10.0 |
| Frozen fish | 3.5 | 15.0 | 14.0 | 20.0 |
| Frozen fish fillet | 3.5 | 15.0 | 20.0 | 20.0 |
| Frozen surimi | 4.2 | 15.0 | 20.0 | 20.0 |
| Frozen shrimp | 1.0 | 4.2 | 13.5 | 20.0 |
| Chilled shrimp | 1.0 | 4.2 | 21.0 | 14.0 |
| Frozen cuttle fish | 3.5 | 2.8 | 15.3 | 10.0 |
| Frozen squid | 3.5 | 4.2 | 15.3 | 10.0 |
| Prepared shrimp | 3.2 | 7.0 | NA | 20.0 |
| Canned fish | - | 20.00 | - | - |
| Canned shrimp | 6.0 | - | - | - |

*Source:* Venkatesan, 2005, p.5.

Table 6.50 shows comparatively higher rates of tariff on most items in EU (except frozen/chilled shrimp and frozen squid and cuttle fish), China and Korea, indicating protective barriers against imports from developing countries like India. Venkatesan further noted that "often there is discrimination in tariff reduction by importing countries especially developed countries. Tariff concession is extended up to zero level to certain countries on political and other consideration. Thus market access is often decided on various grounds other than trade" (ibid. p.5).

Referring to the non-tariff barriers prevailing in the international market for fish, Venkatesan observes that "in many markets, non-tariff barriers continue to present obstacles to imports and are often linked to technical standards or procedures. Trade restrictions largely outside the boundaries of existing international agreements not only exist but also seem to be on the increase. Of late, environmental reasons have been advanced for restricting fish trade" (ibid. p.5).

One of the major non-tariff barriers now operating in the global market arises from the Agreement on Sanitary and Phytosanitary (SPS) measures under the WTO regime which are intended to protect human, animal or plant life or health as practiced in the European Union and HACCP requirements to be met in the US markets. Referring to the impact of SPS and HACCP on the trade of developing countries like India, Venkatesan notes that "the regulations with regard to quality control and assurance for fish and fishery products adopted by major importing countries such as EU and USA, based on own check system or HACCP are today a great hindrance for export from developing countries. Investments needed to bring a fish processing plant upto the standards of a HACCP plan or EU norms are substantial. Thus these regulations serve as a non-tariff barrier for export.

Measures to safeguard human health or to protect the environment are perfectly legitimate ... but at the same time these rules ought to be firmly based on solid science in order to avoid protectionism. Taking refuge under the pretext of protecting human health, several importing countries have imposed stringent quality standards (often without conducting appropriate assessment of risks), which cannot be easily met by exporting nations; e.g. antibiotics residue levels in farmed shrimp fixed by EU sometime back" (ibid. pp.5-7).

The costs of compliance of food safety standards are reported to be quite high and eroding the competitiveness of Indian exporters. The

NCAP reported that "compliance of stringent hygiene and sanitary requirements in developed countries, particularly the provisions concerning the use of HACCP requires significant investment. The investment requirements for HACCP plants are huge, as most of the capital goods related to the plant are to be bought from the developed countries. The installation costs of HACCP plants vary from Rs 10 million to Rs 25 million.

Further, an export processing firm is estimated to spend about 20 lakhs per year on maintenance of a HACCP plant. The Seafood Exporters Association of India claimed to have spent about Rs 1250 million on upgradation of their facilities to meet the regulations. Appropriate training of personnel involved in various stages of production and processing are not included in this cost estimate ...All these ... led to substantial increase in pre-export processing and handling costs" (NCAP 2004, p.43). Table 6.51 gives details of cost of pre-export processing with and without HACCP compliance.

**Table 6.51**

**Cost of pre-export processing with and without HACCP compliance**

*(Rs/Kg.)*

| *Category of firms* | *Without HACCP* | *With HACCP* | *Additional cost due to HACCP* |
|---|---|---|---|
| Small (<10 t/day) | 7.84 | 18.21 | 10.37 |
| Medium (10 – 15 t/day) | 5.23 | 12.41 | 7.18 |
| Large (>15 t/day) | 3.98 | 9.19 | 5.20 |
| Overall | 5.10 | 11.89 | 6.79 |

*Source:* NCAP, 2004, p.44

Table 6.51 makes it apparent that there is marked increase in the cost with HACCP compliance, with small firms having to incur double the expenses of large firms. This has adversely affected the competitiveness of Indian seafood exports.

The NCAP reported that at the aggregate level "the fisheries sector lost competitiveness by about 14 per cent. The magnitude of erosion in export competitiveness varied from as high as 24 percent in the case of Ribbonfish to about 10 per cent in the case of Cuttlefish. The Shrimps and Prawns, the main items of fisheries export, also suffered a serious setback in their export competitiveness" (ibid. p.44).

Kulkarni, while writing for the International Institute for Sustainable Development, reported that "views from exporters in Chennai, Delhi and Mumbai and from regulatory agencies revealed that HACCP is a management system necessary for any company. MPEDA validates exporters complying with HACCP, and HACCP compliance is a mandatory requirement for all exporting units ...

... HACCP has helped the Indian seafood industry in becoming more organised and process-oriented. It is not very difficult for an organisation to introduce HACCP in their unit. Also the costs in many studies are inflated. One study calculates that complying with EU and US regulations increases processing costs from Rs 2 per kilogram to Rs 7 per kilogram. However, the break-up seems less realistic and researchers have often calculated cost difference by comparing zero level of compliance and 100 per cent compliance. Of the 15 exporters selected for intensive interviews, none had complained about the difficulty or cost of HACCP compliance" (Kulkarni, 2005, pp.16-17).

Kulkarni also noted that "Government authorities and exporters are not very concerned about the U.S. bio-terrorism regulation since implementation is not very complex. Registration is online and there are no additional costs of registration, although several exporters in Kerala faced delays in schedules from delayed registration ...

Select exporters have expressed concern about EU process requirements, which often do not result in any risk reduction but impose additional costs such as providing separate chill rooms. The strictness and rigidity of EU requirements concerns some exporters ...There is wide consensus that EU and US product regulations have a negative effect on seafood exports compared to process regulations, since the severity of import regulations are based more on precautionary principles rather than actual food safety concerns ..." (ibid. p.17).

Kulkarni further reported that "the EU version of equivalence is different from that of Codex. To achieve equivalent status with the EU, the exporting country must demonstrate that its 'National Competent Authority' has the capacity to enforce EC... regulations that safe and wholesome products are being produced and sold. EC regulations do not contain a process to develop a MoU-type arrangement, thus equivalence occurs by the EC approving individual countries and companies within them to export to the EC. This sets up a convenient opportunity for the use of equivalency as a non-tariff trade barrier. Since 2004, heavy-metal residue has replaced antibiotic and microbiological contamination as the biggest concern of the future...; an October 2003 study by the European Environmental Agency revealed that, of 153 fishing regions in the EU, ten regions exceeded the EU statutory limit for lead content in mussels. With inadequate environment legislation, monitoring systems and poor environmental compliance by Indian businesses, seawater contamination may increase the rejection of Indian seafood exports. In addition, bio-accumulation increases the concentration of heavy metals in fish ... this creates the need to strengthen India's heavy metal monitoring system" (ibid. pp.17-18).

Chaturvedi and Nagpal observe that "environment and health-related standards and regulations in developed-country markets have the potential to create barriers to trade. However, now it is clear that environment-related non-tariff barriers (ETBs), generally cover all barriers that have been introduced by the importing country to protect the environment, as well as the health and safety of wild life, plants, animals and humans. Developing countries have had to adjust their production processes in response to changing environmental regulations in developed countries ... Measures such as pesticide maximum residue levels (MRL) permitted in food stuffs, emission standards for machines, and packaging requirements have exerted pressure on exporters. However, what remains to be seen is the extent of impact of these measures on trade. It is now widely believed that these technical measures impede the trade of developing countries, either implicitly or explicitly" (Chaturvedi and Nagpal, 2003, p.66).

Referring to the adverse effects of the requirements of adherence to SPS and other standards, Hammer observes that "in many cases, these overly restrictive requirements have become trade barriers and hindered the international food trade" (Hammer, 1999, p.29). Kumar also made similar observations on the working of SPS thus: "The agreement is based on the pillars of harmonisation, equivalence, transparency, scientific judgment and risk assessment. On the face of it, SPS measures provide WTO member countries an opportunity to safeguard their interest in crucial areas of health and hygiene. However, there is a growing apprehension especially in developing countries like India that application of SPS measures are being used as non-tariff barriers" (Kumar, 2004, p.4269).

Salim and Halawai observed that "Indian exporters have to incur large costs if they want to access the upper quality market. This heavy cost burden involves both fixed and variable cost components. Given the small and medium size of most processing units, an additional fixed investment to the tune of Rs 1-2 crores per unit for upgrading, often becomes prohibitively high in the absence of a well-timed and concessional loan facility. These plants, it my be recalled, are not exclusively dedicated plants, and with no assurance of market access even if this kind of large investments are made to upgrade infrastructure, many existing players will find it impossible to continue in the business.

... According to SEAI, the compliance cost for meeting the EC norms is 15-40 per cent of value for new units, with the cost being higher for existing units. It is estimated by MPEDA that only two units in three may be able to upgrade themselves to the EC norms, while the rest would be forced to close down and exit from the business.

Thus, there are issues of sustainability in the marine export business ... SPS measures can and do impede trade in agricultural and food products since in many instances they are incompatible with prevailing systems of production and marketing in developing countries ... The manner in which the SPS agreement has been implemented in the interests of the developed countries is a cause for concern ..." (Salim and Halawai, 2005, p.27).

Even while recognising the positive impacts of HACCP on global seafood production and trade, Carlos, an FAO specialist , noted the threat of new trade barriers emerging from it thus: "For developing countries, the greatest threat is the need of applying HACCP as a compulsory requirement to export their products to major fish importing countries and that it may be used as a new trade barrier to their seafood exports" (Carlos, 1995, p.9).

Writing on the current impediments to international fish trade, Ababouch, et al. observed that "in the international market for fish and fishery products, one of the most serious difficulties faced by exporters is that different standards and designs are being imposed by importing countries on producing countries to ensure that products meet the requirements of the target market. Even after the ratification of the Agreement on Sanitary and Phytosanitary (SPS) measures and the Agreement on Technical Barriers to Trade (TBT), under World Trade Organisation (WTO), differences among various national standards and inspection systems may maintain or create new non-tariff trade barriers ...; many countries have tightened food safety controls, imposing on imports additional costs and requirements that are not always technically or scientifically supportable ...Developing countries have often complained that they are penalised by the complexity of sanitary and quality regulations of major importing countries. In the past, it has been suggested that those regulations have been used as non-tariff barriers" (Ababouch, et al., 2005, pp.1-2).

Another major non-tariff barrier to trade affecting the sustainability of Indian fisheries is the abuse of the agreement on technical barriers to trade (TBT). The agreement on TBT seeks to ensure that technical regulations and standards, including packaging, marking and labelling requirements and procedures for assessment of conformity with technical regulations and standards, do not create unnecessary obstacles to international trade. It is, however, reported that "technical regulations and standards are extensively used in fisheries trade and often constitute distortions or obstacles to trade ... The US testing procedures for imported seafood sometimes takes longer than the shelf-life of the product itself" (Kumar, 2004, p.4269).

Referring to the disadvantage arising from distortions of TBT, Venkatesan notes that "stringent standards discourage developing countries from selling to developed countries. Consequently, exporting countries prefer to sell to less stringent markets, thus resulting in market diversion from premium markets (e.g. sale of seafood by India to Vietnam, Thailand, etc.). Thus TBT makes it difficult to developing countries to sell their products on the global market, especially to premium markets ... It is alleged that often the intent of the importing country is to pay as low prices as possible for raw products on account of quality standards" (Venkatesan, op. cit. p.7). The US ban on import of shrimp from India and other countries without using turtle exclusion devices (TED) was a major case of non-tariff barrier abusing the provisions of agreements on TBT. This is an instance of arbitrarily fixing process and production methods (PPM) on producing and exporting countries.

The possibility of using PPM as a non-tariff barrier has been noted by Tetarwal and Mehta. They observed that "many developing countries are worried about the possibility of PPMs becoming non-tariff barriers. Exporters in developing countries are apprehensive that their products may be denied access or they may have to incur high adjustment costs in order to maintain access to overseas markets. Allowing PPM based trade practices would give many countries greater opportunity to protect their industries unfairly against foreign competition. Under the pretext of environmental concerns some countries might penalise other countries, which do not import certain goods from their domestic industry by enacting new regulations. In this regard the US shrimp-turtle case is of great significance for internationally traded products, which like shrimp, might be subject to environmental standards" (Tetarwal and Mehta, 2001, p.15).

Tetarwal and Mehta also noted that "sustainable development is a larger issue which incorporates efficient allocation of world's resources, actions to protect environment, creation of additional wealth for environmental protection in developing countries, poverty alleviation, and so on. Relationship between trade and sustainable development largely depends on environmental and macro-economic policies.

Environmental policies are enacted to ensure that economic actors comply with international, regional or national environmental standards. In this regard, process and production method (PPM) based measures have been suggested as a possible tool to promote environmental sustainability. However, in many cases PPM based environmental standards are used to create trade barriers and developing countries are denied market access" (ibid. pp.15-17). The turtle protection measure devised by the US, notwithstanding its adverse trade effect on shrimp exporting nations, has been, however, defended by environmental protection agencies and others (Srivastava and Ahuja, 2002, p.3445, and Srinivas, 2003, p.571).

Srivastava and Ahuja noted that "the net effect of the US embargo has been negligible in India. The sanctions have simply resulted in a shift to alternative exports such as cultured shrimps, and hence the impact on exports has been insignificant. Since other exporting destinations such as Japan, did not mandate the use of TEDs, shrimp export to such countries was unaffected.

The use of TED does not impose significant cost for the shrimp industry in India. However, the combined effect of cost of TED, increased fuel cost and the loss of by-catch may result in reluctance among fishermen to use TEDs, and the cost of compliance and enforcement by the government may be significant.

In terms of its systemic implications, the decision in the shrimp-turtle case has virtually mainstreamed environmental requirements in the WTO through its interpretation of the relevant WTO articles. The decision has legitimised the imposition of unilateral trade prohibition and process-related conditions and extra-jurisdictional requirements to protect environment, certainly for transboundary environmental concerns, and may subsequently pave the way for such requirements to be part and parcel of international trade. In future, trade embargo can also be used for protectionist purposes or to make developing countries adhere to certain policies and regulations, which they would otherwise not adopt due to various socio-economic compulsions. It must be noted that trade embargo can only be used effectively by developed countries given the uni-directional export from developing to developed countries. In other words, it is unlikely that trade embargos can ever be used effectively by developing countries for environmental or any other purposes. The question is how far will such measures go? Will they confine themselves to global commons and transboundary environmental problems, or will they gradually extend to other environmental issues since the global common and global shared resource is an evolving concept and may include water, soil, etc. in the future?" (Srivastava and Ahuja, 2002, p.3454).

Referring to the emerging trade impediments, Venkatesan states that "a number of trade impediments are related to environmental issues, since concern over the relationship of fishery with the environment and sustainability has increased significantly in recent years. The most recent, however, are measures aimed at limiting trade to fish coming from a sustainably managed resource. Althouth many address legitimate concerns, these could deliberately or by default, result in increasing trade distortions and difficulties, which might counteract some of the benefits resulting from the Uruguay Round Negotiations. Some of the examples are (1) eco-labelling and (2) certification ...

Mandatory eco-labelling comes clearly within the 'TBT' rules on technical regulations and other relevant WTO rules. Likewise, voluntary labelling standards are subject to the notification provisions of Article 4 and annex 3 (Code of Good Practice) of the TBT agreement ... Under the prevailing chaotic conditions in the Indian marine fishing sector... it would be simply impossible to eco-label any of our fishery in the coming years ... In the absence of proper policies and legislations, we may not be able to get any of our commercially important fisheries certified under eco-labelling. If we fail to manage our fishery resources in a sustainable manner, a stage may come in the future that our marine fish export may loose out to fishes marketed with eco-labels. Thus eco-lablling and certification systems may become an instrument of denial of market access in the coming years. ... Certification of fishery products has already picked up. Spearheaded by Marine Stewardship Council (MSC), about 47 fisheries have so far been certified" (Venkatesan, op. cit. pp. 9-11).

Highlighting on the eco-labelling issue for poor countries, Modayil noted that since "much of the international trade in fish and fishery products is from developing countries to developed countries, the potential of eco-labelling gains in importance as an incentive as well as a trade barrier ...There is increasing acceptance to the argument that eco-labels should not be used for discriminating against those who cannot afford to develop and implement the management protocols needed for sustainable fisheries management ..." (Modayil, 2004, p.41).

One of the recently emerging threat to the sustainability of seafood exports from India is the US charge of dumping and the imposition of anti-dumping duty against Indian exporters, among others. Referring to this issue, Venkatesan noted that "though not extensively used in fisheries sector in the past, anti-dumping measures have become a very serious obstacle to international trade in fish and fishery products. USA is currently spearheading in anti-dumping investigations. It has conducted investigations against a number of fish and fishery products exported from various countries ... The recent shrimp investigations of US have wiped out the business of a good number of exporting companies...

Shrimp anti-dumping investigations undertaken by US ITC were discriminatory too. The investigations were instituted only against top six exporting countries leaving many others who were supplying considerable quantity of shrimp to USA. Mexico was left out from the investigations as it could strike an understanding with the Southern Alliance, which took the case to US ITC on behalf of the American producers of shrimp...

The US law, especially the Byrd Amendment, which helps to pay the anti-dumping duties so collected from exporting countries to the affected local producers, has been held illegal by the WTO.

However, the US is not respecting the WTO rulings in this regard ... The current US Customs Bond requirement, an offshoot of the shrimp anti-dumping rulings, has crippled the export business of hundreds of small exporters in the affected countries. India has filed an appeal in the US Court of International Trade (CIT), challenging the increased bond requirement imposed by the US Bureau of Customs and Border Protection on the import of shrimp from India" (Venkatesan, op. cit, p.7).

Writing on the anti-dumping issue, Modayil notes that "the most recent episode of the United States initiating measures to impose anti-dumping duty against Indian (and a few other countries too) export of shrimps is a classical example of how such measures can affect not only our exports, but also domestic production, markets and economy. The anti-dumping measures under the WTO Agreements on Subsidies and Countervailing Measures, (SCM), also known as the 'Anti-Dumping Agreement', will ultimately affect the poor nations who will be the ultimate victims of stronger WTO rules which prevent those nations from regulating the flood of cheap imports from other countries" (Modayil, op. cit., p .40).

Reviewing the damaging effect of the US anti-dumping duty on Indian shrimp exporters, the Sea Food Export Journal reported in February 2007 thus: "The US anti-dumping duty imposed on Indian shrimp has taken a heavy toll, bringing down shrimp exports to the US by nearly 50 per cent ... The anti-dumping duty of 10.17 per cent coupled with a matching customs bond has seen Indian shrimp exports to the US fall drastically during calendar year 2006. From exports worth $485 million in 2005, exports dipped to worth $252 million during 2006. Trade sources said the industry could not bear the duty and the bonds and so several exporters were forced to keep out of the markets there..." (Sea Food Export Journal, Vol.II, 2007, p.7).

An even more serious threat to the survival of Indian fisheries is emerging from the WTO rules relating to the Agreement on Subsidies and Countervailing Measures (SCM). As per the agreement most assistance to the industry by the governments are prohibited or liable to action through challenge in the multilateral dispute settlement forum of the WTO or through countervailing measures by aggrieved states. It is reported that the European Union has imposed anti-subsidy duties against some Indian exporters allegedly availing 'export subsidies or 'local content subsidies' (Anonymous, 2000, p.43). Some other countries are also allegedly contemplating similar action. Only a few subsidies are 'non-actionable' as they fall under the categories of 'basic research and pre-competitive development subsidies, or 'assistance to disadvantaged regions' or 'assistance to adapt existing facilities to new environment requirements'. Table 6.52 gives details of subsidy granted by MPEDA to the seafood export industry of India from 2003-04 to 2005-06.

**Table 6.52**

**Details of subsidy granted by MPEDA to the seafood export industry of India from 2003-04 to 2005-06**

*(Rs in lakh)*

| *Sl. No.* | *Name of scheme* | *2003-04* | *2004-05* | *2005-06* |
|---|---|---|---|---|
| 1 | All processing machinery and equipments | 335.19 | 273.35 | 203.21 |
| 2 | Flake ice making machinery | 56.14 | 32.87 | 35.47 |
| 3 | Upgradation of cold storages | 17.66 | 28.05 | 25.15 |
| 4 | Insulated fish boxes | 40.28 | 54.10 | 33.71 |
| 5 | Generator sets | 23.16 | 10.71 | 24.25 |
| 6 | Interest subsidy | 120.29 | 78.01 | 63.08 |
| 7 | Chill room | 38.30 | 32.75 | 25.41 |
| 8 | Water purification system | 19.22 | 16.94 | 10.09 |
| 9 | Effluent plant | 47.10 | 28.51 | 25.47 |
| 10 | Acquisition of refrigerated truck/container | 11.67 | 13.40 | 7.00 |
| 11 | New cold storage | 74.76 | 167.22 | 155.07 |
| | All | 783.77 | 735.82 | 607.91 |

*Source:* MPEDA Fact Sheet, 2006.

Table 6.52 shows a decreasing trend in the total volume of subsidies granted by MPEDA under various schemes.

Appendix 6.5 gives details of grants under various subsidy schemes provided by MPEDA to the fisheries sector of India. It may be noted that the abolition of many of these and other subsidies, including the subsidy on fuel is likely to affect the viability of the fishery sector of India. As already noted in chapter four, the global fishing industry is heavily subsidised leading to overcapitalisation and unsustainability. Abolition of subsidies in the short run will have adverse consequences in all branches of the industry, particularly on small producers. One of the earliest non-tariff barriers which is quite frequently used by countries to limit access to foreign goods is by introducing quantitative restrictions on imports which is restricted under the present regime of the WTO. Many countries counter this restriction by resorting to anti- dumping duties and other technical barriers to trade (TBT), as already noted.

Many other forms of non-tariff barriers like import licensing, preferential treatment to foreign competitors (discriminatory trade policy), variable levies by importing countries, meeting labour standards, customs valuation and pre-shipment inspection, and rules of origin, are also reported to be working as constraints on the domestic industry, setting at naught the comparative advantage which it enjoyed earlier and now leading to unsustainable situation (Choudhuri and Chatterjee, 2001, p.37). There is also the fear that some of the provisions of TRIP and TRIM regulations, the Convention on Biological Diversity (CBD) and several of the international fishery instruments (treaties) will be putting additional burden on the domestic industry making it a complex task to achieve sustainable development in the near future.

### 6.3.7. Meagre Contribution to the GDP

One of the economic criteria put forward by the FAO for assessing the economic importance and sustainability of fisheries is the contribution of fisheries to GDP of the country (FAO, 1999b, p.18). Looking at the Indian scenario, it is found that the relative (%) contribution of fisheries to the GDP has been almost static during recent years, although the absolute (actual) contribution has increased significantly. Table 6.53 presents the contribution of fisheries sector to the Gross Domestic Product (GDP) of India from 1993-94 to 2003-04.

Table 6.53 shows that the average contribution of fisheries to GDP remained at 1.15 per cent during the first period (from 1993-94 to 1998-99) as well as in second period (1999-00 to 2003-04). The actual contribution of fisheries, however, increased from an average of Rs 13443 crores (from 1993-94 to 1998-99) to an average of Rs 24303 crores (from 1999-00 to 2003-04). The contribution (share) of fisheries to the GDP from agriculture and related sectors during this period, nevertheless, showed some increase, i.e. from 4.00 per cent during the first period to 4.81 per cent during the second period, indicating comparatively better performance of the fisheries sector and perhaps its sustainability. However, looking at the performance of the sector during the last year (2003-04), the picture emerging is quite dismal with the relative contribution of fisheries to the GDP and to the agricultural sector falling.

**Table 6.53**

**Contribution of fisheries to the Gross Domestic Product (GDP) of India from 1993-94 to 2003-04**

*(Rs in crores)*

| *Year* | *Total GDP* | *GDP from agriculture, forestry and fisheries* | *GDP from fisheries* | *GDP from fisheries as % of* | |
|---|---|---|---|---|---|
| | | | | *Total GDP* | *GDP from agriculture, forestry and fisheries* |
| 1993-94 | 781345 | 241967 | 8679 | 1.11 | 3.59 |
| 1994-95 | 917058 | 278773 | 10602 | 1.16 | 3.80 |
| 1995-96 | 1073271 | 303102 | 11866 | 1.11 | 3.91 |
| 1996-97 | 1243547 | 362606 | 14083 | 1.13 | 3.88 |
| 1997-98 | 1390148 | 387008 | 17269 | 1.24 | 4.46 |
| 1998-99 | 1598127 | 442494 | 18156 | 1.14 | 4.10 |
| Average | 1167249 | 335992 | 13443 | 1.15 | 4.00 |
| 1999-00 | 1761838 | 461964 | 20017 | 1.14 | 4.33 |
| 2000-01 | 1902998 | 468480 | 22535 | 1.18 | 4.81 |
| 2001-02 | 2081474 | 510568 | 24843 | 1.19 | 4.87 |
| 2002-03 | 2254888 | 507863 | 27093 | 1.20 | 5.33 |
| 2003-04 | 2519785 | 575283 | 27026 | 1.07 | 4.70 |
| *Average* | 2104197 | 504832 | 24303 | 1.15 | 4.81 |

*Source:* Department of Animal husbandry, Dairying and Fisheries, 2005, p. 146.

Table 6.54 shows the trend in the contribution of fisheries to the gross state domestic product and the domestic agricultural product of states during 1980-81,1990-91 and 2001-02.

It is apparent from table 6.54 that notwithstanding some downswings in the contribution of fisheries to the gross state domestic product in many states, their contribution to the gross domestic agricultural product has increased over the years in most states. These contributions were comparatively high in the states of Andhra Pradesh, Assam, Bihar, Goa, Gujarat, Kerala, Orissa and West Bengal. Maintaining and enhancing these contributions is an issue for sustainable development of fisheries in India.

**Table 6.54**

**Trend in the contribution of fisheries to the Gross State Domestic Product (GSDP) and the Gross Domestic Agricultural Product (Ag. GSDP) of selected states during 1980-81, 1990-91 and 2001-02**

| *States* | *Share of fisheries to GSDP* | | | | | |
|---|---|---|---|---|---|---|
| | *1980-81* | | *1990-91* | | *2001-02* | |
| | *GSDP* | *Ag. GSDP* | *GSDP* | *Ag. GSDP* | *GSDP* | *Ag. GSDP* |
| Andhra Pradesh | 1.20 | 2.60 | 0.60 | 1.70 | 2.14 | 7.69 |
| Assam | 1.90 | 4.00 | 1.60 | 3.90 | 2.05 | 5.84 |
| Bihar* | 1.00 | 1.90 | 1.00 | 2.40 | 1.63 | 4.11 |
| Goa | 2.30 | 9.90 | 2.20 | 15.80 | 2.67 | 23.54 |
| Gujarat | 0.80 | 2.10 | 1.10 | 4.30 | 1.06 | 6.39 |
| Haryana | 0.00 | 0.10 | 0.30 | 0.60 | 0.27 | 1.21 |
| Himachal Pradesh | 0.20 | 0.30 | 0.20 | 0.50 | 0.14 | 0.41 |
| Jammu & Kashmir | 0.40 | 1.00 | 0.50 | 1.20 | 0.48 | 1.50 |
| Karnataka | 0.60 | 1.30 | 0.40 | 1.20 | 0.37 | 1.29 |
| Kerala | 2.00 | 5.20 | 1.80 | 5.00 | 1.93 | 7.81 |
| Madhya Pradesh* | 0.10 | 0.10 | 0.20 | 0.40 | 0.17 | 0.57 |
| Maharashtra | 0.60 | 2.10 | 0.40 | 1.70 | 0.43 | 2.95 |
| Orissa | 1.10 | 2.10 | 2.00 | 5.20 | 2.42 | 7.45 |
| Punjab | 0.00 | 0.10 | 0.10 | 0.20 | 0.37 | 0.94 |
| Rajasthan | 0.20 | 0.50 | 0.00 | 0.10 | 0.07 | 0.26 |
| Tamil Nadu | 0.60 | 2.50 | 0.30 | 1.30 | 0.74 | 4.38 |
| Uttar Pradesh* | 0.20 | 0.30 | 0.30 | 0.70 | 0.52 | 1.51 |
| West Bengal | 3.00 | 9.40 | 3.10 | 9.90 | 3.14 | 11.82 |

*Figures relate to the period prior to the formation of Chattisgarh, Jharkhand and Uttaranchal

*Source:* NCAP, 2004, p.3

## 6.4. Social and Institutional Issues

The fundamental social and institutional issues affecting the sustainability of global fisheries have been discussed in chater four. In this section the major social and institutional problems threatening the sustainability of Indian fisheries are outlined.

### 6.4.1. Social Issues

The major social issues affecting the fishermen community and accordingly the sustainability of the fisheries sector are (1) poor housing, health and sanitation, (2) illiteracy, (3) poverty and indebtedness, and, (4) intrause and interuse conflicts.

#### 6.4.1.1. Poor Houseing, Health and Sanitation

Poor housing, health and sanitation in the fishermen settlements are critical issues affecting the social and economic condition of the fishermen. They determine their material status and well being. Referring to the condition of the fishermen settlements in Thiruvananthapuram district in Kerala in the early nineteen sixties, the 1961 Cnsus reported that "the houses are so crowded that there is not even moving space around them. The dense smell of fish attracts vast swams of flies, which cover the food, cooking utensils and the whole house as it were. During the rainy season, the floor of the houses will be damp and the roof leaky. Facilities for drainage being extremely poor, the colony presents such unhygienic surroundings that during the monsoons it is hardly worthy of human habitation" (Directorate of Census Operations, 1961, p. 154). This description of the fishermen settlements seems to be quite typical of the situation prevailing in most fishermen settlements in the country even at present.

Housing and colonisation of fishermen was indeed one of the major programmes for improving the socio-economic condition of the fishermen during the five year plans in the country, particularly in the coastal areas. Notwithstanding the operation of this programme, it was observed in the late nitneteen seventies that nearly 20 percent of the fishermen households in Kerala were not having 'own' houses which indicates the magnitude of the housing problem (Korakandy, 1994, p. 254). It is also reported that 48 per cent of the houses owned by fishermen were mere huts and 46 per cent *kutcha* houses, in 1979 (Gulati, 1983, p. 52). It is worth noting here that with growing population in the coastal fishing villages, housing and colonisation of fishermen is a continuing problem for the governments concerned and several new schemes are afoot at the national and regional levels (State Planning Board, 2004, p.91).

The limited sanitary and health facilities available to fishermen households in the country is reported by NCAP. Table 6.55 gives details of access to basic amenities to fishermen households in India.

**Table 6.55**

**Details of access to basic amenities to fishermen households in India**

*(in percentage)*

| *Sl. No.* | *Parameter* | *Households* | | |
|---|---|---|---|---|
| | | *Mechanised* | *Motorised* | *Traditional* |
| 1 | Water | | | |
| | (a) Piped | 55.36 | 92.45 | 79.31 |
| | (b) Well | 32.14 | 3.77 | 17.24 |
| | (c) Borewell | 12.50 | 3.77 | 2.45 |
| 2 | Sanitation | | | |
| | (a) Public | 16.07 | 22.64 | 24.14 |
| | (b) Owned | 62.50 | 62.26 | 41.38 |
| 3 | Electricity | 85.71 | 88.68 | 89.66 |
| 4 | Domestic fuel | | | |
| | (a) Firewood | 48.21 | 84.91 | 72.41 |
| | (b) LPG | 41.07 | 11.32 | 13.79 |
| | (c) Other | 10.71 | 3.77 | 13.79 |
| 5 | Entertainment | | | |
| | (a) Radio | 58.93 | 52.83 | 34.48 |
| | (b) Television | 58.93 | 52.83 | 31.03 |
| 6 | Own transport | 28.57 | 9.43 | 0.00 |
| 7 | Proximity to PHC | | | |
| | (a) Within 5 km | 87.50 | 77.36 | 96.55 |
| | (b) Beyond 5 km | 12.50 | 22.64 | 3.45 |

*Source:* NCAP, 2004, p. 61.

Table 6.55, although presenting a quite aggregate (macro) position at the national level, indicate the different levels of accessibility to water supply, sanitation, electricity, domestic fuel, entertainment, own transport and public health centres for mechanised, motorised and traditional fishermen households. The majority of fishermen households of all categories have access to pipe water. Own sanitary facilities are lacking to a good percentage of fishermen. Nearly one third of the traditional fishermen households do not have any sanitary facility. More than 85 per cent of the fishermen households of all categories are found to have access to electricity. Firewood is still the major domestic fuel for the majority of households of all types. Its use as a more sustainable source of energy may have some implications for the health of the households. A large percentage of the traditional fishermen households do not have entertainment facility like radio or television. Own transport facility is found only among a small percentage of mechanised and motorised fishermen households. Interestingly, the largest chunk of fishermen households of all categories are found to have access to public health centres within five kilometers of their residence, indicating improvement in the health service provided by the state.

**6.4.1.2. Illiteracy**

Illiteracy as an indicator of social backwardness and unsustainable social order is believed to be significant in the fishermen community in India. Current information on this parameter is however, limited. Table 6.56 gives details of literate and illiterate marine fishermen population in India during 1980.

Table 6.56 makes it clear that illiteracy was quite high at about 81 per cent among the marine fishermen community in India during 1980. It was even higher in states like Andhra Pradesh and Orissa.

Table 6.57 presents the percentage of illiterate fishermen in selected fishing villages of Maharashtra and Gujarat during 1983.

It is apparent from table 6.57 that the percentage of illiterates were quite high in both the states, although the above rates in Gujarat were slightly lower than the rates reported for it in 1980.

**Table 6.56**

**Details of literate and illiterate marine fishermen population in India during 1980**

| State/UT | Fishermen population | Literate | | | | Illiterate | Illiterate as % of population |
|---|---|---|---|---|---|---|---|
| | | Primay | Secondary | Above secondary | Total | | |
| West Bengal | 83561 | 15606 | 2752 | 452 | 18810 | 64751 | 77.49 |
| Orissa | 117144 | 7618 | 2045 | 359 | 10022 | 107122 | 91.44 |
| Andhra Pradesh | 326304 | 20386 | 3562 | 429 | 24377 | 301927 | 92.53 |
| Tamil Nadu | 395903 | 60075 | 11897 | 3860 | 75832 | 320071 | 80.85 |
| Pondicherry, Karaikal, Mahe and Yanam | 25312 | 4922 | 1370 | 270 | 6562 | 18750 | 74.08 |
| Kerala | 639872 | 119823 | 23514 | 5317 | 148654 | 491218 | 76.77 |
| Karnataka | 112893 | 21596 | 5174 | 1553 | 28323 | 84570 | 74.92 |
| Goa, Daman & Diu | 39912 | 7060 | 2617 | 338 | 10015 | 29897 | 74.91 |
| Gujarat | 152015 | 23901 | 4067 | 911 | 28879 | 123136 | 81.00 |
| Total* | 1892916 | 280987 | 56998 | 13489 | 351474 | 1541502 | 81.44 |

*Excluding Maharashtra

*Source:* CMFRI, 1981, p.4.

**Table 6.57**

**Percentage of illiterate fishermen in selected fishing villages of Maharashtra and Gujarat during1983**

| *State/Villages* | *Illiterate fishermen (%)* |
|---|---|
| **Maharashtra** | |
| Ekdara | 61.9 |
| Alibag Koliwada | 64.4 |
| Mahim Koliwada | 48.1 |
| **Gujarat** | |
| Umbergam | 52.3 |
| Bhimpora | 51.3 |
| Sutrapada Bunder | 70.7 |
| Mangrol Bunder | 74.9 |

*Source:* CMFRI , 1988, pp.44-45.

It is significant to note here that the NCAP has reported improvements in the educational level of fishermen in the country as a whole. Table 6.58 gives a demographic profile of fishermen working in the mechanised, motorised and non-motorised sectors of the fishing industry of India during 2003.

Table 6.58 makes it clear that the percentage of illiterate fishermen was quite low in the mechanised and motorised sectors while it was quite perceptible in the traditional sector, indicating inequality in social empowerment and violation of the principle of intra-generational equity, which is a cardinal criterion of sustainable development. Even among literate fishermen, the number of years of schooling was very low and only half for fishermen in the non-motorised sector as compared to that of the mechanised sector. This also underscores their weak endowments.

The sex ratio of adult members in the mechanised and non-motorised sectors is found to be adverse indicting either high mortality among females or immigration of male members from other regions and in both cases upsetting the social balance of the community. The percentage of active fishermen (actual fishers) was more in the non-motorised sector indicating higher dependence on fishing. This dependence is further proven by the presence of higher percentage of fisherwomen engaged in marketing in this sector and the limited diversification of occupation in this sector as shown in the table.

**Table 6.58**

**Demographic profile of fishermen working in the mechanised, motorised and non-motorised sectors of the fishing industry of India during 2003**

| *Demographic profile* | *Sectors* | | |
|---|---|---|---|
| | *Mechanised* | *Motorised* | *Non-motorised* |
| 1. Average age (years) | 36.89 | 38.94 | 38.79 |
| 2. Education (years) | 8.36 | 6.68 | 4.31 |
| (a) Illiterate (%) | 12.50 | 16.98 | 41.38 |
| (b) Primary (%) | 10.72 | 33.96 | 31.04 |
| (c) Secondary (%) | 69.64 | 45.28 | 27.59 |
| (d) Higher secondary (%) | 7.14 | 3.78 | 0.00 |
| 3. Experience (years) | 18.62 | 21.00 | 23.93 |
| 4. Family size (number) | 6.35 | 7.21 | 5.76 |
| (a) Adult (number) | 4.60 | 4.80 | 4.00 |
| (b) Male (%) | 54.40 | 50.70 | 57.80 |
| (c) Female (%) | 45.60 | 49.30 | 41.90 |
| (d) Children (number) | 1.70 | 2.40 | 1.80 |
| (e) Actual fishers (%) | 26.96 | 27.82 | 35.32 |
| (f) Fish vendors - only women (%) | 1.68 | 3.50 | 6.58 |
| 5. Diversification of occupation | | | |
| (a) Family members staying in other villages (%) | 19.64 | 5.66 | 3.44 |
| (b) Family with other enterprises (%) | 16.07 | 1.79 | 6.89 |

*Source:* NCAP, 2004, p.60.

### 6.4.1.3. Poverty and Indebtedness

Poverty and indebtedness are perpetual problems of the fishing community, which are even now prevailing in the traditional sector with limited access to resources and credit. The vicious cycle of poverty and indebtedness in the industry and the interlinkages of trade and credit perpetuating poverty in the traditional fishing community is the classic example of merchant capitalism working in the industry. The inter-locking of trade and credit mechanism working against the interests of fishermen in India had been reported by Desai and Baichwal (1960) and Platteau, et al., (1985). Panikker and Alagaraja (1981), Sathiadhas and Venkataraman (1983) and many others (CMFRI, 1983; Samal, 2002, etc.) also reported on the incidence of indebtedness among fishermen in India. Table 6.59 gives details of fishing household income, indebtedness and interest in Neendakara and Sakthikulangara in Kerala during 1980.

Table 6.59 reveals that the average household income of fishermen varied between Rs 1100 and Rs 26000 in Neendakara and between Rs 1150 and Rs 135000 in Sakthikulangara in 1980. Between 53 per cent and 100 percent of the households in different income brackets were in debt in Neendakara, while 49 per cent to 100 per cent were in debt in Sakthikulangara. The average debt of the households varied between Rs 981 and Rs 100000 in Neendakara and between Rs 2524 and Rs 197000 in Sakthikulangara. The amount of interest to be paid as percentage of income varied between 20 per cent and 59 per cent among various income groups in Neendakara and between 20 per cent and 63 per cent in Sakthikulangara. The higher indebtedness among higher income brackets is attributed to higher investments on mechanised boats and infrastructure (Sathiadhas and Venkataraman, 1983, p.3).

Samal reported that in the Chilka area of Orissa, "the fishermen are forced to borrow money at higher rates of interest from the money lenders, traders and agents (popularly known as commission agents, *Chingudi* agents, etc.) with a condition to sell the whole catch at a predetermined price which is usually less than the prevailing market price and hence exploitative. This is applicable to both traditional fishermen and those who are engaged in shrimp culture" (Samal, 2002, p.1714).

**Table 6.59**

**Details of fishing household income, indebtedness and interest in Neendakara and Sakthikulangara in Kerala during 1980**

| *Particulars* | *Village** | *Income group (Rs.)* | | | | | | | |
|---|---|---|---|---|---|---|---|---|---|
| | | *< 1200* | *1201-2500* | *2501-5000* | *5001-10000* | *10001-20000* | *20001-30000* | *30001-50000* | *> 50000* |
| Total Number of households | N | 12 | 128 | 205 | 80 | 2 | 2 | - | - |
| | S | 62 | 197 | 470 | 299 | 118 | 28 | 30 | 5 |
| Number of households in debt | N | 8 | 81 | 109 | 61 | 2 | 2 | - | - |
| | S | 34 | 97 | 264 | 202 | 112 | 27 | 29 | 5 |
| Percentage of households in debt | N | 67 | 63 | 53 | 86 | 100 | 100 | - | - |
| | S | 55 | 49 | 56 | 67 | 95 | 96 | 97 | 100 |
| Average debt of indebted households | N | 981 | 2417 | 3554 | 24090 | 55000 | 100000 | - | - |
| | S | 2524 | 3323 | 6712 | 30755 | 75934 | 96541 | 101543 | 197000 |
| Average annual income of the indebted households | N | 1100 | 2000 | 3750 | 8000 | 15000 | 26000 | - | - |
| | S | 1150 | 22200 | 3800 | 8500 | 18570 | 28340 | 45300 | 135000 |
| Annual interest to be paid | N | 221 | 592 | 885 | 4700 | 6350 | 11750 | - | - |
| | S | 713 | 825 | 1458 | 5397 | 10632 | 14423 | 15044 | 27155 |
| Percentge of interest to be paid from income | N | 20 | 30 | 24 | 59 | 42 | 45 | - | - |
| | S | 62 | 38 | 38 | 63 | 57 | 51 | 33 | 20 |

* N = Neendakara; S – Sakthikulangara

*Source:* Sathiadhas and Venkataraman, 1983, p.6.

NCAP reported that the percentage of fishermen below poverty line was 32 per cent in 1999 which is much higher than the national average of 26 per cent (NCAP, 2004, p.117). The fishermen households were also reported to be highly deficient in calorie and protein intake. The calorie deficit and the protein deficit reported in 1999 were 37.7 per cent and 41.4 per cent respectively (ibid, p.117). Much of these indicates the intragenerational inequality prevailing in the fisheries sector of India.

The emergence of intergenerational inequality arising from lack of ownership of the means of production in the fisheries sector can also be perceived. As observed by Sathiadhas and Biradar, "ownership of means of production is one of the most important indicators for assessing the socio-economic status of fishermen communities. During 1997, overall, only 23 per cent of the active fishermen of marine fisheries sector have ownership of fishing implements as compared to 34 per cent in 1980. The active fishermen owning non-mechanised units declined from 39 per cent during 1980 to 24 per cent during 1997. One of the factors responsible for decline in ownership of non- mechanised units is its conversion into motorised units in recent years. Among the fishermen operating motorised units, 19 per cent have their own units at present. The owners among active fishermen in the mechanised sector increased from 17 per cent in 1980 to 24 per cent in 1997..."(Sathiadhas and Biradar, 2001, p.6). What appears from the above observation is a simultaneous increase in the percentage of fishermen owning mechanised units along with a fall in the percentage of fishemen owning non-mechanised units, as a consequence of technological changes in the industry. This observation, however, is not revealing the fact that with the growth of high-tech fishing, the more equitable distribution of ownership that prevailed in the traditional sector in the past has given way to a higher concentration of ownership in the hands of a limited number of owners of large fishing vessel with local, regional, national or global lineage. The implications of this development for local income distribution and sustainability are significant. Excessive outflow of income (profit) from the fisheries sector may apart from impoverishing the local fishermen community, as in colonial times, will also pave way for the degeneration of indigenous fishing communities and cultures and the growth of new radical cultures including global terrorism and subservient gypsy commercialism simultaneously, all of which work against the goal of sustainable development.

#### 6.4.1.4. Intrause and Interuse Conflicts

Another major issue and indicator of unsustainability in the fisheries sector is the growing conflict within the fisheries sector and conflicts between fisheries and other sectors of the local /regional/national/ international economy. The conflicts within the fisheries sector, known as intra-use conflicts, are many in India at present. Most of these conflicts are for the exclusive use of the natural resource base by a single category of users and for excluding other users of the common pool resources. The most predominant of these conflicts is the conflict between traditional fishing craft operators and mechanised /motorised fishing boat operators. This type of conflict has been reported from all coastal states of the country and especially from Goa and Kerala. Referring to the conflict in Kerala, Korakandy wrote: "The conflicts between the traditional fishermen and the mechanised boat operators had its beginning in the early eighties of the last century when the traditional fishermen suffered heavy loss of fish catch and income in the face of growing competition from the mechanised boat operators in the inshore waters of Kerala coast. The conflict manifested itself initially in the form of burning of mechanised boats by traditional fishermen at several places in Cochin and Quilon and in the confiscation of the catch of the mechanised boats by the traditional fishermen. The main complaints of the traditional fishermen were: (1) the mechanised boats destroyed their gear while passing through the fishing ground where they operated, (2) destroyed the juveniles, larvae and egg of the fishes they catch by using indiscriminate fishing techniques and (3) the mechanised boat operators virtually ousted them in the fishing ground and in the market place. The traditional fishermen felt that their survival was at stake" (Korakandy, 2005, p.345-346).

The conflict between the traditional *Rampani* net operators and purse-seine fishermen in Goa were reported by Kurien and Vijayan (Kurien and Vijayan 1980).

Similar forms of intrause conflicts existing between fish-seed collectors and local fishermen in the coastal wetlands of Sunderbans and elsewhere were reported earlier in this chapter.

Development of aquaculture activities is reported to have given rise to seven intrause conflicts in many places. In the Chilka region, where wetlands are leased out to non-fishermen for aquaculture, it has led to severe conflicts. Samal reported that "since a larger area (around 14,000 acres) is given over for shrimp culture to the non-fishermen, it has not only reduced the share of the fishermen in culture but also for capture. Along with this, encroachment of around 20,000 acres mostly by the non-fishermen and declaration of some portion of the lake as a bird sanctuary by the Government have adversely affected the economic condition of most of the fishermen. Poor fishermen feel that their profession is threatened due to the entry of the non-fishermen who have emerged as their strong competitors mostly from upper caste-local Khadayats and Brahmins and Karanas from outside with more money, muscle power and more favour from state power – in to Chilka. Therefore, a psychology of insecurity now prevails among all the fishermen villages. This is a case of potential occupational displacement.

The lease policy by allowing shrimp culture inside Chilka lake has expedited environmental degradation, which in turn, increases, the threat of occupational displacement" (Samal, 2002, p.1716).

Samal also reported that "the fishermen have been agitating against the lease policy as well as consequent environmental deterioration and degradation and achieved success twice. There was a strong people's agitation in early 1990s when the proposed integrated shrimp farm project of Chilka Aquatic Farm ( a joint project by Orissa Marine and Chilka Development Authority (OMCAD) of Government of Orissa and Tata) was being implemented at the cost of about Rs 15 crore at Panaspada covering 400 to 600 hectares of land ... In protest against the Chilka Aquatic Farm, the fishermen of various villages ... launched several actions such as 'dharna', rally, 'padayatra', symbolic breaking of farm embankment and 'gherao' of the state legislative assembly by 8000 protestors. They faced the police brutality and served jail sentences...

... *The Chilka Macchhyajibi Mahasangha*, the organisation of fishermen of Chilka, gave an ultimatum to the Chief Minister on March 29, 1999 to fulfil their nine point demand, particularly to demolish all shrimp *gheris* in Chilka by April 15, 1999 ... The second stage of the movement started from May 29, 1999 ... There was resistance by the fishermen ... This led to firing by the police claiming four lives ... As a result, lease for shrimp culture in Chilka has been suspended since June 1999 by the Government of Orissa. However, the illegal and unauthorised shrimp culture is going on in the lake by the mafias. In the month of December 2001, the fishermen of Chilka started agitation against these illegal and unauthorised shrimp culture in the lake. Thus, the Government of Orissa, has recently banned shrimp culture in Chilka. Now it is to be seen how government orders are observed" (ibid, p.1717).

As is well known, the proliferation of aquaculture enterprises in the east coast of India in the early 1990s had led to severe environmental consequences forcing environmentalists and social workers in Tamil Nadu to file case in the Supreme Court of India seeking ban on aquaculture activities in the coast, which ultimately resulted in the Supreme Court of India order of 11.12.1996 directing the demolition and removal of all aquaculture enterprises in the CRZ of India before 31.3.1997 (Anonymous, 1997, p.15).

Intrause conflicts arising out of aquaculture development in Tamil Nadu have been pointed out by Selvam, et al. in 2000. The adverse economic effects and environmental consequences of aquaculture were responsible for the conflicts. The adverse economic effects were asset depletion, damage to fishing nets, reduction in employment, loss of agricultural production and worsening income distribution. The environmental consequences included distruction of mangrove ecosystem, salinisation of inland areas, land subsidence and fall in water table due to excessive pumping, pollution of adjacent areas by farm effluents, misuse of antibiotics and other chemicals, poor hygiene favouring spread of diseases, and social disruption. (Selvam, et al, 2000, p.306).

Referring to the adverse consequences of aquaculture, Selvam, et al. noted: "One of the serious consequences of shrimp culture is the change in tenurial structure. The farmers who sold their land were comfortable to sell the land to shrimp farmers because (a) they got inflated price to the land, and in some cases (b) these got rid of tenant farmers and share croppers. The undesirable aspect of shrimp culture expansion are the increasing trend of eviction of tenant farmers from land. This eventually led to transformation of the whole socio-economic structure, leading to marginalisation of small and marginal farmers and agricultural labourers" (ibid. p.304).

Outlining the socio-economic fall out of fisheries development in India, Sampath observed that "the standard of living of a vast majority of fishermen is very low and they lack even the basic amenities such as housing, sanitation, clean drinking water, health care, basic and non-formal education.

While the number of fishing units has been steadily increasing over the years, the production, particularly from the near shore areas, has remained more or less constant ... leading to a stagnation or even decline in the earnings of fishermen because of reduction in catch per unit of effort. This has also led to clashes between the traditional and the small-scale mechanised fishing boat owners, between shrimp trawlers and users of purse-seiners, and between other groups competing for the exploitation of the same type of fishery resources.

The emergence of marine products as an important foreign exchange earner, coupled with the mechanisation, paved the way to the entry of individuals (non-fishermen), and companies from big industrial houses, multinationals, etc. into fisheries, resulting in a gradual growth of competition with traditional fishermen" (Sampath, 1998, p.78).

Intrause conflicts are common between full-time and part-time fishermen. Migrant fishermen and recreational fishermen also contribute to the outbreak of intrause conflicts in the fishing industry.

Srinath notes that "with production levels for most of the commercially important resources showing signs of approaching saturation levels, intersectoral conflicts increased due to competition to exploit the common resource" (Srinath, 2003, p.1).

Interuse conflicts which arise when a number of industries/activities located in the same area use the same natural resources base (space) for multiple uses, have become a major threat to the sustainability of fisheries in India. Interuse conflicts exist between fisheries (aquaculture) and agriculture, fisheries and forestry, fisheries and mining, fisheries and tourism, fisheries and transport, fisheries and power production, fisheries and urban development, fisheries and defence, etc. at several locations in the country. Several instances of such conflicts in Kerala have been noted by Korakandy (Korakandy, 2005, pp.345-354). A very recent report in Alakal, the mouth piece of the Kerala Swathanthra Matsyathozhilali Federation (Federation of Independent Fishermen of Kerala), stated that the proposal to introduce a luxury liner between Kasargode and Thiruvananthapuram is likely to create hurdles in the inshore waters of the state and upset the livelihood of hundreds of fishermen in the state (Thiruvananthapuram Fishermen's Union, 2006, p.1). Vernalcular newspapers are abound with news of such inter-use conflicts, all along the coast, as a result of new development initiatives (e.g. Special Economic Zones). The impact of such conflicts on the sustainability of fisheries must be significant.

### 6.4.2. Institutional Crisis

The fisheries sector in India, as in many developing countries, is facing the major crisis of collapse of old social institutions and the failure of 'new' institutions to fill the void created by the disappearance of old institutions. The collapse of traditional community organisations like the *'Kadakkodies'* (Sea Courts) in Kerala had led to serious social crises in communities which find the institutional vacuum eroding the social/ cultural capital of the community. Referring to this process in Kerala, Ramachandran observed: "The social homogeneity of the Araya fisher community, which has been acting as a bulwark against the onslaughts of various structural challenges – like prevalence of the state legal system, growth in literacy, support from state sponsored social security mechanisms, impact of Gulf-money, etc., that could have helped to weaken the hold of the court over a 'newly empowered' fisherfolk, is now being challenged by technological heterogeneity.

The use of different technologies like OBMs on their traditional crafts, new gears like ring seines, ...practices like night fishing, has polarised the community technologically and later economically vitiating the solidarity they used to enjoy as long as they remained traditional fishers in the true sense ...The practice of night fishing during monsoon was a taboo till some of the fishermen found it irrational not to practice the same when they discovered that it was night trawling introduced by mechanised boats that caused a dwindling in their daily catch. Since the *Kadakkody* had no means for prevailing its authority over the mechanised fishers as they came from other places, the fishers perceived that the institution was incapable to provide stability, which is the fundamental role of any institution.

The *Kadakkody* found it impossible to contain the internal dissention, which led to an erosion of trust in it and this was found to be the major reason for disintegration of many *Kadakkodies* in the region" (Ramachandran, 2004, pp.95-96).

Technological changes in the fishing industry and diversification of the coastal economy, including developments in aquaculture have created wide chasm in the social relations and institutions leading to breakdown of community organisations of fishermen. The institutions created by state machinery, including various types of co-operatives have not succeeded in building the 'solidarity' and social capital needed or sustainable fishery systems.

These institutions dominated by corrupt politicians and corrupt bureaucracy without peoples' participation often stand as 'white elephants' heralding the apex of institutional failure. They also speak of 'policy failure' and failure to correct 'market failures'. Such institutions also collude with the market forces and torpedo the public interest in favour of narrow private or sectarian interests. Commenting on the (social) labour unrest in the fishing community, Krishna observed that "the social inequality and imbalances posed challenges to the very existence of the labour group. Irregularity and uncertainty of income being a peculiar feature, survival became a great struggle to many fishermen.

In the inland sector too, the social imbalance resulting from the new technologies is the major cause of unrest. Scientitific shrimp farming has interfered with the custom of leaving the shrimp filtration field after harvest to the local fishermen and their fishing rights in the inland water bodies ... the fishermen feel that their employment opportunities in such areas are reduced as scientific shrimp farming takes place in a more closed system with restricted labour intake ... Shrimp farming amidst paddy fields is also resisted by paddy farmers as well as the labourers as incursion of saline water affects the growth of paddy. Water logging due to creation of bunds blocking water drainage around the houses situated among shrimp farms pose health hazard to people living there. Other ecological problems affecting the inland fishing communities include the pollution due to fish processing wastes, factory effluents and household garbage ... The increasing occurrence of weeds such as water hyacinth is a big menace to inland fisheries" (Krishna, 1997, p.17).

The institutional crises in the fisheries sector is broadly conveyed by Sathiadhas, et al. when they observed that "the pace of economic development of our coastal belt is not commensurate with other regions and the over-all socio-economic status of fishermen are comparatively lower than other backward sectors of our economy. Overcapitalisation of the small scale mechanised sector and marginalisation of artisanal fishermen, rampant under-employment and low per capita earnings, lack of alternate and supplementary job opportunities, seasonal migration and absence of mobility of labour to other sectors and high rate of illiteracy and indebtedness are some of the major problems faced by the huge population depending on this industry. The multispecies open access marine fishery further faces the problem of selective overexploitation and possible extinction of certain varieties and also create conflicts among the fishermen over the area of operation of different fishing techniques and in sharing the benefits" (Sathiadhas, et al. 1989, p.55).

Similarly the material progress and economic development achieved through commercialisation of the resource base, which is often dominated by external agents have also led to marked dichotomy and class antagonism in the fishermen community leading to loss of faith in the traditional social institutions. Immigration and emigration of labour have further accentuated this process. The ongoing process of globalisation is also expected to strengthen this transformation. The net result of this development as already evident is institutional failure, where the traditional and modern institutions are not able to exercise any control over natural resource exploitation and the sharing of value of output. Its implication for sustainability, especially from the ecological and social point of view appears to be great. It is bound to violate the ethical principles of intragenerational and intergenerational equity by failing to share the resources equitably in the present and not preserving it for use by future generations through conservation. Ironically, the clamour, at present, is to ensure economic viability (sustainability) through institutional change, by limiting access to the common pool resources through privatisation as advocated by free market economists in the past and advocates of liberalisation at present. The implications of approving this demand for privatisation of the 'commons' would be another faltering step towards the mirage of unsustainable development of fisheries in India with heavy social costs to the entire community in the present and in the future.

### 6.5. Technological Issues

As noted earlier in chapter four and elsewhere in this chapter, most of the sustainability issues, especially biological overfishing, overcapitalisation, biodiversity loss, etc. have their roots in the technological 'inappropriateness' or 'non-neutrality' of technology with respect to economy, environment and society. Adoption of new technology of trawling and purse- seining for enhancing production has simultaneously resulted in environmental degradation, biodiversity loss and intrause conflicts in the industry, all manifestations of unsustainable development of the industry. The expansion of aquaculture in the country, while enhancing production, has produced externalities, which are negative and quite unsustainable. Reporting on the negative externalities of shrimp culture in Andhra Pradesh and Tamil Nadu, Selvam, et al. wrote: "The development of shrimp farms in the coastal areas has created an external cost of about Rs 555,968 per hectare of shrimp farming, to the society. The private net benefit from shrimp farming was about Rs 519,293 per hectare. In this study, the annualised external cost per hectare of shrimp farm was Rs 36,675 higher than the private net benefit derived from per hectare shrimp farming. NEERI had assessed the total damage due to aquaculture to be Rs 6305 crores in Andhra Pradesh as against an earning of Rs 1498 crores. In Tamil Nadu, the damage was estimated at Rs 423 crores against an income of Rs 280 crores. That is, the cost of ecological and social damage far exceeds the benefits that accrue out of coastal aquaculture activity. NEERI estimated that the annualised external cost due to the development of shrimp farm was about 3.78 times higher than benefits from shrimp farming in Tamil Nadu and Andhra Pradesh" (Selvam, et al., 2000, p.308).

The major externalities caused by aquaculture technology included loss of potable water, salinisation of adjacent lands, loss of human health, loss of fishing income, loss of fishing nets, loss of man power due to non-approachability of fishermen to seashore directly, and loss of agricultural production (Selvam, et al, 2000 p.312).

Technological externalities are quite predominent in the fish processing sector as well. Technological advancements in the seafood processing industry, has apart from resulting in the ruin of the domestic traditional fish curing industry leading to unemployment of fisher-women folk has also led to environmental pollution. Water and air pollution have been reported from major fish processing centers in the country. The backwaters in the Aroor-Chandiroor belt in Kerala is reported to be polluted by seafood processing plants dumping their wastes in the nearby canals.

The impact of the introduction of new technology of HACCP based processing and adherence to EU and USFDA norms in the domestic seafood processing industry has been noted in section 6.3.6. It is found to affect the viability and sustainability of the seafood export sector.

### 6.6. Other Versions (dimensions) of Sustainability

Another major threat to the sustainability of Indian fisheries, as commonly noted in the global context, is the presence of many occupational hazards. Many consider fishing as the 'occupation of last resort' because of the high risk to life involved in it. In spite of all technological advancements, the number of accidents and casualties in the course of fishing operations are reported to be increasing. Table 6.60 presents the number of casualties/beneficiaries assisted by Kerala Fishermen Welfare Fund Board between 1993-94 and 1999-2000.

Table 6.60 highlights on the critical issue of accidents and the occupational hazards involved in fishing in Kerala which is one of the premier fishing states of India. It may perhaps also explain the reluctance on the part of the younger generation from the fishermen community to take up fishing as a career and their strong preference for less strenuous jobs and the current aversion to a highly hazardous employment. No doubt, many from the younger generation are reported to be migrating from the home turf seeking other jobs in remote towns in the country or abroad. This is likely to cause labour shortage in marine fishing, as reported by FAO in countries of the European Union. There are already reports of the presence of over-aged fishermen in the Indian fishing fleet. Apart from the hazardous nature of the job dissuading many in the new generation from seeking employment in the catching sector, there are other considerations of health and hygiene which may keep many workers not inclined to work in other sectors as well. It is reported that in many developed countries, the educated technical personnel do not like to work in labour intensive low-paid food processing industries. Tharakan notes that in advanced countries, the seafood industry, like other food processing industries is considered as a 'dirty' or polluting industry that they wanted to relocate in other countries like, Thailand, Chinaor Indonesia (Tharakan, 1998, p.19). With the prevailing preference for 'clean' job among the new generation of workers, the fishery sector in India may face the problem of labour shortage, which is likely to affect its sustainability.

**Table 6.60**

**Number of casualties/beneficiaries assisted by Kerala Fishermen Welfare Fund Board between 1993-94 and 1999-2000**

| Sl.No. | Name of scheme | Year | | | | | | |
|---|---|---|---|---|---|---|---|---|
| | | *1993-94* | *1994-95* | *1995-96* | *1996-97* | *1997-98* | *1998-1999* | *1999-2000* |
| 1. | Accidental death | 98 | 102 | 85 | 71 | 62 | 104 | 96 |
| 2. | Permanent total disability | 28 | 32 | 59 | 39 | 57 | 60 | 5 |
| 3. | Permanent partial disability | 28 | 32 | 59 | 39 | 2072 | 2 | 48 |
| 4. | Temporary disability due to accident | 1216 | 1052 | 805 | 1092 | 1384 | 1367 | 1717 |

*Source:* Department of Fisheries, 2002, pp.162-163.

A similar threat to the sustainability of Indian fisheries is likely to arise from its failure to meet the labour standards and conditions of labour fixed by the ILO and other agencies. The working conditions in the Indian fishing vessels may not be as per ILO standards and the vessels may not be carrying life-saving and fire-appliances as per Merchant Shipping Rules or IMO regulations.

The working conditions in the seafood processing plants are reported to be unsatisfactory. Sathiadhas, et al. noted that "the working conditions are poor and the wage rates received by the women are comparatively low. The average monthly wage of a peeling worker is about Rs 300 in Mumbai whereas it varies from Rs 100 to Rs 1000 for those working in Kerala" (Sathiadhas, et al., 1999, p.55).

Warrier reported that 'they (women workers) are provided neither minimum wages nor the basic minimum facilities stipulated by the government through different pieces of legislation specifically meant for contract labour and interstate migrant labour.

The problems of the unorganised sector have become more significant today when liberalisation and globalisation have come centre-stage. The proponents of the new eonomic policy hail it as an attempt to make the economy more productive and globally competitive. However, it is by now fairly obvious that it is only capital that has been provided with a liberal climate, the same cannot be seen to have taken shape for labour. The structural adjustment programme (SAP) 'reforms' in the Indian context have not provided an amenable environment for work to the vast majority of the workers who are in the unorganised sector. In fact the reverse is happening in the case of labour - capital is responding to the imperative of competition by resorting to employment of casual and contract workers. In fact it is the norm in industry today to do so, to minimise labourers... They can be made to work for long hours without anyone raising questions about the propriety of such work ..." (Warrier, 2001, pp.3556–3557, words in parentheses added).

The unsustainability of such operations is further highlighted by Warrier when she wrote: "Such organisation of production in the fish processing units resembles not any modern capitalist enterprise, but more pre-modern practices, prevalent in the early phase of industrialisation when apprendices stayed along with the master craftsmen to learn skills from him ... The women are forced by the nature of their work to handle frozen raw material for long stretches of time. It involves long hours of work in damp, cold rooms ..., the most common ailments reported by the women were malaria, chickenpox, jaundice and severe diarrhoea. In addition, most of them complain of aches and pains, of the head, of the body and particularly of the chest. All these come from their long hours of continuous work ... Very few units systematically follow the rules prescribed by the MPEDA and other regulatory agencies for the minimum requirements of a clean hygienic environment of production ...The non-availability of clean potable water is invariably the reason for the large number of incidents of stomach ailments and jaundice afflicting the workers ... Thus an occupational hazard of the work environment results in loss of wages – and savings – instead of compensation for the severe injury sustained. This reveals the unprotected nature of employment of these workers" (ibid. pp. 3560-3561).

A semi-empirical spin-off version of sustainability of Indian fisheries presented by Datta and Chakrabarti has taken note of the 'crowding externality' with respect to their ecological, economic and social impacts on capture and culture activities. It has tried to build a bridge between global and national approaches for sustainable development planning in Indian fisheries (Datta and Chakrabarti, 2004).

A different listing of sustainability issues of Indian marine fisheries included issues like (1) fish stock decline, (2) exploitation of juveniles, (3) discards utilisation/reduction, (4) environmental degradation, (5) natural and man-made disasters, (6) biodiversity decline, (7) increasing fishing cost and diminishing returns, (8) underexploitation of oceanic stock, (9) inter and intra sectoral conflicts, (10) inefficient internal marketing system, (11) ineffectrive regulatory measures and (13) resistance to regulation (Srinath, 2006, pp.17-19). Most of these issues fall in the range of topics already discussed in this chapter.

### 6.7. Summary

This chapter discussed the major sustainability issues of Indian fisheries by looking at selected indicators of unsustainable development. The major sustainability issues discussed were classified under five main groups: viz. (1) ecological, (2) economic, (3) social and institutional, (4) technological, and (5) other versions (dimensions) of unsustainable development. The major ecological issues discussed included (1) biological overfishing, (2) environmental pollution, (3) habitat destruction,

(4) biodiversity loss, and (5) climate change. All these factors were found to impact adversely on the natural resource base of the industry and lead to unsustainable development.

The economic issues affecting the sustainability of Indian fisheries were discussed under seven categories. They are: (1) stagnation in production, (2) overcapitalisation, (3) uneconomic operations, (4) declining employment, (5) static or declining consumption, (6) unstable global market for fish and barriers to trade and (7) meagre contribution to the GDP. All these factors except the third were found to lead to unsustainability of fisheries in India.

The major social issues threatening the sustainability of Indian fisheries included (1) poor housing, health and sanitation, (2) illiteracy, (3) poverty and indebtedness, (4) intrause and interuse conflicts.

This chapter also noted the presence of institutional crisis in the industry including the collapse of traditional community organisations and the failure of state-sponsored institutions, both leading to lack of control over natural resource exploitation and sharing of output by the society, resulting in unsustainable development of the industry.

This chapter also found that much of the sustainability issues of Indian fisheries were the consequence of the adoption of inappropriate technology having adverse effects on ecology, economy and society.

Other issues of sustainability noted included occupational hazards, labour shortage, etc. A spin-off version (model) of sustainability of Indian fisheries found in the literature is also noted in this chapter. A different listing of sustainability issues of marine fisheries of India found in the literature was also noted in this chapter.

Over all, this chapter leads to the conclusion that most of the ecological, economic, social /institutional, and technological issues/ indicators studied point to the unsustainable development of fisheries in India.

# 7

# FISHERIES DEVELOPMENT IN INDIA—THE POLITICAL ECONOMY OF UNSUSTAINABLE DEVELOPMENT

## 7.1. Introduction

A scrutiny of many of the ecological, economic, social, institutional, technological and other (issues) indicators made in the last chapter has shown that fisheries development in India is not sustainable at present. The objective of this chapter is to present the components of the contemporary strategy for sustainable development of fisheries in India which is an adjunct of the global prescriptions for sustainable development and to examine the feasibility of this strategy in the given political economy situation in India. The various components of the proposed strategy for the sustainability of Indian fisheries are discussed under the following heads: (1) ecological solutions, (2) economic solutions, (3) institutional solutions, and (4) technological solutions. This chapter, however, casts some doubt about the seriousness of the sustainability debate, especially in view of the global developments in market economy (capitalism) and democracy (consumerism). It, nevertheless, prescribes the radical option of limiting population, production, consumption and trade, all of which are quite pessimistic and not exclusive to fisheries sector but applicable to all economic activities. A concluding section presents the summary of main points discussed in this chapter.

## 7.2. Ecological Solutions

The fundamental ecological problem being overexploitation of the natural resource base and damage to the biodiversity of the stock due to pollution, habitat loss, etc. which lead to nonavailability of ecological resources for future use, the ecological solutions seek to protect the natural environment and conserve the stock for steady availability (supply) in the future. The ecological solutions prescribed and popularised by the

FAO and now in the agenda for implementation in India as well are (1) code of conduct for responsible fisheries, (2) precautionary principle, (3) biodiversity conservation, (4) ecosystem based fisheries management and (5) integration of fisheries management with coastal zone management. A brief description of these solutions is given in this section.

### 7.2.1. Code of Conduct for Responsible Fisheries

The Code of Conduct for Responsible Fisheries was adopted by the twenty-eighth session of the FAO Conference in Resolution 4/95 on 31 October 1995. The code sets out principles and international standards of behaviour for responsible practices with a view to ensuring the effective conservation, management and development of living aquatic resources with due respect for the ecosystem and biodiversity. The code recognises the nutritional, economic, social, environmental and cultural importance of fisheries and the interests of all those concerned with the fishery sector. The code takes into account the biological characteristics of the resources and their environment and the interests of the consumers and other users. States and all those involved in fisheries are encouraged to apply the code and give effect to it. The code also provides principles and standards applicable to the conservation, management and development of all fisheries. It also covers the capture, processing and trade of fish and fishery products, fishing operations, aquaculture, fisheries research and the integration of fisheries into coastal area management (FAO, 1995b, pp.1-2).

The code of conduct consists of five introductory articles, viz. nature and scope of the code; objectives of the code; relationship with other international instruments; implementation, monitoring and updating, and special requirements of developing countries. These introductory articles are followed by an article on general principles, which is followed by six thematic articles on (*a*) fisheries management, (*b*) fishing operations, (*c*) aquaculture development, (*d*) integration of fisheries into coastal area management, (*e*) post-harvest practices and trade and (*f*) fisheries research (FAO, 1999b, p.2).

The basic objectives of the code as contained in article two are directed to:

(*a*) Establish principles, in accordance with the relevant rules of international law, for responsible fishing and fisheries activities, taking into account all their relevant biological, technological, economic, social, environmental and commercial aspects;

(*b*) Establish principles and criteria for the elaboration and implementation of national policies for responsible conservation of fisheries resources and fisheries management and development;

(*c*) Serve as an instrument of reference to help states to establish or to improve the legal and institutional framework required for the exercise of responsible fisheries and in the formulation of appropriate measures;

(*d*) Provide guidance which may be used where appropriate in the formulation and implementation of international agreements and other legal instruments, both binding and voluntary;

(*e*) Facilitate and promote technical, financial and other cooperation in conservation of fisheries resources and fisheries management and development;

(*f*) Promote the contribution of fisheries to food security and food quality, giving priority to the nutritional needs of local communities;

(*g*) Promote protection of living aquatic resources and their environments and coastal areas;

(*h*) Promote the trade of fish and fishery products in conformity with relevant international rules and avoid the use of measures that constitute hidden barriers to such trade;

(*i*) Promote research on fisheries as well as associated ecosystems and relevant environmental factors; and

(*j*) Provide standards of conduct for all persons involved in the fisheries sector (FAO, 1995b, pp.3-4).

The general principles of the code as enunciated in article six contain nineteen basic principles that are listed below.

1. States and users of living aquatic resources should conserve aquatic eco-systems. The right to fish carries with it the obligation to do so in a responsible manner so as to ensure effective conservation and management of the living aquatic resources.

2. Fisheries management should promote the maintenance of quality, diversity and availability of fishery resources in sufficient quantities for present and future generations in the context of food security, poverty alleviation and sustainable development.

Management measures should not only ensure the conservation of target species but also species belonging to the same ecosystem or associated with or dependent upon the target species.

3. States should prevent overfishing and excess fishing capacity and should implement management measures to ensure that fishing effort is commensurate with the productive capacity of the fishery resources and their sustainable utilisation. States should take measures to rehabilitate populations as far as possible and when appropriate.
4. Conservation and management decisions for fisheries should be based on the best scientific evidence available, also taking into account traditional knowledge of the resources and their habitat, as well as relevant environmental, economic and social factors. States should assign priority to undertake research and data collection in order to improve scientific and technical knowledge of fisheries including their interaction with the ecosystem. In recognising the transboundary nature of many aquatic ecosystems, states should encourage bilateral and multilateral cooperation in research, as appropriate.
5. States and sub regional fisheries management organisations should apply a precautionary approach widely to conservation, management and exploitation of living aquatic resources in order to protect them and preserve the aquatic environment, taking account of the best scientific evidence available. The absence of adequate scientific information should not be used as a reason for postponing or failing to take measures to conserve target species, associated or dependent species and non-target species and their environment.
6. Selective and environmentally safe fishing gear and practices should be further developed and applied, to the extent practicable, in order to maintain biodiversity and to conserve the population structure and aquatic ecosystems and protect fish quality. Where proper selective and environmentally safe fishing gear and practices exist, they should be recognised and accorded a priority in establishing conservation and management measures for fisheries. States and users of aquatic ecosystems should minimise waste, catch of non-target species, both fish and non-fish species, and impacts on associated or dependent species.

7. The harvesting, handling, processing and distribution of fish and fishery product should be carried out in a manner which will maintain the nutritional value, quality and safety of the products, reduce waste and minimise negative impacts on the environment.
8. All critical fisheries habitats in marine and freshwater ecosystems, such as wetlands, mangroves, reefs, lagoons, nursery and spawning areas, should be protected and rehabilitated as far as possible and where necessary. Particular effort should be made to protect such habitats from destruction, degradation, pollution and other significant impacts resulting from human activities that threaten the health and viability of the fishery resources.
9. States should ensure that their fisheries interests, including the need for conservation of the resources, are taken into account in the multiple uses of the coastal zone, and are integrated into coastal area management, planning and development.
10. Within their respective competences and in accordance with international law, including within the framework of subregional or regional fisheries conservation and management organisations or arrangements, states should ensure compliance with and enforcement of conservation and management measures and establish effective mechanism, as appropriate, to monitor and control the activities of fishing vessels and fishing support vessels.
11. States authorising fishing and fishing support vessels to fly their flags should exercise effective control over those vessels so as to ensure the proper application of this code. They should ensure that the activities of such vessels do not undermine the effectiveness of conservation and management measures taken in accordance with international law and adopted at the national, subregional, regional or global levels. States should also ensure that vessels flying their flags fulfil their obligations concerning the collection and provision of data relating to their fishing activities.
12. States should, within their respective competences and in accordance with international law, cooperate at subregional, regional and global levels through fisheries management organisations, other international agreements or other arrangements to promote conservation and management, ensure effective conservation and protection of living aquatic resources

through out their range of distribution, taking into account the need for compatible measures in areas within and beyond national jurisdiction.

13. States should to the extent permitted by national laws and regulations, ensure that decision making processes are transparent and achieve timely solutions to urgent matters. States, in accordance with appropriate procedures, should facilitate consultation and the effective participation of industry, fish workers, environmental and other interested organisations in decision-making with respect to the development of laws and policies related to fisheries management, development, international lending and aid.

14. International trade in fish and fishery products should be conducted in accordance with the principles, rights and obligations established in the World Trade Organisation (WTO) Agreement and other relevant international agreements. States should ensure that their policies, programmes and practices related to trade in fish and fishery products do not result in obstacles to this trade, environmental degradation or negative social, including nutritional impacts.

15. States should cooperate in order to prevent disputes. All disputes relating to fishing activities and practices should be resolved in a timely, peaceful and co-operative manner, in accordance with applicable international agreements or as may otherwise be agreed between the parties. Pending settlement of a dispute, the state concerned should make every effort to enter into provisional agreements of a practical nature, which should be without prejudice to the final outcome of any dispute settlement procedure.

16. States recognising the paramount importance to fishers and fish farmers of understanding the conservation and management of the fishery resources on which they depend, should promote awareness of responsible fisheries through education and training. They should ensure that fishers and fish farmers are involved in the policy formulation and implementation process, also with a view to facilitating the implementation of the code.

17. States should ensure that fishing facilities and equipment as well as all fisheries activities allow for safe, healthy and fair working

and living conditions and meet internationally agreed standards adopted by relevant international organisations.

18. Recognising the important contributions of artisanal and small-scale fisheries to employment, income and food security, states should appropriately protect the rights of fishers and fish workers, particularly those engaged in subsistence, small-scale and artisanal fisheries, to a secure and just livelihood, as well as preferential access, where appropriate, to traditional fishing grounds and resources in the waters under their national jurisdiction.

19. States should consider aquaculture, including culture-based fisheries, as a means to promote diversification of income and diet. In so doing, states should ensure that resources are used responsibly and adverse impacts on the environment and on local communities are minimised (FAO, 1995b, pp.8-13).

Article four of the code dealing with implementation, monitoring and updating requires that all members and non-members of FAO, fishing entities and relevant subregional, regional and global organisations, whether governmental or non-governmental, and all persons concerned with the conservation, management and utilisation of fisheries resources and trade in fish and fishery products should collaborate in the fulfilment and implementation of the objectives and principles contained in this code (ibid. p.6).

The importance of the need for promoting responsible fisheries development in India has been noted by the Working Group for Revalidating the Potential of Fishery Resources in the Indian EEZ in 2000 (Silas, 2000, p.20).

The basic objective of the code, viz. promoting sustainable development of fisheries, was accepted by the Government of India and incorporated in the tenth five year plan (2002-07). The 'Comprehensive Marine Fishing Policy', a document prepared by the Government of India in 2004 noted that "the policy objectives are: (1) augment marine fish production of the country up to the sustainable level in a responsible manner so as to boost export of seafood from the country and also to increase per capita fish protein intake of the masses, (2) to ensure the socio-economic security of the artisanal fishermen whose livelihood solely depends on this vocation, (3) to ensure sustainable development of marine fisheries with due concern for ecological integrity and biodiversity"

(Ministry of Agriculture, 2004, p.3). It also called for measures dealing with harvest and post-harvest operations, resource management, fishermen welfare, environmental issues, infrastructure development, legislative support, etc. in consonance with the provisions of the code of conduct for responsible fisheries (ibid, pp.3-10). It appears that many of the new and ongoing schemes of the central and state Governments are in keeping with the provisions of the code. It is, however, extremely doubtful that the industry will be achieving sustainable development with the prevailing ecological, economic, social, (institutional) and technological constraints. As rightly conveyed by Caddy and Griffiths, "it is, however, clear that the achievement of sustainable development will involve a long struggle, with many hard lessons learned by each country as it attempts to apply general principles to its specific circumstances" (Caddy and Griffiths, 1995, p.3).

**7.2.2. Precautionary Principle**

Principle 15 of the Rio Declaration of the UN Conference on Environment and Development states that "in order to protect the environment, the precautionary approach shall be widely applied by states according to their capabilities. Where there are threats of serious or irreversible damage, lack of full scientific certainty shall be not used as a reason for postponing cost-effective measures to prevent environmental degradation" (FAO, 1996 a, p.3).

The general principles and article 7.5 of the FAO code of conduct for responsible fisheries prescribe a precautionary approach to all fisheries, in all aquatic systems, and regardless of their jurisdictional nature, recognising that most problems affecting the sector result from insufficiency of precaution in management regimes when faced with high levels of uncertainty.

Article 7.5 makes it clear that "states should apply the precautionary approach widely to conservation, management and exploitation of living aquatic resources in order to protect them and preserve the aquatic environment. The absence of adequate scientific information should not be used as a reason for postponing or failing to take conservation and management measures.

In implementing the precautionary approach, states should take into account, *inter alia,* uncertainties relating to the size and productivity of the stocks, reference points, stock condition in relation to such reference points, levels and distribution of fishing mortality and the impact of fishing activities, including discards, on non-target and associated or dependent species as well as environmental and socio-economic conditions.

States and subregional or regional fisheries management organistions and arrangements should, on the basis of the best scientific evidence available, *inter alia,* determine:

(*a*) stock specific target reference points, and at the same time, the action to be taken if they are exceeded; and

(*b*) stock specific limit reference points and, at the same time, the action to be taken if they are exceeded; when a limit reference point is approached, measures should be taken to ensure that it will not be exceeded.

In the case of new or exploratory fisheries, states should adopt as soon as possible cautious conservation and management measures, including, *inter alia*, catch limits and effort limits. Such measures should remain in force until there are sufficient data to allow assessment of the impact of the fisheries on the long-term sustainability of the stocks, where upon conservation and management measures based on that assessment should be implemented. The latter measures should, if appropriate, allow for the gradual development of the fisheries.

If a natural phenomenon has significant adverse impact on the status of living aquatic resources, states should adopt conservation and management measures on an emergency basis to ensure that fishing activity does not exacerbate such adverse impact. States should also adopt such measures on an emergency basis where fishing activity presents a serious threat to the sustainability of such resources. Measures taken on an emergency basis should be temporary and should be based on the best scientific evidence available" (ibid. pp.22-23).

The UN Conference on Straddling Fish Stocks and Highly Migratory Fish Stocks (New York, 1992-1995) also evolved a consensus on the need to introduce or strengthen the precautionary approach to fishery management, embedding the concept in the draft text of its outcome, and outlining elements for its implementation. FAO also reported that "because uncertainty affects all elements of the fishery system in varying degrees, some degree of precaution is required at all levels of the system: in development planning, management, research, technology development and transfer, legal and institutional frame works, fish capture and processing, fisheries enhancement and aquaculture" (ibid. p.3).

The precautionary principle has been further elaborated by the FAO particularly in relation to fisheries management, fisheries research, and fishery technology and species introduction. Referring to its application to fisheries management, it reported thus: "Management according to the precautionary approach exercises prudent foresight to avoid unacceptable or undesirable situations, taking into account that changes in fisheries systems are only slowly reversible, difficult to control, not well understood, and subject to change in the environment and human values …

The precautionary approach gives due concern to long term effects in the specification of management objectives and in the development of management frameworks, procedures, and measures. The consequences of management and fishery development are evaluated to reduce the possibilities of changes that are not potentially reversible on a two to three decade time scale. Processes for determining acceptable changes and impacts are used to support the precautionary approach. Thus, a precautionary approach links fisheries management intimately with general environmental management.

A precautionary management involves explicit considerations of undesirable and potentially unacceptable outcomes and provides contingency and other plans to avoid or mitigate such outcomes. Undesirable or unacceptable outcomes include over- exploitation of resources, overdevelopment of harvesting capacity, loss of biodiversity, major physical disturbances of sensitive biotopes, or social or economic dislocations. Undesirable conditions can also arise when a fishery is negatively influenced by other fisheries or other activities and when management fails to take action in the face of shifts in the external conditions affecting, for example, the productivity of the fish stocks …

The precautionary approach is included in all stages of the management process. Thus, precaution should be identifiable in the different stages of management, from planning through implementation, enforcement and monitoring to re-evaluation" (ibid. pp.8-9).

Highlighting the need for a precautionary approach with respect to fisheries research, it noted: "Application of the precautionary approach to fishery management depends on the amount, type and reliability of information about the fishery and how this information is used to achieve management objectives … Research to increase information about a fishery usually increases potential benefits while reducing the risk to the resource …

There is a valid scientific role in helping managers develop objectives, so that scientific input to the overall management process is as effective as possible in achieving management intent. The precautionary approach requires continuing and anticipatory evaluation of the consequences of management actions with respect to management objectives. Scientific evaluation of consequences with respect to management objectives requires explicit definition of quantifiable criteria for judgement ...

Research is needed to help formulate biological objectives, targets and constraints regarding the protection of habitat, to avoidance of fishing that significantly reduces population reproductive capacity, and reduces the effects of fishing on other (e.g. non-target) species. Combined with biological research, research on socio-economics and the structure of fishing communities is needed to formulate management objectives.

Until stock specific research leads to the establishment of alternative operational target based on research and practical experiences, a precautionary approach would seek to: (*a*) maintain the spawning biomass at a prudent level (i.e., above 50 percent of its unexploited level), (*b*) keep the fishing mortality rate relatively low (i.e., below the natural mortality rate), (*c*) avoid intensive fishing on immature fish, (*d*) protect the habitat" (ibid. pp.16-17).

Elaborating the precautionary approach with respect to fishery technology, the FAO noted thus: "Recognising that many aquatic resources are overfished and that the fishing capacity presently available jeopardise their conservation and rational use, technological changes aimed solely at further increasing fishing capacity would not generally be seen as desirable. Instead, a precautionary approach to technological changes would aim at: (*a*) improving the conservation and long-term sustainability of living resources, (*b*) preventing irreversible or unacceptable damage to the environment, (*c*) improving the social and economic benefits derived from fishing, and (*d*) improving the safety and working conditions of fishery workers. Fishery technology consists of the equipment and practices used for finding, harvesting, handling, processing and distributing of aquatic resources and their products.

Different fishery technologies will have different effects on the ecosystem, the social structure of fishing communities, the safety of fishery workers and the ease, effectiveness and efficiency of management of the fishery. It is the amount and context in which fishery technology is used (e.g. when, where and by whom) that influence whether the objectives of fisheries management are reached, and not the technology.

For instance, the current overfishing of many aquatic resources is the product of both the efficiency of the finding and catching technologies and of the amount used ...

A precautionary approach should be adopted for the development of new technologies or the transfer of existing technologies to other fisheries to avoid unplanned abrupt changes in fishing pressure or social structures. Certain technologies will be considered undesirable, if they create unacceptable effects (e.g. poison or explosives) or if their adoption leads to wasteful use (e.g. at sea, sorting machines have been banned where they might increase discarding).

Fishery technology produces side effects on the environment and on the non-target species. These effects have often been ignored but, in the context of a precautionary approach, some technologies may warrant a review. Similarly, a precautionary approach would encourage careful consideration of the side effects of new fishery technologies before they are introduced.

A precautionary approach would provide for a process of initial and on-going review of the effects of fishery technology as it is introduced or evolves in local practice. However, the extent to which a precautionary approach can be applied to the management of technological changes depends on the existing level of management. In some cases, education of fishermen and consumers towards responsible practices may be the only possible approach. Where elaborate research, management and enforcement systems are in place, a wider variety of options are available for application of the precautionary approach. However, although some gears and practices are prohibited, they may continue to be used. The adoption of a precautionary approach to the management of new fishery technology depends on the ability to achieve compliance through education and /or enforcement" (ibid. pp.23-25).

Observing the importance of the precautionary approach to species introduction, the FAO noted: "Because of the high probability that impacts of species introduction be of irreversible and unpredictable impacts, many species introductions are not precautionary. Therefore, a strictly precautionary approach would not permit deliberate introductions and would like strong measures to prevent unintentional introductions. Recognising the difficulties with introductions, the objectives of a precautionary approach to species introductions in relation to capture fisheries should be to reduce the risk of adverse impacts of introductions on capture fisheries, to establish corrective or mitigating procedures (as a contingency plan) in advance of actual adverse effects, and to minimise unintended introductions to wild ecosystems and associated capture fisheries.

In relation to aquaculture, experience has shown that animals will usually escape the confines of a facility. As a consequence, the introduction of aquatic organisms for aquaculture should be considered as a purposeful introduction into the wild, even though the quarantine/hatchery facility may be a closed system …

Potential impacts of some introductions on the fishery sector included changes in the distribution and abundance of fishery resources through disease, changes in predator- prey relationships, changes in competition, mixing of bad (maladapted) genes, and habitat modifications. There may also be second and third order changes that affect the ecosystem. Changes in fishing strategy and the fishing community may also require changes in fishing gear and season to allow for a newly introduced species to establish itself or to avoid potential side issues associated with the new fishery. Climate changes may also have significant consequences that may modify the environment, making it more suitable for introductions of either useful or harmful species.

The use of introduced species, including genetically modified and genetically selected organisms, may allow or continued or increased production from habitats that have been so altered or degraded that native fisheries are no longer viable. Care should be taken not to use this potential productivity from introduced species as justification for further abuse of habitat or for delaying their restoration" (ibid. pp.29-30).

The significance of adopting a precautionary approach for the sustainability of Indian fisheries is quite obvious from the findings of the last chapter, where the problems of overfishing, overcapitalisation, habitat loss, threat to the biodiversity, etc. were noted and the need for a more cautious and corrective approach was recognised.

### 7.2.3. Biodiversity Conservation

The threat to the biodiversity, both marine and inland, affecting the sustainability of Indian fisheries has been noted in the last chapter. It is, therefore, imperative that the conservation of biodiversity of marine and inland fish resources is achieved as per the guidelines of the UN Convention on Biodiversity.

The UN Convention on Biodiversity, which was signed on 5 June 1992, and entered into force on 23 December 1993, provides an international framework for the conservation and ecologically sustainable development and use of biodiversity (Aqorau, 2003, p.28). The convention does not address the fisheries issues specifically but has implications as it addresses the terrestrial and marine biodiversity issues.

The objectives of the Convention are "the conservation of biological diversity, the sustainable use of its components and the fair and equitable sharing of the benefits arising out of the utilisation of genetic resources, including by appropriate access to genetic resources and by appropriate transfer of relevant technologies, taking into account all rights over these resources and to technologies, and by appropriate funding" (UN 1992b).

The Convention requires "the states (contracting parties) to (*a*) develop national strategies, plans or programmes for the conservation and sustainable use of biological diversity or adapt for this purpose existing strategies, plans or programmes which shall reflect, *inter alia*, the measures set out in this convention relevant to the contracting party concerned; and (*b*) integrate as far as possible and as appropriate, the conservation and sustainable use of biological diversity into relevant sectoral or cross–sectoral plans, programmes and policies" (ibid. )

The Convention *inter alia* requires the states to adopt policies for *in situ* and *ex situ* conservation of biodiversity. Referring to *in situ* conservation it requires that "each contracting party shall, as far as possible and as appropriate,

(*a*) establish a system of protected areas or areas where specia measures need to be taken to conserve biological diversity;

(*b*) develop, where necessary, guidelines for the selection establishment and management of protected areas or areas wher special measures need to be taken to conserve biological diversity

(*c*) regulate or mange biological resources important for th conservation of biological diversity whether within or outsid protected areas, with a view to ensuring their conservation an sustainable use;

(*d*) promote the protection of ecosystems, natural habitats and th maintenance of viable populations of species in natura surroundings;

(*e*) promote environmentally sound and sustainable development i areas adjacent to protected areas with a view to furtherin protection of these areas;

(*f*) rehabilitate and restore degraded ecosystems and promote the recovery of threatened species *inter alia*, through the development and implementation of plans or other management strategies;

(*g*) establish or maintain means to regulate, manage or control the risks associated with the use and release of living modified organisms resulting from biotechnology which are likely to have adverse environmental impacts that could affect the conservation and sustainable use of biological diversity, taking also into account the risks to human health;

(*h*) prevent the introduction of, control or eradicate those alien species which threaten ecosystems, habitats or species;

(*i*) endeavour to provide the conditions needed for compatibility between present uses and the conservation of biological diversity and the sustainable use of its components;

(*j*) subject to its national legislation, respect, preserve and maintain knowledge; innovations and practices of indigenous and local communities embodying traditional life styles relevant for the conservation and sustainable use of biological diversity and promote their wider application with the approval and involvement of the holders of such knowledge, innovations and practices and encourage the equitable sharing of the benefits arising from the utilisation of such knowledge, innovations and practices;

(*k*) develop or maintain necessary legislation and/or other regulatory provisions for the protection of threatened species and populations;

(*l*) where a significant adverse effect on biological diversity has been determined ..., regulate or manage the relevant processes and categories of activities; and

(*m*) cooperate in providing financial and other support for *in situ* conservation outlined in sub paragraphs (*a*) to (*l*) above, particularly to developing countries" (ibid).

Outlining *ex-situ* conservation, it noted that "each contracting party shall, as far as possible and as appropriate, and predominantly for the purpose of complementing *in situ* measures:

(*a*) adopt measures for the *ex-situ* conservation of components of biological diversity, preferably in the country of origin of such components;

(*b*) establish and maintain facilities for *ex-situ* conservation of and research on plants, animals and micro-organisms, preferably in the country of origin of genetic resources;

(*c*) adopt measures for the recovery and rehabilitation of threatened species and for their reintroduction into their natural habitats under appropriate conditions;

(*d*) regulate and manage collection of biological resources from natural habitats for *ex situ* conservation purposes so as not to threaten ecosystems and *in situ* populations of species, except where special temporary *ex-situ* measures are required;

(*e*) cooperate in providing financial and other support for *ex-situ* conservation outlined in sub paragraphs (a) to (d) above and in the establishment and maintenance of *ex-situ* conservation facilities in developing countries" (ibid).

Making it explicit that the sustainable use of the components of biological diversity is desirable it noted that "each contracting party shall, as far as possible and as appropriate:

(*a*) integrate consideration of the conservation and sustainable use of biological resources into national decision-making;

(*b*) adopt measures relating to the use of biological resources to avoid or minimise adverse impacts on biological diversity;

(*c*) protect and encourage customary use of biological resources in accordance with traditional cultural practices that are compatible with conservation or sustainable use requirements;

(*d*) support local populations to develop and implement remedial action in degraded areas, where biological diversity has been reduced; and

(*e*) encourage cooperation between its governmental authorities and its private sector in developing methods for sustainable use of biological resources" (ibid).

The convention, *inter alia*, requires each contacting party (states) to provide incentives and mechanisms for the conservation and sustainable use of components of biological diversity, for research and training, for public education and awareness generation, for impact assessment and minimising adverse impacts, for access to genetic resources, for access to and transfer of technology, for exchange of information, for technical and scientific cooperation and for the effective use of biotechnology and the distribution of its benefits.

The Jakarta Ministerial Conference (COP 2) issued the Ministerial Statement on the Implementation of the Convention on Biological Diversity (Jakarta Mandate on Coastal and Marine Biodiversity) in November 1995. The mandate specifically linked the conservation, the use of biodiversity and fishing activities, and established a new global consensus on the importance of marine and coastal biodiversity (Aqorau, 2003, p.30).

It is only mandatory for the Government of India, as a signatory to the CBD, to adopt policies and programmes for the conservation of the aquatic biodiversity of the country and to contribute to the sustainable development of fisheries in India.

### 7.2.4. Ecosystem-based Fisheries Management

A holistic approach to the sustainable development of fisheries has been put forward by the FAO since the adoption of the code of conduct for responsible fisheries. It is known as the ecosystem approach to fisheries management or the ecosystem-based fisheries management (EBFM). Highlighting the background and need for an ecosystem-based fisheries management, Sinclair and Valdimarsson reported that "while the conventional single-stock resources management approach has shown its limitations, it cannot be considered the primary cause of past management failures. These can be attributed to a series of factors, including unwillingness to make politically difficult decisions on the allocation, sharing and use of the resources; massive fleet over capacities; and insufficient scientific knowledge about interactions both between species and between species and the environment in the ecosystem. There is, however, justified hope that the move towards an ecosystem-based fisheries management (EBFM) approach might be able to unlock some of the impediments that conventional management has experienced, not only the science of allocating fisheries resources but also the practical implementation. One reason is that this more holistic and integrative approach also calls for strong stakeholder participation, which brings firmly into focus human behaviour as the central management dimension.

However, there are additional forces and issues that underlie the call for a transition to EBFM. Those involved in fishing and dependent on it have recognised that resources must be managed sustainably with a long-term view. Society has developed much greater awareness concerning environmental impacts of unsustainable development, and demands a change of course. Consumers from the main markets, mobilised by non-governmental organisations (NGOs), are becoming aware of the role they could play through expressing their preferences in their purchasing behaviour. A number of eco-labelling schemes are being proposed, tested or even implemented, and they represent both an opportunity and threat if equity cannot be ensured. The question of competition between top predators and man is being asked from ethical as well as ecological points of view, broadening the question of ecosystem resources utilisation and ecosystem management objectives beyond the conventional limits. The request is for a broadening of the framework of all development activities, particularly fisheries, to encompass not only the marketed resource and some elements of its environment or accompanying species, but also the whole ecosystem" (Sinclair and Valdimarsson, 2003, p.393).

Referring to the shift in policy approaches needed while moving to an EBFM, Sinclair and Valdimarsson observe that "the changes required in the transition to EBFM may entail considerable sacrifices and costs to the fisheries sector, particularly in the short run. However, these are likely to be compensated for in the medium term and it can be taken for certain that all interested parties are going to gain large benefits in the long term. The time span for these evolutions will vary greatly depending on the current state of the fishery resources and of the ecosystem they are part of, and they will therefore have to be assessed from case to case. It will be important to ensure that costs are not shouldered solely by the fishery sector, but that they are borne equitably by all those participating in the use of the ecosystem and who are therefore beneficiaries of the additional welfare that will be created. Again this will vary greatly between regions and situations depending on the relative importance of the fishery sector and of other uses of coastal and marine areas. The need to asses the role and responsibility of other sectors should of course not detract from the urgent need for fisheries to correct the problems attributable to ineffective fisheries management practices" (ibid. pp.393-394).

Outlining the marine ecosystem characteristics for EBFM, these authors noted that "the marine ecosystem is highly productive and is used successfully by humans as a source of recreation, food, pharmaceuticals and livelihood in general. These uses have an impact on the ecosystem, and forecasting and controlling the fisheries impacts is one of the key tasks of science-based fisheries management. This task is made more complicated by uncertainties arising from difficulties in observing and measuring ecosystem components and properties, and by the enormous natural variability at a range of time scales in, *inter alia*, the distribution, age and species composition, and abundance of fisheries resources. On a longer time sale, the ecosystem is affected by global climate change, which will probably affect many aspects of fish distribution and dynamics. The marine ecosystem is also significantly affected by pollution and other degradation, which are usually beyond the control of fishery authorities. Responsible fisheries management requires recognising these various impacts and adjusting to them, taking remedial steps where necessary, if the production of ecosystem is to be maintained" (ibid. p.397).

Writing on the state of the ecosystem, Sinclair and Valdimarsson noted that "little attention has been focused in the past on evaluating the status of marine ecosystems as a whole, and there is little information available. In general, marine ecosystems are less perturbed and damaged than inland and terrestrial ecosystems. However, human impacts are still very noticeable, particularly in coastal areas, and impacts have been noted nearly everywhere, from the Arctic to the Antarctic Oceans and extending to the open ocean. Pollution is important, reaching the oceans through rivers, aquifers, sewage (point sources), drainage (non-point sources) and the atmosphere (wind and rain) ...; a global assessment in 2001 ... indicated that, aside from overfishing, the ecosystem is affected by alteration and destruction of coastal habitats and ecosystems, including coral reefs, mangroves and wetlands; industrial pollution, e.g., persistent pollutants (POPs) , heavy metals and hormone-disrupting substances; pollution by sewage, leading to contamination of seafood (e.g., cholera and typhoid); pollution by nutrients, notably fertilisers, leading to widespread and increased eutrophication, contributing to destruction of sea-grass beds and stimulation of toxin-producing algal blooms: changes (increases or decreases) in sediment flows due to deforestation, bad cultural practices, public works, etc.; global warming ...; and the direct impact of fishing on the environment" (ibid. p.397).

Focusing on the impacts of the above on fisheries, these authors noted that "the impacts of land-based and coastal alterations on the marine ecosystem affect the livelihood of coastal fishing communities and industries, and the food security of the poorest sector. They lead to loss of economic opportunities and compound the effects of unsustainable fishery development strategies" (ibid..397).

Pointing out the fishing-related impacts on the ecosystem, these authors noted that "impacts of fisheries on ecosystems are sometimes difficult to separate from environmental effects, but nevertheless have been stressed repeatedly. They are widespread, and include direct impacts of overfishing, modifying community species composition and genetic diversity through selective targeting of species and particular size classes; impacts on non-target species through low selectivity of certain gears; incidental mortality from lost or abandoned gear (ghost fishing); direct impact on the seabed through gear such as trawls and dredges; and destructive illegal fishing techniques, such as dynamite and poisoning. The discarding of about 20 million tonnes of unwanted catch represents wastage of potentially valuable resources. Progress has been made in addressing some of these, for example through development of more selective gear and more effective zoning practices, including the use of marine protected areas. However, the net effect is still frequently inadequate, and frustrated by problems such as open access and excess fishing capacity" (ibid. p.398).

Noting the challenges for implementing the EBFMs Sinclair and Valdimarson observed that "implicit in all initiatives for management of the ecosystem is recognition that man cannot manage the ecosystem as such, but only human activities using it. It follows that fisheries authorities on their own have neither the full mandate nor authority for ecosystem management and that a prerequisite for effective ecosystem management is coordination between all sectors using or affecting marine ecosystems. Nevertheless, much can be achieved by fisheries management agencies in adopting EBFM ... A first step in moving towards EBFM is to identify and describe the different ecosystems and their boundaries, and then to consider each as a discrete entity for the purposes of management. Thereafter, ecosystem management objectives must be developed. The central objective of EBFM is to obtain optimal benefits from all marine ecosystems in a sustainable manner. This requires the maintenance (or rebuilding) of the ecosystem, its habitats and biodiversity to a status capable of supporting all species at levels of maximum production. In pursuing this central objective, many, if not most, of the main conventional fishery management objectives and constraints remain inescapable, even though subject to ecosystem constraints, namely improvements in fishing technology (which should not be stopped); maximal production (to match growing demand for food); maximum employment (particularly in highly populated and poor areas, long coastal deserts, etc.); and minimisation of conflict within fisheries, but also among different sectors). Equitable allocation of resources through systems of rights remains a central challenge" (ibid. p.400).

Sinclair and Valdimarsson further made it clear that there are several other objectives of EBFM that are not different from those enunciated in the code of conduct for responsible fisheries but forming an integral part of it. They noted that "there are many other objectives referred to in the code, including: protection of critical habitats such as wetlands, mangroves, reefs, lagoons, nursery and spawning areas from degradation, pollution, etc. arising from human activities, and their restoration; maintenance of the quality, diversity and availability of resources; restoration or rehabilitation of populations and stocks; conservation of biodiversity and population structure; protection of endangered species; and others. Other important objectives, such as maintaining rural livelihoods or contributing to the foreign exchange balance, will also continue to be considered" (ibid. p.400).

To realise these objectives, it is necessary, that "all potential conflicts and inconsistencies need to be reconciled to arrive at a set of simultaneously attainable objectives encompassing biological, ecological, economic, social and institutional concerns. As in conventional single species fisheries management, the objectives must be formulated and reconciled in full consultation with all legitimate interested parties to ensure that their collaboration is obtained in achieving responsible fisheries" (ibid. pp.400-401).

Finally, for the success of EBFM, Sinclair and Valdimarsson observed that it is essential, *inter alia*, "to establish appropriate reference points ... and/or sustainability indicators, reflecting the objectives and elements of particular interest in the ecosystem, to assist in monitoring the state of the ecosystem and the performance of management efforts. These sustainability indictors must be based on the best scientific evidence available ..." (ibid. p.401).

It is worth noting here that since the aquatic ecosystem supporting the fisheries sector of India is beset with multiple problems of biological overfishing, pollution, habitat loss, biodiversity destruction, overcapitalisation, intrause and interuse conflicts, etc, it is advisable to adopt the ecosystem based approach to fisheries management as outlined above.

### 7.2.5. Integration of Fisheries Management with Coastal Zone Management

The basic need for the integration of fisheries management with coastal zone management is conveyed by the FAO when it noted thus:

> "Marine fisheries, as well as fisheries in large lakes, depend on the coastal area in a variety of ways. Most capture fisheries are based

on coastal stocks, others exploit offshore stocks which spend part of their lives in inshore waters, e.g. in a nursery or feeding area. Fish stocks also rely on primary productivity in the coastal area as an important part of the food chain. Coastal aquaculture is also heavily dependent on the coastal area for space and resources. This dependency of the marine fisheries sector on the coastal area makes it particularly susceptible to activities which result in coastal environmental changes which may have major impacts on the sector. At the same time, the fisheries sector can affect other coastal activities, e.g., through competition for space. The need is apparent, therefore, to consider the development and management of the fisheries sector within the context of coastal area management and development planning, i.e., in the context of the protection and management of resources, the environment and the activities of the coastal area" (FAO, 1996b, p.iv).

Article 10 of the FAO code of conduct for responsible fisheries deals with the integration of fisheries into coastal management to assist in achieving the rational use of scarce coastal resources. In particular they address "the issue of how the fisheries sector can be integrated into coastal management planning so that interactions between the fisheries sector and other sectors can be taken into account in the establishment of management policy and practice with regard to coastal resources" (ibid. p.iv).

The code offers guidelines for (*a*) institutional framework, (*b*) policy measures, (*c*) regional cooperation and (*d*) implementation. The institutional framework requires that:

1. States should ensure that an appropriate policy, legal and institutional framework is adopted to achieve the sustainable and integrated use of the resources, taking into account the fragility of coastal ecosystems and the finite nature of their natural resources and the needs of coastal communities.
2. In view of the multiple uses of the coastal area, states should ensure that representatives of the fisheries sector and fishing communities are consulted in the decision-making processes and involved in other activities related to coastal area management planning and development.
3. States should develop, as appropriate, institutional and legal frameworks in order to determine the possible uses of coastal

resources and to govern access to them taking into account the rights of coastal fishing communities and their customary practices to the extent compatible with sustainable development.

4. States should facilitate the adoption of fisheries practices that avoid conflict among fisheries resources users and between them and other users of the coastal area.

5. States should promote the establishment of procedures and mechanisms at the appropriate administrative level to settle conflicts, which arise within the fisheries sector and between fisheries resource users and other users of the coastal area (FAO, 1995a, pp.45-46).

The FAO, while elaborating the provisions of the code relating to the integration of fisheries into costal area management, *inter alia*, emphasises that "in considering the integration of fisheries into the broader coastal area management, the first requirement is for the state to establish policy, legal and institutional frameworks for the integrated management of coastal areas" (FAO, 1996b, p.2).

It is also noted that "in setting up an effective management framework, an institutional analysis is necessary in which, *inter alia*, the roles and responsibilities of different agencies should be analysed and, if necessary, revised, so that, on the one hand, over- lapping or conflicting jurisdiction is minimised, and on the other, there are no important issues for which there is not a responsible agency. An institutional mechanism for ICM, therefore will ensure the following: first, that appropriate sectoral responsibilities are defined; second, that appropriate coordinating/ integrating arrangements are established, and third, that agencies at all levels are kept informed of coastal area policies to ensure coherence in policy implementation" (ibid. pp.3-4).

As a note of caution to fisheries managements, FAO also reminds that "the nature of the sector which makes it especially susceptible to environmental changes resulting from on-shore activities may result in different and conflicting interests with land-based sectors such as the agriculture sector. Moreover, the issues facing capture fisheries, and to a lesser extent aquaculture, are not the same as those facing the agricultural sector. In particular, the agricultural production model – in which increased inputs result in higher production – cannot be applied to the fisheries sector. There may, therefore, be persuasive arguments why a fisheries agency should not be part of another Ministry or

Department where there may arise situations of conflicting interests" (ibid. p.4).

Applying this logic to the existing institutional set up in India, at the national level, would require the dismantling of the Department of Animal Husbandry, Dairying and Fisheries, and the establishment of a separate Ministry for Fisheries, which is a longstanding demand of the fisheries sector in India. Sustainable development of fisheries in India legitimately demands an independent ministerial set up at the national level.

The policy measures listed by the code include the following:

1. States should promote the creation of public awareness of the need for the protection and management of coastal resources and the participation in the management process by those affected.
2. In order to assist decision-making on the allocation and use of coastal resources, states should promote the assessment of their respective value taking into account economic, social and cultural factors.
3. In setting policies for the management of coastal areas, states should take due account of the risks and uncertainties involved.
4. States, in accordance with their capabilities, should establish or promote the establishment of systems to monitor the coastal environment as part of the coastal management process using physical, chemical, biological, economic and social parameters.
5. States should promote multidisciplinary research in support of coastal area management, in particular on its environmental, biological, economic, social, legal and institutional aspects (FAO, 1995a, pp.46-47).

While elaborating the policy perspectives as noted above, the FAO, *inter alia* suggests that "in the fisheries sector, it is appropriate that the fisheries authority identify potential threats and ensure that the appropriate action to protect fisheries interest is taken. The appropriate response is to attempt to protect the fisheries sector from damage by pre-emptive action. Where such damage does occur, e.g., resulting from a pollution incident, or where a conscious decision is taken at government level that costs to a fisheries sector are offset by benefits occurring elsewhere, action should be taken to rehabilitate the system and there should be adequate compensation to the stakeholders in the fisheries sector"(FAO, 1996b, p.10).

Measures of regional cooperation for ICM suggested in the code include the following:

1. States with neighbouring coastal areas should cooperate with one another to facilitate the sustainable use of coastal resources and the conservation of the environment.
2. In the case of activities that may have an adverse transboundary environmental effect on coastal areas, states should:
   (*a*) Provide timely information and, if possible, prior notification to potentially affected states;
   (*b*) Consult with those states as early as possible.
3. States should cooperate at the sub-regional and regional level in order to improve coastal area management.

Concerning the implementation of ICM programmes, the code requires the following:

1. States should establish mechanisms for cooperation and coordination among national authorities involved in planning, development, conservation and management of coastal areas.
2. States should ensure that the authority or authorities representing the fisheries sector in the coastal management process have the appropriate technical capacities and financial resources.

The coastal zones of India which house multiple coastal activities, ranging from fishing, forestry, agriculture, aquaculture, mining, manufacturing, ports, tourism, transport, defence, power production, etc. to housing, urban development, water supply, waste dumping, etc. have also become theatres of mounting conflict of interests, necessitating ICM for sustaining these activities. The need for integrating fisheries management with coastal zone management is quite pressing in India as the fisheries sector is the one most seriously affected by many externalities created by other sectors.

The idea of integration of fisheries management with coastal zone management is, however, likely to raise serious political economy type of questions. The basic objective of coastal zone management being the maximisation of the economic value of the social product by preventing conflict or through harmonisation of the multiple and often conflicting activities through dialogue based primarily on economic rationale, the frequency of the fishery sector loosing in the changed scenario of global business alternatives is significant and posing potential threat to the sustainability of the sector. Doubts had been cast in the past on the possibility of the fishery sector not getting adequate representation and voice in the negotiating tables. As reported by Nadia, "where conflicts arise between fishing and alternative resource uses, the chances are that fishing will be seen as an activity of marginal economic importance. Yet the resource on which fishing is based is in fact very valuable. Fisheries represent a renewable gold mine, provided they are managed correctly" (Nadia, 1998, p.156).

The complexity of the integration process in coastal area management has been noted by Caddy and Griffiths as well. They observed that "the objectives of ICAM in a given place, time and socio-economic context are multiple and often conflicting: thus, as for fishery development itself, these objectives must be clear-cut and related to the political, ecological, and socio-economic objectives of the responsible government and local authorities in such a way as to maximise the common good. The public perception of this good may not be constant, but it must also be related to the time-scale on which human social development proceeds: that is, decadal. This common good must, in the current climate of social thinking, have sustainable development as its main objective ..." (Caddy and Griffiths, 1995, p.72). Notwithstanding this consensus, it is often the market driven (profit oriented) demand induced (consumerist) political economy (democratic) choices that compromise the interests of traditional sectors like fisheries and pose potential threat to their sustainability. With or without ICM, the political economy of fisheries development has been one of loosing ground to other coastal activities. This process is likely to be aggravated in the era of liberlisation, privatisation and globalisation with greater investments planned in the country for shipping, tourism, transport, mining, etc. in the coast.

### 7.3. Economic Solutions

The major economic issues affecting the sustainability Indian fisheries discussed in the last chapter are (1) stagnation in production, (2) overcapitalisation, (3) economic loss, (4) unemployment, (5) static or declining consumption, (6) unstable market for fish and barriers to trade and (7) meagre contribution of fisheries to the GDP. The economic solutions proposed in this section are presented under three categories: (a) market solutions, (b) non-market solutions and (c) strengthening of central planning for sustainable development.

### 7.3.1. Market Solutions

As most of the economic problems affecting the fisheries sector are attributed to market failure or market not giving proper signals to the industry for sustained growth or sustainable development, much reliance is now placed on correcting the market failure and making it efficient to automatically regulate the industry to work at optimum levels. This is considered to be the best option in the era of liberalisation, privatisation and globalisation, where the industry can be left to operate on its own based on free market economic principles and least interference by the state and the state expected to play only an umpire's or regulator's role. The state, at best, needs to offer only the infrastructure and level-playing ground for the private sector dictated by market forces of supply, demand and price.

The major corrections sought as part of the market solutions are removal of all restrictions on trade and investments in the industry, especially, in aquaculture and deep sea (offshore) fishing, where the potential for growth is considered to be significant. The aquaculture sector in India has been long demanding the removal of all restrictions on intensive and semi-intensive aquaculture introduced following the introduction of CRZ notification in 1991 and the Supreme Court directive on coastal aquaculture in 1996. There is also growing pressure to open up and liberalise the aquaculture sector for foreign direct investment to facilitate the transfer of technology and marketing tie up, all of which are expected to contribute to higher levels of production in the short run. Their impact on long-term sustainability, especially through their effects on habitat and biodiversity needs to be considered, however. The demand to open up the deep-sea fisheries sector of India for foreign private investment is also potent but resisted by the domestic fishermen and the national fleet owners alike. There is, however, a growing stake in this sector with the new impetus for globalisation. The impact of opening the sector for global participation or partnership and the ultimate effect of this on the sustainability of the domestic industry also needs further scrutiny.

Another major market solution prescribed for the economic ills of the fisheries sector of India today is to introduce free market pricing or cost-pricing of all inputs and outputs and abolish all kinds of subsidies and support to the industry by the state. This is considered important for overcoming the overcapitalisation problem in the industry which is a major threat to the sustainability of the industry, caused by the presence of various kinds of subsidies/financial support to the industry in the past and continuing even now in some measure. Much of the excess capacity prevailing in the fisheries sector world-wide is attributed to the public policy of granting support to the industry in the developing stages and their continuation even later, which works as an incentive for overinvestment in the sector which ultimately leads to overcapitalisation, over- fishing and collapse of the industry. It is also considered advisable for the state to insist on all industries to include the pollution abatement costs in their pricing policy to recover the full cost of pollution control and to minimise the damage to the environment. This in effect means the adoption of the 'polluter-pay-principle' for protecting to fishery environment for sustainability.

The impact of subsidy as a barrier to trade has been noted in the last chapter. It has the potential to distort free trade and to work as a protectionist tool. It is, however, significant to note here that in the era of globalisation, where new and artificial barriers to trade are being erected by developed and developing countries alike, a blanket removal of all support/subsidy to the domestic industry by the state will do more harm to the industry, making it uncompetitive all on a sudden in the global market, paving way for the complete ransacking of the domestic industry by foreign firms. It is prudent to be cautious and follow a precautionary approach in this regard, notwithstanding other compulsions of free trade and liberalisation.

The practical difficulty of abolishing subsidies has been made clear by Lesser, *et al.* when they observed that "eliminating subsidies is, of course, not easy, as the beneficiaries have strong incentives to maintain them. In many developing countries, subsidies are also used to justify national goals such as food self-sufficiency or rapid industrialisation. Such goals will remain elusive in the long-run as long as subsidies continue" (Lesser, *et al.* 1997, p.612).

Another major economic solution suggested for minimising the pressure on the limited stock and to overcome the unemployment problem in the fisheries sector is to diversify the coastal economy, including the fisheries sector. This suggestion has been put forward by the FAO and other international agencies. Development of the coastal economy with provision for training and absorption of local fishermen in alternative occupations is considered desirable for sustaining the fisheries sector.

The feasibility of this proposal is, however, suspected when the prevailing socio-economic situation prevent the fishermen from competing with other better-equipped segments of the society.

One plausible suggestion to overcome the crisis arising from the undue dependence on the fluctuating international market for fish is to develop the domestic market for fish, which will also promote the domestic consumption of fish contributing the greater sustainability of the sector. As noted in chapter six, the per capita consumption of fish in India is much below that of China and other countries. The per capita consumption was found to be extremely low in interior areas. Developments of domestic market with better infrastructure and value addition can contribute to greater sustainability of the industry. It can also enhance the contribution of the sector to the GDP of the country, which is just above one per cent at present indicating poor sustainability in the national economic rating of the sector.

It is also noted here that the common proposal to import fish to overcome the excess capacity issue in the processing sector is not going to bring back sustainability in the domestic industry, as it corresponds to 'imported' sustainability and not fulfilling the 'strong' sustainability criteria of maintaining natural capital in tact and meeting the intragenerational equity requirements.

Another economic prescription of the neo-classical school for sustainability is to invest in natural capital, which can partially reduce the natural resource constraint in the long run (Daly, 2005, pp.481-494). The Government of India may devise programame for rebuilding the fish stock through stock enhancement programmes as popularised by the FAO for both marine and inland fisheries.

A further economic proposal of the neo-classical school is to monitor the damage and loss to natural capital by accounting the changes (depletion) in the natural resource base in the National Income Accounting which will be reflected in the national income estimates, following which states may take precautionary or preventive measures to protect the natural resource base (Gilpin, 2000, pp.107-109). In tune with this proposal, Government of India may introduce a system of natural resource accounting or 'green accounting' for fisheries management and sustainability.

Similarly, a system of natural capital depletion tax and ecological tariffs along with the application of the precautionary-polluter-pay-principles (4P) as proposed by Costanza, *et al.* (1987, p.207), and as reported in chapter three may also be thought of as economic tools for regulating the market mechanism within the fisheries sector.

Yet another major economic solution for achieving sustainability of the industry, especially at the level of global trade is to insist for the adherence to the provisions of the FAO code of conduct for responsible fisheries by industry and trading partners. Article 11 of the code relating to responsible international trade prescribes the following measures.

1. The provisions of this code should be interpreted and applied in accordance with the principles, rights and obligations established in the World Trade Organisation (WTO) Agreement.
2. International trade in fish and fishery products should not compromise the sustainable development of fisheries and responsible utilisation of living aquatic resources.
3. States should ensure that measures affecting international trade in fish and fishery products are transparent, based when applicable, on scientific evidence, and are in accordance with internationally agreed rules.
4. Fish trade measures adopted by states to protect human or animal life or health, the interests of consumers or the environment, should not be discriminatory and should be in accordance with internationally agreed trade rules, in particular the principles, rights and obligations established in the Agreement on the Application of Sanitary and Phytosanitary Measures and the Agreement on Technical Barriers to Trade of the WTO.
5. States should further liberalise trade in fish and fishery products and eliminate barriers and distortions to trade such as duties, quotas and non-tariff barriers in accordance with the principles, rights and obligations of the WTO Agreement.
6. States should not directly or indirectly create unnecessary or hidden barriers to trade that limit the consumer's freedom of choice of supplier or that restrict market access.
7. States should not condition access to markets to access to resources. This principle does not preclude the possibility of fishing agreements between states which include provisions referring to access to resources, trade and access to markets, transfer of technology, scientific research, training and other relevant elements.

8. States should not link access to markets to the purchase of specific technology or sale of other products.
9. States should cooperate in complying with relevant international agreements regulating trade in endangered species.
10. States should develop international agreements for trade in live specimens where there is a risk of environmental damage in importing or exporting states.
11. States should cooperate to promote adherence to, and effective implementation of relevant international standards for trade in fish and fishery products and living aquatic resources conservation.
12. States should not undermine conservation measures for living aquatic resources in order to gain trade or investment benefits.
13. States should cooperate to develop internationally acceptable rules or standards for trade in fish and fishery products in accordance with the principles, rights, and obligations established in the WTO Agreement.
14. States should cooperate with each other and actively participate in relevant regional and multilateral fora, such as WTO, in order to ensure equitable, non-discriminatory trade in fish and fishery products as well as wide adherence to multilaterally agreed fishery conservation measures.
15. States, aid agencies, multilateral development banks and other relevant international organisations should ensure that their policies and practices related to the promotion of international fish trade and export production do not result in environmental degradation or adversely impact the nutritional rights and needs of people for whom fish is critical to their health and well being and for whom other comparable sources of food are not readily available or affordable (FAO, 1995b, pp.50-53).

The code also requires states to adhere to laws and regulations relating to fish trade. Specifically it requires:

1. Laws, regulations and administrative procedures applicable to international trade in fish and fishery products should be transparent, as simple as possible, comprehensible and, when appropriate, based on scientific evidence.

2. States, in accordance with their national/laws, should facilitate appropriate consultation with and participation of industry as well as environmental and consumer groups in the development and implementation of laws and regulations related to trade in fish and fishery products.
3. States should simplify their laws, regulations and administrative procedures applicable to trade in fish and fishery products without jeopardising their effectiveness.
4. When a state introduces changes to its legal requirements affecting trade in fish and fishery products with other states, sufficient information and time should be given to allow the states and producers affected to introduce, as appropriate the changes needed in their processes and procedures. In this connection, consultation with affected states on the time frame for implementation of the changes would be desirable. Due consideration should be given to requests from developing countries for temporary derogations from obligations.
5. States should periodically review laws and regulations applicable to international trade in fish and fishery products in order to determine whether the conditions that give rise to their introduction continue to exist.
6. States should harmonise as far as possible the standards applicable to international trade in fish and fishery products in accordance with relevant internationally recognised provisions.
7. States should collect, disseminate and exchange timely, accurate and pertinent statistical information on international trade in fish and fishery products through relevant national institutions and international organisations.
8. States should promptly notify interested states, WTO and other appropriate international organisations on the development of and changes to laws, regulations and administrative procedures applicable to international trade in fish and fishery products (ibid, pp.53-54).

Another neo-classical economic solution for sustainability commonly prescribed is to enhance the productivity of the industry by substituting the less productive or less abundant factor by the more productive or abundant factor. The substitution of the scarce natural capital by man-made capital, e.g., knowledge and other physical capital, has been proposed by environmental and ecological economists of the neo-classical vintage for achieving sustainability. This proposition, i.e. the 'weak-sustainability hypothesis', explained in chapter three, is still in currency as a possible economic solution to achieve sustainability. The feasibility of this alternative is, however, suspected when there is the overall constraint of non-availability of complementary natural resource inputs and their substitution possibilities are limited. It is worth noting here that the neoclassical market models are not going to help much in solving the problem of unsustainability. As noted by Heal "markets have not performed notably well in conserving our planet's environment. Indeed, they have done quite the opposite ...; markets may not be able to do the entire job of maintaining ecosystem services and the stock of natural capital. Direct regulation will be needed as well ..." (Heal, 2000, p.427).

### 7.3.2. Non-Market Solutions

Non-market solutions to the sustainability crises involve primarily recourse to the conventional regulatory techniques of fisheries management. These include the adoption of two broad sets of controls on fishery activities to achieve specific goals of fisheries management. The two broad sets of controls are (1) blanket controls on input and output of the catching, culture, processing and marketing breaches of the industry and (2) selective controls on input and output of all branches of the industry (Korakandy, 1996, pp.134-141). The former limits the number/volume/quantity of inputs used and output produced in the various branches or sectors of the industry to accomplish pre-determined objectives while the latter prescribe standards of quality/size/other norms for inputs used and output produced by the various sectors for realising specific goals of management. The synchronised application of these controls can accomplish the diverse goals of conservation (protection) of stock, prevention of economic waste (overcapitalisation), economic efficiency (viability), prevention of conflict, and intragenerational and intergenerational equity.

Corresponding to the above controls on inputs, fisheries managements (administration) in India can limit the number of fishing units, fish farms, fish processing plants and marketing units through a system of licensing (limited entry) to accomplish single or multiple objectives of sustainable development. Similar controls on the magnitude of output of these sectors (quota system) can also be introduced. Selective controls with respect to time (season), place (location) gear (trawling), species (threatened/ depleted), etc. can also be introduced to accomplish specific goals of management. These restrictions should correspond to the common controls on fishing ground (area restrictions), fishing seasons (breeding /monsoon), fishing techniques (banned gear), controls on processing and marketing of notified (protected/endangered species), product quality (HACCP/SPS), etc. The use of TED, BED, etc, also form part of these controls. These non-market solutions generally work outside the cost-price mechanism and they rely on legal sanctions and compliance by the industry.

It is well known that many of these controls are presently operating in the fisheries sector of India, but with only partial success. Rigorous implementation of these measures may further help in improving their outcome.

### 7.3.3. Strengthening of Central Planning for Sustainable Development

Sustaining fisheries development in India calls for a revamping of central planning with concrete objectives, targets, policies, programmes and strategies, at the local, regional and national levels. The significance of planning for sustainable development has been emphasised by Jacobs. Jacobs noted that "understood as a process of ecological restructuring, therefore, sustainability will require detailed government involvement: in setting environmental-economic objectives, in choosing techniques, and in the use of instruments. This must be described as a form of planning" (Jacobs, 1999, p.94).

Since much of the ecological, economic, social/cultural, technological and institutional problems of unsustainability are the result of the absence of effective and integrated central planning, there is a dire need for strengthening the national economic planning machinery with corresponding improvements at the regional and local levels. The fisheries management plan of the country, both developmental and regulatory should be in harmony with other sectoral plans of the economy and should be planned in such a way as to reap maximum complementarities and to minimise the risk of negative externalities which lead to unsustainability. This is particularly important in the context of development of inland fisheries and aquaculture where the potential for development is considered to be significant. It is also worth noting here that the planners in India should follow the FAO code of conduct for responsible aquaculture development while planning for its development. Article 9 of the code prescribes norms for the responsible development of aquaculture including culture-based fisheries in (1) areas under national jurisdiction and (2) transboundary aquatic ecosystems.

With regard to the first category of area it requires:

1. States should establish, maintain and develop an appropriate legal and administrative framework which facilitates the development of responsible aquaculture.

2. States should promote responsible development and management of aquaculture, including an advance evaluation of the effects of aquaculture development on genetic diversity and ecosystem integrity, based on the best available scientific information.

3. States should produce and regularly update aquaculture development strategies and plans, as required, to ensure that aquaculture development is ecologically sustainable and to allow the rational use of resources shared by aquaculture and other activities.

4. States should ensure that the livelihoods of local communities and their access to fishing grounds are not negatively affected by aquaculture developments.

5. States should establish effective procedures specific to aquaculture to undertake appropriate environmental assessment and monitoring with the aim of minimising adverse ecological changes and related economic and social consequences resulting from water extraction, land use, discharge of effluents, use of drugs and chemicals, and other aquaculture activities (FAO, 1995b, pp.40-41).

With regard to the second category of area it requires:

1. States should protect transboundary aquatic ecosystems by supporting responsible aquaculture practices within their national jurisdiction and by cooperation in the promotion of sustainable aquaculture practices.

2. States should, with due respect to their neighbouring states and in accordance with international law, ensure responsible choice of species, siting and management of aquaculture activities, which could affect transboundary aquatic ecosystems.

3. States should consult with their neighbouring states, as appropriate, before introducing non-indigenous species into transboundary aquatic ecosystems.

4. States should establish appropriate mechanisms, such as databases and information networks to collect, share and disseminate data related to their aquaculture activities to facilitate cooperation on planning for aquaculture development at the national, sub-regional, regional and global level.

5. States should cooperate in the development of appropriate mechanisms, when required to monitor the impacts of inputs used in aquaculture (ibid, pp.41-42).

The guidelines relating to the use of aquatic genetic resources for the purposes of aquaculture including culture-based fisheries given by the code are:

1. States should conserve genetic diversity and maintain integrity of aquatic communities and ecosystems by appropriate management. In particular, efforts should be undertaken to minimise the harmful effects of introducing non-native species or genetically altered stocks into waters under the jurisdiction of other states as well as waters under the jurisdiction of the state of origin. States should, whenever possible, promote steps to minimise adverse genetic disease and other effects of escaped farmed fish on wild stocks.

2. States should cooperate in the elaboration, adoption and implementation of, international codes of practice and procedures for introductions and transfers of aquatic organisms.

3. States should, in order to minimise risks of disease transfer and other adverse effects on wild and cultured stocks, encourage adoption of appropriate practices in the genetic improvement of brood stocks, the introduction of non-native species, and in the production, sale and transport of eggs, larvae or fry, brood stock or other live materials. States should facilitate the preparation and implementation of appropriate national codes of practice and procedures to this effect.

4. States should promote the use of appropriate procedures for the selection of brood stock and the production of eggs, larvae and fry.
5. States should, where appropriate, promote research and, when feasible the development of culture techniques for endangered species to protect, rehabilitate and enhance their stocks, taking into account the critical need to conserve genetic diversity of endangered species (ibid, pp.42-44).

The other guidelines of the code for responsible aquaculture at the production level include:

1. States should promote responsible aquaculture practices in support of rural communities, producer organisations and fish farmers.
2. States should promote active participation of fish farmers and their communities in the development of responsible aquaculture management practices.
3. States should promote efforts, which improve selection and use of appropriate feeds, feed additions and fertilisers, including manures.
4. States should promote effective farm and fish health management practices favouring hygienic measures and vaccines. Safe, effective and minimal use of therapeutants, hormones and drugs, antibiotics and other disease control chemicals should be ensured.
5. States should regulate the use of chemical inputs in aquaculture, which are hazardous to human health and the environment.
6. States should require that the disposal of wastes such as offal, sludge, dead or diseased fish, excess veterinary drugs and other hazardous chemical inputs does not constitute a hazard to human health and the environment.
7. States should ensure the food safety of aquaculture products and promote efforts which maintain product quality and improve their value thorough particular care before and during harvesting and onsite processing and in storage and transport of the products (ibid. pp.44-45).

Fisheries management in India should necessarily follow the relevant provisions of the FAO code of conduct for responsible fisheries while planning for fisheries development in India. Article 7 of the Code prescribes, among other things, that "states and all those engaged in fisheries management should, through an appropriate policy, legal and institutional framework, adopt measures for the long-term conservation and sustainable use of fishery resources. Conservation and management measures, whether at local, national, sub-regional or regional levels, should be based on the best scientific evidence available and be designed to ensure the best long term sustainability of fishery resources at levels which promote the objective of their optimum utilisation and maintain their availability for present and future generations; short-term considerations should not compromise these objectives" (FAO, 1995b, p.14).

A recent report of the FAO noted that "further efforts should therefore be made to ensure the effective integration of fisheries into key national policy documents relating to poverty reduction and rural development, paying particular attention to gender issues and internationally recognised fishery development instruments such as the Code of Conduct for Responsible Fisheries" (FAO, 2004, p.40).

It is also significant to note here that as a precautionary measure, the planners in India should assess the environmental/ecological impacts on fisheries, of major schemes like inter linking of rivers in the country and the *Sethusamudram* coastal dredging project. This is considered important as the fish habitat and biodiversity of the area are expected to be threatened by these projects.

Planning for sustainable development of fisheries in India requires fundamental long-term structural changes in the economy. As pointed out by Jacobs, "sustainability, it is clear, requires long term structural change in economy and society: changes not just in the demands for a wide variety of goods and services, but in technologies, infrastructures, lifestyles ... But these conditions are precisely those which do not hold for the kind of shifts required by sustainability ... Planning for sustainability ... requires changes in the conditions in which markets currently operate: the prices given to them by the regimes (and by the structure of other markets), the infrastructure in which they are embedded, their legal framework, even their social (cultural and moral) context. This is not a question of 'adding' such conditions: markets are already 'bounded' and 'structured' in these ways, both by cultural-historical legacies and deliberate policy ... In this sense current environmental outcomes are already 'determined', if only by omission. Altering the outcomes by changing these conditions will redefine many markets, reducing the scale of some, enlarging others; new markets will be created ... Planning for sustainability will involve negotiations with transnational corporations wielding significant economic power. In many fields, the process may be less one of trying to change a 'market' than simply trying to influence a small number of very large companies ... The dynamic nature of structural change, the idea of sustainability being a direction rather than a condition, suggests that the process is more one of *steering*" (Jacobs, *op. cit.* pp. 90, 94-95).

This process of *steering ecological restructuring* and changing the direction of the economy and society requires active intervention by the state power since the free market forces have miserably led to this pause. And as Jacobs asserts "markets cannot guarantee, and are in practice almost certainly unable to achieve, major reductions in environmental impacts. Since the most important environmental goods are in- escapably public and collective in character, only states can regulate their condition: only states have the coercive power which can overcome the free-riding problem of individual choice" (ibid. p.95). The suggestion for strengthening central planning may sound 'odd' in the era of post-modern reconstruction of free markets and capitalism, but 'strong' sustainability of Indian fisheries and the national economy demands rethinking on the new role of central planning.

Central planning is needed to allocate the scarce resources of the economy between people, areas and sectors overtime to extricate the economy from the labyrinths of unsustainablity enmeshed by free markets and developments in global capitalism. Sustainability requires intensive care in the working of the economy by state and its people without allowing it to be hijacked by profit-seeking enterprises under the incense of 'incentive mechanism' now touted by the liberal school.

A framework for sustainable growth and development planning has been given by Bartelmus (Bartelmus, 1994). Table 7.1 gives details of the framework of sustainable growth and development offered by Bartelmus.

The framework given in table 7.1 essentially focuses on local and national development with eco-development and sustainable economic growth as objectives, assisted by strategic functions of statistical assessment, research and analysis, policy planning and support services. Adopting this framework for planning for sustainable development of fisheries in India is advisable.

**Table 7.1**

**Framework for sustainable growth and development**

| | 1. Local development | | 2. National development | |
|---|---|---|---|---|
| Development paradigms / Strategic functions | 1.1 Regionally sustainable economic growth | 1.2 Eco-development | 2.1 Sustainable economic growth | 2.2 Sustainable development |
| A. Assessment | Integrated regional (monetary) accounting | a. Environmental statistics<br>b. Regional (physical) resource accounting<br>c. Statistical ecology | Integrated environmental accounting | a. Environmental statistics<br>b. Natural (physical) resource accounting<br>c. National development reports |
| B. Research and analysis | Modelling spatial disparities in income and growth | a. Modelling eco-development<br>b. Modelling carrying capacity<br>c. Development of eco-techniques | Integrated micro-meso-macro economic analysis and modelling | Models of integrated (physical) planning and development |

| | | | | |
|---|---|---|---|---|
| C. Planning and policies | Regional planning and policies of sustainable economic growth | Eco-development planning and administration (decentralised planning and strategies) | a. Reorientation of macro- economic policies towards sustainability<br>b. Policies of structural change | a. Integrated (physical) planning and project formulation<br>b. Demographic policies on population, resources, environment and development |
| | | | c. Economic (dis) incentives for micro-economic planning and management | c. Programmes of human needs satisfaction |
| D. Support | a. Extension service | | a. Public awareness building and participation | |
| | b. Technical assistance for local-level projects | | b. Programmes and projects of education, training and public information | |
| | c. Public awareness building and participation (support to grass-roots movements/organisations) | | c. Institution-building and environmental law/regulations | |
| | | | d. Technical cooperation, including transfer (import) of environmentally sound technology and capacitybuilding. | |

*Source:* Adapted from Bartelmus, 1994, pp.82-83.

A framework for sustainable development of fisheries given by the FAO International Conference on the Sustainable Contribution of Fisheries to Food Security held at Kyoto, Japan, during December 1995 noted the following principles as essential components of the strategy: (1) maintenance of ecological systems, (2) improvement in economic and social well-being, (3) intergenerational equity, (4) intragenerational equity, and (5) adoption of the precautionary approach (Government of Japan and FAO, 1995a, p.43).

### 7.4. Institutional Solutions

Another major set of solutions suggested for the sustainable development of fisheries, worldwide, and available for consideration in India as well, is institutional solutions. The institutional solution for sustainability has often been suggested by neo-classical environmental/ ecological economists and by international organisations like the FAO and the World Bank. The UNCED (1992) also had advocated the institutional 'way out' for sustainability. The neo-liberal school is very much in favour of institutional changes to achieve sustainable development of fisheries, globally.

The major institutional solutions suggested are discussed under the following heads in this section: (1) Privatisation, (2) Globalisation, (3) Public-Private-Partnership, (4) Capacity-building, (5) Co-management and (6) Use of traditional knowledge.

#### 7.4.1. Privatisation

One of the frequently cited reasons for the mismanagement of fisheries which lead to overcapitalisation and overfishing and the resulting unsustainability is the 'open access' or common property characteristics of fisheries. To overcome this situation, the neo-classical fishery economists have suggested the introduction of 'private property' or 'sole' ownership rights over the common property or open access marine fisheries (Christy and Scott, 1965). Finding the practical difficulties of vesting exclusive private property rights in open access marine fisheries in advanced countries, Christy and Scot, among others, have suggested a system of 'limited entry' by licensing to prevent over- capitalisation and to minimise the economic waste. The idea of 'sole ownership' has been since modified and presented in the form of 'self management' and territorial use rights in fisheries (TURF) by Christy and others, with exclusive use rights assigned to right holders. The 'right' holders are expected to manage the resources efficiently allocating them taking into account the marginal costs and benefits or their profitability. Thus, privatisation of the 'commons' or common property fisheries is now sought as a solution for the unsustainability issue. The (private) property rights in fisheries with its variants like the 'tradeable permits' and 'individual transferable quotas' are expected to achieve the benefit of an institutional solution through the price mechanism. It is partly a market solution to the problem of overcapitalisation or economic inefficiency arising from the weakness of the common property system.

The neo- liberal institutional school, now out-rightly advocates privatisation calling it as governance reform. Advocating such reforms, Sutinen and Soboil noted that "one obvious way to avoid government failure is to privatise the fishery resource. Privatisation of government-owned and operated industries has been carried out in several countries for several industries, including railways, utilities, and communications and energy industries. Complete privatisation of fisheries is rare. However, there is a recent trend to devote more management responsibility down to users, in effect privatising many management functions" (Sutinen and Soboil, 2003, p.307).

Opschoor and Jongma note that "institutional changes such as introduction of property rights are necessary to correct for market and government failures that hamper the realisation and maintenance of sustainability" (Opschoor and Jongma, 1999, pp. 523-524).

As noted in chapter three, privatisation has been suggested by Pearson also. Pearson observes that "a further step toward sustainable development is for government to establish, clarify, or enforce private property rights, or to strengthen communal property rights" (Pearson, 2000, p.480).

The privatisation solution has been however, questioned by Collet. Collet observes that "the privatisation of access and use-rights, granting the individual rights to a given proportion of the harvestable resource to be regulated by the market, would seem to offer a promising solution for the management of resources challenged by over exploitation and the threat of depletion. Once the political problems associated with the initial distribution of rights have been resolved, the system should certainly provide the most efficient means for allocating resources based on the highest bidder and so involving those best placed to maximise the value of production. But this so-called 'radical' form of management in fact belongs to a long tradition of the enclosure of common or communal property which accelerated during the 18th and 19th centuries; it is a process of exclusion which not infrequently leads to violence, as regularly portrayed in the imagery of the Holywood 'western'. It is a system burdened by heavy social costs and one that takes little or no account of the specificity of the marine environment. Despite the assumption that privatisation will involve the internalisation of management costs, the burden of management responsibility still falls largely on the state.

As in other areas of economic activity, private enterprise tends naturally to externalise the environmental and social costs in order to maximise short-term profits. The allocation of transferable use rights is expected, at least in theory, to create for its beneficiaries the incentive to protect the long-term capital value of the resource base, as in the case of privately held farm land in the western world. But, in truth, private land ownership for agricultural or extractive use has not prevented erosion of the soil, the depletion of its productive capacity and, under conditions of the chemicalisation of agriculture as in the USA, the virtual desertification of farmland. In Europe, the effects of nutrient overload are one of the principal reasons for the deterioration of the fragile coastal ecosystems. From purely economic perspective, the exhaustion of certain natural resources with slow growth and replacement rates might be seen as an optimal strategy. Once the resource has been exhausted, the short term profits so earned can be reinvested elsewhere in order to earn higher interest rates than those previously generated by the exploitation of the resource. The translocation of investment has already characterised the recent history of fisheries development. There is, therefore, no real guarantee that the allocation of fishery resources to quasi-private owners will not recreate the same process that led to the degradation of agricultural resources" (Collet, 1999, p.123).

Collet also noted that "this allegedly 'radical' and 'promising' management regime only addresses questions of economic efficiency but at the cost of drastic social change involving the loss of jobs, the disintegration of family enterprises ... and the concentration of wealth and power in the hands of 'sea barons' ... The social externalities that result from this game of 'monopoly' are deferred to the state, which act as a social 'stretcher-bearer', or to informal care institutions. Social justice and the conservation of the resource, which should be the central concerns of any management system, are left to their own devices ..." (ibid, p.124).

Nadia observes that "the existence of private or common property or exclusive use rights may lead to undesirable environmental and other impacts. For example, the holding of private property rights by entrepreneurs investing in shrimp cultivation in some coastal areas of south and southeast Asia and of Latin America has, in some cases, resulted in destructions of wetland forests, water pollution, and the marginalisation and dislocation of resource poor people. Where population pressure increases, through migration for instance, and pure survival is the issue, it will often be difficult to ensure compliance, with various property regimes that endeavours to exclude one group or another" (Nadia 1998, p.14). Nadia further thinks that "owing to the difficulty of accounting for the environmental goods and services of a given resource, especially in the long-term, and the social values placed upon them by different user groups, the market will be a poor guide to management decisions ..." (Nadia, 1998, p.14).

Datta and Chakrabarti are found to argue for the introduction of some form of stakeholder ownership in Indian fisheries. They observed that "there is no denial of the fact that fixation of property rights to the stakeholders is one fundamental criterion for ensuring sustainability of any fisheries unit. This is because such fixation makes the owner(s)/ lease holder(s) responsible for minimising the extent of possible externalities generated out of his/her/their enterprises as they can be easily caught and made to compensate the victims as per the 'polluter pays' principle ... In respect of riverine, big reservoir and estuarine fishery segments also, suitable contractual agreements in respect of property rights arrangements have to be ensured either at individual or group levels ..."(Datta and Chakrabarti, 2004, pp.399-400). Such arrangements, no doubt, will promote private investments in wetlands, as in the Chilka lake in Orissa, and lead to serious intrause conflicts as reported in chapter six. The faith in the responsible and law abiding behaviour of stakeholders (enterprises) leading to minimisation of externalities as upheld by these authors is mere academic illusion of the neo-classical type.

The NCAP, however, reported that "privatisation of the fishing rights in riverine fisheries would accelerate the process of social disequilibria and broaden income inequalities" (NCAP, 2004, p.21).

Privatisation as a solution for unsustainability has been questioned by Symes in the European Community contest. Symes observed that "certain moral questions may well arise over the alienation of hitherto common use rights for the benefit of privileged individuals and over the social inequity induced by capitalist models of development in the fishing industry. In seeking to solve the market failure attributed to the condition of *res communis*, common or shared interests within the local communities have been very largely ignored. However, the key question is whether the neo-liberal agenda of privatisation, accumulation and concentration of use rights, which increasingly lies at the heart of most restrictive management systems, is necessarily the best way of securing the sustainability of the physical resource base, especially within the emerging imperative of a precautionary approach to fisheries management. There may be clear benefits in terms of a more efficient and profitable industry, but cannot the dual objectives of fisheries management – abundant and sustainable commercial fish stocks within a diverse and sustainable marine ecosystem – be secured through a system that seeks to preserve social equity in terms of access to resources and thereby guarantee the future of fishing opportunities in most, if not all, fishing dependent regions? Sustainable development does not rule out trade-offs between economic efficiency and social equity in the quest for the greater common good; on the contrary, it insists on the implementation of precisely this kind of economic and social cost-benefit analysis at the regional level. There is something faintly paradoxical about a common fisheries policy (CFP) that lays so much emphasis on the need to maintain relative stability among its member states but that seemingly ignores the growing inequity in the distribution of access to fishing resources between different regions, user groups and individual fishermen" (Symes, 2000, pp.210-211). The fact that privatisation of the resource base is not going to achieve sustainability has been conveyed by Costanza, *et al,* when they observed that "western neo-classical economists, including resource and environmental economists, addressed questions of the efficient allocation of resources, leaving the initial distribution of resources among people as a given, not to be questioned. We now recognise that the initial distribution of right to resources and to the services of the environment is critically important to resource and environmental conservation and the prospects of sustainability ..." (Costanza, *et al.* 1997, p.33). Sustainability demands fair distribution of assets (wealth) and access to common pool resources or public goods to all.

Looking at the domestic context, it is necessary to note that the Government of India should not tamper with the traditional fishing rights of the indigenous fishermen while promoting greater investment and faster growth in capture and culture fisheries under private initiative. Disempowering the traditional fishermen will only aggravate the unsustainability situation.

### 7.4.2. Globalisation

Globalisation, defined as the growing integration of world economy through the process of liberalisaltion of trade and investment in goods and services and factor inputs such as labour, capital, know-how and technology is considered as a practical solution to the problem of unsustainability. It is presumed to promote production and trade from developing countries through the liberal flow of capital, know-how and technology to different sectors from the developed world. Such benefits are expected from foreign direct investments in aquaculture, deep-sea fishing and post-harvest operations. Advocates of globalisation believe that trade induced investment in developing countries by rich countries would promote sustained growth in poor countries and lead to sustainable development in the long run.

The above expectations have seldom materialised since the poor countries have inherent weaknesses constraining their development, the chief among them being their heavy dependence on natural resource (agriculture), unfavourable terms of trade, deficiency of capital, uncertainty of markets and negative externalities of trade. Referring to the first factor, Dragun noted that "a feature of the movement of some poor countries towards development and a higher quality of life over the last 50 years is that few of the success stories have been based on the development and export of natural resources or agriculture, the notable exception being in the oil sector ...

Very few poorer countries, which rely heavily on their natural resources, have been overly successful in improving their economies and quality of life for their citizens. And this pattern of specialisation seems to be endemic in the poor countries where comparative advantage, if it exists, might only be found in a substitutable natural resource" (Dragun, 1999,p.10).

Referring to the second factor, Dragun wrote "international markets have been characterised over the last several decades by reasonably consistent and strong trends against natural resource markets. That is the terms of trade for natural resource markets (against other traded goods) have consistently declined. To the extent that the areas of comparative advantage for many poorer countries in the south is in the agricultural and natural resource sectors, they may be at considerable disadvantage as the performance of their specialised markets does not live up to the initial prospect. This might have significant effects where the financing of development and infrastructure are concerned over the long run …" (ibid. pp.10-11).

With respect to the third factor, it is pointed out that "a feature of many of the new large natural resource developments in poorer countries in recent years, has been the exceptionally large scale of financial investment. Unfortunately, much of this investment is beyond the scope of many of the poor countries involved and in many cases it has been the importing countries which have been responsible for arranging the finance for the poorer countries. This has created an unavoidable dependence on behalf of the poor countries and in many cases, where the capital investment was perhaps a little 'over optimistic' it has also created a 'liability' which the poorer countries find very difficult to recover from. The situation of Mexico, Brazil and Indonesia are typical …" (ibid. p.11).

Writing on the uncertainty of markets, Dragun noted that "an issue which concerns …is that free trade, while implying greater specialisation for less diversified poor countries, also creates a dependence and uncertainty that they were previously not accustomed to. It is probably the case that many poorer countries have had complex and possibly sustainable agricultural systems. However, when such countries attempt to specialise, to be competitive, much of that sustainability and complexity can be lost yielding a very insecure and uncertain food base.

Such poorer countries subsequently become dependent on the international market system and given local 'perturbations' the new simplified food systems might fail with disastrous results. The current difficulties in the African continent might be seen to be partially a consequence of such circumstances" (ibid. p.11).

Referring to the negative externalities of trade liberalisation (globalisation) which poor countries are forced to bear, Dragun states that "as a function of the lack of quality of life, the institutional structure as well as public exposure to environmental issues, it is easier to hide externalities in poorer countries than in richer countries. It is a fact that given the high levels of corruption, lack of political and media transparency and the 'daily fight for survival' in poor countries, the environmental conservation is seen as a western luxury, which can't be afforded. In the light of the 'flight of capital' from richer to poorer countries to produce consumer goods for western citizens, it is convenient to ignore the negative environmental consequences of such an arrangement.

In fact, in some quarters such an arrangement is seen to be wholeheartedly beneficial for poorer countries, where the value of human life can be very low or negligible. Laurence Summers, a chief economist, with the World Bank in the early 1990s, actually articulated that orgnisations such as his should actively encourage the transfer of externalities from richer countries to poor countries where the monetary impact was much less ..." (ibid. pp.11-12).

Outlining the over all biological and environmental effects of trade liberalisation, Dragun noted that "a general theoretical expectation is that in the setting of the poor countries, trade liberalisation will lead to a reduction in the range of food crops produced and thus in a general loss of biodiversity. In fact the crops produced under a regime of comparative advantage may not be indigenous at all, being tailored to the needs of the competitive market (usually for wheat or corn) – this also has local implications in terms of diet and health. The co-evolutionary link in this change in biodiversity is also of relevance in complex ecosystems that may have existed in reasonable stability with humans for some considerable time. At an institutional level the needs of broad scale homogeneous agriculture calls for a rapid centralisation of land, which runs counter to the informal but complex indigenous rights relationships which might be in existence" (ibid. p.17).

Commenting on the polarisation taking place as the aftermath of trade liberalisation (globalisation) Dragun observes: "The process of international trade liberalisation and globalisation, which has begun and which is probably now irreversible, will no doubt create a wide range of benefits for many citizens of the new world of the third millennium. There are some reasons to be optimistic that certain of the processes of trade liberalisation will lead to improvements in environmental quality and the enhancement of biological diversity – in some places.

But there are grounds to believe that the processes of trade liberalisation will not be uniform and in fact there is no reason, from the theory, that this should be so, given the ecological and institutional diversity of the nations of the world ... In this setting there is a pressing need for serious analysis and policy initiative in a wide range of settings, particularly where the risk of environmental deterioration and social dislocation in the poorer countries of the world is clearly very high. Fundamentally, it could be the case that poorly conceived trade liberalisation (globalisation) certainly threatens the sustainability of many individual countries, thus rendering the purported benefits rather corrupt" (ibid. p.19; word in parentheses added).

Criticising the way in which global trade and market institutions are working, Costanza, *et al.* observed "economists have long argued that trade is good, more of it is even better, and governments should not intervene to constrain market transactions. Based on the logic of exchange, economists have provided strong justification for and generally favoured the globalisation of the world's economies through the expansion of the institution of the market ... The problem of market failure exists when these transaction costs are prohibitively high and those external parties experiencing benefits or costs from the exchange remain external and do not affect the exchange. Similarly for common institutions, it is the transaction costs of communicating and agreeing between individuals and enforcing agreements which ultimately determine whether commons institutions arise and are sustained for the management of environmental resources and the attainment of other collective goals …

… The geographic expansion of exchange increases physical distance. With greater distance, it is more difficult for people to see the consequences of their actions. Those who see the consequences are in one place, those who can do something about are in another, and the distance between them makes communicating and agreeing on a collective solution difficult.

Specialisation, which goes along with increased trade, increases social distancing by reducing shared experiences and ways of seeing the world. The parable started with a world of generalist farmers and ended with a world of academics distanced by their own disciplines, bankers with amazing international cameraderie, communications specialists who care little about the substance of their message, doctors and dentists with specialities of their own, engineers who think physics can and should be used to override ecological and sociological problems, and so on through the alphabet. Specialisation not only makes communications difficult, specialisation makes it difficult to perceive problems that defy specialities … And as trade expands, existing national and cultural borders are crossed, further compounding the difficulties" (Costanza, *et al.*, 1997, pp.164-165).

Costanza, *et al.* further note that "as trade expands, it creates new problems and challenges the communication systems of existing groups. Existing commons institutions becomes obsolete as the geographic scope of effects beyond the market that they managed expands beyond their existing boundaries. Thus, communities that have some autonomy, that are not constantly being challenged by strong external forces but rather are evolving largely through internal dynamics, are more likely to develop and sustain viable institutions to encourage individuals to transfer appropriate levels of assets. Such autonomy has not been a characteristic of the past few centuries of globalisation. Thus there is good reason to be concerned that the rise of trade and geographic expansion of economic activity has broken-down the institutions of many separate communities which facilitated asset transfer. This globalisation has also worsened the conditions for new institutions to arise as the expanding number of people who must come to terms geometrically increases the cost of coming to a new agreement.

In summary, the increased material consumption of current generations attributed to the gains from trade may well have been facilitated by the breakdown of commons, which facilitated the transfer of assets to future generations and the absence of their replacement on a larger scale. While economists' promotion of exchange and specialisation advances the markets for particular goods, it increases transaction costs and promotes the conditions for externalisation of other goods through the failure of existing commons institutions and through a net increase in the externalisation of environmental and other goods. Economics, by not using its own understanding of transaction costs more fully and acknowledging the problem of distancing, has unwittingly promoted two inextricably linked phenomena, both of which lead to more consumption in the present, but one of which results in less consumption in the future. There no doubt are gains from specialisation and expansion of the market for the particular goods traded. At the same time, both specialisation and geographic expansion increase the transaction costs for effects associated with exchange but prevented from being included in determining the exchange by the very same increased transaction costs.

... To the extent that externality resolving institutions have not expanded in scope and adjusted as fast as have trading patterns, the gains from trade are less than expected, perhaps even negative, because the economy is working less efficiently than presumed. Equally important, however, is the absence of discussions concerning intergenerational equity and institutions to facilitate transfers of assets to future generations. The term 'environmental externality' is now very much a part of the vocabulary of international discourse, though the international institutions designed to deal with externalities are far too weak. ... The concepts of intergenerational commons and the transfer of assets to future generations are not even part of trade negotiations" (ibid, pp.166-167).

Noting the impossibility of globalisation meeting the challenges of sustainability, Rees observes: "in the light of the second scientific revolution, the contemporary socio-cultural revolution seems perversely enigmatic. While the new science reveals a world of dynamic complexity and sudden surprises, the material philosophy of our globalising society assumes vapid simplicity and practical certainty. The past twenty years have witnessed the unprecedented homogenisation of the world's economic system. The most visible manifestation is the near-universal collapse of state socialism in all its historical forms and its rapid substitution by market-based economies. However, this shift represents more than the mere triumph of 'capitalism' over alternative approaches to production and consumption. It heralds an era in which simplistic economic considerations have come to over ride all other objectives in the arenas of public policy and international development: The economic ideology, the dominant intellectual framework in the world today, has reduced practically every human value to the category of economics: production and consumption, basic needs and satisfiers, human rights, scarcity, nature, energy systems, Cartesian time and space, the assumption that all things are measurable and comparable ... Virtually all major governments, corporations; and international institutions, particularly the UN, the World Bank and International Monetary Fund, the Organisation for Economic Cooperation and Development (OECD), and their offspring such as the World Trade Organisation (WTO), have made economic development their central preoccupation following the urging of US President Roosevelt and the experience of the Marshall Plan ...

Accordingly global commerce is increasingly governed by regional alliances and trade treaties aimed at increasing economic output in both rich and poor countries. Such agreements confer greater freedom and power on corporations and on international tribunals while restricting the authority of electorally accountable governments" (Rees, 1999, pp.112-113).

The fear that globalisation will produce more negative effects on poor economies has been expressed by Tisdell and Dragun. Tisdell and Dragun observed that "not only is there little evidence for the proposition that globalisation will generate positive consequences for global agriculture and environment, there is some concern that a diminishing level of research will be directed to the problem of the poor and developing countries, where the negative impacts of globalisation might be most severely realised ... With the very sustainability of humanity of concern, it is important to consider the environmental impact of globalised agriculture and the proposition that globalisation will be an international win-win game ..." (Tisdell and Dragun, 1999,p.2).

The greater possibility of globalisation of trade and investment in poor countries adding to unsustinability is indicated by Pearson when he wrote, as reported in chapter three that: "A country is unlikely to achieve sustainable development by selling its products in world markets at less than social costs or by inviting foreign investment to plunder its environment ...

... Just as trade separates production and consumption in a spatial sense, transnational externalities separate the activities that generate the externality from those individuals, groups, or countries that bear the burden ... Thus it is possible that one country, in internalising the full social cost to itself of its production or correcting for the external cost to itself of its consumption, may fail to include international interests in its calculus ... This problem is compounded because there is no environmental agency to protect the broader international interest, and international environmental law is not well developed. In this context, international trade may exacerbate unsustainable production and consumption activities by increasing total world output and consumption. It is also possible that trade (globalisation) shifts the location of production towards countries less inclined to internalise international externalities, or countries with open – access natural resource regimes and excessive exploitation levels. For example U.S. restrictions on domestic logging, mining and oil exploration and development or Japan's domestic forest conservation practices may shift resource exploitation pressure to developing countries. This would be the raw material analogue of industrial relocation to pollution havens, about which there has been much speculation. In general, however, the environmental costs of such shifts would be borne by the country of production ... When transnational pollution is present, however, one cannot rely on narrow national interest, and some control on relocating polluting activity through trade and foreign investment may be justified. Also, governments (in poor countries) are tempted toward policies that shift social costs onto future generations and under these circumstances trade and foreign investments (globalisation) can contribute to unsustainability" (Pearson, 2000, pp.482-483; words in parentheses added).

A further possibility arising from globalisation is the loss of national sovereignty for poor countries and their inability to manage their economies sustainably. As noted by Miller, "third world marine and coastal management options are constrained by fluid sovereignty. In the absence of changes to the structure of global economy, environmental regimes will have limited effectiveness, and sovereignty bargains will not enhance states' control over their environment. Third world states will continue to find that the net result of their fluid sovereignty is a diminished ability to sustainably manage their costal and marine resources" (Miller, 2000, p.252). The impact of globalisation on labour migration and the resulting social tensions both in the receiving and sending countries are critical for sustainability and needs to be studied.

The imminent threats to sustainability arising out of globalisation has been pointed out by Achim Steiner, UNEP Executive Director, when he said: "If rising living standards and efficient methods of production and consumption intensify pressure on nature's natural resources – from fish, freshwater and the atmosphere to forests and fragile lands – globalislation could become a spectacular failure rather than saviour" (Seafood Export Journal, 2007, p.15). Steiner also noted that: "Globalisation is one of the defining issues of our time. Wealth is being generated on an unprecedented scale and millions are being lifted out of poverty. But a big question mark hangs over its future and its sustainability for current and future generations" (ibid. p.15).

In the light of the above authentic observations by reputed scholars, the approach to globalisation for sustainable development of fisheries in India needs to be cautious and tempered by a precautionary approach to fisheries management.

### 7.4.3. Public-Private Partnership

Yet another institutional solution suggested for the sustainable development of fisheries world wide, by the neo-liberal school, and considered suitable for application in the Indian context as well is the introduction of public-private partnership in the management and development of fisheries sector. Public-private partnership is considered to be an alternative to both the top-down type of centrally planned (controlled) public sector dominated management (development) of the sector as practiced in the hither to socialist/communist economies and the bottom-up decentralised planning as practiced in liberal democracies of the west. It is expected to combine the benefits of public sector control where it is necessary and private sector initiative where it is lacking.

Public-private partnerships is considered more useful where the state cannot independently raise the required resources for the development of the industry or when it cannot implement the various regulatory measures in isolation without the cooperation or participation of the private sector players. In view of the failure of the state in regulating the industry in the past especially in the open access marine fisheries sector and the need for ensuring private sector participation for the development of the inland fisheries sector, a policy favouring public-private partnership is now advocated worldwide by FAO and other agencies like the World Bank

It is, however, significant to note here that the advocates of public-private partnership have the ultimate aim of promoting privatisation and globalisation of trade and investment in the sector. It is feared that the argument for public-private partnership is largely a strategic move to get entry into state/public sector dominated economies as a starting point or as a foothold, and then to penetrate and finally to dominate the sector by dictating its own terms to the weak governments of the 'banana' republics or 'puppet' democracies of the southern hemisphere.

The above argument may sound realistic especially where the state (public sector) is exercising strong control over all matters relating to planning and development of the industry both at the national and the regional (state) level as in India and the private sector is only a silent (weak) partner in policy making. Moreover the entry of global capital needs a dominant cooperating private sector and to accomplish that objective the promotion of public-private partnership as a policy measure is a strategic move on the part of global business interests. When sustainability demands protection of the common (community) property rights of the fishermen and the maintenance of intra-generational and intergenerational equity, the adoption of public-private partnership as a hidden agenda for privatisation and globalistion should be viewed more cautiously. Failure to do so will only help in sabotaging the goal of sustainability, with the state (public sector) becoming a mere spectator of the private sector extracting rent/profit from the community of producers and consumers of fish. Considering this possibility it is best to proceed on a precautionary basis, even if it means inaction on the part of the state on this account. It is worth noting here that the partnership idea is part of the global intrusive diplomacy followed by imperialist powers to circumvent the developing country aspirations as exemplified in the India-US Nuclear agreements and the intimidating postures taken by the US on the Indo-Iranian oil dealings (The Hindu 6.5.2007).

### 7.4.4. Co-management

Co-management or collaborative management defined as "the sharing of power and responsibility between the government and local resource users" is another institutional solution suggested for reversing the unsustainability situation prevailing in global fisheries and sought for application in the Indian context as well. Co-management is sought where a maximum of people's participation is essential for the success of the management programme.

Highlighting the need for public participation in ICZM planning, Clark observed that "in most countries a priority goal of coastal management should be to arrange for the most extensive participation possible ...; consultations should be held with all relevant agencies of central and local government, with developers, with resource users and other interests that would be affected by ICZM (fishermen, farmers, etc.), environmental advocacy groups and investment sources (including international donor institutions).

Coastal areas and costal resource systems are governmentally complex because of the degree of shared jurisdiction and the amount of common property resources involved. Therefore resource management programmes need to involve all levels from national to village governments regardless of the particular institutional arrangement at the central level" (Clark, 1996, p.170).

Participation of the people is considered valuable for several reasons. Quoting Renard, Clark lists them into four, as follows:

1. Participation is a way to ensure that popular knowledge and experience is indeed integrated into the planning and management process.

2. Participation gives a better guarantee for the quality of the solution identified and for adaptation to a particular condition.

3. Participation in planning and problem identification promotes involvement in the actual implementation of decisions.
4. Participation ensures that all needs and priorities are taken into account in the formulation of management decisions (ibid. p.171).

Stressing the need for community participation for the success of ICZM programmes, Hildebrand noted that "community-based coastal management represents a new form of partnership between government and community-based organisations. In essence, it is about 'power-sharing' in the integrated planning and management of coastal zones. There is growing evidence of the desire, if not demand by local stakeholders to be more actually and meaningfully involved in what have been traditionally, government decisions. Traditional forms of 'public consultation' are no longer adequate. Yet there is still debate over the degree of public involvement that is desirable and feasible" (Hildebrand, 1997, pp.1-2).

Hildebrand also emphasised that "genuine participation is only achieved when power is shared. This means that citizens, through community organistions, are making planning decisions with government that have meaningful consequences. Involvement in implementation and subsequent running of the management programme can give resource users and local stakeholders real power, if they play a central role in decision- making about management actions" (ibid, p.2).

Emphasising the need for people's participation in the ICZM context, Clark further noted that "ICZM programmes require high levels of participation. Most likely, people who live along the coast and have traditionally used coastal resources will be greatly affected by any new rules and procedures. Therefore, if they are to support the programme, they must have a voice in the formation of coastal policies and rules on resource use. Broad participation will also provide an opportunity to resolve conflicting points of view among various stakeholders so that later the ICZM programmes will meet lesser political resistance" (Clark, 1996, p.47).

Clark also pointed out that "the stakeholders should be encouraged to go beyond dialogue and to participate to the maximum possible in goal setting, data collection, conflict identification and so forth. The decision-making and implementation process must be shared with the people and their organisers, requiring efficient communication and effective dialogue through participatory planning" (ibid, p.47).

Quoting other sources, Clark further reported that "public participation is a tool available to the entire management community (resource users, public agencies, non-governmental organisations, etc.) to ensure the quality and effectiveness of the management solutions that will be implemented. Participation is also a duty because the issue remains above all, one of human development and because people are not the object of that development, but the subject of development and the makers of their own destiny" (ibid. p.47).

Referring to the concept of co-management, Charles observes that "the essential idea of co-management is the sharing of decision-making and management functions between government and stakeholders in the fishery. More formally, co-management can be defined as the creation and implementation of suitable management arrangements through which a set of agreed stakeholders, i.e., fishers and their organisations, work jointly with government to develop and enforce fishery regulations and management measures" (Charles, 2001, p.265).

The two underlying motivations for co-management initiatives noted by Charles are: "First, there is the desire to reduce conflict between stakeholders (particularly fishery users) and government, as well as between stakeholders themselves. By clearly defining rights and responsibilities, by providing an institutional forum for discussion among the decision makers, and by ensuring that the management simultaneously serves the public interest and operates inclusively, co-management can encourage fishers to support the process and provide a vehicle to help in resolving conflicts.

Second, and closely related to the first, is the need in the fishery for a conservation ethic, i.e., a fundamental conservation perspective within the 'belief-system of fishery participants. The manner by which the management system is structured, and who is able to participate, can affect the presence or absence of this conservation ethic among fishers since, for fishers to want to conserve the fish, they must 'buy into' management. A co-management approach is a means to accomplish this, bringing fishers and others into the decision-making process, and at the same time ensuring that they share responsibility with government for sustainability in the fishery" (ibid. p.266).

The success of co-management institutions is, however, believed to depend upon several factors, the chief among them being the small number of resource users and the relatively small and clearly defined area. As Nadia presents it,"local management will have all the more chance of success when the area devolved or under co-management is relatively small and clearly defined, with a relatively small number of resource users and where rights of ownership or use are exclusive" (Nadia, 1998, p.45).

The fishery sector of India being so large and with multiple use conflicts prevailing in the coast, the scope for introducing co-management as an institutional solution for achieving sustainability seems to be limited. Moreover, as noted by Nadia, "local managers require a constant flow of information on which they can base their management decisions and, frequently, they require support in the form of enforcement by government, especially to stop encroachment by 'outsiders'. In most situations, the institutions responsible for implementation of management require considerable training and technical support. For these reasons, the recognition of the role of line ministries by resource users is important, especially as certain vital functions can be fulfilled only by the public sector ..." (ibid. p.45). This further justifies the need for establishing an exclusive ministry for fisheries and strengthening the central planning machinery as noted earlier in this chapter.

### 7.4.5. Capacity Building

With the growing emphasis on globalisation, it is now very fashionable to talk of 'capacity building' as a prerequisite for the success of all policy measures. This is applicable in the context of sustainable development planning as well. Referring to the need for capacity building in the context of ICZM, Chua noted that "professional and technical support staff of organisations must be given appropriate formal education and training in CAM, dealing with issues and problems, and developing effective strategies among others. Their capacity must be further enhanced based on knowledge of the coastal resources and the environmental, social and cultural and economic systems; and understanding of present and future solutions through an integrated management approach" (Chua, 1991, p.83). The need for capacity building (human and institutional capacity) has been identified in Agenda 21 of the UNCED, as well as by a number of international institutions, as essential for integrated coastal management and sustainable development in developing coastal nations (Korakandy, 2005, p.431).

The declaration of Agenda 21 of the UNCED 1992 made the need for capacity building for sustainable development of fisheries explicit. Item 17.95 of the Agenda noted that "coastal states, with the support of relevant sub-regional, regional and global agencies, where appropriate should: (a) develop research capacities for assessment of marine living resource populations and monitoring; (b) provide support to local fishing communities, in particular those that rely on fishing for subsistence, indigenous people and women, including, as appropriate, the technical and financial assistance to organise, maintain, exchange and improve traditional knowledge of marine living resources and fishing techniques, and upgrade knowledge on marine ecosystems; (c) establish sustainable aquaculture developing strategies, including environmental management in support of rural fish farming communities; (d) develop and strengthen, where the need may arise, institutions capable of implementing the objectives and activities related to the conservation and management of marine living resources" (UN, as quoted by Caddy and Griffiths, 1995, p.166). Item 17.96 states that "special support, including cooperation among states, will be needed to enhance the capacities of developing countries in the areas of data and information, scientific and technological means and human resource development in order to enable them to participate effectively in the conservation and sustainable use of marine living resources under national jurisdiction" (ibid. p.166).

The Cancun declaration of 1992 as well as the FAO code of conduct for responsible fisheries adopted by the UN in 1995 had recognised the importance of the capacity building exercise for sustainable development of fisheries.

Loucks, *et al.* note that "sustainable system design and operation strongly depends on the capacity building infrastructure available in the region where it is located. Knowledgeable, well-trained and motivated individuals are the backbone of sustainable development. The people who can best manage a system effectively and efficiently are those who know what a system is supposed to accomplish and understand how it functions ... 'Capacity building' is one of the most essential and important long-term conditions for sustainable development" (Loucks, *et al.* 1999, p.22).

The global position in this regard has been summarised by Crawford, *et al.* thus: "The UNCED Earth Summit identified coastal management as a priority issue for the near future. Meeting this demand will require significant emphasis to be placed on institutional strengthening and human resource development. Coastal management already has become a priority for many low-income nations, where planning and implementation effort are under way. Even modest estimates for the demand for individuals and organisations indicate that a large investment in capacity building is required to meet the objectives of Agenda 21" (Crawford, *et al.* 1993, p.333).

Referring to the capacity building exercise, Sicin-Sain and Knecht noted the need for four types of capacity which included:

(*a*) Legal and administrative capacity - to designate a coastal zone, to develop and carry out coastal plans, to regulate development in vulnerable zones, and to designate areas of particular concern.

(*b*) Financial capacity – adequate financial resources to carry out the planning and implementation of coastal management efforts.

(*c*) Technical capacity – information gathering and monitoring of coastal marine ecosystems and processes, patterns of human use, and the effectiveness of government coastal management programmes, establishment and maintenance or coastal data base and information system.

(*d*) Human resource capacity – personnel with interdisciplinary training in social sciences (including law and planning), natural and physical sciences and engineering. Also public awareness and understanding of the coastal ocean development and the problems and opportunities it offers (Cicin-Sain and Knecht, 1998, pp.60-61).

Nadia reported that "the institutions contributing to ICAM should have the collective capacity to allocate resources according to the goals and strategic approach adopted. The engine to drive the process includes well-trained and experienced staff. The capacity to manage the processes can be developed as part of the strategy. Not all individual participating organisations will - or should be able to-satisfy this requirement, but it is important that the system as a whole is able to deliver the following services: (a) an equitable and efficient decision-making process; (b) use of best available knowledge about how the relevant ecosystem functions, (c) participation of resource users, and all those affected by management decisions, in the decision- making process; (d) capacity to resolve differences of interests; (e) ability to employ economic policy instruments strategically; (f) integrated, simple and effective regulatory instruments, (g) public investment for the protection of coastal ecosystems and management of renewable resources" (Nadia, 1998, pp.48-50).

Nadia also made it explicit that "because coastal problems involve a range of actors and a multiplicity of complex interrelated issues, an institutional capacity to resolve conflicts and institutional supervision will be required to manage the participation and relationships of interested parties and the different interests represented, as well as to identify suitable options and agree on objectives and means to attain them. Depending on local circumstances (traditional practices and principles), consideration should also be given to establishing funding mechanisms for conflict resolution ( in order to cover the costs of appointing mediators or experts, or simply of running negotiations) and providing training and education for third parties to mediate, facilitate or arbitrate in disputes. Administrative procedures and dispute resolution offices or commissions might also be established to anticipate and resolve conflicts arising within and between institutions" (ibid. pp, 50-51).

It is worth noting here that much of the institutional issues and practical problems associated with ICAM noted above are applicable to the context of sustainable development planning as well. The dearth of institutional capacity, especially legal institutions for achieving sustainability at the international level has been pointed out by Sands. Sands noted that "the application of 'sustainable development' itself raises broader issues … There is clearly a need for greater policy coordination on the approach which international bodies should take to this question, as indicated by the current debate on whether, and if so to what extent, commercial growing of genetically modified seeds should be permitted. The differences of approach - even between Europe and the United States - suggest that there may not be room for a single approach, that risk taking and risk assessment must be determined in the specific cultural and social context in which they are being applied. To that extent, 'globalisation' remains something of a misnomer. This, of course raises the related question concerning the proper level for decision making in the areas of economic and environmental relations.: is it to be sub-national, national, regional or global or a combination of these different levels? This issue is not peculiar to international law making and development, but applies equally within single states (the United States) and economic agglomerations of states (the European Union). However, it is clear that much greater thought will have to be given to the appropriateness of different levels of decision-making in the fields of environment and sustainable development, and the factors, which should be taken into account in determining the right level. This in turn raises issues about the current arrangement for international legislative efforts in this field, and the need to avoid duplicative or even incompatible or inconsistent efforts at law development.

Over arching each of these issues is an even bigger question, and one which is central to the law of sustainable development; how are the different areas of intetrnational law (trade, human rights, environment, and so on) to intersect and inter relate?...the technique of international law designed to achieve an integrated approach are rudimentary, to say the least. The prospects for a more integrated approach are scarcely assisted by the fragmentary and disunited arrangements the international community has put in place to ensure compliance and resolve disputes.

Each of these matters suggests that the law of sustainable development is still finding its feet. The international community, such as it exists, has at its disposal a system of international law which can hardly be expected, at this time at least, to master the complex societal, technical, and cultural matters which will have to be balanced in the quest to attain 'sustainable development'. The fact that they are now being addressed holistically for the first time as a result of the emergence of 'sustainable development' indicates the contribution the term might make to the development of international law. But it has to be recognised that these are still early days, and we cannot expect too much from a legal system and its institutional structure which remains basic, certainly as compared to arrangements within certain - but by no means all – national jurisdictions" (Sands, 2000, pp.408-409).

The fallacy of the appeal for capacity building by the liberal school for sustainable development is obliquely conveyed by Gilpin when he observed that "despite enormous material progress ... the world at the social level remains substantially tribal and barbaric. Certainly, democratic forms of government have made substantial progress while a variety of dictatorships have collapsed. Society remains, however, relatively primitive; it is the area of least progress. Progress seems at times to come by chance, or through the actions of a small number of heroic people. People seem to find it easier to hate than to love, particularly in respect of people who look or sound different ..." (Gilpin, 2000, p.97).

The state of society being such as it is, there is added reason for capacity building for sustainable development of fisheries in India. This is especially important for the country where the Directive Principles of State Policy (Article 48-a) prescribe that the "state shall endeavour to protect and improve the natural environment and safeguard the forest and wild life in the country" (Government of India, 1999, p.19). Article 51A(g) of the Constitution of India also provides that "it shall be the duty of every citizen of India to protect and improve the natural environment including forests, lakes, rivers and wildlife and to have compassion for living creatures" (ibid. p.19). Thus a holistic approach to development and sustainability is implicit in the Constitution and it is explicit that the country develop its capacity for sustainable use of its natural resources including fish stock. There is, however, a pinch of salt in the prescription when the capacity building exercise is directed exclusively to promote marketisation of the traditional subsistence sectors of the economy like fisheries and the proposal is synchronised with the suggestion for privatisation of the 'commons' by conferring of property rights as a requirement for sustainability. The granting of tradeable permits for fishing will certainly land the ownership of domestic fisheries in the hands of international fishing cartels which will be against the tenets of sustainable development which requires bequeathing the assets (natural capital) to future generations to meet their own needs. This in other words means creating conditions leading to the failure to meet the intergenerational equity criterion of sustainability. Sustainable development of fisheries in India needs to protect the rights of the traditional stake holders, and all capacity building exercise should be directed to that end. It is advisable for fisheries governance system in India to heed to this caution.

### 7.4.6. Use of Traditional Knowledge

Another institutional solution suggested for achieving sustainability in Indian fisheries is to make use of indigenous traditional knowledge systems for managing the fisheries. This suggestion is significant in the context of globalisation where homogenisation of management techniques is not producing the expected results. Outlining the need for drawing on traditional knowledge, the FAO observed that "one solution to the constraints imposed by the diffuse nature of the resource is to use local and traditional knowledge. Most rivers, reservoirs and lakes are fished and fishers are well aware of the general biology of the fish species involved, their breeding seasons, migration patterns, responses to fishing methods, etc. Equally, traditional systems have been developed in many parts of the world for management of fisheries, integrating local experience and needs of various participant groups. Unfortunately, the pace of change over the past decades has destroyed many of the traditional management and knowledge systems. Efforts are needed to study and document surviving local management systems and knowledge bases so that they can be improved, adapted and applied to the changing conditions ..." (FAO, 1997 c, pp.8-9).

Article 17.75 (b) of Chapter 17 of Agenda 21 of the UNCED 1992, prescribes that states should "take into account traditional knowledge and interests of local communities, small-scale artisanal fisheries and indigenous people in development and management programmes" (Caddy and Griffiths, 1995, p.162).

The relevance of indigenous knowledge has been pointed out by Nadia as well. Nadia noted that "in the past, resources were always community-managed. It is therefore not surprising that community-based resource management still tends to succeed today, when properly set up.

When devolving management responsibility on local communities, it is always advisable to draw on indigenous knowledge and resource management practices. In some cases, it may be necessary to adopt enabling legislation. Similarly, assistance may be needed for communities to develop managerial and organisational skills adapted to current conditions" (Nadia, 1998, p.47).

Pitcher and Pauly also emphasised the value of traditional environmental knowledge. They pointed out "that historical records and indigenous knowledge can help tune the rebuilding models and define management objectives. The value of historical records of abundance and species composition is high ... If we look at the management goals of indigenous and aboriginal peoples, we see that a goal related directly to primal abundance strikes an immediate chord ... Moreover, traditional environmental knowledge (TEK) can, through the cultural shadow cast by past abundances, help with the construction, tuning and validation of our scientific models of natural ecosystems" (Pitcher and Pauly, 1998, pp.320-321).

The importance of local knowledge for transforming the local economy on the sustainable path has been recognised by Jenkins. Jenkins observed that "by making the best use of local resources such as people and local knowledge, endogenous development is often thought likely to create more employment than modernist development forms. ... and to result in positive approaches to environmental conservation and the quality of products, in the efficiency of resource use, and in the retention of value generated locally" (Jenkins, 1998, p.503).

Charles outlines the challenges of using TEK thus: "while it is important to acknowledge the existence of TEK and related fishermen's knowledge, perhaps the key challenge lies in integrating this knowledge with modern fishery science and management, which have developed largely without recognition that fishers and others hold valuable ecological and resource management knowledge ...

Given this potential to improve the performance of fishery management, and at the same time to improve the interaction between fishers and communities on the one hand, and scientists and managers on the other, increasing attention can be anticipated (and indeed is urged) to the many strong bases of local knowledge (whether it is considered 'traditional', 'indigenous' or simply 'fisherman's' knowledge) that are now understood to exist around the world. Obviously, such efforts do not guarantee successful management in the future, but at the same time, to neglect any available sources of knowledge is to court disaster" (Charles, 2003, pp.330,332).

The prevalence of a rich tradition of ecological knowledge of fishermen in India had been reported by many including Kurien (1998), Korakandy (2000), and Ramachandran (2004). The practical value and applicability of this knowledge system (*the pedagogy of the oppressed*) in the changed socio-cultural and techno-economic context of the country at present is however, suspected. As noted by this author elsewhere, "the indigenous systems which are sought to be resurrected have lost their existence value in the changed scenario of exploding population and depleted alternatives" (Korakandy, 2002, p.27). It is however, worth trying to protect this knowledge system giving it institutional status and making it mandatory for conservation of the stock and preventing conflict in the industry. But there is a lurking danger and limitation in it. As noted by Sarkar, "many eco alternative activists and theorists romanticise traditional cultures. Many of them also romanticise what they call traditional, vernacular, or people's knowledge systems ...such experience and knowledge is limited to their own lives and immediate surroundings. With such knowledge and experience we cannot tackle today's problems. They can be useful only in certain circumstances and only to complement modern knowledge ... In the eco alternative movement, one often finds a romanticisation of nature alongside a romanticisation of traditional and indigenous cultures and knowledge systems ..." (Sarkar, 1999, p.57-58).

### 7.5. Technological Solutions

Technological solutions involve the introduction of new technology as a neo-classical solution for sustainability. They refer to the use of new production procedures or processes which minimise the need for scarce inputs or maximise the output by using the same inputs. In the former case, the factor-factor ratios are changed while in the latter, the factor-product ratios are altered. In both cases the production function changes and the overall input requirements are altered. By minimising the use of scarce inputs, the sustainability constraint is overcome. Hence technological changes which help in increasing or maintaining the output at steady levels by substituting scarce inputs by abundant inputs or by changing the processes are considered as a viable solution for achieving sustainability.

In the real context of fisheries management, it may involve the adoption of improved or modified gears, which enhance the output while reducing the fishing effort or the use selective gears which help in avoiding the by-catch and juveniles and hence in protecting the stock and conserving the biodiversity of the ecosystem. In the former case, it seeks to achieve economic sustainability while in the latter, ecological sustainability is the goal. The use of TED, BED, etc. and the ban on trawl or other environmentally hazardous gear/devices may also be prescribed as technological solutions for unsustainable fishing operations.

An assortment of measures, some of which are not technological, followed worldwide to achieve sustainability, have been listed by Garcia and Moreno. They note that several technical measures have been tested, including: (1) modified gear design or introduction of selective grids, panels and square meshes to reduce by-catch and discards; (2) bans on discards; (3) flexible exclusion zones to protect juveniles; (4) limits on the authorisations to fish; (5) reduction or suppression of subsidies; (6) attempts to deal with fisheries within coastal area management plans; (7) reserved areas for small-scale fisheries; and (8) artificial reefs as enhancement and anti-trawl devices (Garcia and Moreno, 2003, p.15). These writers also point out that "in general, in the absence of improved systems of user rights, these measures have been ineffective in the long run. Zoning, including through marine protected areas (MPAs), has been used conventionally, for example, to protect biodiversity and to keep trawlers away from vulnerable coastal habitats and small scale fisheries. In general, zoning, alone, will not be effective in a context of over-capacity. MPAs have become fashionable, particularly as a biodiversity conservation device, and if properly enforced, may be more effective, particularly if fishing capacity could be controlled or reduced. Control and surveillance has been improved with the use of on-board observers and the development of electronic (satellite-based) VMS" (ibid. p.15).

Apart from the above, the country may also explore methods to improve the aquaculture production systems to enhance output/ productivity and to minimise damage to the natural environment and to achieve social harmony. It may also seek measures to improve the quality of marine products exported from the country and to adhere to the quality norms prescribed by importing countries. Adherence to good management practices (GMP), safe minimum standards (SMS), HACCP, eco-labelling, traceability, sanitary and phyto-sanitary (SPS) regulations, etc. are also suggested by the international trade lobby. Technological solutions with suitable infrastructure and institutional support have been proposed by the NCAP (NCAP, 2004, pp.118-119).

It is, however, worth noting here that the technological solutions sought are not going to bring permanent solutions to the basic sustainability issues since the substitution possibilities are limited and the new technology adopted will be costly and producing additional externalities which will be ultimately affecting the natural and the social environment, nullifying their long-term compatibility. As noted by Sarkar "one very popular illusion is that further development of science and technology and more intensive use of both would enable humanity to overcome the ecological crisis, save industrial society and enable the South accomplish sustainable development. Indeed, there is a lot of talk of a technological and/or efficiency revolution. Another popular illusion is that some economic innovations like pollution certificates, ecological tax reform, and so on, would make the transformation of present day capitalism into ecological capitalism possible ..." (Sarkar, 1999, p.3). Ecological capitalism is apparently a transformed version of capitalism ridden of ecological ills by adopting the ecological solutions prescribed by the neo-classical liberal school of ecological economists. Technological solutions are only part of the neo-classical strategy for sustaining the free market economy of capitalism. It is prudent to be conscious of the liberal agenda of technology transfer and the impending dangers to the natural environment arising from privatisation and globalisation.

## 7.6. Rethinking on Sustainable Development

There is a lingering doubt about the viability of many of the solutions prescribed above for achieving sustainability. Many of the solutions prescribed have originated from the neo-classical economic thinking, which finds the genesis of the crisis of un- sustainability in market failure, institutional failure, governance failure, etc. all of which prompted it to recommend corresponding solutions which are quite simple, but of doubtful value. Moreover, the neo-classical thinking has its own inherent limitation in so far as it believes in infinite resource substitution possibilities ('weak sustainability' hypothesis) and considers unsustainability only as a short run problem. It holds that the natural resource constraint can be overcome by the substitution by man-made capital and through technological changes and market/institutional corrections. The neo-classical theorising has also failed to take note of the over- population problem as a constraint for sustainability since it was extraneous to the model postulated by it. So also, believing in the freedom of the consumers, it did not find any need to check consumerism for achieving long-term sustainability. It is indeed the consumerism promoted by democracy and free market economy promoted by capitalism that breeds unsustainability. The neo-liberal economics, however, ignores this or fails to recognise it.

It is not surprising then that the unsustainability issue remains as crucial as before and even more pressing now looking for urgent solutions. But interestingly and not surprisingly, it is also noted here that the very same concept of sustainable development has been questioned and ridiculed by many western writers. O'Riordan, writing on the 'real politics of sustainability' observes that "sustainability appears to be accepted as the mediating term designed to bridge the gulf between 'developers' and 'envrironmentalists'. Its beguiling simplicity and apparently self-evident meaning have obscured its inherent ambiguity. Its survival attests to the fact that the developmental interests now recognise that much more serious attention must be paid to incorporating a thorough understanding of environmental processes into project investment calculus, if for no other reason that failure to do so may result in environmental side effects that carry economic losses. But the perseverance of the concept goes far beyond that. Developers now realise that under the guise of sustainability almost any environmentally sensitive programme can be justified. They thereby seek to exploit the very ambiguities that give sustainability its staying power. Similarly, environmentalists abuse sustainability by demanding safeguards and compensatory investments that are not always economically efficient or socially just. It may only be a matter of time before the metaphor of sustainability becomes so abused as to be meaningless, certainly as a device to straddle the ideological conflicts that pervade contemporary environmentalism. Once the notions that underline sustainability are politicised, the concept is effectively devalued ... Sustainability, on the other hand, is politically treacherous since it challenges the status quo ... One can only be cautious about an effective future role for the concept of sustainability. It is probably going to languish as a 'good idea' which cannot sensibly be put into practice - like 'democracy' and 'accountability'. Its advantage is that it establishes a useful moral position, which can be exploited by reformists. Its disadvantage is that it can be manipulated into tinkering adjustments to the status quo by established interests which, in order to retain respectability, have to make certain relatively minor concessions. The real threat is that the concept becomes widely misunderstood, it is confined to the flow rates of depletion and replenishment, it remains essentially regarded as a scientific and managerial device, and it has no role either in institutional reform, mobilisation of new power relationships, or in the extension of a more pragmatic eco-morality" (O'Riordan, 1991, pp.29-30, 48-49).

Symes, probing the future for fisheries dependent regions of Europe, notes that "the sustainable development paradigm has become the modern template for development policy. With the adoption of the Treaty of Amsterdam, sustainable development becomes an explicit objective of the European Union (EU). The problem is, however, that there is no single uncontested interpretation of sustainable development beyond the notion that it some how links resource use, economic growth, social and cultural development and environmental sustainability in a holistic manner. As Redclift suggests, sustainable development may be concerned with 'meeting human needs, or maintaining economic growth, or conserving natural capital, or about all three'. Something of this uncertainty of meaning is apparent in the infiltration of sustainable development rhetoric into the revised objectives of the Common Fisheries Policy (CFP)"(Symes, 2000, p.209).

Emphasising the vagueness of the concept and quoting other sources, Symes further reports that, "not surprisingly, in view of its elasticity of meaning, sustainable development proves difficult to substantialise ... the concept is now widely used to legitimate, uphold and promote a wide variety of different agendas and activities .... many analysts have come to regard it as *an insubstantial and clichéd platitude unworthy of further interest* ... Certainly its very ambiguity, allied to its apparent high moral tone, has enhanced its political appeal and tended to convert it into a 'flag of convenience' ..." (ibid. p.209, emphasis added).

Pearson considers the concept of sustainable development as 'fashionable' and at one level a 'clever term' (Pearson, 2000, p.461).

Loucks, *et al.*, however, think that "when the history of natural resource management during the last quarter of the 20th century is written, sustainability may well prove to be the major unifying concept that was advanced, discussed, promoted and accepted, even at the highest levels of government through out most of the world. This is rather amazing, given the fact that as yet there is no consensus on its precise meaning or even how to measure it ..." (Loucks, *et al.* 1999, p.6).

Gilpin remarks a bit sarcastically, "sustainability, like apple pie and motherhood, is everyone's favourite. Business people are very keen on sustainable profits, sustainable growth, and sustainable investments; academics may search for sustainable arguments; designers may seek sustainable performances. In the end sustainability simply means keeping things going for a long period of time, perhaps indefinitely" (Gilpin, 2000, p.111).

Arancibia thinks that "the term, is in fact, so vague that it has been used not only by advocates of precaution to refer to the environmental sustainability of economic activity but also by advocates of growth to refer to the sustainability of economic expansion ... Because of misunderstandings there is a tendency in official gatherings and agency programmes to focus upon areas of consensus and very specific missions ... Issues of controversies are swept aside, and the operating principle is that continued economic growth and new technology will solve problems of poverty and environment for all peoples" (Arancibia, 1999, pp. 83-84).

Arancibia further observes that "the term, is in fact so vague that it has been used not only by advocates of precaution to refer to the environmental sustainability of economic activity but also by advocates of growth to, refer to the sustainability of economic expansion" (Arancibia, 1999, p.83). Achterberg considers it a 'protean' term (Achterberg, 1999, p.128).

Some writers have also expressed fears about the tendency to narrow down the broad objectives of sustainability or sustainable development to specific individual goals of quality assurance or market access which are no doubt goals but remain far from the core issues of sustainability, like conservation of natural capital, population stabilisation, technology transfer, efficient use of natural resources, waste reduction, prevention of conflict, protection of social and cultural values, etc. (ibid, p.85).

Cicin-Sain and Knecht noted that "lately, however, we have observed a disquieting trend – the beginning of a tendency to undo the careful job of aggregation done in chapter 17 of Agenda 21 – to disaggregate the integrated framework into discrete areas of biodiversity, land-based sources, and so forth. This has been evident both among governments and among some NGOs. These tendencies need to be held in check; the integrated vision of Chapter 17 and of the preamble of the Law of the Sea Convention must be retained – otherwise, we are back to the beginning" (Cicin-Sain and Knecht, 1996, p.302).

The emerging conclusion from these observations is that sustainable development is an 'oxymoron' concept (Rees, 1997), which can be conveniently used by vested interests to promote narrow national, regional, local or parochial interests, sacrificing its unifying or integrating mission. The fact remains to be that in the globalised market economy which is fast getting privatised under liberal public (government) protection, world-wide, the concept of sustainable development is a mere hogwash for the academics to consume and to propagate.

The latest proof of disbelief in the concept has come from the recently held annual meeting of the UN Commission on Sustainable Development, where developed and developing nations accused each other of not fulfilling their commitments to promote sustainable development. Brundtland, who attended the meting noted that the mission has failed due to 'deep-rooted lack of trust' between developed and developing countries (The New Indian Express, 11.5.2007).

### 7.6.1. Weakness of the 'Weak Sustainability' Hypothesis

The major weakness of the sustainable development thinking is its adherence to the neo-classical 'weak sustainability' hypothesis which believes in the infinite substitution possibility of 'man-made' capital for 'natural' capital and the resulting devaluation of the importance of natural capital (resources) for future production and their transfer to future generations for meeting the future needs. The blind faith in the infinite substitution possibility has emboldened Nobel Laurette economist, Robert Solow to pronounce that "... the world can, in effect, get along without natural resources" (as quoted by Daly, 2005, p.493).

In spite of this assertion by the neo-classical school, the fact remains to be one of importing sustainability by engaging in natural resource imports from poor countries or 'outsourcing' production in third world countries which are considered as 'pollution havens'.

As reported by Pearce, *et al.*, "it is perfectly possible for a single nation to secure a sustainable development path, but at the cost of non-sustainability in another country. Thus many countries, including the UK, rely on imports of natural resources from developing countries. It is a distinctive feature of their international 'footprint'. This latter group frequently contains countries which do not have any other ('value added', semi-processed or fully-processed manufactured goods) alternative products to sell in international markets. The danger is that these 'primary commodity' exporting countries will maximise, over the short run, the revenue available from the exploitation of forests or other natural resources. In doing so they run the risk of reducing the stock available in the future - unsustainable development. The widespread concern in Europe about the use of imported tropical hardwoods is a good example of possible 'imported sustainability' at the expense of non-sustainability in other nations. Some analysts have also expressed concern that trade policy could be used as a mechanism to import sustainability by setting high environmental standards at home and importing cheap products from 'pollution havens' abroad ..." (Pearce, *et al.* 1993, Reprint 1996, p.24).

The weakness of the 'weak sustainability' hypothesis upheld by the neo-classical school is not confined to its promotion of wanton exploitation of natural resources from third-world countries based on the comparative advantage principle, but it also extends to its blind faith in technological solutions for natural resource constraints and its plea for improvements in efficiency (productivity). The limitations of the technological solutions for sustainability have been effectively conveyed by Daly, and reported in chapter three. The 'weak sustainability' hypotheses is also notorious for its neglect of the complementary character of natural capital and its disbelief of the need for transfer of assets (natural capital) to future generations for meeting the ' intergenerational' equity criterion of sustainable development. This disbelief has emboldened Gilpin to assert that "if the past is any guide, future generations will be substantially better off than those living at present. The future will inherit the present with all its progress in electronics and advanced technologies. To hand over a planet in fairly good trim is all that is morally required from the present.

Intergenerational equity remains a noble concept which cannot be translated into useful and practical policies other than the pursuit of responsible management of resources to serve the interest of current generations. There is every reason to believe that problems with population growth, forestry, fisheries, biodiversity, global warming, the ozone layer and world food supplies, will be resolved, while material progress continues to surge forward through out many parts of the world. There is no evidence to the contrary" (Gilpin, 2000, pp.98, 101). This author, further, argues that "the present owes the future nothing. First, the needs of future generations cannot be predicted. Secondly, the future automatically inherits the scientific and technical achievements of the present. What we achieve now adds to the inheritance of future generations. They need nothing more" (ibid. p.111).

It is apparent that the believers in 'weak sustainability' hypothesis are promoting the culture of 'business as usual' (BAU) or reckless pursuit of economic growth and consumerism with scant regard for sustainability, as presently understood.

Pearce and Turner question the neo-classical view of substitution of 'natural capital' by manufactured (man-made) capital for the following reasons: (1) manufactured capital is not independent of natural capital. The latter is often needed to make the former, (2) natural capital fulfils other economic functions, including basic life support; it is multifunctional to an extent not shared by manufactured capital, (3) because of the above, it is not always possible to substitute manufactured capital (as quoted by Victor, 1997, p.427). These authors also question the faith in new technology saying that "new technology is not necessarily less polluting" and it is unlikely that a backstop technology will always emerge as an "indefinitely renewable resource which eventually takes over when exhaustible resources have gone" (ibid. p.428). It is advisable that planners in India understand this message while planning for natural resource exploitation.

### 7.6.2. Strong Sustainability Needed

Strong sustainability holds that there is very little possibility of substitution of natural capital by man-made capital and its stock should be kept steady or increasing for serving the essential function of the life-support system and for meetings the needs of the future generations. It rejects the neo-classical logic of 'weak sustainability', which permits depletion of natural capital and its substitution by man-made capital. 'Strong sustainability' principle assumes that natural capital and man-made capital are complements rather than substitutes and there are limits to their substitution possibility. This being the case, maintaining or increasing the stock of natural capital is vital for sustaining the economic system.

Some authors have also cited other reasons for favouring strong sustainability. As noted by Pearce, *et al.* "(1) there is excessive *uncertainty* about the way in which natural capital stock work. We do not understand the full workings of ecological systems. Uncertainty is always a reason for being cautious, unless society can be deemed to be indifferent to risk or positively welcome it ('risk neutrality' and 'risk-loving'). Indeed, this uncertainty lies at the foundation of the precautionary principle whereby decision-makers do not wait for full scientific certainty before making decisions. The precautionary approach is especially important if the scale of damage from natural capital loss is likely to be large. (2) when natural capital assets are lost, it may not be possible to recreate them. This is the problem of *irreversibility*. Once lost, such assets are lost for ever. By contrast, man-made capital can be run down and then recreated, as can human capital (although the conservation of indigenous knowledge and crafts, for example, is important). For these and other reasons, conserving natural capital (strong sustainability) is especially important to sustainable development" (Pearce, *et al.* 1996, p.17, words in parentheses added).

Victor reports three other factors highlighted by Pearce and Turner, which are also important for adopting a strong sustainability hypothesis. They are: (1) in some circumstances, such as a rural setting in a developing country, more natural capital can mean more resilience to shocks and hence a more sustainable society; (2) considerations of intergenerational equity demand that the resource stock be maintained so as to ensure broadly equal access to it by different generations; and (3) preservation of natural capital is consistent with a world view which recognises the rights of other species to co-exist with humans (Victor, 1997, p.428).

Strong sustainability requires the protection of life-supporting natural resources like water and air, and other common pool resources like the forests and fisheries. It indirectly favours the transference of these resources to future generations as common heritage or as public goods. Viewed in this perspective, strong sustainability upholds and helps in fulfilling the objective of meeting intergenerational equity which is a major requirement (criterion) of sustainable development. Weak sustainability, on the other hand, seems to favour the conversion of common pool natural resources which are part of the life-support system into man-made capital, amenable to private ownership and available for infinite substitution for natural capital along with 'human' capital, 'knowledge' systems and other artefacts under the free market regime, promoted by globalisation and liberalisation. This undoubtedly is the aim of the liberal school which is funded by global business and is orchestrating and synchronising the plea for institutional changes and property rights corrections, favoring private property relations, all in the name of economic efficiency and comparative advantage.

The fact that 'weak sustainability' is falling short of meeting the criterion of inter- generational equity and maintaining the life-support systems for sustaining life in this planet and is also promoting privatisation which is solely concerned with extraction of economic rent and short-run profits is enough proof that it is no guarantee for strong sustainability. Sustainable development needs strong sustainability promoted by the 'strong sustainability' hypothesis. It is advisable that (fisheries development) planners in India follow this principle.

**7.6.3. Limit Population**

Another major weakness of the neo-classical notion of sustainability is its treatment of population as an exogenous variable having no impact on sustainability. It simply considers that an increase in population will lead to an increase in the demand for goods and services which will be followed by an increase in their supplies by employing more of the variable inputs of labour and (man-made) capital, even if there is a constraint of shortage of natural capital. As already noted elsewhere , it considers that man-made capital can be easily substituted for natural capital and the natural resource constraint for sustainability averted. Moreover, it also stipulates that technological advancements will remove any remaining constraint for sustainability. All these hypotheses (expectations) have proved wrong with the overwhelming increase in global population, and the crisis of unsustainability is looming large, especially in poor countries, where the overpopulation problem is critical and unsustainability is staring.

Referring to the critical issue of overpopulation threatening sustainability, Costanza, *et al.* note that "while all countries must worry about both population and per capita consumption, it is evident that the South needs to focus more on population, and the North more on per capita consumption. This fact will likely play a major role in all North/South treaties and discussions"(Costanza, *et al.* 1997, p.175). Highlighting the need for arresting the growth in population, Costanza, *et. al.* further noted quoting Mc Neil that "reducing rates of population growth is an essential condition to achieve sustainability. This is as important if not more so, in industrial countries as it is in developing countries ..." (ibid. p.14).

Outlining the magnitude of the overpopulation problem and its impact on sustainability, Sarkar notes thus: "Unless population decreases, per capita availability of resources will be much lower than today. But we see that the global population continues to grow. The most important contribution of the third world countries towards global sustainability should therefore, be an early end to population growth, while that of the industrial countries should be a drastic reduction in total resource consumption ..." (Sarkar, 1999, p.137). Sarkar further observes that "in countries with a growing population, the most important and urgent task is to stop population growth, for which state action would be necessary" (ibid. p.202).

But the irony today, found in both 'mature democracies' and 'banana republics' alike, is the indifference on the part of the administration to arrest population growth. This indifference is perhaps the consequence of the vote bank politics played by communal parties and coalition governments in these countries ignoring the impact of such games on sustainable development or the very survival of the society. The disincentive and the current approach of the politicians to sustainable development is conveyed by Costanza, *et al.* thus: "the current political incentives are such that politicians have to be more concerned with generating policies that secure the short term goal of re-election rather than tackling the inevitably fraught transition towards more sustainable development. Ironically, it is probably democracy itself that is the greatest political barrier to a truly sustainable future ..." (Costanza, *et al.* 1996, p.185).

It is further felt that the 'growth-oriented' global capitalist business economies favour population growth for promoting and maintaining 'effective demand' for their products. Similarly, the so-called 'democracies' governed by 'puppet' political alliances and 'proxy' politicians may be more conscious of the need to promote their communal vote banks and less inclined to check population growth and achieve sustainable development in their countries. The political hierarchy in these countries also seems to be guided by a time serving intelligentsia least bothered about sustainability. This situation, corresponds to the one portrayed by Bates, a biologist, who has been quoted by Daly thus: "Then we come to man and his place in the system of life. We could have left man outplaying the ecological game of 'let's pretend man does n't exist'! But this seems as unfair as the corresponding game of the economists, let's pretend that nature does n't exist'. The economy of nature and ecology of man are inseparable and attempts to separate them are more than misleading, they are dangerous. Man's destiny is tied to nature's destiny and the arrogance of the engineering mind does not change this. Man may be a very peculiar animal, but he is still a part of the system of nature" (Daly, 1997, p.22).

What is more apparent from this question is the critical point of the economists ignoring the totality of the reality and trying to theorise based on incomplete variables leading to dangerous consequences for the economy. The need to arrest population growth has been emphasised by Costanza, *et al.* Costanza, *et al.* state that "... the sustainable development imperative is far more important and can be achieved only with strong growth of capital stocks, technological change and a slowing of population growth. Rapid population growth is a formidable threat to sustainable development" (Costanza, *et al.* 1996, p.23).

Costanza, *et al.* further assert that "the welfare of the poor, and indeed of the rich as well, depends much more on population control, consumption control, and redistribution than on the technical fix of 5 to 10 fold increase in total factor productivity" (Costanza, *et al.* 1997, p.103).

In the current situation, the growth-at all costs-mania is bound to backfire and lead to the critical situation of unsustainable development, perhaps corresponding to the Malthusian overpopulated, below subsistence, food starved economy. Overpopulation today leading to mass exodus of people from poor countries reminds one about the pastoral or gypsy way of life, making a mockery of the so-called 'civil-society' of the post-modern, liberalised market economy, promoted by agents of growth and globalisation. This happens inside the pale of democracies, while outside it is the slaughter of men and genocide that is committed for building democracies and free- market economies, both of which remind one about the dark ages. It is high time to check the growth in national and global population and to educate it of 'humane' ways of living. There is no choice for humanity other than restricting its number to avert itself from falling to the state of lower animals and becoming its own predator.

### 7.6.4. Limit Production, Consumption and Trade

Since sustainable development is basically a question of meeting the needs of the present without compromising the ability of the future generations to meet their own needs, it requires that current production and consumption are modified in such a way that there is less conflict and more harmonisation of the interests of the present and future generations. With the prevailing scarcity of natural resources and other inputs acting as constraints for production and consumption now and in the future, it becomes imperative on the part of the present generation to restrict the production and consumption of non-essential goods, irrespective of the 'strong preferences' of the developed countries and the rich elites in third world countries to consume many articles of ostentation or sheer luxury. It is also noted here that the free market (capitalist) economy produces many articles which remain unsold in the market, indicating the serious misallocation of resources or market failure. There is an absolute need to restrict the production of such goods with out leaving it to the caprice of the 'hidden hand' or individual choice in the free market. This is essential for meeting the essential needs of the present and future generations. There need not be any doubt about the essential needs of the future generation as made out in some of the current writings on sustainable development. Such doubts are only in the realm of the thinking of highly innovative, creative entrepreneurs who are engaged in 'creative destruction' of existing wants for new ones and concerned solely with business profits. The new world has little resource to squander for the production of unwanted and unsold goods as one finds in the free market economy. Sustainability requires preservation of all resources, especially the natural resources by minimising wasteful production and consumption. Sustainability demands rationing of all 'inputs' and 'outputs' to both producers and consumers. The 'growth' argument based on the 'trickle down' process is irresponsible, ignoring its social and environmental consequences and is purely guided by the logic of the free-market and short-run benefits, having scant regard for long-term sustainability and survival.

The need for conservation is more pressing in the case of non-renewable resources. As noted by Sarkar "as far as non-renewables are concerned, even zero growth is no solution. If consumed at a lower rate, they will be available for longer, that is all. We cannot bequeath to the next generation as much of them as we inherited unless we totally refrain from consuming them ..." (Sarkar, 1999, p.137).

The necessity of an alternative approach to production and consumption is reported by Rees. Rees, quoting Heuting states that "the world has conceived an approach to international development that can only exacerbate the 'environmental crisis' – existing levels of production and consumption are the proximate cause of global ecological change. Not only is this fixation of economic growth ecologically deluded, it is also a perversion of economic theory. Economic theory starts from the assumption that people want to maximise their welfare, but welfare comprises more than greater production and rising incomes. If, at the margin, we value safe communities, public health or local ecosystems more than production, and if preserving community and the environment leads to less production, then less production actually improves welfare. In short, to the extent that our global credo of progress is equated with production growth (at least in high income countries), we are up against a deep-rooted, erroneous notion that is threatening our planet" (Rees, 1999, p.114).

Another reason for limiting the scale of production and consumption as indicated by Daly is that "scale has become important because the economic subsystem has grown to the point where its physical demands on the ecosystem are far from trivial. We have moved from a relatively empty world to a relatively full world from the point of view of human beings. Since scale can no longer be considered as infinitesimal, its dismissal now rests on the view that it is total, and that the ecosystem is not the containing natural matrix of the economy, but just one more sector within the all-inclusive economy waiting for its due allocation of resources according to individual willingness to pay for its service or product. To put it starkly, in the neo-classical view, the economy contains the ecosystem; in the view advocated here ... the ecosystem contains the economy to which it supplies a throughput of matter-energy taken from in *natura* uses according to some rule of sustainable yield rather than according to individual willingness to pay"( Daly, 1999, p.202).

A further justification for limiting production and consumption in the economy is to carry on the economic activity with in the 'carrying capacity' of the environment or the ecosystem. As noted by Jacobs, "sustainability requires economic activity to remain within biophysical limits" (Jacob, 1999, p.96).

The need for restricting global trade for achieving sustainability is conveyed by Pearson. As already noted elsewhere in this chapter, Pearson observes: "this problem (trade and sustainability) is compounded because there is no environmental agency to protect the broader international interest, and international environmental law is not well developed. In this context, international trade may exacerbate unsustainable production and consumption activities by increasing total world output and consumption. It is also possible that trade shifts the location of production towards countries less inclined to internalise international externalities, or countries with open-access natural resource regimes and excessive exploitation levels ... Trade and sustainability are linked in yet another way. Trade increases specialisation of production within countries and regions of countries. Specialisation promotes monocultures and the spatial concentration of industry. Monocultures are the antithesis of ecological sustainability – the diversity and resiliency of ecosystems. Concentration and specialisation in production is more likely to overwhelm local assimilative capacity. Industrial scale farming of poultry and hogs is a good example. Some concentration of production result from purely domestic trade, but international trade is an increasingly important factor. The long-term implications for environmental sustainability from globalisation of trade and investment remains an open question" (Pearson, 2000, pp. 483-484, words in parentheses added).

Repeating the adverse effects of global trade, Costanza, *et al.* note: "It is perfectly possible for a single country to secure a sustainable development path, but at the cost of non-sustainability in another country. Thus many countries, including the UK, rely on imports of natural resources from developing countries. It is a distinctive feature of their international 'foot print'. This latter group frequently contains countries which do not have any other ('value added' or semi-processed or fully-processed manufactured goods) alternative products to sell in international markets. The danger is that these 'primary commodity' exporting countries will maximise, over the short run, the revenue available from exploitation of forests or other natural resources. In doing so they run the risk of reducing the stock available in the future – unsustainable development. The widespread concern in Europe about the use of imported tropical hardwood is a good example of possible 'imported sustainability' at the expense of nonsustainability in other nations ...trade policy could be used as a mechanism to import sustainability by setting high environmental standards at home and importing cheap products from 'pollution havens' ..." (Costanza, *et al.* 1996, p.24). The much touted business - process - outsourcing (BPO) policy of advanced countries now is nothing short of 'importing sustainability' and exporting unsustainability to poor countries. Third world countries have to be cautious of its consequences for sustainability. Advocates of globalisation may pry at this game.

While suggesting limits to production, consumption and trade, it is necessary to look at the feasibility of their operation. It is unlikely that present day consumers will voluntarily abstain from the consumption of many non-essential goods, since many of the goods add to their comforts and it is fashionable to use them for social status or for other false notions of being up to date and elitist. Many are ignorant of the poor quality of the products but still use them, as in the case of many 'repelling' perfumes (pesticides?) in rich and poor countries alike. The reason is simple. As noted by Rees, "we must also remember that politically powerful vested interests benefit in various ways from the continued expansion of consumption. In the wealthy countries, in order to ensure that demand remains high, a multimillion dollar advertising industry is dedicated to exploiting people's natural insecurities. By undermining our sense of self worth, by creating and emphasising symbols of social status, this industry helps stimulate material consumption far beyond the requirement for a good life ..." (Rees, 1999, p.119).

One may still appeal to the public to voluntarily abstain from the consumption of many non-essential goods and educate the masses about the social, cultural, economic and ecological impacts of their consumption and their effects on sustainability. This approach which is essentially Gandhian, i.e. 'moralsuation', to accept voluntary poverty as a way of preserving the natural resources for posterity and to live like a 'trustee' for the present and the future generations and to hope that the future generations will also be adopting this principle or practice, is ethically sound but very unlikely to prevail in the changed scenario of modernisation and globalisation.

Globalisation has changed and is changing the life styles of people everywhere and sustainability has been threatened in all fronts: ecological, economic, social, cultural, political and institutional. One cannot now think of the *Rama Rajya,* the self-sufficient village economy conceived by Mahatma Gandhi, to be reconstructed by any country or polity in the changed scenario. Reconstructing or reviving indigenous community systems of 'self-management'. or 'co-management' as visualised by many NGOs and international agencies is only wishful thinking or pure academic dreams propagated by foreign funding agencies which will never materialise. Many of these 'project-games' only help in brokering information to global exchange through the academic conduit. It is also the thinking that with global business cartels dictating terms to puppet national governments, the probability of nation states regulating production and consumption as practised in the socialist/communist states in the cold-war era is going to be a mere speculation. Jacobs raises the greater question thus: "in a globalised economy are national states powerful enough, or are supranational states or state structures, required?" (Jacobs, 1999, p.96). Jacobs, however, thinks that "sustainability requires considerable government intervention" (ibid. p.96).

With the collapse of 'socialism' and the triumph of capitalism following the *Peristroika/Glasnost* and the end of the 'cold war', state power is being snatched by global agencies like World Bank, IMF and WTO through the down-sizing of national governments and the liberalisation of trade and administration. Notwithstanding these developments, sustainability still requires effective state control on production and consumption and public policy affecting trade and investment. As noted by Costanza, *et al.* "the nation state certainly has many historical sins to atone for, but it is where community exists in the sense that it is the main unit in which policies are taken for the common good. To say that national boundaries are just lines on the map, and that we should all be environmental earth citizens is nice rhetoric, but not very realistic. Given the urgency of action and the reality of transnational corporate power eager to take over, we have no alternative but to work within the existing institution of nation state. Certainly population and per capita consumption will not be controlled at the global level. It will be done by nations. But the nations will have to cooperate and make binding international agreements" (Costanza, *et al.* 1997, p.175)

It is also worth repeating the advice and questions raised by Costanza, *et al.* that "while all countries must worry about both population and per capita consumption, it is evident that the South needs to focus more on population, and the North more on per capita consumption. This fact will likely play a major role in all North/South treaties and discussions.

Why should the South control its population if the resources saved thereby are merely gobbled up by Northern over-consumption? Why should the North control its over-consumption if the saved resources will merely allow a larger number of people to subsist at the same level of misery? Global problems are indeed global, but their solutions require national policies supported by international treaties. Nations have to be able to meet and enforce national policies agreed to in international treaties. If a nation's borders are porous to the flow of goods and services, capital and labour, then that country is in a poor position to carry out any national policy including those it agreed to in international treaties" (ibid. p.175).

The fundamental point is that sustainability needs state control on the 'scale' of economic activity. Unfortunately in the era of globalistion and privatisation states are forced to follow a *laissez-faire* policy and to exercise least control over business. It is unlikely that the free market economy will come to a 'steady' state of sustainable development, where everything will go on smoothly over and over again. Economic history has proved otherwise and it has been a history of war and terror imposed by powerful nations over poor countries for capturing more raw materials or natural resources for sustaining their domestic consumption at higher levels.

As noted by Opschoor, *et al.* "it could easily happen that increasing scarcity will lead nations to devote more rather than less resources to weapons, in order to appropriate by force the remaining resources from other countries. With proliferation of nuclear weapons to underdeveloped countries, however, this may become an expensive conquest" (Opschoor, *et al.,* 1999, p.88). The underpinning of this statement is probably to disarm all poor but resisting nations. The frequent warnings and reminders by the US to India on its economic ties with Iran and its arm-twisting on the nuclear treaty with the US also bespeak of its global approach to sustainable development and the third world's inanity in protecting the national sovereignty. All these indicate the little chance for poor countries to achieve sustainable development, reminding one about the working of the 'impossibility theorem' (Opschoor, 1999, pp.82-83).

### 7.6.5. Sustainable Development, a Myth, an Utopia

In the light of the current global developments, especially relating to global trade, investment and information technology and national economies aspiring for double digit growth rates, it is unlikely that the global economy is going to apply any break on its production and consumption or growth pattern. It is more likely that global economic growth will be promoted further and the gap between the North and the South, and the rich and the poor nations will only be widened, and in this process, the limits to growth' will be achieved sooner than later. With no check on population, production and consumption and with no institutional mechanism to protect the environmental quality and to fulfil intragenerational and intergenerational equity in the economy, sustainable development will be more a pype-dream of academics and politicians than a concrete reality. This is clear from the many criticisms levelled against this concept as noted earlier in this section. It is indeed a 'clever term' a 'mediating' term, popularised by neo-classical (hybrid) ecological-economists to accommodate the joint-interests of business to promote economic growth and the ecological interests of sustainability. With global business exerting full control over national governments everywhere and international organisation playing second fiddle to business interests, it is the business as usual (BAU) approach that is prevailing over environmental issues, and that is threatening the sustainability of most societies. It being so, the concept of sustainable development is an attractive academic myth of the late 20th century neatly laced with the texture of ecology, economics and ethics, making it appealing to every interest group, but remaining as utopian as socialism or communism in the last century. The steady state of sustainable development visualised by Daly is indeed an Utopia; where 'more' of everything is obtained for 'less' of resources as a result of technical improvements and qualitative changes in the economy. This is certainly a neo-classical myth. As Sarkar observes: "Miracles happen only in storybooks. We cannot imagine a car needs no energy. And oil tankers are not becoming smaller and smaller while transporting more and more oil" (Sarkar, 1999, p.176).

Many writers have cast doubts about the feasibility of achieving sustainable development. Pearce, *et al.* noted that 'it is still doubtful whether even the very basic needs of at least one billion, of the world's poorest people can really be met without an enormous convulsion in the denial of expectations over future consumption of materials and energy amongst the very wealthy. Moreover, existing experience provides little support for the hope that it is technically possible to bring the existing global population up to the living standards of, say France, without environmental disruptions on an enormous scale. At the very least, there would need to be serious and prolonged commitment to technology transfer, to scientific and managerial capacity building in the south and fundamental adjustments to the international systems of trade, debt and aid ... Any shift towards sustainability will inevitably be slow, taking generations, not years. Full sustainable development involves a cultural shift, not just economic and political tinkering. The goal is elusive, so we must learn to experiment and adjust towards sustainability, shedding failure and misunderstanding and capitalising on success and support for well-intentioned trials ..." (Pearce, *et al.* 1996, pp. 184-185).

The fact of the matter being such as it is, one is inclined to think that all appeals to sustainable development are mere rhetorics and part of the new 'dialectics of denial' of opportunity for development in poor countries and a strategy for maintaining high levels of consumption in advanced countries . The philosophical appeal of the concept to intragenerational and intergenerational equity with out any check on population, production, consumption and trade, world-wide, is purely utopian or mythical, just as it was destined with socialism and communism in the last century. The concept of sustainable development, however, gives hope to the poor countries to remove poverty and inequality. For this they are persuaded to promote growth, which ultimately leads to unsustainability. This, in essence, is the political economy of unsustainable development, keeping the third world engaged in the trajectory of growth.

### 7.6. Summary

This chapter presented the standard ecological, economic, institutional, and technological solutions for achieving sustainable development of fisheries in India. The ecological solutions prescribed included (1) implementation of the FAO code of conduct for responsible fisheries, (2) adoption of the precautionary principle for fisheries management, (3) biodiversity conservation, (4) eco-system based fisheries management and (5) integration of fisheries management with coastal zone management.

The major economic solutions prescribed included (a) market solutions, (b) non-market solutions and (c) strengthening of central planning for sustainable development.

The institutional solution suggested included (1) privatisation, (2) globalisation, (3) public-private partnership, (4) capacity-building, (5) co-management and (6) use of traditional knowledge.

The technological solutions suggested included the adoption of new inputs and processes to improve the performance of all branches of the industry.

Notwithstanding the above, a rethinking on the concept of sustainable development made in this chapter has raised serious doubts about the feasibility of various prescriptions for sustainability and the credibility of the concept of sustainable development itself. It has further noted the weakness of the 'weak sustainability' hypothesis upheld by the neo-classical thinking and suggested the need for adopting the 'strong sustainability' hypothesis for achieving sustainable development of the economy. This chapter also argued for limiting population, production, consumption and trade at all levels for achieving sustainability. Finally, this chapter also came to the conclusion that the concept of sustainable development is a mere academic myth or utopia and its rhetorics is part of the new 'dialectics of denial' of opportunity for development in poor countries and a strategy for maintaining high levels of consumption in advanced countries through trade with poor countries. This in essence is the political economy of unsustainable development.

# 8

# SUMMARY AND CONCLUSION

## 8.1. Summary

Chapter one of this book made clear the theme and background of the study, the need for the study, its objectives and scope, hypotheses and methodology, database and limitations, and utility of the study.

This chapter essentially noted the critical situation prevailing in the fisheries sector of India and indicated the need for the present study.

The primary objective of this study was to make clear the political economy of unsustainable development of fisheries in India. In tune with this objective, the study had sought to identify, assess (measure) and discuss the impact of critical ecological, economic, social, cultural, institutional and technological factors (issues) affecting the sustainability of Indian fisheries. *Ipso facto*, this study also suggested and reviewed the measures for promoting sustainable development of fisheries in India. The scope of this study extended from a theoretical exposition of the concept of sustainable development to its application to the fisheries sector of India in particular and world fisheries in general.

The main hypothesis put forward in this study was that the sustainability of Indian fisheries is currently threatened by a number of ecological, economic, social, cultural, institutional and technological factors (issues) which act as constraints for the working of the industry. It further held that the sustainable development of fisheries in India required the removal of these constraints, which is, however, not quite easy given the many interactions, interdependencies and externalities working in the sector, and against the sector, reminding one about working of the 'impossibility theorem' in poor countries.

The methodology noted in this chapter consisted of identifying the major ecological, economic, social, cultural, institutional and technological factors (issues) which act as constraints for the working of the industry and also measuring the extent of their operation and their implication for sustainability.

The data base noted consisted of published materials and information from national and international sources.

One major limitation noted in this chapter was that it did not make any 'single' composite index of unsustainability prevailing in the industry. This chapter, however, noted that the various sustainability indicators studied were sufficient to represent the nature and extent of unsustainability situation prevailing in the industry and this approach was very much in tune with the global approach to the study of sustainable development. The practical value of this study as noted in this chapter is its novelty in making a significant academic exercise to study the sustainability issues of Indian fisheries and its possibility of giving some food for thought to the intellectuals and policy makers.

Chapter two took note of the general theoretical literature relating to sustainable development and the applied fisheries literature relating to sustainable development of fisheries, both domestic and international. The domestic literature, both general and applied, were found to be quite scanty and underdeveloped in its structure and composition. The limited domestic literature on sustainable development of fisheries discussed predominantly the sustainability of aquaculture and the need for promoting specific aquaculture systems for sustainability. Some of this literature also discussed the sustainability issues of marine fisheries with respect to their environment, technology, output, costs, etc. Quite a few of these studies also dealt with coastal fishermen and their social life. The most shocking aspect of the domestic literature, however, was that scarcely any of them had discussed the sustainability issues systematically following or evolving some practical criteria for sustainable development.

The international theoretical literature on sustainable development is found to be quite advanced and expanding. Its origin may be traced in the writings of Adam Smith, David Ricardo, T.R. Malthus, J.S.Mill, Karl Marx, John Maynard Keynes, Joseph, A.Schumpeter, Alwin Hansen, and so on. The global theoretical literature, however, had its boom in the writings of contemporary ecological economists and other institutional writers attached to OECD, World Bank, International Institute for Sustainable Development, etc. The contemporary international literature focused mainly on definition, measurement, developing criteria and indicators, mechanisms (systems and institutions) for sustainable development and in establishing linkages between environment (ecology), economy (economics) and society (culture). The global literature is found to have developed in some good progression in its mission, mode and strategy.

The international applied literature on sustainable development of fisheries is also found to be extensive and growing. The global literature is quite outstanding in the variety of topics handled as well. It ranged from the sustainability of capture fisheries to aquaculture and environment, responsible fisheries, food safety and security, global economic structure, trade and sustainability, FAO/World Bank strategy for sustainable development of fisheries, WTO, globalisation and sustainable development, and a whole host of other issues.

The global literature, especially institutional literature, originating from FAO, World Bank, OECD, etc. is found to be quite advanced in its formulation of indicators, criteria and measurement of sustainable development of fisheries. It is found to focus on ecological, economic, social, institutional and technological criteria of sustainable development. This literature is, however, generally silent on the unsustainable development of fisheries in developing countries. Notwithstanding the developed country-centric treatment of sustainable development issues in the global literature, its comprehensive coverage of ecological, economic, social, technological and institutional issues of production, processing, marketing and management of the industry makes it amenable for adoption and adaptation by developing countries as well for the sustainable development planning of their fisheries.

The myriad of definitions and observations on sustainable development made in chapter three of this book pointed to the failure of (1) the ecological systems in providing inputs and services (source and sink) for production and consumption on a sustained basis, (2) the economic system in providing optimum condition for sustained production and consumption for want of proper signals and incentives from the market mechanism and (3) the social systems in meeting the requirements of intragenerational and intergenerational equity, all leading to unsustainable development. The basic approach to sustainability indicated in most definitions was to modify the producing and consuming systems with suitable changes in technology and social organisatons.

A review of development of the concept of sustainable development made in this chapter traced its origin and growth through the classical, Marxian, neo-classical, modern and post-modern thoughts. The classical economists, notably Smith, Malthus, Ricardo and Mill had anticipated the emergence of 'stationary state' arising out of scarcity of land, over-population and diminishing returns in the economy. Improvements in the art of production (technological change) and extension of markets (including colonies) for raw materials and products were considered as possible solutions. The Marxian school viewed the capitalist mode of production as quite unsustainable due to capitalist exploitation of labour, changing organic composition of capital, the resulting disproportionality crisis (falling demand), class struggle, etc. The capitalist system sought to impart sustainability through technological improvements and colonial trade.

The neo-classical writers of the early twentieth century had recognised the sustainability issues and the economy slipping to crises of 'unemployment' and 'secular stagnation'. Later neo-classical writers were optimists who considered that the natural resource constraint could be overcome by the substitution of scarce natural capital (resources) by abundant ones and by man-made capital.

The modern view of sustainable development which had its origin in the 'conservation movement' of the USA at the beginning of the last century had its flowering in the last decades of the last century with the World Conservation Union and many ecologists highlighting the threat to natural resources and global environment. The implications for global sustainability was made clear by the ecological school which underscored the role of the 'environment' as a 'source' of raw material, and as a 'sink' for wastes of production and consumption. This school recognised the 'limits' to growth and called for saving 'critical natural resources and environment' and making sufficient investments in 'natural capital' for conservation and sustainable development.

The post-modern view, which is predominantly a post-cold war, and post-UNCED development, focused initially on creating a just and equitable society where there is harmony between rich and poor nations, between North and South and between developed and developing countries. It had while upholding the principles of intra-generational and intergenerational equity as popularised by the WCED and Rio declarations, sought to reform global economic relations, policies and institutions to achieve the goal of sustainable development. However, with the rising tide of liberalisation, privatisation and globalisation of the world economy, it appears that sustainable development as a high moral principle has lost sight of its practical utility as conveyed in the Brundtland Report. This is evident from the growing conflicts of interests of the rich and poor nations at the global trade negotiating fora and the visible 'business-as-usual attitude of world business, having scant regard for environmental protection or for fulfilling the criteria of intragenerational and intergenerational equity.

This chapter also recognised the need for measuring sustainable development and noted the criteria and indicators for sustainable development. They were discussed under three categories; neo-classical, modern and post-modern.

This chapter further noted the major factors behind unsustainable development. They included market failure, government failure, institutional failure and information failure.

Some of the policy recommendations for sustainable development made outside the fold of the UN, notably by the OECD and other scholars were also cited in this chapter. These prescriptions were, however, found to be predominantly pro-advanced country, based on neo-classical economic thinking. The conclusion thus emerging from these theoretical positions was that developing countries have to rework and redesign their own models of sustainable development taking into account the supply and demand for natural, human and physical resources and the prevailing ecological, economic, social, political, institutional and technological constraints for sustainable development.

Chapter four discussed the major sustainability issues facing global fisheries. These issues were classified as (1) ecological, (2) economic, (3) social/institutional, (4) technological, and (5) other versions. The major ecological issues threatening the sustainability of global fisheries noted are (1) biological overfishing, (2) environmental pollution, (3) habitat loss, (4) biodiversity loss and (5) climate change. The economic issues outlined are (1) decline/stagnation in production, (2) stagnation in consumption, (3) overcapitalisation, (4) uneconomic operations, (5) decline in employment and productivity, (6) poverty and (7) barriers to trade.

The social and institutional issues identified included (1) institutional crisis involving the collapse of indigenous community organisations, (2) socio-economic conflicts (intrause and interuse conflicts) and (3) occupational hazards. The social and institutional issues are considered as both the cause and consequence of ecological and economic issues. Many of the technological changes that took place in the catching, culture, processing and marketing sectors of the industry are also noticed to cause problems for the sustainability of the industry. This casts doubt on the technological solutions for sustainability as conceived by the neo-classical school.

A different version of sustainability issues reported in the literature and noted in this chapter included lack of good governance, inappropriate incentives, high demand for limited resources, poverty and lack of alternatives, complexity and lack of knowledge and interactions of the fisheries sector with other sectors and the environment.

Chapter five of this book identified and discussed the major resources available for fisheries development in India at present. It took note of the natural, human, physical and social capital available to the industry. The natural resources (capital) available to the industry consisted of the marine ecosystem and the living resources spread over the coastal zones and the continental shelf of the country and the inland water ecosystems of the rivers, reservoirs, canals, tanks and ponds, flood plain lakes and derelict water bodies, and brackish water areas.

The human resources available to the fisheries sector noted in this chapter consisted of the active fishermen, fish farmers, workers engaged in the fish processing industry, people engaged in storage, transportation and distribution (marketing) of fish, workers engaged in ancillary industries, personnel involved in research and development (R & D) activities in the industry, personnel involved in fisheries education and training and personnel engaged in fisheries administration and governance (management).

The physical (man-made) capital investments in the industry consisted of investments in fishing vessels, fishing harbours, fish farming infrastructure, fish processing plants, fish marketing infrastructure and ancillary industries.

The social (institutional) capital for fisheries development in India noted included the traditional community organisations and the modern specialised functional organisations created by the state machinery and other voluntary, national and international organisations.

This chapter also noted the significant investments made by the state (public) sector for fisheries development in India during the five year plans. Notable public sector investments were made in strategic fields like infrastructure for the development of capture, culture, processing and marketing of fish, research and development (R & D) in the industry, fisheries education and training, technological changes in all branches of the industry, and in institution-building for fisheries development.

Chapter six of this book discussed the major sustainability issues of Indian fisheries by looking at selected indicators of unsustainable development. The major sustainability issues discussed were classified under five main groups, viz. (1) ecological, (2) economic, (3) social and institutional, (4) technological and (5) other versions (dimensions) of unsustainable development. The major ecological issues discussed included (1) biological overfishing, (2) environmental pollution, (3) habitat destruction, (4) biodiversity loss, and (5) climate change. All these factors were found to impact adversely on the natural resource base of the industry leading to un-sustainable development.

The economic issues affecting the sustainability of Indian fisheries were discussed under seven categories, viz. (1) stagnation in production, (2) overcapitalisation, (3) un-economic operations, (4) declining employment, (5) static or declining consumption, (6) unstable global markets and barriers to trade, and (7) meagre contribution to the GDP. All these factors, except the third, were found to lead to unsustainability of fisheries development in India.

The major social issues threatening the sustainability of Indian fisheries included (1) poor housing, health and sanitation, (2) illiteracy, (3) poverty and indebtedness and (4) intrause and interuse conflicts.

This chapter also noted the presence of institutional crisis in the industry, including the collapse of traditional community organisations and failure of state sponsored institutions, both leading to lack of control over natural resource exploitation and the sharing of output by the society, resulting in conflicts and unsustainable development of the industry.

This chapter also found that much of the unsustainability issues of Indian fisheries were the consequence of the adoption of inappropriate technology, having adverse effects on ecology, economy and society.

Other issues of sustainability noted in this chapter included occupational hazards, labour shortage, etc. A spin-off version (model) of unsustainability of Indian fisheries found in the literature is also noted in this chapter. A different listing of sustainability issues affecting the marine fisheries sector of India, found in the literature, is also noted.

Overall, this chapter led to the conclusion that most of the ecological, economic, social/institutional and technological indicators studied pointed to the unsustainable development of fisheries in India.

Chapter seven presented the standard (global) ecological, economic, institutional and technological solutions (prescriptions) for sustainable development of fisheries in India. The ecological solutions prescribed included (1) implementation of the FAO code of conduct for responsible fisheries, (2) adoption of the precautionary principle for fisheries management, (3) biodiversity conservation, (4) ecosystem - based fisheries management and (5) integration of fisheries management with coastal zone management.

The major economic solutions prescribed included (a) market solutions, (b) non-market solutions and (c) strengthening of central planning for sustainable development.

The institutional solutions suggested included (1) privatisation, (2) globalisation, (3) public-private partnership, (4) capacity-building, (5) co-management and (6) use of traditional knowledge.

The technological solutions suggested included the adoption of new inputs and processes (technological changes) to improve the performance of all branches of the industry.

A simultaneous review of the various prescriptions made in this chapter has raised serious doubts about the feasibility of many of the solutions due to the many interactions, interdependencies and externalities involved, reminding one about the working of the 'impossibility theorem' in poor countries.

It has further noted the weakness of the 'weak sustainability' hypothesis held by the neo-classical thinking and suggested the need for adopting the 'strong sustainability' hypothesis for achieving sustainable development of the economy. This chapter also argued for limiting population, production, consumption and trade at all levels for achieving sustainability.

Finally, a rethinking on sustainability made in this chapter led to the conclusion that the concept of sustainable development is a mere academic myth or utopia and its rhetorics are part of the new 'dialectics of denial' of opportunity for development in poor countries and a strategy for maintaining high levels of consumption in advanced countries. This in essence is the political economy of unsustainable development.

## 8.2. Conclusion

Sustainable development of fisheries in India is threatened by a number of ecological, economic, social, cultural, institutional and technological factors (issues). The many criteria and indicators of sustainable development observed in this study proved the presence of unsustainable conditions in the industry. The standard (global) solutions prescribed for sustainable development of fisheries in India are unlikely to produce substantial changes in the industry due to many interactions and externalities prevailing in the industry/economy, all of which remind one about the working of the 'impossibility theorem' in poor countries. Any policy for 'sustainability' in general (including fisheries) requires drastic checks on population, production, consumption and trade in the economy, administered by far sighted governments acting as trustees for the future and promoting intragenerational and intergenerational equity. These checks are required as no plundering of resources from within or other countries or other planets can satisfy the greed (tastes) of the multitude of the so called 'civil societies' (democracies) and call it sustainable.

Sustainability demands 'limits' to growth world-wide and absolute controls on population growth and consumerism. Global capitalism and free-market economies (democracies) are, however, not going to promote any of these policies and it is only likely that militant consumerism and patent terrorism will make this planet a hell or a 'paradise lost' for the future. The responsibility for this tragedy has to be placed squarely on capitalism (free market economy) and democracy (consumerism). It is time to tell the world that democracy is sowing the seeds of its own destruction through market expansion and promoting consumerism and terrorism simultaneously. With faint hope, it is still suggested here that fisheries development planners in India should follow a policy of promoting 'strong sustainability' principle by conserving the natural resource base by limiting fishing effort, fishing capacity, seasonal closure of fishing, establishing marine protected areas and introducing various other forms of 'blanket' and 'selective' controls on all branches of the industry. In all these efforts, the focus should be on intragenerational and intergenerational equity principles which are fundamental to sustainability in all senses - ecological, economic and social.

# Appendix 3.1
# The Principles of Sustainable Society

1. A duty of care for other people and other forms of life, now and in the future; to share fairly the benefits and costs of resource use and environmental conservation. This is an ethical principle.

2. The direction of development and economic growth towards the improvement of the quality of human life in the broadest sense.

3. The conservation of life-support systems and biodiversity, ensuring that the uses of renewable resources are sustainable, that is within the capacity of the resource for renewal.

4. Minimising depletion of non-renewable resources such as minerals, oil, gas and coal, through recycling, economical use, and switching to renewable substitutes.

5. Keeping within the carrying capacity of the Earth. Human numbers and life styles should be kept within the carrying capacity of the Earth, while that capacity is expanded by careful management.

6. A re-examination of values and adjustments of behaviour to support the new ethic, discouragement of values that are incompatible with a sustainable way of life.

7. Encourage local communities to care for their environments, taking part in decision-making processes and active discussions.

8. A national framework for integrating development and conservation involving all interests, seeking to identify and prevent problems before they occur.

9. A firm alliance between all countries to achieve global sustainability; global and shared resources, especially the atmosphere, oceans, major ecosystems, and endangered species need to be managed on the basis of common purpose and resolve.

*Source:* Gilpin, 2000, p. 92, as derived from *Caring for the Earth: A Strategy for Sustainable Living* (1991) IUCN, UNEP, WWF, Gland, Switzerland.

# Appendix 3.2
# The Rio Declaration

Having met at Rio de Janeiro from 3 to 14 June 1992,

Reaffirming the Declaration of the United Nations Conference on the Human Environment, adopted at Stockholm on 16 June 1972, and seeking to build upon it,

With the goal of establishing a new and equitable global partnership through the creation of new levels of cooperation among states, key sectors of societies and people,

Working towards international agreements which respect the interests of all and protect the integrity of the global environmental and developmental system,

Recognising the integral and interdependent nature of the Earth, our home,

Proclaims that:

**Principle 1**

Human beings are at the center of concerns for sustainable development. They are entitled to a healthy and productive life in harmony with nature.

**Principle 2**

States have, in accordance with the Charter of the United Nations and the principles of international law, the sovereign right to exploit their own resources pursuant to their own environmental and developmental policies, and the responsibility to ensure that activities within their jurisdiction or control do not cause damage to the environment of other states or of areas beyond the limits of national jurisdiction.

**Principle 3**

The right to development must be fulfilled so as to equitably meet developmental and environmental needs of present and future generations.

**Principle 4**

In order to achieve sustainable development, environmental protection shall constitute an integral part of the development process and cannot be considered in isolation from it.

**Principle 5**

All states and all people shall cooperate in the essential task of eradicating poverty as an indispensable requirement for sustainable development, in order to decrease the disparities in standards of living and better meet the needs of the majority of the people of the world.

**Principle 6**

The special situation and needs of developing countries, particularly the least developed and those most environmentally vulnerable, shall be given special priority. International actions in the field of environment and development should also address the interests and needs of all countries.

**Principle 7**

States shall co-operate in a spirit of global partnership to conserve, protect and restore the health and integrity of the Earth's ecosystem. In view of the different contributions to global environmental degradation, states have common but differentiated responsibilities. The developed countries acknowledge the responsibility that they bear in the international pursuit of sustainable development in view of the pressures their societies place on the global environment and of the technologies and financial resources they command.

**Principle 8**

To achieve sustainable development and a higher quality of life for all people, states should reduce and eliminate unsustainable patterns of production and consumption and promote appropriate demographic policies.

**Principle 9**

States should cooperate to strengthen endogenous capacity building for sustainable development by improving scientific understanding through exchanges of scientific and technological knowledge, and by enhancing the development, adaptation, diffusion and transfer of technologies, including new and innovative technologies.

**Principle 10**

Environmental issues are best handled with the participation of all concerned citizens, at the relevant level. At the national level, each individual shall have appropriate access to information concerning the environment that is held by public authorities, including information on hazardous materials and activities in their communities, and the opportunity to participate in decision-making processes. States shall facilitate and encourage public awareness and participation by making information widely available. Effective access to judicial and administrative proceedings, including redress and remedy, shall be provided.

**Principle 11**

States shall enact effective environmental legislation. Environmental standards, management objectives and priorities should reflect the environmental and developmental context to which they apply. Standards applied by some countries may be inappropriate and of unwarranted economic and social cost to other countries, in particular developing countries.

**Principle 12**

States should co-operate to promote a supportive and open international economic system that would lead to economic growth and sustainable development in all countries, to better address the problems of environmental degradation. Trade policy measures for environmental purposes should not constitute a means of arbitrary or unjustifiable discrimination or a disguised restriction on international trade. Unilateral actions to deal with environmental challenges outside the jurisdiction of the importing country should be avoided. Environmental measures addressing transboundary or global environmental problems should, as far as possible, be based on an international consensus.

**Principle 13**

States shall develop national law regarding liability and compensation for the victims of pollution and other environmental damage. States shall also cooperate in an expeditious and more determined manner to develop further international law regarding liability and compensation for adverse effects of environmental damage caused by activities within their jurisdiction or control to areas beyond their jurisdiction.

**Principle 14**

States should effectively cooperate to discourage or prevent the relocation and transfer to other states of any activities and substances that cause severe environmental degradation or are found to be harmful to human health.

**Principle 15**

In order to protect the environment, the precautionary approach shall be widely applied by states according to their capabilities. Where there are threats of serious or irreversible damage, lack of full scientific certainty shall not be used as a reason for postponing cost-effective measures to prevent environmental degradation.

**Principle 16**

National authorities should endeavour to promote the internalisation of environmental costs and the use of economic instruments, taking into account the approach that the polluter should, in principle, bear the cost of pollution, with due regard to the public interest and without distorting international trade and investment.

**Principle 17**

Environmental impact assessment, as a national instrument, shall he undertaken for proposed activities that are likely to have a significant adverse impact on the environment and are subject to a decision of a competent national authority.

**Principle 18**

States shall immediately notify other states of any natural disasters or other emergencies that are likely to produce sudden harmful effects on the environment of those states. Every effort shall be made by the intentional community to help states afflicted.

**Principle 19**

States shall provide prior and timely notification and relevant information to potentially affected states on activities that may have a significant adverse transboundary environmental effect and shall consult with those states at an early stage and in good faith.

**Principle 20**

Women have a vital role in environmental management and development. Their full participation is therefore essential to achieve sustainable development.

**Principle 21**

The creativity, ideals and courage of the youth of the world should be mobilised to forge a global partnership in order to achieve sustainable development and ensure better future for all.

**Principle 22**

Indigenous people and their communities and other local communities have a vital role in environmental management and development because of their knowledge and traditional practices. States should recognise and duly support their identity, culture and interests and enable their effective participation in the achievement of sustainable development.

**Principle 23**

The environment and natural resources of people under oppression, domination and occupation shall be protected.

**Principle 24**

Warfare is inherently destructive of sustainable development. States shall therefore respect international law providing protection for the environment in times of armed conflict and cooperate in its further development, as necessary.

**Principle 25**

Peace, development and environmental protection are interdependent and indivisible.

**Principle 26**

States shall resolve all their environmental disputes peacefully and by appropriate means in accordance with the Charter of the United Nations.

**Principle 27**

States and people shall cooperate in good faith and in a spirit of partnership in the fulfilment of the principles embodied in this Declaration and in the further development of international law in the field of sustainable development.

---

Source: United Nations, 1993, *Report of the United Nations Conference on Environment and Development*, Rio-de Jeneiro, 3-14, June 1992, Resolutions adopted by the Conference, United Nations , New York.

# APPENDIX 3.3
# Priorities for Sustainable Development

1. A transition to population stability, to reduce the need for growth everywhere.

2. Poverty reduction will require considerable growth and development in developing countries, balanced by negative growth for the richer countries.

3. The large-scale transfer of resources from the richer to the poorer countries.

4. Higher prices for the exports of the poorer countries.

5. Markets will have to learn to function without expansion, without wars, without waste and without advertising.

6. Economic policy will have to suppress certain activities in order to allow others to expand, so that the sum total remains within biophysical budget.

7. The transition to renewable energy will need to accelerate.

8. The upgrading of human capital through education and training and adequate employment, job creation in preference to automation.

9. The alleviation of poverty by direct amelioration and targeted aid.

10. Major technological transfer from rich to poor.

11. The limitation, arrestation and even reduction of economic activities in the richer countries.

12. In conflicts between biophysical realities and political realities, the latter must eventually give ground.

13. As economic stability in the richer countries may depress the terms of trade and lower economic activity in developing countries, additional large-scale transfers to the poorer countries will be needed.

14. The primary need is for income redistribution and population stability.

15. Exceptional political wisdom and leadership will be required; political resolve will be the scarcest resource.

16. Other criteria include no net increase in the concentration of greenhouse gases in the atmosphere; no net increase in acidification in surface

waters and soils; no net increases in toxic chemical and heavy metal concentrations in soil and water; no net top soil erosion; no net depletion of aquifers; the preservation of all or most remaining natural forests, estuarine areas, coral reefs, and other ecologically critical biomes of ecosystems; no further humanly induced extinctions of other species; the reduction of the energy intensity of GDP; an increase in the proportion of energy from renewable resources; an increase in recycling; avoidance of overgrazing.

17. Part of the proceeds from consuming non-renewables should be allocated to research in pursuit of sustainable substitutes.

18. The harvest rates of renewable resource inputs should be within the regenerative capacity of the natural system that generates them.

19. If a non-renewable resource has no renewable substitute, its use may be shared over some ethically determined number of generations.

---

Source: Goodland, Daly and El Serafy (1992), quoted by Gilpin, 2000, p. 93.

# APPENDIX 3.4
# WCED Perspective (Policy Directions) for Sustainable Development

1. Population and human resources:
2. Food security – sustaining the potential:
   - increase of food crops in developing countries
   - reduction of food surplus in industrialised countries
   - promotion of ecologically-sound farming
   - land reform and protection of vulnerable subsistence activities (integrated rural development)
3. Species and ecosystems – resources for development:
   - increases in protected areas
   - establishment of a 'Species Convention'
4. Energy-choices for environment and development:
   - energy efficiency policies
   - research and development: environmentally sound and safe energy alternatives
   - 'conservation pricing' of energy commodities
5. Industry–producing more with less:
   - export control of hazardous chemicals
   - control of hazardous waste dumping
   - technology assistance to developing countries
6. The urban challenge:
   - settlement strategies for urban control
   - decentralisation policies
7. International cooperation:
   - technical assistance for environmentally sound projects and policies;
   - incorporation of environmental concerns into international commodity arrangements
   - disarmament and use of peace dividend

Source: WCED (1987), quoted in Bartelmus, 1994, p. 80.

# Appendix 3.5
# Ecological, Socio-economic/Community and Institutional Indicators of Sustainability

| *Sustainability criteria* | *Indicators* | *Range* | *Indicators at minimum if* |
|---|---|---|---|
| *Ecological sustainability indicators* | | | |
| Catch level | MSY-catch/MSY | –α to 1 | Catch exceeds maximum sustainable yield |
| Biomass | Biomass (relative to historical average) | 0 to α | Total biomass or spawning stock biomass below a critical low level |
| Biomass trend | Multi-year average annual percentage rate of change | –1 to 1 | Biomass declining rapidly or predicted to do so due to lack of recruitment |
| Fish size | Average fish size (relative to historical average) | 0 to α | Average size at capture very low relative to optimal capture size |
| Environmental quality | Quality (relative to historical average) + (% rate of change) | 0 to α | Environmental quality low and declining |
| Diversity (harvested species) | (No. of species)/ (hist. avg.) + (diversity)/ (hist. avg.) | 0 to α | No. of species in catch and diversity index both low relative to historical levels. |
| Diversity (eco-system) | (No.of species)/ (hist. avg.) + (diversity)/ (hist. avg.) | 0 to α | No. of species and diversity index both low and declining |
| Rehabilitated areas | Area rehabilitated as % of total area | 0 to 1 | Increasing area closed due to contamination, etc. |
| Protected areas | Area protected as % of total area | 0 to 1 | Decrease in areas protected from exploitation |
| Ecosystem understanding | Level of understanding relative to full knowledge (subjective) | 0 to 1 | No clear understanding of resource and its ecosystem |
| *Socio-economic/community sustainability indicators* | | | |
| Community resiliency | Index of diversity in employment | 0 to 1 | Lack of livelihood alternatives/ low diversity of employment |

| *Sustainability criteria* | *Indicators* | *Range* | *Indicators at minimum if* |
|---|---|---|---|
| Community independence | Percentage of economic activity locally | 0 to 1 | High dependence on external economic forces |
| Human carrying capacity (livelihood) | Current (or potential) sustainable employment (relative to population) | 0 to 1 | Sustainable economic or employment base is substantially below current (or predicted population) |
| Human carrying capacity (environment) | Natural absorptive capacity/ human waste production | 0 to α | Generation of human waste far exceeds the absorptive capacity of the environment |
| Equity | Ratio of historical to current Gini coefficients of income and/or food distribution | 0 to α | Dispersion in income and or food supply is substantially above traditional norms |
| Sustainable fleet capacity | Ratio of capacity for harvesting at MSY to current capacity | 0 to α | Current capacity exceeds that required to harvest at MSY |
| Appropriate investment | Investment capacity (when stock < optimal) | –1 to 1 | Investment above replacement level when stock is fully exploited, or > 0 when stock is declining. |
| Food supply | Food supply per capita (relative to minimum nutritional needs) | 0 to α | Food available per person is below minimum nutritional requirement |
| Long term food security | Probability of sufficient food being available for next 10 years | 0 to 1 | Stability of food supply is low, or food supply is declining rapidly |
| *Institutional sustainability indicators* | | | |
| Management effectiveness | Level of success of stated management and regulatory policies | 0 to 1 | Existing management structures are insufficient to control exploitation levels and regulate resource users |
| Use of traditional methods | Extent of utilisation | 0 to 1 | Traditional resource and environmental manage-ment methods not utilised |
| Incorporating local input | Extent of incorporation | 0 to 1 | Management planning activity does not incorporate local socio-cultural factors (tradition, community decision- making, ecological knowledge, etc.) |
| Capacity building | Extent of capacity-building efforts | 0 to 1 | Lack of capacity building within relevant organisations |

| *Sustainability criteria* | *Indicators* | *Range* | *Indicators at minimum if* |
|---|---|---|---|
| Institutional viability | Level of financial and organisational viability | 0 to 1 | Management organisation lack long-term financial viability, or there is a lack of political will to support such structures. |

Source: Adapted from Charles, 2001, pp. 193-195.

# APPENDIX 4.1
# Types of Threat to Marine Eco-systems, Drivers and Possible Policy Responses

| *Types of threat* | *Drivers* | *Policy responses* |
|---|---|---|
| *Habitat loss or conversion* | | |
| Coastal development (ports, urbanisation, tourism-related development, industrial sites) | Population growth, poor siting due to undervaluing and lack of knowledge, poorly developed industrial policy, tourism demand, environmental refugees and internal migration | Requirement for environmental impact assessment (EIA), technology transfer and training in planning, tourism policies, identification of ecologically critical areas, marine protected areas (MPAs) |
| Destructive fisheries (dynamite, cyanide, other poison-fishing, bottom trawling) | Shift to market economies, demand for aquaria fish and live food fish, increasing competition in light of diminishing resources | MPAs, training for alternative methods, green-labelling and certification policies, cost-benefit analyses and awareness raising |
| Coastal deforestation (especially mangrove deforestation) | Lack of alternative materials, increased competition, poor national policies | Access to and training in use of alternative materials, cost-benefit analyses and awareness raising |
| Mining (coral, sand, minerals, maintenance dredging) | Lack of alternative materials, global commons perceptions | Cost-benefit analyses, technology transfer for employing alternatives |
| Civil engineering works | Transport and energy demands, poor public policy, lack of knowledge about impacts and their costs | Mainstreaming marine conservation into national policy, cost-benefit analyses, awareness raising |

| *Types of threat* | *Drivers* | *Policy responses* |
|---|---|---|
| Environmental change brought about by war and conflict | Increased competition for scarce resources, political instability, inequality in wealth distribution | Social policy reform, policies to deal with immigrants, limited access (in special cases), mainstreaming marine conservation into foreign policy |
| Aquaculture-related habitat conversion | International demand for luxury items and regional demand for fish food, decline in wild stocks and decreased access to fisheries (or inability to compete) | International security of trade and its impacts, international agreements, training in environmentally sensitive aquaculture, certification |
| **Habitat degradation** | | |
| Eutrophication from land-based sources (LBS) (agricultural waste, sewage, fertilisers) | Urbanisation, lack of sewage treatment or use of combined storm and sewer systems (CSS), unregulated agricultural development, loss of wetlands and other natural controls | Regional agreements involving both sources and sinks, common policies and actions on waste treatment, adequate financing for waste treatment and run-off mitigation (river basin and watershed management), artificial wetlands construction and stricter protection of existing wetlands |
| Pollution: toxics and pathogens from LBS | Lack of awareness, increasing pesticide and fertiliser use (especially as soil quality diminishes), unregulated industry | International standards and compliance on toxics, awareness raising |
| Pollution: dumping and dredge spoils | Lack of alternative disposal methods, increased enforcement and stiffer penalties for land disposal, belief in unlimited assimilative capacities, waste as a commodity | Technology transfer and training in appropriate methods for dumping, enforcement of treaties (LDC and MARPOL), financing and construction of waste-accepting stations in ports of call |

| *Types of threat* | *Drivers* | *Policy responses* |
|---|---|---|
| Pollution: shipping-related | Sub-standard shipping regulations, no investment in safety, policies promoting flags of convenience, increases in ship-based trade. | International regulations on ship hulls and safety measures, establishment of Sensitive Sea Areas (SSAs) |
| Salinisation of estuaries due to decreased fresh-water inflow | Demand for electricity and water, territorial disputes | Cost-benefit analyses, technology transfers for water re-use |
| Alien species invasions | Lack of regulations on ballast discharge, increased aquaculture-related escapes, lack of international agreements on deliberate introduc-tions | Ballast water discharge regulations, active controls against spreading of invading species |
| Global warming and sea level rise | Controls on emissions lacking, poorly planned development (vulnerable development), stressed ecosystems less able to cope | Adherence to emission standards, sea-level rise defences |
| **Over-exploitation** | | |
| Directed take (low value, high volume) exceeding sustainable levels | Demand for subsistence and market (food and medicinal), industrialisation of fisheries, improved fish-finding technology, poor regional agreements, breakdown of traditional regulation systems, lack of enforcement subsidies | International agreements (global codes of conduct, regional management) and enforcement, consumer awareness, quotas, limited access |
| Directed take for luxury markets (high value, low volume) exceeding sustainable levels | Demand for specialty foods and medicines, aquarium fish and curios, lack of awareness or concern about impacts, technological advances, commodification | International pressure on key demand hot spots, trade embargoes, quotas, limited access, MPAs |

| *Types of threat* | *Drivers* | *Policy responses* |
|---|---|---|
| Incidental take or by-catch | Subsidies, by-catch has no cost | Regulations on gear, MPAs for critically important habitats, seasonal closures |
| Directed take at commercial scales, decreasing availability of resources for subsistence and artisanal use | Un-empowered local peoples, breakdown of traditional structures | MPAs, campaign to highlight the problem, artisanal fishing cooperatives |

Source: Agardy, T, 2003, pp.73-74.

# APPENDIX 4.2
# Impact of El Nino on Fisheries

The *El Nino* phenomenon of 1997-98 is considered to be the second strongest 'warm event' in the tropical and sub-tropical Pacific Ocean this century. At the time of its maximum strength, it was not as strong as the 1982-83 event, but lasted a little longer and had two peaks of maximum warming - one almost immediately after its onset, during May-September 1997, and another in January-April 1998. It was preceded by a cold episode in the Eastern Pacific, lasting from the end of 1995 to the beginning of 1997. To some extent, this turn around from a cold to a warm episode might have magnified the negative impacts that this latest *El Nino* has had on certain fish resources.

From the point of view of fisheries, the Eastern Pacific, and particularly the area off Western South America, is the area that is most negatively affected by *El Nino* warming events, and this case was no exception. Rising coastal sea temperatures and a weakening of the up-welling environment process caused a severe decline in biomass and total production of small schooling palagics and other coastal resources that are otherwise readily available off the western coast of South America. This has caused, and is still causing, large losses to the fisheries sectors in the area and a world-wide shortage of fish meal and fish oil.

Anchoveta fish stocks have declined to very low levels in Peru and Chile. The main direct causes of this decline are: recruitment failure, with at least two consecutive year classes either missing or being much less abundant; poor somatic growth with significant loss in average weight; and possible increase in fishing and natural mortality. The region's anchoveta population might take several years to recover. In the same area, important sardine stocks were already declining before the onset of the *El Nino* phenomenon and, although slightly warmer-than-normal conditions are known to favour sardines in this area, prospects of a recovery are likely to have been offset or even lowered owing to the extreme strength of this warming event.

Total production of horse mackerel has also been much lower in 1997-98 than in previous years. This is probably due to an offshore and poleward displacement of existing concentrations, but an actual decline in the total biomass of horse mackerel as a result of heavy fishing, together with the prevailing environmental conditions, cannot be excluded.

So far, the 1997-1998 *El Nino* is known to have produced a 10 to 20 per cent decline in total production from this area in 1997. This is a significant drop, as the region usually produces nearly 20 per cent of total world fish landings. An even larger decline is foreseen for 1998. Catches of other small and medium-sized pelagics, coastal demersals and other species (including salmon, tuna and some invertebrates) have also been affected throughout the Eastern Pacific, from Canada to Chile. While heavy rain and flooding, caused by *El Nino* in some areas, have resulted in reduced shrimp culture activities and smaller landings of otherwise abundant and common fish species, catches of other, more tropical, pelagic species (e.g., dolphin fish, tropical sharks and tuna) have increased in the tropical and subtropical Eastern Pacific. This is because stocks experienced a poleward displacement at the onset of *El Nino*. Both types of effect have retreated or are expected to retreat more rapidly with the phasing out of the event.

In some areas, total production of some wild shrimp stocks and shellfish has also increased as a result of the warmer temperatures. In other regions of the world, minor or less dramatic negative effects of *El Nino* have been reported, for example coral bleaching in the Indian Ocean and tropical and Western Pacific. Even though declines in the production of some tropical fish stocks might be compensated by an increase in production in other areas, a possible reduction of 5 to 10 per cent in total marine fish capture could be attributed to the 1997-1998 *El Nino*.

---

Source: FAO, 1999, p. 85.

# APPENDIX 4.3

## Details of Catch of Principal Capture Fisheries of the World From 1999 to 2003

(in million tonnes)*

| *Principal species* | *1999* | *2000* | *2001* | *2002* | *2003* |
|---|---|---|---|---|---|
| *(1)* | *(2)* | *(3)* | *(4)* | *(5)* | *(6)* |
| Anchovieta (Peruvian anchovy) | 8.72 | 11.28 | 7.21 | 9.70 | 6.20 |
| Alaska pollock (Wall eye poll) | 3.28 | 2.94 | 3.14 | 2.65 | 2.69 |
| Blue whiting (Poulassou) | 1.32 | 1.47 | 1.82 | 1.57 | 2.39 |
| Skipjack tuna | 1.97 | 1.97 | 1.82 | 2.00 | 2.11 |
| Japanese anchovy | 1.82 | 1.73 | 1.84 | 1.85 | 2.09 |
| Atlantic herring | 2.41 | 2.39 | 1.95 | 1.87 | 1.96 |
| Chub mackerel | 1.95 | 1.44 | 1.82 | 1.48 | 1.85 |
| Chilean jack mackerel | 1.42 | 1.54 | 2.51 | 1.75 | 1.74 |
| Yellow fin tuna | 1.21 | 1.18 | 1.32 | 1.33 | 1.48 |
| Large head hair tail | 1.42 | 1.48 | 1.48 | 1.46 | 1.45 |
| Capelin | 0.90 | 1.48 | 1.67 | 1.98 | 1.15 |
| European pilchard (Sardine) | 0.91 | 0.94 | 1.13 | 1.09 | 1.05 |
| Atlantic cod | 1.09 | 0.94 | 0.94 | 0.91 | 0.85 |
| California pilchard | 0.41 | 0.55 | 0.69 | 0.72 | 0.69 |
| Atlantic mackerel | 0.62 | 0.69 | 0.72 | 0.77 | 0.69 |
| Akiami paste shrimp | 0.60 | 0.64 | 0.58 | 0.59 | 0.64 |
| European sprat | 0.68 | 0.66 | 0.65 | 0.62 | 0.63 |
| European anchovy | 0.63 | 0.62 | 0.66 | 0.65 | 0.55 |
| Gulf menhaden | 0.69 | 0.59 | 0.53 | 0.58 | 0.52 |
| Japanese flying squid | 0.50 | 0.57 | 0.53 | 0.50 | 0.49 |
| Round sardinella | 0.41 | 0.36 | 0.46 | 0.44 | 0.48 |
| Argentina shortfin squid | 1.15 | 0.93 | 0.74 | 0.53 | 0.48 |
| Pacific saury | 0.19 | 0.31 | 0.38 | 0.34 | 0.45 |
| Japanese Spanish mackerel | 0.60 | 0.54 | 0.52 | 0.55 | 0.44 |
| Golden threadfin bream | 0.25 | 0.30 | 0.29 | 0.31 | 0.44 |

| *(1)* | *(2)* | *(3)* | *(4)* | *(5)* | *(6)* |
|---|---|---|---|---|---|
| Southern rough shrimp | 0.40 | 0.31 | 0.25 | 0.23 | 0.43 |
| Big eye tuna | 0.43 | 0.43 | 0.41 | 0.43 | 0.42 |
| Cape horse mackerel | 0.40 | 0.42 | 0.35 | 0.39 | 0.40 |
| Saithe (Pollock) | 0.34 | 0.31 | 0.33 | 0.39 | 0.39 |
| Northern prawn | 0.34 | 0.37 | 0.34 | 0.38 | 0.38 |
| Jumbo flying squid | 0.13 | 0.19 | 0.22 | 0.39 | 0.38 |
| Argentina hake | 0.37 | 0.24 | 0.31 | 0.41 | 0.38 |
| Pink (hump back) salmon | 0.39 | 0.29 | 0.35 | 0.27 | 0.38 |
| Pacific cod | 0.40 | 0.37 | 0.33 | 0.33 | 0.38 |
| Chum (Keta-Dog) salmon | 0.28 | 0.28 | 0.31 | 0.31 | 0.36 |
| Indian oil sardine | 0.22 | 0.42 | 0.46 | 0.36 | 0.36 |
| Yesso scallop | 0.31 | 0.31 | 0.29 | 0.31 | 0.35 |
| Japanese mackerel | 0.23 | 0.27 | 0.24 | 0.23 | 0.33 |
| Pacific sandlance | 0.08 | 0.07 | 0.09 | 0.07 | 0.32 |
| Gazami crab | 0.28 | 0.35 | 0.35 | 0.37 | 0.32 |
| Southern African pilchard | 0.18 | 0.16 | 0.20 | 0.26 | 0.31 |
| Dagger tooth pike conger | 0.25 | 0.24 | 0.26 | 0.27 | 0.31 |
| Pacific herring | 0.47 | 0.46 | 0.41 | 0.32 | 0.31 |
| Araucanian herring | 0.78 | 0.72 | 0.32 | 0.35 | 0.30 |
| American sea scallop | 0.13 | 0.20 | 0.25 | 0.28 | 0.29 |
| Nile perch | 0.31 | 0.30 | 0.28 | 0.26 | 0.29 |
| Yellow croaker | 0.26 | 0.30 | 0.25 | 0.27 | 0.29 |
| Haddock | 0.25 | 0.21 | 0.23 | 0.27 | 0.28 |
| Southern African anchovy | 0.18 | 0.27 | 0.29 | 0.25 | 0.26 |
| Nile tilapia | 0.23 | 0.25 | 0.25 | 0.25 | 0.26 |
| Giant tiger prawn | 0.26 | 0.25 | 0.21 | 0.21 | 0.25 |
| Okhotsk atka mackerel | 0.21 | 0.22 | 0.21 | 0.21 | 0.23 |
| Albacore | 0.25 | 0.22 | 0.23 | 0.24 | 0.23 |
| Japanese pilchard. | 0.52 | 0.31 | 0.34 | 0.24 | 0.22 |
| Atlantic horse mackerel | 0.32 | 0.23 | 0.25 | 0.22 | 0.21 |
| Bluegrenadier | 0.28 | 0.28 | 0.26 | 0.21 | 0.21 |
| Patagonian grenadier | 0.45 | 0.23 | 0.30 | 0.26 | 0.21 |

| *(1)* | *(2)* | *(3)* | *(4)* | *(5)* | *(6)* |
|---|---|---|---|---|---|
| Hilsa shad | 0.22 | 0.22 | 0.23 | 0.23 | 0.21 |
| Atlantic menhaden | 0.21 | 0.21 | 0.26 | 0.21 | 0.20 |
| Bonge shad | 0.18 | 0.16 | 0.18 | 0.19 | 0.19 |
| Gold stripe sardinella | 0.16 | 0.17 | 0.19 | 0.18 | 0.19 |
| Indian mackerel | 0.30 | 0.19 | 0.16 | 0.18 | 0.19 |
| Blue swimming crab | 0.15 | 0.16 | 0.17 | 0.15 | 0.18 |
| Madeiran sardinella | 0.13 | 0.14 | 0.13 | 0.13 | 0.18 |
| Narrow barred Spanish mackerel | 0.17 | 0.19 | 0.18 | 0.19 | 0.17 |
| Ocean quahog | 0.14 | 0.12 | 0.15 | 0.16 | 0.17 |
| Indian scad | 0.16 | 0.18 | 0.17 | 0.19 | 0.17 |
| Atlantic surf clam | 0.14 | 0.17 | 0.17 | 0.18 | 0.17 |
| American cupped oyster | 0.13 | 0..22 | 0.18 | 0.16 | 0.17 |
| Long tail tuna | 0.11 | 0.14 | 0.14 | 0.12 | 0.16 |
| Flat head grey mullet | 0.14 | 0.14 | 0.15 | 0.14 | 0.15 |
| 71 species (listed above) | 47.48 | 49.42 | 47.03 | 47.90 | 46.25 |
| Other species | 46.25 | 46.05 | 45.78 | 45.10 | 43.97 |
| World Total | 93.73 | 95.48 | 92.81 | 93.00 | 90.22 |

*Total will not tally as individual figures were rounded to two digits after decimal.
Source: FAO, 2005a, p.41

# APPENDIX 5.1
# Estimated Potential Yield of Major Marine Fishery Resources of the EEZ of India

(in '000 tonnes)

| *Sl. No.* | *Group of fishes* | *Potential yield* |
|---|---|---|
| 1. | Elasmobranchs | 71 |
| 2. | Eels | 9 |
| 3. | Catfish | 51 |
| 4. | Oil sardine | 295 |
| 5. | Other sardines | 101 |
| 6. | Anchovies | 142 |
| 7. | Other clupeids | 79 |
| 8. | Bombay duck | 116 |
| 9. | Lizard fish | 28 |
| 10. | Perches | 227 |
| 11. | Croakers | 273 |
| 12. | Ribbon fish | 194 |
| 13. | Carangids | 238 |
| 14. | Silver bellies | 67 |
| 15. | Pomfrets | 46 |
| 16. | Mackerel | 295 |
| 17. | Seer fish | 62 |
| 18. | Tunnies | 65 |
| 19. | Flat fish | 47 |
| 20. | Penaeid shrimps | 194 |
| 21. | Non-Penaeid shrimps | 139 |
| 22. | Cephalopods | 101 |
| 23. | Priacanthus | 28 |
| 24. | Black ruff | 27 |

| *Sl. No.* | *Group of fishes* | *Potential yield* |
|---|---|---|
| 25. | Indian drift fish | 8 |
| 26. | Deeep sea shrimps | 2 |
| 27. | Deep sea lobster | 1 |
| 28. | Oceanic tunas | 213 |
| 29. | Bill fishes | 5 |
| 30. | Others | 810 |
| | Total | 3934 |

Source: Silas, 2000, Table 10b.

# APPENDIX 5.2

# Location and Cost of Minor Fishing Harbours and Landing Centres Constructed/ Commissioned in India by 2004

| Location | | FH/FLC* | Sanctioned cost (Rs lakhs) |
|---|---|---|---|
| Andhra Pradesh | | | |
| 1. | Kakinada | FH | 973.170 |
| 2. | Nizamapatnam | FH | 157.660 |
| 3. | Bhaavanapadu | FH | 340.000 |
| 4. | Calingapatnam | FLC | 60.350 |
| 5. | Mangipudi | FLC | 17.000 |
| Goa | | | |
| 1. | Cortalim | FLC | 0.510 |
| 2. | Malim | FLC | 89.250 |
| Gujarat | | | |
| 1. | Veraval | FH | 900.000 |
| 2. | Mangrol Stage-I | FH | 200.000 |
| 3. | Porbandar | FH | 276.000 |
| 4. | Mangrol Stage-II | FH | 701.000 |
| 5. | Jafrabad | FLC | 25.000 |
| 6. | Jakhau-1 | FLC | 5.000 |
| 7. | Nansi-borsi | FLC | 16.000 |
| 8. | Kosamba | FLC | 13.000 |
| 9. | Mandvi | FLC | 16.000 |
| 10. | Salaya | FLC | 5.000 |
| 11. | Umarsadi | FLC | 5.000 |
| 12. | Jakhau | FLC | 5.000 |
| 13. | Sachana | FLC | 20.000 |
| 14. | Madhavad | FLC | 17.760 |

| *Location* | | *FH/FLC** | *Sanctioned cost (Rs lakhs)* |
|---|---|---|---|
| 15. | Surjbari | FLC | 27.900 |
| 16. | Magod Dungari | FLC | 38.740 |
| 17. | Dholai | FLC | 54.660 |
| 18. | Chorwad | FLC | 46.120 |
| 19. | Port Onjal | FLC | 42.000 |
| 20. | Rajpara | FLC | 43.450 |
| 21. | Umergaon | FLC | 1.000 |
| 22. | Kolak | FLC | 4.150 |
| 23. | Hirakot | FLC | 0.710 |
| 24. | Navapur | FLC | 0.610 |
| Karnataka | | | |
| 1. | Karwar | FH | 30.000 |
| 2. | Honnavar | FH | 75.000 |
| 3. | Tadri | FH | 4.590 |
| 4. | Mangalore | FH | 33.000 |
| 5. | Malpe Stage -I | FH | 426.000 |
| 6. | Malpe Stage –II | FH | 1146.700 |
| 7. | Coondapur | FLC | 1.000 |
| 8. | Kagal Heni | FLC | 0.600 |
| 9. | Gangolli | FLC | 3.700 |
| 10. | Belikeri | FLC | 0.990 |
| 11. | Keni | FLC | 0.990 |
| 12. | Bhatkal | FLC | 6.000 |
| 13. | Moolky | FLC | 0.100 |
| 14. | Sadasivgad | FLC | 0.990 |
| 15. | Belambar | FLC | 0.990 |
| 16. | Kodibengre | FLC | 55.000 |
| Kerala | | | |
| 1. | Vizhinjam Stage I | FH | 208.000 |
| 2. | Puthiappa | FH | 962.000 |
| 3. | Munambam | FH | 1167.200 |
| 4. | Vizhinjam Stage II | FH | 764.000 |

| *Location* | | *FH/FLC** | *Sanctioned cost (Rs lakhs)* |
|---|---|---|---|
| 5. | Neendakara | FH | 585.000 |
| 6. | Chombal | FH | 556.000 |
| 7. | Mopla Bay | FH | 816.000 |
| 8. | Thangassery | FH | 1930.500 |
| 9. | Kasaragode | FLC | 13.000 |
| 10. | Cannanore | FLC | 1.459 |
| 11. | Neeleswaram | FLC | 15.000 |
| 12. | Munakkadavu | FLC | 19.000 |
| 13. | Beypore | FLC | 2.100 |
| 14. | Palacode | FLC | 19.000 |
| 15. | New Mahe | FLC | 24.590 |
| 16. | Vellayil Beach | FLC | 22.000 |
| 17. | Vallikunnu | FLC | 17.900 |
| 18. | Chettuvai | FLC | 19.500 |
| 19. | Arthungal | FLC | 32.220 |
| 20. | Ponnani | FLC | 8.000 |
| 21. | Baliapatnam | FLC | 13.000 |
| 22. | Thottappally | FLC | 30.000 |
| 23. | Cheruvathur | FLC | 18.000 |
| 24. | Dharmadom | FLC | 21.000 |
| 25. | South Paravoor | FLC | 24.940 |
| 26. | Vizhinjam South | FLC | 19.100 |
| 27. | Vizhinjam North | FLC | 19.100 |
| 28. | Chalil Gopalpettah | FLC | 25.000 |
| 29. | Quilandy | FLC | 23.000 |
| 30. | Punnapra | FLC | 36.800 |
| 31. | Kattor Pollathai | FLC | 50.250 |
| Maharashtra | | | |
| 1. | Ratnagiri | FH | 1840.500 |
| 2. | Karanja | FLC | 11.000 |
| 3. | Navalgaon | FLC | 0.034 |

| *Location* | | *FH/FLC** | *Sanctioned cost (Rs lakhs)* |
|---|---|---|---|
| 4. | Borli Mandla | FLC | 0.520 |
| 5. | Nandgaon | FLC | 0.095 |
| 6. | Murud | FLC | 0.034 |
| 7. | Revadanda | FLC | 0.007 |
| 8. | Anjarle | FLC | 0.003 |
| 9. | Ade-Uttambar | FLC | 0.016 |
| 10. | Agrao | FLC | 0.549 |
| 11. | Boria | FLC | 0.029 |
| 12. | Burondi | FLC | 0.049 |
| 13. | Bagamandla | FLC | 1.000 |
| 14. | Datiware | FLC | 0.922 |
| 15. | Dahanu | FLC | 0.990 |
| 16. | Dakti-Dahanu | FLC | 0.994 |
| 17. | Khardanda | FLC | 0.822 |
| 18. | Ekdara | FLC | 0.012 |
| 19. | Mandavi | FLC | 0.508 |
| 20. | Mulgaon | FLC | 1.860 |
| 21. | Navapur | FLC | 0.200 |
| 22. | Onni-Bhatti | FLC | 0.027 |
| 23. | Thumvadi | FLC | 0.160 |
| 24. | Thal | FLC | 0.547 |
| 25. | Utton | FLC | 0.020 |
| 26. | Vashi | FLC | 0.311 |
| 27. | Wadrai | FLC | 0.739 |
| 28. | Rajpuri | FLC | 0.536 |
| 29. | Jeevne Bundar | FLC | 0.536 |
| 30. | Mahim Causeway | FLC | 23.070 |
| 31. | Alibagh Koliwada | FLC | 32.530 |
| 32. | Tarkarli | FLC | 53.340 |
| 33. | Taramumbri | FLC | 97.020 |
| 34. | Achara Peerwada | FLC | 95.160 |
| 35. | Rajpuri Koliwada | FLC | 73.960 |
| 36. | Ekdara Koliwada | FLC | 38.660 |

| | Location | FH/FLC* | Sanctioned cost (Rs lakhs) |
|---|---|---|---|
| Orissa | | | |
| 1. | Gopalpur | FH | 805.300 |
| 2. | Dhamra | FH | 70.000 |
| 3. | Naugarh (Astrang) | FH | 507.000 |
| 4. | Chandipur | FLC | 15.000 |
| 5. | Pathara | FLC | 2.500 |
| 6. | Nairi Stage-I | FLC | 5.410 |
| 7. | Nairi Stage II | FLC | 6.000 |
| 8. | Jamboo | FLC | 73.030 |
| 9. | Palaur | FLC | 17.000 |
| 10. | Kansabansa | FLC | 65.100 |
| 11. | Soran | FLC | 9.970 |
| 12. | Sabelia | FLC | 2.420 |
| 13. | Chudamani | FLC | 14.060 |
| 14. | Panchubisa | FLC | 32.680 |
| 15. | Talchua | FLC | 110.700 |
| 16. | Kharanasi | FLC | 99.900 |
| 17. | Chandrabhaga | FLC | 8.320 |
| 18. | Rushikulya | FLC | 9.400 |
| 19. | Tantiapal | FLC | 99.060 |
| 20. | Sorala | FLC | 70.280 |
| 21. | Bandara | FLC | 160.500 |
| 22. | Khandiapatana | FLC | 105.830 |
| 23. | Bhusandpur Baliapatpur | FLC | 108.600 |
| 24. | Bahabalpur | FLC | 98.040 |
| Tamil Nadu | | | |
| 1. | Tuticorin | FH | 210.000 |
| 2. | Mallipatnam | FH | 10.600 |
| 3. | Kodiakarai | FH | 14.400 |
| 4. | Vallinokkam | FH | 77.000 |
| 5. | Tondi | FH | 56.560 |
| 6. | Pazhayar | FH | 67.000 |

| Location | | FH/FLC* | Sanctioned cost (Rs lakhs) |
|---|---|---|---|
| 7. | Chinnmuttom | FH | 684.000 |
| 8. | Cuddalore | FLC | 12.000 |
| 9. | Rameshwaram | FLC | 10.000 |
| 10. | Kottaipatnam | FLC | 22.000 |
| 11. | Muttom | FLC | 12.600 |
| 12. | Vallapalam | FLC | 7.140 |
| 13. | Vallavillai | FLC | 7.500 |
| 14. | Nagapattinam | FLC | 0.750 |
| 15. | Palk Bay | FLC | 1.000 |
| 16. | Erawadi | FLC | 26.000 |
| 17. | Poompuhar | FLC | 7.870 |
| 18. | Kodimurai | FLC | 7.500 |
| West Bengal | | | |
| 1. | Fraser Ganj | FH | 452.320 |
| 2. | Digha Stage-I | FH | 139.000 |
| 3. | Digha Stage-II | FH | 492.520 |
| 4. | Sultanpur (Diamond Harbour) | FH | 473.470 |
| 5. | Namkhana | FLC | 7.060 |
| 6. | Jalda | FLC | 9.500 |
| 7. | New Jalda | FLC | 5.000 |
| 8. | Kharpai | FLC | 6.300 |
| 9. | Kalinagar | FLC | 7.130 |
| 10. | Bamanagar | FLC | 4.180 |
| 11. | Ganeshpur | FLC | 5.310 |
| 12. | Akhoynagar | FLC | 3.080 |
| 13. | Junapat | FLC | 9.800 |
| 14. | Soula | FLC | 13.270 |
| 15. | Madanganj | FLC | 9.600 |
| 16. | Brajobalapur | FLC | 9.650 |
| A & N Islands | | | |
| 1. | Phoenix Bay | FH | 67.000 |

| *Location* | | *FH/FLC** | *Sanctioned cost (Rs lakhs)* |
|---|---|---|---|
| Lakshadweep | | | |
| 1. | Kavaratti | FLC | 11.000 |
| 2. | Minicoy | FLC | 15.520 |
| 3. | Agathi | FLC | 5.000 |
| Pondicherry | | | |
| 1. | Pondicherry | FH | 423.000 |
| 2. | Mahe | FLC | 0.040 |
| Daman & Diu | | | |
| 1. | Ghoghla | FLC | 52.120 |
| 2. | Vanakbara | FLC | 43.800 |

*FH: Fishing Harbour; FLC: Fish Landing Centre
Source: Department of Animal Husbandry, Dairying and Fisheries, 2005, pp.76-77.

# APPENDIX 5.3
# Location and Cost of Fishing Harbours Under Construction in 2004

| Location | | FH/FLC* | Sanctioned cost (Rs. lakhs) |
|---|---|---|---|
| Andhra Pradesh | | | |
| 1. | Machililipatnam | FH | 470.88 |
| 2. | Baruva | FLC | 83.60 |
| 3. | Gondisamudram | FLC | 88.86 |
| 4. | Isakapalli Patapupalem | FLC | 85.62 |
| 5. | Thatichetlapalem | FLC | 84.86 |
| 6. | Nuvvalarevu | FLC | 79.35 |
| 7. | Bandaruvanipeta | FLC | 79.00 |
| 8. | Chintapalli | FLC | 79.77 |
| 9. | Mukkam | FLC | 79.77 |
| 10. | Pudimadakara | FLC | 78.00 |
| 11. | Mypadu | FLC | 81.16 |
| 12. | Atimoga | FLC | 61.57 |
| 13. | Vodarevu | FLC | 92.47 |
| 14. | Kothapatanam | FLC | 92.84 |
| Goa | | | |
| 1. | Cortalim Stage-II | FLC | 89.31 |
| 2. | Cutbona | FLC | 89.20 |
| Gujarat | | | |
| 1. | Jakhau | FH | 1143.60 |
| 2. | Navabunder | FLC | 33.91 |
| 3. | Dhamlej | FLC | 31.00 |
| Karnataka | | | |
| 1. | Mangalore Stage-II | FH | 75.00 |
| 2. | Gangolli | FH | 13.12 |

| Location | | FH/FLC* | Sanctioned cost (Rs. lakhs) |
|---|---|---|---|
| 3. | Hejmadikodi | FLC | 95.00 |
| 4. | Alvekodi | FLC | 89.53 |
| 5. | Belikeri Stage-II | FLC | 67.40 |
| Kerala | | | |
| 1. | Vizhinjam Stage-III | FH | 1366.00 |
| 2. | Muthalapozhy | FH | N.A |
| 3. | Ponnani | FH | 2759.40 |
| 4. | Kayamkulam | FH | 624.00 |
| 5. | Thottappally | FH | 1458.30 |
| 6. | Moylali Kadappuram | FLC | 85.20 |
| 7. | Kanhangad | FLC | 28.42 |
| 8. | Thikkodi | FLC | 49.25 |
| 9. | Poovar | FLC | 26.99 |
| 10. | Kadapra | FLC | 18.52 |
| Maharashtra | | | |
| 1. | Agaro | FH | 414.00 |
| 2. | Sarjekote | FLC | 30.00 |
| Orissa | | | |
| 1. | Dhamra Stage-II | FH | 640.00 |
| 2. | Bahabalpur | FH | 1080.00 |
| 3. | Kirtania | FLC | 84.00 |
| 4. | Panthakata | FLC | 80.20 |
| 5. | Talasari | FLC | 98.24 |
| 6. | Gopalpur-on-Sea | FLC | 96.00 |
| 7. | Hata Baradi | FLC | 62.00 |
| 8. | Balugaon | FLC | 235.50 |
| 9. | Nairi Stage-III | FLC | 38.86 |
| Tamil Nadu | | | |
| 1. | Arcottuthurai | FLC | 122.00 |
| 2. | Pulicat | FLC | 132.32 |
| 3. | Punnakayal | FLC | 132.32 |
| 4. | Soliakudi | FLC | 132.32 |

| Location | | FH/FLC* | Sanctioned cost (Rs. lakhs) |
|---|---|---|---|
| 5. | Mandapam North | FLC | 132.32 |
| 6. | Jagathapattinam | FLC | 132.32 |
| 7. | Nagapattinam | FLC | 132.32 |
| 8. | Sethupavasatram | FLC | 132.32 |
| West Bengal | | | |
| 1. | Harwood Point | FH | 1350.00 |
| Andaman & Nicobar Islands | | | |
| 1. | Dairy Farm (Junglighat) | FLC | 368.00 |

*FH: Fishing Harbour; FLC: Fish Landing Centre

Source: Department of Animal Husbandry, Dairying and Fisheries, 2005, p.78.

# APPENDIX 5.4
# Location of FFDAs in States and Union Territories of India in 2004

| *State/UT* | *No. of FFDAs* | *Location (District)* |
|---|---|---|
| Andhra Pradesh | 22 | Karimnagar, Kurnool, Medak, Krishna, Nalgonda, East Godavari, West Godavari, Mehboobnagar, Nizamabad, Chittoor, Khammam, Srikakulam, Vijayanagaram, Visakapattanam, Guntoor, Prakasham, Nellore, Warangal, Adilabad, Anantpur, Cuddapah and Rangareddy |
| Arunachal Pradesh | 2 | Regional FFDA at Itanagar and Siang |
| Assam | 23 | Darrang, Kamrup, Naowgang, Sibsagar, Cachar, Lakhimpur, Sonitpur, Karimganj, Karbi, Anglong, Dibrugarh, Kokrajhar, Dhubri, Barpeta, Goalpara, Jorhat, Bongaigaon, Nalbari, Morigaon, Golaghat, Tinsukia, Dhemaji, Hailakandi and N.C. Hills District. |
| Bihar | 33 | East Champaran, West Champaran, Siwan, Gopalganj, Saran,Vaishali, Muzaffarpur, Sitamarhi, Gaya, Purnea, Khagaria, Patna, Madhubani, Darbhanga, Munger, Samastipur, Begusarai, Saharsa, Aurangabad, Katihar, Madhepura, Nalanda, Bhagalpur, Rohtas, Bhojpur, Nawada, Jahanabad, Buxar, Supaul, Ataria, Kishanganj, Banka, and Jamul. |
| Jharkhand | 16 | Ranchi, Hazaribagh, Gumla, Dhanbad, Giridih, Godda, Dumka, Palamu, Lohardaga, Bokaro, Chatra, Deoghar, Gadhwa, Sahebganj, Singhbhum and Jamshedpur. |
| Goa | 1 | Regional FFDA at Panaji |
| Gujarat | 21 | Surat, Panchmahal, Bulsar, Kheda, Jamnagar, Bharoch, Surendranagar, Sabarkantha, Vadodhara, Ahemedabad, Rajkot, Bhavnagar, Kutch, Junagarh, Amreli, Banaskantha, Mehsana, Navsari, Anand, Dahod, Narmada. |

| *State/UT* | *No. of FFDAs* | *Location (District)* |
|---|---|---|
| Haryana | 18 | Karnal, Rohtak, Sonepat, Gurgaon, Faridabad, Sirsa, Mahindergarh, Ambala, Kurukshetra, Hissar, Bhiwani, Jind, Rewari, Panipat, Kaithal, Yamunanagar, Jhajjar, Fatehabad |
| Himachal Pradesh | 2 | Regional FFDAs at Bilaspur and Mandi |
| Jammu & Kashmir | 2 | Regional FFDAs at Jammu and Kashmir |
| Karnataka | 18 | Mysore, Dharwar, Shimoga, Kolar, Raichur, Bidar, Bangalore, Chickmangalur, Hassan, Chitradurga, Gulbarga, Belgaum, Bijapur, Madikeri, Uttara-Kannada, Mandya, Tumkur and Dakshin-Kannada |
| Kerala | 14 | Palghat, Quilon, Trichur, Cannanore, Alleppey, Trivandrum,. Ernakulam, Kottayam, Malappuram, Kozhikode, Pathanamthitta, Idukki, Wayanad, and Kasargode. |
| Maharashtra | 29 | Nagpur, Chandrapur, Bhandara, Yeotmal, Gadchirolli, Pune, Satara, Sangli, Thana, Sholapur, Kolhapur, Aurangabad, Parbhani, Latur, Beed, Amravati, Buldhana, Akola, Ratnagiri, Kolaba, Bombay, Nandid, Jalgaon, Ahmednagar, Nasik, Jalna, Usmanabad, Vardha, Dhulia |
| Madhya Pradesh | 38 | Rewa, Shahdol, Seoni, Balaghat, Sagar, Chatarpur, Satna, Jabalpur, Sidhi, Shivpuri, Tikamgarh, Dhargaona, Dhar, Betul, Shehore, Raisen, Mandla, Chhindwara, Bhind, Guna, Gwalior, Hoshangabad, Damoh, Ujjain, Khandwa, Mandsour, Dewas, Indore, Jhabua, Panna, Shajapur, Ratlam, Morena, Datia, Rajgarh, Vidisha, Narsinghpur and Bhopal |
| Chattisgarh | 7 | Raipur, Durg, Rajanandgaon, Bilaspur, Raigarh, Jagdalpur (Bastar), Sarguja (Ambikapur) |
| Manipur | 8 | Central Manipur, South Manipur, Bishanpur, Ukhrul, Tamenglong, Chandel, Sanepati and Thoubal |
| Meghalaya | 2 | Regional FFDAs at Shillong and Baghmare |
| Mizoram | 5 | Aizwal (East), Lunglai, Chhimtuiphi, Aizwal (West) and Kolasib |

| *State/UT* | *No. of FFDAs* | *Location (District)* |
|---|---|---|
| Nagaland | 8 | Kohima, Zunheboto, Tuensang, Mon, Pheak, Wokha, Mokokchung and Dimapur |
| Orissa | 30 | Cuttack, Puri, Balasore, Ganjam, Phulbani, Bolangir, Sambalpur, Dhenkanal, Mayurbhanj, Kalahandi, Koraput, Sundergarh, Keonjhar, Gajapati, Rayagadas, Nawarangpur, Malkanagiri, Bhadrak, Jajpur, Kendrapara, Jagarsinghpur, Khurda, Nayagarh, Angul, Bargarh, Nuapara, Sonepur, Jharsuguda, Boudh, and Deogarh |
| Punjab | 17 | Gurdaspur, Amritsar, Ludhiana, Sangrur, Jallundur, Patiala, Ropar, Hoshiarpur, Bhatinda, Kapurthala, Ferozpur, Faridkot, Mansa, Fatehgarh Saheb, Mooga, Muktsar and Navasher |
| Rajasthan | 15 | Ajmer, Alwar, Bhilwara, Bharatpur, Dungarpur, Jaipur, Tonk, Udaipur, Kota, Chittorgarh, Banswara, Jhalawad, Sewaimadhopur, Pali and Sriganganagar |
| Sikkim | 1 | Regional FFDA at Gangtok |
| Tamil Nadu | 17 | Thanjavur, Madurai, South Arcot, Periyar, Tiruchirapalli, Dharmapuri, Changalpattu, Kamarajar, Anna, Tirunelveli, North Arcot, Kanyakumari, Madras, Pudukottai, Posumpam-Mutthuramalingam, Kattabomman and Chidambaranar |
| Tripura | 4 | West Tripura, South Tripura , North Tripura and Dhala |
| Uttar Pradesh | 53 | Allahabad, Kanpur, Fatehpur, Varanasi, Jaunpur, Balia Gazipur, Mirjapur, Basti, Gorakhpur, Deoria, Azamgarh, Lucknow, Unnao, Banda, Gonda, Raibareilly, Moradabad, Sitapur, Hardoi, Lakhimpur-Kheri, Faizabad, Sultanpur, Prtapgarh, Barabanki, Bahraich, Meerut, Badaun, Etah, Aligarh, Jalaun, Etawah, Agra, Farukhabad, Mainpuri, Muzzffarnagar, Bulandshahar, Saharanpur, Gaziabad, Jhansi, Lalitpur, Hamirpur, Bareilly, Shahjahanpur, Pilibhit, Rampur, Bijnaur, Mathura, Firozabad, Sidharthnagar, Mau, Sonabhadra, Maharajgarh. |

| *State/UT* | *No. of FFDAs* | *Location (District)* |
|---|---|---|
| Uttaranchal | 3 | Hardwar, Dehradoon (Regional FFDA for Garhwal Division) and Nainital (Regional FFDA for Kumaon Division) |
| West Bengal | 18 | Bankura, Nadia, Howrah, West Dinajpur, Hooghly, Birbhum, Darjeeling, North 24-Parganas, Malda, Murshidabad, Cooch-Behar, Jalpaiguri, Burdwan, Midnapur, Purulia, South 24-Parganas, Siliguri Sub Division of Darjeeling District and Uttar Dinajpur |
| Pondicherry | 2 | Regional FFDAs at Karaikal and Pondicherry |
| Total | 429 | |

Source: Department of Animal Husbandry, Dairying and Fisheries, 2005, pp.149-150.

# APPENDIX 5.5
## Trend in Fish Seed Production in States and Union Territories of India from 1994-95 to 2003-04

(in million fry)

| Sl. No. | State/UT | 1994-95 | 1995-96 | 1996-97 | 1997-98 | 1998-99 | 1999-2000 | 2000-01 | 2001-02 | 2002-03 | 2003-04 |
|---|---|---|---|---|---|---|---|---|---|---|---|
| (1) | (2) | (3) | (4) | (5) | (6) | (7) | (8) | (9) | (10) | (11) | (12) |
| 1. | Andhra Pradesh | 700.00 | 709.00 | 711.00 | 700.00 | 752.40 | 899.00 | 920.50 | 214.90 | 178.90 | 351.64 |
| 2. | Arunachal Pradesh | 19.95 | 21.00 | 21.00 | 24.00 | 24.50 | 24.40 | 25.00 | 25.00 | 25.10 | 25.00 |
| 3. | Assam | 2386.95 | 2547.54 | 2634.48 | 2245.57 | 1703.06 | 2114.14 | 1485.68 | 1801.55 | 1902.00 | 2228.41 |
| 4. | Bihar | 321.16 | 332.21 | 492.00 | 405.49 | 451.39 | 449.11 | 358.57 | 329.95 | 367.99 | 346.11 |
| 5. | Goa | - | 0.03 | - | - | 0.45 | 0 | 0 | 4.95 | 0.15 | 0.50 |
| 6. | Gujarat | 161.78 | 191.17 | 199.40 | 670.00 | 469.50 | 469.07 | 359.55 | 496.33 | 414.40 | 114.56 |
| 7. | Haryana | 102.22 | 200.73 | 147.30 | 151.69 | 168.00 | 177.00 | 177.60 | 180.50 | 204.00 | 243.06 |
| 8. | Himachal Pradesh | 20.14 | 23.10 | 21.97 | 23.35 | 23.21 | 23.63 | 25.77 | 27.53 | 16.99 | 19.47 |
| 9. | Jammu & Kashmir | 11.82 | 12.60 | 12.60 | 13.07 | 10.65 | 11.20 | 12.30 | 13.90 | 14.55 | 15.62 |
| 10. | Karnataka | 165.30 | 164.34 | 208.30 | 202.12 | 42.47 | 183.91 | 230.27 | 206.37 | 155.26 | 135.35 |
| 11. | Kerala | 20.26 | 20.26 | 20.26 | 5.18 | 9.50 | 19.02 | 19.02 | 11.20 | 12.60 | 12.70 |

| (1) | (2) | (3) | (4) | (5) | (6) | (7) | (8) | (9) | (10) | (11) | (12) |
|---|---|---|---|---|---|---|---|---|---|---|---|
| 12. | Madhya Pradesh | 523.40 | 564.20 | 612.36 | 584.94 | 495.10 | 610.60 | 339.70 | 359.30 | 263.20 | 384.40 |
| 13. | Maharashtra | 270.00 | 293.00 | 270.00 | 242.00 | 241.00 | 208.00 | 207.00 | 275.00 | 187.00 | 169.04 |
| 14. | Manipur | 81.00 | 90.50 | 101.00 | 110.05 | 98.20 | 115.10 | 115.00 | 116.00 | 117.00 | 117.00 |
| 15. | Meghalaya | 4.00 | 0.97 | 0.97 | 0.98 | 0.78 | 1.12 | 1.12 | 1.15 | 0.87 | 0.96 |
| 16. | Mizoram | 0.56 | 0.31 | 0.50 | 2.70 | 5.80 | 14.00 | 13.00 | 9.12 | 10.30 | 13.20 |
| 17. | Nagaland | 50.00 | 50.00 | 50.00 | 50.00 | 50.00 | 50.00 | 50.00 | 47.00 | 47.00 | 40.00 |
| 18. | Orissa | 188.67 | 186.69 | 211.82 | 234.20 | 261.71 | 346.00 | 274.03 | 365.28 | 439.86 | 497.39 |
| 19. | Punjab | 42.00 | 44.00 | 54.00 | 60.05 | 71.97 | 71.00 | 71.90 | 91.73 | 89.43 | 97.69 |
| 20. | Rajasthan | 150.00 | 175.00 | 169.00 | 220.00 | 167.31 | 238.51 | 231.00 | 286.00 | 423.34 | 303.00 |
| 21. | Sikkim | 1.25 | 2.50 | 2.50 | 2.50 | 3.60 | 2.50 | 2.50 | 2.50 | 2.50 | 2.50 |
| 22. | Tamil Nadu | 536.59 | 467.43 | 638.00 | 561.05 | 542.44 | 814.36 | 591.91 | 627.14 | 686.59 | 413.05 |
| 23. | Tripura | 170.10 | 172.00 | 208.95 | 210.03 | 211.12 | 209.90 | 209.80 | 220.92 | 229.54 | 272.26 |
| 24. | Uttar Pradesh | 479.15 | 546.62 | 618.79 | 680.10 | 730.54 | 806.52 | 882.81 | 959.92 | 975.44 | 1053.58 |
| 25. | West Bengal | 8126.14 | 8180.00 | 8435.00 | 8500.00 | 8610.00 | 8725.00 | 8850.00 | 9000.00 | 9100.00 | 11910.00 |
| 26. | A & N Islands | 0.17 | 0.57 | 0.35 | 0.47 | 0.14 | 0.49 | 0.45 | 0.57 | 0.76 | 0.55 |
| 27. | Chandigarh | 1.62 | 0.63 | 0.63 | - | 6.60 | 0 | 0.70 | 0.70 | 0.70 | 1.10 |
| 28. | Dadra & Nagar Haveli | - | - | - | - | - | 0 | 0 | 0 | 0 | 0 |
| 29. | Daman & Diu | - | - | - | - | - | 0 | 0 | 0 | 0 | 0 |

| (1) | (2) | (3) | (4) | (5) | (6) | (7) | (8) | (9) | (10) | (11) | (12) |
|---|---|---|---|---|---|---|---|---|---|---|---|
| 30. | Delhi | 3.80 | 3.82 | 3.82 | 4.10 | 4.25 | 3.20 | 3.20 | 3.17 | 2.33 | 2.00 |
| 31. | Lakshadweep | - | - | - | - | - | 0 | 0 | 0 | 0 | 0 |
| 32. | Pondicherry | 9.00 | 7.00 | 6.97 | - | - | 2.40 | 0.50 | 0 | 0 | 0 |
| 33. | Chattisgarh | - | - | - | - | - | - | 23.30 | 0.01 | 327.17 | 367.82 |
| 34. | Uttaranchal | - | - | - | - | - | - | 51.60 | 51.66 | 33.30 | 29.01 |
| 35. | Jharkhand | - | - | - | - | - | - | 74.54 | 28.27 | 104.30 | 64.50 |
| | India | 14547.03 | 15007.22 | 15852.97 | 15903.64 | 15155.69 | 16589.18 | 15608.32 | 15757.62 | 16332.57 | 19231.47 |

Source: Department of Animal Husbandry, Dairying and Fisheries, 2005, p.57.

# APPENDIX 5.6
# Distribution of Active Fishermen in States and Union Territories of India during 1993 and 1994

| Sl. No. | State/UT | Year | Full-time | Part-time | Occasional | Total |
|---|---|---|---|---|---|---|
| 1 | Andhra Pradesh | 1993 | 151425 | 132320 | 212986 | 496731 |
| | | 1994 | 151425 | 132320 | 212986 | 496731 |
| 2 | Arunachal Pradesh | 1993 | 0 | 4610 | 954 | 5564 |
| | | 1994 | 0 | 4751 | 965 | 5716 |
| 3 | Assam | 1993 | 362819 | 112181 | 0 | 475000 |
| | | 1994 | 362819 | 112181 | 0 | 475000 |
| 4 | Bihar | 1993 | 288034 | 475736 | 322101 | 1085871 |
| | | 1994 | 295235 | 487629 | 330154 | 1113018 |
| 5 | Goa | 1993 | 15709 | 2439 | 688 | 18836 |
| | | 1994 | 15709 | 2439 | 688 | 18836 |
| 6 | Gujarat | 1993 | 52388 | 24051 | 63769 | 140208 |
| | | 1994 | 52388 | 24051 | 63769 | 140208 |
| 7 | Haryana | 1993 | 6814 | 5046 | 3940 | 15800 |
| | | 1994 | 7090 | 5094 | 3890 | 16034 |
| 8 | Himachal Pradesh | 1993 | 3300 | 5801 | 4220 | 13321 |
| | | 1994 | 3294 | 3718 | 1443 | 8455 |
| 9 | Jammu & Kashmir | 1993 | 8302 | 2449 | 2249 | 13000 |
| | | 1994 | 8302 | 2449 | 2249 | 13000 |
| 10 | Karnataka | 1993 | 20688 | 9849 | 779931 | 810468 |
| | | 1994 | 20688 | 9849 | 779931 | 810468 |
| 11 | Kerala | 1993 | 345913 | 107352 | 143137 | 596402 |
| | | 1994 | 412091 | 127891 | 170520 | 710502 |
| 12 | Madhya Pradesh | 1993 | 28856 | 88916 | - | 117772 |
| | | 1994 | 130982 | - | - | 130982 |
| 13 | Maharashtra | 1993 | 67930 | 46042 | 311680 | 425652 |
| | | 1994 | 67930 | 46042 | 311680 | 425652 |
| 14 | Manipur | 1993 | 14961 | 8362 | 8677 | 32000 |
| | | 1994 | 18675 | 8112 | 5563 | 32350 |

| *Sl. No.* | *State/UT* | *Year* | *Full-time* | *Part-time* | *Occasional* | *Total* |
|---|---|---|---|---|---|---|
| 15 | Meghalaya | 1993 | 2291 | 3667 | 4531 | 10489 |
| | | 1994 | 2321 | 3836 | 4940 | 11097 |
| 16 | Mizoram | 1993 | 0 | 0 | 600 | 600 |
| | | 1994 | 0 | 600 | - | 600 |
| 17 | Nagaland | 1993 | 80200 | 0 | 82140 | 162340 |
| | | 1994 | 90100 | 0 | 95250 | 185350 |
| 18 | Orissa | 1993 | 99074 | 69352 | 29723 | 198149 |
| | | 1994 | 101000 | 72760 | 28352 | 202112 |
| 19 | Punjab | 1993 | 1100 | 2050 | 950 | 4100 |
| | | 1994 | 1200 | 2050 | 950 | 4200 |
| 20 | Rajasthan | 1993 | 6576 | 4853 | 1654 | 13083 |
| | | 1994 | 6170 | 4649 | 2738 | 13557 |
| 21 | Sikkim | 1993 | 0 | 300 | 250 | 550 |
| | | 1994 | 0 | 300 | 250 | 550 |
| 22 | Tamil Nadu | 1993 | 111449 | 111449 | 222897 | 445795 |
| | | 1994 | 267309 | - | - | 267309 |
| 23 | Tripura | 1993 | 18561 | 16786 | 14463 | 49810 |
| | | 1994 | 18853 | 16815 | 15287 | 50955 |
| 24 | Uttar Pradesh | 1993 | 30042 | 71089 | 59692 | 160823 |
| | | 1994 | 30042 | 71089 | 59692 | 160823 |
| 25 | West Bengal | 1993 | 298590 | 298590 | - | 597180 |
| | | 1994 | 298590 | 298590 | - | 597180 |
| 26 | A & N Islands | 1993 | 2940 | 510 | 200 | 3650 |
| | | 1994 | 2960 | 518 | 200 | 3678 |
| 27 | Chandigarh | 1993 | 200 | 0 | 50 | 250 |
| | | 1994 | 200 | - | 50 | 250 |
| 28 | Dadra & Nagar Haveli | 1993 | 120 | 10 | 0 | 130 |
| | | 1994 | 120 | 10 | 0 | 130 |
| 29 | Daman & Diu | 1993 | 14500 | 3150 | 12950 | 30600 |
| | | 1994 | 14520 | 3150 | 13330 | 31000 |
| 30 | Delhi | 1993 | 1030 | 344 | 0 | 1374 |
| | | 1994 | 1030 | 400 | 15000 | 16430 |
| 31 | Lakshadweep | 1993 | 3600 | 800 | 1300 | 5700 |
| | | 1994 | 3700 | 830 | 1470 | 6000 |
| 32 | Pondicherry | 1993 | 8293 | 1116 | 0 | 9409 |
| | | 1994 | 9871 | 1100 | - | 10971 |
| | Total | 1993 | 2045705 | 1609220 | 2062835 | 5717759 |
| | | 1994 | 2394574 | 1443223 | 2121347 | 5959144 |

Source: Department of Agriculture and Cooperation, 1996, pp.136-137

# APPENDIX 5.7

## Distribution of Fishermen Population and Working Fishermen in States and Union Territories of India during 2003

| Sl. No. | State UT | Fishermen population | | | | Fishermen engaged in fishing | | | | | | Fishermen engaged in other activities | | |
|---|---|---|---|---|---|---|---|---|---|---|---|---|---|---|
| | | | | | | Full-time | | | Part-time | | | | | |
| | | Male | Female | Children | Total | Male | Female | Total | Male | Female | Total | Male | Female | Total |
| (1) | (2) | (3) | (4) | (5) | (6) | (7) | (8) | (9) | (10) | (11) | (12) | (13) | (14) | (15) |
| 1. | Andhra Pradesh | 249386 | 250877 | 393102 | 893365 | 91038 | 26422 | 117460 | 124967 | 25768 | 150735 | 155208 | 149685 | 304893 |
| 2. | Arunachal Pradesh | 1650 | 1376 | 1373 | 4399 | 0 | 0 | 0 | 1099 | 843 | 1942 | 0 | 0 | 0 |
| 3. | Assam | 131312 | 97986 | 161082 | 390380 | 66120 | 39568 | 105688 | 42746 | 23676 | 66422 | 48814 | 12282 | 61096 |
| 4. | Bihar | 1391166 | 1266997 | 2301353 | 4959516 | 25503 | 11576 | 37079 | 43347 | 14942 | 58289 | 32234 | 14468 | 46702 |
| 5. | Chattisgarh | 621607 | 529697 | 760064 | 1911368 | 4828 | 2805 | 7633 | 32905 | 13719 | 46624 | 18201 | 12206 | 30407 |
| 6. | Goa | 5521 | 4863 | 3586 | 13970 | 1844 | 355 | 2199 | 1116 | 566 | 1682 | 923 | 1477 | 240 |
| 7. | Gujarat | 134475 | 129900 | 228880 | 493255 | 77653 | 6024 | 83677 | 26601 | 10383 | 36984 | 18479 | 33219 | 51698 |
| 8. | Haryana | 5910 | 3322 | 7259 | 16491 | 2527 | 174 | 2701 | 1002 | 433 | 1435 | 108306 | 415 | 108721 |
| 9. | Himachal Pradesh | 1537 | 1372 | 2713 | 5622 | 421 | 207 | 628 | 547 | 27 | 574 | 554 | 4 | 558 |
| 10. | Jammu & Kashmir | 9628 | 7593 | 13232 | 30453 | 2876 | 467 | 3343 | 1244 | 717 | 1961 | 3480 | 1732 | 5212 |

| (1) | (2) | (3) | (4) | (5) | (6) | (7) | (8) | (9) | (10) | (11) | (12) | (13) | (14) | (15) |
|---|---|---|---|---|---|---|---|---|---|---|---|---|---|---|
| 11. | Jharkhand | 577908 | 571584 | 781428 | 1930920 | 4329 | 914 | 5243 | 17100 | 4341 | 21441 | 18362 | 3913 | 22275 |
| 12. | Karnataka | 55809 | 52898 | 50245 | 158952 | 13640 | 770 | 14410 | 8669 | 1207 | 9876 | 40948 | 13805 | 54753 |
| 13. | Kerala | 224007 | 317758 | 206072 | 747837 | 110953 | 3803 | 114756 | 26515 | 6213 | 32728 | 36599 | 39027 | 75626 |
| 14. | Madhya Pradesh | 213888 | 200607 | 302479 | 716974 | 4699 | 751 | 5450 | 13743 | 4125 | 17868 | 8245 | 2776 | 11021 |
| 15. | Maharashtra | 63354 | 46603 | 61873 | 171830 | 14587 | 5019 | 19606 | 38280 | 11397 | 49677 | 40029 | 9101 | 49130 |
| 16. | Manipur | 25009 | 24091 | 21368 | 70468 | 2516 | 451 | 2967 | 2003 | 2090 | 4093 | 2225 | 2957. | 5182 |
| 17. | Meghalaya | 525 | 504 | 1354 | 2383 | 2 | 0 | 2 | 346 | 148 | 494 | 0 | 2 | 2 |
| 18. | Mizoram | 5498 | 5312 | 7097 | 17907 | 116 | 29 | 145 | 1150 | 201 | 1351 | 1163 | 440 | 1603 |
| 19. | Nagaland | 5762 | 5519 | 3581 | 14862 | 43 | 0 | 43 | 0 | 0 | 0 | 0 | 0 | 0 |
| 20. | Orissa | 70971 | 48334 | 60721 | 180026 | 27331 | 7973 | 35304 | 26322 | 12499 | 38821 | 40784 | 20547 | 61331 |
| 21. | Punjab | 2150 | 1874 | 5061 | 9085 | 1528 | 28 | 1556 | 898 | 386 | 1284 | 3001 | 718 | 3719 |
| 22. | Rajasthan | 2638 | 1693 | 2985 | 7316 | 654 | 21 | 675 | 881 | 93 | 974 | 1060 | 124 | 1184 |
| 23. | Sikkim | 9893 | 8353 | 8568 | 26814 | 536 | 609 | 1145 | 87 | 207 | 294 | 182 | 0 | 182 |
| 24. | Tamil Nadu | 171992 | 156107 | 148519 | 476618 | 63232 | 6111 | 69343 | 35280 | 7790 | 43070 | 50140 | 33071 | 83211 |
| 25. | Tripura | 15966 | 13177 | 17590 | 46733 | 2934 | 541 | 3475 | 145 | 5424 | 5569 | 6160 | 2488 | 8648 |
| 26. | Uttar Pradesh | 70373 | 48892 | 59799 | 179064 | 11316 | 3148 | 14464 | 12718 | 3100 | 15818 | 10571 | 6794 | 17365 |
| 27. | Uttaranchal | 32 | 23 | 35 | 90 | 43 | 9 | 52 | 109 | 73 | 182 | 103 | 23 | 126 |
| 28. | West Bengal | 587214 | 205198 | 119210 | 911622 | 267944 | 0 | 267944 | 446517 | 0 | 446517 | 364618 | 0 | 364618 |
| 29. | Andaman & Nicobar | 9859 | 7693 | 0 | 17552 | 2630 | 0 | 2630 | 7191 | 0 | 7191 | 746 | 429 | 1175 |
| 30. | Chandigarh | 198 | 109 | 172 | 479 | 168 | 18 | 186 | 97 | 44 | 141 | 344 | 7 | 351 |

| (1) | (2) | (3) | (4) | (5) | (6) | (7) | (8) | (9) | (10) | (11) | (12) | (13) | (14) | (15) |
|---|---|---|---|---|---|---|---|---|---|---|---|---|---|---|
| 31. | Dadra & Nagar Haveli | 0 | 0 | 0 | 0 | 0 | 0 | 0 | 0 | 0 | 0 | 0 | 0 | 0 |
| 32. | Daman & Diu | 7649 | 7756 | 10080 | 25485 | 4404 | 22 | 4126 | 895 | 481 | 1376 | 2901 | 1341 | 1632 |
| 33. | Delhi | 485 | 475 | 1555 | 2515 | 253 | 0 | 253 | 262 | 8 | 270 | 184 | 0 | 184 |
| 34. | Lakshadweep | 10408 | 2621 | 0 | 13029 | 4231 | 19 | 4250 | 2807 | 1003 | 3810 | 1448 | 0 | 1448 |
| 35. | Pondicherry | 12378 | 12799 | 12797 | 37974 | 4352 | 339 | 4691 | 2187 | 399 | 2586 | 3613 | 4416 | 8029 |
| | Total | 4696158 | 4033963 | 5755233 | 14485354 | 814951 | 118173 | 933124 | 919776 | 152303 | 1072079 | 1017015 | 367467 | 138482 |

Source: Department of Animal Husbandry, Dairying and Fisheries, 2005, p.141.

# APPENDIX 5.8
# Details of Outlay and Expenditure for Fisheries Development under Central and Centrally-Sponsored Schemes during the Fifth Five Year Plan (1974-79)

(Rs. in lakhs)

| *Sl. No.* | *Name of Scheme* | *Outlay* | *Expenditure* |
|---|---|---|---|
| I. | *Central Schemes* | | |
| 1. | Exploratory Fisheries Project | 350.16 | 161.42 |
| 2. | Integrated Fisheries Project | 359.18 | 323.78 |
| 3. | Central Institute of Fisheries Nautical & Engineering Training | 150.11 | 85.17 |
| 4. | Pelagic Fisheries Project | 149.87 | 96.54 |
| 5. | Pre-Investment Survey of Fishing Harbour Projects | 49.88 | 35.22 |
| 6. | Central Fisheries Corporation, Calcutta | 100.00 | 55.00 |
| 7. | Provision for Landing & Berthing Facilities at Major Ports | 1799.60 | 1210.40 |
| 8. | Subsidy for Indigenous Vessels | 700.00 | 4.90 |
| 9. | Trawler Development Fund | - | 1230.13 |
| 10. | Development of Aquaculture (FFDA) | 500.43 | 310.87 |
| 11. | Development of Brackish Water Fisheries | 70.00 | 71.70 |
| 12. | Development of Reservoir Fisheries | 2.00 | - |
| 13. | Central Assistance to State Fisheries Corporation | 180.00 | 217.14 |
| 14. | Refrigerated Rail Vans | 199.63 | 58.46 |
| 15. | Project for Survey of Marine Fisheries Resources on North-West Coast and East Coast | 164.93 | 62.58 |
| 16. | Establishment of Cold-Chains | 149.58 | 13.96 |
| 17. | Other Schemes | 179.44 | 55.82 |
| | Total | 5104.81 | 3993.09 |

| *Sl. No.* | *Name of Scheme* | *Outlay* | *Expenditure* |
|---|---|---|---|
| II. *Centrally-Sponsored Schemes* | | | |
| 18. | Landing & Berthing Facilities at Minor Ports | 1200.00 | 320.56 |
| 19. | Development of Infrastructural Facilities for Coastal Fishing Villages | 400.00 | 71.95 |
| 20. | Strengthening of Organisation of Fisheries Extension Work | 100.00 | 14.36 |
| | Total | 1700.00 | 406.87 |
| III. *Grand Total (I & II)* | | 6804.81 | 4399.96 |

Source: Department of Agriculture and Cooperation, 1996, p.107.

# APPENDIX 5.9

# Details of Outlay and Expenditure for Fisheries Development under Central and Centrally-Sponsored Schemes during the Annual Plans 1978-79 and 1979-80

(Rs. in lakhs)

| *Sl. No.* | *Name of Scheme* | *1978-79* | | *1979-80* | |
|---|---|---|---|---|---|
| | | *Outlay* | *Expenditure* | *Outlay* | *Expenditure* |
| 1 | Exploratory Fisheries Project | 694.04 | 711.88 | 700 | 653.42 |
| 2 | Fish Processing & Marketing (Integrated Fisheries Project) | 154.48 | 45.65 | 75 | 55.97 |
| 3 | Central Institute of Fisheries Nautical and Engineering Training | 257.09 | 90.00 | 600 | 2.44 |
| 4 | Pelagic Fisheries Project | 30.00 | 32.1[illegible] | 10 | 10.73 |
| 5 | Pre-investment Survey of Fishing Harbour Projects | 9.00 | 7.4[illegible] | 10 | 7.84 |
| 6 | Central Fisheries Corporation, Calcutta | 1.00 | 33.41 | 1 | 15.75 |
| 7 | Landing & Berthing Facilities for Fishing Crafts at Major Ports | 500.00 | 308.44 | 550 | 206.05 |
| 8 | Trawler Development Fund | 2550.00 | 11.31 | 2000 | 2.54 |
| 9 | Development of Aquaculture (FFDAs) | 300.00 | 31.73 | 6 | 0.6 |
| 10 | Development of Brackish Water Aquaculture | 200.00 | 49.55 | * | * |
| 11 | Development of Reservoir Fisheries | 1.00 | - | * | * |
| 12 | Central Assistance to State Fisheries Corporation | 300.00 | 103.[illegible]5 | * | * |
| 13 | Refrigerated Rail Vans | - | 0.46 | - | - |
| 14 | Project for Survey of Marine Fisheries Resources | - | 19.14 | - | - |
| 15 | Landing & Berthing Facilities for Fishing Crafts at Minor Ports | 600.00 | 393.58 | - | 0.55 |
| 16 | Development of Infrastructural Facilities for Coastal Fishing Villages | 200.00 | 89.34 | 22 | - |
| 17 | Other Schemes | 74.39 | 49.20 | 29 | 15.85 |
| | Total | 5871.00 | 1977.55 | 4312 | 1471.74 |

*Transferred to states

Source: Department of Agriculture and Cooperation, 1996, p.108.

# APPENDIX 5.10
# Details of Outlay and Expenditure for Fisheries Development under Central and Centrally-Sponsored Schemes during the Sixth Five Year Plan (1980-85)

(Rs in lakhs)

| *Sl. No.* | *Name of Scheme* | *Outlay* | *Expenditure* |
|---|---|---|---|
| I. | *Central Schemes* | | |
| 1. | Exploratory Fisheries Project (now Fishery Survey of India) | 4800.00 | 2157.77 |
| 2. | Integrated Fisheries Project (Fish Processing & Marketing Project) | 285.00 | 618.07 |
| 3. | Central Institute of Fisheries Nautical & Engineering Training (CIFNET) | 700.00 | 848.81 |
| 4. | Central Institute of Coastal Engineering for Fisheries | 75.00 | 51.36 |
| 5. | Fishing Harbour at Major Ports | 1700.00 | 1320.08 |
| 6. | All India Fish Marketing Survey | 41.00 | 22.90 |
| 7. | Assistance to SDFC for Trawler Development Fund | 5000.00 | 1922.05 |
| 8. | Strengthening of Organisation at Fishery Head Quarters | 25.00 | 16.85 |
| 9. | Programmes for Fish Seed Production | 800.00 | 317.33 |
| 10. | Augmentation of Slipway Facilities at Goa Shipyard | 165.00 | - |
| 11. | Pilot Project on Reservoir Fisheries with World Bank Assistance | 19.00 | 18.00 |
| 12. | Development of Inland Fisheries Statistics | 100.00 | 11.85 |
| 13. | Andaman & Lakshadweep Islands Corporation | - | - |
| 14. | Enforcement of Maritime Zones of India Rules | - | - |
| 15. | Assessment of Marine Fisheries Resources and Training | - | 2.37 |

| *Sl. No.* | *Name of Scheme* | *Outlay* | *Expenditure* |
|---|---|---|---|
| 16. | Project Preparation for IDA Assistance (Pilot Project) for Inland Fisheries | - | - |
| 17. | National Welfare Fund for Fishermen | - | - |
| 18. | National Fisheries Development Corporation | - | - |
| 19. | Schemes for Wooden Hull Development | | 83.20 |
| 20. | Development of Small Scale Fisheries under Japanese Aid | - | 162.00 |
| | Total | 13710.00 | 7553.24 |
| II. | *Centrally-Sponsored Schemes* | | |
| 21. | Development of Aquaculture (FFDA) | 500.00 | 369.52 |
| 22. | Fishing Harbours at Minor Ports | 1900.00 | 1795.10 |
| 23. | Establishment of Prawn Hatcheries & Prawn Farming | 500.00 | 113.00 |
| 24. | Inland Fisheries Project with World Bank Assistance | 762.00 | 522.76 |
| 25. | Techno-Socio-Economic Survey of Fisheries/ Construction of Dry Docks | - | 17.85 |
| 26. | Group Insurance Scheme for Active Fishermen | - | 32.57 |
| 27. | Development of Botanical Garden near Fisheries Harbour | - | 10.00 |
| 28. | Introduction of Beach Landing Crafts for Small Fishermen | - | 19.46 |
| | Total | 3662.00 | 2880.26 |
| III. | *Grand Total* | 17372.00 | 10433.50 |

Source: Department of Agriculture and Cooperation, 1996, p. 110.

# APPENDIX 5.11

## Details of Outlay and Expenditure for Fisheries Development under Central and Centrally-Sponsored Schemes during the Seventh Five Year Plan (1985-90)

(Rs in lakhs)

| *Sl. No.* | *Name of Scheme* | *Outlay* | *Expenditure* |
|---|---|---|---|
| *I. Central Schemes* | | | |
| 1. | Integrated Fisheries Project (IFP) | 700.00 | 490.93 |
| 2. | Central Institute of Fisheries Nautical & Engineering Training | 700.00 | 831.82 |
| 3. | Central Institute of Coastal Engineering for Fisheries | 75.00 | 95.91 |
| 4. | Training/Seminar, etc. | 50.00 | 32.07 |
| 5. | Fishery Harbours at Major Ports | 1700.00 | 1684.40 |
| 6. | Development of Inland Fisheries Statistics | 80.00 | 56.48 |
| 7. | National Fisheries Development Board | 500.00 | - |
| 8. | Wooden Hull Trawler | 30.00 | - |
| 9. | Strengthening of Technical Wing | 160.00 | 30.19 |
| | Total | 3995.00 | 3221.80 |
| *II. Centrally-Sponsored Schemes* | | | |
| 10. | Fish Seed Development Programme | 550.00 | 364.49 |
| 11. | FFDA | 1550.00 | 1701.29 |
| 12. | Development of Derelict Water Bodies | 165.00 | 112.00 |
| 13. | Development of Reservoir Fisheries | 400.00 | 14.35 |
| 14. | Development of Coastal Marine Fisheries | | |
| | (*i*) Motorisation of Traditional Craft | - | - |
| | (*ii*) Introduction of Improved Beach Landing Craft | 300.00 | 278.84 |
| | (*iii*) Introduction of Plywood Boats | - | - |
| | (*iv*) Development of Offshore Pelagic Fishing | - | - |

| *Sl. No.* | *Name of Scheme* | *Outlay* | *Expenditure* |
|---|---|---|---|
| | (*v*) Reimbursement of Excise Duty on HSD Oil used by Mechanised Fishing Boats | - | - |
| | (*vi*) Assistance to States for Enforcement of Marine Fishing Regulations | - | - |
| 15. | Integrated Brackish Water Fish Farming Development | 500.00 | 479.93 |
| 16. | Minor Fishery Harbours including Fishery Industrial Estates | 1900.00 | 2168.86 |
| 17. | Welfare Schemes | | |
| | (*i*) Group Accident Insurance Scheme for Active Fishermen | 150.00 | 140.01 |
| | (*ii*) National Welfare Fund for Fishermen | 400.00 | 266.28 |
| | (*iii*) Savings-Cum-Relief Scheme | - | |
| | Total | 5915.00 | 5526.05 |
| III. | *Grand Total* | 9910.00 | 8747.85 |

Source: Department of Agriculture and Cooperation, 1996, p. 111.

# APPENDIX 5.12

## Details of Outlay and Expenditure for Fisheries Development under Central and Centrally-Sponsored Schemes and Externally Aided new Schemes during the Eighth Five Year Plan

(Rs.in lakhs)

| Sl. No. | Name of scheme | VIII Plan 1992-97 | Annual Plan 1992-93 | | Annual Plan 1993-94 | | Annual Plan 1994-95 | | Annual Plan 1995-96 | | Annual plan 1996-97 |
|---|---|---|---|---|---|---|---|---|---|---|---|
| | | | Outlay | Expenditure | Outlay | Expenditure | Outlay | Expenditure | Outlay | Expenditure | Outlay |
| (1) | (2) | (3) | (4) | (5) | (6) | (7) | (8) | (9) | (10) | (11) | (12) |
| *A.* | *Central Schemes* | | | | | | | | | | |
| 1. | Central Institute of Fisheries Nautical and Engineering Training | 1500 | 170 | 135 | 180 | 342 | 465 | 203 | 435 | 345 | 449.50 |
| 2. | Central Institute of Coastal Engineering for Fisheries | 400 | 49 | 98 | 12 | 35 | 20 | 8 | 122 | 89 | 19.50 |
| 3. | Integrated Fisheries Project | 1000 | 260 | 109 | 2300 | 2352 | 594 | 257 | 578 | 211 | 564.00 |
| 4. | Fishing Harbour Facility at Major Ports | 5400 | 800 | 1279 | 1400 | 1200 | 1000 | 1000 | 1100 | 751 | 913.00 |
| 5. | Training and Fisheries Extension | 200 | 70 | 68 | 30 | 11 | 250 | 36 | 35 | 38 | 48.00 |
| 6. | Inland Fisheries Statistics | 230 | 50 | 21 | 55 | 49 | 50 | 38 | 60 | 50 | 70.00 |
| 7. | Central Fisheries Harbour Authority | 500 | 1 | 0 | 10 | 0 | 210 | 0 | 10 | 0 | 0 |
| | Total (A) | 9230 | 1400 | 1710 | 3987 | 3989 | 2589 | 1542 | 2340 | 1484 | 2064.00 |

| (1) | (2) | (3) | (4) | (5) | (6) | (7) | (8) | (9) | (10) | (11) | (12) |
|---|---|---|---|---|---|---|---|---|---|---|---|
| *B. Externally Aided Project* | | | | | | | | | | | |
| 8. | Central Project Unit for Shrimp & Fish Culture | 770 | 0 | 0 | 170 | 236 | 250 | 216 | 105 | 95 | 155.00 |
| | Total (B) | 770 | 0 | 0 | 170 | 236 | 250 | 216 | 105 | 95 | 155.00 |
| C. *Centrally-Sponsored Schemes* | | | | | | | | | | | |
| 9. | Minor Fishing Harbours | 4700 | 600 | 601 | 700 | 675 | 1100 | 1110 | 1125 | 1167 | 1150.00 |
| 10. | Fresh Water Aquaculture | 6000 | 749 | 515 | 900 | 856 | 900 | 895 | 929 | 1020 | 1005.00 |
| 11. | Integrated Brackishwater Fish Farm Development | 2500 | 400 | 199 | 450 | 221 | 500 | 257 | 575 | 293 | 480.00 |
| 12. | Development of Coastal Marine Fisheries | | | | | | | | | | |
| | a) Motorisation of Traditional Craft | 1000 | 1000 | – | 210 | – | 261 | 302 | 350 | – | – |
| | b) Introduction of Plywood Craft | 200 | 10 | 457 | 20 | 641 | 30 | 23 | 45 | 825 | 1300.00 |
| | c) Introduction of Intermediate Craft | 400 | 100 | – | 10 | – | 200 | 25 | 105 | – | – |
| | d) Re-imbursement of Excise duty on HSD Oil | 5000 | 1000 | – | 1000 | – | 900 | 797 | 900 | – | – |
| 13. | Welfare of Fishermen | | | | | | | | | | |
| | a) Group Accident Insurance | 200 | 45 | – | 48 | – | 48 | 46 | 48 | – | – |
| | b) Model Fishermen Villages | 2000 | 300 | 792 | 327 | 959 | 500 | 485 | 500 | 1242 | 800.00 |
| | c) Savings-cum-Relief | 2000 | 455 | – | 528 | – | 622 | 724 | 500 | – | – |
| 14. | Assistance for Strengthening Fish Marketing | 2500 | 300 | 355 | 750 | 500 | 700 | 318 | 633 | 328 | 700.00 |

| (1) | (2) | (3) | (4) | (5) | (6) | (7) | (8) | (9) | (10) | (11) | (12) |
|---|---|---|---|---|---|---|---|---|---|---|---|
| 15. | Enforcement of Marine Fishing Regulation Act and Resource Enhancement for Artificial Reefs | | | | | | | | | | |
| | a) Marine Fishing Regulation Act | 3000 | 540 | 0 | 500 | 600 | 800 | 795 | 850 | 547 | 900.00 |
| | b) Resource Enhancement Through Artificial Reef | 500 | - | 0 | 100 | 0 | 100 | - | - | - | - |
| | c) Development of Derelict Water Bodies | 0 | 0 | 45(scheme transferred to states) | | | 0 | - | - | - | - |
| | d) Net Making | 0 | 0 | 900(book adjustment) | | - | 900 | - | - | - | - |
| | Total (C) | 30000 | 4600 | 3864 | 5543 | 4452 | 6661 | 6677 | 6560 | 5422 | 6335.00 |
| | Total (A+B+C) | 40000 | 6000 | 5574 | 9700 | 8677 | 9500 | 8435 | 9005 | 7001 | 8554.00 |
| *D. New Schemes* | | | | | | | | | | | |
| 16. | Fisheries Development in Floodplain Lakes | - | - | - | - | - | - | - | 100 | - | 50.00 |
| 17. | Integrated Fisheries Development of Reservoirs | - | - | - | - | - | - | - | 50 | - | 25.00 |
| 18. | Omnibus Scheme for Fishery Development | - | - | - | - | - | - | - | 50 | - | 25.00 |
| 19. | Fishnet-making Machine | - | - | - | - | - | - | - | 100 | - | |
| 20. | Acquisition of Dredging Equipments for Fishery Harbours & Fish Landing Centres Under Japanese Assistance | - | - | - | - | - | - | - | - | - | 1.00 |
| F. | Grand total (A+B+C+D) | 40000 | 6000 | 5574 | 9700 | 8677 | 9500 | 8435 | 9305 | 7001 | 8655.00 |

Source: Department of Agriculture and Cooperation, 1996, pp. 112-114.

# APPENDIX 5.13
## Developmental Thrust and Expenditure for Fisheries during the Various Five Year Plans

(Rs in millions)

| *Plan* | *Period** | *Outlay* | *Expenditure* | *Development thrust* |
|---|---|---|---|---|
| *(1)* | *(2)* | *(3)* | *(4)* | *(5)* |
| I | 1951-1956 | 51.3 | 27.8 | Inland fisheries and collection of spawn and fry from natural sources; some states passed legislation for bringing neglected water under fish culture |
| II | 1956-1961 | 122.6 | 90.6 | Programmes initiated in the First Plan continued during the Second Plan with added thrust on development of marine fisheries |
| III | 1961-1966 | 282.7 | 233.2 | Thrust on increased fish production, mechanisation of fishing vessels and programames for improvement in the condition of fishermen; schemes for development of infrastructure for landing and berthing facilities for fishing vessels introduced. |
| IV | 1969-1974 | 826.8 | 541.1 | Develoment of export potential, including setting up of an autonomous authority for export promotion; allocation of separate outlay for fisheries research; setting up of special Trawler Development Fund; setting up of Fish Farmers' Development Agencies to promote inland aquaculture |

| *(1)* | *(2)* | *(3)* | *(4)* | *(5)* |
|---|---|---|---|---|
| V | 1974-1979 | 1512.4 | 1152.1 | Development of brackishwater fisheries; survey of marine fisheries resources; development of infrastructure facilities for coastal fishing villages, etc. |
| VI | 1980-1985 | 3711.4 | 2869.5 | Assistance for acquisition of trawlers for deep-sea fishing; development of inland fisheries statistics; establishment of prawn hatcheries and prawn farming. |
| VII | 1985-1990 | 5465.2 | 4775.9 | Motorisation of traditional fishing craft; National Welfare Fund for development of fishing villages; conservation of marine resources through closed season; initiation of new Deep-Sea Fishing Policy. |
| VIII | 1992-1997 | 12053.9 | 11184.6 | Strengthening of inland fish marketing; resource enhancement through artificial reefs; fisheries training and extension; setting up of large number of minor harbours and fish landing centers; setting up of Aquaculture Development Authority for regulation of shrimp farming |
| IX | 1997-2002 | 20697.8 | 14141.0 | Acquisition of survey vessels for strengthening Fishery Survey of India; modernisation of fishing harbours and fish landing centres. |

*The period 1996-1969, 1978-1980 and 1990-1992 were considered as annual plans.

Source: 1. Yadava, 2004, p.100.

2. Department of Animal Husbandry, Dairying and Fisheries, 2005, p.89.

# APPENDIX 6.1
# Dimensions and Criteria/Indicators of Sustainable Development of Fisheries

| *Dimensions* | *Criteria* |
|---|---|
| Economic | Harvest<br>Harvest value<br>Fisheries' contribution to GDP<br>Fisheries exports value (compared with total value of exports)<br>Investment in fishing fleets and processing facilities<br>Taxes and subsidies<br>Employment<br>Income<br>Fishery net revenues |
| Social | Employment/participation<br>Demography<br>Literacy/education<br>Protein/consumption<br>Income<br>Fishing traditions/culture<br>Indebtedness<br>Gender distribution in decision-making |
| Ecological | Catch structure<br>Relative abundance of target species<br>Exploitation rate<br>Direct effects of fishing gear on non-target species<br>Indirect effects of fishing: trophic structure<br>Direct effect of gear on habitats<br>Biodiversity (species)<br>Change in area and quality of important or critical habitats<br>Fishing pressure – fished-versus-unfished area |
| Governance | Compliance regime<br>Property rights<br>Transparency and participation<br>Capacity to manage |

Source: FAO, 1999b, p.18.

# APPENDIX 6.2
## State-wise Details of Production of Shrimp and Scampi in India from 2002-03 to 2005-06

| Sl. No. | State | 2002-03 | | | 2003-04 | | | 2004-05 | | | 2005-06 | | |
|---|---|---|---|---|---|---|---|---|---|---|---|---|---|
| | | Area under culture (ha) | Production (MT) | Productivity (MT ha Yr) | Area under culture ha) | Production (MT) | Productivity (MT ha Yr) | Area under culture ha) | Production (MT) | Productivity (MT ha Yr) | Area under culture ha) | Production (MT) | Productivity (MT ha Yr) |
| 1. | West Bengal | 53150 | 30410 | 0.57 | 534375 | 32149 | 0.59 | 54610 | 38625 | 0.71 | 54758 | 46087 | 0.84 |
| 2. | Orissa | 11995 | 10690 | 0.89 | 12586 | 12840 | 1.02 | 10218 | 10366 | 1.01 | 11560 | 10419 | 0.90 |
| 3. | Andhra Pradesh | 93000 | 86210 | 0.93 | 96924 | 85209 | 0.88 | 89525 | 96150 | 1.07 | 91268 | 107772 | 1.18 |
| 4. | Tamil Nadu | 3800 | 5120 | 1.35 | 3373 | 6203 | 1.84 | 3876 | 6818 | 1.76 | 5452 | 7641 | 1.40 |
| 5. | Kerala | 14510 | 7770 | 0.54 | 14915 | 6699 | 0.45 | 11708 | 7841 | 0.67 | 15122 | 7247 | 0.47 |
| 6. | Karnataka | 3205 | 2800 | 0.87 | 3291 | 1943 | 0.59 | 1693 | 1426 | 0.84 | 3406 | 1886 | 0.55 |
| 7. | Goa | 930 | 710 | 0.76 | 963 | 700 | 0.73 | 295 | 534 | 1.81 | 331 | 659 | 1.99 |
| 8. | Maharashtra | 4880 | 930 | 0.19 | 7596 | 1287 | 0.17 | 567 | 1129 | 1.99 | 881 | 917 | 1.04 |
| 9. | Gujarat | 1240 | 1130 | 0.91 | 2443 | 1616 | 0.66 | 895 | 1502 | 1.68 | 1337 | 3362 | 2.51 |
| | Total | 186710 | 145770 | 0.78 | 196470 | 148650 | 0.76 | 173380 | 164390 | 0.95 | 184115 | 185990 | 1.01 |

Source: Marine Products Export Development Authority, Files ( 2006).

# APPENDIX 6.3
# Number of Households per 1000 Households Reporting Consumption of Fish in Rural and Urban Areas of States and Union Territories of India during 1999-2000

| *Sl. No.* | *States/Union territories* | *Rural area* | *Urban area* |
|---|---|---|---|
| 1. | Andhra Pradesh | 250 | 205 |
| 2. | Arunachal Pradesh | 487 | 638 |
| 3. | Assam | 894 | 862 |
| 4. | Bihar | 454 | 421 |
| 5. | Goa | 957 | 934 |
| 6. | Gujarat | 64 | 59 |
| 7. | Haryana | 119 | 267 |
| 8. | Himachal Pradesh | 305 | 11 |
| 9. | Jammu & Kashmir | 621 | 42 |
| 10. | Karnataka | 116 | 139 |
| 11. | Kerala | 916 | 838 |
| 12. | Madhya Pradesh | 190 | 153 |
| 13. | Maharashtra | 196 | 287 |
| 14. | Manipur | 708 | 909 |
| 15. | Meghalaya | 810 | 677 |
| 16. | Mizoram | 411 | 283 |
| 17. | Nagaland | 685 | 779 |
| 18. | Orissa | 701 | 717 |
| 19. | Punjab | 211 | 286 |
| 20. | Rajasthan | 169 | 256 |
| 21. | Sikkim | 141 | 411 |
| 22. | Tamil Nadu | 322 | 379 |
| 23. | Tripura | 963 | 965 |
| 24. | Uttar Pradesh | 165 | 63 |
| 25. | West Bengal | 938 | 878 |
| 26. | A & N Islands | 920 | 878 |

| (1) | (2) | (3) | (4) | (5) | (6) | (7) |
|---|---|---|---|---|---|---|
| 27. | Chattisgarh | | | 82 | | 426 |
| 28. | Dadra & Nagar Haveli | | | 229 | | 271 |
| 29. | Daman & Diu | | | 591 | | 718 |
| 30. | Delhi | | | 254 | | 74 |
| 31. | Lakshadweep | | | 882 | | 895 |
| 32. | Pondicherry | | | 829 | | 757 |
| | All India | | | 336 | | 285 |

Source: Department of Animal Husbandry, Dairying and Fisheries, 2005, pp.144-145.

# APPENDIX 6.4

# Trend in the Export of Marine Products from India between 1961-62 and 2003-04

| *Year* | *Quantity (Tonnes)* | *Change over 1961-62 (%)* | *Value (Rs Crores)* | *Change over 1961-62 (%)* | *Unit value (Rs/tonne)* | *Change over 1961-62 (%)* |
|---|---|---|---|---|---|---|
| *(1)* | *(2)* | *(3)* | *(4)* | *(5)* | *(6)* | *(7)* |
| 1961-62 | 15732 | - | 3.92 | - | 2491.74 | - |
| 1962-63 | 11161 | 29.05 | 4.20 | 7.14 | 3763.10 | 51.02 |
| 1963-64 | 19057 | 21.13 | 6.09 | 55.36 | 3195.68 | 28.25 |
| 1964-65 | 21122 | 34.26 | 7.14 | 82.14 | 3380.36 | 35.66 |
| 1965-66 | 15295 | -2.78 | 7.06 | 80.10 | 4615.89 | 85.25 |
| 1966-67 | 21116 | 34.22 | 17.37 | 343.11 | 8225.99 | 230.13 |
| 1967-68 | 21907 | 39.25 | 19.72 | 403.06 | 9001.69 | 261.26 |
| 1968-69 | 26811 | 70.42 | 24.70 | 530.10 | 9212.64 | 269.73 |
| 1969-70 | 31695 | 101.46 | 33.46 | 753.57 | 10556.87 | 323.68 |
| 1970-71 | 35883 | 128.08 | 35.07 | 794.64 | 9773.43 | 292.23 |
| 1971-72 | 35523 | 125.80 | 44.55 | 1036.47 | 12541.17 | 403.31 |
| 1972-73 | 38903 | 147.29 | 59.72 | 1423.46 | 15351.00 | 516.08 |
| 1973-74 | 52279 | 232.31 | 89.51 | 2183.41 | 17121.60 | 587.14 |
| 1974-75 | 45099 | 186.67 | 68.41 | 1645.15 | 15168.85 | 508.77 |
| 1975-76 | 54463 | 246.19 | 124.53 | 3076.78 | 22865.06 | 817.64 |
| 1976-77 | 66750 | 324.29 | 189.12 | 4724.48 | 28332.58 | 1037.06 |
| 1977-78 | 56967 | 262.10 | 180.12 | 4494.89 | 31618.31 | 1168.93 |
| 1978-79 | 86894 | 452.34 | 234.62 | 5885.20 | 27000.71 | 983.61 |
| 1979-80 | 86401 | 449.21 | 248.82 | 6247.44 | 28798.28 | 1055.75 |
| 1980-81 | 75591 | 380.49 | 234.84 | 5890.81 | 31067.19 | 1146.81 |
| 1981-82 | 70105 | 345.62 | 286.01 | 7196.17 | 40797.38 | 1537.31 |
| 1982-83 | 78175 | 396.92 | 361.36 | 9118.36 | 46224.50 | 1755.11 |
| 1983-84 | 92187 | 485.98 | 373.02 | 9415.81 | 40463.41 | 1523.90 |
| 1984-85 | 86187 | 447.85 | 384.29 | 9703.31 | 44587.93 | 1689.43 |
| 1985-86 | 83651 | 431.73 | 398.00 | 10053.06 | 47578.63 | 1809.46 |
| 1986-87 | 85843 | 254.96 | 460.67 | 11651.78 | 53664.25 | 2053.69 |

| *(1)* | *(2)* | *(3)* | *(4)* | *(5)* | *(6)* | *(7)* |
|---|---|---|---|---|---|---|
| 1987-88 | 97179 | 517.71 | 531.20 | 13451.02 | 54662.02 | 2093.73 |
| 1988-89 | 99777 | 534.22 | 597.85 | 15151.27 | 59918.62 | 2303.69 |
| 1989-90 | 110843 | 604.59 | 634.99 | 16098.72 | 57287.33 | 2199.09 |
| 1990-91 | 139419 | 786.21 | 893.37 | 22690.05 | 64078.07 | 2471.62 |
| 1991-92 | 171820 | 992.16 | 1375.89 | 34999.23 | 80077.41 | 3113.72 |
| 1992-93 | 209025 | 1228.66 | 1768.56 | 45016.32 | 84609.97 | 3295.62 |
| 1993-94 | 243960 | 1450.72 | 2503.62 | 63767.85 | 102624.20 | 4018.58 |
| 1994-95 | 307337 | 1853.57 | 3575.27 | 91105.87 | 116330.61 | 4568.66 |
| 1995-96 | 296277 | 1783.28 | 3501.11 | 89214.03 | 118170.16 | 4642.48 |
| 1996-97 | 378199 | 2304.29 | 4121.36 | 105036.73 | 108973.32 | 4273.39 |
| 1997-98 | 385818 | 2352.44 | 4697.48 | 119733.67 | 121753.78 | 4786.30 |
| 1998-99 | 302934 | 1825.59 | 4626.87 | 117932.39 | 152735.25 | 6029.67 |
| 1999-00 | 343031 | 2080.48 | 5116.67 | 130427.29 | 149160.57 | 5886.21 |
| 2000-01 | 440473 | 2699.85 | 6443.89 | 164284.95 | 146294.78 | 5771.20 |
| 2001-02 | 424470 | 2598.13 | 5957.05 | 151865.56 | 140340.90 | 5532.25 |
| 2002-03 | 467297 | 2870.36 | 6881.31 | 175443.62 | 147257.74 | 5809.84 |
| 2003-04 | 412017 | 2518.97 | 6091.95 | 155306.89 | 147856.76 | 5833.87 |

Source: Department of Animal Husbandry, Dairying and Fisheries, 2005, p.65.

# APPENDIX 6.5
## Details of Various Subsidy Schemes Provided by MPEDA to the Fishery Sector of India

| Sl. No. | Name of the scheme | Objective | Quantum of subsidy |
|---|---|---|---|
| *I. Export production – capture fisheries* | | | |
| 1. | Installation of Turtle Exclusion Devices (TED) in fishing trawlers | To protect Turtles during fishing as a conservation measure | Supply of TED, free of cost to mechanised trawlers |
| 2. | Financial assistance for installation of fish finders, GPS, radio telephone & fish-holds onboard-mechanised fishing vessels | To increase the efficiency of large mechanised vessels to fish in deeper waters | 30% of the cost of eligible items (Fish finder, Global Positioning System & Radio Telephone) & installation charges subject to a maximum of Rs 50,000/- per vessel |
| 3. | Grant from Ministry of Food Processing Industries for setting up of new processing plant/pre-processing plant or modernisation of existing processing/ pre-processing plant. | To encourage modernisation of existing units or to set up new units | Grant to the extent of 25% of cost of the technical, civil work and machinery, limited to Rs 50 lakhs in the case of units in general area and 30% of the cost, limited to Rs 75 lakhs in the case of difficult areas |
| *II. Export production – culture fisheries* | | | |
| 4. | Financial assistance for new farm development in undeveloped areas | Assistance is given to shrimp/scampi farmers for setting up of new farms for augmenting production | 25% of the capital cost or @ Rs. 50,000/ha water spread area. A farmer is eligible to avail maximum subsidy of Rs 2.50 lakhs for culturing shrimp/scampi in 5.00 ha. water spread area. |

| *Sl. No.* | *Name of the scheme* | *Objective* | *Quantum of subsidy* |
|---|---|---|---|
| 5. | Promotion of comercial hatcheries for seed production of exportable species | Assistance for setting up of hatcheries for production of healthy and quality seeds for aquaculture | a) 25% of capital cost, to the maximum of Rs 3.00 lakhs/ hatchery for a small-scale hatchery of 10 to 30 million post-larvae production capacity. b) 25% of capital cost, to the maximum of Rs 6.00 lakhs/ hatchery for a medium scale hatchery of 30 million and above post-larvae production capacity. |
| 6. | a) Financial assistance for establishment of effluent treatment system (ETS) in shrimp farms | ETS is mandatory for shrimp farms above 5 ha water area. Hence, this scheme was introduced to assist farmers to set up ETS in their farms. | 25% of the capital cost or Rs 1.5 lakh, whichever is less per unit of 5 ha area, subject to a maximum of Rs 6.00 lakh per beneficiary. |
| | b) Financial assistance for establishment of effluent treatment system (ETS) in shrimp natchery | ETS in hatchery also considered mandatory from pollution control point of view and hence the scheme was introduced to assist hatchery operators to set up ETS. | 25% of the capital cost, subject to a maximum of Rs 1.5 lakh per unit (One unit per hatchery) |
| 7. | Development assistance for setting up of PCR labs in private hatcheries | To ensure quality of shrimp seed PCR labs are required in hatcheries. Hence, this scheme was introduced to screen any viral infection in seeds/ brooders. | 50% of capital cost with the maximum of Rs 5.00 lakh per unit. |
| 8. | Financial assistance to setting up of chill room facilities in shrimp farming areas | In order to help the farmers to market their produce in fresh condition for obtaining better prices, this scheme was introduced. | 25% of the cost of establishment, subject to a maximum of Rs 3.00 lakh per beneficiary. |

| *Sl. No.* | *Name of the scheme* | *Objective* | *Quantum of subsidy* |
|---|---|---|---|
| 9. | Financial assistance for purchase of water quality testing equipment | To help the farmers for better management of their farms, this scheme envisages extending financial assistance for purchase of water quality testing equipment. | 25% of the cost of water testing kits/equipment subject to a maximum of Rs 30,000/- per beneficiary. |
| *III. Induction of new technology, modernisation of processing facilities and development of infrastructure facilities* | | | |
| 10. | Subsidy for acquisition of all processing machinery and equipments for production of value-added marine products | To assist seafood processors to acquire machinery & equipments for production of value-added marine products | 25% of the cost of machinery and equipment, subject to a maximum of Rs 17.50 lakhs |
| 11. | Subsidy for acquisition of machinery for tuna cannery / processing of value-added tuna product | To assist seafood processors to set up tuna cannery / processing facilities for value-added tuna products | 25% of the cost of machinery and equipment, subject to a maximum of Rs 62.25 lakhs |
| 12. | Subsidy for automatic flake/chip/ tube-ice making machine | To assist seafood processors to install machines for production of quality ice required for in-plant use | 25% of the cost of the machine subject to a maximum of Rs 2.25 lakhs. The assistance would be available for maximum of two flake-ice making machine. Maximum eligible subsidy per processing plant under the scheme is Rs. 4 lakhs. |
| 13. | Subsidy for upgrading deficient cold storage | To enable seafood processors to upgrade their storage so as to maintain optimum temperature | 25% for improving insulation and 25% for upgrading the existing diffusers, subject to a maximum of Rs 3.50 lakhs (eligible for existing units). |

| *Sl. No.* | *Name of the scheme* | *Objective* | *Quantum of subsidy* |
|---|---|---|---|
| 14. | Assistance for establishment of Chill Room facility in seafood processing plants | To assist seafood processors to set up Chill Room facilities in their processing plants for preserving the quality of the raw material at proper temperature starting from harvest till processing | 25% of the costs of establishment of Chill Room facility, subject to a maximum of Rs 3.00 lakhs per Chill Room and the assistance would be available for a maximum of two Chill Rooms in a plant. Maximum eligible subsidy per processing plant under the scheme is Rs. 6.00 lakhs. |
| 15. | Financial support for acquisition of Refrigerated Trucks/ Containers | To encourage seafood processors to acquire Refrigerated Trucks/ Containers for transportation of raw material/ finished products | 25% of the cost of Refrigerated Truck/ Container, subject to a maximum of Rs 3.50 lakhs. |
| 16. | Financial assistance to set up large Cold Storages | To encourage individuals to establish cold storages for keeping the surplus seafood | 25% of the cost of cold-storage, subject to the maximum of Rs 60.00 lakhs |
| 17. | Subsidised distribution of insulated fish boxes | For proper preservation of raw materials in iced condition on board fishing vessels, in shrimp farms, peeling sheds and processing plants | Moulded synthetic insulated fish boxes of various capacity are distributed at 50% subsidy: to the following category of units with maximum amount in brackets.<br>1. Small mechanised boat/ country craft (less than 32 ft. OAL) (Rs.4500)<br>2. Mechanised boat owners (above 32 ft. OAL) (Rs.15000)<br>3. Peeling shed/ pre-processing plants (Rs. 50000) |

| *Sl. No.* | *Name of the scheme* | *Objective* | *Quantum of subsidy* |
|---|---|---|---|
| | | | 4. Processing plants (Rs. 100000)<br>5. Shrimp farmers 5 ha. & less (Rs.35000)<br>6. Shrimp farmers above 5 ha. (Rs.50000)<br>7. Fresh/Chilled Fish Handling Centres (Rs.100000) |
| 18. | Assistance for the setting up of new/ modern ice plants/ renovation of existing ice plants | For ensuring quality ice for fish preservation | A maximum of Rs 22 lakhs for new units and Rs 12 lakhs for renovation |
| 19. | Subsidy for generator sets | To assist the seafood processing units to have captive power as stand-by arrangement | 25% of the cost of generator set or Rs 2.50 lakhs whichever is less |
| 20. | Assistance for installation of Water Purification System in seafood processing plants | To assist seafood processors to establish suitable water purification system in their processing plants for compliance with EU/GOI norms for water quality | 25% of the cost of installation of water purification system, subject to a maximum of Rs 7.50 lakhs per unit |
| 21. | Assistance for setting up of effluent treatment plants in seafood processing plants | To encourage seafood processors to provide effective effluent treatment plant in their processing units for achieving compliance with EU/GOI norms | 25% of the cost of setting up of effluent treatment plant, subject to a maximum of Rs 7.00 lakhs per unit |

| *Sl. No.* | *Name of the scheme* | *Objective* | *Quantum of subsidy* |
|---|---|---|---|
| 22. | Interest subsidy assistance for seafood units to facilitate upgradation | To subsidise a part of the interest payable by the plant owners to their bank/financial institutions for the loans availed by them for modernisation of their plant to achieve conformity with EU standards | The subsidy eligibility will be restricted to a maximum of 7% of the interest charged by the bank/financial institutions over and above the international interest of 7% or actual rate of interest over and above the international interest; i.e. 7% whichever is less subject to a maximum of Rs 15 lakhs |
| 23. | Assistance for establishment of Chill Room facility in seafood processing plants | To assist seafood processors to set up Chill Room facilities in their processing plants for preserving the quality of the raw material at proper temperature, starting from harvest till processing | 25% of the cost of establishment of Chill Room facility subject to a maximum of Rs 3.00 lakhs per Chill Room and the assistance would be available for a maximum of two Chill Rooms in a plant. |
| 24. | Subsidy for setting up Mini Laboratory | For effective implementation of in- process quality control | 25% of the cost of mini-laboratory subject to a maximum of Rs 1,50,000/- per unit |
| 25. | Assistance to seafood processors for construction/ renovation of Captive Pre-processing Centres with upgraded facilities | To bring the pre-processing activities under the control of processors and upgrade the facilities on par with HACCP/ EU Regulations | 50% of the cost of eligible expenditure on the above items, subject to a maximum of Rs 15 lakhs for new construction and 45% of the cost subject to a maximum of Rs 13.50 lakhs for renovation for captive PPCs, which is again linked to the number of and the area of the pre-processing hall. |

| *Sl. No.* | *Name of the scheme* | *Objective* | *Quantum of subsidy* |
|---|---|---|---|
| 26. | Financial assistance to pre-processors for construction/ renovation of independent pre-processing centres with up-graded facilities | To upgrade the facilities on par with HACCP/EU regulations and thereby improve the handling practices in the entire pre-processing sector | 50% of the cost of eligible expenditure on the above items subject to a maximum of Rs 27 lakhs for new construction and 45% of the cost subject to a maximum of Rs 24.3 lakhs for renovation for independent PPCs, which is again linked to the number of workers and the area of the pre-processing hall. The subsidy is further restricted to maximum limits fixed for individual items. |
| 27. | Financial assistance for procurement of quick testing kit for anti-biotics | GOI has made mandatory for all EU approved units to procure and install Quick Testing Kit for testing antibiotics residues. Non-EU approved units can also procure and install the Quick Testing Kit. | The quantum of assistance is 33.3 % of the cost of the Microwell Reader and five test kits as well as other accessories, subject to a maximum of Rs 1 lakh per unit. |
| 28. | Assistance for setting up of Ornamental Fish Breeding Units | To set up small-scale ornamental fish breeding units to enhance the domestic production | 50% of the capital cost for the infrastructure specified, subject to a maximum of Rs 75,000/- per unit, linked to export |
| *IV. Market promotion* | | | |
| 29. | Assistance to seafood exporters and prepro-cessors for setting up chill storage either at their premises or near the landing centre/air port | Promotion of export of fresh / chilled marine products | 25% of actual cost subject to a maximum of Rs 3.00 lakhs per beneficiary |

| *Sl. No.* | *Name of the scheme* | *Objective* | *Quantum of subsidy* |
|---|---|---|---|
| 30. | Airfreight support scheme for live marine products | India's share of live marine products in the international market is not even one per cent of the world trade. This negligible percentage needs to be increased. The scheme has been formulated with a view to give a boost to the export of live marine products. | a) Asian countries (other than Japan) - 10% of the per kg airfreight of Rs 55/- or 10% of airfreight rate approved by IATA , whichever is less.<br>b) Europe, countries of American continents, Japan, etc. – 15 % of the per kg airfreight of Rs 120/- or 15% of airfreight approved by the IATA, whichever is less.<br>c) The assistance will be limited to Rs 15 lakhs per exporter per annum |
| 31. | Developmental assistance for export of ornamental/aquarium fishes | To give a thrust to the export of ornamental fish from the country and to fetch better unit value by competing with our neighbouring countries | 10% of f.o.b. value of export subject to the ceiling of Rs 3 lakhs per exporter per year |
| 32. | Financial assistance for extending insurance coverage to workers employed in the fish processing units | The insurance scheme is envisaged for workers employed in seafood processing units with a terminal benefit of Rs 1 lakh for the insured, medical expenses (hospitlisation) reimbursement upto Rs 10,000 for the insured or his/her parents or dependants and also to insure household articles against calamities either natural or man- made upto Rs 20,000/- | The premium of the insurance will be paid by the employer, employee and MPEDA in a ratio of 50%, 25% and 25%.<br><br>The annual premium works out to Rs 281 per worker. |

Source: MDEDA, Data Sheet, 2006.

# BIBLIOGRAPHY


Ababouch, A., Gandini, G. and Ryder, J., 2005, *Causes of Detentions and Rejections in International Fish Trade*, FAO Fisheries Technical Paper, 473, Food and Agriculture Organisation, Rome.

Abidi, S.A.H. and Biradar, R.S., 2001, 'Changing Needs of Fisheries Education in India', Pandyan, T.J. (ed.) *Sustainable Indian Fisheries*, National Academy of Agricultural Sciences, New Delhi, pp.281-305.

Achterberg, W., 1999, 'From Sustainability to Basic Income', Kenny, M. and Meadowcroft, J., *Planning Sustainability*, Routledge, London, pp. 128-147.

Allen, R., 1980, *How to Save the World*, Barnes and Noble Books, Totowa, New Jersey.

Ammini, P.L., Khambatkar, L.L. and Burman, B.K., 2004, 'A Review of the Marine Fisheries of West Bengal during 2000', *Marine Fisheries Information Service*, T & E Series, No.180, CMFRI, Cochin, pp.7-10.

Anderson, L.G., 1995, 'Privatising Open Access Fisheries: Individual Transferable Quotas', Bromley (ed.), *Handbook of Environmental Economics*, Blackwell Science, Oxford, pp.453-474.

Andy, T. and Elizabeth, B., 2000, 'Latin American Fisheries, Globalisation and the Sustainability Debate: A Relocation of Boundaries?' Sumaila, *et al.*, 2000, *Proceedings of the INCO-DC International Workshop on Markets, Global Fisheries and Local Development,* Brussels, pp. 47-72.

Annick, V.H., 2004, 'Compliance with International Fisheries Law', Swan, J. and Greboval, D. (eds.), *Report and Documentation of the International Workshop on the Implementation of International Fisheries Instruments and Factors of Unsustainability and Overexploitation in Fisheries*, Mauritius, 3-7 February 2003, FAO, Rome, pp.285-294.

Anonymous, 1997 , 'Ecology Based Fishery Management in Aliyar Reservoir'. *Bulletin No.72,* Central Inland Capture Fisheries Research Institute, Barrackpore, West Bengal.

Anonymous, 2000a, *Australian Commonwealth Government Guidelines for the Assessment of Sustainable Fisheries*, http:// www.gov.au/coasts/fisheries/assessment/guidelines.html.

Anonymous, 2000b, 'World Trade Organisation and its Implications for Industry', *Seafood Export Journal*, Vol.31, No.6, pp.41-49.

Anonymous, 2002, 'Indian Shrimp Culture Scenario: State-wise Status; Expert Consultation: Development of Sustainable Shrimp Farming in India,' held at Chennai, 28-29, August, *Fishing Chimes*, 22, (7), 10.

Appleyard, D.R. and Field, Jr., 1998, *International Economics* (3[rd] edition), Irwin McGraw Hill, New York.

Appolonio, S., 1994, 'The Use of Ecosystem Characteristics in Fisheries Management', *Review of Fisheries Science*, 2(2), 157-180.

Aqorau, T., 2003, 'Obligations to Protect Marine Ecosystems Under International Conventions and Other Legal Instruments', Sinclair,M.and Valdimarsson,G.(eds.),*Responsible Fisheries in the Marine Ecosystem*, FAO, Rome and CABI Publishing, Oxon, pp.25-40.

Arancibia, A.Y.,1999, 'Terms of Reference Towards Coastal Management and Sustainable Development in Latin America: Introduction to Special Issue on Progress and Experiences', *Ocean and Coastal Management*, (42), 77-104.

Archibugi, F. and Nijkamp, P. (eds.), 1990, *Economy and Ecology: Towards Sustainable Development,* Kluwer Acadmic Publishers, Dordrecht.

Archibugi, F., Nijkamp, P. and Soeteman, F.J., 1990, 'The Challenge of Sustainable Development', Archibugi, F. and Nijkamp, P. (eds.), *Economy and Ecology: Towards Sustainable Development*, Kluwer Academic Publishers, Dordrecht, pp.1-2.

Arumugham, G., Balalsubramanian, T.S. and Rajapakiam, S., 1993, 'The Impact of Cyclone along the Tuticorin Coasts', *Marine Fisheries Information Service*, No.122, Central Marine Fisheries Research Institute, Cochin.

Asian Development Bank (ADB) and Network of Aquaculture Centres in Asia-Pacific (NACA), 1998, *Aquaculture Sustainability and the Environment – Report on a Regional Study and Workshop*, ADB/NACA, Bangkok.

Atkinson, G., Dubourg, R., Hamilton, K., Munasinghe, M., Pearce, D. and Young, C. 1997, *Measuring Sustainable Development: Macroeconomics and the Environment,* Edward Elgar, Cheltenham.

Ayres, R. and Weaver, P.M. (eds.), 1998, *Eco-Restructuring: Implications for Sustainable Development*, United Nations University Press, New York.

Ayyappan, S. and Jena, J.K., 1998, 'Carp Culture in India – A Sustainable Farming Practice', Natarajan, P., Dhevendran, K., Aravindhan, C.M. and Rita Kumari, S.D. (eds.), *Advances in Aquatic Biology and Fisheries, Vol.II*, Department of Aquatic Biology and Fisheries, University of Kerala, Trivandrum,pp.125-153.

Ayyappan, S. and Jena, J.K., 2001, 'Sustainable Freshwater Aquaculture in India', T.J. Pandian (ed.), *Sustainable Indian Fisheries*, National Academy of Agricultural Sciences, New Delhi, pp.88-133.

Ayyappan, S. and Srinath, M., 2005, 'Sustainability of Marine Fisheries in India – Issues and Approaches', Kurup, *et al.* (eds.), *Souvenir, Sustain Fish 2005*, School of industrial Fisheries, Cochin University of Science and Technology, Cochin, p.11.

Baba, M., Shamsudhin, M. and Thomas, K.V., 1995, *Coastal Zone management Plan of Kerala,* (Mimeo), Centre for Earth Science Studies, Trivandrum.

Bagarino, T.U. and Flores, E.C.C., 1995, *Towards Sustainable Aquaculture in South East Asia and Japan*, SEAFDEC Aquaculture Department, Iloilo, Philippines.

Baily, C., 1988, 'The Political Economy of Fisheries Development', *Agriculture and Human Values,* 5, 35-48.

Baldwin, R., 1995, 'Does Sustainability Require Growth?', Ian Goldin and Alan Winters (eds.), *The Economics of Sustainable Development*, Organisation for Economic Cooperation and Development, Paris.

Barbier, E.B., 1987, 'The Concept of Sustainable Economic Development', *Environmental Conservation*, Vol.14, No.2, pp.101-110.

Barbier, E.B., 1998, *The Economics of Environment and Development.* Edward Elgar, Cheltenham, U.K.

Barbier, E.B. and Markandya, A., 1990, 'The Conditions for Achieving Environmentally Sustainable Development', *European Economic Review*, 34, 659-669.

Barbier, E.B., Burgess, J.C. and Folke, C., 1994, *Paradise Lost? The Ecological Economics of Biodiversity*, Earth Scan, London.

Barg, U.C. 1992, *Guidelines for the Promotion of Environmental Management of Coastal Aquaculture Development.* FAO Fisheries Technical Paper No.328, FAO, Rome.

Barg, U.C. and Phillip, J., 1997, *Environmental Sustainability*, FAO Fisheries Circular, 886, 4(1), 55-59.

Barnett, H.J. and Chandler, M., 1963, *Scarcity and Growth*, John Hopkins University Press, Resources for the Future, Baltimore.

Barret, P., 2004, 'Man's Extinction in 100 years?' *The New Indian Express*, Kochi, 10.11.2004,

Bartelmus, P., 1986, *Environment and Development*, Allen and Unwin, Boston.

Bartelmus, P., 1994, *Environment, Growth and Development : The Concepts and Strategy of Sustainability*, Routledge, London.

Bavenik, M., 2001, 'Marine Resource Management: Conflict and Regulation in the Fisheries of the Coromandel Coast' *Livelihood and Environment*, No.5, Sage Publications, New Delhi.

Beaton, R. and Maser, C., 1999, *Reuniting Economy and Ecology in Sustainable Development,* Lewis Publishers, Washington, DC.

Beckerman, W. 1994, 'Sustainable Development : Is it a Useful Concept?', *Environmental Values*, 3:, 191-209.

Beckerman, W., 1996, 'A Sceptical View of Sustainable Development', *Global Agricultural Science Policy for the Twenty-first Century*, Conference Proceedings, Department of Natural Resources and Environment, Melbourne.

Beltratti, A., Chichilnisky, G. and Heal, G.M., 1995, 'Sustainable Growth and the Green Golden Rule', Ian, G. and Alan, W. (eds.), *The Economics of Sustainable Development,* Cambridge University Press, Cambridge.

Bergh, J.C., Vanden, J.M., 1996, *Ecological Economics and Sustainable Development: Theory, Methods and Applications*, Edward Elgar, Cheltenham.

Berkes, F. (ed.), 1989, *Common Property Resources: Ecology and Community – Based Sustainable Development,* Belhaven Press, London.

Berkes, F., Folke, C. and Gadgil, M., 1993. *Traditional Ecological Knowledge, Biodiversity, Resilience and Sustainability*, Beijer Discussion Paper Series 31, Swedish Academy of Sciences.

Berkes, F. and Folke, C., 1994, 'Investing in Cultural Capital for Sustainable Use of Natural Capital', Jansson, A.M., Hammer, M., Folke, C. and Costanza, R. (eds.), *Investing in Natural Capital: The Ecological Economics Approach to Sustainability,* Island Press, Washington, DC., pp.128-149

Bhatta, R., 2001, 'Production, Accessibility and Consumption Patterns of Aquaculture Products in India', in FAO, *Production, Accessibility, Marketing and Consumption Patterns of Freshwater Aquaculture Products in Asia – A Cross Country Comparison*, FAO, Rome, pp.147-189.

Bigg, T. (ed.), 2001, *Survival for a Small Planet: The Sustainable Development Agenda*, Earth Scan, London.

Bishop, R.C., 1993, 'Economic Efficiency, Sustainability and Biodiversity', *Ambio*, 22, 69-73.

Boopendranath, M.R., Badonia, R., Sankar, T.V., Pravin, P. and Saly, N. Thomas (eds.), 2003, *Sustainable Fisheries Development: Focus on Gujarat,* Society of Fishery Technologists (India), Cochin.

Boopendranath, M.R., Mathew, P.T., Gupta, S., Pravin, P. and Jeeva, J.C, 2005, *Sustainable Fisheries Development : Focus on Andhra Pradesh*, Society of Fishery Technologists (India), Cochin.

Bordal, B.O., 2003, 'Incorporating Ecosystem Considerations into Fisheries Management: Large Scale Industry Perspectives', Sinclair,M.and Valdimarsson,G. (eds.), *Responsible Fisheries in the Marine Ecosystem.* FAO, Rome, and CABI Publishing, Oxon, pp.41-46.

Boulding, K.E., 1966, 'The Economics of the Coming Spaceship Earth', Henry Jarret (ed.), *Environmental Quality in a Growing Economy*, Resources for the Future/

John Hopkins University, Baltimore, MD pp.3-14, Reprint in Costanza, R., Perring, C. and Cleveland, C, J.(eds.), 1997, *The Development of Ecological Economics*, An Elgar Reference Collection, Cheltenham, UK, pp.3-14.

Boulding, K.E., 1985, *World as a Total System*, Sage Publications, Beverly Hills, C.A.

Bromley, D. (ed.), 1995, *The Handbook of Environmental Economics*, Basil Blackwell, Oxford.

Bromley, D.W., 1999. *Sustaining Development: Environmental Resources in Developing Countries*, Edward Elgar, Cheltenham, UK.

Brooks, H., 1992, 'Sustainability and Technology', *Science and Sustainability*, HASA, Luxemburg, Austria.

Brown, B.J., 1987, 'Global Sustainability: Towards Definition', *Environmental Management*, Vol.11, No.6, pp.713-719.

Brown, L., Flavin, C. and Postel, S., 1992, *Saving the Planet: How to Shape an Environmentally Sustainable Global Economy*? Earth Scan, London.

Bruce, J.P., Hoe-Song Yi, P. and Haites, E.F. (eds.), 1996, *Climate Change 1995: Economic and Social Dimensions of Climate Change,* Inter-Governmental Panel on Climate Change, Working Group, III, Cambridge University Press for the Inter-Governmental Panel on Climate Change, Cambridge.

Burness, H.S. and Cummings, R.G., 1986, 'Thermodynamic and Economic Concepts as Related to Resource Use Policies: Reply', *Land Economics*, Vol.62, No.2, pp.323-324.

Caddy, J.F. and Griffiths, R.C., 1995, *Living Marine Resources and Their Sustainable Development: Some Environmental and Institutional Perspectives,* FAO, Fisheries Technical Paper No.353, FAO, Rome.

Caddy, J.F. and Mahon, R., 1995, *Reference Points for Fishery Management*, FAO Fisheries Technical Paper 347, FAO, Rome.

Carlo, C. and Domenico S., 1995, 'Policy Coordination for Sustainability: Commitments, Transfers and Linked Negotiations', Ian, G. and Alan, W. (eds), *The Economics of Sustainable Development*, Cambridge University Press, Cambridge.

Carlos, A.L.S., 1995, 'Impact of HACCP on Seafood International Production and Trade', *Seafood Export Journal*, Vol.25, No.10, pp.5-13,

Carson, R., 1962, *Silent Spring*, Houghton Mifflin, Boston.

Central Marine Fisheries Research Institute, 1981, *All India Census of Marine Fishermen, Crafts and Gear; 1980.* Marine Fisheries Information Service, T.& E. Series, No.30, CMFRI, Cochin.

Central Marine Fisheries Research Institute, 1988, 'An Evaluation of Fishermen Economy in Maharashtra and Gujarat : A Case Study', *CMFRI Special Publication No.44*, CMFRI, Cochin.

Charles, A.T., 1994, 'Towards Sustainability: The Fishery Experience', *Ecological Economics,* 11, 201-211.

Charles, A.T., 1995, 'Sustainability Assessment and Bio-Socio-Economic Analysis: Tools for Integrated Coastal Development', Junio-Menez, M.A. and Newkirk,G (eds.), *Philippines Coastal Resources Under Stress,* Coastal Resources Research Network, Halifax, Canada and Marine Sciences Institute, Quezon City, Philippines, pp.115-125,

Charles, A.T., 1997a, *Sustainability Indicators: An Annotated Bibliography with Emphasis on Fishery Systems, Coastal Zones and Watersheds,* Strategy for International Fisheries Research, Ottawa.

Charles, A.T., 1997b, 'The Path to Sustainable Fisheries', Borgesa, E.M. (ed.), *Peace in the Oceans: Ocean Governance and the Agenda for Peace,* Proceedings of Pacem in Maribus XXIII, Costa Rica, 3-7 December 1995, Inter-Governmental Oceanographic Commission, Technical Series, 47, UNESCO, Paris, pp.201-213,

Charles, A.T., 2000, *Sustainability Assessment for Nova Scotia's Fisheries: Towards a Genuine Progress Index,* GPI, Atlantic, Halifax, Canada.

Charles, A.T., 2001, *Sustainable Fishery Systems,* Blackwell Science, Oxford.

Charles, Anthony, 2004, 'Some Ideas Relating to Fishery Sustainability', Swan, J. and Greboval, D., (eds.), *Report and Documentation of the International Workshop on the Implementation of International Fisheries Instruments and Factors of Unsustainability and Overexploitation in Fisheries,* Mauritius, 3-7, February *2003,* FAO, Rome, pp. 295-297.

Chaturvedi, S. and Nagpal, G., 2003, 'WTO and Product-Related Environmental Standards : Emerging Issues and Policy Options', *Economic and Political Weekly,* Vol.38, No.1, pp.66-74.

Chesson, J. and Clayton, H.A., 1998, *A Framework for Assessing Fisheries With Respect to Ecologically Sustainable Development,* Bureau of Rural Sciences, Canberra.

Choudhuri, R. and Chatterjee, B., 2001, 'Trade Liberalisation, Market Access and Non-Tariff Barriers', *Seafood Export Journal,* Vol.32, No5, pp.37-44.

Christensen, P., 1991, 'Driving Forces, Increasing Returns, and Ecological Sustainability', Jansson, A.M., Hammer, M., Folke, C. and Costanza, R., (eds.), *Investing in Natural Capital: The Ecological Economics Approach to Sustainability,* Island Press, Washington, DC.

Christie, W.J., 1993, 'Developing the Concept of Sustainable Fisheries', *Journal of Aquatic Ecosystem & Health,* 2, 99-109.

Christy, F.T. (Jr.), and Scott, A., 1965, *The Commonwealth in Ocean Fisheries: Some Problems of Growth and Economic Allocation,* John Hopkins University Press, Baltimore.

Chua, T.E. (ed.), 1991, *Coastal Area Management Education in the ASEAN Region,* ICLARM Conference Proceedings, 29, ICLARM, Manila.

Cicin-Sain, B., 1993, 'Sustainable Development and Integrated Coastal Management', *Ocean and Coastal Management*, 21 (1-3), 11-43.

Cicin-Sain, B. and. Knecht, R.B., 1998, *Integrated Coastal Zone Management: Concepts and Practices*, Island Press, Washington, DC.

Clark, C.W. and Munn, R.E., 1986, *Sustainable Development of the Biosphere,* Cambridge University Press, Cambridge.

Clark, J.R., 1996, *Coastal Zone Management : Handbook*, Lewis Publishers, Washington, DC.

Clayton, A.M.H. and Radclife, N.J., 1996, *Sustainability: A Systems Approach*, Earth Scan, London.

Cline, W.R., 1992, *The Economics of Global Warming*, Institute for International Economics, Washington, DC.

Cochrane, K.L., 2000, 'Reconciling Sustainability, Economic Efficiency and Equity in Fisheries: The One that Got Away?' *Fish and Fisheries*, 2000, 1.

Coffey, C., 2000, 'European Funding for Sustainable Development of Fisheries Dependent Regions', David Symes (ed.), *Fisheries Dependent Regions*, Fishing News Books, London, pp.164-173.

Collet, S., 1999, 'From Sustainable Resource Use to Governance of Marine Ecosystem: Functions and Role of the Ethic of the Sea', David Symes (ed.). *Alternative Management Systems for Fisheries*, Fishing News Books, London, pp.117-126.

Commission of the European Communities (CEC), 1992, *Towards Sustainability: A European Community Programme of Policy and Action in Relation to the Environment and Sustainable Development', Vol.II,* Commission of the European Communities, Brussels.

Committee on Fisheries (COFI), 1991, *Environment and Sustainability in Fisheries,* COFI, FAO, Doc, COFI/91/3, (Mimeo).

Common, M., 1995, *Sustainability and Policy: Limits to Economics*, Cambridge University Press, Sydney.

Common, M. and Perrings, C., 1992, 'Towards an Ecological Economics of Sustainability', *Ecological Economics*, 6, 7-34.

Common Wealth of Australia, 1992, *National Strategy for Ecologically Sustainable Development*, Australian Government Publishing Service, Canberra.

Coomer, J.C., 1979, 'The Nature of the Quest for a Sustainable Society', Coomer, J.C., (ed.), *Quest for a Sustainable Society*, Pergamon Press, New York.

Corbin, J.S. and Young, L.G.L., 1997, 'Planning, Regulation and Administration of Sustainable Aquaculture', Brdrach, S.J.E. (ed), *Sustainable Aquaculture*, John Wiley & Sons, New York.

Costanza, R. (ed.), 1991, *Ecological Economics: The Science and Management of Sustainability*, Columbia University Press, New York.

Costanza, R. and Daly, H.E., 1992, 'Natural Capital and Sustainable Development', *Conservation Biology*, 6(1), 37-46, Reprinted in Costanza, R. Perrings, C. and Cleveland, C., (eds.), 1997, *The Development of Ecological Economics*, An *Elgar Reference Collection*, Cheltenham, U.K., pp.455-475.

Costanza, R. and Patten, B.C., 1995, 'Defining and Predicting Sustainability', *Ecological Economics*, 15, 193-196.

Costanza, R., Segura, O. and Martinez, A.J. (eds.), 1996, *Getting Down to Earth: Practical Applications of Ecological Economics,* Island Press, Washington, DC.

Crawford, B.R., Cobb, J.S. and Friedman, A., 1993, 'Building Capacity for Integrated Coastal Management in Developing Countries', *Ocean and Coastal Management*, 21(1-3), pp.311-337.

Crean, K. and Symes, D. (eds.), 1996, *Fisheries Management in Crisis*, Fishing News Books, Blackwell Science, Oxford.

Cropper, M. and Griffiths, C., 1994, 'The Interactions of Population Growth and Environmental Quality' *American Economic Review*, 84, 250-254.

Cumberland, J. 1991, 'Inter-generational Transfers and Ecological Sustainability', Costanza,R., *Ecological Economics: The Science and Management of Sustainability*, Columbia University Press, New York, pp. 355-366.

Cumberland, J.H., 1994, 'Ecology, Economic Incentives and Public Policy in the Design of Transdisciplinary Pollution Control Instruments', van der Bergh, J.C.J.M. and van der Straitem,J.(eds.), *Towards Sustainable Development,* Island Press, Washington, DC.

Cunningham, S., and Bostock, T., (eds.), 2004, *Papers Presented at the Workshop and Exchange of Views on Fiscal Reforms for Fisheries to Promote Growth, Poverty Eradication and Sustainable Management*, Rome, 13-15 October, 2003, FAO Fisheries Report No.732, Supplement, FAO, Rome.

Daily, G.C. and Ehrlich, P.R., 1992, 'Population, Sustainability and Earth's Carrying Capacity', *Bio-science*, 42(10), November, 761-771, Reprinted in Costanza, R., Perrings, C. and Cleveland, C. J.(eds.), 1997, *The Development of Ecological Economics,* An Elgar Reference Collection, Cheltenham, UK, pp. 465-475.

Daly, H.E., 1968, 'On Economics as a Life Science', *Journal of Political Economy*, 76, 392-406, Reprinted in Costanza, R., Perrings, C. and Cleveland, C.J. (eds),1997, *The Development of Ecological Economics*, An Elgar Reference Collection, Cheltenham, UK, pp.15-29.

Daly, H.E., 1987, 'The Economic Growth Debate: What Some Economists Have Learned But Many Have Not', *Journal of Environmental Economics and Management, Vol.14, No.4, pp.323-336.*

Daly, H.E., 1990a, 'Towards Some Operational Principles of Sustainable Development', *Ecological Economics*, 2, 1-6.

Daly, H.E., 1990b, 'Steady State and Growth Concepts for the Next Century', Archibugi, F. and Nijkamp, P. (eds.), *Economy and Ecology. Towards Sustainable Development,* Kluwer Academic Publishers, Dordrecht, pp.73-87.

Daly, H.E., 1991a, 'Ecological Economics and Sustainable Development', Rossi and Tiezzy, E. (eds.), *Ecological, Physical Chemistry,* Elsevier, Amsterdam, pp. 185-201

Daly, H.E., 1991b, 'Sustainable Development: From Conceptual Theory Towards Operational Principles', *Population and Development Review,* 16 (Supplement).

Daly, H.E., 1992a, *Steady State Economics,* Earth Scan, London.

Daly, H.E., 1992b, 'Allocation, Distribution and Scale: Towards an Economics that is Efficient, Just and Sustainable', *Ecological Economics,* 6, 185-193. Reprinted in Costanza, R., Perrings, C. and Cleveland, C.J. (eds.), 1997, *The Development of Ecological Economics,* An Elgar Reference Collection, Cheltenham, UK, pp.200-208.

Daly, H.E., 1993, 'The Perils of Free Trade', *Scientific American,* November, 50-57.

Daly, H.E., 1994a, 'Operationalising Sustainable Development by Investing in Natural Capital', Janson, A.M., *et al.* (ed.) *Operationalising Sustainable Development by Investing in Natural Capital,* Island Press, Washington, DC, pp.22-37.

Daly, H.E., 1994b, 'Fostering Environmentally Sustainable Development: Four Parting Suggestions for the World Bank', *Ecological Economics,* 10, 183-187.

Daly, H.E., 1995, 'On Wilfred Beckerman's Critique of Sustainable Development', *Environmental Values* ,4, 49-55.

Daly, H.E., 1996, *Beyond Growth: The Economics of Sustainable Development,* Beacon Press.

Daly, H.E., 1997, 'Allocation, Distribution and Scale: Towards an Economics that is Just and Sustainable', Costanza, R., Perrings, C., and Cleveland, C.J. (eds.), *The Development of Ecological Economics,* An Elgar Reference Collection, Cheltenham, U.K., pp.200-208.

Daly, H.E., 1999, 'Steady-State Economics: Avoiding Uneconomic Growth', Van den Bergh, J.C.J.M. (ed.), *Handbook of Environmental and Resource Economics,* Edward Elgar, Cheltenham, U.K., pp.635-642.

Daly, H.E. 2005, *'Operationalising Sustainable Development by Investing in Natural Capital'* (Reprint), Sahu, N.C. and Choudhury, A.K. (eds.), Universities Press, Hyderabad, 2005, pp.481-494.

Daly, H.E. and Cobb, J.B. Jr., 1994, *For the Common Good: Redirecting the Economy Towards Community, Environment and a Sustainable Future,* Beacon Press.

Daly, H.E. and Goodland, R., 1994, 'An Ecological-Economic Assessment of Deregulation of International Commerce Under GATT', *Environment,* 15, 399-427, 477-503.

Das Gupta, P.S. and Heal, G.M., 1979, *Economic Theory and Exhaustible Resources,* Cambridge University Press, Cambridge.

Das, M.K. and Das, R.K., 1995, 'Fish Disease in India: A Review', *Environ. Ecol.*, 13: 533-541.

Das, P., De, S.P., Bhowmick, R.M., Nandy, A.C., Pandit, P.K., Sengupta, R.C. and Thakurta, S.C., 2004, 'Diminishing Trend of Fish Species Diversity in West Bengal: Field Study', *Fishing Chimes*, Vol.24, No.1, pp.73-76.

Datta, S.K. and Chakrabarti, M., 2004, 'A Management Perspective for Sustainable Marine Fisheries Under Globalised Market Conditions: The Indian Scenario', Somvanshi, V.S., (ed.) *Large Marine Ecosystems: Exploration and Exploitation for Sustainable Development and Conservation of Stocks*, Fishery Survey of India, Government of India, Mumbai.

Deadman, D. and Turner, R.K., 1991, 'Resource Conservation, Sustainability and Technical Change', Turner, R.K. (ed.), *Sustainable Environmental Management: Principles and Practice,* CBS Publishers and Distributors, New Delhi, pp.. 67-101.

Dean, J.M., 1992, 'Trade and the Environment: A Survey of the Literature', Patric,L. (ed.), *International Trade and the Environment*, Discussion Paper, World Bank, Washington, DC.

Dean, J.M., 1995, 'Export Bans, Environment and Developing Country Welfare', *Review of International Economics*, 3(3), 319-329.

Dean, J.M. and Gangopadhyay, S., 1997, 'Export Bans, Environmental Protection and Unemployment', *Review of Development Economics*, 1(3), 324-336.

Deere, C., 1999, *Eco-labelling and Sustainable Fisheries*, IUCN, Washington and FAO, Rome.

Deere, C., 2000, *Net Gains: Linking Fisheries Management, International Trade and Sustainable* Development, The World Conservation Union, Washington, DC.

de Groot, R., 1994, 'Functions and Values of Protected Areas: A Comprehensive Framework for Assessing the Benefits of Protected Areas to Human Society', Munasinghe, M. and McNeely, J., (eds.), *Protected Area Economics and Policy: Linking Conservation and Sustainable Development*, World Bank and World Conservation Union (IUCN), Washington, DC.

Delgado, C.L., Nikolas, W., Mark, W. R., Siet, M. and Mahfuzuddin, A., 2003, *Fish 2020: Supply and Demand in Changing Global Markets*, International Food Policy Research Institute (IFPRI), Washington DC and World Fish Centre, Penang.

Department of Agriculture, 1973, *Report of the Working Group on Fifth Five Year Plan (1974-79), Fisheries,* Ministry of Agriculture, Government of India, New Delhi.

Department of Agriculture and Co-operation, 1996, *Handbook on Fisheries Statistics, 1996,* Government of India, New Delhi.

Department of Animal Husbandry and Dairying, 2000, *Report of the Working Group for Revalidating the Potential of Fishery Resources in the Indian EEZ*, Government of India, New Delhi.

Department of Animal Husbandry and Dairying, 2001, *Handbook on Fisheries Statistics, 2000*, Government of India, New Delhi.

Department of Animal Husbandry, Dairying and Fisheries, 2005, *Handbook on Fisheries Statistics 2004,* Government of India, New Delhi.

Department of Fisheries, *Kerala Fisheries – Facts and Figures – 2000*. Government of Kerala, Thiruvananthauram, 2002.

Desai, M.B. and Baichwal, P.R., 1960, 'Economic Survey of Fishing Industry in Thane District, Bombay State, India', Szczepanik, E.F. (ed.), *The Economic Role of Middlemen and Co-operatives in Indo-Pacific Fisheries*. FAO, Rome, pp.3-78.

Devadasan, K., 2005, 'CIFT Initiatives in Responsible Fishery Operations', Kurup, *et al.* (eds.), *Souvenir, Sustain. Fish. 2005*, School of Industrial Fisheries, Cochin University of Science and Technology, Cochin, pp.59-63.

Devaraj, M., 1997, 'The Need for Promoting Eco-friendly Mariculture', *National Aquaculture Week Souvenir 1997*, ICAR & Aquaculture Foundation of India, Madras.

Devaraj, M., 1998, 'Sustained Development of Marine Fisheries and Marine Culture in India', Qasim, S.Z. and Roonwal, G.S., (eds.), *Living Resources of India's Exclusive Economic Zone*, Omega Scientific Publishers, New Delhi, pp.50-64.

Devaraj, M., Menon, N.G., Pillai, V.K. and Balachandran, K., 1999, 'Coastal Zone Governance in Kerala in Relation to National and International Situations', *Marine Fisheries Information Service*, 162: 1-22.

Devaraj, M., Murthy, V.S.R., Sathiadhas, R., and Joshi, K.K., 1998, 'The New Economic Policy and Perspectives for Marine Fisheries Research and Development in India', *Fishing Chimes,* 18(5), 18-29.

Devaraj, M. and Vivekanandan, E., 1999, 'Marine Capture Fisheries of India: Challenges and Opportunities', *Current Science*, 76, 314-332.

Dey, M.M., Paraguas, F.J. and Alam, M.F., 2001, 'Cross-Country Syntheses',FAO, *Production, Accessibility, Marketing and Consumption Patterns of Freshwater Aquaculture Products in Asia*, FAO, Rome, pp. 1-53.

Dey, P.B. and Dan, S.S., 1989, 'The Impact of Cyclone Along the West Bengal Coast in November 1988'. *Marine Fisheries Information Service,* No.97, Central Marine Fisheries Research Institute, Cochin.

Directorate of Census Operations, 1961, *Village Survey Monographs of Trivandrum District*, Government of Kerala, Trivandrum.

Diwan, A.D., Biradar, R.S., George, J.P. and Iftekhar, M.B., 2004, 'Need for New Dimensions in Marine Fisheries Development for Sustainable Management', Somvanshi, V.S. (ed.), *Large Marine Ecosystems: Exploration and Exploitation for Sustainable Development and Conservation of Fish Stocks*, Fishery Survey of India, Government of India, Mumbai, pp.271-278.

Dixitulu, J.V.H. and Paparao, G., 1994, *Handbook on Fisheries*, Global Fishing Chimes Pvt. Ltd., Visakhapatnam.

Dobon, A., 1996, 'Environmental Sustainabilities: An Analysis and a Typology', *Environmental Politics*, 5, 401-428.

Doeringer, P.B. and Terkla, D.G., 1995, *Troubled Waters: Economic Structure, Regulatory Reform and Fisheries Trade*, University of Toronto Press, Toronto.

Downes, D. and Brennan, V.D., 1998, *Fisheries Conservation and Trade Rules: Ensuring that Trade Law Promotes Sustainable Fisheries*, Centre for International Environmental Law and Green Peace, Washington, DC.

Dragun, A.K., 1999, 'Trade Liberalisation, Agriculture and Sustainability', Dragun, A.K. and Tisdell, C. (eds.), *Sustainable Agriculture and Environment: Globalisation and the Impact of Trade Liberalisation*, Edward Elgar, Cheltenham, U.K., pp. 7-21.

Dragun. A.K., and Tisdell, C., (eds.), 1999, *Sustainable Agriculture and Environment: Globalisation and the Impact of Trade Liberalisation*, Edward Elgar, Cheltenham, UK.

Drummond, I. and Symes, D., 1996, 'Rethinking Sustainable Development: The Realistic Paradigm', Otterstad, O. and I, Drummond (eds.), *Sustainable Fisheries 2 (Special issue), Social. Ruralis*, 36(2), 152-162.

Dunn, E., 1996, 'Fisheries and the Development of Sustainability Indicators', *North Sea Monitor*, June 1996, pp. 13-19.

Durning, A.T., 1992, *How Much is Enough? The Consumer Society and the Future of the Earth*, Norton, New York.

Dyer, C.L. and McGoodwin, T.R., 1994, *Folk Management in the World's Fisheries: Lessons for Modern Fisheries Management*, University Press of Colorado, Niwot, CO.

Edward, S.F., 1999, 'Influence of a Century of Macro-economic Change on U.S. Fisheries Production', *North American Journal of Fisheries Management*, Vol. 19, Feb. 1999, No.1, pp. 1-17.

Ehrenfield, D., 1978, *The Arrogance of Humanism*, Oxford University Press, Oxford.

Ehrlich, P., 1989, 'The Limits of Substitution: Meta-resource Depletion and a New Economic – Ecologic Paradigm', *Ecological Economics*, 1, 9-16.

Ekins, P., 1992, 'A Four-Capital Model of Wealth Creation', Ekins, P. and Max-Neef, M. (eds.), *Understanding Wealth Creation*, Routledge, London, pp. 147-155.

Ekins, P., 1995, *Harnessing Trade to Sustainable Development*, Green College Centre for Environmental Policy and Understanding, Oxford.

Ekins, P. and Jacobs, M., 1994, 'Are Environmental Sustainability and Economic Growth Compatible?', *Energy-Environment – Economy Modelling Discussion Paper No.7*, Department of Applied Economics, University of Cambridge, Cambridge.

Ekins, P. and Jacobs, M., 1995, 'Environmental Sustainability and the Growth of GDP: Conditions for Compatibility', Baskerville,G. and Glym. A. (eds.), *The North, the South and the Environment*, Earth Scan, London.

Ekins, P.A., 1993a, 'Limits to Growth and Sustainable Development: Grappling with Ecological Realities', *Ecological Economics*, 8, 269-288.

Ekins, P.A., 1993b, 'Trading off the Future: Making World Trade Environmentally Sustainable', *New Economics Foundation'*, London, September.

El Serafy, S., 1991, 'The Environment as Capital', Costanza, R., (ed.), *Ecological Economics: The Science and Management of Sustainability*, Columbia University Press, New York, pp. 168-175.

El Serafy, S., 1996, 'Influence of Weak Sustainability: A Response to Beckerman' *Environmental Values*, 5, 75-81.

El Serafy, S. and Lutz, E., 1989, 'Environmental and Resource Accounting: An Overview', Ahmed, Y., El Serafy, S. and Lutz, E. (eds.), *Environmental Accounting for Sustainable Development: Selected Papers from Joint UNEP/World Bank Workshops,* World Bank, Washington, DC.

Eskeland, G.S. and Harrison, A.E., 1997, *Moving to Greener Pastures? Multinationals and the Pollution-Haven Hypothesis*, Policy Research, Working Paper 1744 (March), The World Bank, Washington, DC.

Expert Committee, 1985, *Report of the Expert Committee on Marine Fisheries in Kerala (Mimeo)*, Central Institute of Fisheries Education, Versova, Bombay.

Expert Committee, 2000, *Report of the Expert Committee for Fisheries Management Studies, Kerala,* Directorate of Fisheries, Thiruvananthapuram.

Faber, M., Manstetten, R., Proops, J. and Jost, F.,1996, 'Sustainable Development: The Role of Science and Ethics', Faber, M., Manstetten, R. and Proops, J. (eds.), *Ecological Economics: Concepts and Methods*, Edward Elgar, Cheltenham, UK, pp. 75-92.

Fancheux, S., Pearce, D. and Proops, J., 1996, *Models of Sustainable Development,* Edward Elgar, Cheltenham, U.K.

Fegan, D.F., 1996, 'Sustainable Shrimp Farming in Asia: Vision or Pipedream', *Aquaculture Asia*, Oct. – Dec. 1996, 22-28.

Flint, M., 1997, 'Biological Diversity and Developing Countries', Markandya, A. and Richardson, J. (eds.), *Environmental Economics* (1997 Reprint), Earth Scan Publications Ltd., London, pp. 437-469.

Folke, C. and Kautsky, N., 1992, 'Aquaculture with its Environment: Prospects for Sustainability', *Ocean and Coastal Management*, 17( ), 5-24.

Folke, C., Hammer, M., Costanza, R. and Jansson, A.M., 1994, 'Investing in Natural Capital –Why, What and How', Jansson, A.M., Hammer, M., Folke, C. and Costanza, R., (eds.), *Investing in Natural Capital: The Ecological Economics Approach to Sustainability,* Island Press, Washington, DC.

Folke, C., Jansson, A.M., Larsson, J., and Costanza, R., 1997, 'Ecosystem Appropriation by Cities', *Ambio,* 26, 167-172.

Folke, C., Kautsky, N., Berg, H., Jansson, A.M. and Troel , M., 1998, 'The Ecological Footprint Concept for Sustainable Seafood Production: A Review', *Ecological Applications* , 8 (Suppl.), S63-S71.

Food and Agriculture Organisation, 1984, *Report of the FAO World Conference on Fisheries Management and Development*, FAO, Rome.

Food and Agriculture Organisation, 1990, 'Sustainable Development and Natural Resource Management', *The State of Food and Agriculture, 1989*, Part 3, FAO, Rome.

Food and Agriculture Organisation, 1993 a, *Marine Fisheries and the Law of the Sea: A Decade of Change,* FAO Fish. Cir. 853, FAO, Rome.

Food and Agriculture Organisation, 1993 b, *Conservation and Rational Utilisation of Living Marine Resources With Special Reference to Responsible Fishing,* COFI Document 93/5 FAO, Rome.

Food and Agriculture Organisation, 1993 c, *UNCED and its Implications for Fisheries,* COFI Document/93/Inf.8. FAO, Rome.

Food and Agriculture Organisation, 1995 a, *Precautionary Approach to Fisheries – Part-1: Guidelines on the Precautionary Approach to Capture Fisheries and Species Introduction*, FAO, Fisheries Technical Paper No.350, Part l, FAO, Rome.

Food and Agriculture Organisation, 1995 b, *Code of Conduct for Responsible Fisheries,* FAO, Rome.

Food and Agriculture Organisation, 1996 a, *Precautionary Approach to Capture Fisheries and Species Introduction,* FAO, Technical Guidelines for Responsible Fisheries, No.2, FAO, Rome.

Food and Agricultural Organisation, 1996b, *Integration of Fisheries into Coastal Area Management*, FAO, Technical Guidelines for Responsible Fisheries, No.3, FAO, Rome.

Food and Agriculture Organisation, 1997a, *Review of the State of World Fisheries Resources: Marine Fisheries*, FAO Fisheries Circular No.920, FIRM/C920, Marine Resources Service, Fisheries Resources Division, Fisheries Department, FAO, Rome.

Food and Agriculture Organisation, 1997b, *Fisheries Management*, FAO Technical Guidelines for Responsible Fisheries, No.4, FAO, Rome.

Food and Agriculture Organisation, 1997c, *Inland Fisheries*, FAO Technical Guidelines for Responsible Fisheries, No.6, FAO, Rome.

Food and Agriculture Organisation, 1999a, *The State of World Fisheries and Aquaculture 1998,* FAO, Rome.

Food and Agriculture Organisation, 1999b, *Indicators for Sustainable Development of Marine Capture Fisheries*, FAO, Technical Guidelines for Responsible Fisheries, No.8, FAO, Rome.

Food and Agriculture Organisation, 2000a, *The State of World Fisheries and Aquaculture 2000*, FAO, Rome.

Food and Agriculture Organisation, 2000b, *Globalisation and Implication for International Fish Trade and Food Security* (Item 6 of the Provisional Agenda) Committee on Fisheries, Sub-Committee on Fish Trade, Seventh Session, FAO, Bremen.

Food and Agriculture Organisation, 2000c, *Demographic Change in Coastal Fishing Communities and its Implications for the Coastal Environment,* Tjetze, U., Groenevold, G and Marconx, A (eds.), FAO Fisheries Technical Paper No.403, FAO, Rome.

Food and Agriculture Organisation, 2001a, *Ecosystem Based Fisheries Management: Opportunities and Challenges for Co-ordination Between Marine Regional Seas Conventions*, RFB/11/2001/7/FAO, Rome.

Food and Agriculture Organisation, 2001b, *Production, Accessibility, Marketing and Consumption Patterns of Freshwater Aquaculture Products in Asia, A Cross-Country Comparison,* FAO Fisheries Circular No.973, FAO, Rome.

Food and Agriculture Organisation, 2002, *The State of World Fisheries and Aquaculture, 2002*, FAO, Rome.

Food and Agriculture Organisation, 2004, *The State of World Fisheries and Aquaculture 2004,* http: //www.fao.org/sof/sofia.

Food and Agriculture Organisation, 2005a, *FAO Yearbook, Fishery Statistics : Capture Production*, Vol.96/1, 2003, FAO, Rome.

Food and Agriculture Organisation, 2005b, *FAO Yearbook, Fisheries Statistics: Aquaculture Production,* Vol.96/2/, 2003, FAO, Rome.

Food and Agriculture Organisation and Government of Japan, 1995, *International Conference on the Sustainable Contribution of Fisheries to Food Security,* Kyoto, Japan 4-9, December 1995, FAO, Rome/Government of Japan, Kyoto.

Frank, A. and Pascal, B., 2000, 'Fisheries and Internationalisation of Markets', Sumaila, *et.al., Proceedings of the INCO-DC International Workshop on Markets, Global Fisheries and Local Development,* Brussels, pp. 4-18.

Garcia, S.M., 1994a, 'The Precautionary Principle: Its Implication in Capture Fisheries Management', *Ocean and Coastal Management*, 22, 99-125.

Garcia, S.M., 1994b, *The Precautionary Approach to Fisheries With Special Reference to Straddling Fish Stocks and Highly Migratory Fish Stocks*, FAO Fish. Circ. 871, FAO, Rome.

Garcia, S.M., 1996, *The Precautionary Approach to Fisheries and its Implications for Fishery Research, Technology and Management: An Updated Review,* FAO Fisheries Technical Paper 350(2)1-75, FAO, Rome.

Garcia, S.M., 1997, *Indicators of Sustainable Development of Fisheries, Land Quality Indicators and Their Use in Sustainable Agriculture and Rural Development,* FAO Land and Water Bulletin No.5, pp.131-162, FAO, Rome.

Garcia, S.M., 2000, 'The FAO Definition of Sustainable Development and the Code of Conduct for Responsible Fisheries: An Analysis of the Related Principles, Criteria and Indicators', *Marine and Freshwater Research*, 51, 535-541.

Garcia, S.M., 2003, *The Ecosystem Approach to Fisheries*, FAO Fisheries Technical Paper 443, FAO, Rome.

Garcia, S.M. and Grainger, R.J.R.,1997, 'Fisheries Management and Sustainability: A New Perspective of an Old Problem?', Hancock, D.A.., Smith, D.O., Grant, A. and Beumer, J.P. (eds.), *Developing and Sustaining World Fisheries Resources: The State of Science and Management,* Proceedings of the 2nd World Fisheries Congress, pp. 631-654, CSIRO, Australia.

Garcia, S.M. and Newton, C, 1997, 'Current Situation, Trend and Prospects in Capture Fisheries'. Pikitch, E.K., Huppert, D.D. and Sissenwine, M.P. (eds.), *Global Trends in Fisheries Management*, American Fisheries Society Symposium 20, American Fisheries Society, Bethesda, M.D., pp.3-27.

Garcia, S.M., Kochrane, K., van Santen, G and Christy, F., 1999, 'Towards Sustainable Fisheries: A Strategy for FAO and the World Bank', *Ocean and Coastal Management*, 42: 369-398.

Garcia, S.M. and Stapples, D.J., 2000, 'Sustainability Reference Systems and Indicators for Responsible Marine Capture Fisheries: A Review of Concepts and Elements for a Set of Guidelines', *Marine Fisheries Research (Special Issue),* 51, 385-426.

Garcia, S.M., Stapples, D.J. and Chesson, J., 2000, 'The FAO Guidelines for the Development and Use of Indicators for Sustainable Development of Marine Capture Fisheries and an Australian Example of their Application', *Ocean and Coastal Management*, 43, 537-556.

Garcia, S.M. and Moreno, I.L. 2003, 'Global Overview of Marine Fisheries', Sinclair, .M., and Valdimarsson ,G (eds.), *Responsible Fisheries in the Marine Ecosystem,* Food and Agriculture Organisation, Rome, and CABI Publishing, Oxon, 1-24.

Georgescu-Roegen, N., 1971, *The Entropy Law and the Economic Process*, Harward University Press, Cambridge, MA.

Ghosh, P. and Jaitly, A., (eds.) 1994, *The Road from Rio: Environment and Development Policy Issues in Asia,* Tata Energy Research Institute, New Delhi.

Ghosh, P. and Malhotra A., 1994, 'The Implications of Agenda 21 - An Overview', Ghosh, P. and Jaitly, A.(eds.), *The Road from Rio: Environment and Development Policy Issues in Asia,* Tata Energy Research Institute, New Delhi, pp.68-83.

Gill, R.T., 1972, *Evolution of Modern Economics,* Prentice Hall of India Private Limited, New Delhi.

Gimbel, K.L. (ed.), 1994, *Limiting Access to Marine Fisheries: Keeping the Focus on Conservation*, Centre for Marine Conservation and World Wildlife Fund, US, Washington, DC.

Gilpin, A., 2000, *Environmental Economics: A Critical Overview*, John Wiley & Sons, Ltd., New York.,

Gladstone, W., Tawfiq, N., Nasar, D., Andersen, I., Cheung, C., Drammah, H., Krupp, F. and Lintner, S., 1999, 'Sustainable Use of Renewable Resources and Conservation in the Red Sea and Gulf of Aden: Issues, Needs and Strategic Actions' *Ocean and Coastal Management*, Vol. 42, No.8, pp. 671-698.

Golding, R. and Triplett, T., 1997, *Murky Waters: Environmental Effects of Aquaculture in the US*, Environmental Defence Fund, Washington, DC.

Goodland, R., 1991, 'The Case that the World has Reached Limits', Goodland, R., Daly, H.E., El Serafy, S. and von Droste, B. (eds.), *Environmentally Sustainable Economic Development: Building on Brundtland*, UNESCO, Paris.

Goodland, R., 1994, *Environmental Sustainability*, World Bank Working Paper, World Bank, Washington, DC.

Goodland, R., 1995, 'The Concept of Environmental Sustainability', *Annals of Ecology and Systematics*, 26, 1-24.

Goodland, R., 1997a, 'Biophysical and Objective Sustainability', Dragun, A.K. and Jakobsson, K.M. (eds.), *Sustainability and Global Environmental Policy: New Perspectives,* Edward Elgar, Cheltenham, UK.

Goodland, R., 1997b, 'Environmental Sustainability: Universal and Rigorous', Dragun, A.K. and Jakobsson, K.M. (eds.), *Sustainability and Global Environmental Policy: New Perspectives,* Edward Elgar, Cheltenham, U.K.

Goodland, R. and Ledec, G., 1987, 'Neoclassical Economics and Principles of Sustainable Development', *Ecological Modelling*, Vol.38, pp.19-46.

Goodland, R., Daly, H.E. and El Serafy, S., 1991, *Environmentally Sustainable Economic Development: Building on Brundtland*, World Bank Environmental Working Paper No.46, World Bank, Washington, DC.

Goodstein, E.S., 2002, *Economics and the Environment* (3rd ed.), John Wiley and Sons, Inc., New York.

Gopakumar, K., 1999, 'Strategies for Increasing Inland Fish Production in India', *Souvenir*, Central Inland Capture Fisheries Research Institute, Barrackpore,

Gopal, N., Annamalai, V., Remesan, M.P. and Premkumar, 2001, 'Marketing Efficiency of Fresh Fish Trade in Cochin and Veraval', *Fishery Technology*, Vol. 38(2), pp. 129-132.

Gordon, H.S., 1954, 'The Economic Theory of a Common Property Resource', *Journal of Political Economy*, 62, 124-142.

Government of India, 1999, *The Constitution of India*, Government of India, New Delhi.

Government of Japan and Food and Agriculture Organisation, 1995a, *Safeguarding Future Fish Supplies: Key Policy Issues and Measures*; International Conference on the Sustainable Contribution of Fisheries to Food Security, Kyoto, Japan, 4-9 December 1995, Government of Japan and FAO.

Government of Japan and Food and Agriculture Organisation,1995b, *Demand and Supply of Fish and Fish Products in Selected Areas of the World: Perspectives and Implications for Food Security*, International Conference on Sustainable Contribution of Fisheries to Food Security, Kyoto, Japan, 4-9 December 1995, Government of Japan and FAO.

Greboval, D., (ed.), 2002, *Report and Documentation of the International Workshop on Factors Contributing to Unsustainability and Overexploitation in Fisheries, Bangkok, Thailand, 4-8 February 2002*, FAO Fisheries Report No.672, FAO, Rome.

Greiner, R., Young, M.D., McDonald, A.D. and Brooks, M., 2000, 'Incentive Instruments for the Sustainable Use of Marine Resources' *Ocean and Coastal Management,* 43, 29-50.

Grossman, G.M., 1995, 'Pollution and Growth: What do We Know?' Goldin, I. and Winters, L. (eds.), *The Economics of Sustainable Development*, Cambridge University Press, Cambridge, pp. 977-987.

Gudmudsson, E.and Wessells, C.R. 2000, 'Eco-labelling Seafood for Sustainable Production: Implications for Fisheries Management', *Marine Resources Economics,* 15, 97-113.

Gulati, L., 1983, *Fishing Technology and Women (Part-1),* CDS Working Paper No.155, (Mimeo), Centre for Development Studies, Trivandrum.

Haimes, Y.Y., 1992, 'Sustainable Development: A Holistic Approach to Natural Resources Management', *IEEE Transactions on Systems, Man and Cybernetics,* SMC 3, pp. 413-417.

Hammer, M., 1998, 'The Adoption of an Ecosystem Approach to the Conservation and Sustainable use of Biological Diversity : The Malawi Principles', *Workshop on the Ecosystem Approach to the Management and Protection of the North Sea,* Oslo, Norway, 15-17 June, Nordic Council of Ministers, Copenhagen, pp. 51-53.

Hammer, M., Jansson, A.M. and Jansson, B., 1993, 'Diversity, Change and Sustainability: Implications for Fisheries' *Ambio*, 22, 97-105.

Hammer, W.C.K., 1999, 'International Food Trade and World Trade Organisation Agreements', *Seafood Export Journal*, Vol.30, No.1, pp.19-33.

Hammond, A., Adrianse, A., Rodenburg, E., Bryant, D. and Woodward, R., 1995, *Environmental Indicators: A Systematic Approach to Measuring and Reporting on Environmental Policy Performance in the Context of Sustainable Development,* World Resources Institute, Washington, DC.

Hancock, D.A. (ed.), 1993, *Sustainable Fisheries Through Sustaining Fish Habitat,* CSIRO, Canberra, Australia.

Hancock, D.A., Smith, D.C., Grant, A. and Beumer, J.P. (eds.), 1997, *Developing and Sustaining World Fisheries Resources: The State of Science and Management,* 2nd World Fisheries Congress Proceedings, CSIRO, Collingwood, Australia.

Hanley, N., Shogren, J.F. and White, B., 1999, *Environmental Economics in Theory and Practice,* Macmillan, Reprinted in India by Macmillan India, New Delhi.

Hansen, A., 1951, *Business Cycles and National Income*, Norton, New York.

Harden J.F.R., 1994, *Fisheries : Ecologically Sustainable Development*, Institute of Antarctic and Southern Ocean Studies (IASOS), Hobart, Tasmania.

Hardin, G., 1968, 'The Tragedy of the Commons', *Science*, 162. 1243-1248.

Hart, P.J.B. and Pauly, D., 'Reinventing Fisheries Management', Pitcher, T.J., Hart, P.J.B. and Pauly, D., (eds.), *Reinventing Fisheries Management*, Kluwer Academic Publishers, Dordrecht, pp.3-17.

Hatcher, A. and Robinson, K.,1999, *Over Capacity, Over Capitalisation and Subsidies in European Fisheries*, University of Portsmouth, Portsmouth.

Hawaken, P., 1993, *The Ecology of Commerce: A Declaration of Sustainability,* Harper Business, New York.

Heal, G., 1998, *Valuing the Future: Economic Theory and Sustainability*, Columbia University Press, New York.

Heal, G., 2000, 'Markets and Sustainability', Revesz, R.L., Sands, P. and Stewart, R.B., (eds.), *Environmental Law, The Economy and Sustainable Development,* Cambridge University Press, New York.

Higgins, B., 1976, *Economic Development, Principles, Problems and Policies*, Central Book Depot, Allahabad.

Hildebrand, L.P., 1997, 'Introduction to the Special Issue on Community - Based Coastal Management', *Ocean and Coastal Management, 36 (1-3), Special issue, Community-based Coastal Management,* pp.1-10.

Hodgsen, G. and Dixon, J.A., 1992, 'Sedimentation Damage to Marine Resources: Environmental and Economic Analysis', March, J.B. (ed.) *Resources and Environment,* Taylor and Francis, New York.

Holden, M., 1994, *The Common Fisheries Policy: Origin, Evaluations and Future,* Fishing News Books, Oxford.

Hotelling, H., 1931, 'The Economics of Exhaustible Resources', *Journal of Political Economy*, 39, 137-175.

Howarth, R.B. and Norgaard, R.B., 1992, 'Environmental Valuation Under Sustainable Development', *American Economic Review*, 82, 473-477.

Howe, C.W., 1979, *Natural Resource Economics : Issues, Analysis and Policy*, John Wiley and Sons, NewYork.

http:www. world fish centre.org/news/press/tsunami/jan18,2005 – India.pdf.

Hueting, R., 1990, 'The Brundtland Report : A Matter of Conflicting Goals', *Ecological Economics*, 2, 109-118.

Indo-Pacific Fisheries Commission (IPFC), 1991, *Symposium on Artificial Reefs and Fish Aggregating Devices as Tools for the Management and Enhancement of Marine Fishery Resources.* FAO Regional Office for Asia and the Pacific (RAPA), 1991(11).

Infofish, 1996, 'Extracts on Kyoto Declaration and Plan of Action on the Sustainable Contribution of Fisheries to Food Security' *Infofish International*, 1, 13.

Ins, P. and Jacobs, M., 1995, 'Environmental Sustainability and the Growth of GDP: Conditions for Compatibility', Baskerville,G. and Glym, A. (eds.), *The North, the South and the Environment*, Earth Scan, London.

Institution of Engineers, Australia, 1989, *Policy on Sustainable Development*, Barton, ACT, Australia.

International Institute for Sustainable Development,1996, *The World Trade Organisation and Sustainable Development: An Independent Assessment*, IISD, Winnipeg.

IUCN, 1980, *World Conservation Strategy: Living Resources Conservation for Sustainable Development*, IUCN-UNEP-WWF, Gland.

Iyer, K.H., Srinivsa Rao, P., Unnithan, G.R., Kesavan Nair, A.K. and Nair, R.G., 1981, 'Survey on the Idle Capacity of Fish Processing (freezing) Plants in India – I. West Coast', *Fishery Technology*, Vol.18, pp.109-115.

Iyer, K.H., Srinivasa Rao, P., Unnithan, G.R., Kesavan Nair, A.K. and Nair, R.G., 1982, 'Survey on the Idle Capacity of Fish Processing (freezing) Plants in India - II, East Coast', *Fishery Technology*, Vol. 19, pp.9-14.

Jacob, J., 2007, 'CPM Against Sending IAS Officers to US', *The New Indian Express*, Cochin, 13.4.2007.

Jacobs, M., 1995, 'Sustainable Development, Capital Substitution and Economic Humility: A Response to Beckerman', *Environmental Values*, 14, 57-68.

Jacobs, M., 1999, 'Sustainability and Markets: On the Neo-Classical Model of Environmental Economics'. Kenny, M. and Meadowcroft, J. (eds.), *Planning Sustainability*, Routledge, London, pp. 78-100.

Jagadish, I., Menon, N.G., and Shanmughavel, A., 2004, 'Observations on the Effect of Bottom Trawling on Dislocation of Non-edible Biota in the Palk Bay and Gulf of Mannar, South East Coast of India', Somvanshi, V.S. (ed.), *Large Marine Ecosystems: Exploration and Exploitation for Sustainable Development and Conservation of Fish Stocks*, Fishery Survey of India, Mumbai.

Jaitly , A., 1994, An Overview of Post-Rio Political Economy Issues', Ghosh, P. and Jaitly, A., (eds.), *The Road from Rio: Environment and Development Policy Issues in Asia*, Tata Energy Research Institute, New Delhi, pp. 27-56.

James, D.E., Nijkamp, P. and Opschoor, J.B., 'Ecological Sustainability and Economic Development', Archibugi, F. and Nijkamp, P. (eds.), *Economy and Ecology: Towards Sustainable Development*, Kluwer Academic Publishers, Dordrecht, pp.27-48.

James, P.S.B.R., 1999, 'Shrimp Farming Development in India : An Overview of Environment, Socio-Economic, Legal and Other Implications', *Aquaculture Magazine*,Online, http://www.ioa com/aquamag/html/featart. html.

Jansen, K., 1991, 'Structural Adjustment and Sustainable Development', *International Spectator*, November, 1991.

Jansson, A.M., Hammer, M., Folke, C. and Costanza, R. (eds.), 1994, *Investing in Natural Capital: The Ecological Economics Approach to Sustainability*, Island Press, Washington, DC.

Jayashree, B. and Subbaiah, A., 2001, 'Mapping Fish Research in India', Pandyan, T.J. (ed.), *Sustainable Indian Fisheries*, National Academy of Agricultural Sciences, New Delhi, pp.306-320.

Jenkins, T.N., 2005, 'Socio-Cultural Dimensions of Ecological Economics and Sustainable Rural Development', Sahu, N.C. and Choudhury, A.K. (eds.), *Dimensions of Environmental and Ecological Economics*, Universities Press, Hyderabad, pp.495-510.

Jentoft, S. and McCay, B.J., 1995, 'User Participation in Fisheries Management: Lessons Drawn From International Experience', *Marine Policy*, 19, 227-246.

Jesdapipat, S. and Piyawadee, C., 1997, 'Eco-Tax, Shrimp Farming and Mangrove', Paper presented at the *Sixth National Workshop on Mangrove Protection and Conservation,* 28 August, Haad Yai, Thailand.

Jevons, W.S., 1865, *The Coal Question: An Inquiry Concerning the Progress of the Nation, and the Probable Exhaustion of Our Coal Mines,* Macmillan, London.

Jhingran,V.G., 1991, *Fish and Fisheries of India*, Hindustan Publishing Corporation (India), Delhi.

Joint Group of Experts on the Scientific Aspects of Marine Pollution , 1991, *Reducing Environmental Impacts of Coastal Aquaculture,* IMO/FAO.UNESCO-IOC/WMO/ WHO/IAEA/UN/UNEP/GESAMP, Report and Studies , 47, FAO, Rome.

Joint Group of Experts on the Scientific Aspects of Marine Pollution , 2001, *Planning and Management for Sustainable Coastal Aquaculture Development*, GESAMP Reports and Studies No.68.

Jones, G.E., Davies, B. and Hussain, S., 2000, *Ecological Economics*, Blackwell, Sciences Ltd., Oxford.

Joseph, K.O., Gupta, V.P., Alavandi, S.V., Mishra, S.S. and Sivakumar, G., 1995, 'Impacts of Shrimp Farming on the Environment : A Case Study', *Proceedings of the National Workshop on Transfer of Technology for Sustainable Shrimp Farming*, 9-10 Jan. 1995, Chennai, pp.127-134.

Jyothisi, A. and Parthasarathy, R., 2007, 'Reservoir Fisheries Management: Experience of Tawa in Madhya Pradesh', *Economic and Political Weekly*, Vol.42, No.5, pp.409-415.

Kadekodi, G.K. and Nayampalli, A., 2005, 'Reversing Biodiversity Degradation : A Case of Chilka Lake', Sahu, N.C. and Choudhury, A.K. (eds.), *Dimensions of Environmental and Ecological Economics,* Universities Press, Hyderabad, pp. 527-545.

Kageson, P.,1998, *Growth Versus the Environment: Is there a Trade-off?* Kluwer Academic Publishers, Boston.

Kaladharan, P. and Jayasankar, R., 2003. 'Seaweeds', Modayil, M.J. and Jayaprakash, A.A. (eds.), *Status of Exploited Marine Fishery Resources of India*, Central Marine fisheries Research Institute, Cochin, pp.228-238.

Kaladharan, P., Nandakumar, A., Rajagoalan, M. and George, J.P., 2005, 'Mangroves of India: Biodiversity, Conservation and Management', *Marine Fisheries Information Service,* Central Marine Fisheries Research Institute, Cochin, pp.8-14,

Karunakaran, B., 2001, 'Mangroves Fast Depleting in State Due to Urbanisation and Pollution', *The New Indian Express*, Cochin, 23.3.2001.

Kasim, M.H., 2003, 'Carangids', Modayil, M.J., and Jayaprakash, A.A.. (eds.), *Status of Exploited Marine Fishery Resources of India*, Central Marine Fisheries Research Institute, Cochin, pp.66-75..

Katherine, R., 2003, 'Anthropogenically Induced Changes in the Environment: Effect on Fisheries'; Sinclair, M. and Valdimarsson, G., (eds.), *Responsible Fisheries in the Marine Ecosystem,* FAO, Rome and CABI Publishing, Oxon, pp.275-290.

Katiha, P.K. and Bhatta, R., 2002, 'Production and Consumption of Aquacultural Products in India: Past Trends, Present Status and Future Prospects', Paper presented at the Special Session on *Strategies and Options for Sustainable Aquacultural Development at World Aquaculture Congress*, 23-27, April, Beijing, China.

Keith, S. and Sumaila, U.S., 2003, 'Incorporating Ecosystem Objectives into Management of Sustainable Marine Fisheries, including Best Practice, Reference Points and use of Marine Protected Areas', Sinclair, .M. and Valdimarsson, G. (eds.), *Responsible Fisheries in the Marine Ecosystem*, FAO, Rome, and CABI Publishing, Oxon, pp.343-362.

Kenny, M. and Meadowcroft, J., (eds.), 1999, *Planning Sustainability*, Routledge, London.

Kerala Gazetteers Department, 1989, *Kerala State Gazetteer, Vol. III*, Government of Kerala, Trivandrum.

Kerr, M., Marothia, D.C., Singh, K., Ramasamy, C. and Bently, W.R., 1997, *Natural Resource Economics: Theory and Application in India*, Oxford and IBH Publishing Co., Pvt. Ltd., Delhi.

Keynes, J.M., 1936, *The General Theory of Employment, Interest and Money,* Harcourt Brice and Co. Inc, New York.

Kohr, M., 2002, *Globalisation and Sustainable Development: Challenges for Johannesburg*, http://www.tunside.org.sg./twr 139a-htm

Koli, P.A., 2005, 'Are Environmental Laws Sufficient for Sustainable Development?', Sahu, N.C. and Choudhury, A.K. (eds.), *Dimensions of Environmental and Ecological Economics*, Universities Press, Hyderabad, pp.546-555.

Korakandy, R., 1994, *Technological Change and the Development of Marine Fishing Industry in India,* Daya Publishing House, Delhi.

Korakandy, R., 1996, *Economics of Fisheries Management: A Critique in Third World Perspective*, Daya Publishing House, Delhi.

Korakandy, R., 2000, *Recreational Fisheries Development in India*, Daya Publishing House, Delhi.

Korakandy, R., 2002, 'Sustainability of Indian Fisheries', *Seafood Export Journal*, Vol. 33, No.1, Jan. 2002, pp.23-27.

Korakandy, R., 2005a, *Coastal Zone Management in India: The Political Economy of Sustainable Development*, Vol. I & II, Kalpaz Publications, Delhi.

Korakandy, R., 2005b, 'Sustainable Development of Indian Fisheries : Some Comments', Kurup, *et al.* (eds.), *Souvenir, Sustain Fish 2005*, School of Industrial Fisheries, Cochin University of Science and Technology, Cochin, pp.25-27.

Korakandy, R., 2005c, 'Sustainable Development of Indian Fisheries' *Souvenir,* issued on the occasion of the 42nd Anniversary of CIFNET, 18-19 March 2005, CIFNET, Cochin, pp.31-34.

Kripa, V. and Appukuttan, K.K., 2003, 'Marine Bivalves', Modayil, M.J. and Jayaprakash, A.A., (eds.), *Status of Exploited Marine Fishery Resources of India,* Central Marine Fisheries Research Institute, Cochin, pp.211-220.

Krishna, S., 1995, 'Technology Transfer for Sustainable Shrimp Farming'. *Proceedings of the Workshop on Technology Transfer for Sustainable Shrimp Farming,* Central Institute of Brackish Water Aquaculture, Madras, pp.146-153.

Krishna, S, 1997, 'Labour Unrest in Fisheries Sector', *Fishing Chimes*, Vol. No.17, No.9, p.17.

Krishna, S., Manpal, S., Kartha, P.N.R., and Mohanan, A.N., 2000, 'Group Farming for Sustainable Aquaculture', *Ocean and Coastal Management*, 43: 557-571.

Krishna, S., Menon, S.J., Gopal, N., Thomas, M., Edwin, L., Meenakumari, M., Unnithan, G.R., Balasubrahmaniam, S. and Annamalai, V., 2002, 'Unemployment and Labour Redeployment among Trawler Workers during Trawl Ban Period', *Fishing Chimes*, Vol. 22, No.1., pp.137-139.

Kuik, O. J. and Verbruggen, H., 1991, *In Search of Indicators of Sustainable Development,* Kluwer, Dordrecht.

Kuik, O.J., and Gilbert, A.J., 1999, 'Indictors of Sustainable Development', van den Bergh, J.C.J.M (ed.), *Hand Book of Environmental and Resource Economics*, Edward Elgar, Cheltenham, U.K., pp.722-730.

Kulkarni, P., 2005, *The Marine-Seafood Export Supply Chain in India,* International Institute for Sustainable Development, Winnipeg, Manitoba, Canada.

Kumar, A., Joshi, P.K. and Birthal, S.P., 2001, 'Fisheries Sector in India: An Overview of Performance, Policies and Programmes', *International Workshop on Strategies and Options for Increasing and Sustaining Fisheries Production to Benefit Poor Households in Asia,* 22-25 August, ICLARM, Penang, Malalysia.

Kumar, A. and Kumar, P., 2003, 'Food Safety Measures: Implications for Fisheries Sector in India', *Indian Journal of Agricultural Economics*, 58(3), 366-374.

Kumar, A., 2004, 'Export Performance of Indian Fisheries : Strengths and Challenges Ahead', *Economic and Political Weekly*, September 18, 2004, pp. 4264-4270.

Kumar, H.D., 2003, *Sustainability and Management of Aquaculture and Fisheries*, Daya Publishing House, Delhi.

Kummer, K., 1994, *Transboundary Movements of Hazardous Wastes at the Interface of Environment and Trade,* United Nations Environment Programme, Geneva.

Kurian, A., 2003, 'Bombay-Duck', Modayil, M.J. and Jayaprakash, A.A. (eds.), *Status of Exploited Marine Fishery Resources of India*, Central Marine Fisheries Research Institute, Cochin, pp.88-91.

Kurien, J., 1998, 'Traditional Ecological Knowledge and Ecosystem Sustainability: New Meaning to Asian Coastal Proverbs', *Ecological Applications*, 8(Suppl.), S2-S5.

Kurien, J., 2005, 'Fisheries Co-management: Some Different Perspectives', Kurup, *et al.* (eds.), *Souvenir, Sustain Fish 2005*, School of Industrial Fisheries, Cochin University of Science and Technology, Cochin, pp.71-74.

Kurien, J. and Vijayan, A.J., 1980, *Capitalist Relations in Traditional Fishing – The Case of the Goan 'Rampon'*, Fisheries Research Cell, Trivandrum.

Kurup, K.N. and Devaraj, M., 2000, 'Estimates of Optimum Fleet Size for the Exploited Indian Shelf Fisheries', *Marine Fisheries Information Service*, No.165, Central Marine Fisheries Research Institute, Cochin, pp.2-12.

Kurup, M.B., *et al.* (eds.), 2005, *Souvenir, Sustain Fish 2005*, School of Industrial Fisheries, Cochin University of Science and Technology, Cochin.

Kurup, M.B. and Manojkumar, T.G., 2005, 'Habitat Conservation: The Ultimate Impulsion of Fisheries Sustainability', Kurup, *et al.* (eds.) *Souvenir, Sustain - Fish 2005*, School of Industrial Fisheries, Cochin University of Science and Technology, Cochin, pp.75-83.

Kutty, M.N., 1995, 'Aquaculture Development and Sustainability in South East Asia', Bagario, T.U. and Flores, E.C.C. (eds.), *Towards Sustainable Aquaculture in South East Asia and Japan, SEAFDEC*, Aquaculture Department, Iloilo, Philippines, pp.91-108.

Kutty, M.N., 1999a, 'Aquaculture Development of India from a Global Perspective', *Current Science*, 76, 333-341.

Kutty, M.N., 1999b, 'Aquaculture Development and Sustainable Environment', Sukumarn, N., (ed.), *'Sustainable Environment'*, M.S.University, Sri-Paramakalyani Centre for Environmental Sciences, Alwarkurichi, Tamil Nadu, p.11.

Kutty, M.N., 2005, 'Development of Sustainable Aquaculture Systems', Kurup, *et al.* (eds.), *Souvenir, Sustain Fish 2005*, School of Industrial Fisheries, Cochin University of Science and Technology, Cochin, pp.19-24.

Lafferty, W., 1996, 'The Politics of Sustainable Development. Global Norms for National Implementation', *Environmental Politics*, 5, 185-208.

Lakshmanan, P.T., Liju, F., Prafulla, V. and Mukundan, M.K., 2001, 'Effect of Environmental Hazards on the Seafood Export of India', *Seafood Export Journal*, Vol. 32, No.2, pp. 35-42.

Lane, D.E. and Stephenson, R.L., 1995, 'Fisheries Management Science: The Framework to Link Biological, Economic and Social Objectives in Fisheries Management', *Aquatic Living Resources*, 8, 215-221.

Larkin, P.A., 1977, 'An Epitaph for the Concept of Maximum Sustainable Yield', *Trans. Amer. Fish. Soc.*, 106, 1-11.

Laureti, E., 1998, *Fish and Fishery Products: World Apparent Consumption Statistics Based on Food Balance Sheets (1961-1995)*, FAO, Rome (Reprint, Daya Publishing House, Delhi, 2001).

Legault, L.J.H., 1971, 'The Freedom of the Seas: A Licence to Pollute?', *University of Toronto Law Journal*, 21(2), 211-221.

Lery, J.M., Prado, J. and Tietze, U., 1999, *Economic Viability of Marine Capture Fisheries*, FAO, Technical Paper 377, FAO, Rome.

Lesser, J.A., Dodds, D.E., and Zerbe (Jr.), R.O., 1997, *Environmental Economics and Policy,* Addison-Wesley, New York.

Levin, S.A., (ed.),1993, 'Forum: Perspectives on Sustainability' *Ecological Applications,* 3, 545-589.

Lombardini, S., 1990, 'Economics Versus Ecology', Archibugi, F. and Nijkamp, P. (eds.), *Economics and Ecology: Towards Sustainable Development*, Kluwer Academic Publishers, Dordrecht, pp.139-148.

Long, A., 1999, 'The Marine Stewardship Council Initiative: The Development of a Market Incentive Approach to Achieving Sustainable Fisheries', Symes, D., (ed.), *Alternative Management Systems for Fisheries*, Fishing News Books, London, pp. 145-156.

Loucks, L., Charles, A.T. and Butler, M. (eds.), 1998, *Managing our Fisheries, Managing Ourselves*, Gorsebrook Research Institute, Halifax, Canada.

Loucks, P. and Gladwell, J. S., (eds.), 1999, *Sustainability Criteria for Water Resource Systems,* Cambridge University Press, Cambridge.

Low, P. and Yeats, A., 1992, 'Do Dirty Industries Migrate?', Low, P.(ed.), *International Trade and the Environment*, World Bank Discussion Paper 159, IBRD/The World Bank.

Luther, G. and Sastry, Y.A., 1993, 'Occurrence of Spawners, Juveniles and Young Fish in Relation to the Fishery Seasons of Some Major Fishery Resources of India :A Preliminary Study'. *The Marine Fisheries Information Service* No.122, Central Marine Fisheries Research Institute, Cochin.

Lutz, E., 1998, *Agriculture and the Environment: Perspectives on Sustainable Rural Development,* World Bank, Washington, DC.

Lux, K., 1990, *Adam Smith's Mistake: How a Moral Philosopher Invented Economics and Ended Morality,* Shambhala, Boston.

Mace, P.M., 1997, 'Developing and Sustaining World Fisheries Resources: The State of Science and Management' (Keynote Presentation), Hancock, D.A., Smith, D.C., Grant, A. and Beumer, J.P. (eds.), *Developing and Sustaining World Fisheries Resources: The State of Science and Management,* Proceedings of the Second World Fisheries Congress, CSIRO Publishing, Australia, pp.1-20.

Macintosh, D.J., 1996, 'Mangroves and Coastal Aquaculture: Doing Something Positive for Environment', *Aquaculture Asia*, 1, 3-4.

Mac Neill, J., 1989, 'Strategies for Sustainable Development', *Scientific American*, 261(3), 154-165.

Mac Neill, J., 1990a, 'Sustainable Development, Economics, and the Growth Imperative', *Workshop on the Economics, of Sustainable Development*, Background Paper No.3, Washington, DC.

Mac Neill, J., 1990b, 'Our Common Future': Sustaining the Momentum', Archibugi, F, and Nijkamp, P. (eds.), *Economy and Ecology: Towards Sustainable Development*, Kluwer Academic Publishers, Dordrecht, pp.15-25.

Malthus, T.R., 1820, *Principles of Political Economy Considered With a View to Their Practical Applications,* London.

Manonmoney, N., 2005, 'Management of Ecological (Common Property) Resources in Developing Countries', Sahu, N.C. and Choudhury, A.K., (eds.), *Dimensions of Environmental and Ecological Economics*, Universities Press, Hyderabad, pp.521-526.

Marine Products Export Development Authority, 2005, *Statistics of Marine Products Exports 2003*, Marine Products Export Development Authoriity, Cochin.

Marine Stewardship Council, 1998, *Principles and Criteria for Sustainable Fishing: Arlie House Draft* , www.msc.org/october.

Markandya, A. and Pearce, D.W., 1988, 'Natural Environment and the Social Rate of Discount', *Project Appraisal*, Vol.3, No.1, pp.2-12.

Markandya, A. and Richardson, J. (eds.), 1997, *Environmental Economics* (Reprint), Earth Scan Publications Ltd., London.

Marshall, A., 1890, *Principles of Economics* (8th edition, 1972), Mac Millan, London.

Marvasti, A., 1998, 'An Assessment of the International Technology Transfer Systems and the New Law of the Sea', *Ocean and Coastal Management*, 39, 197-210.

Marx, K. and Engels, E., 1867, *Capital*, Vol. III, Progress Publishers (1971 ed.), Moscow.

Mc Allister, D.E., 1999, 'The Crises of Aquatic Biodiversity', Pullin, R,.S.V., Froese, R. and Casal, C.M.V. (eds.), *Proceedings of the Conference on Sustainable Use of Aquatic Biodiversity: Data, Tools and Co-operation,* Lisbon, Portugal, 3-5, September 1998, pp.25-28.

Mc Connell, R.L., 'History of Aquatic Biodiversity', Pullin, R.S.V., Froese, R., and Casal, C.M.V. (eds.), *Proceedings of the Conference on Sustainable Use of Aquatic Biodiversity: Data, Tools and Co-operation, Lisbon, Portugal, 3-5,* September 1998, pp.29-33.

Mc Goodwin, J.R., 1990, *Crisis in the World Fisheries: People, Problems and Policies,* Stanford University Press, Stanford, California.

Mc Goodwin, J.R., 1995, *Culturally Based Conflicts in the Use of Living Marine Resources and Suggestions for Resolving or Mitigating Such Conflicts,* International Conference on Sustainable Contribution of Fisheries to Food Security, Kyoto, Japan, 4-9 December 1995, Government of Japan and Food and Agriculture Organisation.

Mc Mahon, G.F., and Mrozek, J.R., 1996, 'Economics, Entropy and Sustainability' *Hydrologic Sciences Journal*, 42(4), 501-538.

Mc Neely, J.A.,1999, 'Current Approaches to the Sustainable Use of Biodiversity: Key Implications for Fisheries Research' Pullin, R.S.V., Froese, R. and Casal, C.M.V. (eds.), *Proceedings of the Conference on Sustainable Use of Aquatic Biodiversity: Data, Tools and Co-operation,* Lisbon, Portugal, 3-5, September 1998, pp.34-39.

Meadowcroft, J., 1997, 'Planning, Democracy and the Challenge of Sustainable Development', *International Political Science Review*, 18 167-190.

Meadowcroft, J., 1999a, 'The Politics of Sustainable Development: Emergent Trends and the Challenge for Political Science', *International Political Science Review*, 20, 223-242.

Meadowcroft, J., 1999b, 'Planning for Sustainable Development: What Can be Learned from the Critics?' Kenny, M. and Meadowcroft, J. (eds.), *Planning Sustainability*, Routledge, London.

Meadows, D.H., 1996, 'Envisioning a Sustainable World', Costanza, R., Olman, S. and Alier, J.M., (eds.), *Getting Down to Earth: Practical Applications of Ecological Economics*, Island Press, Washington, DC, pp. 117-126

Meadows, D.H., Meadows, D.L., Randers, J. and Behrens- III,W.W., 1974, *Limits to Growth*, Report for the Club of Rome's Project on the Predicament of Mankind, 2nd edition, Universe Books, New York.

Meadows, D.H., Meadows, D.L. and Randers, J., 1993, *Beyond the Limits: Confronting Global Collapse, Envisioning a Sustainable Future*, Chelsea Green Publishing Co.

Meffe, G.K., 1992, 'Techno-Arrogance and Halfway Technologies: Salmon Hatcheries on the Pacific Coast of North America', *Conservation Biology*, 6(3), 350-354.

Menon, A.G.K., Singh, H.R., and Goelkumar, N., 2000, 'Present Ecological Status of Coldwater Fish and Fisheries', Singh, H.R., and Lakra, W.S., (eds.), *Coldwater Aquaculture and Fisheries*, Narendra Publishing House, Delhi, pp.1-36.

Menon, N.G., 2003, 'Catfishes', Modayil, M.J. and Jayaprakash, A.A., (eds.), *Status of Exploited Marine Fishery Resources of India*, Central Marine Fisheries Research Institute, Cochin, pp.110-119.

Mesarovic, M. and Pestel, E.,1974, *Mankind at the Turning Point*, The Second Report to the Club of Rome, Dutton, New York.

Milbrath, L.,1989, *Envisioning a Sustainable Society: Learning Our Way Out*, State University of New York Press, New York.

Miles, E.L., 1998, 'The Concept of Ocean Governance: Evolution Towards the 21st Century and the Principle of Sustainable Ocean Use', *Coastal Management*, 27, 1-30.

Mill, J.S., 1848, *Principles of Political Economy*, edited by Winch, D., Penguin Books, (1970), Harmondsworth.

Miller, D. (ed.), 1974, *The Political Economy of Capitalism*, Progress Publishers, Moscow.

Miller, M.A.L., 2000, 'Third World States and Fluid Sovereignty: Development Options and the Politics of Sustainable Ocean Management', *Ocean and Coastal Management*, 43, 235-253.

Ministry of Agriculture and Irrigation, 1976, *Report of the National Commission on Agriculture 1976, Part VIII, Fisheries*, (mimeo), Government of India, New Delhi.

Ministry of Agriculture, 2004, *Comprehensive Marine Fishing Policy*, Government of India, New Delhi.

Mitlin, D., 1992, 'Sustainable Development: A Guide to Literature', *Environment and Urbanisation,* 4, 111-124.

Modayil M.J., 2004, 'Impact of Globalisation on Indian Marine Fisheries', *Fishing Chimes*, Vol. 24, No.1, pp.38-42.

Modayil, M.J., 2005, 'How Do We Ensure Sustainability in the Open Access Marine Fisheries of India?' Kurup, *et al.* (eds.), *Souvenir, Sustain Fish 2005,* School of Industrial Fisheries, Cochin University Science and Technology, Cochin, pp.55-57.

Modayil, M.J. and Jayaprakash, A.A. (eds.) 2003, *Status of Exploited Marine Fishery Resources of India*, Central Marine Fisheries Research Institute, Cochin.

Mooney, H., 1998, 'Ecosystem Management for Sustainable Marine Fisheries' *Ecological Applications*, l8(1), S1

Munasinghe, M.C., 1993, *Environmental Economics and Sustainable Development,* World Bank Environment Paper No.3, The World Bank, Washington, DC.

Munasinghe, M. and Mc Neely, J.,1995, 'Key Concepts and Terminology of Sustainable Development', Munasinghe, M. and Shearer, W. (eds*.), Defining and Measuring Sustainable Development: The Biophysical Foundations*, The United Nations University and the World Bank, Washington DC.

Munasinghe, M. and Shearer, W., (eds.) 1995, *Defining and Measuring Sustainable Development: The Biophysical Foundations,* The United Nations University and the World Bank, Washington, DC.

Munn, R.E., 1990, 'Towards Sustainable Development: An Environmental Perspective', Archibugi, F. and Nijkamp, P. (eds.), *Economy and Ecology: Towards Sustainable Development*, Kluwer Academic Publishers, Dordrecht, pp.49-72.

Muttiah, C., Pillai, N.G.K., Mohammed, K.H. and. Bhat, U.S. 2003, 'Seerfishes', Modayil, M.J. and Jayaprakash, A.A., (eds.), *Status of Exploited Marine Fishery Resources of India*, Central Marine Fisheries Research Institute, Cochin, pp.45-50..

Nadia, S., (ed.), 1998, *Integrated Coastal Area Management and Agriculture, Forestry and Fisheries*, FAO Guidelines, Environment and Natural Resource Service, FAO, Rome.

Naem, S., Thomson, L.J., Lawler, S.P., Lawton, J.M., and Woodfin,R.M., 1994, 'Declining Biodiversity Can Alter the Performance of Ecosystem', *Nature,* 368, 734-737.

Nagpal, T. and Folke, C., 1995, *Choosing our Future: Visions of Sustainable World,* World Resources Institute, Washington, DC.

Naik, B.K., Kunnel, L.B., and Basavkumar, M., 2000, 'Economics of Brackishwater Prawn Farming in Coastal Belt: A Case Study of Uttar Kannada Coast in Karnataka State', Sathiadhas, R. and Venkateshwaran, K., (eds.), *Proceedings of the National Conference on Fisheries Economics, Extension and Management,* 5-6, January, 2000, CIFE, Mumbai,pp.107-113.

Nair, N.B., 1989, *Summary Report of the Expert Committee on Marine Fishery Resources Management in Kerala,* Expert Committee on Marine Fishery Resources Management in Kerala, Trivandrum.

Nair, N.B., 1991, *Report of the Fisheries Expert Committee on Ban on Monsoon Trawling in Kerala,* Fisheries Expert Committee on Monsoon Trawling in Kerala, Thiruvananthapuram.

Nair, R. and Prakasan, D., 2003, 'Ribbon fishes', Modayil, M.J. and Jayaprkash, A.A. (eds.), *Status of Exploited Marine Fisheries Resources of India*, Central Marine Fisheries Research Institute, Cochin, pp.76-87.

Nair, V.R., 2004, 'Environmental Impact Assessment : A Management Tool for Conservation of Large Marine Ecosystems', Somvanshi, V.S. (ed.), *Large Marine Ecosystems: Exploration and Exploitation for Sustainable Development and Conservation of Fish Stocks*, Fishery Survey of India, Mumbai, pp.433-447.

Nanda, S. and Mohapatra, B.C., 1995, 'Distribution of Heavy Metals on Coastal Waters of India', *Fishing Chimes*, Vol.15, No.8, pp.21-23.

Nandakumar, D., and Muraleekrishna, M., 1998, *Mapping the Extent of Coastal Zone Violations of the Indian Coast,* National Fish Workers' Forum, Thiruvananthapuram.

Nandakumar, G., and Maheswarudu, G., 2003, 'Penaeid Shrimps', Modayil, M.J. and Jayaprakash, A.A. (eds.), *Status of Exploited Marine Fishery Resources of India,* Central Marine Fisheries Research Institute, Cochin, pp.176-182.

Narayankumar, R., Suryaprakash, S. and Seenappa, D., 2000, 'Economics of Different Marine Fishing Crafts in Tamil Nadu', Sathiadhas, R. and Venkateshwaran, K., (eds.) *Proceedings of the National Conference on Fisheries Economics, Extension and Management,* January 5-6, 2000, Central Institute of Fisheries Education, Mumbai, pp.80-91.

National Centre for Agricultural Economics and Policy Research (NACP) and World Fish Centre, 2004, *Strategies and Options for Increasing and Sustaining Fisheries and Aquaculture Production to Benefit Poor Households in India,* NCAP, New Delhi and World Fish Centre, Penang.

National Fisheries Institute, 2000, *Fisheries Industry Principles for Responsible Fisheries*, http://www.nfi.organisations/rfs-prf.htm.

National Marine Fisheries Service , 1999, *Ecosystem-based Fishery Management:* A Report to the Congress by the Ecosystems Principles Advisory Panel. http://www.nmfs.noaa.govt/sfa/reports.html.

National Research Council, 1999, *Sustaining Marine Fisheries*, National Academy Press, Washington, DC.

National Round Table on Environment and Ecology , 1998, *Sustainable Strategy for the Oceans: A Co-management Guide*, NRTEE, Ottawa.

Nazeer, M., 1997, 'Mangrove Destruction Despite Protests', *The Hindu*, Thiruvananthapuram, 1.1.1997.

New, M., 1990, 'Shrimp Farming Experiences Environmental Problems', *Fisheries Cooperation Bulletin*, 3(3), European Commission.

New, M.B.,1999, 'Sustainable Shrimp Farming in the Tropics: Third Generation Farming Technology', *World Aquaculture*, 30, 34-43.

Nielson, J.R. and Vedsmand, T., 1997, 'Fishermen's Organisations in Fisheries Management: Perspectives for Fisheries Co-management Based on Danish Fisheries', *Marine Policy*, 21, 277-288.

Norgaard, R.B., 1994, *Development Betrayed: The End of Progress and a Co-evolutionary Re-visioning of the Future*, Routledge, London.

Norgaard, R.B. and Howarth, R.B., 1991a, 'Economics, Ethics and the Environment', Costanza, R. (ed.), *Ecological Economics: Science and Management of Sustainability*, Columbia University Press, New York.

Norgaard, R.B. and Howarth, R.B., 1991b, 'Sustainability and Discounting the Future', Costanza, R. (ed.), *Ecological Economics: The Science and Management of Sustainability, Columbia* University Press, New York, pp. 88-101.

Norton, B., 1992, 'Sustainability, Human Welfare and Ecosystem Health', *Environmental Values*, 1, 97-111.

Norton, B.G. and Toman, M.A., 1995, *Sustainability: Ecological and Economic Perspectives*, Resources for the Future, Discussion Paper 95/34(July).

Norton, B.G. and Toman, M.A., 1997, 'Sustainability: Ecological and Economic Perspectives', *Land Economics*, 73, 553-568.

Nunes, A.J.P. and Parsons, G.J., 1998, 'Dynamics of Tropical Coastal Aquaculture Systems and the Consequences of Waste Production', *World Aquaculture*, 29, 27-37.

O'Connor, M. (ed.), 1995, *Is Capitalism Sustainable: Political Economy and the Politics of Ecology*, Guilford Press, New York.

O'Riordan, T., 1988, 'The Politics of Sustainability', Turner, R.K., (ed.), *Sustainable Environmental Management: Principles and Practice*, Belhaven Press, London.

O'Riordan, T., 1991, 'The Politics of Sustainability', Turner, R. K. (ed.), *Sustainable Environmental Management: Principles and Practice*, CBS Publishers and Distributors (P) Ltd., New Delhi, pp.29-50.

Opschoor, J.B., Button, K. and Nijkamp, P., 1999, 'Developing Economies and the Steady State', Opschoor, J.B., Button, K. and Nijkamp, P. (eds.), *Environmental Economics and Development*, An Elgar Reference Collection, Cheltenham, U.K.

Opschoor, J.B. and Jongma, S.M., 1999, 'Brettonwoods Intervention Programmes and Sustainable Development', Reprinted in Opschoor, J.B., Button, K. and Nijkamp, P. (eds.), *Environmental Economics and Development*, An Elgar Reference Collection,. Cheltenham, U.K., pp. 506-525.

Organisation for Economic Co-operation and Development, 1994, *The Environmental Effects of Trade*, OECD, Paris.

Organisation for Economic Co-operation and Development , 1997, *Towards Sustainable Fisheries: Economic Aspects of the Management of Living Marine Resources*, OECD, Paris.

Organisation for Economic Cooperation and Development, 2000, *Tansition to Responsible Fisheries: Economic and Policy Implications*, OECD, Paris.

Orrego, V.F., 1993, 'Toward an Effective Management of High Seas Fisheries and the Settlement of Pending Issues of the Law of the Sea'. *Ocean Development and International Law*, 24(1), 81-92.

Owens, S., 1994, 'Land, Limits and Sustainability: A Conceptual Framework and Some Dilemmas for the Planning System', *Transactions of the Institute of British Geographers,* NS, 19, 439-456.

Page, T., 1977, *Conservation and Economic Efficiency: An Approach to Materials Policy,* Johns Hopkins University Press, for Resources for the Future, Baltimore.

Pajack, P., 2000, 'Sustainability, Ecosystem Management and Indicators: Thinking Globally and Acting Locally in the 21st Century', *Fisheries,* 25(12), 16-30.

Panayotou, T., 1993, *Green Markets: The Economics of Sustainable Development*, ICS Press, San Francisco.

Panayotou, T., 1994, *Economic Instruments for Environmental Management and Sustainable Development,* International Environmental Programame, Harward Institute for International Development, Harward University, Massachusetts.

Panayotou, T., 1995, 'Environmental Degradation at Different Stages of Economic Development', Ahmed, I. and Doelman, J.A. (eds.), *The Environmental Crisis and Sustainable Livelihood in the Third World*, Houndmills and Macmillan, London, pp.13-36.

Panayotou, T., 2000, 'Environment and Growth', CID Working Paper 56, Harward University Centre for International Development, Cambridge, M.A. (also at http://www.cid.harward.edu/cidw/o/056.htm).

Pandian, T.J., 2001, 'A Prelude for Indian Fisheries Policy', T.J. Pandian (ed.), *Sustainable Indian Fisheries*, National Academy of Agricultural Sciences, New Delhi, pp.321-327.

Panikkar, K.K.P. and Alagaraja, K., 1981, 'Socio-economic Status of Fishermen Community of Calicut Area', *Marine Fisheries Information Service*, No.33, CMFRI, Cochin.

Panikkar, K.K.P., Sathiadhas, R. and Jacob, T., 1990, 'Comparative Economic Efficiency of Different Types of Mechanised Fishing Units Operating Along the Kerala Coast', *Journal of Marine Biological Association of India*, Vol. 32, No.2, pp. 97-106.

Parikh, J., 1994, *Trade and Environmental Linkages: A Case Study of India*,(Mimeo) , Indira Gandhi Institute of Development Research, Bombay, for UNDP/ UNCTAD.

Parritt, J., 1984, *Seeing Green: The Politics of Ecology Explained*, Basil Blackwell, Oxford.

Parthasarathi, G. and Nirmala, K.A., 2000, 'Economics and Environmental Issues of Brackish Water Aquaculture', Krishnan, M. and Birthal, P.S., (eds.), *Aquaculture Development in India: Problems and Prospects*, National Centre for Agricultural Economics and Policy Research, New Delhi, pp. 32-51.

Pattnaik, B.C., 2000, 'Marketing of Traditional Value-Added Fish Products: A Profitable Venture', *Fishing Chimes*, Vol. 20, No.6, pp.52-54.

Paul Raj, R.,Gopalan, M.R., Vijayakumaran, M., Vivekanandan, E., and Sathiadhas,R., 1998, 'Environmental and Social Issues in Coastal Aquaculture: A Case Study', *Bay of Bengal News*, 11, 15-18.

Pauly, D. and Christensen, V., 1995, 'Primary Production Required to Sustain Global Fisheries', *Nature*, 374, 255-257.

Pearce, D.W., 1987, 'Foundations of an Ecological Economics', *Ecological Modelling,* 38, 9-18.

Pearce, D.W., 1991, 'The Sustainable Use of Natural Resource in Developing Countries', Turner, R.K. (ed.), *Sustainable Environmental Management: Principles and Practices*, CBS, Publishers and Distributors, New Delhi, pp. 102-117.

Pearce, D.W., 1993, 'Valuing the Environment: Past Practice, Future Prospect', *Paper presented at the First Annual International Conference on Environmentally Sustainable Development*, IBRD, Washington, DC, September 30-October 1.

Pearce, D.W., 1997, 'Economics and the Global Environmental Challenge', Markandya, A. and Richardson, J. (eds.), *Environmental Economics* (1997 Reprint), Earth Scan Publications Ltd., London, pp.391-406.

Pearce, D.W., 1998, *Economics and Environment: Essays on Ecological Economics and Sustainable Development,* Edward Elgar, Cheltenham, U.K.

Pearce, D.W., Barbier, E.B. and Markandya, A., 1988, 'Sustainable Development and Cost-Benefit Analysis', *LEEC Paper*, 88-03, London Environmental Economics Centre, University College, London.

Pearce, D.W., Barbier, E.B. and Markandya, A., 1990, *Sustainable Development: Economics and Environment in Third World*, Edward Elgar, London.

Pearce, D.W. and Atkinson, G, 1992, *Are National Economies Sustainable? Measuring Sustainable Development*, CSERGE Working Paper GEC 92-11, Centre for Socio-Economic Research on the Global Environment, University College, London.

Pearce, D.W. and Warford, J.J.,1992, *World Without End: Economics, Environment and Sustainable Development,* Oxford University Press for the World Bank, Oxford.

Pearce, D.W. and Atkinson, G., 1993a, 'Measuring Sustainable Development', *Ecodecision*, 9, 64-66.

Pearce, D.W. and Atkinson, G., 1993 b, 'Capital Theory and Measurement of Sustainable Development: An Indicator of 'Weak' Sustainability', *Ecological Economics*, 8( 2) ,103-108.

Pearce, D. W., Turner, R.K., O'Riordan, T., Adger, N., Atkinson, G., Brisson, I , Brown, K., Dubourg, R., Fankhauser, S., Jordan, A., Maddison, D., Moran, D. and Powell, J., (eds.), 1993, *Blueprint: Measuring Sustainable Development*, (Reprint, 1996) Earth Scan Publications, Ltd., London.

Pearce, D.W. and Atkinson, G, 1994, 'What is Sustainable Development' *Annual Review of Energy*, 19, 457-474.

Pearce, D.W. and Moran, D., 1994, *The Economic Value of Biodiversity,* Earth Scan, London

Pearce, D.W. and Atkinson, G, 1995, 'Measuring Sustainable Development', Bromley, D.W. (ed.), *Handbook of Environmental Economics,* Blackwell, Oxford, pp.166-181.

Pearce, D.W., Atkinson, G. and Hamilton, K., 1998, 'The Measurement of Sustainable Development', van den Bergh, J.C.J.M. and Hofkes,. M.W. (eds.), *Theory and Implementation of Economic Models for Sustainable Development.* Kluwer Academic Publishers.

Pearson, C., 1982, *Environmental Policies and Their Trade Implications for Developing Countries with Special Reference to Fish, Shellfish, Fruits and Vegetables,* United Nations Conference on Trade and Development, UNTCAD/ST/MD/26 (October).

Pearson, C.S., 2000, *Economics and the Global Environment,* Cambridge University Press, Cambridge.

Peet, J., 1992, *Energy and the Ecological Economics of Sustainability,* Island Press, Washington, DC.

Peet, J. and Peet, K., 1990, 'With People's Wisdom: Community Based Perspectives on Sustainable Development', *Paper Presented at the Ecological Economics of Sustainability Conference,* 21-23, May World Blank, Washington, DC.

Perman, R., Ma Yue and Mc Gilvray, J., 1996, *Natural Resource and Environmental Economics,* Longman, London.

Perrings, C., 1991, 'Reserved Rationality and the Precautionary Principle: Technological Change, Time and Uncertainty in Environmental Decision Making', Costanza, R.(ed.), *Ecological Economics: The Science and Management of Sustainability,* Columbia University Press, New York, pp.153-166.

Pezzey, J., 1989, *Economic Analysis of Sustainable Growth and Sustainable Development,* Environment Department Working Paper 18, World Bank, Washington, DC.

Pezzey, J., 1992, *Sustainable Development Concepts: An Economic Analysis,* The World Bank, Washington, DC.

Pezzey, J.C.V. 1997, 'Sustainability Constraints Versus Optimality Versus Inter-temporal Concerns and Axioms Versus Data', *Land Economics,* 73, 448-466.

Philippe, C., 2004, 'The Case of Developing Countries' Swan, J. and Greboval, D. (eds.), *Report and Documentation of the International Workshop on the Implementation of International Fisheries Instruments and Factors of Un-sustainability and Overexploitation in Fisheries,* Mauritius, 3-7 February *2003,* FAO, Rome, pp.265-281.

Phillips, M.J., 1995, 'Shrimp Culture and the Environment', Bagarino, T.U. and Flores, E.C.C. (eds.), *Towards Sustainable Aquaculture in Southeast Asia and Japan,* SEAFDEC Aquaculture Department, Iloilo, Philippines, pp.37-62.

Pigou, A.C., 1932, *The Economics of Welfare,* (4th ed.), Macmillan, London.

Pillai, N.G.K., Ganga, U. and Jayaprakash, A.A., 2003, 'Indian Oil-Sardine', Modayil, M.J. and Jayaprakash, A.A., (eds.), *Status of Exploited Marine Fishery Resources of India,* Central Marine Fisheries Research Institute, Cochin, pp.18-24.

Pillai, P.P. and Gopakumar, G., 2003, 'Tunas', Modayil, M.J. and Jayaprakash, A.A. (eds.), *Status of Exploited Marine Fishery Resources of India*, Central Marine Fisheries Research Institute, Cochin, pp.51-59.

Pinkerton, E. and Weinstein, M., 1995, *Fisheries That Work: Sustainability Through Community-Based Management*, David Zuzuki Foundation, Vancouver.

Pirages, D.C., 1977. 'A Social Design for Sustainable Growth', Pirages, D.C., (ed.,), *The Sustainable Society : Implications for Limited Growth*, Praeger, New York.

Pitcher, T.J. and Pauly, D., 1998, 'Rebuilding Ecosystems, Not Sustainability as the Proper Goal of Fishery Management', Pitcher, T.J., Hart, P.J.B., and Pauly, D., (eds.), *Re-inventing Fisheries Management*, Kluwer Academic Publishers, Dordrecht, pp.311-329.

Pitcher, T.J., Hart, P.J.B. and Pauly, D., (eds.), 1998, *Re-inventing Fisheries Management*, Kluwer, Dordrecht.

Pitcher, T., 2001, 'Ecosystem Goals Can Reinvigorate Fisheries Management, Help Dispute Resolution and Encourage Public Support', *Fish and Fisheries*, 1, 99-103.

Planning Commission, 1981, *Sixth Five Year Plan, 1980-85*, Government of India, New Delhi.

Planning Commission, 1985, *Seventh Five Year Plan, 1985-90, Vol. II, Sectoral Programmes of Development*, Government of India, New Delhi.

Planning Commission, 1992, *Eighth Five Year Plan*, 1992-97, *Vol. II, Sectoral Programmes of Development*, Government of India, New Delhi.

Planning Commission, 2001, *Report of the Working Group on Fisheries for the Tenth Five Year Plan (2002-2007)*, Government of India, New Delhi.

Planning Commission, 2002, *Tenth Five Year Plan, (2002-2007)*, Government of India, New Delhi.

Platteau, J.P., Murikan,J. and Delbar, E. 1985, *Technology, Credit and Indebtedness in Marine Fishing*, Hindustan Publishing Corporation (Ltd.) India, Delhi.

Pomeroy, R.S., 1995, 'Community-Based and Co-management Institutions for Sustainable Coastal Fisheries Management in South-east Asia', *Ocean and Coastal Management*, 27, 143-162.

Porritt, J., 1984, *Seeing Green : The Politics of Ecology Explained*, Basil Blackwell, Oxford.

Prakash, C.P., Sinha, S.R.K. and Reddy, A.K. , 1990, 'Economic Viability of Aquaculture in Sewage', *J. Environ. Biol.*, 11, 7-14.

Prakash, T.N. and Pearce, D.W., 1993, *Sustainability as Resilience: Measuring Sustainable Development*, (mimeo), Centre for Social and Economic Research on the Global Environment, University of East Anglia and University College, London.

Prendergast, J., 1993, 'Engineering Sustainable Development' *Civil Engineering*, 63(10), 39-42.

Prescot-Allen, R., 1996, *Barometer of Sustainability: What it's for and How to Use it*, The World Conservation Union (IUCN), Gland, Switzerland.

Primavera, J.H., 1989, 'The Social, Ecological and Economic Implications of Intensive Prawn Farming', *Asian Aquaculture*, 11, 1-6.

Pullin, R.S.V., 1991, *An Overview of Environmental Issues in Developing Country Aquaculture Development*, ICLARM Conference Proceedings, 31, International Centre for Living Aquatic Resource Management (now World Fisheries Centre), Manila.

Pullin, R.S.V., Froese, R. and Casal, C.M.V. (eds.), 1999, *Proceedings of the Conference on Sustainable Use of Aquatic Biodiversity: Data, Tools and Co-operation*, Lisbon, Portugal, *3-5*, September 1998, ACP-EU Fish. Res. Rep., (6).

Purandhara, C., 1993, 'Report on the Set-back Suffered by Marine Fishing Sector on Dakshina Kannada Coast, Karnataka, due to the Cyclone during November 1992', *Marine Fisheries Information Service*, No.121, Central Marine Fisheries Research Institute, Cochin.

Radhakrishnan,E.V. and Manisseri, M.K., 2003, 'Lobsters', Modayil, M.J. and Jayaprakash, A.A. (eds.), *Status of Exploited Marine Fishery Resources of India*, Central Marine Fisheries Research Institute, Cochin, pp.195-202.

Radhakrishnan, E.V. and Vijayakumaran, M., 2004, 'The Status of Lobster Fishery in India and Options for Sustainable Management', Somvanshi, V.S. (ed.), *Large Marine Ecostystems: Exploration and Exploitation for Sustainable Development and Conservation of Stocks*, Fishery Survey of India, Mumbai.

Raghu, K.V., 2002, 'Impact of Coastal Aquaculture on Environment and its Management', *Proceedings of the National Seminar on Current Environmental Problems and Management*, Irinjalakuda, Kerala.

Rajagopalan, M. and Menon, N.G., 2003, 'Marine Turtles and Mammals', Modayil, M.J. and Jayaprakash, A.A., (eds.), *Status of Exploited Marine Fishery Resources of India*, Central Marine Fisheries Research Institute, Cochin, pp.240-245.

Rajan, K.N., Nandakumar, G. and Chellappan, K., 2000, 'Innovative Exploitation of Deep Sea Crustaceans Along the Kerala Coast', *Marine Fisheries Information Service*, No.168, Central Marine Fisheries Research Institute, Cochin, pp.1 –11.

Rajasenan, D., 2005, 'Marine Fishing in Kerala: Dynamics and Challenges', Rajasenan, D. and de Groot, G. (eds.), *Kerala Economy: Trajectories, Challenges and Implications*, Directorate of Publications, Cochin University of Science and Technology, Cochin, pp.149-167.

Raje, S.G. and Joshi, K.K., 2003, 'Elasmobranchs', Modayil, M.J. and Jayaprakash, A.A. (eds.), *Status of Exploited Marine Fishery Resources of India*, Central Marine Fisheries Research Institute, Cochin, pp.92-101.

Ramachandran, M., 2004, *Teaching not to F(in)ish? A Constructivist Perspective on Reinventing a Responsible Marine Fisheries Extension System*, CMFRI, Cochin.

Rao, G.R.M and Ravichandran, P., 2001, 'Sustainable Brackish Water Aquaculture', Pandyan, T.J. (ed.), *Sustainable Indian Fisheries*, National Academy of Agricultural Sciences, New Delhi, pp. 134-151.

Rao, S.G., 2004, 'Deep Sea Shrimp Fishery Along the Northeast Coast of India: A Critical Appraisal', Somvanshi, V.S. (ed.), *Large Marine Ecostystems: Exploration and Exploitation for Sustainable Development and Conservation of Stocks*, Fishery Survey of India, Mumbai, pp.668-682.

Redclift, M., 1984, *Development and the Environmental Crisis: Red or Green Alternatives,* Methewn, London.

Redclift, M., 1991, 'Economic Models and Environmental Values: A Discourse on Theory', Turner, R.K., (ed.), *Sustainable Environmental Management: Principles and Practice*, CBS Publishers and Distributors, New Delhi, pp.52-66.

Redclift, M., 1992, 'The Meaning of Sustainable Development', *Geoforum*, 23, 395-403.

Redclift, M., 1999, 'Pathways to Sustainability: Issues, Policies and Theories', Kenny, M. and Meadowcroft, J. (eds.), *Planning Sustainability*, Routledge, London.

Reddy, G.P., Sontakki, B., Shenoy, N.S.,.Rao, V.K.J., and Soam, S.K., 2004, *Prioritisation of Fisheries Research in India*, Indian Council of Agricultural Research/National Academy of Agricultural Research Management, Rajendra Nagar, Hyderabad.

Rees, W.E., 1988, 'Defining Sustainable Development', Background Paper for the Conference, *Planning for Sustainable Development*, School of Community and Regional Planning, University of British Columbia, Vancouver.

Rees, W.E., 1990, 'The Ecology of Sustainable Development', *The Ecologist,* 20, 18-23.

Rees, W.E., 1995, 'Achieving Sustainability: Reform or Transformation', *Journal of Planning Literature*, 9, 343-361.

Rees, W.E., 1996, 'Revisiting Carrying Capacity : Area-based Indicators of Sustainability', *Population and Environment,* 17, 195-215.

Rees, W.E., 1997, 'Is Sustainability an Oxymoron?' *Local Environment,* 2, 303-310.

Rees, W.E., 1999, 'Scale, Complexity and the Conundrum of Sustainability', Kenny, M. and Meadowcroft, J. (eds.), *Planning Sustainability*, Routledge, London, pp. 101-127.

Rees, W.E. and Wackernagel, M., 1994, 'Ecological Foot-prints and Appropriated Carrying Capacity: Measuring the Natural Capital Requirements of the Human Economy', Jansson, A.M., Hammer, M., Folke, C. and Costanza, R. (eds.), *Investing in Natural Capital: The Ecological Economics Approach to Sustainability,* Island Press, Washington, DC.

Rees, W.E. and Wackernagel, M. 1996, 'Urban Ecological Foot-prints; Why Cities Cannot be Sustainable and Why They are a Key to Sustainability' *Environmental Impact Assessment Review*, 16, 223-248.

Regier, H. and Baskerville, G., 1986, 'Sustainable Redevelopment of Regional Ecosystems Degraded by Development', Clark, W. and Munn, R., (eds.), *Sustainable Development of the Biosphere*, Cambridge University Press, Cambridge.

Reid, D., 1995, *Sustainable Development: An Introduction*, Earth Scan, London.

Rennings, K. and Wiggering, H., 1997, 'Steps Towards Indicators of Sustainable Development: Linking Economic and Ecological Concepts', *Ecological Economics*, 2, 25-36.

Repetto, R., 1985, *The Global Possible : Resources, Development and the New Century,* Yale University Press, New Haven.

Resources for the Future, 1996, 'Rights Based Fishing: Transition to a New Industry', *Resources,* 124.

Ricardo, D., 1817, *Principles of Political Economy and Taxation.*

Ridmontri, C., 1996, 'Shrimp Import Ban Could be Good for Resources', *Bangkok Post*, 17th March.

Riedel, W.V., 1993, *Biodiversity Prospecting: Using Genetic Resources for Sustainable Development*, World Resources Institute, Washington, DC.

Rik, C.B., 1998, 'World Fisheries are in Crisis? We Must Respond!' Pitcher, T.J., Hart, P.J.B. and Pauly, D. (eds.), *Re-inventing Fisheries Management*. Kluwer Academic Publishers, Dordrecht, pp.3-17.

Roberts, C.M., 1997, 'Ecological Advice for the Global Fisheries Crisis', *Trends in Ecology and Evolution*, 12, 35-38.

Robinson, J., Francis, G, Legge, R. and Lerner, S., 1990, 'Defining Sustainable Society, Values, Principles and Definitions', *Alternatives,* 17, 36-46.

Rogers, R.A., 1995, *The Oceans are Emptying: Fish Wars and Sustainability*, Black Rose Books, Montreal.

Rohit, P., Gupta, A.C. and Bhat, U.S., 1993, 'Increased Exploitation of Juvenile Fish Population by Bull Trawlers during the early Post-monsoon Fishing Season of 1992 along the Dakshina Kannada Coast, Karnataka', *Marine Fisheries Information Service*, No.122, Central Marine Fisheries Research Institute, Cochin.

Rojer, S.V., Pullin D., Bartley, M. and Kooiman, J., 1997, *Towards Policies for Conservation and Sustainable Uses of Aquatic Genetic Resources*, FAO and ICLARM.

Roshada, H., 2005, 'Sustaining Aquaculture Development: The Feeds and Feeding Connection', Kurup, *et al.*, (eds.), *Souvenir, Sustain Fish (2005)*, School of Industrial Fisheries, Cochin University of Science and Technology, Cochin, pp.37-43.

Ruddle, K., 1994, 'Local Knowledge in the Folk Management of Fisheries and Coastal Marine Environment', Dyer, C.L. and McGoodwin, J.R. (eds.), *Folk Management in the World's Fisheries: Lessons for Modern Fisheries Management*, University of Colorado Press, Niwot, Co., pp. 161-206

Sakthivel, M., 2001a, 'Challenging Tasks for Sustainable Fisheries Development in the Millennium 2000', Pandyan, T.J. (eds.), *Sustainable Indian Fisheries*, National Academy of Agricultural Sciences, New Delhi, pp.6-18.

Sakthivel, M., 2001b, 'Need for Legal Framework for Sustainable Aquaculture', Pandyan, T.J., (ed.), *Sustainable Indian Fisheries*, National Academy of Agricultural Sciences, New Delhi, pp. 225-231.

Salih, M.M.A., 2001, 'Globalisation, Sustainable Development and Environment: A Balancing Act', Schuurman, F.J. (ed.), *Globalisation and Development Studies: Challenges for the 21st Century*, Vistar Publications, New Delhi, pp. 117-134.

Salim, S. and Halawai, B.K., 2005, 'Capture and Culture Fisheries of India : Impact of Sanitary and Phyto-sanitary Measures in Relation to Exports', *Fishing Chimes*, Vol. 24, No. 12, pp.24-28.

Salim, S.S. and Palanisami, K., 2006, 'Export Growth and Instability of Indian Seafood Export in the Post-WTO Era', *Seafood Export Journal*, Vol. 36, No.3, 9-19.

Samal, K.C., 2002, 'Shrimp Culture in Chilka Lake : Case of Occupational Displacement of Fishermen', *Economic and Political Weekly*, Vol.37, No.18, pp.1714-1718.

Sampath, V., 'Sustainable Fisheries and the Environment', Qazim, S.Z. and Roonwal, G.S. (eds.), 1998, *Living Resources of India's, Exclusive Economic Zone*, Omega Scientific Publishers, New Delhi, pp. 65-85.

Sands, P., 2000, 'Environmental Protection in the Twenty-first Century: Sustainable Development and International Law', Revesz, R.L., Sands, P. and Stewart, R.B. (eds.), *Environmental Law, The Economy and Sustainable Development*, Cambridge University Press, New York.

Sankar, U. (ed.), 2001, *Environmental Economics*, Oxford University Press, New Delhi.

Sanwal, M., 2004, 'Sustainable Development and the Evolution of International Policy and Law', Ghosh, P. and Jaitly, A., (eds.), The *Road from Rio: Environment and Development Policy in Asia*, Tata Energy Research Institute, New Delhi, pp.57-67.

Sarkar, S., 2000, *Ecosocialism or Ecocapitalism?: A Critical Analysis of Humanity's Fundamental Choices*, Orient Longman Limited, New Delhi

Sathiadhas, R., and Venkataraman, G., 1983, 'Indebtedness and Utilisation of Fisheries Credits in Sakthikulangara and Neendakara, Kerala : A Case Study', *The Marine Fisheries Information Service*, No. 54, CMFRI, Cochin, pp.1-6.

Sathiadhas, R.,Kumar, R.N. and Reghu, R., 1995, *Marine Fisheries Management for Sustainable Development*, CMFRI Technology Transfer Series 2, CMFRI, Cochin.

Sathiadhas, R., 1996, 'Economic Evaluation of Marine Fisheries of India for Sustainable Production and Coastal Zone Development', *Naga*, The ICLARM Quarterly, 19(3), 54-56.

Sathiadhas, R., Reghu, R. and Immanuel, S., 1999, 'Human Resource Utilisation, Productivity and Earnings in Indian Marine Fisheries', *Seafood Export Journal*, Vol. 30, No.4, pp. 51-55.

Sathiadhas, R. and Biradar, S., 2000, 'Fisheries in the Development of Indian Economy', Sathiadhas R. and Venkateswaran (eds.), *Proceedings of the National Conference on Fisheries Economics, Extension and Management*, January 5-6, 2000, CIFE, Mumbai, pp.1-20.

Schmidt, C.C., 2000, 'Traceability and Fisheries: Consumer Wants and Government Needs – Lessons Learned from Past Experience', *Paper Presented at the International Conference on Fisheries Monitoring, Control and Enforcement, Brussels, 24-27, October.*

Schumpeter, J.A., 1939, *Business Cycles*, McGraw Hill, New York..

Schrank, W.E., 2003, *Introducing Fisheries Subsidies*, FAO Fisheries Technical Paper No.437, FAO, Rome.

Scott, M., 1995, 'What Sustains Economic Development?' Ian, G. and Alan, W. (eds.), *The Economics of Sustainable Development*, Cambridge University Press, Cambridge.

Seafood Export Journal, 2007a, 'Anti-dumping Duty Slashes Shrimp Exports to US by 50 per cent' *Seafood Export Journal*, Vol.37, No.2, p.7.

Seafood Export Journal, 2007b, 'UN Ecology Agency Calls for Better Global Management to Prevent Collapse of Fish Stocks' *Seafood Export Journal*, Vol.37,No.2, p.15.

Selvam, S., Pouchepparadjou, A. and Ramasamy, C., 2000, 'The Social, Ecological and Economic Implications of Shrimp Farming in Coromandel Coast of South India', Sathiadhas, R. and Venkateswaran, K. (eds.), *Proceedings of the National Conference on Fisheries Economics, Extension and Management*, January 5 - 6, 2000, Mumbai, pp.298-312.

Selvan, S. and Ramaswamy, C., 2000, 'Socio-Economic and Environmental Impacts of Shrimp Farming', Krishnan. M. and Birthal, P.S. (eds.), *Aquaculture Development in India: Problems and Prospects*, National Centre for Agricultural Economics and Policy Research (NCAP), New Delhi.

Senthilathiban, R., Venkataramanujam, K., Selvaraj, P. and Sanjeevraj, G., 1997, 'Costs and Earnings of Trawlers Operating at Tuticorin, Tamil Nadu', *Fishery Technology*, Vol. 34(2), pp.31-34.

Serageldin, I, 1993, 'Making Development Sustainabile' *Finance and Development*, pp.6-10.

Serageldin, I., 1996, *Sustainability and the Wealth of Nations, First Step in an Ongoing Journey*, Monograph Series No.5, World Bank, Washington DC.

Sherman, K., 1993, 'Large Marine Eco-Systems as Global Units for Marine Resources Management : An Ecological Perspective', Sherman, K., Alexander, L.M. and Gold, B.D. (eds.), *Large Marine Ecosystems: Stress, Mitigation and Sustainability*, AAAS Press, Washington, DC, pp. 3-14

Sherman, K., and Duda, A.M., 1999, 'Large Marine Ecosystems: An Emerging Paradigm for Fishery Sustainability', *Fisheries*, 24(12), 15-26.

Shiva, V. and Karir, S., 1997, *Towards Sustainable Aquaculture (Chemmeen kettu)*, Research Foundation for Science, Technology and Ecology, New Delhi.

Shrybman, S., 1991, 'Trading Away the Environment', *World Policy Journal*, 9(1), 93-110.

Siebert, H., 1977, 'Environmental Quality and the Gains from Trade', *Kyklos*, 30(4), 657-673.

Silas, E.G., (ed.), 1977, *Indian Fisheries, 1947-'77*, Marine Products Export Development Authority, Cochin.

Silas, E.G, 2000, *Report of the Working Group for Revalidating the Potential of Fishery Resources in the Indian EEZ,* Department of Animal Husbandry and Dairying, New Delhi.

Simonis, U.E., 1990, *Beyond Growth: Elements of Sustainable Development*, Sigma Edition, Berlin.

Simov, D., 1989, 'Sustainable Development: Theoretical Construct or Attainable Goal?', *Environmental Conservation*, 16(1), 41-48.

Sinclair, M. and Valdimarsson, G. (eds.), 2003a, *Responsible Fisheries in the Marine Ecosystem*, FAO, Rome and CABI Publishing, Oxon.

Sinclair, M. and Valdimarsson, G, 2003b, 'The Reykjavik Declaration on Responsible Fisheries in the Marine Ecosystem', Sinclair, M. and Valdimarsson, G. (eds.), *Responsible Fisheries in the Marine Ecosystem*, FAO, Rome and CABI Publishing, Oxon, pp.409-412.

Sinclair, M. and Valdimarsson, G., 2003c, 'Towards Ecosystem Based Fisheries Management', Sinclair, M., and Valdimarsson, G., (eds.), *Responsible Fisheries in the Marine Ecosystem*, FAO, Rome and CABI Publishing, Oxon, pp.393-404.

Sinden, J.A. and Worrell, A.C., 1979, Un-*priced Values: Decisions Without Market Prices,* Wiley, New York.

Singh, H.R. and Lakra, W.S. (eds.), *Coldwater Aquaculture and Fisheries,* Narendra Publishing House, Delhi.

Singh, V.V. and Raje, S.G, 1989, 'Squally Weather Disrupted Fishing Activities along Maharashtra Coast in September, 1988', *Marine Fisheries Information Service,* No.98, Central Marine Fisheries, Research Institute, Cochin.

Sinha, P.C., 2004, 'Large Marine Ecosystems (LMEs), Ecologically Critical Areas (ECAs), and Sustainable Management of India's Marine Biodiversity: A Conceptual Analysis', Somvanshi, V.S. (ed.), *Large Marine Ecostystems: Exploration and Exploitation for Sustainable Development and Conservation of Fish Stocks*, Fishery Survey of India, Mumbai, pp.448-481.

Sissenwine, M.P. and Rosenberg, A.A., 1993, 'Marine Fisheries at a Critical Juncture', *Fisheries,* 18(10), 6-13.

Sissenwine, M.P. and. Mace, P.M., 2003, 'Governance for Responsible Fisheries: An Ecosystem Approach', Sinclair, M. and Valdimarsson, G. (eds.), *Responsible Fisheries in the Marine Ecosystem,* FAO, Rome and CABI Publishing, Oxon, *pp.363-392.*

Sivadas, M., 2004, 'Economics of Tuna Pole and Line Operation in Minicoy, Lakshadweep', Somvanshi, V.S. (ed.), *Large Marine Ecosystems: Exploration and Exploitation for Sustainable Development and Conservation of Fish Stocks*, Fishery Survey of India, Mumbai, pp 683-686.

Sivakami, S., Vivekanandan, E., Raje, S.G., Shobha, J.K. and Rajkumar, U., 2003, 'Lizard Fishes, Pomfrets and Bulls Eye', Modayil, M.J. and Jayaprkash, A.A., (eds.), *Status of Exploited Marine Fishery Resources of India*, Central Marine Fisheries Research Institute, Cochin, pp.141-157.

Smith,A., 1776, *An Enquiry into the Nature and Causes of The Wealth of Nations*, The Modern Library (1937 edn.), New York.

Smith, A., 1776, *The Wealth of Nations* (ed. by Skinner, A.), Penguin Books (1970), Harmondsworth.

Solow, R.M., 1986, 'On the Intergenerational Allocation of Natural Resources', *Scandinavian Journal of Economics*, Vol.88, No.1, pp.141-149.

Solow, R.M., 1992, *An Almost Practical Step Toward Sustainability*, Resources for the Future, Washington, DC.

Solow, R.M., 1993a, 'Sustainability: An Economist's Perspective', Dorfman, R. and Dorfman, N., (eds.), *Economics of the Environment: Selected Readings*, W.W.Norton Company, New York, pp.179-187.

Solow, R.M., 1993b, 'An Almost Practical Step Toward Sustainability, *Resources Policy*, 19 (September), 162-172.

Somvanshi, V.S., 1999, 'Resource Potential and Conservation Measures in Capture Fisheries', *Seafood Export Journal*, 30, 25-39.

Somvanshi, V.S., 2001, 'Problems and Prospects of Deep Sea and Far Sea Fishing', Pandyan , P.J. (ed.), *Sustainable Indian Fisheries*, National Academy of Agricultural Sciences, New Delhi, pp.71-87.

Somvanshi, V.S., 2003, 'Indian Experience on Assessment, Measurement and Monitoring of Fishery Resources and Fishing Capacity', Pascoe, S. and Greboval, D. (eds.), *Measuring Capacity in Fisheries*, FAO Fisheries Technical Paper No.445, FAO, Rome, pp.113-119.

Somvanshi, V.S. (ed.), 2004, *Large Marine Ecosystems: Exploration and Exploitation for Sustainable Development and Conservation of Fish Stocks*, Papers Presented at the International Symposium on Large Marine Ecosystem: Exploration and Exploitation for Sustainable Development and Conservation of Fish Stocks, held at Cochin, during 25-27 November 1998, Fishery Survey of India, Mumbai.

Somvanshi, V.S., 2005, 'Advances in Exploratory Survey and Fish Stock Assessment in the Seas Around India', Kurup, *et al.* (2005), *Souvenir, Sustain Fish 2005*, School of Industrial Fisheries, Cochin University of Science and Technology, Cochin, pp.67-70.

Springer, A.L., 1997, 'The Canadian Turbot War with Spain: Unilateral Action in Defence of Environmental Interests', *Journal of Environment and Development*, 6(1), 26-60.

Srinath, M., 2003, 'An Appraisal of the Exploited Marine Fishery Resources of India', Modayil, M.J. and Jayaprakash, A.A. (eds.), *Status of Exploited Marine Fishery Resources of India*, Central Marine Fisheries Research Institute, Cochin, pp.1-17.

Srinath, M. and Balan, K., 2003, 'Potential Yield from Indian EEZ', Modayil, M.J. and Jayaprakash, A.A. (eds.), *Status of Exploited Marine Fishery Resources of India,* Central Marine Fisheries Research Institute, Cochin, pp.286-290.

Srinath, M. and Pillai, N.G.K., 2006, 'Marine Fisheries in India : An Approach to Responsible Fisheries Management', *Seafood Export Journal*, Vol. 36, No.5, pp.11-31.

Srinivas, K.R., 2003, 'Turtles, Trade and Unilateral Measures', *Economic and Political Weekly,* Vol. 38, No.6, pp.571-576.

Srivastava, J. and Ahuja, R., 2002, 'Shrimp-Turtle Decision in WTO - Economic and Systemic Implication for Developing Countries', *Economic and Political Weekly,* Vol. 37, No.33, pp.3445-3455.

State Planning Board, 2004, *Economic Review, 2003*, State Planning Board, Thiruvananthapuram.

Stern, D.I., Common, M.S. and Barbier, E.B., 1996, 'Economic Growth and Environmental Degradation: The Environmental Kuznets Curve and Sustainable Development'*: World Development*, 24, 1151-1160.

Strutt, A. and Anderson, K., 1998, *Will Trade Liberalisation Harm Environment?: The Case of Indonesia to 2020*, World Bank Conference on Trade, Global Policy and the Environment, 21-22 April, Washington, DC.

Subash Babu, K.K., John, T. and Sreekumr, S., 2002, 'The Species Diversity of Fish Fauna of Muriyad Wetlands', *Proceedings of National Seminar on Current Environmental Problems and Management,* Irinjalakuda, Kerala, 1-3 August 2002, pp.59-63.

Subba Rao, N., 2004, 'The Impact of Cyclonic Disasters on the Life and Economy of Marine Fishing Communities of Andhra Pradesh', *Fishing Chimes*, Vol. 24, No.3, pp.26-30.

Sugunan, V.V. and Sinha, M. 2001 'Sustainable Capture and Culture-Based Fisheries in Freshwaters', Pandyan, T.J. (ed.), *Sustainable Indian Fisheries*, National Academy of Agricultural Sciences, New Delhi, pp. 43-76.

Sukumaran, N. (ed.), 1999, *Sustainable Environment*, M. S. University, Sri Paramakalyani Centre for Environmental Sciences, Alwarkurichi, Tamil Nadu.

Sumaila, U.R., Chuenpagdee, R. and Vasconcellos, M. (eds.), 2000, *Proceedings of the INCO-DC (International Cooperation in Science and Technology with Developing Countries), Workshop on Markets, Global Fisheries and Local Development,* Bergen, Norway, 22-23 March 1999, ACP-EU Fish. Res. Rep. (7), Brussels.

Supreme Court of India, 1996, *Coastal Aquaculture: Writ Petition*, (Civil No. 9661 of 1994) , S.Jagannathan versus Union of India and Others: S.C. Judgement dated 11.12.1996. Extract of Operative Part reported in *Fishing Chimes*, January, 1997, pp.15-16.

Sutinen, J.G. and Soboil, M., 2003, 'The Performance of Fisheries Management Systems and the Ecosystem Challenge', Sinclair, M. and Valdimarsson, G. (eds.), *Responsible Fisheries in Marine Ecosystem*, FAO, Rome, and CABI Publishing, Oxon.

Sutton, M., 1998, 'Harnessing Market Forces and Consumer Power in Favour of Sustainable Fisheries', Pinter, T.J., Hart, P.J.B. and Pauly, D. (eds.), *Re-inventing Fisheries Management*, Kluwer, Dordrecht, pp. 125-135.

Svedin, U., 1988, 'The Concept of Sustainability', *Perspectives of Sustainable Development,* Stockholm Studies in Natural Resources Management, No.1, Stockholm, pp.1-18.

Swan, J. and Greboval, D. (eds.), 2004, *Report and Documentation of the International Fisheries Instruments and Factors of Unsustainability and Overexploitation in Fisheries,* Mauritius, 3-7, February 2003, FAO, Fisheries Report No.700, FAO, Rome.

Symes, D., 2000, 'The Future for Fisheries Dependent Regions', Symes, D. (ed.) *Fisheries Dependent Regions*, Fishing News Books, London.

Talbot, L.M., 1984, 'The World Conservation Strategy', Thibodeau, F.R., and Field, E., (eds.), *Sustaining Tomorrow : A Strategy for World Conservation and Development,* University Press of New England.

Tamanaha, B.Z., 1993, 'The Folly of the Social Scientific Concept of Legal Pluralism', *Journal of Law and Society*, 20(2), 192-217.

Tetarwal, S.K. and Mehta, P.S., 2001, 'Process and Production Methods (PPMs): Implications for Developing Countries', *Seafood Export Journal*, Vol.32, No.3, pp.15-25.

Thailand Environment Institute, 1994a, *The Internal Linkages Between Trade and Environment: Thailand*, Report Submitted to UNCTAD/UNDP, June.

Thailand Environment Institute, 1994b, *Applying Polluter-Pays-Principle: Time for Action*, Research Paper Presented at Thailand Environment Institute Annual Conference, 29, July.

Tharakan, A.J., 1998, 'Seafood Industry : Reasons for Impasse and Solutions', *Seafood Export Journal*, Vol.29, No.4, pp.5-22.

The Hindu, 2007, 'U.S.Congressmen Attack India's Relations with Iran: Link this to Nuclear Deal' , *The Hindu*, Mangalore, 6.5.2007, p.8.

The New Indian Express,2007, 'Suspicions Among Nations Hold Back Climate Pacts', *The New Indian Express*, Cochin, 11.5.2007.

Thiruvananthapuram Fishermen's Union, 2005, 'The Proposed Luxury Liner Damaging to Fishermen', *Alakal*, Book, 3, Vol.28, October, 1-15, 2006, p.1.

Throsby, D., 2001, *Economics of Culture*, Cambridge University Press, Cambridge.

Tinbergen, J. and Hueting, R., 1991, 'GNP and Market Prices: Wrong Signals for Sustainable Economic Development that Disguise Environmental Destruction', Goodland, R., Daly, H.E. and El Serafy, S. (eds.), *Population, Technology and Lifestyle: The Transition to Sustainability*, Island Press, Washington, DC, pp.52-62.

Tisdell, C., 1999a, 'Conditions for Sustainable Development: Weak and Strong', Dragun, A.K. and Tisdell, C. (eds.), *Sustainable Agriculture and Environment,* Edward Elgar, Cheltenham, U.K., pp.23-36.

Tisdell, C., 1999b, 'Economics, Aspects of Ecology and Sustainable Agriculture Production', Dragun, A.K. and Tisdell, C. (eds.), *Sustainable Agriculture and Environment,* Edward Elgar, Cheltenham, U.K.

Tisdell, C., and Dragun, A.K., 1999, 'Agriculture and Sustainability: The Impact of Trade Liberalisation', Dragun, A.K., and Tisdell, C., (eds.), *Sustainable Agriculture and Environment*, Edward Elgar, Cheltenham, U.K., pp.1-6.

Tisdell, C.A., 1982, 'Environmental Conservation: Economics, Ecology and Ethics', *Environmental Conservation*, 10, 107-112.

Tietenberg, T., 1984, *Environmental and Natural Resource Economics*, Scott Foresman and Co., Glenview, Illionois.

Tietenberg, T., 1988, *Environmental and Natural Resource Economics*, (2nd ed.) Harper Collins Publishers, New York.

Tolba, M.K., 1987, *Sustainable Development: Constraints and Opportunities,* Butterworths, London.

Toman, M.A. and Crosson, *O., 1991, Economics and Sustainability: Balancing Trade-offs and Imperatives,* ENR 91-05, Resources for the Future, (mimeo), Washington, DC.

Toman, M.A., Pezzey, J. and Krautkraemer, J., 1995, 'Neo-Classical Economic Growth Theory and Sustainability', Bromley, D.W. (ed.), 1995, *Handbook of Environmental Economics,* Blackwell, Oxford, pp.139-165.

Tonn, B.E., 1988, 'Philosophical Aspects of 500 – Year Planning,' *Environment and Planning*, A.20, pp.1507-1522.

Tsamenyi, M. and Alistair, M.I., 1999, *International Environmental Instruments: The Effect on the Fishing Industry*, (2nd edition), Fisheries Research and Development Corporation, Australia.

Turner, R.K., 1987, 'Sustainable Global Futures, Common Interest, Inter-dependency, Complexity and Global Possibilities', *Futures,* Vol.19, No.5, pp.574-582.

Turner, R.K., 1988, 'Sustainability, Resource Conservation, and Pollution Control:An Over-View', Turner, R.K. (ed.), *Sustainable Environmental Management: Principles and Practice*, Belhaven Press, London.

Turner, R.K., (ed.), 1991a, *Sustainable Environmental Management: Principles and Practice,* CBS Publishers and Distributors (P) Ltd., New Delhi.

Turner, R.K., 1991b, 'Sustainability, Resource Conservation and Pollution Control: An Overview', Turner, R.K. (ed.), *Sustainable Environmental Management: Principles and Practice*, CBS Publishers and Distributors (P) Ltd., New Delhi, pp.1-25.

Turner, R. K. (ed.), 1993, *Sustainable Environmental Economics and Management*, Belhaven Press, London.

United Nations, 1992a, *Agenda-21: Programme of Action for Sustainable Development*, UN, New York.

United Nations, 1992b, *Convention on Biodiversity*, United Nations, New York.

United Nations, 1996, *Agreement for the Implementation of the Provisions of the United Nations Convention on the Law of the Sea of 10 December 1982, Relating to the Conservation and Management of Straddling Fish Stock and Highly Migratory Fish Stocks,* United Nations General Assembly, New York.

United Nations Conference on Environment and Development, 1992, *Agenda 21 Chapter 17: Protection of the Ocean, All kinds of Seas, including Enclosed and Semi-enclosed Seas and Coastal Areas and the Protection, Rational Use and Development of Their Living Resources* (mimeo), Rio Conference, 1992, UNCED, Conches, Switzerland.

United Nations Environment Programme (UNEP), 1994, *The Impacts of Climate on Fisheries,* UNEP Environment Library, Issue No.13.

Unnithan, G.R., Kesavan Nair, A.K., Iyer, K.H. and Annamalai, V., 1998, 'Capacity Utilisation in the Fish Processing Plants in Kerala', *Fishery Technology*, Vol. 35(2), pp.120-126.

Unnithan, G.R., Nikita, G. and Nair, R.V., 2004, 'Economics of Operation of 18 m Fuel Efficient Steel Trawlers of CIFT Design', *Fishery Technology*, Vol.41(1), pp.71-76.

Unnithan, G.R., Nikita, G., Nair, R.V. and Nassar, M., 2005, 'Fuel Consumption Pattern by the Mechanised Fishing Sector in Kerala', *Fishery Technology*, Vol. 42(1), pp.77-82.

van den Bergh, J.C.J.M. and Jan van der Straeten (eds.), 1994, *Towards Sustainable Development: Concepts, Methods and Policy*, Island Press, Washington, DC.

van den Bergh, J.C.J.M. and Hofkes, M.W., 1998, 'A Survey of Economic Modelling of Sustainable Development', van den Bergh, J.C.J.M. and Hofkes, M.W., (eds.), *Theory and Implementation of Economic Models for Sustainable Development*, Kluwer Academic Publishers, Dordrecht.

van Grasstek, C., 1992, 'The Political Economy of Trade and the Environment in the United States', Low, P. (ed.), *International Trade and the Environment*, World Bank Discussion Paper 159, IBRD/The World Bank, Washington, DC.

van Kooten, G.C. and Bulte, E.H., 2000, *The Economics of Nature: Managing Biological Assets*, Blackwell Publishers, Massachusetts, USA.

Velayudhan, T.D., 2005, 'Status of Fresh Water Prawn Farming in Kerala with Special Reference to Sustainable Development', Kurup, *et al.* (eds.), *Souvenir, Sustain Fish 2005*, School of Industrial Fisheries, Cochin University of Science and Technology, Cochin, pp. 111-118.

Venkatesan, V., 2005, 'Trade Barriers in the International Trade of Fish and Fishery Products with Special Reference to India', *Seafood Export Journal*, Vol.35, No.7 & 8, pp.3-11.

Verghese, P.U., 1995, 'Aquaculture Production to Augment Export of Marine Products from India' *Souvenir*, INDAQUA, 1995, MPEDA, Cochin, pp.13-15.

Vhora, N.A., 1998, 'Trends of Fisheries Development in Gujarat', *Fishing Chimes* 18(4), 35-38.

Victor, P., Hanna, E. and Kubursi, A., 1994, *How Strong is Weak Sustainability?* (mimeo). Ontario Ministry of Environment,

Victor, P.A., 1991, 'Indicators of Sustainable Development: Some Lessons from Capital Theory', *Ecological Economics*, 4, 191-213.

Victor, P.A., 1997, 'Indicators of Sustainable Development: Some Lessons from Capital Theory, Costanza, R., Perrings, C., and Cleveland, C,.J. (eds.). *The Development of Ecological Economics,* An Elgar Reference Collection, Cheltenham, U.K.

Vijayan, K.K., Alavandi, S.V., Kalaimani, K. and Santiago, T.C., 2005, 'Disease Related Crop Failures and Factors Affecting the Sustainability of Shrimp Aquaculture in India,' Kurup, *et al.* (eds.), *Souvenir, Sustain-Fish 2005*, School of Industrial Fisheries, Cochin University of Science and Technology, Cochin pp.119-125.

Vincent ,J.R., Panayotou, T. and Hartwick, J.M. 1997, 'Resource Depletion and Sustainability in Small Open Economies', *Journal of Environmental Economics and Management*, 33(3), 274-286.

Vivekanandan, E., 2001, 'Sustainable Coastal Fisheries for Nutritional Security', Pandyan, T.J., (ed.), *Sustainable Indian Fisheries*, National Academy of Agricultural Sciences, New Delhi, pp.19-42.

Vivekanandan, E., Rajkumar, U., Nair, R.J., and Gandhi, N., 2003, 'Goat Fishes', Modayil, M.J. and Jayaprakash, A.A., (eds.), *Status of Exploited Marine Fishery Resources of India*, Central Marine Fisheries Research Institute, Cochin, pp.158-163.

Vivekanandan, E., Zacharia, P.U., Ferozkhan, M. and Nair, R.J., 2003, 'Flat Fishes', Modayil, M.J. and Jayaprakash, A.A. (eds.), *Status of Exploited Marine Fishery Resources of India*, Central Marine Fisheries Research Institute, Cochin, pp. 164-170.

Vivekanandan, E., Zacharia, P.U. and Mahadevaswamy, H.S., 2003, 'White Fish', Modayil, M.J. and Jayaprakash, A.A. (eds.), *Status of Exploited Marine Fishery Resources of India*, Central Marine Fisheries Research institute, Cochin. 171-175.

von Moltke, K., 1994a, 'The World Trade Organisation: Its Implication for Sustainable Development', *Journal of Environment and Development*, 3(1).

von Moltke, K., 2004, 'Trade and Sustainable Development in the Doha Round', Moore Mike (ed.), *Doha and Beyond: The Future of the Multilateral Trading System,* Cambridge University Press, New York, pp. 1-18.

Ward, B. and Dubois, R.,1972, *Only One Earth: The Care and Maintenance of a Small Planet,* Norton, New York.

Ward, J.M., Kirkley, J.E., Metzner, R., Pascoe, S., 2004, *Measuring and Assessing Capacity in Fisheries (1), Basic Concepts and Management Options*, FAO Fisheries Technical Paper No. 433/1, Rome.

Warrier, S.M.V., 2001, 'Women at Work: Migrant Women in Fish Processing Industry', *Economic and Political Weekly*, Vol.36, No.37, pp. 3554-3562.

Weiss, E.B., 1989, *In Fairness to Future Generations: International Law, Common Patrimony and Intergenerational Equity.* Translation Publishers, Ardsley-on-Hudson, New York.

Wessells, C.R., Cochrane, K., Deere, C., Wallis, P. and Willmann, R., 2001, *Product Certification and Ecolabelling for Fisheries Sustainability*, FAO Fisheries Technical Paper No. 422, FAO, Rome.

White, L., 1967, 'The Historical Roots of Our Environmental Crisis', *Science*, 155, 1203-1207.

Wilen, J.E., 1976, *Common Property Resources and Dynamics of Overexploitation: The Case of the North Pacific Fur Seal,* University of British Columbia, Resources Paper No.3, University of British Columbia.

Williams, M.J., 1999, 'Factoring Fish into Food Security: Policy Issues', Ahmed, M., Delgado, C., Sverdrup-Jenson, S., and. Santas, R.A.V. (eds.), *Fisheries Policy Research in Developing Countries: Issues, Priorities and Needs*, ICLARM Conference Proceedings, 60.

Willmann, R., 1997, *Certification and Ecolabelling in Marine Fisheries: A Preliminary Assessment*, Unpublished mimeograph, FAO, Rome.

Willmann, R., and Insull, D., 1993, 'Integrated Coastal Fisheries Management', *Ocean and Coastal Management*, 21, 285-302.

Wilson, S.J., 2000, *The Development Challenge in Trade: Sanitary and Phyto-Sanitary Standards*, 21-22, June, W.T.O. Geneva.

World Bank, 1987, *Environment, Growth and Development*, Development Committee Pamphlet 14, World Bank, Washington D.C.

World Bank, 1990, *Adjustment Lending Policies for Sustainable Growth*, World Bank Country Economics Department Policy and Research Series No.14, Washington, DC.

World Bank, 1992, *A Study of International Fisheries Research*, Policy and Research, Series 19, World Bank, Washington, DC.

World Bank, 1994, *Making Development Sustainable*, World Bank, Washington, DC.

World Commission on Environment and Development, 1987, *Our Common Future, (The Brundtland Report),* Oxford University Press.

World Humanity Action Trust, 2000, *Governance for a Sustainable Future, II: Fishing for the Future*, WHAT, London.

World Resources Institute, 1998, *Building a Safe Climate, Sound Business Future,* World Resources Institute's Climate Protection Initiative, WRI, Washington, DC.

WTO, 1998a, *Trade and Environment in the WTO: Background to WTO Work in Trade and Environment*, (www.wto.org).

WTO, 1998b, *Market Access Impact of Ecolabelling Requirements,* WT/CTE/W/79, Geneva.

Yadava, Y.S., 2004, 'Fiscal Reforms for Fisheries in India : A Case Study', Cunningham, S. and Bostock, T., (eds.), *Paper Presented at the Workshop and Exchange of Views on Fiscal Reforms for Fisheries to Promote Growth, Poverty Eradication and Sustainable Management*, Rome, 13-15, October 2003, FAO, Rome, pp. 79-100.

Yohannan, T.M. and Sivadas, M , 2003, 'Indian Mackerel', Modayil, M.J. and Jayaprakash, A.A. (eds.), *Status of Exploited Marine Fishery Resources of India*, Central Marine Fisheries Research Institute, Cochin. pp. 60-65.

Young, M.D., 1992, *Sustainable Investment and Resource Use: Equity, Environmental Integrity and Economic Efficiency*, UNESCO Man and the Biosphere Series, Vol. 9, UNESCO and Parthenon Publishing Group, Paris, France.

Young, M.D., 2005, 'Sustainable Use of Renewable Natural Resources: Are There Necessary or Desirable Institutional Conditions?', Sahu, N.C. and Choudhury, A.K. (eds.), *Dimensions of Environmental and Ecological Economics*, Universities Press, Hyderabad, pp. 511-570.

# INDEX

**F**